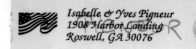
THIRD EDITION

Decision Support and Expert Systems:
Management Support Systems

EFRAIM TURBAN
Eastern Illinois University

Macmillan Publishing Company
New York

Maxwell Macmillan Canada
Toronto

Maxwell Macmillan International
New York   Oxford   Singapore   Sydney

Editor: Charles Stewart
Production Editor: Mary M. Irvin
Art Coordinator: Lorraine Woost
Cover Designer: Thomas Mack
Production Buyer: Pamela D. Bennett

This book was set in Palatino by Compset and was printed and bound by Bookpress. The cover was printed by Lehigh Press.

The Publisher offers discounts on this book when ordered in bulk quantities. For more information, write to: Special Sales Department, Macmillan Publishing Company, 445 Hutchinson Avenue, Columbus, OH 43235, or call 1-800-228-7854.

Macmillan Publishing Company
866 Third Avenue
New York, New York 10022

Macmillan Publishing Company is part of the
Maxwell Communication Group of Companies.

Maxwell Macmillan Canada, Inc.
1200 Eglinton Avenue East, Suite 200
Don Mills, Ontario M3C 3N1

Library of Congress Cataloging-in-Publication Data
Turban, Efraim.
    Decision support and expert systems : management support systems /
Efraim Turban.
        p.   cm.
    Includes index.
    ISBN 0-02-421691-7
    1. Management—Data processing.   2. Decision support systems.
3. Expert systems (Computer science)   I. Title.
HD30.2.T87   1993
658.4'03'0285633—dc20   92-39523
                                                                  CIP

Printing: 2 3 4 5 6 7 8 9   Year: 3 4 5 6 7

Dedicated to
my daughters Daphne and Sharon,
with love

Preface

Overview

Computer applications for management support are on the rise. The microcomputer revolution made computers available on many managers' desks. Managers may now access thousands of databases all over the country. Most organizations, private and public, use computerized analysis in their decision making. The cost of hardware and software is declining, whereas the capabilities of information systems and networks continue to increase.

Corporations are developing distributed systems that enable easy accessibility to data stored in multiple locations. Various information systems are being integrated with each other and/or with other automated systems. Managers can make better decisions because they have more accurate information at their fingertips.

However, despite all these technological developments, many managers are not using computers at all, or are using them primarily to support simple decisions. Decision Support Systems (DSS), Group Decision Support Systems (GDSS), Executive Information Systems (EIS), Expert Systems (ES) and Artificial Neural Networks (ANN) are the major technologies designed to change this situation.

The purpose of this book is to introduce the reader to these technologies, which we call collectively *management support systems* (MSS). This book presents the fundamentals of the techniques and the manner in which they are being constructed and used.

DSS and ES courses and portions of courses are recommended by ACM and DPMA. This course is designed to cover the material of CIS/86-11 (Decision Support and Expert Systems) of the DPMA model curriculum for computer information systems. It actually covers more than what is recommended. A secondary objective is to provide the practicing manager with the foundations

v

of DSS, GDSS, EIS, neural computing and ES. In addition, the book can be used as a sourcebook for MSS hardware and software.

The Third Edition

The third edition presents the material in a more structured manner and adds many new developments. Specifically:

- New Chapter 4: deals with data and its management
- Modified Chapter 5: consolidates all the material related to modeling and model management
- Modified Chapter 6: consolidates all the material related to user interface
- New Chapter 8: presents advanced DSS topics such as organizational DSS (ODSS) and intelligent DSS
- New Chapter 9: provides an extensive overview of Group DSS
- Old Chapter 14 divided into two new chapters:
     Chapter 14: Knowledge Representation
     Chapter 15: Knowledge Inferencing
- New Chapter 17: Neural Computing and Genetic Algorithms
- New Appendix: Harvard Business School case studies (one on Executive Information Systems, one on Expert Systems)
- The text was streamlined and updated.

The Instructional Materials

The instructional package consists of several components:

- **Instructor's Manual.** This manual includes:
  a. Learning objectives for the entire course and for each chapter.
  b. Answers to the questions, problems and exercises at the end of the chapters.
  c. Teaching suggestions (including instructions for projects).
- **Software Guide.**
  a. How to use EXSYS.
  b. How to use IFPS.
  c. How to use VP EXPERT.
  d. How to use Expert Choice.
  e. How to use LightShip.
- **Test Bank.** The test bank includes multiple choice questions for all the chapters with answers and many test exercises for both DDS and Expert Systems with solutions.
- **Transparency Masters.**
- **Free Development Software.**   The following software development packages are provided to the instructor. Unlimited copies of each package can be made without any charge. The packages are:
  a. EXSYS EL (with 50-rule limit)

  b. EXSYS Professional (with 50-rule limit)
  c. VP Expert (student version)
  d. IFPS/Personal (student version)
  e. Expert Choice (student version)
  f. LightShip (Demo and Development)
  g. NeuroShell (runtime and demo)

  The documentation is available in part in the Instructor's Manual and in part on the disks (as tutorials). A detailed presentation of IFPS is provided in Appendix A of this book.

- **Free Demonstration Software.**   These demos are basically a "slide show" type. They include: IFPS/Plus, The Executive Edge (an EIS), IdeaFisher, PMSS, Simfactory II and more.
- **Harvard Business Cases.**   Two Harvard Business Cases are appended to the book.
- **Demonstration Student Projects.**   Two student projects are appended to the book.

Acknowledgments

Many individuals provided suggestions and criticisms since the initiation of the first edition. Dozens of students participated in class testing of various chapters and problems and assisted in collecting material. It is not possible to name all of the many who participated in this project; thanks go to all of them. However, certain individuals made significant contributions and they deserve special recognition for the first edition.

First, those individuals who provided formal reviews. For the first edition: Robert Blanning (Vanderbilt University), Charles Butler (Colorado State), Warren Briggs (Suffolk University), Sohail S. Chaudry (University of Wisconsin, LaCrosse), Joyce Elam (University of Texas), Anand S. Kunnathur (Florida International University), Hank Lucas (NYU), Dick Mason (SMU), Benjamin Mittman (Northwestern University), Larry Moore and Loren Rees (Virginia Polytechnic and State University), Roger Alan Pick (University of Wisconsin), and John VanGigch (California State University at Sacramento).

The second edition reviewers are: Orv Grynhold (University of Denver), Steve Ruth (George Mason University), David Russell (Western New England College), Randy Smith (University of Virginia), Jung Shim (Mississippi State University), and Steve Zanakis (Florida International University).

The third edition reviewers are: Joey George (University of Arizona), Paul Gray (Claremont Graduate School), Leonard Jessup (California State University at San Marcos), Jane Mackay (Texas Christian University), Ido Millet (Bentley College), Jung P. Shim (Mississippi State University), James T. C. Teng (University of Pittsburgh), David Van Over (University of Georgia), and Paul R. Watkins (University of Southern California at Los Angeles).

Second, several individuals contributed material to the text or the supporting material. Major contributors are: Lou Frenzel (an independent consultant) who collaborated with me in my book *Expert Systems and Applied Artificial Intel-*

ligence (Macmillan, 1992). Considerable material from his books: *Crash Course in Artificial Intelligence and Expert Systems*, and *Understanding of Expert Systems* (both published by Howard W. Sams & Company of New York, 1987), is embedded in this text; Glen Gray (California State University at Northridge), who wrote the VP Expert Guide; Paul Gray (Claremont Graduate School), who wrote the IFPS Appendix; Larry Medsker (The American University), who contributed most of the material on organizational DSS and reviewed the chapter.

Third, the book benefitted greatly from efforts of many individuals who contributed advice and interesting material (e.g., problems), gave feedback on material, or helped in class testing. These individuals are: Warren Briggs (Suffolk University), Frank DeBalough (University of Southern California), Neil Dorf (Xerox Corporation), George Easton (California State University, San Diego), Janet Fisher (California State University, Los Angeles), Janet Francis (United States International University), David Friend (Pilot Executive Software), Dustin Huntington (EXSYS Inc.), David King (Execucom Systems Corporation), Jim Ragusa (Unviersity of Central Florida), Elizabeth Rivers (University of Southern California), Alan Rowe (University of Southern California), Steve Ruth (George Mason University), Ron Swift (independent consultant, on leave from IBM Corporation), Merril Warkentin (George Mason University), Paul Watkins (University of Southern California), Richard Watson (University of Georgia), and Mark Wood (Execucom Systems Corporation).

Fourth, many students helped in literature searches, condensing material, class testing, and proofreading. Most valuable was the help of: Janet Francis (United States International University), Rocky McClain (Eastern Illinois University), Lisa Sandoval (California State University, Long Beach), and Scott Singer (California State University, Long Beach).

Fifth, several vendors cooperated by providing development and/or demonstration software. They are: Comshare Corporation (Ann Arbor, MI), Expert Choice Inc. (Pittsburgh, PA), EXSYS Inc. (Albuquerque, NM), Pilot Executive Software (Boston, MA), Ward Systems Group, Inc. (Frederick, MD), FisherIdea Systems, Inc. (Irvine, CA), Wordtech Systems (Orinda, CA), and CACI Products Company (LaJolla, CA). Also, the Defense Systems Management College (Fort Belvoir, VA) provided their PMSS.

Sixth, many individuals helped me in administrative matters, in editing, and in proofreading. To begin with, Jack Repcheck (a former Macmillan editor) who initiated this project with the support of Hank Lucas (from New York University), the series editor, who provided many valuable suggestions. Help in the tedious job of proofing was provided by my friend Gerry Bedore and my daughter Sharon. Last, but not least, is Judy Lang, who played a major role in various tasks related to this book including the preparation of the Testbank and the Instructor's Manual.

Finally, the Macmillan Publishing Company team needs to be commended. Charles Stewart orchestrated this project. Contributions by the following team members ia also appreciated: Mary Irvin, who coordinated the production, and Pam Bennett. Also, Vernon Anthony, a former Macmillan editor, provided continuous support and help during the initial stages of the revision.

Contents

Part 2   Decision Support Systems   81

Chapter 3   Decision Support Systems: An Overview   83

Chapter 4   Data Management   131

Chapter 5   Modeling and Model Management   159

Chapter 6   User Interface   223

Chapter 10   Executive Information and Support Systems   391

Part 4   Fundamentals of Artificial Intelligence and Expert Systems   431

Chapter 11   Applied Artificial Intelligence: An Overview 433

Chapter 14   Knowledge Representation   553

Chapter 15   Inferences, Explanations, and Uncertainty 585

Chapter 16   Building Expert Systems: Process
and Tools   631

Part 6   Cutting Edge Technologies   679

Chapter 17   Neural Computing and Other Machine
Learning Technologies   681

Part 1

Introduction

Management Support Systems refers to a collection of computerized technologies whose objective is to support managerial work and especially decision making. In Part 1, two topics are presented. First, an overview of the book is given, including the rationale for the technologies and a brief description of each (Chapter 1). In Chapter 2, we present the fundamentals of decision making, including terminology and an overview of the decision-making process.

Chapter 1

Management Support Systems—An Overview

This book is about emerging computer technologies for managers: decision support systems, group decision support systems, executive information systems, expert systems, and neural computing. We are already seeing evidence that leads us to believe that these technologies will change the manner in which organizations are being structured and managed. Furthermore, these technologies may create a synergy with even greater potential impact on the effectiveness of managerial decision making. This introductory chapter provides an overview of the book and covers the following topics:

3

1.1 Managers and Computerized Support

A 1984 study of top corporate executives in Fortune 500 companies revealed that one-third of these executives *personally* use computers when making critical decisions. About one-quarter of these executives also used computers in their homes. A 1989 study of chief executive officers (CEOs) in the Fortune 500 indicated that 21 percent of them use computers. (See [21].) These figures are only one of many signals indicating that we are indeed in the information age. The impact of computer technology on organizations and society is increasing as new technologies evolve and existing technologies expand. The interaction and cooperation between people and machines is rapidly growing to cover more and more aspects of organizational activities. From traditional uses in payroll and bookkeeping functions, computerized systems are now penetrating complex managerial areas ranging from the design and management of automated factories to the evaluation of proposed mergers and acquisitions.

Some clerks and technicians have been using computers for as long as four decades to support routine jobs; in contrast, most managers use computers very infrequently to support their decision-making and other activities. This situation began to change in 1982. The driving forces of this change are the availability of microcomputers, the concepts of distributed computing and client/server computing, and the introduction of relatively easy-to-use software. These innovations enable managers not only to use general-purpose programs (application programs) but also to build their own computerized systems with easy-to-use construction tools. The first construction tool for micros was the spreadsheet technology, which received lots of attention in 1979 because of VisiCalc (see Figure 1.1). The construction tools and application programs are assisting managers in building, analyzing, and utilizing models, graphs, and charts; managing time and projects; and electronically writing memos and reports. Furthermore, managers can perform these tasks by themselves on their PCs instead of waiting for data processing* to do them. The executive is discovering that the computer is like a very reliable staff assistant; it works endlessly without pay, complaints, mistakes, or criticisms of other people.

Management now realizes that desktop computers are not "just another fad." Executives are recognizing that computers can provide value-added com-

---

*The terms *data processing* (DP) and *data processing people* and *departments* are being replaced with the term *information systems* or *services* (IS). The two terms are used interchangeably in this book.

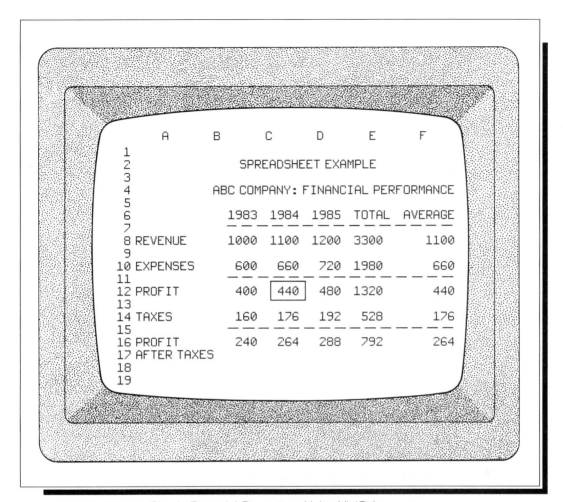

FIGURE 1.1 Simple Financial Statement Using VisiCalc.

puting power to existing large-capacity computing and that computers are here to stay. These executives have started asking such questions as "What can we do with all these micros?" [9]. Technological developments in hardware, software, and telecommunications are providing answers to this and similar questions by introducing products that can assist executives in their jobs. Computer applications are moving from transaction (or "backroom") processing and monitoring activities (which dominated the industry in the 1960s and 1970s) to problem analysis and solution applications in the 1990s. There is also a trend to provide managers with integrated packages that can assist them in their most important task—making decisions.

Computer-based technologies are being developed to improve the effectiveness of managerial decision making (see Box 1.1), especially in complex tasks.

Box 1.1: Wide Use of Computers in Business

Nine of ten senior executives say U.S. companies have successfully made computers a vital part of their business.

Interviews with 320 chief executives, chief operating officers, and strategic planners, conducted in 1991 under the sponsorship of Digital Equipment Corporation, indicate that computers are now an integral factor in major U.S. corporations, with applications ranging beyond such early uses as data processing.

The results of the survey show that today's top executives believe that computers play significant roles throughout their enterprise. Moreover, executives believe that they personally have a role in the management of their company's computers as a strategic resource.

Among highlights of the poll:

- Nine of ten respondents said U.S. companies have been "somewhat" or "very" successful in integrating computer technology in all areas of their business.
- An overwhelming majority—98 percent—said senior executives must understand computers and "their business impact."
- 81 percent said computer networks are "critical" to doing business abroad.
- 88 percent said they are using computers to increase communications, while 87 percent said computers have already cut the time needed to develop products.

Box 1.2: Management Support Systems Technologies

1. Decision Support Systems (DSS)
2. Group Decision Support Systems (GDSS)
3. Executive Information Systems (EIS)
4. Expert Systems (ES)
5. Artificial Neural Networks (ANN)

Such technologies—decision support systems (DSS),* group DSS, executive information systems (EIS), expert systems (ES), and neural computing (also referred to as artificial neural networks, or ANN)—are the subject of this book (see Box 1.2). They are collectively known as computerized *management support systems*. These technologies appear as independent systems but they are sometimes integrated.

1.2 Managerial Decision Making and Management Information Systems

To better understand management support systems, let us examine two important topics: managerial decision making and management information systems (MIS).

Management is a process by which certain goals are achieved through the use of resources (people, money, energy, materials, space, time). These resources are considered to be inputs, and the attainment of the goals is viewed as the output of the process. The degree of success of a manager's job is often measured by the ratio between outputs and inputs. This ratio is an indication of the organization's **productivity.**

$$\text{Productivity} = \frac{\text{outputs (products, services)}}{\text{inputs (resources)}}$$

Productivity is a major concern for any organization because it determines the well-being of the organization and its members. Productivity is also one of the most important issues at the national level. National productivity is the sum of the productivity of all organizations and individuals, and it determines the standard of living, the employment level, and the economic well-being of a country.

The level of productivity, or the success of management, depends on the execution of certain managerial functions like planning, organizing, directing, and controlling. To carry out these functions, managers are engaged in a continuous process of making decisions.

All managerial activities revolve around decision making. The manager is first and foremost a decision maker. Organizations are filled with decision makers at various levels (see Box 1.3).

For years, managers have considered decision making a pure art—a talent acquired over a long period of time through experience (learning by trial and error). Management was considered an art because a variety of individual styles could be used in approaching and successfully solving the same type of managerial problems in actual business practice. These styles are often based on crea-

---

*The abbreviations DSS, EIS, ES, and other support technologies are used for both the singular and plural form throughout this text.

Box 1.3: Ability to Make Decisions Rated First in Survey

In almost any survey of what constitutes good management, you are likely to find prominently mentioned the ability to make clear-cut decisions when needed.

It is not surprising, therefore, to hear that the ability to make crisp decisions was rated first in importance in a study of 6,500 managers in more than 100 companies, many of them large, blue-chip corporations.

As managers entered a training course at Harbridge House, a Boston-based firm, they were asked how important it was that managers employ certain management practices. They also were asked how well, in their estimation, managers performed these practices.

It was from a statistical distillation of these answers that Harbridge ranked "making clear-cut decisions when needed" as the most important of ten management practices.

And it was from these evaluations they concluded that only 20 percent of the managers performed "very well" on any given practice.

Ranked second in managerial importance was "getting to the heart of problems rather than dealing with less important issues," a finding that seems to show up in all such studies. Most of the remaining eight management practices were related directly or indirectly to decision making.

(*Source:* Condensed from *Stars and Stripes*, May 10, 1987.)

tivity, judgment, intuition, and experience, rather than on systematic quantitative methods based on a scientific approach.

However, the environment in which management must operate today is changing very rapidly. Business and its environment are more complex today than ever before, and the trend is toward increasing complexity. Figure 1.2 shows the changes in major factors (on the left) that have had an impact on managerial decision making. The results (on the right) indicate that decision making today is more complicated than in the past. It is more difficult to make decisions for two reasons. First, the number of available alternatives is much larger today than ever before, owing to improved technology and communication systems. Second, the cost of making errors can be very large, owing to the complexity and magnitude of operations, automation, and the chain reaction that an error can cause in many parts of the organization. By the same token, the benefits can be extremely large if correct decisions are being made.

As a result of these trends and changes, it is very difficult to rely on a trial-and-error approach to management, especially in decisions involving the factors shown in Figure 1.2. Managers must become more sophisticated—they must

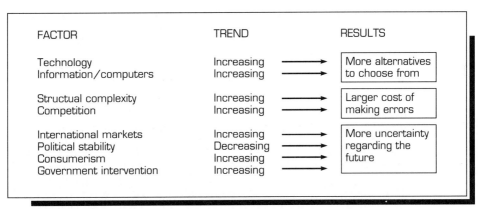

FACTOR	TREND		RESULTS
Technology	Increasing	⟶	More alternatives
Information/computers	Increasing	⟶	to choose from
Structual complexity	Increasing	⟶	Larger cost of
Competition	Increasing	⟶	making errors
International markets	Increasing	⟶	More uncertainty
Political stability	Decreasing	⟶	regarding the
Consumerism	Increasing	⟶	future
Government intervention	Increasing	⟶	

FIGURE 1.2 Factors Affecting Decision Making. (*Source:* Adapted from Turban and Meredith [17].)

learn how to use new tools and techniques that are being developed in their field. Many of these techniques use a quantitative analysis approach; they are grouped into a discipline called **management science** (or **operations research**). (For further details, see Turban and Meredith [17].)

1.3 A Framework for Decision Support

Before defining the specific management support technologies, it will be useful to present a classical framework for decision support. This framework will provide us with several major concepts that are used in the definitions. It will also help us in discussing several additional issues, such as the relationship among the technologies and the evolution of computerized systems. This framework was proposed by Gorry and Scott-Morton [6], who combined the work of Simon [16] and Anthony [2]. The details of this framework are as follows:

The first half of the framework is based on Simon's idea that decision-making processes fall along a continuum that ranges from highly structured (sometimes referred to as *programmed*) to highly unstructured (*nonprogrammed*) decisions. **Structured** processes refer to routine and repetitive problems for which standard solutions exist. **Unstructured** processes are "fuzzy," complex problems for which there are no cut-and-dried solutions. Simon also described the decision-making process as a three-phase process: intelligence, design, and choice.

- Intelligence—searching for conditions that call for decisions.
- Design—inventing, developing, and analyzing possible courses of action.
- Choice—selecting a course of action from those available.

An *unstructured problem* is one in which none of the three phases are structured. Decisions where some, but not all, of the phases are structured are referred to as **semistructured** by Gorry and Scott-Morton.

In a structured problem, the procedures for obtaining the best (or at least a good enough) solution are known. Whether the problem involves finding an appropriate inventory level or deciding on an optimal investment strategy, the objectives are clearly defined. Frequent objectives are cost minimization or profit maximization. The manager can use the support of clerical, data processing, or management science models. Management support systems such as DSS and ES can be useful at times. In an unstructured problem, human intuition is frequently the basis for decision making. Typical unstructured problems include planning of new services to be offered, hiring an executive, or choosing a set of research and development projects for next year. The semistructured problems fall between the structured and the unstructured, involving a combination of both standard solution procedures and individual judgment. Keen and Scott-Morton [8] give the following examples of semistructured problems: trading bonds, setting marketing budgets for consumer products, and performing capital acquisition analysis. Here, a decision support system can improve the quality of the information on which the decision is based (and consequently the quality of the decision) by providing not only a single solution but a range of alternate solutions. These capabilities, which are described later, allow managers to better understand the nature of the problems so they can make better decisions.

The second half of this framework is based on Anthony's taxonomy [2], which defines three broad categories that encompass all managerial activities: (1) strategic planning—the long-range goals and the policies for resource allocation; (2) management control—the acquisition and efficient utilization of resources in the accomplishment of organizational goals; and (3) operational control—the efficient and effective execution of specific tasks.

Anthony and Simon's taxonomies are combined in a nine-cell decision support framework (see Figure 1.3). The right-hand column and the bottom row indicate the technologies needed to support the various decisions. Gorry and Scott-Morton suggested, for example, that for the semistructured and unstructured decisions, the conventional MIS and management science approaches are insufficient. They proposed the use of a supportive information system, which they called *decision support system* (DSS). Expert systems (ES), which were introduced several years later, are most suitable for tasks requiring expertise.

The more structured and operational control-oriented tasks (cells 1, 2, and 4) are being performed by low-level managers, whereas the tasks in cells 6, 8, and 9 are the responsibility of top executives. This means that DSS, EIS, neural computing, and ES are more often applicable for top executives and professionals tackling specialized, complex problems.

Type of Decision	Type of Control			
	Operational Control	Managerial Control	Strategic Planning	Support Needed
Structured	Accounts receivable, order entry **1**	Budget analysis, short-term forecasting, personnel reports, make-or-buy analysis **2**	financial management (investment), warehouse location, distribution systems **3**	MIS, Operations research models, Transaction processing
Semistructured	Production scheduling, inventory control **4**	Credit evaluation, budget preparation, plant layout, project scheduling, reward systems design **5**	Building new plant, mergers and acquisitions, new product planning, compensation planning, quality assurance planning **6**	DSS
Unstructured	Selecting a cover for a magazine, buying software, approving loans **7**	Negotiating, recruiting an executive, buying hardware, lobbying **8**	R & D planning, new technology development, social responsibility planning **9**	DSS ES Neural Networks
Support Needed	MIS, Management science	Management science, DSS, ES, EIS	EIS, ES, Neural Networks	

FIGURE 1.3 Decision Support Framework.

Computer Support for Structured Decisions

Structured and some semistructured decisions, especially of the operational and managerial control type, have been supported by computers since the 1960s. Decisions of this type are being made in *all functional areas*, especially in finance and production (operations management).

Such problems, which are encountered fairly repeatedly, have a high level of structure. It is therefore possible to abstract and analyze them and classify them into prototypes. For example, a "make-or-buy" decision belongs to this category. Other examples are capital budgeting (e.g., replacement of equipment), allocation of resources, distribution problems, procedures, planning, and inventory control. For each type of problem, a prescribed solution was developed through the use of some mathematical formulas. This approach is called management science.

Management Science

The management science approach adopts the view that managers can follow a fairly systematic process for solving problems. Therefore, it is possible to use a scientific approach to managerial decision making. This approach involves the following steps:

1. Defining the *problem* (a decision situation which may deal with some *trouble* or with an *opportunity*).
2. Classifying the problem into a standard category.
3. Constructing a mathematical model that describes the real life problem.
4. Finding potential solutions to the modeled problem and evaluating them.
5. Choosing and recommending a solution to the problem. This process is centered around *modeling*.

Modeling involves the transformation of the real-world problem into the prototype structure. As will be seen later, modeling is going to be used also in less structured problems. The use of computers was designed to help in finding the solution for the problem in a quick and efficient manner. Although structured problems can be solved with the aid of standard quantitative models, the less structured ones can be handled by decision support systems or other MSS. Finally, future consequences of decisions are more difficult to predict because of increased uncertainty.

1.4 Decision Support Systems

The concepts involved in DSS were first articulated in the early 1970s by Scott-Morton under the term *management decision systems*. He defined such systems as "interactive computer-based systems, which help decision makers utilize *data* and *models* to solve unstructured problems" [15]. Another classical definition of DSS, provided by Keen and Scott-Morton [8] follows:

> Decision support systems couple the intellectual resources of individuals with the capabilities of the computer to improve the quality of decisions. It is a computer-based support system for management decision makers who deal with semi-structured problems.

The DSS definition will be revisited and expanded in Chapter 3. It should be noted that DSS, like MIS and other MSS technologies, is content-free expression (i.e., it means different things to different people). There is no universally accepted definition of DSS.

Now, let us examine a typical case of a successfully implemented DSS, as shown in Box 1.4.

Box 1.4: The Houston Minerals Case

Houston Minerals Corporation was interested in a proposed joint venture with a petrochemicals company to develop a chemical plant. Houston's executive vice president responsible for the decision wanted analysis of the risks involved in the areas of supplies, demands, and prices. Bob Sampson, manager of planning and administration, and his staff built a DSS in a few days by means of a specialized planning language. The results strongly suggested the project should be accepted.

Then came the real test. Although the executive vice president accepted the validity and value of the results, he was worried about the potential downside risk of the project, the chance of a catastrophic outcome. As Sampson tells it, his words were something like this:

> I realize the amount of work you have already done, and I am 99 percent confident with it. I would like to see this in a different light. I know we are short of time and we have to get back to our partners with our yes or no decision.

Sampson replied that the executive could have the risk analysis he needed in less than an hour's time. Sampson concluded, "within 20 minutes, there in the executive boardroom, we were reviewing the results of his 'what-if?' questions. Those results led to the eventual dismissal of the project, which we otherwise would probably have accepted."

The case demonstrates some of the major characteristics of a DSS. The risk analysis performed first was based on the decision maker's initial definition of the situation using a management science approach. Then the executive vice president, using his experience, judgment, and intuition, felt that the model should be modified. The initial model, although mathematically correct, was incomplete. With a regular simulation system, a modification would have taken a long time, but the DSS provided a very quick analysis. Furthermore, the DSS was flexible and responsive enough to allow managerial intuition and judgment to be incorporated in the analysis.

How can such a thorough risk analysis be performed so quickly? How can the judgment factors be elicited, quantified, and worked into the model? How can the results be presented meaningfully and convincingly to the executive? What is meant by "what-if" questions? The answers to these questions are provided in Chapters 3 through 10.

Why Use a DSS?

Firestone Tire & Rubber Co. explained its reasons for implementing a DSS in *Computerworld* (September 27, 1982). The major reasons were that:

- The company was operating in an unstable economy.
- The company was faced with increasing foreign and domestic competition.
- The company encountered increasing difficulty in tracking the numerous business operations.
- The company's existing computer system did not support the objectives of increasing efficiency, profitability, and entry into profitable markets.
- The DP Department could not begin to address the diversity of the company's needs or management's ad hoc inquiries, and business analysis functions were not inherent within the existing systems.

A survey conducted by Hogue and Watson [7] identified six main reasons why major corporations started large-scale DSS:

Factors	Cited by (percent)
Accurate information is needed.	67
DSS is viewed as an organizational winner.	44
New information is needed.	33
Management mandated the DSS.	22
Timely information is provided.	17
Cost reduction is achieved.	6

Another reason for the development of DSS is the end-user computing movement. End-users are not programmers and therefore they require easy-to-use construction tools and procedures. These are provided by DSS.

The overall results of using a DSS can be very impressive, as indicated by the Pfizer case (see Box 1.5).

1.5   Group Decision Support Systems

Many major decisions in organizations are made by groups, collectively. Getting a group together in one place and at one time can be difficult and expensive. Furthermore, group meetings can take a long time and the resulting decisions may be mediocre.

Attempts to improve the situation with the aid of information technology appear under several names, such as Groupware, electronic meeting systems, collaborative systems, and group decision support systems. Of special interest in this book is the area of group DSS (see Box 1.6).

Box 1.5: DSS at Pfizer Pharmaceutical, Inc.

As of 1973, Rachelle Laboratories, Inc. (Long Beach, CA), a competitor of Pfizer, began selling an antibiotic called Doxychel, which was the same drug as Pfizer's Vibramycin. Pfizer contended that its patent had been violated.

The disagreement came to a head in the winter of 1983 in a district court in Honolulu. Throughout the six-week trial, however, Pfizer had an edge over Rachelle. Pfizer had a DSS. Jeffrey Landau, manager of DSS at Pfizer, recalls: "We put together a team of lawyers, system-staff professionals, and others, and built a model." The model, he says, looked at one key "what-if." If Rachelle hadn't started selling Doxychel, how much more money would Pfizer have made? The answer, of course, depended on two assumptions. One was that all Rachelle's sales were at Pfizer's expense. The other was that, without Rachelle as a competitor, Pfizer could have sold its antibiotic at a higher price.

Armed with these assumptions, the Pfizer team set up, three blocks from the courthouse, a DSS war room, complete with terminals, printers, plotters, and high-speed communication to a DEC System-10 mainframe in Connecticut. With the system in place, the opposition could not stall for time by requesting additional information. Pfizer's system accessed the requested information instantly.

When the trial got under way, however, Pfizer's decision support system was really put to the test. "We could measure the impact of claims witnesses made about the market. Using the information provided, the lawyers would yield on points that were determined to be insignificant. If the other side made a claim that had big monetary implications, our lawyers would fight it." In effect, the Pfizer team used the model to plan its legal tactics.

The result: On June 30, 1983, Judge Martin Pence, who frequently alluded to Pfizer's model, awarded Pfizer $55.8 million. It was the largest judgment on a patent-infringement suit in U.S. history.

(*Source:* Condensed from M. Lasden, *Computer Decisions*, Nov. 1983, pp. 254–58.)

1.6   Executive Information (or Support) Systems

Executive information systems are being developed primarily for the following objectives:

- Serve the information needs of executives.
- Provide extremely user friendly interface for the executive.
- Meet individual executives' decision styles.

Box 1.6: Total Quality Management (TQM) at IBM

The Malcolm Baldridge National Quality Award is granted annually to those companies and individuals in the U.S. that show excellence in persuing TQM programs. The prestigious award is based on assessment of 32 criteria organized in the following categories: leadership, information and analysis, strategic quality planning, human resource utilization, quality assurance, and customer satisfaction.

At IBM Boulder (Colorado), TQM has a high priority. Although management does not believe that at the present time the organization is ready for the Baldridge Award, they would like to apply for IBM's internal quality award, as well as to identify potential improvement areas. The problem is that there is a diversity of opinion on the current accomplishment level of each of the 32 criteria of quality. Thus, there are disagreements on priorities and the resulting allocation of resources of improving quality.

To arrive at the appropriate decision, IBM used its own decision room and software (TeamFocus) to support the process of group work. This approach, called group DSS, enabled IBM to achieve consensus, to learn more about TQM, to assess where the company is, and to determine where it needs to go to achieve excellence in TQM.

(*Source:* Condensed from R. L. and J. J. Mozeliak, "TeamFocus: Experiences with Malcolm Baldridge Self-Assessment," in *DSS-91 Transactions*, Mahattan Beach, California, June 1991.)

- Provide timely and effective tracking and control.
- Provide quick access to detailed information behind text, numbers, or graphics (drill-down capability).
- Filter, compress, and track critical data and information.
- Identify problems (opportunities).

Executive information systems, which started in the mid 1980s in large corporations (see Box 1.7), are becoming affordable to smaller companies and are serving many managers as enterprise-wide systems. See Watson et al. [19].

1.7   Expert Systems

When an organization has a complex decision to make or problem to solve, it often turns to experts for advice. These experts have specific knowledge and experience in the problem area. They are aware of the alternatives, the chances of success, and the costs the business may incur. Companies engage experts for advice on such matters as which equipment to buy, mergers and acquisitions, and advertising strategy. The more unstructured the situation, the more spe-

Box 1.7: Executive Information System at Hardee's

At Hardee's (Rocky Mount), the EIS primarily provides status access, according to John Wilson, chief financial officer. Point of sale terminals at over 3,000 Hardee's restaurants accumulate detailed sales information, which the corporate mainframe collects automatically each night. Financial analysts extract and analyze information from the mass of data using Express (a DSS generator listed in Chapter 7). This information is transformed to the EIS database.

The database also holds information on Hardee's competitors and other financial information from online information services. Five top executives, including the chairman and Wilson, tap the EIS with their own IBM PCs. The executives use a mouse to select graphs and reports from menus. Much of their work with the system involves devising and tracking marketing strategies. For example, if the figures show that sales in a region are falling off during a particular time of day, local advertising might have to be refocused.

At Hardee's, the EIS's analyst is tailoring the information to executives' needs and desires. The analyst puts together a basic package of reports and graphs. As the five users familiarize themselves with the available information and possible formats, they are requesting new reports and modifications of standing ones. Wilson expects to add more sophisticated features that the executives consider critical, like automatic exception reporting and the tracking of situations. The system was developed with the Command Center software (see Chapter 10). "It takes no time at all to learn the system," Wilson says. "Everyone was up to speed in five minutes."

(*Source:* Condensed from *Computer Decisions*, Dec. 17, 1985.)

cialized (and expensive) is the advice. Expert systems are an attempt to mimic human experts.

Typically, an expert system is a decision-making and/or problem-solving package of computer hardware and software that can reach a level of performance comparable to—or even exceeding that of—a human expert in some specialized and usually narrow problem area.

Expert systems are a branch of applied **artificial intelligence** (AI). From applications in medical diagnosis, mineral exploration, and computer configurations, expert systems are spreading into complex business applications like managing assets and liabilities, corporate planning, tax advice, competitive bid preparations, internal control evaluations, and fault analysis.

The basic idea behind ES is simple. **Expertise** is transferred from the human to the computer. This knowledge is then stored in the computer and users call on the computer for specific advice as needed. The computer can make inferences and arrive at a specific conclusion. Then, like a human consultant, it advises the nonexperts and explains, if necessary, the logic behind the advice. (See Turban [18].)

Illustrative Case

When Elf Aquitaine, the French oil company, has a drill bit stuck thousands of feet below the earth's surface, they no longer call their top troubleshooter to fix this costly problem. Instead, the drilling rig foreman calls a computer for help. The computer asks the foreman questions, just as an expert would. Once it gathers the information it needs from the foreman, the computer, by using its inferencing capabilities, makes a recommendation on how to retrieve the drill bit. The computer can also explain to the foreman why a certain action is less effective than the recommended one. The recommendation is made by drawing images on the computer screen.

To build this system, the builders interviewed Elf Aquitaine's top troubleshooter, Jacques-Marie Courte, and then programmed his answers into the computer. Thus, the computer replicates the expert's knowledge.

This case illustrates some of the distinct capabilities and characteristics of expert systems, such as their ability to:

- Capture and preserve perishable expertise from one or several experts.
- Apply this expertise to solve complex problems effectively and efficiently by using inferencing capabilities.
- Solve problems by providing answers instead of data.
- Provide an explanation of how solutions are derived.

Expert systems are used today in thousands of organizations and they support many tasks (see Box 1.8). These capabilities can provide companies with improved productivity levels and increased competitive advantages.

1.8 Neural Computing (Artificial Neural Networks)

The application of all the previous technologies was based on the use of *explicit* data, information, or knowledge, which was stored in a computer and manipulated as needed. However, in the complex real world we may not have explicit data, information, or knowledge. Yet, people must make decisions that are based on partial, incomplete, or inexact information. Such conditions are created, for example, in rapidly changing environments. Decision makers are using their experiences to handle these situations; i.e., they are recalling experiences and *learning* from their experiences what to do with new similar situations for which *exact* replicas are unavailable.

Box 1.8: How Expert Systems Can Perform Useful Tasks

Suppose you manage an engineering firm that bids on many projects. Each project is, in a sense, unique. You can calculate your expected cost, but that's not sufficient to set up your bid. You have background information on your likely competitors and their bidding strategies. Something is known about the risks—possible technical problems, political delays, material shortages, or other sources of trouble. An experienced proposal manager can put all this together and, generally, arrive at a sound judgment concerning terms and bidding price. However, you do not have that many proposal managers who have the time to concentrate on preparing and negotiating major proposals. This is where expert systems become useful. An expert system can capture the lines of thinking the experienced proposal managers can follow. It can also catalog information gained on competitors, local risks, etc. and can incorporate your policies and strategies concerning risk, pricing, and terms. It can help your younger managers work through to an informed bid consistent with your policy.

Suppose you are a life insurance agent and you are a very good one; however, your market has changed. You are no longer competing only with other insurance agents. You are also competing with banks, brokers, money market fund managers, and the like. Your company is now pushing a whole array of products, from universal life insurance to venture capital funds. Your clients have the same problems as ever, but they are more inquisitive, more sophisticated, and more conscious of tax avoidance and similar considerations. How can you give them advice and put together a sensible package for them when you are more confused than they are?

Financial planning systems and estate planning guides have been part of the insurance industry's marketing kit for a long time. However, sensible financial planning takes more skill than the average insurance agent has or can afford to acquire. This is one reason why the fees of professional planners are as high as they are. A number of insurance companies are currently investing heavily in artificial intelligence techniques in the hope that these techniques can be used to build sophisticated, competitive, knowledge-based financial planning support systems to assist their agents in helping their clients.

(*Source:* Publicly disclosed project description of Arthur D. Little, Inc.)

In all the previous technologies, there was no element of learning by the computer. A technology that attempts to close this gap is called *neural computing* or **artificial neural networks** (ANN). The technology, which employs a pattern recognition approach, has been used successfully in some business applications

Box 1.9: Neural Computing Identifies More Heart Attacks Than Doctors Do

Emergency room doctors instantly identified 78 percent of patients with heart attacks in an experiment involving 331 patients complaining of chest pains at a San Diego hospital emergency room. The sooner a heart attack is diagnosed, the better is the chance of saving the patient's life.

Dr. Baxt of the University of California, San Diego Medical Center, reported in the December 1991 issue of the *Annals of Internal Medicine* that a new computerized technology, called neural computing, instantly and correctly identified 97 percent of the same patients. Furthermore, as compared to the doctors, the computer program did very well when important information was missing.

The capability of neural computing to work despite missing data is one of the greatest advantages of this emerging technology, which has been used successfully in several financial management applications.

(see Box 1.9), but much research and development is still needed. (See Zeidenberg [20].)

1.9 The Evolution of Computerized Decision Aids

Computers have been used as tools to support managerial decision making for over three decades. Table 1.1 presents a summary of the development of computerized procedures used as aids in decision making.

The computerized tools or decision aids displayed in Table 1.1 can be grouped into seven categories (see Kroeber and Watson [10]):

- Transaction processing systems (TPS)
- Management information systems (MIS)
- Office automation systems (OAS)
- Decision support systems (DSS) and group DSS (GDSS)
- Expert systems
- Executive information systems (EIS)
- Artificial neural networks (ANN).

There are several opinions about the evolution of management support systems (MSS) and their relationship to the other systems. A common view is that the recommendations and advice provided by MSS to the manager can be considered as information needed for final decisions made by humans. If we accept this approach, we can consider MSS as sophisticated, high-level types of infor-

TABLE 1.1   Aids in Decision Making.

Phase	Description	Examples of Tools
Early	Compute, "crunch numbers," summarize, organize.	Calculators, early computer programs, statistical models, simple operations research models.
Intermediate	Find, organize, and display decision-relevant information.	Database management system, MIS, filing systems.
Current	Perform decision-relevant computations on decision-relevant information; organize and display the results. Query-based and user-friendly approach. "What-if" analysis.	Financial models, spreadsheets, trend exploration, operations research models, CAD systems, decision support systems.
	Interact with decision makers to facilitate formulation and execution of the intellectual steps in the process of decision making.	Expert systems; executive information systems.
Just beginning	Complex and fuzzy decisions situations, expanding to collaborative decision making and to machine learning.	Second generation of expert systems, group DSS, neural computing.

mation systems that can be used in addition to traditional transaction processing systems, office automation, and MIS.*

The evolutionary view of computer-based information systems (CBIS), presented in Figure 1.4, has a strong logical basis. First, there is a clear-cut sequence through time: EDP systems appeared in the mid-1950s, MIS followed in the 1960s, OAS was developed mainly in the 1970s, and DSS is a product of the 1970s and expanded in the 1980s. Commercial applications of expert systems and executive information systems and expert systems emerged in the 1980s. In the 1990s we see neural computing emerging as well as many **integrated computer systems.** Second, there is a common technology linking the various types of CBIS: the computer, which itself has evolved considerably over time. And third, there are systemic linkages in the manner in which each system processes data into information. Additional support for the evolutionary view is presented in Figure 1.5. This figure lists the attributes of TPS, MIS, DSS, EIS, and ES classified into several dimensions. Only the most sophisticated attributes of each level are listed. Several lesser attributes can be found (although not listed) in most of the CBIS.

The relationship among TPS, MIS, DSS, EIS and ES and other technologies that are not shown in the table can be summarized as follows:

- The technologies can be viewed as being unique classes of information technology.

---

*All these systems are supported by telecommunications and networks, a topic outside the framework of this book.

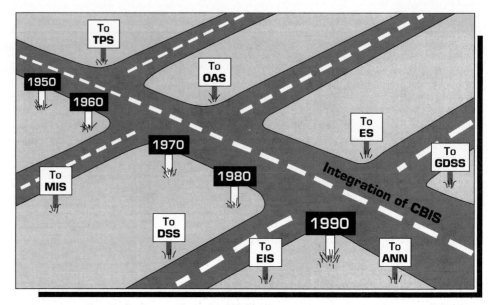

FIGURE 1.4 The Evolutionary Path of CBIS. (*Source:* Kroeber and Watson [10]; modified.)

- They are interrelated, and they each support some aspects of managerial decision making.
- The evolution and creation of the newer tools help expand the role of information technology for the betterment of management in organizations.
- The interrelationship and coordination between these tools is still evolving.

The classification of CBIS does not imply that real world computer systems must belong to only one category. On the contrary, an MIS system may be coupled with a transaction processing system. A DSS may be combined with an MIS and integrated with an ES. The interactions among CBIS occur along two dimensions: technology (hardware, software, processes) and applications (personnel management, scheduling, inventory control).

An illustration of CBIS in a personnel department is provided in Appendix A at the end of the chapter.

1.10 Some Differences Between MIS and DSS

The DSS definitions, performance characteristics, and examples clearly indicate that there are differences between DSS and MIS. We notice that the differences are real and merit our attention. What can be expected from a DSS is less typi-

Dimension	Transactions Processing Systems (TPS)	Management Information Systems (MIS)	Decision Support Systems (DSS)	Expert Systems (ES)	Executive Information Systems (EIS)
Applications	Payroll, inventory, record keeping, production and sales information	Production control, sales forecasting, monitoring	Long-range strategic planning, complex integrated problem areas	Diagnosis, strategic planning, internal control planning, maintenance strategies. Narrow domain	Support to top management decision, environmental scanning
Focus	Data Transactions	Information	Decisions, flexibility, user-friendliness	Inferencing, Transfer of expertise	Tracking, control "Drill down"
Database	Unique to each application, batch update	Interactive access by programmers	Database management systems, interactive access, factual knowledge	Procedural and factual knowledge; knowledge base (facts, rules)	External (online) and corporate
Decision Capabilities	No decision, or simple decision models	Structured routine problems using conventional operations research tools	Semistructured problems, integrated OR models, blend of judgment and structured support capabilities	The system makes complex decisions, unstructured; use of rules (heuristics)	None
Manipulation	Numerical	Numerical	Numerical	Symbolic	Numeric (mainly) some symbolic
Type of information	Summary reports, operational	Scheduled and demand reports, structured flow, exception reporting	Information to support specific decisions	Advice and Explanations	Status access, exception reporting, key indicators
Highest organizational level served	Submanagerial, low management	Middle management	Top management	Top management and specialists	Senior executives (only)
Impetus	Expediency	Efficiency	Effectiveness	Effectiveness and expediency	Timeliness

FIGURE 1.5 Attributes of the Major Computerized Support Systems.

cally possible with an MIS (see Box 1.10). This does not mean that an MIS cannot have these features; rather, they are simply not common to most management information systems. The Houston Minerals Case (Box 1.4) illustrates these differences.

Specifically, a DSS can be used to address ad hoc, unexpected problems. The proposed joint venture described in Box 1.4 was possibly a once-in-a-lifetime decision-making situation. Most MIS decision support is supplied by structured information flows in the form of summary and exception reports. An exception report singles out items that require special attention. Structured reports are of limited value for unique problems. Either the needed information is not provided or it is in the wrong format.

A DSS can provide a valid representation of a complex real world system. In this example, the decision maker accepted the validity of the model and the value of the results; the model builders were able to develop a model that could be trusted. The way many models are embedded in an MIS does not engender such trust, because they are frequently built by the management science group and left for the user as the management scientist moves on to other projects. Over time, the models become out-of-date and either are not used or are used and provide potentially misleading, outdated information.

A DSS can supply decision support within a short time frame. A model for the proposed joint venture was completed and working within days. A request

Box 1.10: Management Information Systems

A management information system (MIS) is a formal, computer-based* system, intended to retrieve, extract, and integrate data from various sources in order to provide timely information necessary for managerial decision making. MIS has been most successful in providing information for routine, structured, and anticipated types of decisions. In addition, it has been successful in acquiring and storing large quantities of detailed data concerning transaction processing. MIS has been less successful in supporting complex decision situations. This is because of a lack of capabilities necessary for such support, and MIS traditionally has not been easy enough to be developed or even used by managers. Furthermore, as managers climb the corporate ladder, they must increasingly deal with matters outside the organization. Most MIS are built with a focus on the internal organization. Hence, the support of the traditional MIS decreases as the organizational level increases. The computerized management support systems discussed in this book are intended to complement both management science and MIS because they address those tasks that are nonroutine and require managerial judgment in addition to formal analysis.

*A management information system may be in operation without a computer. However, in this book an MIS should always be thought of as computer-based.

TABLE 1.2 DSS Features

- A DSS can be used to address ad hoc, unexpected problems.
- A DSS can provide valid representation of the real world system.
- A DSS can provide decision support within a short time frame.
- A DSS can evolve as the decision maker learns more about the problem.
- DSS can be developed by non-data processing professionals.

for risk analysis was satisfied within one hour. In an MIS, if the model is not already available, the lead time for writing programs and getting answers is often too long to help many decision situations.

A DSS can evolve as the decision maker learns more about the problem. In many cases, managers cannot specify in advance what they want from computer programmers and model builders. In our example, the request for risk analysis occurred *after* the model was built. Many computerized applications are developed in a way that requires detailed specifications to be formalized in advance. This requirement is not reasonable in many semistructured and unstructured decision-making tasks.

A DSS is often developed by non-data processing (DP) professionals. In the Houston case, the planning and administration group created the model with no outside help. This was possible because of the software package that was available. Most MIS applications and systems are developed by data processing professionals.

These distinguishing DSS features are summarized in Table 1.2. Keen and Scott-Morton also have noted the distinctive nature of DSS. Table 1.3 summarizes the differences that they see among MIS, operations research/management science (OR/MS), and DSS.

Another way to look at the relationships between DSS and MIS is provided by McLean [12], who uses Anthony's framework. The three levels of organizational activities are shown as a triangle with an added level for transaction processing. Transaction processing is done mainly at the operational level.

MIS, in theory, was to serve all levels of managerial activities. As such, DSS can be considered a subset of MIS (see Figure 1.6). In practice, MIS has fallen far short of this objective. The proponents of decision support systems therefore argued that their approaches were better suited to the upper two layers of decision making.

Similar to McLean's point of view is the notion that MIS is an umbrella that supports all managerial activities. DSS is viewed as the portion that deals with unstructured situations, while management science deals with structured problems.

Note: For a discussion on the differences between DSS and EIS, see Chapter 10.

1.11 The Decision Support–Expert Systems Connection

DSS and ES seem to be completely different and unrelated computerized systems. As can be viewed in Table 1.4, there are significant philosophical, tech-

TABLE 1.3   The Characteristics of MIS, OR/MS, and DSS.

Management Information Systems
- The main impact has been on structured tasks, where standard operating procedures, decision rules, and information flows can be reliably predefined
- The main payoff has been in improving efficiency by reducing costs, turnaround time, and so on, and by replacing clerical personnel
- The relevance for managers' decision making has mainly been indirect, for example, by providing reports and access to data

Operations Research/Management Science
- The impact has mostly been on structured problems (rather than tasks), where the objective, data, and constraints can be prespecified
- The payoff has been in generating better solutions for given types of problems
- The relevance for managers has been the provision of detailed recommendations and new methodologies for handling complex problems

Decision Support Systems
- The impact is on decisions in which there is sufficient structure for computer and analytic aids to be of value but where managers' judgment is essential
- The payoff is in extending the range and capability of computerized managers' decision processes to help them improve their effectiveness
- The relevance for managers is the creation of a supportive tool, under their own control, that does not attempt to automate the decision process, predefine objectives, or impose solutions

Source: Keen and Scott-Morton [8] p. 1.

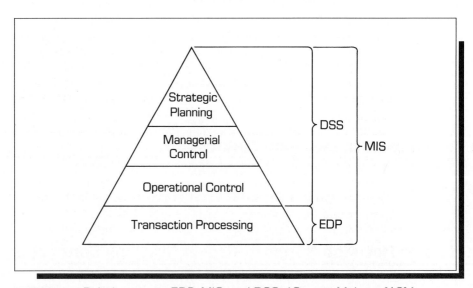

FIGURE 1.6   Relation among EDP, MIS, and DSS. (*Source:* McLean [12].)

TABLE 1.4 Differences Between DSS and ES.

	DSS	ES
Objective	Assist human decision maker	Replicate (mimic) human advisers and replace them
Who makes the recommendations (decisions)?	The human and/or the system	The system
Major orientation	Decision making	Transfer of expertise (human-machine-human) and rendering of advice
Major query direction	Human queries the machine	Machine queries the human
Nature of support	Personal, groups, and institutional	Personal (mainly), and groups
Manipulation method	Numerical	Symbolic
Characteristics of problem area	Complex, integrated, wide	Narrow domain
Type of problems	Ad hoc, unique	Repetitive
Content of database	Factual knowledge	Procedural and factual knowledge
Reasoning capability	No	Yes, limited
Explanation capability	Limited	Yes

nological, and managerial differences between the two tools. These differences are discussed in detail in Chapter 18 when the integration of the tools is examined.

The disciplines of ES and DSS grew up along parallel, but largely independent, paths. Only recently has the potential of integrating the two been recognized. As a matter of fact, because of the different capabilities of the two tools, they can complement each other, creating a powerful, integrated, computer-based system that can considerably improve managerial decision making.

1.12 Support of Decision Making

The technologies discussed in this book can be used to support managers as independent, stand alone tools, or they can be integrated. The manner in which they are applied depends on the nature of the decision, the nature of the organization, and the individuals involved in the decision making (see Box 1.11). To show the potential support of the techniques discussed in this book we revisit Simon's decision-making process, discussed earlier. The process is shown in Figure 1.7 (slightly modified). We also show the potential support of MSS technologies.

Box 1.11: Benefits of Computerized Decision Support

To summarize and reinforce some of the ideas expressed in this chapter, we present representative quotations from several practitioners:

- Our bank, the nation's fourth largest, would hardly make a major decision without marshalling the facts and figures in computer-generated presentations.
- The PC has become an essential part of the CEO's business life, as essential as the company telephone.
- Managers now have a more broadly perceived need for decision support, and in many cases, a belief that computer systems can be a valuable source of help.
- The basic function of innovational technology is replacement and amplification of mental labor.
- We've got information coming out of our ears and what we need now is some way to make sense of it.
- About $30 billion of DP funds in the U.S.A. goes to support $450 billion of managerial/professional activities, while $50 billion of DP dollars go to support $150 billion of clerical activities. It is time for a change.
- A study of DP departments by IBM indicates that in major companies there is an average 2.5-year backlog for major system applications, with 15 percent experiencing more than 4 years of backlog.
- Information consumers might want to help themselves to information instead of being spoon-fed by professionals.
- Expert systems provide direct answers to questions, not merely information. Furthermore, they are capable of using incomplete or even inconsistent input data to infer a conclusion.

The steps of the process are:

Step A. Problem (Opportunity) Finding. This step involves the collection of information from various sources in order to identify problems and opportunities.

An ES can help in the design of the flow of information to the executive (e.g., what to monitor, when) and in the interpretation of the collected information. Because some of the information is fuzzy, a combination of ES and ANN can be very helpful. The entire area of scanning, monitoring, forecasting (e.g., trends) and interpretation can be greatly helped by computerization. Also, natural language processors (NLP) can be useful in summarizing information.

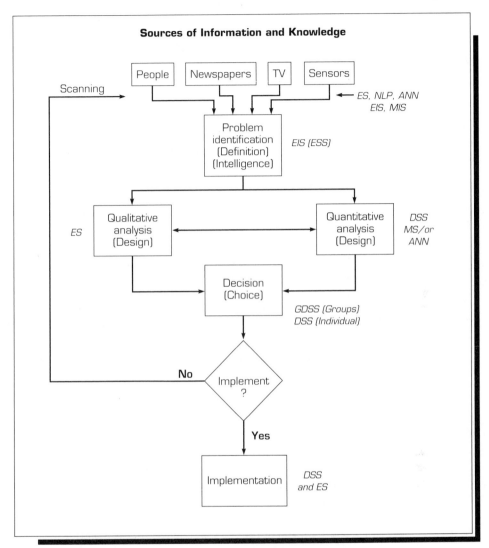

FIGURE 1.7 Computerized Support to the Decision-Making Process.

Step B. Analysis. Once the problem (opportunity) has been identified, a question is posed: what to do about it? At this step an analysis is called for. The analysis can be qualitative or quantitative (or combined). The quantitative analysis can be supported by a DSS and by structured quantitative analysis tools. The qualitative analysis can be supported by an ES.

Step C. Choice. In this step, a decision is made regarding the problem (or opportunity) based on the results of the analysis. The step can be supported by a DSS (if the decision maker is an individual) or by a GDSS (if the decision is made by a group).

Step D. Implementation. In the event that the decision is to implement a proposed solution a DSS and/or ES can provide the support.

Chapter Highlights

- The rate of computerization is increasing rapidly and so is its use by managers.
- Management support systems is a family of technologies that can be used independently or in combination.
- Computerized support for managers is essential, in many cases, for the survival of organizations.
- Managerial decision making is getting complex. Therefore intuition and trial-and-error methods may not be sufficient.
- A framework of decision support divides decision situations into nine categories, depending on the degree of structuredness and managerial activities. Each category is supported differently by computers.
- Structured decisions are supported by standard quantitative analysis methods such as management science and capital budgeting.
- Decision support systems (DSS) is an analytical technology that employs models for the solution of semistructured and unstructured problems.
- All MSS technologies are interactive.
- Most benefits of MSS are intangible.
- Group DSS is a technology that supports the process of making decisions in a group.
- Executive information systems is a technology for supporting executives by providing them with timely, detailed, and easy-to-visualize information.
- Expert systems are advisory systems that attempt to mimic experts.
- The main features of expert systems are the application of knowledge and the use of reasoning.
- Neural computing is a technology that attempts to exhibit learning and pattern recognition.
- All MSS technologies have distinct features, yet their content is debatable and so are their definitions.

Key Words

artificial intelligence
artificial neural
   networks (ANN)
decision support
   systems (DSS)

executive information
   systems (EIS)
expertise
expert systems (ES)
integrated computer
   systems

group DSS (GDSS)
management
   information systems
   (MIS)
management science
   (MS)

management	management support	semistructured
information systems	systems (MSS)	decisions
(MIS)	operations research	structured decisions
management science	(OR)	unstructured decisions
(MS)	productivity	

Questions for Review

1. What caused the latest revolution in management use of computers? List at least two causes.
2. What is a computer-based information system (CBIS)?
3. List the three phases of the decision-making process (according to H.A. Simon).
4. Define DSS.
5. Discuss the major characteristics of DSS.
6. List five major benefits of DSS.
7. Management is often equated with decision making. Why?
8. Discuss the major trends that impact managerial decision making.
9. Define management science.
10. Define MIS and relate it to the decision-making process.
11. Relate MIS and DSS to the degree of structuredness of managerial decisions.
12. Define structured, semistructured, and unstructured decisions.
13. Categorize managerial activities (according to Anthony).
14. Define expert systems.
15. Define expertise.
16. List the major benefits of ES.
17. Trace the evolution of MIS through DSS to ES.
18. Discuss the major differences between MIS and DSS.
19. Discuss the major differences between DSS and ES.
20. Describe the objectives and characteristics of EIS.
21. Describe GDSS.
22. Define EIS and its major functions.
23. Define neural computing.

Questions for Discussion

1. Give additional examples for each cell in Figure 1.3.
2. Read *MIS Week* of September 8, 1982, p. 23, for an article by Hiller titled "Personal Computer Revolution: How to Manage It." Answer the following questions:
   a. How are information centers, office automation, personal computers, and DSS interrelated?
   b. How can the personal computer revolution impact a DSS?

3. Design a computerized system for a brokerage house that trades in securities, conducts research on companies, and provides information and advice to customers (e.g., "buy," "sell," "hold"). In your design, clearly distinguish five parts: transaction processing, MIS, office automation, DSS, and ES. Be sure to deal with input and output information.
   For extra credit: List the hardware and the software that you recommend. List all your assumptions.
   Note: Assume that the brokerage company is a small one with only 20 branches in four different cities. (Submit this special assignment at the end of the semester.)
4. Survey the literature of the last six months to find one application each of DSS, EIS, GDSS, and ES. Summarize the applications on one page and submit it with a photocopy of the article.
5. Observe an organization that you are familiar with. List five decisions it makes in each of the following categories: strategic planning, management control (tactical planning), and operational planning and control.
6. What capabilities are provided by ANN and not by another MSS?

CASE STUDY 1.1:   The Ohio Association of Realtors (OAR)

The OAR headquarters, an organization with 27 employees, serves 33,000 members in Ohio. The association has been using computers since 1970. In 1985 the system was upgraded to a network of mini- and microcomputers that provide the following services and capabilities: (1) Electronic mail is now available in the office. (2) A list (tracking) of all members is updated monthly. (3) Word processing is done. (4) Several periodical reports are generated. (5) Bookkeeping is done. (6) Information about educational activities is mailed to members. (7) Standard mortgage evaluation models are accessed. (8) Executive calendars and calendars of activities are produced. (9) A statistical analysis of home sales is compiled monthly. (10) Standard management science models (like PERT/CPM) are available on the system. A telecommunications package is available for receiving information from commercial databases.

The system is centered around IBM minicomputers and it includes IBM PCs, Compaqs, and a Macintosh. (The Macintosh is used to create flyers, charts, and graphs.) The association uses spreadsheet software for modeling purposes.

Case Questions

1. What kind(s) of CBIS exist at OAR? (Refer to Figure 1.4.)
2. What attributes of DSS or ES can be found in this system? (Be specific!)
3. Can EIS be useful to this organization? Why or why not?

CASE STUDY 1.2:   A Management Support System
Helps the Balsams Grand Resort Hotel

Problem

Providing personalized service is essential in the hospitality industry, especially in expensive hotels and restaurants.* However, labor costs are increasing constantly and so is competition among hotels and restaurants. Thus, personalized service is essential, yet expensive, if provided manually.

Grand Resort Hotel (Dixville Notch, NH)

The Balsams has been a posh resort for 113 years. Located on 15,000 acres just 15 miles from Canada, it's a sprawling 232-room hotel that offers golf, tennis, swimming, ice skating, skiing, dancing, and more. It's the only resort hotel in New England rated Four Stars by Mobil, and Four Diamonds by the AAA. Its managing director, Stephen Barba, is considered a hotelier's hotelier.

Guests at the Balsams are all treated as VIPs, and occupancy consistently runs close to 100 percent during the summer season. But true champions are never satisfied. Management felt they could sell even more effectively if their reservationists could quickly match a specific room (each room is unique) to each guest's preferences (during one brief phone call), and also reserve tee times on the golf course, make other special arrangements, and send the guest a written confirmation the same day. They also knew that such a system could help them avoid the one- and two-day gaps in a room's occupancy that often occur with manual systems. Resort hotels rarely have short-stay guests, so these gaps are frequently left unsold.

The Solution

In January 1986, the Balsams installed an MSS. This highly flexible and versatile system helps to service inquiries, make reservations, assign rooms, generate confirmations and other correspondence, handle deposits, do market analysis, and create management reports. The physical system includes eight Macintosh Plus personal computers and several printers connected to an Explorer workstation. The software is an integrated package composed of an expert system (the first to be used by any hotel in the U.S.), MIS, and multimedia.

The Explorer AI computer has optical disk storage that can hold up to a million guest histories. Presently, it holds information on Balsams guests and stays since 1971—so a reservationist might tell a caller, "I can give you the same

---

Source: Condensed from *Artificial Intelligence Letter* (September 1987), published by Texas Instruments, Data Systems Group, Austin, TX.

room you had in 1981, if you liked it." Only the best concierges in Europe have memories like that.

The system rests on three foundations: the continually updated history of guest stays, complete characteristics of each room, and management's strategies and policies for running the hotel.

In practice, when a guest calls, the reservationist quickly types the guest's name and the display shows all previous stays and the guest's preferences. As soon as a bit of conversation has made the guest "feel at home," the reservationist can switch to a display form and enter the guest's needs and wants—in plain English, an important feature of this easy-to-use system.

Information entered includes dates of stay, rate class, bed type, number of adults and children, section of the hotel preferred, view preferred, and the like. When this is complete, the reservationist enters the one-touch command "Suggest Rooms." The computer reviews its inventory of rooms available on those dates, selects the ones that best fit the guest's wishes *and* the hotel's need to avoid gaps, and lists them in descending rank—with the recommendations that will make everybody happy at the top.

Each room on the recommended list is described, so the reservationist can say, "We can give you room 262, which is our superior class, has a king-size bed, has handicap access as you requested, has a door to room 263, and has a lovely view of our flower gardens, the pool, and the tennis courts." The reservationist is also informed by the display that this stay will fit perfectly between two others, without a gap. Other matching possibilities show gaps, and they're left to guests whose stays will leave no gaps.

Once the guest makes the final decision, the reservationist prints out a confirmation form that's ready to go out in the next mail. It confirms the basic reservation, as all hotels do, but also confirms all the other special arrangements being made for the guest's convenience and enjoyment—and it's signed personally by the reservationist.

Jerry Owen, reservation manager, says, "We're offering the guests better service by meeting their requests and handling the paperwork. And we have much better business forecasts than ever before. I sleep better at night." Owens reports that the system has eliminated the hotel keeper's nightmare, accidental double booking, that is, promising the same room for the same night to two different guests. But the big profit maker is the feature of gap reduction: In the first season, the system cut single-night vacancies more than 50 percent, which translates into roughly six extra guest-nights a day, which means almost $1,000 added profit per day. Management estimates that the system produced $50,000 in its first season. The second season, with the system in full use, looked even better (saving almost $3,000 added profit per day).

The system is popular with the reservationists, too. With the old manual system and a welter of practices, procedures, special rate discounts, and frequent changes, it typically took two months to train a new reservationist. The first reservationist to start work after the system was installed became proficient in a week. Probably more important, reservationists are now free to concentrate on extending gracious and creative hospitality rather than being preoccupied with the hectic business of making the manual scheduling system work.

The artificial intelligence component makes the system easy to learn. Also it is easy to change the computer program as the market changes (without the need for a programmer). Management can easily modify rates, introduce new packages, modify minimum stays, adjust deposit policies, and try new room assignment guidelines. Owen says, "We can quickly make changes. It doesn't take long, and it doesn't screw up existing operations."

Balsams management is known for creative marketing skill, and the system serves marketing well. To cite just one of many examples, management is seeking to increase group business. The system is an excellent tool for this, because it provides an excellent database for cross-marketing—identifying which social guests may be contacts for obtaining group business, and which group guests to invite back as social guests.

There's a nice symmetry to this application of artificial intelligence: The most human-oriented computer concept is now serving one of the most human-oriented businesses, and delighting all the humans it touches.

Some additional facts:

1. This is a typical integrated MSS. The major components are DSS, an expert system, and a traditional MIS reporting system (e.g., accounting).

2. The system is rule based, written in Texas Instrument's shell. This allows hotel management to maintain the system; there is no need for a programmer.

3. The total development cost of the system is estimated to be about $100,000.

4. The initial needs assessment for the system pointed out a possibility of automating food-service management. A good food-service manager is "worth" between $200,000 and $400,000 in profit in hotels. AI technology was not found to be appropriate, however, since there are many restaurant computer systems on the market that are fairly useful.

Case Questions

1. Identify the various MSS technologies used in this system.
2. Identify the multimedia portions of the system.
3. Why is there a need for both the Macintosh Plus and the Explorer machines?
4. List the benefits to the customers.
5. List the benefits to the company.
6. What type of system is this?
7. The system increases the productivity of the reservationists. Why are they happy with the system?
8. Discuss the decision support opportunities in this system.
9. Why is AI considered the "most human-oriented computer concept"?
10. Discuss the relationship between the software vendor and the Balsams.

11. It is said that the system provides tight control yet more flexibility to management. Explain.
12. Why is AI inappropriate for food-service management?

References and Bibliography

1. Andriole, S. J. *Handbook of Decision Support Systems.* Summit, PA: TAB Professional Books, 1989.
2. Anthony, R. N. *Planning and Control Systems: A Framework for Analysis.* Cambridge, MA: Harvard University Graduate School of Business, 1965.
3. Chung, C. "A Network of Management Support Systems." *Omega,* Vol. 13, No. 4, 1988.
4. Coll, R., et al. "The Effect of Computerized Decision Aids on Decision Time and Decision Quality." *Information and Management,* February 1991.
5. Forgionne, G. A. "Decision Technology Systems: A Step toward Complete Decision Support." *Information Systems Management,* Fall 1991.
6. Gorry, G. M., and M. S. Scott-Morton. "A Framework for Management Information Systems." *Sloan Management Review,* Fall 1971.
7. Hogue, J. T., and H. J. Watson. "Management's Role in the Approval and Administration of Decision Support Systems." *MIS Quarterly,* June 1983.
8. Keen, P. G. W., and M. S. Scott-Morton. *Decision Support Systems, An Organizational Perspective.* Reading, MA: Addison-Wesley, 1978.
9. Keen, P. G. W., and L. A. Woodman. "What to Do With All Those Micros?" *Harvard Business Review,* 1984.
10. Kroeber, D. W., and H. J. Watson. *Computer-based Information Systems: A Management Approach.* 2nd ed. New York: Macmillan, 1988.
11. Martin, J. *Applications Development Without Programmers.* Englewood Cliffs, NJ: Prentice-Hall, 1982.
12. McLean, E. R. *Decision Support Systems and Managerial Decision Making.* Working paper 1–83, Graduate School of Management, UCLA, Los Angeles, CA, 1982.
13. Olson, D. L., and J. F. Courtney. *Decision Support Models and Expert System.* New York: Macmillan, 1992.
14. Rockart, J. F., and D. W. DeLong, *Executive Support Systems.* Homewood, IL: Dow-Jones, Irwin, 1988.
15. Scott-Morton, M. S. *Management Decision Systems: Computer-Based Support for Decision Making.* Cambridge, MA: Division of Research, Harvard University, 1971.
16. Simon, H. *The New Science of Management Decision.* Englewood Cliffs, NJ: Prentice-Hall, 1977.
17. Turban, E., and J. Meredith. *Fundamentals of Management Science.* 6th ed. Homewood, IL: Irwin, 1994.
18. Turban, E. *Expert Systems and Applied Artificial Intelligence.* New York: Macmillan, 1992.

19. Watson, H. J., et al. (eds). *Executive Support Systems*. New York: Wiley and Sons, 1992.

20. Zeidenberg, M. *Neural Computing in Artificial Intelligence*. Englewood Cliffs, NJ: Prentice-Hall, 1990.

21. *Personal Computing*, April 1989.

APPENDIX 1-A: Computer-Based Information Systems in a Personnel Department

The purpose of this appendix is to illustrate the content of typical CBIS in a personnel department. The classification is somewhat arbitrary since we do not have information on the content of each task. In reality these tasks can be placed in different categories or one task can be classified in two categories, since the boundaries of the categories are not precise and several real-life systems combine several of the categories.

Category	Task
Transaction Processing	Keep inventory of personnel. Prepare payroll; compute salaries and incentive plans.
Management Information System	Prepare summary reports (e.g., average salaries in town). Conduct performance tracking of employees, labor budget. Do preparation, monitoring, and analysis. Perform short-term scheduling. Match positions and candidates. Monitor positions control systems. Do fringe benefits monitoring and control.
Decision Support Systems	Prepare special reports (e.g., safety records, equal opportunity achievements). Do long-range planning for human resources. Design a compensation plan. Provide quantitative support of labor-management negotiation.
Expert Systems	Obtain advice on legal and tax implications during management-labor negotiations. Develop a social responsibility plan. Select training media. Design comprehensive training programs.

Office Automation	Do online job interviews and recruiting, schedule meetings, maintain mailing lists, schedule training, use for electronic mail, receive labor news and statistics online, prepare training materials.
Executive Information System	Exists at the corporate level only. Will measure key performance indicators of the department (such as dollar per employee).
Group DSS	Can be used for controversial major decisions (e.g., personnel policies).
Neural Computing	Screen applicants for jobs. Analyze reasons why people leave the company (find pattern).

Chapter 2

Decision Making, Systems, Modeling, and Support

The major focus of this book is computerized support of decision making. The purpose of this chapter is to provide the necessary conceptual foundations regarding decision making and systems approach, and how support is provided. This chapter covers the following topics:

2.1   Decision Making*

Decision making is a process of choosing among alternative courses of action for the purpose of attaining a goal or goals. According to Herbert A. Simon [18], managerial decision making is synonymous with the whole process of management. To illustrate the idea, let us examine the important managerial function of planning. Planning involves a series of decisions, for example, What should be done? When? How? Where? By whom? Hence, planning implies decision making. Other functions in the management process like organizing and controlling can also be viewed as decision making.

Decision Making and Problem Solving

Much confusion exists between the terms *decision making* and *problem solving*. One way to distinguish between them is to examine the phases of the decision process. These phases are (1) intelligence, (2) design, (3) choice, and (4) implementation. One school of thought considers the entire process (steps 1–4) as problem solving; the choice step is considered decision making. Another viewpoint is that steps 1–3 constitute decision making that ends with a recommendation—whereas problem solving additionally includes implementation of the recommendation (step 4). The terms decision making and problem solving are used here interchangeably.

2.2   Systems

The names DSS, GDSS, EIS, and ES include the term *systems*. A system is a collection of objects such as people, resources, concepts, and procedures intended to perform an identifiable function or to serve a goal. A clear definition of that function is most important for the design of MSS. For instance, the purpose of an air defense system is to protect ground targets, not just to destroy attacking aircraft or missiles.

The notion of levels (or a hierarchy) of systems reflects that all systems are actually subsystems, since all are contained within some larger system. For example, a bank includes such subsystems as (1) the commercial loan department, (2) the consumer loan department, (3) the savings department, and (4) the operations department. The bank itself may also be a subsidiary of a holding corporation, such as Bank of America, which is a subsystem of the California banking system, which is a part of the national banking system, which is a part of the national economy, and so on. The interconnections and interactions among the subsystems are termed *interfaces*.

---

*Some of the material in this chapter was adapted, with permission, from Turban and Meredith [21].

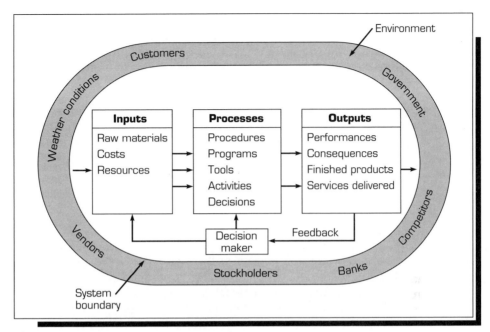

FIGURE 2.1   The System and Its Environment.

The Structure of a System

Systems are divided into three distinct parts: inputs, processes, and outputs. They are surrounded by an environment (Figure 2.1) and frequently include a feedback mechanism. In addition, a human, the decision maker, is considered a part of the system.

Inputs. Inputs include those elements that enter the system. Examples of inputs are raw materials entering a chemical plant, patients admitted to a hospital, or data input into a computer.

Processes. All the elements necessary to convert or transform the inputs into outputs are included in the processes. For example, in a chemical plant a process may include heating the materials, using operating procedures, employing the materials handling subsystem, and using employees and machines. In a hospital the process may include conducting tests and performing a surgery. In a computer a process may include activating commands, executing computations, and storing information.

Outputs. Outputs describe the finished products or the consequences of being in the system. For example, fertilizers are one output of a chemical plant, cured people are an output of a hospital, and reports may be the output of a computerized system.

Feedback. There is a flow of information from the output component to the decision maker concerning the system's output or performance. Based on this information the decision maker, who acts as a control, may decide to modify the inputs or the processes, or both. This flow, which appears as a closed loop (Figure 2.1), is termed *feedback*.

The Environment. The environment of the system is composed of several elements that lie outside it in the sense that they are not inputs, outputs, or processes. However, they have an impact on the system's performance and consequently on the attainment of its goals. One way to identify the elements of the environment is by answering two questions as suggested by Churchman [4]:

1. Is the element matter relative to the system's goals?
2. Is it possible for the decision maker to significantly manipulate this element?

If and only if the answer to the first question is *yes*, but the answer to the second is *no*, the element should be considered part of the environment. Environmental elements can be social, political, legal, physical, and economical. For example, in the case of a chemical plant the suppliers, competitors, and customers are elements of the environment. In a decision support system that deals with capital budgeting, the Dow-Jones database, the manufacturing system of the company, a telecommunications network, and the personnel department may represent some elements of the environment.

The Boundary. A system is separated from its environment by a boundary. The system is inside the boundary whereas the environment lies outside. Boundaries may be physical (e.g., the system is a department in Building C), or the boundary may be some nonphysical factor. For example, a system can be bounded by time. In such a case we may analyze an organization for a period of only one year.

When systems are studied it is often necessary to arbitrarily define the boundaries in order to simplify the analysis. Such boundaries are related to the concepts of closed and open systems.

Closed and Open Systems. Because every system can be considered a subsystem of another, the application of system analysis may never end. Therefore it is necessary, as a matter of practicality, to confine the system analysis to defined manageable boundaries. Such confinement is termed *closing* the system.

A *closed system* represents one extreme along a continuum (the *open system* is at the other extreme), which reflects the degree of independence of systems. A closed system is totally independent, whereas an open system is very dependent on its environment (and/or other systems). The open system accepts inputs (information, energy, materials) from the environment and may deliver outputs into the environment.

When determining the impact of decisions on an open system, we must check the environment, the related systems, and vice versa. In a closed system, however, it is not necessary to conduct such checks because it is assumed that the system is isolated. Traditional computer systems like transaction processing systems (TPS) are considered to be closed systems. Many management science models are also confined to closed systems.

A special type of closed system is called the *black box*. In such a system inputs and outputs are well defined but the process itself is not specified. Many managers like to treat computer systems as a black box; in other words, they do not care how the computer works. They consider it as they would consider a telephone or an elevator. They use these devices but do not care how they operate.

Decision support systems attempt to deal with systems that are fairly open. Such systems are complex, and during their analysis it is necessary to check the impacts on and from the environment. To illustrate the difference between a DSS and a management science approach, let us look at an inventory system (Table 2.1), which compares a well-known inventory model, the economic order quantity (EOQ) model, with a hypothetical DSS for an inventory system.

System Effectiveness and Efficiency

Systems are evaluated and analyzed with two major classes of performance measurement: effectiveness and efficiency.

Effectiveness is the degree to which goals are achieved. It is therefore concerned with the results or the outputs of a system. These outputs may be total sales of a company or of a salesperson, for example.

Efficiency is a measure of the use of inputs (or resources) to achieve results; for example, how much money is used to generate a certain level of sales.

An interesting way to distinguish between the two terms was proposed by Peter Drucker, who makes the following distinction:

Effectiveness = doing the "right" thing
Efficiency = doing the "thing" right

An important characteristic of DSS and ES is their emphasis on the effectiveness, or "goodness," of the decision produced, rather than on the compu-

TABLE 2.1 A Closed versus an Open Inventory System

Management Science, EOQ (Closed System)	DSS (Open System)
Constant demand, constant per unit cost, constant lead time.	Variable demand influenced by many factors; cost can be changed any day; lead time varies and is difficult to predict.
Vendors and users are excluded from the analysis.	Vendors and users are being considered.
Weather and other environmental factors are ignored.	Weather conditions could determine both demand and lead time.

tational efficiency, which is usually a major concern of a transaction processing system.

In many managerial systems, and especially those involving the delivery of human services (such as education, health, or recreation), the measurement of the system's effectiveness and efficiency is a major problem. The reason for the difficulty is due to the existence of several often nonquantifiable, conflicting goals. In addition, indirect costs may be involved. For further discussion and references, see Van Gigch [23].

2.3 Models

A major characteristic of decision support systems is the inclusion of a modeling capability. The basic idea is to execute the DSS analysis on a model of reality rather than on reality itself.

A *model* is a simplified representation or abstraction of reality. It is usually simplified because reality is too complex to copy exactly and because much of the complexity is actually irrelevant to the specific problem. The characteristics of simplification and representation are difficult to achieve simultaneously in practice (they *contradict* each other). For example, the EOQ model of Table 2.1 is simple but inadequately representative of many real life inventory systems.

The representation of systems or problems through models can be done at various degrees of abstraction; therefore models are classified, according to their degree of abstraction, into three groups.

Iconic (Scale) Models. An iconic model—the least abstract model—is a physical replica of a system, usually based on a different scale from the original. Iconic models may appear to scale in three dimensions such as that of an airplane, car, bridge, or production line. Photographs are another type of iconic scale model but in only two dimensions. Object-oriented programming (Chapter 14) is another example of the use of icons.

Analog Models. An analog model does not look like the real system but behaves like it. It is more abstract than an iconic model and is considered a symbolic representation of reality. These are usually two-dimensional charts or diagrams: that is, they could be physical models, but the shape of the model differs from that of the actual system. Some examples:

- Organization charts that depict structure, authority, and responsibility relationships
- A map where different colors represent water or mountains
- Stock market charts
- Blueprints of a machine or a house
- A speedometer
- A thermometer.

A special class of analog modeling is symbolic logic. This topic is revisited in Chapter 11.

Mathematical (Quantitative) Models. The complexity of relationships in many organizational systems cannot be represented with icons or analogically, or such representation may be cumbersome and time-consuming. Therefore a more abstract model is used with the aid of mathematics. Most DSS analysis is executed numerically with the aid of mathematical or other quantitative models.

The Benefits of Models

The following are the major reasons why an MSS employs models:

1. The cost of the modeling analysis is much lower than the cost of a similar experimentation conducted with a real system.
2. Models enable the compression of time. Years of operations can be simulated in minutes of computer time.
3. Manipulation of the model (changing variables) is much easier than manipulating a real system. Experimentation is therefore easier to conduct and it does not interfere with the daily operation of the organization.
4. The cost of making mistakes during a trial-and-error experiment is much less when models are used rather than real systems.
5. Today's environment involves considerable uncertainty. The use of modeling allows a manager to calculate the risks involved in specific actions.
6. The use of mathematical models enables the analysis of a very large, sometimes infinite number of possible solutions. With today's advanced technology and communications, managers frequently have a large number of alternatives to choose from.
7. Models enhance and reinforce learning and enhance training.

Note: With recent advances in computer graphics, there is an increased tendency to use iconic and analog models to complement mathematical modeling in MSS. For example, visual simulation (see Chapter 6) combines the three types of models.

2.4   The Modeling Process—A Preview

Ma-Pa Groceries is a small neighborhood food store on the West Side of New York City. Bob and Nancy, the owners, are very sensitive to their clients' wishes. They also are concerned with the financial viability of the store. A major product they sell is bread. Bread causes them headaches. Some days there is not enough bread; other days bread is overstocked so they have to sell it the next day at a loss. Their problem is simple: How much bread to stock each day?

Bob and Nancy can apply several solution approaches to the problem. Four such approaches are: trial-and-error, simulation, optimization, and heuristics.

a. Trial and Error with the Real Systems. In this approach the owners try to learn from experimentation. Namely, they change the quantities of bread stocked and observe what happens. If they find they are short on bread too often, they will increase the quantities ordered. If they find that too much bread is left, they will decrease the quantities ordered. Sooner or later they will find out how much bread to order.

Although this approach may be very successful for Bob and Nancy, it may fail in many other cases. Trial-and-error may not work if one or more of the following conditions exists:

1. There are too many alternatives ("trials") to experiment with.
2. The cost of making errors (which is part of the trial-and-error approach) is very high.
3. The environment itself keeps changing. Therefore learning from experience is difficult or even impossible. By the time you have experimented with all the alternatives, the environmental conditions have changed—you have a new "ball game" to deal with.

In such cases Nancy and Bob can try modeling approaches; instead of dealing with the real system, they will deal with a model of it. Two common types of modeling approaches they can use are simulation and optimization.

b. Simulation. In this case Nancy and Bob play a make-believe game. They ask themselves a question: *If* we order 300 loaves of bread, *what* will the results be? The results of course will depend on the demand, which may be constant or may vary. Simulation can deal with both situations. The model that represents Ma-Pa Groceries is used to calculate results like total profit (or loss), percentage of unsatisfied customers, and amount of leftovers. A big advantage of modeling is that months of operations can be simulated in seconds (if a computer is used). Next, Nancy and Bob change the order quantity to 350, 400, 200, 250, and so on. They "run the store" with each order quantity for several months and calculate the results. Finally, they compare the results of each order quantity and decide how much to order.

The problem with the simulation approach is that once the experiment is completed, there is no guarantee that the selected order level is the best one. It will be the best of all levels experimented; but it is possible that the true best level (the optimal one) is 675, a level not checked in the experiment. Another problem with the simulation is that Nancy and Bob will need professional help to design the simulation study, to program it on a computer, and to statistically interpret the results. The cost may not be justified. However, if Nancy and Bob learned DSS they could probably do the job by themselves.

c. Optimization. A more sophisticated solution approach to the problem is to use an optimization model. Ideally such a model will generate in seconds an optimal (best) order level, say, 675. Usually there is a very user-friendly software to conduct such an analysis. The limitation of optimization is that it will work only if the problem is very structured. Specifically, such a model will specify the required input data and the mathematical relationship in a precise manner. Obviously if reality differs significantly from the model optimization cannot be used.

As stated earlier, DSS deals with unstructured problems. Does this preclude optimization? Not necessarily. Many times it is possible to break a problem into subproblems, some of which are structured enough to justify optimization. Also, optimization can be combined with simulation for the solution of complex problems.

d. Heuristics. Nancy and Bob can use some rules of thumb. For example, they can order today the average daily quantity demand over the last seven days. Another rule that they can use is to order each day the quantity demanded on the same day one week before.

The Decision-Making Process. To better understand the modeling process, it is advisable to follow the decision-making process which, according to Simon [18], involves three major phases: intelligence, design, and choice. A fourth phase, implementation, was added later. A conceptual picture of the modeling process is shown in Figure 2.2. There is a continuous flow of activities from intelligence to design to choice (bold lines), but at any phase there may be a return to a previous phase.

The modeling process starts with the intelligence phase where reality is examined and the problem is identified and defined. In the design phase a model that represents the system is constructed. This is done by making assumptions that simplify reality and by writing the relationships among all variables. The model then is validated and criteria are set for the evaluation of the alternative courses of action that are also being identified. The choice phase includes a proposed solution of the model (not of the problem that it represents). This solution is being tested "on paper" (that is, in the modeling framework). Once the proposed solution seems to be reasonable, it is ready for the last phase—implementation. Successful implementation results in solving the original problem. Failure leads to a return to the modeling process. Detailed discussion of the process is given in the following sections.

2.5   The Intelligence Phase

Intelligence entails scanning the environment, either intermittently or continuously. It includes several activities aimed at identifying problem situations or opportunities.

Finding the Problem. The intelligence phase begins with the identification of organizational goals and objectives. Problems arise out of dissatisfaction with the way things are going. Such dissatisfaction is the result of a difference between what we desire and what is (or is not) happening. In this phase, one attempts to find out if a problem exists, find the symptoms of the problem, find

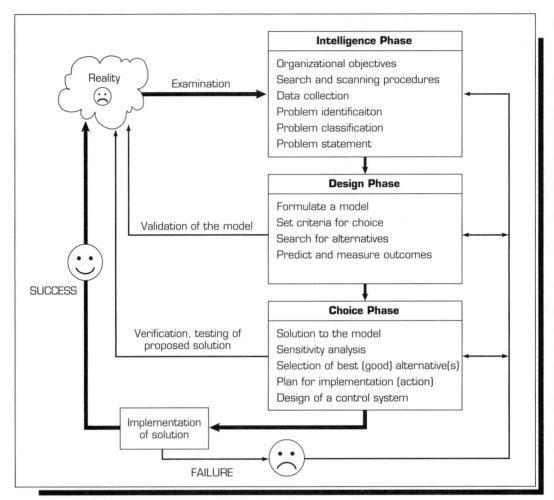

FIGURE 2.2   The Decision-Making/Modeling Process.

its magnitude, and define the problem. Often what is described as a problem (e.g., excessive costs) may be only a symptom of a problem (e.g., improper inventory levels). Because so-called real world problems are usually complicated by many interrelated factors, it is sometimes difficult to distinguish between the symptoms and the real problem.

The existence of a problem in an organization can be appraised by monitoring and analyzing the organization's (or department's) productivity level. The measurement of productivity, as well as the construction of the model, are based on data. The collection of existing data and the estimation of future data is one of the most difficult steps in the analysis. Following are some of the issues that may arise during data collection and estimation:

1. Outcome (or results) may occur over an extended period of time. As a result, revenues (or profits) and expenses will be recorded at different

points in time. To overcome this difficulty a present-value approach should be used.

2. It is often necessary to use a subjective approach to data estimation.
3. It is assumed that future data will be similar to historical ones. If not, it is necessary to predict the nature of the change and include it in the analysis.

Once the preliminary investigation is completed it is possible to determine whether a problem really exists, where it is located, and how significant it is (i.e., what is the priority of the problem). In addition, the intelligence phase may involve other activities such as problem classification, problem decomposition, and determination of problem ownership.

The Classification. This activity is the conceptualization of a problem in an attempt to classify it into a definable category. An important classification is according to the degree of structuredness evident in the problem.

Programmed versus Nonprogrammed Problems. Herbert A. Simon [18] has distinguished two extreme situations regarding structuredness of decision problems. At one end of the spectrum are the well-structured problems that are repetitive and routine, and for which standard models have been worked out. Simon termed these *programmed problems.* Examples of such problems are weekly scheduling of employees and monthly determination of cash flow and selection of an inventory level for a specific item. At the other end of the spectrum are the poorly structured (called *nonprogrammed* by Simon) *problems,* which are novel and nonrecurrent. For example, acquisition and merger decisions, undertaking a complex research and development project, reorganizing a corporation, and opening a university are all nonstructured problems.

Problem Decomposition. Many complex problems can be broken apart into subproblems. Solving the simpler subproblem may help in solving the complex problem. Such an approach also facilitates communication between the people involved in the solution process.

To Whom a Problem Belongs. In the intelligence phase, it is important to establish the "ownership" of the problem. A problem exists in an organization only if the organization has the capability to solve it. For example, many companies feel that they have a problem because interest rates are too high. Since interest rate levels are determined at the national level and most companies can do nothing about them, high interest rates are the problem of the federal government and not of a specific company. The problem that companies face is how to operate in an environment in which the interest rate is high. For the individual company the interest rate level is an uncontrollable factor.

The intelligence phase ends with a problem statement. At that time the design phase can be started.

2.6   The Design Phase

The design phase involves generating, developing, and analyzing possible courses of action. This includes activities such as understanding the problem and testing solutions for feasibility. Also in this phase, a model of the problem situation is constructed, tested, and validated.

Modeling involves the conceptualization of the problem and its abstraction to a quantitative and/or qualitative form. In case of a mathematical model, the dependent and independent variables are identified and the equations describing their relationships are established. Simplifications are made, whenever necessary, through a set of assumptions. For example, a relationship between two variables may be assumed to be linear. It is necessary to find a proper balance between the level of simplification of the model and the representation of reality. A simpler model leads to easier manipulations and faster solution, but is also less representative of the real problem.

The task of modeling involves a combination of art and science. The following topics of modeling are presented here as they relate to quantitative models (mathematical, financial, etc.):

- The components of the model
- The structure of the model
- Selection of a principle of choice (criteria for evaluation)
- Developing (generating) alternatives
- Predicting outcomes
- Measuring outcomes
- Scenarios.

The Components of Quantitative Models

All models are comprised of three basic components: decision variables, uncontrollable variables (and/or parameters), and result (outcome) variables (see Figure 2.3). These components are connected by mathematical relationships. In a nonquantitative model the relationships are symbolic or qualitative.

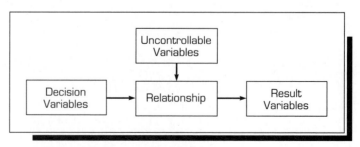

FIGURE 2.3   The General Structure of a Model.

TABLE 2.2 Examples of the Components of Models.

Area	Decision Variables	Result Variables	Uncontrollable Variables and Parameters
Financial investment	Investment alternatives and amounts Period of investment Timing of investment	Total profit Rate of return Earnings/share Liquidity	Inflation rate Prime rate Competition
Marketing	Advertising budget Product lines	Market share Customer satisfaction	Customers' income Competitors' actions
Manufacturing	Products and amounts Inventory levels Compensation program	Total cost Quality level Employee satisfaction	Machine capacity Technology Materials prices
Accounting	Use of computers Audit schedule Depreciation schedule	Data processing cost Error rate	Computer technology Tax rates Legal requirements
Transportation	Shipments schedule	Total transport cost	Delivery distance Regulations
Services	Staffing levels	Customer satisfaction	Demand for services

As can be seen in Figure 2.3, the results (or outcome) of decisions are determined by (1) the decision being made; (2) other factors that are uncontrollable by the decision maker; and (3) by the relationships among variables.

Result Variables. These variables reflect the level of effectiveness of the system; that is, they indicate how well the system performs or attains its goals. Examples of result variables are shown in Table 2.2. The result variables are considered to be dependent variables.*

Decision Variables. Decision variables describe the alternative courses of action. For example, in an investment problem, investing in bonds is a decision variable. In a scheduling problem, the decision variables are people and jobs. The values of these variables are determined by the decision maker. Other examples include the number of tellers to use in a bank (more are listed in Table 2.2). Decision variables are classified mathematically as independent variables (or unknown variables). An aim of DSS is to find good enough, or possibly the best, values for these decision variables.

Uncontrollable Variables or Parameters. In any decision situation there are factors that affect the result variables but *are not under the control* of the de-

*A dependent variable means that for the event described by this variable to occur, another event must occur first. In this case the result variables depend on the occurrence of the decision and the uncontrollable variables.

cision maker. These factors can be either fixed, and then they are called parameters, or they can vary, and then they are called variables. Examples are the prime interest rate, a city's building code, tax regulations, and prices of utilities (others are shown in Table 2.2). Most of these factors are uncontrollable because they emanate from the environment surrounding the decision maker. These variables are also classified as **independent variables** since they affect the dependent (result) variables. Some of these variables place limits on the decision maker, and, therefore, are called the *constraints* of the problem.

Intermediate Variables. Intermediate variables are any variables necessary to link the decision variables to the results. Sometimes they reflect intermediate outcomes. For example, in determining machine scheduling, spoilage is an intermediate variable while total profit is the result variable (spoilage determines the total profit).

Another example is employee salaries or wages, which is a decision variable. It determines employees' satisfaction (intermediate outcome), which determines productivity level (result).

The Structure of Quantitative Models

The components of a quantitative model are tied together by sets of mathematical expressions such as equations or inequalities.

A simple financial-type model may look like this: $P = R - C$, where P stands for profit, R stands for revenue, and C stands for cost. Another well-known financial-type model is a present-value model, which may look like this:

$$P = \frac{F}{(1 + i)^n}$$

where:

P = the present value
F = a future single payment in dollars
i = interest rate
n = number of years

Using this model, one can find, for example, the present value of a payment of $100,000, to be made five years from today, considering 10 percent interest rate, to be:

$$P = \frac{100,000}{(1.1)^5} = \$62,110$$

A more complex product-mix model is presented next. This model is a management science optimization model that helps determine the best production plan.

Example: The Product-Mix Model

MBI Corporation makes special computers. A decision must be made: How many computers should be produced next month in the Boston plant? Two types of computers are considered: PC-7, which requires 300 days of labor and $10,000 in materials; and PC-8, which requires 500 days of labor and $15,000 in materials. The profit contribution of PC-7 is $8,000, whereas that of PC-8 is $12,000. Currently, the plant has a capacity of 200,000 working days per month while the material budget is $8,000,000 per month. Marketing requires that at least 100 units of PC-8 be produced while the market will absorb any quantity produced. The problem is how many units of PC-7 and how many units of PC-8 to produce each month to maximize the company's profits.

Modeling. A standard mathematical model used in this case is called **linear programming** (see Box 2.1). It has three components:

Decision variables: X_1 = units of PC-7 to be produced; X_2 = units of PC-8.
Result variable: The total profit.
   The objective is to maximize total profit.
Z = Total profit: $8,000 X_1 + 12,000 X_2$
Uncontrollable constraints:
   Labor constraint: $300 X_1 + 500 X_2 \leq 200,000$ (in days)
   Budget constraint: $10,000 X_1 + 15,000 X_2 \leq 8,000,000$ (in dollars)
   Marketing requirement: $X_1 \geq 100$ (in units)
   This information is summarized in Figure 2.4.
   Solution. The solution to this problem (derived by a computer) is X_1 = 666,667, X_2 = 0, Profit = $5,333,333.

Box 2.1: Linear Programming

Linear programming is perhaps the best-known optimization model. It deals with optimal allocation of resources among competing activities. The allocation problem is presented in the model as follows:

   The problem is to find the value of the decision variables X_1, X_2, and so on (Figure 2.4) such that the value of the result variable Z is maximized, subject to a set of linear constraints that express the technology, market conditions, and other uncontrollable variables. The mathematical relationships are all linear equations and inequalities. Theoretically, there are an infinite number of possible solutions to any allocation problem of this type. Using special mathematical procedures, the linear programming approach applies a unique search procedure that finds the best solution(s) in a matter of seconds. Furthermore, the solution approach provides automatic sensitivity analysis (see Section 2.8).

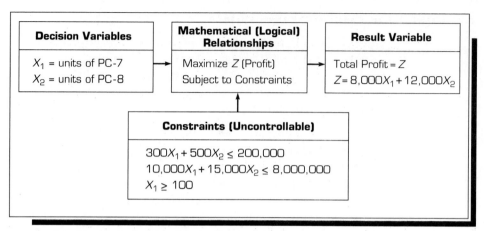

FIGURE 2.4 Mathematical Model of a Product Mix.

The model of the product mix just presented has an infinite number of possible solutions. Assuming that a production plan is not restricted to whole numbers—which is a reasonable assumption in a monthly production plan—finding the one that maximizes total profit was done with linear programming. Determining which model to use relates to the discussion of our next topic, the principle of choice.

The Principle of Choice

The evaluation of alternatives and the final choice depend on the type of criteria we want to use. Are we trying to get the best solution? Or will the "good enough" result be sufficient? This issue is discussed next.

Selection of a Principle of Choice. A principle of choice refers to a decision regarding the acceptability of a solution approach. Is the best possible alternative sought, or will a "good enough" solution do? Are we willing to assume risk or do we prefer a conservative low risk approach? Of the various principles of choice, two are of prime interest: normative and descriptive.

Normative Models. The chosen alternative is demonstrably the best of all possible alternatives. To find it, one should examine all alternatives and *prove* that the one selected is indeed the best. This process is basically what we call optimization (see Box 2.2). In operational terms, optimization can be achieved in one of three ways:

- Get the highest level (maximization) of goal attainment from a given set of resources. For example, which alternative will yield the maximum profit from an investment of $1,000,000?
- Find the alternative with the highest ratio (maximization) of goal attain-

Box 2.2: Optimization Models

- Assignment
- Dynamic programming
- Goal programming
- Investment (maximize rate of return)
- Linear programming
- Maintenance (minimize cost of maintenance)
- Network models
- Nonlinear programming
- Replacement (capital budgeting)
- Simple inventory models (e.g., economic order quantity)
- Transportation

ment to cost (e.g., profit per dollar invested), or in other words, maximize productivity.

- Find the alternative with the lowest cost (or other resources) that will fulfill a required level of goal(s) (minimization). For example, if your task is to build a product to certain specifications, which method will accomplish this goal with the least cost?

Normative decision theory is based on the following assumptions:

- Humans are economic beings whose objective is to maximize the attainment of goals; that is, the decision maker is rational.
- In a given decision situation, all viable alternative courses of action and their consequences, or at least the probability and the values of the consequences, are known.
- Decision makers have an order or preference that enables them to rank the desirability of all consequences of the analysis.

Suboptimization. By definition, optimization requires the decision maker to consider the impact of each alternative course of action on the entire organization. The reason for this is that a decision made in one area may have significant effects in other areas. Take as an example a production department that plans its own schedule. For that department it would be beneficial to produce only a few products but in large quantities to reduce manufacturing costs. However, such a plan may result in large, costly inventories and marketing difficulties owing to the lack of a variety of products.

Using a systems point of view affords consideration of the impact on the entire system. Thus the production department should make its plans in conjunction with other departments. Such an approach, however, may require a complicated, expensive, and time-consuming analysis. As a matter of practice the MSS builder may "close" the system within narrow boundaries, considering only part of the organization under study (the production department in this case). Such an approach is called *suboptimization*.

If a suboptimization decision is made in one part of the organization without consideration of the rest of the organization, then a solution that is optimal from the point of view of that part may be suboptimal from the point of view of the whole. This may produce inferior or even damaging results.

Suboptimization, however, may still be a very practical approach, and many problems are first approached from this perspective. The primary reason for this is that analyzing only a portion of a system allows some tentative conclusions to be made without bogging down the organization in a deluge of details. Once a solution is proposed, its potential effects on the remaining departments of the organization can be checked. If no significant negative effects are found, the solution may then be adopted. This approach fits nicely with the iterative (step-by-step) development approach to DSS.

Descriptive Models. Descriptive models (see Box 2.3) describe things as they are, or as they are believed to be. Such models are extremely useful in DSS for investigating the consequences of various alternative courses of action under different configurations of **inputs** and processes. However, because a descriptive analysis checks the performance of the system for a given set of alternatives (rather than for *all* alternatives), there is no guarantee that an alternative selected with the aid of a descriptive analysis is optimal. In many cases it is only satisfactory or "good enough." Simulation is probably the most recognized example of descriptive modeling.

Good Enough or "Satisficing." Most human decision making, according to Simon [18], whether organizational or individual, involves a willingness to settle for a satisfactory solution, "something less than the best." In a "satisficing" mode the decision maker sets up an aspiration, goal, or desired level of perfor-

Box 2.3: Descriptive Models

- Information flow
- Scenario analysis
- Financial planning
- Inventory management (complex)
- Markov analysis (predictions)
- Environmental impact analysis
- Simulation (different types)
- Technological forecasting
- Waiting line management

mance and then searches the alternatives until one is found that achieves this level. The usual reasons for satisficing are lack of time or ability to achieve optimization as well as unwillingness to pay the price for the required information.

A related concept is that of *bounded rationality*. Humans have a limited capacity for rational thinking; they generally construct a simplified model of the real situation in order to deal with it. Their behavior with respect to the simplified model may be rational. However, it does not follow that the rational solution for the simplified model is rational in the real world situation. Rationality is bounded not only by limitations on human processing capacities but also by individual differences such as age, education, and attitudes. Bounded rationality is the cause of many models being descriptive rather than normative.

Developing (Generating) Alternatives

A significant part of the process of model building is generating alternatives. In optimization models (such as linear programming) the alternatives may be generated automatically by the model. In most DSS situations, however, it is necessary to generate alternatives. This can be a lengthy process that involves search and creativity, and it takes time and costs money. Issues such as when to stop generating alternatives can be very important. Generating alternatives is heavily dependent on the availability and cost of information and requires expertise in the problem area. This is the least formal portion of problem solving. When creativity is used to generate alternatives it can be enhanced by aids like brainstorming, group dynamics sessions, checklists, and special training.

Notice that the search for alternatives usually comes *after* the criteria for evaluating the alternatives were determined. This sequence can reduce the search for alternatives and the efforts involved in the evaluation of the alternatives. Alternatives can be generated by using **heuristics.** For example, real estate is a viable alternative in inflationary periods. Generating alternatives is done manually in most DSS; however, as will be shown in Chapter 9, this activity can be automated.

Predicting the Outcome of Each Alternative

To evaluate and compare alternatives it is necessary to predict the future outcome of each proposed alternative. Decision situations are frequently classified on the basis of what the decision maker knows (or believes) about the forecasted results. It is customary to classify this knowledge into three categories (see Figure 2.5), ranging from complete knowledge, on the left, to ignorance, on the right. Specifically, these categories are

- Certainty
- Risk
- Uncertainty

Decision Making Under Certainty. In decision making under certainty, it is *assumed* that complete information is available so that the decision maker knows

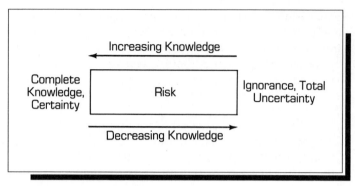

FIGURE 2.5 The Zones of Decision Making.

exactly what the outcome of each course of action will be. The decision maker is being viewed as a perfect predictor of the future, because it is assumed that there is only one outcome for each alternative. For example, the alternative of investing in U.S. Treasury bills is one for which it is reasonable to assume complete availability of information about the future return on the investment. Such a situation is also termed *deterministic*. It occurs most often with structured problems with short time horizons (up to one year). Some problems under certainty are not structured enough to be approached by management science; they thus require a DSS approach.

Decision Making Under Risk (Risk Analysis). A decision made under risk (also known as a probabilistic or stochastic decision situation) is one in which the decision maker must consider several possible outcomes for each alternative, each with a given probability of occurrence. In addition, it is assumed that the long-run probabilities of the occurrences of the given outcomes are known or can be estimated. Under these assumptions, the decision maker can assess the degree of risk assumed (termed *calculated* risk).

Risk analysis is usually executed by computing the expected value of each alternative and selecting the alternative with the best expected value.

Decision Making Under Uncertainty. In decision making under uncertainty,* the decision maker considers situations in which several outcomes are possible for each course of action. In contrast to the risk situation, the decision maker does not know, or cannot estimate, the probability of occurrence of the possible outcomes.

Decision making under uncertainty is more difficult to evaluate because of insufficient information. Modeling of such situations involves the assessment of

---

*The definitions of the terms *risk* and *uncertainty,* as presented here, were suggested by Professor F. H. Knight of the University of Chicago in 1933. Several other definitions are being used by different organizations and authors.

the decision maker's (and/or the organizational) attitude toward risk (e.g., being a conservative or a risk taker).

Measuring Outcomes (Goals' Attainment Level)

The value of an alternative is judged in terms of goals' attainment. Sometimes an outcome is expressed directly in terms of a goal. For example, profit is an outcome, whereas profit maximization is a goal, and both are expressed in dollar terms. In other cases an outcome may be expressed in other terms than that of the goal.

Scenarios

A **scenario** is a statement of assumptions about the operating environment of a particular system at a given time. In other words, a scenario is a narrative description of the *setting* in which the decision situation is to be examined. A scenario describes the decision and uncontrollable variables and parameters for a specific modeling situation. It also may provide the procedures and constraints for the modeling itself.

Scenarios were originated in the field of drama. The term was then borrowed for war gaming and large-scale simulations. More recently scenarios have entered the realm of MSS. For example, a scenario may describe the set of assumptions about the behaviors, intentions, and effects of the various processes represented in a merger proposal to be evaluated by a DSS.

A scenario is especially helpful in simulation and in "what-if" analysis. In both cases we keep changing scenarios. For example, one can change the anticipated demand for hospitalization (which is an input variable for planning), thus creating a new scenario. Then one can measure the anticipated cash flow of the hospital for each scenario.

Scenarios play an important role in MSS because they:

- Help identify potential opportunities and/or problem areas
- Provide flexibility in planning
- Identify the leading edges of changes that management should monitor
- Help *validate* major assumptions used in the modeling
- Help to check the sensitivity of the proposed solutions to changes in the scenarios.

Possible Scenarios. Thousands of possible scenarios may exist for every decision situation. However, the following are of a special value:

- The "worst possible" scenario
- The "best possible" scenario
- The "most likely" scenario.

The scenario sets the context of the analysis (or the evaluation) to be performed, defines many of the inputs, and to a large degree establishes the evaluation criteria.

2.7   The Choice Phase

The boundary between the design and the choice phases is frequently unclear because certain activities may be performed both during the design and the choice phases and because one may return frequently from the choice activities to the design. For example, one may generate new alternatives while performing an evaluation of existing ones. The choice phase includes search, evaluation, and recommending an appropriate solution to the model.

A *solution* to a model is a specific set of values for the decision variables. The solution of the model identifies the alternative selected.

Note: Solving the model is not the same as solving the problem that the model represents. The solution to the model yields a recommended solution to the problem. Only if this recommended solution is successfully implemented is the problem considered to be solved.

Search Approaches

The choice phase involves the search for the appropriate course of action (among those identified during the design phase) that will solve the real problem. Several major search approaches exist, depending on the criteria of choice. For normative models either an analytical approach is used or a complete, exhaustive enumeration (comparing all alternatives to one another) is applied. For descriptive models a comparison of a limited number of alternatives is used, either blindly or by using heuristics. These search approaches are shown in Figure 2.6.

Analytical Techniques. Analytical techniques use mathematical formulas to directly either derive an *optimal solution* or predict a certain result. Analytical techniques are used mainly for solving structured problems, usually of a tactical or operational nature, in areas like allocation of resources or inventory management. For more complex problems that are addressed by MSS the blind or heuristic search approaches are generally used.

Algorithms. Analytical techniques may use algorithms to increase the efficiency of the search. An **algorithm** is a step-by-step search process (see Figure 2.7) for arriving at an optimal solution. Solutions are generated and tested for possible improvements. An improvement is made whenever possible and the new solution is subjected to an improvement test. The process continues until no further improvement is possible.

Blind and Heuristic Search Approaches

In conducting a search, a description of a desired solution may be given. This is called a *goal*. A set of possible steps leading from initial conditions to the goal is viewed as the *search steps*. Problem solving is carried out by searching

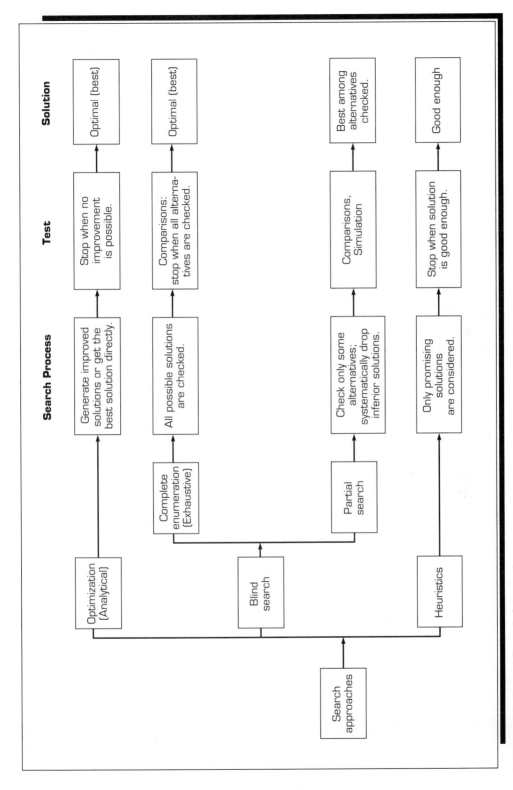

FIGURE 2.6 Formal Search Approaches.

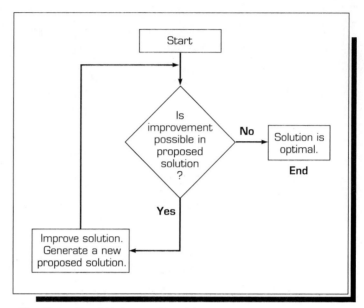

FIGURE 2.7   The Process of Using an Algorithm.

through the space of possible solutions. Two search methods are considered: the blind search and the heuristic search.

Blind Search. Blind search techniques refer to a search approach which is arbitrary and not guided. Two types of blind search exist: *complete enumeration,* in which case all the alternatives are considered, and therefore an optimal solution is discovered; and *incomplete,* partial search, which continues until a "good enough" solution is found.

There are practical limits on the amount of time and computer storage available for blind searches. Although in principle blind search methods can eventually find an optional solution to most search situations, the method is not practical for large problems because too many nodes must be visited before a solution is found.

Heuristic Search. For many applications, it is possible to find specific information to guide the search process and reduce the amount of necessary computations. This is called heuristic information, and the search procedures that use it are called heuristic search methods.

Heuristics (derived from the Greek word for "discovery") are decision rules regarding how a problem should be solved. Heuristics are developed on a basis of solid, rigorous analysis of the problem, sometimes involving designed experimentation. In contrast, "rules of thumb" are usually developed as a result of a trial-and-error experience. Some heuristics were derived from rules of thumb. *Heuristic searches* (or *programming*) are step-by-step procedures that are repeated

TABLE 2.3　Examples of Heuristics and Rules of Thumb.

Sequence jobs through a machine	Do the jobs that require the least time first.
Purchase stocks	Do not buy stocks whose price-to-earnings ratio is larger than 10.
Travel	Do not go on the freeway between 8 and 9 A.M.
Capital investment in high-tech projects	Consider only those projects whose estimated payback period is less than two years.
Purchase of a house	Buy only in a good neighborhood, but buy there only in the lower price range.

until a satisfactory solution is found. In practice, such a search is much faster and cheaper than a blind search, while the solutions can be very close to the best ones. For details see Pearl [14] and Zanakis et al. [25]. Examples of heuristics are given in Table 2.3. For the role of heuristics in modeling see Chapter 5.

2.8　Evaluation: Multiple Goals, Sensitivity Analysis, "What-If," and Goal Seeking

The search process described earlier is coupled with evaluation. The evaluation is the final step that leads to the recommended solution. Several topics are important in the evaluation of MSS solutions: multiple goals, sensitivity analysis, "what-if" analysis, and goal seeking. They are discussed next.

Multiple Goals

The analysis of management decisions aims at evaluating, to the greatest possible extent, how far each alternative advances management toward its goals. Unfortunately, managerial problems are seldom evaluated in terms of a single goal such as profit maximization. Today's management systems are becoming more and more complex, and a single goal is rare. Instead, managers want to attain simultaneous goals, some of which conflict with each other. Therefore it is often necessary to analyze each alternative in light of its potential impact on several goals.

For example, consider a profit-making firm. In addition to making money, the company wants to grow, to develop its products and its employees, to provide job security to its workers, and to serve the community. Managers want to satisfy the shareholders and at the same time enjoy high salaries and expense accounts, while employees wish to increase their take-home pay and fringe benefits. Needless to say, some of these goals complement each other while others are in direct conflict. Add to this social and ethical considerations, and the system of goals begins to look quite complex.

Most quantitative approaches to decision theory are based on comparing a single measure of effectiveness. Therefore, it is necessary to transform, mathematically, the multiple-goal problem into a single-goal problem prior to the final comparison, or to develop another method of comparison.

Several methods of handling multiple goals can be used when working with MSS. The most common ones are:

- Use of utility theory
- Goal programming
- Expression of goals as constraints, using linear programming
- Using a point system.

For further details, see Keeney and Raiffa [9] or Tabucanon [20]. The analysis of multiple goals involves the following difficulties:

1. It is usually difficult to obtain an explicit statement of the organization's goals.
2. Various participants assess the importance (priorities) of the various goals differently.
3. The decision maker may change the importance assigned to specific goals with the passage of time or in different decision situations.
4. Goals and subgoals are viewed differently at various levels of the organization and in various departments.
5. The goals themselves are dynamic in response to changes in the organization and its environment.
6. The relationship between alternatives and their impact on goals may be difficult to quantify.
7. Complex problems are solved by groups of decision makers.

Computerized models are used extensively to support multiple goal decision making. These will be discussed in detail in Chapter 5.

Sensitivity Analysis

Sensitivity analysis attempts to help managers when they are not certain about the accuracy or relative importance of information, or when they want to know the impact of changes in input information of a model on some results or measures of performance.

The topic of sensitivity analysis is extremely important in MSS because (a) it enables flexibility and adaptation to changing conditions and to the requirements of different decision-making situations, and (b) it provides a better understanding of the model and the world it purports to describe. Sensitivity analysis checks relationships such as:

- Effect of uncertainty in estimating external variables
- Effects of different interactions among variables

- Robustness of decisions under changing conditions
- The impact of changes in external (uncontrollable) variables and parameters on the outcome variable(s)
- The impact of changes in the decision variables on the outcome variable(s).

Sensitivity analyses are used to:

- Revise models to eliminate too large sensitivities
- Add details about sensitive variables or scenarios
- Obtain better estimates of sensitive external variables
- Alter the real-world system to reduce actual sensitivities
- Live with a sensitive (and hence vulnerable) real world, monitoring actual results continuously and closely.

Two types of sensitivity analysis exist: automatic and trial and error.

Automatic Sensitivity Analysis. This kind of analysis is provided with some standard quantitative models such as linear programming. It tells the manager, for example, the range within which a certain input variable (e.g., unit cost) can vary without any significant impact on the proposed solution. Automatic sensitivity analysis is usually limited to one change at a time, and only for certain variables. It is, however, very powerful because of its ability to establish ranges and limits very fast (and with little or no additional computational efforts).

Trial and Error. The impact of changes in any variable, or in several variables, can be determined through a trial-and-error approach. One simply changes some input data and resolves the problem. By repeating the changes several times, better and better solutions are discovered. Such experimentation appears in two forms: "what-if" and goal seeking.

"What-If" Analysis. A model builder makes predictions and assumptions regarding the input data, many of which deal with the assessment of uncertain futures. When the model is solved, the results depend, of course, on these data. Sensitivity analysis attempts to check the impact of a change in the input data on the proposed solution (the result variable). This type of sensitivity analysis is called "what-if" analysis, because it is structured as "*What* will happen to the solution *if* an input variable, an assumption, or a parameter value is changed?"
Examples include the following:

- *What* will happen to the total inventory cost *if* the cost of carrying inventories increases by 10 percent?
- *What* will be the market share *if* the advertising budget increases by 5 percent?

Assuming the appropriate user interface, managers can easily ask the computer these types of questions. Furthermore, they can repeat the question and change the percentage or change any other data in the question, as desired.

Figure 2.8 shows a "what-if" query in the case of five years' financial planning (a portion of a DSS). The user asks "what if" material cost equals $22.00 (this figure is different from the original material cost). Then the user commands the computer to calculate (all the affected data). Once the computer informs the user that the computation is completed, the user commands the computer to print any desired data (in this case, projected gross income for the next five years). "What-if" analysis can be executed with expert systems as well. Users are given the opportunity to change their answers to some of the computer's questions; then a revised recommendation is shown and compared to the previous one.

Goal Seeking. Goal seeking analysis checks the inputs necessary to a desired level of an output (goal). It represents a "backward" solution approach. For example, let us say that our initial analysis yielded a profit of $2 million. Management might then want to know what sales volume would be necessary to generate a profit of $2.2 million.

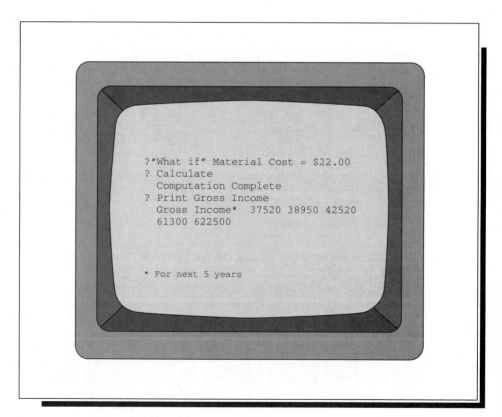

```
?"What if" Material Cost = $22.00
? Calculate
  Computation Complete
? Print Gross Income
  Gross Income*  37520 38950 42520
  61300 622500



* For next 5 years
```

FIGURE 2.8 "What-If" Analysis (? preceeds the user's input). (Screen generated by IFPS.)

Other examples of goal seeking are:

- What is the annual R&D budget needed for an annual growth rate of 15 percent by 1996?
- How many nurses are needed to reduce the average waiting time of a patient in the emergency room to less than 10 minutes?
- How many auditors are needed to complete the audit by November 15?

A computer printout of goal-seeking dialogs is shown in Figure 2.9. The user wants to determine the per unit price necessary to achieve a profit of $100,000 the first year and $5,000 more in each of the following years. The computer calculates the necessary price (per unit) for each of the five years in a planning document.

Computing a Break-even Point Using Goal Seeking. An interesting application of goal seeking for computing break-even points is available in some computer packages. This application can be done by finding what quantity needs to be produced in order to generate zero profit.

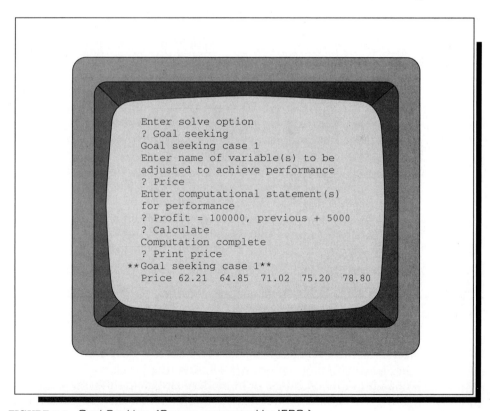

FIGURE 2.9   Goal Seeking. (Screen generated by IFPS.)

Sensitivity analysis is important because it can be used to improve confidence in the model and thus increase the rate of application and implementation of quantitative analysis. In many regular computer-based decision systems, it is difficult to conduct such an analysis because the prewritten routines usually present only a limited opportunity for "what-if" questions. In a DSS the "what-if" and the goal seeking options are easy to execute and provide ample opportunity for flexibility and adaptability.

2.9   Critical Success Factors

The final issue that relates to "choice" is the technique of critical success factors. Critical success factors (CSF) is a diagnostic technique (see Rockart [16]) for identifying the factors that are the most critical to the achievement of organizational objectives. The process involves conducting interviews with individual executives, followed by a structured group discussion for the purpose of identifying success factors and agreeing on their importance. The identification of such factors is essential both for determining the information needs required by management to achieve their objectives and for prioritizing the criteria used in evaluating alternative courses of action.

Once the critical factors are determined, it is possible to identify information gaps, that is, to find out which critical factors are not being adequately supported by the current information system. The lack of such information prevents management from measuring the effectiveness of areas that are critical to the organization. Therefore it is necessary to identify the critical factors and structure the appropriate information system before developing the MSS. In addition to its use in determining information requirements, CSF has been used in feasibility studies of MSS and in other phases of the development process of these techniques as well as information systems in general. For example, it was used in DSS software selection (Shank et al. [17]). The CSF approach can be applied to many other decision-making situations.

Once the choice phase has been completed, the recommended solution must be implemented. This issue is discussed next.

2.10   Implementation

What is implementation? Machiavelli astutely noted more than 400 years ago that there was "nothing more difficult to carry out, nor more doubtful of success, nor more dangerous to handle, than to initiate a new order of things." The implementation of a proposed solution to a problem is, in effect, the initiation of a new order of things, or in modern language—the introduction of a change.

The definition of implementation is somewhat complicated because implementation is a long and involved process whose boundaries are vague. In a simplistic manner, it may be defined as putting a recommended solution to work.

Many of the generic issues of implementation, such as resistance to change, degree of support of top management, and user's training, are important in dealing with MSS.

The decision-making process described in Sections 2.5 through 2.10 is conducted by people, but it can be improved if supported by computers. The manner in which such support can be provided is the subject of the next section.

2.11   How Decisions Are Being Supported

The discussion in this chapter has centered so far on decisions and systems; equally important is the notion of *support* in MSS. Chapter 1 illustrated, in general terms, how computers have supported management decisions since the early 1950s (Table 1.1). Now that we are familiar with the decision process, we will discuss the support from this point of view. Simon's phases of intelligence, design, and choice will be used as a framework, with the addition of the implementation phase.

As noted by Sprague and Carlson [19], a DSS could support all phases of the decision-making process (see Figure 2.10). In contrast, MIS supports mainly the intelligence phase, whereas management science supports mainly the choice

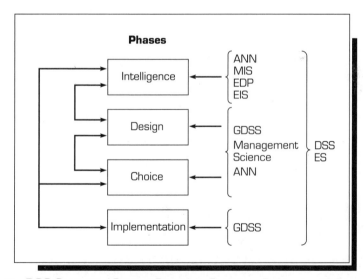

FIGURE 2.10   DSS Support. (*Source:* Based on Sprague, R. H., Jr., "A Framework for the Development of DSS." *MIS Quarterly* [Dec. 1980], Fig. 5, p. 13. Reprinted by special permission of the *MIS Quarterly.* © 1980 by the Society for Information Management and the Management Information Systems Research Center at the University of Minnesota.)

phase. EIS would support the intelligence phase while ES can support any of the phases.

Support for the Intelligence Phase

The primary requirement of decision support for the intelligence phase is the ability to scan external and internal databases for opportunities and problems and interpretation of what the scanning discovers. Computerized systems store large volumes of information. An EIS, as will be described later, helps in accessing databases rapidly and efficiently. Furthermore, a DSS through its modeling capabilities can analyze data very fast. That is, the scanning done during the intelligence phase can be executed much faster with the aid of a DSS and EIS.

Another area of support is that of reporting. Both routine and ad hoc reports can aid in the intelligence phase. For example, regular reports can be designed to assist in the problem-finding activity by comparing expectations with current and projected performance. Table 2.4 lists report elements that can assist in problem finding.

The major purpose of an EIS is to support the intelligence phase. This is done by continuously monitoring both internal and external information, looking for early signs of problems and/or opportunities. For example, EIS will detect

TABLE 2.4 Report Elements. (Condensed from Brookes [3].)

Report Element	Problem-Finding Use
Summarization	Current performance is summarized by expectations provided by the user of the report.
Comparison	The report has explicit comparisons with current performance expectations: Comparison with plans, budgets, or standards. Variance (from standards) reports. Comparison with competitors, industry averages, and other extraorganizational standards and measures. Exceptions reports.
Prediction	Forecasts of future performance: Prediction based on budget or planning model or historical ratios. Prediction based on seasonally adjusted (or other method) data. Forecast of current performance to the end of the planning period.
Confirmation	Data items that allow the user to validate or audit the report to provide assurance that it corresponds to underlying detail or other data available to the user. Confirmation may use historical data, planning data, or data from elsewhere in the organization.

below normal performance and through a detailed investigation will attempt to pinpoint its sources.

Finally, ES can render advice regarding the nature of the problem, its classification, its seriousness, and the like. ES can advise on the suitability of a solution approach and on the likelihood of successfully solving the problem. One of the primary areas of ES success, as will be shown later, is in *interpretation* of information and in *diagnosing* problems. This capability can be utilized during the intelligence phase.

The phase of intelligence, according to a study conducted by Lucas [10], is a primary target for DSS and other computer-based information systems that deal with nonstructured problems.

Support for the Design Phase

The design phase involves generating alternative courses of action, discussing the criteria for choice and their relative importance, and forecasting the future consequences of using various alternatives. Several of these activities could use standard models provided by the DSS (e.g., forecasting). Generation of alternatives for structured problems could be provided by a DSS through the use of either standard or special models. However, generation of alternatives for complex problems requires expertise that could be provided by a human, an idea generation software, or an expert system. Information about technology, availability of resources, market conditions, and the like could be provided to the decision maker by the computer's database. This information is essential for the development of alternative solutions to the problems and for the prediction of decision consequences. Most DSS have forecasting capabilities while an added-on ES can assist with qualitative methods of forecasting as well as with expertise required in applying quantitative forecasting models.

Support for the Choice Phase

A decision support system, by definition, recommends but does not make a choice. In addition to the use of models that rapidly identify the best or "good enough" alternative, a DSS can support the choice phase through the "what-if" and goal seeking analyses. Different scenarios can be tested for the selected option to reinforce the final decision. An ES can be used to assess the desirability of certain solutions as well as to recommend an appropriate solution.

Support for the Decision Implementation

Interviews conducted by Mittman and Moore [13] suggest that the DSS benefits provided during implementation are frequently as important or more important than those mentioned in the previously discussed phases. Respondents reported numerous uses of DSS in implementation activities like decision communication, explanation, and justification. For example, a copy containing DSS results was frequently sent to parties who were both internal and external to companies. The recipients included senior managers' peers and subordinates, the board of directors, bankers and financial analysts, customers and clients, suppliers, and others from whom cooperation and coordination are needed.

Benefits of DSS in the implementation phase are due in part to the vividness and detail of the analysis and resulting output. For example, one CEO gives subordinates and external parties not only the aggregate financial goals and cash needs for the near term, but includes the calculations, intermediate results, and statistics used in determining the aggregate figures. In addition to communicating the financial goals unambiguously, the CEO signals other messages. Subordinates know that the CEO has thought through the assumptions behind the financial goals and is serious about their importance and attainability. Bankers and directors are shown that the CEO was personally involved in analyzing cash needs, and is aware of and responsible for the implications of the financing requests prepared by the finance department. Each of these messages improves decision implementation in some way.

The evidence just discussed indicates that senior managers are using computers primarily in support of the implementation aspects of the decision process—explaining, justifying, and communicating decisions. Numerous indications of the DSS role in decision implementation appear in other studies (e.g., see Alter [1] and Keen and Scott-Morton [8]).

All phases of the decision-making process can be supported by improved communication in cases of *group decision making*. Computerized systems can facilitate communication by allowing people to explain and justify their suggestions and opinions, usually with graphic support. Quantitative support can also be quickly provided for various possible scenarios while a meeting is in session.

Decision implementation can also be supported by ES. Some ES include, like a DSS, a "what-if" mechanism that intends to increase the *confidence* in the system. Furthermore, an ES can be used as an advisory system regarding implementation problems (e.g., resistance to change). Finally, an ES can provide training that may smooth the course of implementation.

2.12 Human Cognition and Decision Styles

Cognition Theory. Cognition refers to the activities by which an individual resolves differences between an internalized view of the environment and what actually exists in that same environment. In other words, it is the ability to perceive and understand information. Cognitive models are attempts to explain or understand various human cognitive processes. For instance, they explain how individuals revise previous opinions to conform with a particular choice after they have made that choice.

Cognitive Style. Cognitive style refers to the subjective process through which individuals perceive, organize, and change information during the decision-making process. Cognitive style may be important because in many cases it determines peoples' preference for human-machine interface. For example, should data be raw or aggregate, should they be detailed or summarized, should they be tabulated or presented as graphs? Furthermore, cognitive styles impact on preferences for qualitative versus quantitative analysis as well as on the preferences for decision-making aids.

The research on cognitive styles is directly relevant to the design of management information systems. MIS and transaction processing systems tend to be designed by individuals who perceive the decision-making process to be systematic. Systematic managers are generally willing to use such systems; they are typically looking for a standard technique and view the system designer as an expert with a catalog of methods. However, such systems do not conform to the natural style of a heuristic decision maker. For this individual, a system should allow for exploration of a wide range of alternatives, permit changes in priorities or in processing, allow the user to shift easily between levels of detail, and permit some user control over the output form (e.g., visual, verbal, graphic, and so on). And this is precisely what DSS is attempting to do. Other interesting implications of cognitive style will be presented when MSS implementation is discussed.

Although cognitive style is a useful concept, it may be overemphasized in the MIS literature. There are difficulties in applying it to information systems and decision making (see Huber [7]). For one thing, cognitive style is a continuous variable. Many people are not completely heuristic nor analytic, but are somewhere in between. Related to the cognitive styles is the concept of decision styles.

Decision Styles. The manner in which decision makers think and react to problems, the way they perceive, their cognitive response, their values and beliefs vary from individual to individual and from situation to situation. As a result people make decisions differently. Although there is a general process of decision making, it is far from being linear. People do not follow the same steps of the process in the same sequence, nor do they use all of the steps. Furthermore, the emphasis, time allotment, and priorities given to each step vary significantly—not only from one person to another, but also from one situation to the next. The manner in which managers make decisions (and the way they interact with other people) describes their decision style. Because decision styles depend on the factors described earlier, there are many decision styles. For example, Gordon et al. [6] identified 40 processes in looking at nine types of decisions, and Mintzberg [12] identified seven basic styles with many variations.

In addition to the heuristic and analytic styles discussed earlier, one can distinguish autocratic versus democratic styles; another style is consultative (with individuals or groups). Of course, there are many combinations and variations of styles. For example, one can be analytic and autocratic, or consultative (with individuals) and heuristic. For further details on how decision styles relate to DSS and the provided support, see Wedley and Field [24].

For a computerized system to successfully support a manager, it should fit the decision situation as well as the decision style. Therefore the system should be flexible and adaptable to different users. The capability of asking "what-if" and goal seeking questions provides flexibility in this direction. Availability of graphics is also desirable in supporting certain decision styles. If an MSS is to support varying styles, skills, and knowledge, it should not attempt to enforce a specific process. Rather, the MSS should help decision makers use and develop their own styles, skills, and knowledge.

Different decision styles require different types of support. A major factor that determines the type of required support is whether the decision maker is an individual or a group.

2.13   Making Decisions in Groups

The discussion of decision making in this chapter is basically centered around a rational approach to decision making, which is usually considered a normative model for an individual decision maker. However, many complex decisions are being made in organizations by groups. Computerized technologies that are being developed to support such decisions, under the name of group DSS (GDSS), are described in Chapter 9. Several aspects of group decision making processes are described there as well.

However, computer support can be provided even at a broader level that surpasses the group, moving up to departments, divisions, and even organizations. Such support requires specialized architecture and procedures and it is labeled *organizational DSS*. For details see Chapter 8.

Chapter Highlights

- Managerial decision making is synonymous with the whole process of management.
- Problem solving also refers to opportunity's evaluation.
- Systems are composed of inputs, outputs, processes, and a decision maker.
- All systems are separated from their environment by a boundary.
- Systems can be open, interacting with their environment, or closed.
- DSS deals with open systems.
- Models are used extensively in MSS; they can be iconic, analog, or mathematical.
- Models enable fast and inexpensive experimentation with systems.
- Modeling can employ simulation, optimization, or heuristic techniques.
- Decision making involves four major phases: Intelligence, design, choice, and implementation.
- In the intelligent step, the problem (opportunity) is identified, classified, and decomposed (if needed).

- In the design phase, a model of the system is built, criteria for selection are agreed open, alternatives are generated, results are predicted, and decision methodology is created.
- In the choice phase, alternatives are compared and a search for the best (good enough) is launched. Many search techniques are available.
- In evaluating alternatives, one should consider multiple goals and sensitivity analysis issues.
- "What-if" and goal seeking are the two most common sensitivity analysis approaches.
- Critical success factors is a methodology for diagnosing problems and identifying information requirements.
- Computers can support all phases of decision making by automating many of the required tasks.
- Humans' decision styles need to be recognized in complementing MSS.
- Decisions can be made by individuals or by groups.

Key Words

algorithm	implementation	risk analysis
analog model	independent variables	satisfice
analytical approach	inputs	scenario
cognitive style	linear programming	sensitivity analysis
critical success factors	mathematical	simulation
decision styles	(quantitative) model	suboptimization
descriptive models	normative models	system
effectiveness	optimization	uncertainty
efficiency	outputs	uncontrollable
goal seeking	principle of choice	variables
heuristics	problem solving	"what-if" analysis
iconic model	programmed problems	

Questions for Review

1. What is the difference between making decisions and solving problems?
2. Define a system.
3. List the major components of a system.
4. Explain the role of feedback in a system.
5. Define an environment of a system.
6. Define open and closed systems. Give an example of each.
7. What is meant by a "black box"?
8. Define efficiency and contrast it with effectiveness.
9. Define the phases of intelligence, design, and choice.
10. Define a problem and distinguish it from the symptoms of the problem.
11. Define programmed versus unprogrammed problems; give one example

of each in each of the following areas: accounting, marketing, personnel administration.
12. List the major components of a mathematical model.
13. Define optimization and contrast it with suboptimization.
14. Compare and contrast normative versus descriptive approaches to decision making.
15. Why do people have a bounded rationality?
16. Distinguish between decision making under risk and under uncertainty.
17. What is the major advantage of optimization?
18. What is the major disadvantage of complete enumeration?
19. Define heuristics.
20. Why is a heuristic search superior to a blind one?
21. Compare decision style to cognitive style.
22. Discuss the various types of computerized support.
23. Define "what-if" analysis and provide an example.
24. Define goal seeking analysis and provide an example.
25. Define critical success factors (CSF) and describe the steps in this process.
26. Define implementation.
27. Define a scenario. How is it used in decision making?
28. Define cognition and cognitive style.
29. Compare simulation and optimization.
30. Define sensitivity analysis.

Questions for Discussion

1. Specify in a table the inputs, process, and output of the following systems:
   a. post office
   b. elementary school
   c. social service agency
   d. paper mill.
2. List possible modes of feedback for the systems in the previous question.
3. A hospital includes dietary, radiology, housekeeping, and nursing (patient care rooms) departments, and an emergency room. List four system interfaces between pairs of these departments.
4. How would you measure the productivity of:
   a. a letter carrier
   b. a salesperson
   c. a professor
   d. a social worker.
5. Give an example of five elements in the environment of a university.
6. Analyze a managerial system of your choice and identify the following:
   a. the components, inputs, and outputs
   b. the environment

    c. the process

    d. the system's goals

    e. the feedback.

7. What are some of the "measures of effectiveness" in a manufacturing plant, a restaurant, an educational institution, and the U.S. Congress?

8. What are some of the controllable and uncontrollable variables in the following systems: automotive manufacturing, hospital, courthouse, airline, restaurant, hotel, bank, oil refinery, atomic power plant? Specify a typical decision in each of the above.

9. Assume a marketing department is an open system. How would you "close" this system?

10. What could be the major advantages of a mathematical model that would be used to support a major investment decision?

11. Your company is considering opening a branch in China. List typical activities in each phase (intelligence, design, choice, implementation).

12. Many farm equipment manufacturers have had major losses in recent years because farmers have had no money to purchase farm equipment. What is the problem that the manufacturing companies are faced with?

13. You are about to sell your car. What criteria (or principles of choice) are you most likely to employ in deciding about accepting or rejecting offers? Why?

14. You are about to decide on driving to work via the freeway or via the parallel road. There is no immediate traffic information. Is your decision under certainty? risk? uncertainty? Why?

15. There are $n!$ (n factorial) ways to schedule n jobs through one machine. You have 50 jobs to schedule. You must decide which job to run first, second, etc. There is no analytical solution to the problem. What type of search would you use in your analysis and why?

16. List five heuristics (or rules of thumb) that are being used in your company, a university, a bank, or a fast-food restaurant.

17. A hospital desires to know what level of demand for its services will guarantee an 85 percent bed occupancy. What type of sensitivity analysis should the hospital use and why?

18. Apply the method of critical success factors to determine which computer to buy for your home. Assume that at least three people will use the computer and you can afford only one PC.

19. The use of scenarios is becoming popular in computerized decision making. Why? For what type of decisions is this technique most appropriate?

20. Explain how cognitive style relates to decision style. How might these concepts impact the development of information systems?

21. Discuss the major issues related to group decision making.

22. Explain, through an example, the support given to decision makers by computers in each phase of the decision process.

23. Some experts believe that the major contribution of DSS is to the implementation of the decision and not to the intelligence, design, or choice. Why is this so?

TABLE 2.5 Cognitive-style Decision Approaches.

Problem-solving Dimension	Heuristic	Analytic
Approach to learning	Learns more by acting than by analyzing the situation and places more emphasis on feedback.	Employs a planned sequential approach to problem solving; learns more by analyzing the situation than by acting and places less emphasis on feedback.
Search	Uses trial and error and spontaneous action.	Uses formal rational analysis.
Approach to analysis	Uses common sense, intuition, and feelings.	Develops explicit, often quantitative, models of the situation.
Scope of analysis	Views the totality of the situation as an organic whole rather than as a structure constructed from specific parts.	Reduces the problem situation to a set of underlying causal functions.
Basis for inferences	Looks for highly visible situational differences that vary with time.	Locates similarities or commonalities by comparing objects.

Source: G. B. Davis; *Management Information Systems: Conceptual Foundations, Structure, and Development.* New York: McGraw-Hill, 1974, p. 150.

24. Table 2.5 shows the differences between heuristic and analytic cognitive styles.
    a. Would you consider yourself heuristic or analytic? Why?
    b. Read Huber's article [7] (*Management Science,* May 1983). Do you agree with Huber's position? Why or why not?
    c. Assume you are making a presentation to two managers—one heuristic, the other analytic—regarding a decision about adding a service by the bank you work for. How would you appeal to their cognitive styles? (Be specific.)
25. How is the term *model* used in this text? What are the strengths and weaknesses of modeling?
26. Most managers are capable of utilizing the telephone without understanding or even considering the electrical and magnetic theories involved. Why then is it necessary for managers to understand analytic tools to use them wisely?
27. Decision-making styles vary from analytical to heuristic-intuitive. Does a decision maker consistently use the same style? Give examples from your own experience.

References and Bibliography

1. Alter, S. L. *Decision Support Systems: Current Practice and Continuing Challenge.* Reading, MA: Addison-Wesley, 1980.

2. Bell, D. E., et al. *Decision Making.* New York: Cambridge University Press, 1988.

3. Brookes, C. H. P. "A Framework for DSS Development." Information Systems Forum Research Report, Department of Information Systems, University of New South Wales, Sydney, Australia, 1984.

4. Churchman, C. West. *The Systems Approach.* Rev. ed. New York: Delacorte, 1975.

5. Etzioni, A. "Humble Decision Making." *Harvard Business Review,* July-August 1989.

6. Gordon, L. A., et al. *Normative Models in Managerial Decision Making.* New York: National Association of Accounting, 1975.

7. Huber, G. P. "Cognitive Style as a Basis for MIS and DDS Designs: Much Ado About Nothing?" *Management Science,* Vol. 29, No. 5, May 1983.

8. Keen, P. G. W., and M. S. Scott-Morton. *Decision Support Systems: An Organizational Perspective.* Reading, MA: Addison-Wesley, 1978.

9. Keeney, R., and H. Raiffa. *Decisions with Multiple Objectives, Preferences, and Value Tradeoffs.* New York: Wiley, 1976.

10. Lucas, H. C. "Top Management Problem Solving and Information Systems," Working Papers CRIS #11, Center for Research on Information Systems; New York University, 1980.

11. McKenney, J. L., and P. G. W. Keen. "How Managers' Minds Work." *Harvard Business Review,* May–June 1974.

12. Mintzberg, H. *The Nature of the Managerial Work.* New York: Harper & Row, 1973.

13. Mittman, B. S., and J. H. Moore. *Senior Management Computer Use: Implications for DSS Design and Goals.* Paper presented at the DSS-84 meetings, Dallas, Texas, April 1984.

14. Pearl, J. *Heuristics: Intelligent Search Strategies for Computer Problem Solving.* Reading, MA: Addison-Wesley, 1984.

15. Robbins, S. R. *Management,* 3rd ed. Englewood Cliffs, NJ: Prentice-Hall, 1991.

16. Rockart, J. F. "Chief Executives Define Their Own Data Needs." *Harvard Business Review,* July–August 1981.

17. Shank, M. E., et al. "Critical Success Factor Analysis as a Methodology for MIS Planning." *MIS Quarterly,* June 1985.

18. Simon, H. *The New Science of Management Decisions.* Rev. ed. Englewood Cliffs, NJ: Prentice-Hall, 1977.

19. Sprague, R. H., and E. D. Carlson. *Building Effective Decision Support Systems.* Englewood Cliffs, NJ: Prentice-Hall, 1982.

20. Tabucanon, M. T. *Multiple Criteria Decision Making in Industry.* New York: Elsevier, 1989.

21. Turban, E., and J. Meredith. *Fundamentals of Management Science*. 6th ed. Homewood, IL: Richard D. Irwin, 1994.
22. Tylor, A. *Applied Decision Analysis*. Boston, MA: PWS-Kent, 1991.
23. Van Gigch, J. P. *Applied General Systems Theory*. 2nd ed. New York: Harper & Row, 1978.
24. Wedley, W. K., and R. H. C. Field. "A Predecision Support System." *Academy of Management Review*, October 1984.
25. Zanakis, S. H., et al., "Heuristic Methods and Applications: A Categorized Survey." *European Journal of Operations Research*, No. 43, 1989.

Part 2

Decision Support Systems

In this part we concentrate on DSS technology in its narrow definition. Chapter 3 provides an overview of the technology: the characteristics, the structure, the methodology, and the types of DSS. The three major components of DSS are presented in Chapter 4 (Data Management), Chapter 5 (Modeling and Model Management), and Chapter 6 (User Interface). Much of the material in Chapters 4 and 6 is relevant to other MSS technologies. Chapter 7 deals with the development process of DSS and Chapter 8 ends the presentation with a discussion of more advanced DSS topics.

Chapter 3

Decision Support Systems: An Overview

In Chapter 1, we introduced DSS and claimed that a DSS is superior to earlier types of computer systems like electronic data processing (EDP) and MIS for supporting the solution of complex problems. The support of managerial decision making was stressed, and the methodology of decision making was presented in Chapter 2. In this chapter, we show how DSS superiority is achieved by examining its capabilities, structure, and classification. The following sections are presented:

3.1   The Case of Gotaas-Larsen Shipping Corp. (GLSC)*

Strategic planning is one of the most difficult tasks of modern management. It involves all functional areas in an organization and several relevant outside factors, a fact that complicates the planning process, especially when one deals with the uncertainties of the long run. As such, strategic planning is clearly not a structured decision situation; therefore it is a potential candidate for DSS applications.

GLSC, a subsidiary of International Utilities (IU), operates cargo ships all over the world. The company developed a comprehensive decision support system for executing both short- and long-term planning in the mid-1970s. The system is composed of two major parts: data and models.

The data include both external data (port or canal characteristics, competitors' activities, and fares) and internal data (existing plans, availability of resources, and individual ships' characteristics). In addition, users can utilize their own data or express their attitudes (e.g., add their own risk preferences).

The models include routine standard accounting and financial analysis models (like cash flow computations and pro forma income and expenses) organized on a per ship, per voyage, per division, and per entire company basis. These models permit elaborate financial analyses. A simulation model is used to analyze short- and long-term plans and to evaluate the desirability of projects. In addition, the system interfaces with a commercially available time-sharing application program for analyzing individual voyages (time-charter analysis).

A highly decentralized, 15-month operational planning and control document is prepared within the framework of the long-term strategic plan. This 15-month document is used as the basis for detailed goal formation for the various ships and the individual voyages. A detailed monitoring and control mechanism is also provided, including a regular variance report and diagnostic analysis. In addition, a detailed performance tracking report is executed (by voyage, ship, division, and entire corporation).

Once the assessment of the opportunity of individual projects (such as contracting a specific voyage) is examined by a charter analysis, an aggregation is performed. The objective is to determine whether a series of individually profitable projects adds up to a feasible and effective long-range plan. The DSS utilizes a simulation model that examines various configurations of projects in an attempt to conduct a "fine tuning" of the aggregate plan. Specifically, when several projects are executed, the resources (like labor and finance) might be insufficient for all the projects. Therefore modifications in scheduling and financial arrangements might be necessary. This fine tuning provides a trial-and-error approach to feasibility testing and sensitivity analyses. The "what-if" capabilities of the DSS are especially important in this case. The strategic plan of GLSC is very detailed and accurate because of the contractual nature of both the sales

---

*For a complete description, see Alter [1].

and some of the expenses. The model is geared to a traditional business policy structure, which helps in assessing the threats and risks in the general operating environment and makes possible an examination of the impacts of new opportunities on existing plans.

The GLSC case is an example of large-scale DSS. We refer to this case in the forthcoming sections.

3.2 Introduction

The early definitions of a DSS identify it as a system intended to support managerial decision makers in semistructured decision situations. DSS were meant to be an adjunct to decision makers, to extend their capabilities but not to replace their judgment. They were aimed at decisions where judgment was required, or decisions that could not be completely supported by algorithms. Not specifically stated, but implied in the early definitions, was the notion that the system would be computer-based, would operate on-line, and preferably would have graphic-output capabilities.

The early definitions were open to several interpretations. Soon several other definitions appeared that occasioned considerable disagreement as to what a DSS is. Some skeptics even suggested that DSS was just another buzz word. The purpose of this chapter is to show that this is not the case, and that there is a significant amount of content behind the label DSS. To do so we present the essential characteristics that could help in determining whether a system is a DSS or not. Also, the structure of DSS is presented as well as the various types of systems. Let us begin by reviewing some definitions (based on Ginzberg and Stohr [5]) and then delve into the DSS content and structure.

3.3 What Is a DSS?

A refinement of Gorry and Scott-Morton's DSS definition (in Chapter 1) was provided by Little [11], who defines DSS as a "model-based set of procedures for processing data and judgments to assist a manager in his decision making." He argues that in order to be successful, such a system must be (1) simple, (2) robust, (3) easy to control, (4) adaptive, (5) complete on important issues, and (6) easy to communicate with. Implicit in this definition, too, is the assumption that the system is computer-based and serves as an extension of the user's problem-solving capabilities.

Throughout most of the 1970s, definitions of DSS, like those just presented, were accepted by practitioners and researchers. By the end of the decade, however, new definitions began to emerge. Alter [1] defines DSS by contrasting them with traditional EDP systems on five dimensions, as shown in Table 3.1.

Three other definitions of DSS were offered by Moore and Chang [14], Bonczek, Holsapple, and Whinston [3], and Keen [8]. Moore and Chang argue

TABLE 3.1 DSS versus EDP.

Dimension	DSS	EDP
Use	Active	Passive
User	Line and staff management	Clerical
Goal	Effectiveness	Mechanical efficiency
Time Horizon	Present and future	Past
Objective	Flexibility	Consistency

that the "structuredness" concept, so much a part of early DSS definitions (i.e., that DSS can handle semistructured and unstructured situations), is not meaningful in general; a problem can be described as structured or unstructured only with respect to a particular decision maker (i.e., structured decisions are structured because we choose to treat them as such). Thus, they define DSS as (1) extendable systems, (2) capable of supporting ad hoc data analysis and decision modeling, (3) oriented toward future planning, and (4) used at irregular, unplanned intervals.

Note: Computerized systems for decision support are being developed today by end-users on microcomputers for dealing with fairly structured problems for which commercial software is not available. The advantage here is that the user can build systems with little or no help from information systems people.

Bonczek et al. [3] define a DSS as a computer-based system consisting of three interacting components: (1) a language system—a mechanism to provide communication between the user and other components of the DSS, (2) a knowledge system—the repository of problem domain knowledge embodied in DSS, either as data or procedures, and (3) a problem-processing system—the link between the other two components, containing one or more of the general problem-manipulatory capabilities required for decision making.

Note: The concepts provided by this definition are important for understanding the structures of DSS and ES and the interrelationship between the two technologies.

Finally, Keen [8] applies the term DSS "to situations where a 'final' system can be developed only through an **adaptive process** of learning and *evolution*." Thus, he defines DSS as the product of a developmental process in which the DSS user, the DSS builder, and the DSS itself are all capable of influencing one another, resulting in an evolution of the system and the pattern of its use.

These definitions are compared and contrasted by examining the types of concepts employed to define DSS (see Table 3.2). It seems that the basis for defining DSS has been developed from the perceptions of what a DSS does (e.g., support decision making in unstructured problems) and from ideas about how the DSS's objective can be accomplished (e.g., components required, appropriate usage pattern, and the necessary development processes).

TABLE 3.2 Concepts Underlying DSS Definitions.

Source	DSS Defined in Terms of
Gorry and Scott-Morton [6]	Problem type, system function (support)
Little [11]	System function, interface characteristics
Alter [1]	Usage pattern, system objectives
Moore and Chang [14]	Usage pattern, system capabilities
Bonczek et al. [3]	System components
Keen [9]	Development process

One result of these definitions is a narrowing of the population of systems that each author would identify as DSS. For example, Keen would exclude systems built without following an evolutionary strategy, and Moore and Chang would exclude systems used at regular, planned intervals to support decisions about current operations. The narrowing of a population is indeed a proper function of a definition. By dealing with a smaller population of objects, we can identify those characteristics that the population members have in common, as well as characteristics that differentiate one population from another.

Unfortunately, these definitions of DSS do not provide a consistent focus, because each tries to narrow the population in a different way. Furthermore, they collectively ignore the central issue in DSS; that is, support and improvement of decision making. There seems to have been a retreat from the consideration of outputs, and a focus on the inputs instead. A very likely reason for this change in emphasis is the difficulty of measuring the outputs of a DSS (e.g., decision quality).

A major DSS book should provide its own definition. Thus, we provide in Box 3.1 a working definition that basically defines a range, from a basic to an ideal DSS. It is much more beneficial, however, to deal with the characteristics and capabilities of DSS, which are presented next.

Box 3.1: What Is a DSS?—A Working Definition

It depends. At minimum we can say: A DSS is an interactive, flexible and adaptable CBIS, specially developed for supporting the solution of a particular management problem for improved decision making. It utilizes data, it provides easy user interface, and it allows for the decision maker's own insights.

The most sophisticated DSS definition will add to this: DSS also utilizes models (either standard and/or custom-made), it is built by an iterative process (frequently by end-users), it supports all the phases of the decision making, and it includes a knowledge base.

3.4   Characteristics and Capabilities of DSS

Because there is no consensus on what a DSS is, there is obviously no agreement on the characteristics and capabilities of DSS. Therefore we label the list in Figure 3.1 as an ideal set. Most DSS have only *some* of the listed features.

1. DSS provides support for decision makers mainly in semistructured and unstructured situations by bringing together human judgment and computerized information. Such problems cannot be solved (or cannot be solved conveniently) by other computerized systems, such as EDP or MIS, nor by management science.
2. Support is provided for various managerial levels, ranging from top executives to line managers.
3. Support is provided to individuals as well as to groups. Many organizational problems involve group decision making. The less structured problems frequently require the involvement of several individuals from different departments and organizational levels.
4. DSS provides support to several interdependent and/or sequential decisions. (See Section 3.12 for definitions.)
5. DSS supports all phases of the decision-making process: intelligence, design, choice, and implementation.
6. DSS supports a variety of decision-making processes and styles; there is a fit between the DSS and the attributes of the individual decision makers (e.g., the vocabulary and decision style).
7. DSS is adaptive over time. The decision maker should be reactive, being able to confront changing conditions quickly and adapt the DSS to meet these changes. DSS are flexible so users can add, delete, combine, change, or rearrange basic elements (providing fast response to unexpected situations). This capability makes possible timely and quick ad hoc analyses.
8. DSS is easy to use. Users must feel "at home" with the system. User-friendliness, flexibility, strong graphic capabilities, and an English-like dialog language can greatly increase the effectiveness of DSS. This ease of use implies an interactive mode.
9. DSS attempts to improve the effectiveness of decision making (accuracy, timeliness, quality), rather than its efficiency (cost of making the decision, including the charges for computer time).
10. The decision maker has complete control over all steps of the decision-making process in solving a problem. A DSS specifically aims to support and not to replace the decision maker. The decision maker can override the computer's recommendation at any time in the process.
11. DSS leads to learning, which leads to new demands and the refinement of the system, which leads to additional learning, and so forth, in a continuous process of developing and improving the DSS.

12. DSS are relatively easy to construct. End-users should be able to construct simple systems by themselves. Larger systems could be built in users' organizations with only minor assistance from information systems (IS) specialists.

13. A DSS usually utilizes models (standards, custom-made). The modeling capability enables experimenting with different strategies under different configurations. Such experimentations can provide new insights and learning.

14. Advanced DSS are equipped with a knowledge component that enables the efficient and effective solution of very difficult problems.

The characteristics and capabilities of DSS (see Figure 3.1) provide some major benefits (see Box 3.2).

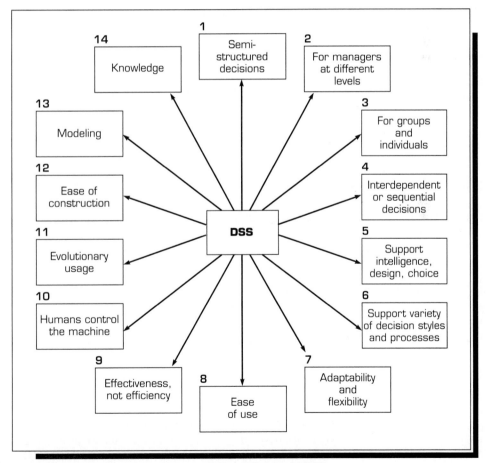

FIGURE 3.1 The Characteristics and Capabilities of DSS.

Box 3.2: The Major Benefits of DSS

1. Ability to support the solution of complex problems.
2. Fast response to unexpected situations that result in changed conditions. A DSS enables a thorough, quantitative analysis in a very short time. Even frequent changes in a scenario can be evaluated objectively in a timely manner.
3. Ability to try several different strategies under different configurations, quickly and objectively.
4. New insights and learning. The user can be exposed to new insights through the composition of the model and an extensive sensitivity "what-if" analysis. The new insights can help in training inexperienced managers and other employees as well.
5. Facilitated communication. Data collection and model construction experimentations are being executed with active users' participation, thus greatly facilitating communication among managers. The decision process can make employees more supportive of organizational decisions. The "what-if" analysis can be used to satisfy skeptics, in turn improving teamwork.
6. Improved management control and performance. DSS can increase management control over expenditures and improve performance of the organization.
7. Cost savings. Routine applications of a DSS may result in considerable cost reduction, or in reducing (eliminating) the cost of wrong decisions.
8. Objective decisions. The decisions derived from DSS are more consistent and objective than decisions made intuitively.
9. Improving managerial effectiveness, allowing managers to perform a task in less time and/or with less effort. The DSS provides managers with more "quality" time for analysis, planning, and implementation.

3.5   Components of DSS

DSS is composed of the following:

1. Data Management. The data management includes the database(s), which contains relevant data for the situation and is managed by software called database management systems (DBMS).
2. Model Management. A software package that includes financial, statistical, management science, or other quantitative models that provide the system's analytical capabilities, and an appropriate software management.

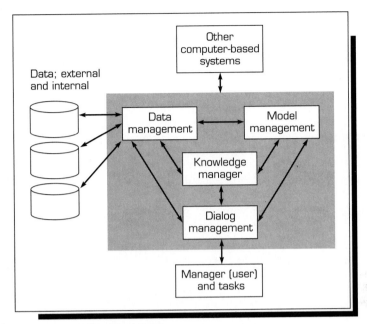

FIGURE 3.2 Conceptual Model of DSS.

3. Communication Subsystem **(dialog subsystem).** The user can communicate with and command the DSS through this subsystem. It provides the *user interface*.
4. Knowledge Management. This optional subsystem can support any of the other subsystems or act as an independent component.

These components constitute the software portion of the DSS. They are housed in a computer and could be facilitated by additional hardware and software pieces. Finally, the user is considered to be a part of the system. Researchers assert that some of the unique contributions of DSS are derived from the interaction between the computer and the decision maker.

A conceptual model of the DSS is given in Figure 3.2. It provides a basic understanding of the general structure and components of a DSS. A more detailed look at each of the components is given in the forthcoming sections and in Chapters 4–6 and 12.

3.6   The Data Management Subsystem

The data management subsystem is composed of the following elements:

- DSS database
- Database management system

■ Data directory
■ Query facility.

These elements are shown schematically in Figure 3.3 (inside the shaded area). The figure also shows the interaction of the data management subsystem with the other parts of the DSS, as well as the interaction with several data sources. A brief discussion of these elements and their function follows.

The Database

A **database** is a collection of interrelated data organized in such a way that it corresponds to the needs and structure of an organization and can be used by more than one person for more than one application. To understand better what a database is, let us consider information kept in separate files.

A file traditionally contains information regarding one application. For ex-

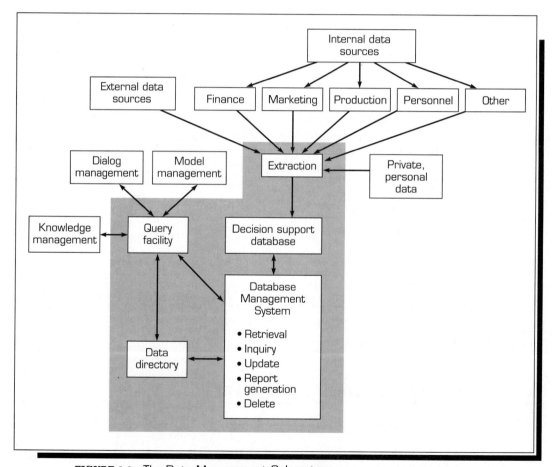

FIGURE 3.3   The Data Management Subsystem.

ample, a company may have a personnel file listing all employees, a customer file listing all customers, and so on. Such files may contain extensive information such as addresses, telephone numbers, and volume of purchases for each customer. In a computerized system, a file can be on an auxiliary storage device, such as a tape or disk.

Example. Let us assume that a company has four files: a parts inventory file, a product file, a parts usage file (quantity used), and a customer file. Although each file has a different purpose, the data within the files are interrelated. For example, the parts usage file is required in preparing the monthly inventory report. And the purchasing data of products recorded in the customer files are used to forecast the demand for these products.

In addition to routine reports, management may require special reports from time to time (called **ad hoc reports**) based on information available in two or more files. In some companies, as much as 80 percent of all reporting is ad hoc and special analysis. In the past, programmers and system analysts had to sort files, create new programs, and manipulate data to meet management's needs, usually at tremendous cost. These needs are now being met quickly and inexpensively by the database and its management. Many times, users can create the reports by themselves.

The data in the database are stored together with a minimum of redundancy to serve multiple applications, so the database is independent of the computer program that uses it and the type of hardware where it is stored. The database is organized so that the firm's files still exist, but they are linked in certain ways so that they form an integrated unit. This arrangement is very important when information is updated. In addition, there could be a considerable savings of storage space.

The data in the DSS database, as shown in Figure 3.3, may include internal transactions, other internal data sources, external data, and private (personal) data belonging to one or more users.

Internal data come from the organization's transaction processing (or data processing) system. Depending on the needs of the DSS, data from functional areas like accounting, finance, marketing, production, and personnel might be included. Transaction data are the major source of information regarding internal company operations. A typical example of such data is the monthly payroll.

Other internal data might also be important to the DSS. Examples include planned dividend rates, machine maintenance scheduling, forecasts of future sales, cost of out-of-stock items, and future hiring plans.

External data may include industry data, marketing research data, census data, regional employment data, government regulations, tax rate schedules, or national economic data. These data might come from the U.S. government, trade associations, marketing research firms, econometric forecasting firms, and the organization's own efforts in collecting external data. Like internal data, the external data may be permanently maintained in the DSS database or may be entered when the DSS is used. External data are provided, in many cases, by computerized online services, a topic discussed in Chapter 4.

Private data may include rules of thumb used by specific decision makers and assessments of specific data and/or situations.

An example of a DSS database for a bank is shown in Figure 3.4.

Organization. The data in the database can be organized in different configurations. For details see Chapter 4. Should a DSS have an independent database? Most large DSS have their own fully integrated, multiple-source DSS database. A separate DSS database does not have to be physically separated from the corporate database. It can be located at the same place as the corporate database for economic reasons. It also can be merged with other databases (see Figure 3.5).

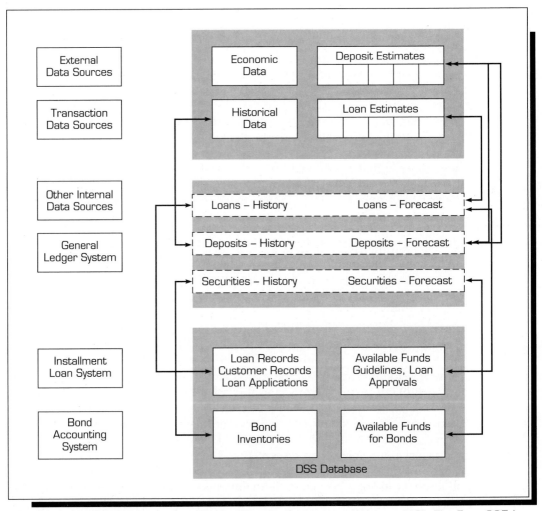

FIGURE 3.4 A DSS Database for a Bank. (*Source:* Sprague and Watson [18], Fig. 5, p. 665.)

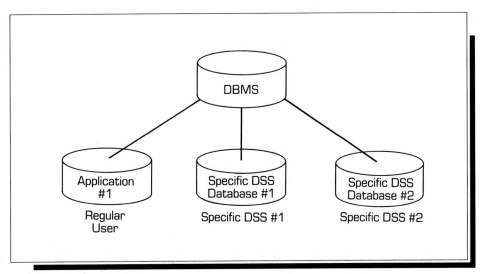

FIGURE 3.5 Database Management System Manages Several Databases.

The major advantages and disadvantages of a separate DSS database are summarized as follows:

Advantages:

1. A greater control exists over the data.
2. A better fit exists with the software that manages the database.
3. Most organizational databases are oriented toward transaction processing; therefore a separate database may be more efficient for a DSS.
4. A DSS may be cross-functional, requiring input from several databases. Once extracted into one database, the use of the data is much more efficient and simpler.
5. Changes and updates are faster, easier, and cheaper.
6. Easier access and data manipulation are provided.
7. Can adopt a database structure that is optimal for the specific DSS use (like relational or object-oriented).

Disadvantages:

1. A special additional database is more expensive to build, secure, and maintain than one database.
2. Separate databases can be individually modified by each user. If redundant data are stored in different places, and if the data are modified differently, we may have inconsistent data in the organization.

Extraction. In order to create a DSS database it is often necessary to capture data from several sources. This operation is called **extraction.** It is basically importing of files, summarization, filtration, and condensation of data. Extraction also occurs when the user produces reports from the data in the DSS database.

Box 3.3: The Capabilities of DBMS in a DSS

- Captures/extracts data for inclusion in a DSS database.
- Quickly updates (adds, deletes, edits, changes) data records and files.
- Interrelates data from different sources.
- Quickly retrieves data from a database for queries and reports.
- Provides comprehensive data security (protection from unauthorized access, recovery capabilities, etc.).
- Handles personal and unofficial data so that users can experiment with alternative solutions based on their own judgment.
- Performs complex retrieval and data manipulation tasks based on queries.
- Tracks usage of data.

The extraction process is managed by the database management system (DBMS).*

Database Management System

The database is created, accessed, and updated by a set of software programs called **database management systems** (DBMS), ranging in price from $99 for a microcomputer to $100,000 for complex mainframe software. DBMS have varied capabilities and are fairly complex so that only a few users can program and develop their own DBMS software. Instead, usually a standard software package is purchased. Examples of micro DBMS are dBASE IV, R base 5000, and ORACLE. On the mainframe one can use DB2. The data management capabilities in DSS (see Box 3.3) are provided by either a standard or a custom made DBMS.

A DBMS performs three basic functions. In enables storage of data in the database, retrieval of data from the database, and control of the database.

Storage. DBMS vary in the configuration of the stored data. Mainframe systems store many large files, each file containing many records, each record containing many data items, and the data items containing many characters. The systems for microcomputers offer more constrained capacities because of limited primary and secondary storage space. (This limitation is becoming less and less of a factor.)

Retrieval. The feature of the DBMS most visible to the user is data retrieval. Current DBMS offer great flexibility in terms of how the information is retrieved

---

*DBMS is both singular and plural (system or systems).

and displayed. With a sophisticated DBMS, the user can specify certain processing of data and customize the output (e.g., reports or graphs) in terms of heading and spacing.

Control. Much of the control activity of the DBMS is invisible to users. The users ask for some information and receive it without knowing the processes that the DBMS has performed. The DBMS can be designed to screen each request for information and determine that (1) the person making the request is indeed an authorized user, (2) the person has access to the requested file, and (3) the person has access to the requested data items in the file. A mainframe DBMS might perform all the control functions very well. The micro DBMS may perform some. This is an area of great variety among the various commercial DBMS.

The manager can obtain information from the DSS in the form of periodic reports, special reports, and output of mathematical models. In all three of these instances, the DBMS serves as a gatekeeper and makes the data available (see Figure 3.6). The periodic reports are frequently prepared by application programs. These programs make requests of the DBMS for data needed from the database. The DBMS might offer a query language that can be manipulated by the user to create special reports. The user enters a few instructions, and this is all that is needed to trigger the preparation of a report.

An effective database and its management can provide support for many managerial activities; general navigation among records, support for a diverse set of data relationships, and report generation are typical examples. However,

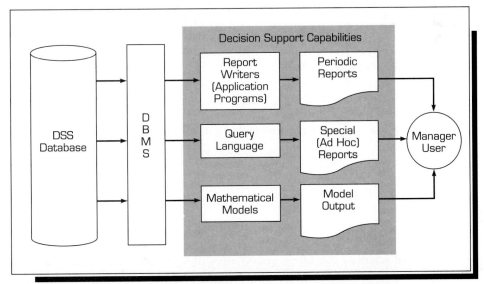

FIGURE 3.6 The Role of DBMS. (*Source:* Adapted from McLeod [12]. Reprinted by permission. Copyright © 1985 by Science Research Associates, Inc.)

the real power of the DSS is provided when the database is integrated with models. The data management subsystem is revisited in Chapter 4.

The Query Facility

The **query facility** element provides the basis for access to data. It accepts requests for data (from other DSS components; see Figure 3.3), determines how these requests can be filled (consulting, if necessary, the data directory), formulates the detailed requests, and returns the results to the issuer of the request. The query facility includes a special query language. Important functions of a DSS query system are the "selection" and "manipulation" operations. For example, the ability to follow an instruction such as "search for all sales in zone B during January 1992 and summarize sales by salesperson."

The Directory (Dictionary)

The data **directory** is a catalog of all the data in the database. It contains the data definitions, and its main function is to answer questions about the availability of data items, their source, or their exact meaning. The directory is especially appropriate for supporting the intelligence phase of the decision-making process by helping to scan data and identify problem areas or opportunities. The directory, as does any other catalog, supports the addition of new entries, deletion of entries, and retrieval of information on entries.

3.7   The Model Management Subsystem

The model management subsystem of the DSS is composed of the following elements:

- Model base
- Model base management system
- Modeling language
- Model directory
- Model execution, integration, and command.

These elements and their **interface** with the other DSS components are shown in Figure 3.7.

The definition and function of each of these elements is described next.

Model Base

A **model base** contains routine and special statistical, financial, management science, and other quantitative models that provide the analysis capabilities in a DSS. (For details see Chapter 5.) The ability to invoke, run, change, combine, and inspect models is a key capability in DSS that differentiates it from the traditional **computer-based information system** (CBIS). The models in the

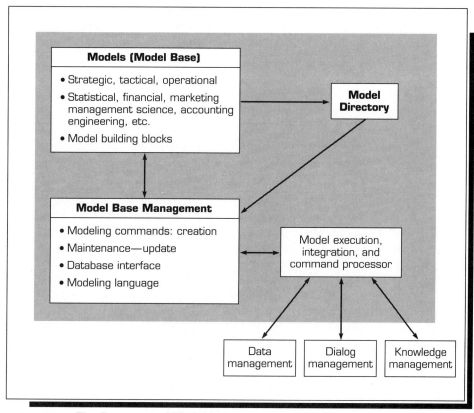

FIGURE 3.7 The Structure of Model Management.

model base can be divided into four major categories: strategic, tactical, operational, and **model building blocks** and subroutines.*

Strategic models are used to support top management's strategic planning responsibilities. Potential applications include developing corporate objectives, planning for mergers and acquisitions, plant location selection, environmental impact analysis, and nonroutine capital budgeting. Strategic models tend to be broad in scope with many variables expressed in a compressed form. The time horizons for these models are expressed in years. The GLSC case includes a long-range planning model. For details regarding planning models, see Naylor [15].

Tactical models are employed mainly by middle management to assist in allocating and controlling the organization's resources. Examples of tactical models include labor requirement planning, sales promotion planning, plant layout determination, and routine capital budgeting. Tactical models are usually

---

*The details of these are based on Kroeber and Watson [10].

applicable only to an organizational subsystem like the accounting department. Their time horizon varies from one month to less than two years. Some external data are needed, but the greatest requirements are for internal data. The GLSC case includes mainly tactical models for their 15-month plan.

Operational models are used to support the day-to-day working activities of the organization. Approving personal loans by a bank, production scheduling, inventory control, maintenance planning and scheduling, and quality control are all examples of operational areas with potential DSS application. Operational models support mainly first-line managers' decision making with a daily to monthly time horizon. The models normally use internal data.

In addition to strategic, tactical, and operational models, the model base could contain model building blocks and subroutines. Examples include a "random number generator mechanism," "curveline fitting routine," "present-value computational routine," or "regression analysis." Such building blocks can be used in several ways. They can be used on their own for applications like data analysis. They can also be employed as components of larger models. For example, a present-value component can be part of a "make or buy" model. Some of these building blocks are used to determine the values of variables and parameters in a model, as in the use of regression analysis to create trend lines in a forecasting model.

The models in the model base can also be classified by functional areas (e.g., financial models, production control models) or by discipline (e.g., statistical models, management science allocation models). A list of representative models is given in Chapter 5. The number of models in a DSS can vary from a few to several hundred. For example, a DSS for a large transportation company includes over 175 models (see Oliff [16]).

DSS holds the potential for reducing or eliminating several typical problems associated with the use of conventional quantitative models in decision making. One such problem is the difficulty of keeping models up-to-date. An all too common situation has been one in which model builders create a model, turn it over to users, and then move on to other projects. Because no easy way exists in a traditional system for updating and changing models, the models eventually become obsolete. Then one of two unfortunate conditions occur. Either the user stops using the model or the user continues to use the model, while the model's output is no longer valid. With a well-thought-out DSS, users have the capability of updating and changing the models by themselves.

Another major problem with quantitative models has been the lack of integration among models. To reduce this problem, models need to be able to "talk" to one another. With a DSS approach to modeling, this integration is accomplished with the help of a software system called model base management system (MBMS). The MBMS facilitates entering and extracting model output in and out of the database. Other problems that are typical of quantitative models and that could be eliminated by using DSS are inadequate tools to support model development, output in a form that is difficult to use, inflexible inputs and outputs, and lack of support for user understanding of large (complex) models.

Modeling Languages

Although some of the models in the model base are standard, it is frequently necessary to write a model. This can be done with high-level languages (COBOL) or better with fourth-generation languages (4GL) and special modeling languages (see Chapters 5 and 7).

The Model Base Management System (MBMS)

The **model base management system** is a software system with the following functions: model creation, using subroutines and other building blocks; generation of new routines and reports; model updating and changing; and data manipulation. The MBMS is capable of interrelating models with the appropriate linkages through a database. (See Box 3.4.)

The Model Directory

The role of the model directory is similar to that of a database directory. It is a catalog of all the models in the model base. It contains the model definitions, and its main function is to answer questions about the availability and capability of the models.

An interesting issue in a DSS might be "Which model should be used for what occasion?" Such model selection cannot be done by the MBMS because it

Box 3.4: Major Functions (or Capabilities) of the MBMS

- Creates models easily and quickly, either from scratch or from existing models or from the building blocks.
- Allows users to manipulate the models so that they can conduct experiments and sensitivity analyses ranging from "what-if" to "goal seeking."
- Stores and manages a wide variety of different types of models in a logical and integrated manner.
- Accesses and integrates the model building blocks.
- Catalogs and displays the directory of models for use by several individuals in the organization.
- Tracks models, data, and application usage.
- Interrelates models with appropriate linkages through the database.
- Manages and maintains the model base with management functions analogous to database management: store, access, run, update, link, catalog, and query.

requires expertise; it is a potential area for a knowledge component "assisting" the MBMS.

Model Execution, Integration, and Command

The following activities are usually controlled by model management:

- Model execution—controlling the actual running of the model.
- Model integration—combining the operations of several models when needed (e.g., directing the output of one model to be processed by another one).

A modeling command processor is used to accept and interpret modeling instructions as they flow out of the dialog component, and to route them to the MBMS, the model execution, or to the integration functions.

The execution of computations with the models requires retrieval of data items from the DSS's or other databases. This activity is performed through a database interface.

3.8 The Knowledge Subsystem

Many unstructured and semistructured problems are so complex that they require expertise for their solution in addition to the regular DSS capabilities. Such an expertise can be provided by an expert system(s). Therefore, the more advanced DSS are equipped with a component that we call knowledge management. Such a component can provide the required expertise for solving some aspects of the problem and/or providing knowledge that can enhance the operation of the other DSS components.

The knowledge management component is composed of one or more expert systems. Like data and model management, knowledge management software provides the necessary execution and integration of the expert system (see Chapter 18). The capabilities of this component are discussed in Chapter 12.

Decision support systems that include such a component are referred to as an intelligent DSS, a DSS/ES, or a knowledge-based DSS.

3.9 The User Interface (Dialog) Subsystem

The dialog component of a DSS is the software and hardware that provides the user interface for DSS. The term **user interface** covers all aspects of the communications between a user and the DSS. It includes not only the hardware and software, but also factors that deal with ease of use, accessibility, and human-machine interactions. Some DSS experts feel that user interface is the most important component because much of the power, flexibility, and ease-of-use characteristics of DSS are derived from this component (e.g., Sprague and Carlson [17, p. 29]). An inconvenient user interface is one of the major reasons why managers have not used computers and quantitative analyses to the extent that these technologies have been available.

Management of the Dialog Subsystem

The **dialog subsystem** is managed by software called **dialog generation and management system (DGMS).** The DGMS is composed of several programs that provide the capabilities listed in Box 3.5.

The Dialog Process

The dialog process for a DSS is shown schematically in Figure 3.8. The user interacts with the computer via an action language processed via the DGMS. In advanced systems the dialog component includes a natural language processor. The DGMS provides the capabilities listed in Box 3.5, and enables the user to interact with the model management and the data management subsystems.

The dialog management subsystem offers a user interface system, which includes the input-output devices and provides the physical means of communication with the DSS; a function that controls the flow of information through the dialog subsystem as data are being inputted and outputted; and a function that transforms the input from the user into languages that can be read by the

Box 3.5: Major Capabilities of DGMS

- Interacts in several different dialog styles.
- Captures, stores, and analyzes dialog usage (tracking), which can be used for improving the dialog system.
- Accommodates the user with a variety of input devices.
- Presents data with a variety of formats and output devices.
- Gives users "help" capabilities, prompting, diagnostic and suggestion routines, or any other flexible support.
- Provides user interface with database and model base.
- Creates data structures to describe outputs (output formatter).
- Stores input and output data.
- Provides color graphics, three-dimensional graphics, and data plotting.
- Has windows to allow multiple functions to be displayed concurrently.
- Can support communication among and between users and builders of DSS.
- Provides training by examples (guiding users through the input and modeling process).
- Provides flexibility and adaptiveness so the DSS will be able to accommodate different problems and technologies.

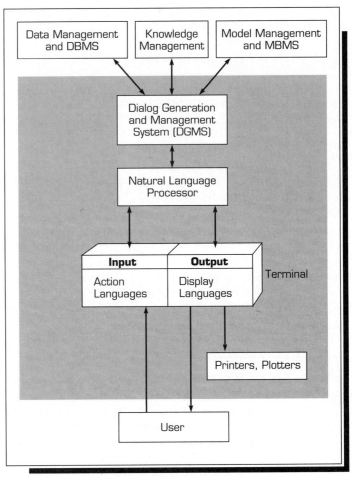

FIGURE 3.8 Schematic View of Dialog Management.

DBMS and the MBMS and that can translate output from the DBMS, the MBMS, and the knowledge management subsystem into a form that can be understood by the user. For further discussion see Chapter 6.

3.10 The User

The person faced with the problem or decision that the DSS is designed to support has been referred to as the *user*, the *manager*, or the *decision maker*.* These terms fail to reflect, however, the heterogeneity that exists among users and the usage patterns (see Box 3.6) of DSS. There are differences in the positions that

---

*The material in Sections 3.10 and 3.11 was adapted from Kroeber and Watson [10].

Box 3.6: DSS Usage Patterns

The ultimate "user" of a decision support system is the decision maker. However, he or she may not actually run the system. Based on his research on 56 decision support systems, Alter ([1], p. 115) identified four distinct usage patterns:

1. *Subscription mode.* The decision maker receives reports generated on a regular basis. Although some data analysis systems or accounting models might be used in this way, it is not typical for decision support systems.
2. *Terminal mode.* The decision maker is the direct user of the system through online access.
3. *Clerk mode.* The decision maker uses the system directly but off line, preparing input on coding forms. The primary difference between this mode and the terminal mode is in the technology employed. This is basically an obsolete mode.
4. *Intermediary mode.* The decision maker uses the system through intermediaries, who perform the analysis and interpret and report the results. The decision maker does not need to know how the intermediary used the system to arrive at the requested information.

The role of an intermediary is common in the use of decision support systems and merits separate attention. The use of an intermediary allows the manager to benefit from the decision support system without actually having to use the keyboard. Some managers resist using the keyboard, and until speech recognition devices become available, there will continue to be some resistance to the terminal mode.

There are three types of intermediaries that reflect different types of support for the manager:

1. *Staff assistant.* This person has specialized knowledge about management problems and some experience with the decision support technology.
2. *Expert tool user.* This person is skilled in the application of one or more types of specialized problem-solving tools. The expert tool user performs tasks that the problem solver does not have the skills or training to perform.
3. *Business (system) analyst.* This person has a general knowledge of the application area, formal business administration education (not computer science), and considerable skill in DSS construction tools.

Note: Another type of intermediary is the facilitator in a group DSS (Chapter 9).

the users hold, the way in which a final decision is reached, the users' cognitive preferences and abilities, and ways of arriving at a decision (decision styles).

A DSS has two broad classes of users: managers and staff specialists. Staff specialists, like financial analysts, production planners, and marketing researchers, outnumber managers by about three to two and are using computers by a much larger ratio. Knowing who will actually have hands-on use of the DSS is important when one is designing it. In general, managers expect systems to be more user-friendly than do staff specialists. Staff specialists tend to be more detail-oriented, are more willing to use complex systems in their day-to-day work, and are interested in the computational capabilities of the DSS. In many cases the staff analysts are the intermediaries between management and the DSS.

Even within the categories of managers and staff specialists, there are important subcategories that influence DSS design. For example, managers differ by organizational level, functional area, education background, and need for analytic support. Staff specialists differ in areas such as education, the functional area that they operate, and relationship to management.

3.11   DSS Hardware and Software

Decision support systems have evolved simultaneously with advances in computer hardware and software technologies. Hardware affects the functionality and the usability of the DSS. Although the choice of hardware may be made before, during, or after the design of the DSS software, in many cases the hardware choice is predetermined by what is already available within the organization. A DSS runs on standard hardware, in contrast to artificial intelligence technologies that may require specially designed hardware. The major hardware options are a time-sharing network, the organization's mainframe computer, a minicomputer, a personal computer, or a distributed system. Each option offers advantages and disadvantages. These are briefly discussed next.

Time-sharing Network

Companies like Boeing Computer Services, Tymshare, and CompuServe offer national time-sharing networks on which DSS software can be placed. In addition, several DSS vendors offer tools for building DSS via time-sharing. Time-sharing is an ideal option if you do not have a mainframe computer, but you need its capabilities. It is also used by companies that already have a mainframe because in some instances better response times can be obtained from a time-sharing network than from an in-house computer system. Another benefit is the quickness with which a DSS can be constructed when the vendor is the DSS builder, because the vendor has experience in using the software and building similar DSS.

Most time-sharing networks have an extensive set of software packages, including a variety of DSS building tools. The more of these that are available, the better the potential fit between the tools and the problem attacked by the DSS. Most organizations can afford to buy only a few of the tools; however, with time sharing one can "rent" the best tool for each specific purpose. Because computing is usually their only business, time-sharing networks tend to keep up with, and use, the latest in both hardware and software.

A time-sharing network also typically offers a variety of support services. These services include training sessions for users, hotlines to answer questions, and management consulting. In addition, some in-house systems do not have network support for strategic businesses in outlying geographic areas (e.g., out of state). A time-sharing vendor helps avoid added telecommunications investment.

Another potential advantage of a time-sharing network is that at a reasonable cost (sometimes at no cost) the user can try the DSS approach on a problem or a set of problems and see whether the approach looks promising. The ability to try out the DSS lowers the risk of a bad investment.

The major disadvantage of a time-sharing network is cost control. If a DSS is frequently used, time-sharing costs can become quite high. What frequently happens in this case is that the DSS is then brought in house.

Mainframe, Workstation, Mini-, or Personal Computer

If the DSS is located in-house, a mainframe, workstation, mini-, or personal computer might be used (or a combination of these if a distributed DSS is used). A variety of factors influence the type of computer used, including what kind of computers are available in-house, the type of decision support to be provided, the data needs of the DSS, the computational power that is needed, the existing network (communication) system, and the software demands of the DSS.

A major reason for placing a DSS in-house is that the required hardware and software may already be available there. However, this situation need not be the limiting consideration. It is not unusual for software and sometimes hardware to be purchased specifically for DSS.

The range of DSS users also influences what hardware is to be used and where it is placed. If the system is to support users throughout an organization, a large mainframe system might be required. On the other hand, if the DSS is to provide decision support for one person, a personal computer might be used (e.g., see Hackathorn and Keen [7]).

The latest developments in the area of super micros and micro-to-mainframe communication and networks of computers could have a major impact on hardware selection.

The data needs of the DSS may also play a role in determining the hardware selection. Some DSS require considerable data from the organization's (corporate) database. Then it may be advantageous to place the DSS on the same system where the database is maintained. However, this may not be as important a consideration as it might first seem. Experience has shown that the data needs of many decision support systems differ considerably from what is maintained in existing databases. Therefore, it may be more practical to download and extract data from the corporate database to the DSS database or even directly to a microcomputer's memory.

Some decision support systems require significant computational power, which necessitates the use of large, fast machines. Some simulation models especially require a large number of calculations. Multidimensional reports constructed from a large number of files also require a significant memory.

In addition to the selection of the computer itself, there is the problem of selecting several additional pieces of hardware that are used to support activities ranging from graphics to auxiliary storage. The selection of specific hardware and peripherals, which requires expertise, is beyond the scope of this book.

The DSS software, as outlined earlier, is composed of the DBMS, MBMS, and dialog management. There may also be additional software for added capabilities (e.g., knowledge-base word processing).

Distributed DSS

An increased number of DSS is available on networks, either LANs and/or wide area networks. The advantages of such systems are the availability of the DSS to users in many locations and the accessibility of the DSS to data and models in many locations. This important topic is revisited in Chapter 4.

3.12   Classifications of DSS and Their Support

There are several classifications of DSS, some of which overlap. The design process, as well as the operation and implementation of DSS, depends in many cases on the type of DSS involved. Several classification schemes are presented next.

Type of Support: Data-oriented versus Model-oriented (Alter [1])

This classification is based on the "degree of action implication of system outputs"; that is, the extent to which system outputs can directly support (or determine) the decision (see Box 3.7). According to this classification, there are seven categories of DSS software (see Table 3.3 on page 110). The first three types are *data-oriented*, performing data retrieval and/or analysis. The remaining four are *model-oriented*, providing either simulation capabilities, optimization, or computations that "suggest an answer." Not every DSS fits neatly into this classification system; some have equally strong data and modeling orientation (e.g., the GLSC case).

Institutional versus Ad Hoc DSS (Donovan and Madnick [4])

This classification is based on the nature of the decision situation that the DSS are designed to support. There are two categories.

Box 3.7: Support Provided by DSS

DSS may provide several types of support. The following structure is based on Alter [1]. Each level of support contains and adds on the previous level (but may also contribute to the previous level).

DSS Provides:	Answers to Questions:
Raw data and status access	What is . . . ?
↓	
General analysis capabilities	What is/Why . . . ?
↓ ↑	
Representation models (financial statements)	What will be . . . ?
Causal models (forecasting, diagnosis)	What will be/ Why . . . ?
↓	
Solution suggestions, evaluation	What if . . . ?
↓	
Solution selection	What is best/What is good enough . . . ?

Institutional DSS. This type of DSS deals with decisions of a *recurring* nature. A typical example is a portfolio management system (PMS), which has been used by several large banks (see Alter [1]). Another example is the GLSC case presented earlier. An **institutional DSS** may be developed and refined over a number of years because the DSS will be used over and over (with appropriate updating of the database and models) to solve identical or similar problems. Institutional DSS deal mainly with operational and management control problems.

Ad Hoc DSS. This type of DSS deals with specific problems that are usually neither anticipated nor recurring. For example, the Houston Minerals DSS was created specifically to evaluate the feasibility of a joint venture. Economic support for this type of situation requires general-purpose software for information retrieval, data analysis, modeling, and the like that can be quickly customized to a specific application. The concept of DSS generators, which will be introduced later, was developed to provide a means for satisfying ad hoc needs for decision-making support. Ad hoc decisions frequently involve strategic planning issues and sometimes management control problems.

Many of the DSS developed up to about 1983 were institutional in nature (see Alter [1] and Meador et al. [13]), mainly owing to the high cost of developing a DSS for nonrecurring use. However, with the increased availability of

TABLE 3.3   Characteristics of Different Classes of Decision Support Systems.

Category	Type of Operation	Type of Task	User	Usage Pattern	Time Frame
File drawer systems	Access data items	Operational	Nonmanagerial line personnel	Simple inquiries	Irregular
Data analysis systems	Ad hoc analysis of files of data	Operational or analysis	Staff analyst or managerial line personnel	Manipulation and display of data	Irregular or periodic
Analysis information systems	Ad hoc analysis involving multiple databases and small models	Analysis, planning	Staff analyst	Programming special reports, developing small models	Irregular, on request
Accounting models	Standard calculations that estimate future results on the basis of accounting definitions	Planning, budgeting	Analyst or manager	Input estimates of activity; receive estimated monetary results as output	Periodic (e.g., weekly, monthly, yearly)
Representational models	Estimating consequences of particular actions	Planning, budgeting	Staff analyst	Input possible decisions; receive estimated results as output	Periodic or irregular (ad hoc analysis)
Optimization models	Calculating an optimal solution to a combinatorial problem	Planning, resource allocation	Staff analyst	Input constraints and objectives; receive answer	Periodic or irregular (ad hoc analysis)
Suggestion models	Performing calculations that generate a suggested decision	Operational	Nonmanagerial line personnel	Input a structured description of the decision situation; receive a suggested decision as output	Daily or periodic

Source: Adapted from Alter [1], p. 90–99.

DSS tools, with their steadily decreasing costs and increasing capabilities, and with the appearance of DSS software for microcomputers, it is probable that relatively more ad hoc DSS are being constructed today.

Degree of Nonprocedurality (Bonczek et al. [3])

This classification is based on the degree of nonprocedurality of the data retrieval and modeling languages provided by the DSS. Procedural languages, such as BASIC and COBOL, require step-by-step specifications of how data are to be retrieved and how computations are to be performed. In nonprocedural languages the system itself is programmed so that programmers are required to specify only what action is needed. There is no need to specify the sequence of execution. At an intermediate level of procedurality are systems that utilize a command language allowing users to call up a desired prespecified report, model, or function. Most DSS users find nonprocedural languages more convenient for both data retrieval and modeling activities. Nonprocedural languages (also called fourth-generation languages) are discussed in Chapter 7.

Personal, Group, and Organizational Support (Hackathorn and Keen [7])

The support given by DSS can be separated into three distinct but interrelated categories:

Personal Support. Here the focus is on an individual user (or a group of users) performing the same activity in a discrete task or decision (e.g., recommending stocks). The task is relatively independent of other tasks.

Group Support. The focus here is on a group of people, each of whom is engaged in separate but highly interrelated tasks. An example is a typical finance department where one DSS may serve most of the employees.

Organizational Support. Here the focus is on organizational tasks or activities involving a *sequence* of operations, different functional areas, and required resources. For example, the GLSC case illustrates a sequence of decisions composed of long-term planning, short-term planning, resource allocation, and job assignment decisions.

Degree of Dependency

There are two types of **interdependent decisions.** *Sequential interdependent* decisions may require a decision maker to make part of a decision and then to pass it on to other decision makers, who make their own contributions to the decision. The GLSC case is an example of such a situation. Decision support systems that support sequential interdependent decision making provide organizational support. Capabilities such as access by multiple users throughout the organization (e.g., using networks) and the ability to store and retrieve data, models, and other users' contributions to the decision are important in providing organizational support. *Pooled interdependent* decisions are made by a group after interaction and negotiation by group members. A DSS for this type of decision making is described as group DSS (GDSS, see Chapter 9).

Note: The term *group support* introduced earlier should not be confused with the concept of **group DSS.** In group support the decisions are made by individuals whose tasks are interrelated. Therefore they should check the impact of their decisions on others, but not necessarily make decisions as a group. In a group DSS each decision (sometimes only one decision) is made by a group.

Individual versus Group DSS

Decision support systems are used by individuals for personal support, or they can use *individually* a DSS or portion of a DSS for organization support. In either case however, the support is given to an individual decision maker. However, many DSS researchers and practitioners (e.g., Keen [8]) point out that the fundamental model of DSS—the lonely decision maker striding down the hall at high noon to make a decision—is true only for minor decisions. In most organizations, be they public or private, Japanese, European, or American, most *major* decisions are made collectively. In making decisions collectively one introduces a new dimension, namely the manner in which the group works together, communicates, and eventually arrives at a decision. This is a complicated process and it can be supported by computers. This is basically what is called group DSS.

Custom-made versus Ready-made Systems

Most DSS are custom made for individual organizations. In such an organization, the problem is nonroutine and not structured. However, a similar problem may exist in a similar organization. For example, hospitals, banks, and universities share many such problems. Similarly, certain nonroutine problems in a functional area (finance, accounting, etc.) can repeat themselves in the same functional area of different organizations. Therefore, it makes sense to build generic DSS that can be used (usually with some modifications) in several organizations of a similar nature. Such DSS are called *ready-made*. They are sold by various vendors and sometimes are available on time-sharing. An example of two such systems is given in Appendix 3-A to this chapter.

3.13   The Big Picture

So far we have introduced you to the fundamentals of DSS. We started the chapter with a discussion of the GLSC case. Now that you have learned about the various components of the DSS, we can superimpose the details of the case on the general structure of the DSS (Figure 3.2 minus the knowledge component). The result is shown in Figure 3.9. Also, we have summarized the major capabilities of the DSS component (excluding the knowledge component) in Figure 3.10.

3.14   Technology Levels

A useful framework for understanding DSS construction issues was devised by Sprague and Carlson [17], who identified **three levels of DSS technology:** specific DSS, DSS generators, and DSS tools. (See Figure 3.11)

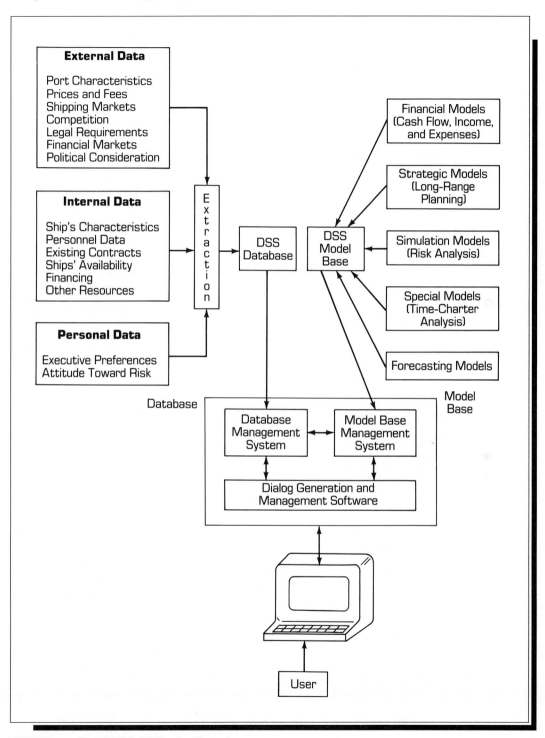

FIGURE 3.9 The GLSC DSS—An Overview.

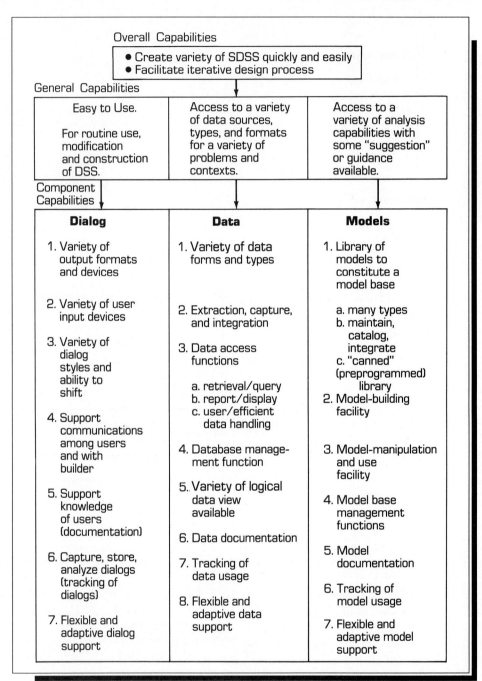

FIGURE 3.10 Summary of DSS Capabilities. (*Source:* Sprague and Carlson [17], p. 313.)

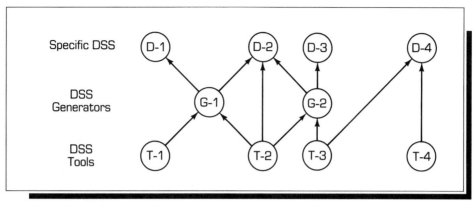

FIGURE 3.11   Technology Levels.

Specific DSS

The "final product," or finished DSS that actually accomplishes the work, is called a **specific DSS** (SDSS). It is used to support a specific application. For example, the Houston Minerals case presented earlier is a specific DSS for analyzing a joint venture.

A well-known example of a specific DSS is the police-beat allocation system, which was implemented by IBM in San Jose, California. This system allows a police officer to display a map outline on a video display terminal and call up data by geographical zones showing police calls for service, response times, and activity level. An officer can manipulate the map, zones, and data, and experiment with a variety of police patrol alternatives. Incidentally, this DSS yielded superior results (in terms of acceptance by users and consistency with the problem requirements) over a solution derived by linear programming.

DSS Generators

A generator (see Box 3.8) is an integrated package of software that provides a set of capabilities to build a specific DSS quickly, inexpensively, and easily. A popular microcomputer-based generator is Lotus 1-2-3. A generator possesses diverse capabilities ranging from modeling, report generation, and graphical display to performing risk analysis. These capabilities, which have been available separately for some time, are integrated into an easy-to-use package.

There has been an evolutionary growth from two directions toward what might be described as an "ideal" DSS generator. One direction is *special-purpose languages* initially developed for the mainframes. In fact, many commercial DSS generators evolved from planning (or modeling) languages, usually with added report generation and graphic display capabilities. Examples of such languages are the Interactive Financial Planning System (IFPS) and Evaluation Planning Systems (EPS). Other types of specialized languages are those initially developed around strong DBMS capabilities. Examples of such languages are Nomad 2,

Box 3.8: DSS Generator

The term *DSS generator* emerged from the concept of application (or program) generator. Application generators are tools used by programmers and system analysts to expedite programming and systems development. For example, an application generator can be used to build an inventory control system.

Application generators add convenience and reduce costs for the creation of programs. The programs produced are not as efficient, in terms of processing throughout, as those coded from scratch by experienced programmers. Therefore generators are more suitable for applications that run infrequently or that do not involve large-volume data processing.

Ramis II, and Focus. The second direction is microbased *integrated software* systems like Lotus 1-2-3, Quattro Pro, and Excel, which are constructed around spreadsheet technology. Both types of generators are discussed in chapter 7.

DSS Tools

At the lowest level of DSS technology are the software utilities or tools. These elements facilitate the development of either a DSS generator or a specific DSS. Examples of **DSS tools** are graphics (hardware and software), editors, query systems, random number generators, and spreadsheets.

Relationships Among the Three Levels

The relationships among the three levels are presented in Figure 3.11. The tools are used to construct generators, which in turn are used to construct specific DSS. However, tools can also be used directly to construct specific DSS. In addition (not shown in the figure), there may be simpler tools for constructing more complicated tools.

The use of DSS generators is extremely helpful in constructing specific DSS and enabling them to quickly adapt to changes. Using generators can save a significant amount of time and money, thus making a DSS financially feasible. Constructing DSS only with tools, without generators, can be a very lengthy and expensive proposition, especially if the tools themselves need to be developed. Although most of the early DSS were developed without generators, this is no longer the usual case.

Significance. The classification of technology levels is not only important for understanding the construction of DSS (and also ES) but also for developing a framework for their use. A field study revealed that DSS generators and tools are extremely useful even for senior managers. There is a wide range of decision situations faced by senior management that require ad hoc DSS. Ad hoc DSS can be developed economically, and in a timely manner, with the aid of generators.

Chapter Highlights

- There are many definitions of DSS.
- At the minimum, DSS is designed to support complex managerial problems that other computerized techniques cannot. DSS is user-oriented, utilizes data, and frequently models.
- It is possible to add a component to the DSS to make it intelligent.
- DSS is frequently built by an iterative approach.
- DSS may provide support to all phases of the decision-making process and to all managerial levels, both for individuals and groups.
- DSS is a user-oriented tool. It can be constructed by end-users.
- DSS can improve the effectiveness of decision making, decrease the need for training, improve management control, facilitate communication, save costs, and allow for more objective decision making.
- The major components of a DSS are: database and its management, model base and its management, and friendly user interface. An intelligent (knowledge) component can be added.
- The data management subsystem includes: a DSS database (optional), a DBMS, a data directory, and a query facility.
- Data are extracted from several sources, internal and external.
- The DBMS provides many capabilities to the DSS, ranging from storage to retrieval and report generation.
- The model base includes standard models and models specifically written for the DSS.
- Custom-made models can be written with third- and fourth-generation languages. End-user DSS are usually written with 4GLs (modeling languages).
- The user interface (or dialog) is of utmost importance. It is managed by a special software that provides the needed capabilities.
- DSS can be used directly by managers (and analysts) or it can be used via intermediaries.
- DSS can be built on all types of hardware and can be placed on networks (distributed DSS).
- DSS can be used by individuals or it can be used to support decisions made by groups.

Key Words

adaptive process	DSS tool	query facility
ad hoc reports	extraction	sequential
computer-based	group DSS	interdependent
information system	institutional DSS	decisions
database	interdependent	specific DSS
database management	decisions	strategic models
system (DBMS)	interface	tactical models
dialog generation and	model base	technology levels
management system	model base	user interface
(DGMS)	management system	
dialog subsystem	(MBMS)	
directory	model building blocks	
DSS generators	operational models	

Questions for Review

1. Give two definitions of DSS.
2. Why do people attempt to narrow the definition of DSS?
3. Give your own definition of DSS.
4. List the major components of DSS and define each of them briefly.
5. How does a database differ from a collection of files?
6. What are the major functions (capabilities) of DBMS?
7. What is meant by "extraction"?
8. What is the function of a query facility?
9. What is the function of a directory?
10. Models are classified as strategic, tactical, or operational. What is the purpose of such classifications? Give an example of each.
11. List some of the major functions of MBMS.
12. What is the major purpose of the user interface system?
13. Define a ready-made DSS.
14. List the major user patterns.
15. What is meant by "dialog style"?
16. What are the major functions of a dialog management system?
17. List the major classes of DSS users.
18. What types of support are provided by DSS?
19. What are the major advantages of time sharing?
20. What are the major disadvantages of time sharing?
21. What are the major software components included in a DSS?
22. Define a procedural computer language and contrast it with a nonprocedural one.
23. Compare a custom-made DSS versus ready-made. List advantages and disadvantages of each.
24. List and discuss the various technology levels.
25. Define DSS "generators" and discuss their objectives.

Questions for Discussion

1. Review the major characteristics and capabilities of DSS. Relate each of them to the three major components of DSS.
2. List some internal data and external data that could be found in a DSS for selection of a portfolio of stocks for an investor.
3. List some internal and external data in a DSS that will be constructed for a decision regarding the expansion of a hospital.
4. Provide a list of possible strategic, tactical, and operational models in a university, in a restaurant, in a chemical plant.
5. Show the similarity between DBMS and MBMS. What is common to both?
6. Compare an individual (specific) DSS to a group DSS.

Exercise

Susan Lopez was promoted to be a director of the transportation department in a medium size university. She controlled the following vehicles: 17 sedans, 15 vans, 3 trucks. The previous director was fired because there were too many complaints concerning not getting vehicles when needed. Susan was told not to expect any increase in budget for the next two years (no replacement or additional vehicles). Susan's major job was to schedule vehicles to employees, and to schedule the maintenance and repair of the vehicles. All this was being accomplished manually.

Your job is to consult with Susan regarding the possibility of using a DSS to improve this situation. Susan has a 386 PC, Lotus, dBase IV, and Harvard Graphics, but she is not using the computer.

Prepare:

1. A justification for the use of this DSS, namely, what this DSS can do to improve Susan's job.
2. What will be included in the major components of the DSS: data management, model management and dialog (interface).
3. What type of support do you expect this DSS to render (consult Table 3.3)?
4. How would you classify this DSS (consult Section 3.12)?

CASE STUDY: Financial Planning at the Louisiana National Bank*

The Louisiana National Bank (LNB) is located in Baton Rouge, Louisiana. In 1958, Charles McCoy became the bank's chief executive officer. Under his lead-

---

*Condensed from Ralph H. Sprague, Jr., and Ronald L. Olson. "The Financial Planning Systems at Louisiana National Bank." *MIS Quarterly*, September 1979, pp. 35–46.

ership, the LNB has developed a reputation for innovation. By 1978 the LNB became the largest bank in Baton Rouge.

In the fall of 1973, the LBN was facing serious problems. Profits had been declining for over a year. Traditional policies for managing the bank were failing. There was a lack of coordination among decision makers. The bank was slow to react to market and regulation changes.

In response to this deteriorating situation, McCoy designated Gil Urban as corporate planner and charged him with the responsibility of developing a system to help analyze the bank's performance and to support top management decision making. Urban was an excellent choice for this position because he had extensive banking experience and a personal interest in planning and analysis activities.

The Development of FPS

After an intensive six-week study, Urban began developing the financial planning system (FPS). The initial system was designed to produce reports of the type and format that top management had been receiving in the past. Over time, management understanding of FPS grew, and the capabilities of the system were refined and expanded.

System Components

FPS has three components: data, reports and analyses, and forecasts. Each component plays an important role in the functioning of FPS.

Data

On a monthly basis, summary data from the bank's general ledger accounting system are extracted and entered into the FPS. The data are added to a matrix of historical data in which the rows are items in the summary chart of accounts and the columns are time periods. The database maintains up to three years of monthly figures and up to 7.5 years of quarterly figures. The database also stores 12 periods of forecast data.

Reports and Analyses

Each month, FPS produces a complete set of summary financial statements, including the balance sheet, the income statement, and standard operating reports. Data from the current month are compared with the forecast, the budget, and the actual data for the previous year. A number of special reports are also generated. Of particular importance to the LNB management are the interest rate-volume-mix analysis and the line-of-business-analysis reports.

Forecasts

The system produced a forecast of the information included in the reports for a period of 12 months. The system contains a built-in linear programming submodel that can be used to optimize projected earnings with respect to yields, subject to constraints or guidelines defined by management.

Use of the System

FPS is employed in several ways. On the first Tuesday of each month, FPS is used to supply the planning committee with reports and graphs that show the previous month's activities and the forecast.

During the meeting of the planning committee, anticipated changes and pending issues are discussed. Frequently, there are questions and possibilities that need to be explored further at the next meeting after additional runs of FPS.

Urban also uses FPS to prepare forecasts for other bank officers who wish to investigate the consequences of possible strategies.

Urban also uses FPS on his own initiative. He investigates areas such as the impact of pending changes in money market rates, banking regulations, market trends, and internal policy changes.

FPS also plays an important role in the bank's budgeting process. Each fall a "grass roots" budget, as it is called, is prepared. It is composed of about 9,000 data items: one for each budget line item, for each of the cost centers, for each of the 12 months of the coming year. Once the tentative budget is prepared, summaries are then extracted and entered into the FPS the same way that actual data are transferred after the end of each month. FPS is then used to assess the combined impact of the budget estimates, to examine the reasonableness of the estimates compared with top management's judgment, and to search for any inconsistencies in interrelated areas. Any adjustments of the tentative budget are made through a process of negotiation between top management and the cost center managers. The detailed final budget is approved by mid-December and is then carried in the automated accounting system, which produces monthly budget variance reports for each cost center during the coming year.

Benefits

The LNB has benefited considerably from the use of FPS. Most important, it has made the bank profitable. After-tax profit grew from 2 to 6 million dollars between 1974 and 1978.

The use of FPS has led to new policies for asset-liability management. An example of this occurred in 1975 when the government authorized consumer certificates of deposit (CDs) in small denominations for four- and six-year maturities. Many banks hesitated to offer these CDs because of the fear that savers would shift their regular savings to higher-paying CDs. By using FPS, the management at the LNB became convinced that the CDs were an excellent way to obtain long-term funds on which to build their consumer loan portfolio. Consequently, they gave heavy promotion to the CDs, which resulted in increased funds, increased loans, and increased profitability in the retail segment of the LNB's business.

FPS has also provided a framework, a structure, and a discipline for unified decision making. Later on, the LNB experienced a growth in credit card loans and decided to sell a large portion of the loans to a New York bank. Without the convincing analysis provided by FPS, this move would have been strongly opposed by several of the bank's managers because of the bank's history as the leading regional credit card lender.

Reporting and negotiating with bank regulators has been facilitated by FPS. In 1978, management noted that FPS forecasted a need for additional capital because of a growing demand for loans. Using FPS, management developed a "balanced growth" plan.

The use of FPS has made it possible to respond to changes faster. In March 1978, after several years of liquidity shortages, the LNB was experiencing an average excess liquidity of 30 million dollars a day. FPS forecasted, however, that loan growth and deposit shrinkage would create liquidity problems by early fall. Based on this forecast, the planning committee set maximum growth goals for all departments and took some other preemptive actions. By October, it was clear that the LNB had averted a major liquidity crisis because of the early warning provided by FPS.

FPS produces the normal monthly reports less expensively than when they were prepared manually. However, the cost of additional runs to explore alternative plans and assumptions more than consumes this saving.

This additional cost does not bother management. As McCoy has said, "FPS clearly paid for itself in helping us generate that first set of strategic plans. Now we don't even think about what it costs, because we couldn't run the bank without it."

Case Questions

1. Discuss the data, models, software interface, and user components in this case.
2. Is the financial planning system at the Louisiana National Bank best categorized as an MIS or a DSS? Why? Is the distinction clear? Why?
3. Decision support systems have the potential for supporting top-, middle-, and lower-management decision making. To what extent is decision making at these levels supported by the decision support systems described in this case?
4. Decision support systems can be used for ad hoc and for repetitive decision making. How would you classify the decision support systems described in this case?

5. Decision support systems have the potential for supporting the intelligence, design, and choice phases of decision making. To what extent are these decision-making phases supported by the decision support systems described in this case?

6. Decision support systems can support independent and sequential interdependent decision making. What kind of decision support is provided by the decision support systems described in this case?

7. Explain the following statement: "Values for the independent variables were entered by management or statistically estimated by FPS with a management override capability." What is the significance of this statement?

8. An evolutionary developmental approach is best for most decision support systems. To what extent was an evolutionary approach used with the decision support systems described in this case? Do you agree with the approaches that were used? Why?

9. The objective of a DSS is to create organizational benefits. Describe the benefits generated by the decision support systems described in this case.

CASE STUDY: Decision Support for Military Housing Managers*

The Problem

The Department of the U.S. Army often enters into agreements for long-term leasing or even building appropriate housing facilities close to or on the bases. The decision where, what, when, and how to build or lease is a complex one, and it requires a formal segmented housing market analysis (SHMA) which costs about $50,000 to prepare and whose purpose is to justify the decision. The SHMA analysis is lengthy and complex. It must meet not only the available budget but also the requirements of several auditing agencies. Furthermore, the analysis takes into account the economy around each base and the existing housing market (e.g., availability of rental units that the military may utilize). The problem is even more complex because there are 20 military ranks (the higher your rank, the nicer accommodations you can get, of course). Housing is available in six sizes ranging from a studio to five bedrooms. Of course, a family's size is a determining factor. The SHMA analysis uses several quantitative models, including econometric models. Execution of such computation, in each of the 200 military installations, is lengthy and is subject to errors, especially when it is done manually using manuals as data sources.

---

*Condensed from G.A. Forgionne, "HANS: A Decision Support System for Military Housing Managers," *Interfaces*, November–December 1991.

The Solution

The DSS which was developed with IFPS (see Appendix A to this book) runs on a PC and is intended to support the SHMA analysis. A simplified diagram of the DSS is shown in Figure 3.12.

The Components of the DSS

On the left side of the figure, two basic components are listed: database and model base.

- The database is composed of:
  a. Off-post data: economic characteristics of the area around the military installation
  b. On-post data: profile of the military personnel seeking housing.

Sources for the internal data are internal databases and reports.

Sources for the external data are Rand McNally's *Places Rated Almanac*, statistical abstracts of the United States, chambers of commerce, banks, real estate boards, and on-line databases.

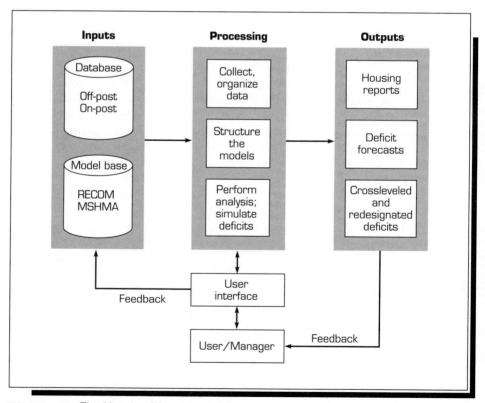

FIGURE 3.12 The Housing Management DSS.

- The model base is composed of two parts:
  a. RECOM (a regional econometric model for the area). This model uses many variables and constraints (such as value of housing, consumer price index, median rent, median per capita income, annual utility bill, and military allowances).
  b. MSHMA (Modified Segmented Housing Market Analysis). This model has many variables, and it also uses on-post and off-post data. The on-post data include: the military share of the housing market, housing available at the base (post), housing occupancy levels, demographics of military people, and housing needs. The off-post data are derived from the RECOM sources, consisting of median selling price, taxes paid, household income, and total population.

Operation

The user receives the DSS on a disk (including all the documentation). The processing starts with data entry. The data are recorded on forms from manuals. The DSS organizes the database, structures the model, and performs analysis (using simulation). All this is done interactively in a user-friendly environment.

The DSS executes all the necessary calculations requested by the housing manager (several options are available). The user can review and modify values as needed.

Outputs

Three major outputs are produced: first, housing reports as desired by army managers (e.g., housing reports that identify market conditions); second, housing deficit (demand over supply) forecasts; and third, cross-leveled and redesignated deficit forecasts. These output are synthesized into two major reports. The output of tested cases was found to be accurate in 95 percent of the cases.

Feedback

Decision making is a continuous process. Managers learn from reality. Thus, corrective actions can take place. As shown in Figure 3.12, there is a feedback from the manager's actions (processing) to the database and the models (adjustment, changes). The second feedback goes from the outputs to the decision maker so that processing can be improved. This feedback may include sensitivity analysis. The DSS can also be used to determine whether a SHMA is needed (from needed to strongly needed).

Sensitivity analysis

The model provides "what-if" and goal-seeking capabilities. These capabilities are built into the IFPS, the tool with which the DSS was constructed.

Benefits

The system provides both monetary and managerial benefits.

a. Monetary benefits. Savings are estimated at about $16,500 per housing project which runs SHMA (or about 2 million dollars per year for the U.S. Army). In addition, there will be a savings of 1 million dollars per year, due to reduced training requirements.

b. Managerial benefits. The tedious manual procedures that often resulted in inaccurate, incomplete, and redundant data were eliminated. The decision-making process has been considerably improved thanks to: quicker analysis of the housing market, impact analysis, error free computation, and rapid sensitivity analyses. In addition, the auditing process has been standardized, and it is done faster, resulting in early releases of funds and alleviation of housing shortages in many locations.

Enhancements

The DSS is being enhanced with an intelligent component, a market-share model, and an improved DBMS.

Case Questions

1. Why was this DSS needed?
2. What factors, in your opinion, contributed to the success of the DSS?
3. Discuss the role of forecasting in the DSS.
4. Discuss the role of sensitivity analysis in this DSS.

References and Bibliography

1. Alter, S. L. *Decision Support Systems: Current Practices and Continuing Challenges.* Reading, MA: Addison-Wesley, 1980.
2. Bennett, J. "User Orientated Graphics, Systems for Decision Support in Unstructured Tasks." In *User-Orientated Design of Interactive Graphic Systems*, S. Treu, ed. New York: ACM, 1977.
3. Bonczek, R. H., C. W. Holsapple, and A. B. Whinston. "The Evolving Roles of Models in Decision Support Systems." *Decision Sciences*, Vol. 11, No. 2, 1980.
4. Donovan, J. J., and S. E. Madnick. "Institutional and Ad Hoc Decision Support Systems and Their Effective Use." *Data Base*, Vol. 8, No. 3, Winter 1977.
5. Ginzberg, M. J., and E. Stohr. "Decision Support Systems: Issues and Perspectives." In *Decision Support Systems*, M. J. Ginzberg et al., ed. Proceedings, NYU Symposium on DSS; New York, 1981. Amsterdam: North-Holland, 1982.
6. Gorry, G. A., and M. S. Scott-Morton. "A Framework for Management Information Systems." *Sloan Management Review*, Vol. 13, No. 1, Fall 1971.

7. Hackathorn, R. D., and P. G. W. Keen. "Organizational Strategies for Personal Computing in Decision Support Systems." *MIS Quarterly*, September 1981.

8. Keen, P. G. W. "Adaptive Design For Decision Support Systems." *Data Base*, Vol. 12, Nos. 1 and 2, Fall 1980.

9. Keen, P. G. W. "Value Analysis: Justifying Decision Support Systems." *MIS Quarterly*, March 1981.

10. Kroeber, D. W., and H. J. Watson. *Computer-Based Information Systems.* 2nd ed. New York: Macmillan, 1986.

11. Little, J. D. C. "Models and Managers: The Concept of a Decision Calculus." *Management Science*, Vol. 16, No. 8, April 1970.

12. McLeod, R., Jr. *Decision Support Software for IBM Personal Computer.* Chicago: SRA, 1985.

13. Meador, C. L., et al. "Setting Priorities for DSS Development." *MIS Quarterly*, June 1984.

14. Moore, J. H., and M. G. Chang. "Design of Decision Support Systems." *Data Base*, Vol. 12, Nos. 1 and 2, Fall 1980.

15. Naylor, T. H. "Strategic Planning Models." *Managerial Planning*, Vol. 30, No. 1, 1983.

16. Oliff, M. D. "FAST Decision Support." *Proceeding Amer. Inst. of Dec. Sciences*, National Meeting, Toronto, Canada, November 1984.

17. Sprague, R. H., Jr., and E. D. Carlson. *Building Effective Decision Support Systems.* Englewood Cliffs, NJ: Prentice-Hall, 1982.

18. Sprague, R. H., Jr., and J. J. Watson. "A Decision Support System for Banks." *Omega*, Vol. 4, No. 6, 1976.

19. Stohr, E. A., and N. H. White. "User Interfaces for Decision Support Systems: An Overview." *Inter. Jour. of Policy Analysis and Infor. Systems*, Vol. 6, No. 4, 1982.

20. Watson H., and Sprague R., (eds.). *Decision Support Systems: Putting Theory into practice*, 3rd ed. Englewood Cliffs NJ: Prentice-Hall, 1993.

APPENDIX 3-A: Examples of Ready-Made Systems

1. Hewlett Packard (HP) Quality Decision Management*

HP Quality Decision Management is an applications software package for analyzing manufacturing processes and product quality. The package provides control and Pareto charts that help production and quality assurance engineers identify and prioritize statistically significant product defects and manufacturing

---

Source: Condensed from "HP Quality Decision Management/1000," Hewlett Packard advertisement brochure, San Jose, CA.

process problems. Engineering departments can use data collected on-line to generate scattergrams, histograms, and tabular reports.

The package differs from conventional MIS application packages because of many added-on DSS capabilities. For example, a menu and prompt/response approach allows engineers without programming experience to configure data collection transactions, specify report and graph formats, archive data, and perform system maintenance functions. The database is designed for workstation-oriented production environments. The system provides data collection, validation, and storage to the database. It also allows "what-if" analysis, sensitivity analysis, and simulation capabilities. Engineers can statistically analyze the data and output the results in tabular or graphical format.

The HP Quality Decision Management System may be used in the following application areas:

1. *Incoming inspection:* displays of inspection instructions, vendor rating reports, control charts of defect rates, and vendor's quality.
2. *Product test:* manual and automatic online data collection, test procedure display, statistical monitoring of defect levels, and decision support graphics and reports.
3. *Statistical process and product monitoring:* on-line data collection from incoming inspection, manufacturing process and test areas, statistical graphs and reports to monitor manufacturing process quality, correlation between product defect data, and defect cause data (in a real-time environment).

2. Equitable Life Insurance—Real Estate Application Via Time Sharing*

The Realty Group of this large insurance company buys, sells, and manages hundreds of real estate properties for the insurance company and for clients. The DSS (Tymcom 370) provides the following capabilities:

1. Database management including preparation of periodic reports and preparation of real estate closing transactions.
2. Cash flow projections (itemized by expense and income categories) for properties that are candidates for acquisitions.
3. Computations of the rate of return on investments and other measures of performance of existing and proposed properties.
4. Access to the corporate database and execution of standard manipulations.
5. User access to the system through telephone lines.

System Benefits. This type of DSS provides several advantages. Latest software and hardware technologies are available to the user. This system, which is

---

Source: Condensed from *Computerworld*, February 22, 1982, p. 34.

several years old, is being constantly updated for increased capabilities and reduced cost.

1. The major benefits reported are reduction of report turnaround time (by as much as 75 percent), capability of making faster (and more consistent) acquisition decisions, downloading of information from the corporate database to PCs for manipulation by decision makers, and comparative analysis of hundreds of managers and properties.
2. Time-sharing is mainly appropriate for infrequent use. With the decreased cost of software and hardware and the increased capabilities of microcomputers, there is a trend away from time-sharing to in-house computing.

Chapter 4

Data Management

Data and its management are the foundation upon which all DSS and many MSS are constructed. Where data come from, how they are collected, and how they are organized are the subject of this chapter. Also we describe the issues of distributed databases and DBMS as they relate to DSS and the new concept of object-oriented databases. The outline of this chapter is:

4.1   Introduction

Databases and their management play a major role (frequently **the** major role) in most DSS. A similar situation is observable in related technologies such as organizational DSS and executive information systems. Data exist in many sources, internal and external. In many cases, they are being extracted to a special database for the specific MSS application.

In the previous chapter, we provided an overview of the data and their management in a DSS. Specifically we showed the internal structure of the data management component and how it is related to the other DSS component. In this chapter we describe where data come from, how they are collected, and how they are organized. Special attention is given to the DBMS and to its operation. Three related topics are also presented: distributed DSS (including databases and DBMS), object-oriented databases, and intelligent databases.

4.2   Sources of Data

Data for the DSS (and MSS) come from three major sources: internal, external, and personal (of the user).

Internal Sources. Data are stored in one or more places in any organization. These data are about people, products, services, and processes. For example, data about the employees and their pay are usually stored in the corporate database. Data about equipment and machinery may be stored in the maintenance department database. Sales data can be stored in several places—aggregate sales data in the corporate database and details at each region.

A DSS may use raw data as well as processed data (e.g., reports, summaries).

External Data. There are many, many sources for external data (see Box 4.1). They range from commercial databases (see Section 4.4) to data collected by sensors and satellites. Data are available on CD-ROMs, as films, and even as music or voices. Pictures, diagrams, atlases, and television are also sources of data. Government reports (either computerized or not) constitute a major source for external data. The Chamber of Commerce, local banks, research institutions, and the like flood the environment with data and information, resulting in information overload for the MSS user. Data may come from around the globe. Most of the external data are irrelevant to the specific MSS. Yet much external data need to be monitored and captured to assure that important data are not overlooked.

Personal Data. The DSS users may contribute their own expertise by creating personal data for the DSS. These include, for example, subjective estimates of sales or opinions about what the competitors are likely to do.

Box 4.1: Sources of External Data—A Sampler

Many sources of data exist in addition to commercial online databases (section 4.4). Common data sources are:

Federal Publications

Business Conditions Digest (Department of Commerce) **(discontinued March 1990)**—monthly report of a number of data series focused on forecasting U.S. GNP

Survey of Current Business (Department of Commerce) **(continues *Business Conditions Digest* in short form)**—monthly, general business conditions

Monthly Labor Review (Department of Labor)—monthly employment statistics (a journal with articles)

Employment and Earnings (Department of Labor)—monthly, more detailed than *Monthly Labor Review*

Other

International Monetary Fund—report of balance of payments, including currency rates, for participating countries

Moody's—a series of manuals including abstracted information and balance sheets of most large U.S. corporations, intended for investors

Standard & Poor's—annual, updated report of financial stability of most U.S. corporations

Advertising Age—marketing newspaper, with a great deal of data on marketing

Annual Editor & Publisher Market Guide—annual report of marketing information by SMSA (standard metropolitan statistical area)

Indexes

Business Information Sources. 1985. Rev. ed., ed. L. M. Daniells. University of California Press. Categorization of databases by functional area of business

Encyclopedia of Business Information Sources. 1988. 7th ed., ed. J. Woy. Gale Research, Inc. Bibliographic guide on about 1,000 business subjects, including online databases

Encyclopedia of Information Systems and Services. 10th ed., ed. A. Lucas. Gale Research, Inc. Descriptive guide to databases in electronic form

The CD-ROM Directory. 1990, 1989. 4th ed., ed. J. Mitchell and J. Harrison. TFPL Publishing. Index of CD-ROM databases

(*Source:* Olson and Courtney [13], p. 119. Used with permission.)

4.3 Data Collection and Data Problems

The availability of data in many internal and external sources complicates the task of DSS building. Sometimes it is even necessary to collect raw data in the field. In other cases it is necessary to elicit data from people. In either case, data need to be validated. A classic expression that sums it up well is "Garbage in, garbage out" (GIGO).

Methods for Collecting Raw Data. Raw data can be collected manually or by instruments and sensors. Representative data collection methods are time studies (during observations), surveys (using questionnaires), observation (e.g. using video cameras), and soliciting information from experts (e.g. interviews, see Chapter 13).

Data Problems. All computer-based systems depend on data. The quality and integrity of the data are critical for the DSS to avoid the GIGO syndrome. MSS are even more dependent on data, because compiled data make up information and knowledge that are the center of any decision-making system.

The major data problems in DSS are summarized in Table 4.1 along with some possible solutions. These problems were observed in large DSS during the mid- to late 1970s. Although some of these problems may be less acute today because of developments in software, hardware, and computer networks, they still present potential problem areas for most MSS.

Data must either be available to the system or the system must include a data acquisition subsystem, which is the case with any specific ES. The data issue should be considered in the planning stage of the system life cycle. If too many problems are anticipated, the project should not be undertaken.

4.4 DSS and Commercial Database Services

An **online (commercial) database** service sells access to large (usually nation-wide) databases. Such a service can add external data to the DSS in a timely manner and at reasonable cost. All that is necessary to retrieve data from such a service is a computer terminal, modem, telephone, password, and some service fees. Sometimes described as a computerized data bank, this form of information supply is becoming extremely popular. Several thousand services* are currently available. For an overview of this business, see Seligman [15]. Table 4.2 lists several representative services.

Directory of Online Databases is a quarterly publication by Cuadra Assoc., Inc., Santa Monica, CA (with Elsevier Publishing Co., New York) that provides current information on commercial databases. This directory is also available online.

TABLE 4.1 Data Problems.

Problem	Typical Cause	Possible Solutions (in Some Cases)
Data are not correct.	Raw data were entered inaccurately.	Develop a systematic way to ensure the accuracy of raw data.
	Data derived by an individual were generated carelessly.	Whenever derived data are submitted, carefully monitor both the data values and the manner in which the data were generated.
Data are not timely.	The method for generating the data is not rapid enough to meet the need for the data.	Modify the system for generating the data.
Data are not measured or indexed properly.	Raw data are gathered according to a logic or periodicity that is not consistent with the purposes of the analysis.	Develop a system for rescaling or recombining the improperly indexed data.
Too many data are needed.	A great deal of raw data is needed to calculate the coefficients in a detailed model.	Develop efficient ways of extracting and combining data from large-scale data processing systems.
	A detailed model contains so many coefficients that it is difficult to develop and maintain.	Develop simpler or more highly aggregated models.
Needed data simply do not exist.	No one ever stored data needed now.	Whether or not it is useful now, store data for future use. (This may be impractical because of the cost of storing and maintaining data. Furthermore, the data may not be found when they are needed.)
	Required data never existed.	Make an effort to generate the data or to estimate them if they concern the future.

Source: Alter [1] p. 30.

TABLE 4.2   Representative Commercial Database (Data Bank) Services.

CompuServe and The Source. Personal computer networks providing statistical data banks (business and financial market statistics) as well as bibliographic data banks (news, reference, library, and electronic encyclopedias). CompuServe is the largest supplier of such services to personal computer users.

Compustat. Provides financial statistics about more than 12,000 corporations.

Data Resources, Inc. Offers statistical data banks in agriculture, banking, commodities, demographics, economics, energy, finance, insurance, international business, and the steel and transportation industries. DRI economists maintain a number of these data banks. Standard & Poor's is also a source. It offers services under the **U.S. Central Data Bank.**

Dow Jones Information Service. Provides statistical data banks on stock market and other financial markets and activities, and in-depth financial statistics on all corporations listed on the New York and American stock exchanges, plus 800 other selected companies. Its Dow Jones News/Retrieval system provides bibliographic data banks on business, financial, and general news from the *Wall Street Journal, Barron's*, the Dow Jones News Service, *Wall Street Week*, and the 21-volume *American Academic Encyclopedia*.

Interactive Data Corporation. A statistical data bank distributor covering agriculture, autos, banking, commodities, demographics, economics, energy, finance, international business, and insurance. Its main suppliers are Chase Econometric Associates, Standard & Poor's, and Value Line.

Lockheed Information Systems. The largest bibliographic distributor. Its DIALOG system offers extracts and summaries of more than 150 different data banks in agriculture, business, economics, education, energy, engineering, environment, foundations, general news publications, government, international business, patents, pharmaceuticals, science, and social sciences. It relies on many economic research firms, trade associations, and governmental groups for data.

Mead Data Central. This data bank service offers two major bibliographic data banks. **Lexis** provides legal research information and legal articles. **Nexis** provides a full-text (not abstract) bibliographic database of over 100 newspapers, magazines, newsletters, news services, government documents, and so on. It includes full text and abstracts from the *New York Times* and the complete 29-volume *Encyclopedia Britannica*. Also provided is the Advertising & Marketing Intelligence (AMI) data bank, and the National Automated Accounting Research System.

Source: Based on Standard & Poor's Compustat Services, Inc., statistics on 6,000 companies, financial reports.

Some of these services also offer time-sharing capabilities for the use of DSS generators like IFPS, EXPRESS, and EPS. Several services use other data banks as a source of information.

4.5   Databases and Database Management Systems— An Introduction

The construction of a DSS may involve the creation of a separate DSS database. In such a case the DSS builder will need help to design the database, to prepare the data, and so on. Later, it will be necessary to administer the database.

The complexity of most corporate databases and/or large-scale independent DSS databases sometimes makes the standard computer operating systems inadequate for an effective and/or efficient interface between the user and the database. A database management system (DBMS) is designed to supplement the standard operating systems by allowing for greater integration of data, complex file structure, quick retrieval and changes, and better data security, to mention a few advantages. Specifically, a DBMS is a software program for entering (or adding) information into a database, updating, deleting, manipulating, storing and retrieving the information. A DBMS combined with a *modeling language* is a typical system development pair, which is used in constructing DSS.

DBMS are designed to handle large amounts of information. Often, data from the database are extracted and put in a statistical, mathematical, or financial model for further manipulation or analysis. This is basically what is happening in a DSS.

Database Software

The DSS builders use procedural (also called high-level or third-generation) and/or nonprocedural programming languages.

Procedural Languages

Procedural languages, which include such well-known names as BASIC, COBOL, FORTRAN, and Pascal, use symbols extensively. They were developed by the late 1950s. As the name implies, with these languages the programmer defines the detailed procedures that the computer is to follow. The main advantage of using procedure-oriented languages is that they are widely known and are available on most computer systems. Their major limitation is that they do not contain features that facilitate the creation and use of MSS.

Certain procedural languages are better suited to DSS than others. Such languages may still require programmers to describe a procedure for the computer to follow, but features have been included in the languages that make them especially attractive for certain applications. Three languages that are used in some large-scale decision support systems are APL, PL/1, and Pascal. APL is especially appropriate for mathematical modeling applications that involve cumbersome mathematical operations like inverting a matrix. Pascal has useful data-handling features.

Nonprocedural Fourth-generation Languages (4GLs)

In contrast to procedural languages, programmers who use a nonprocedural language have to specify only the major steps of the program; there is no need to specify low-level details such as the sequencing of computations or the exact data representation. **Nonprocedural languages** are the backbone of most DSS generators and tools.

The fundamental concept behind a nonprocedural language is to transfer the entire concern about program flow from the programmer to the computer software. With nonprocedural languages the programmer instructs the computer by specifying the desired result, rather than specifying actions needed to achieve that result. To do this it is necessary to use a memory-hungry software to translate the 4GL code into machine language.

For example, assume that a report is desired showing the total units sold for each product, in each month and year, with a subtotal for each customer. In addition, each new customer must start on a new page. A 4GL request would look something like this:

```
TABLE FILE SALES SUM UNITS BY
YEAR BY MONTH BY CUSTOMER BY
PRODUCT ON CUSTOMER SUBTOTAL PAGE BREAK
END
```

The logic flow of the same request, using a procedural language like COBOL, would be represented (for a complex situation) by a flowchart with more than 50 active procedural blocks and could require hundreds of lines of coding. By eliminating most of the programming, nonprocedural languages tend also to improve application reliability by an even larger margin than their program size reduction would suggest.

4GLs are beneficial because:

- They are result-oriented.
- They improve programmers' productivity by at least 5 to 1, and by as much as 300 to 1 for some activities (e.g., see Cobb [4]). In Appendix 4-A we show an example of a program done with FOCUS versus the same programming done in COBOL. The FOCUS programming required 4 lines versus 115 lines in COBOL.
- A large percentage of end-users can build systems with 4GLs without going through intermediaries, because fourth-generation languages are designed for both computer specialists and end-users.

Fourth-generation languages are used to build information systems quickly and inexpensively. Therefore they can be considered effective development tools. In the non-DSS environment they are considered to be efficient applications generators for improving programmers' productivity. In the DSS environment they can be used as follows:

- As one of the tools used when a DSS or a DSS generator is built from scratch.
- As a basis for building other tools or components of a DSS; for example, a DSS DBMS is usually written in 4GL.
- As a DSS generator for building specific DSS.
- They are the ideal tool for the Information Centers being established by corporations today.

Problem-oriented Languages

These languages allow the programmer to describe the characteristics of a problem to be solved rather than a procedure to be followed. A variety of problem-oriented languages has been developed for different types of problems or functions. For example, GPSS (General Purpose Simulation Software, a well-known simulation package) is used to expedite the construction of simulation models and can be used in the construction of a large DSS.

Report Generators and Query Languages

The procedures for preparing a report—performing subtotals and breaks for each group of items, page breaks, page headings on first and subsequent pages, page numbering, grand totals, and the like—can be quite complex. Yet they follow fairly regular rules. The regularity of the procedures and rules for report layout are the basis for **report generators.**

Using a report generator, the programmer describes the format of the report and characteristics of the data. The detailed procedures are generated by the software. An older but rather widely used report generator is RPG (Report Program Generator, with new versions coming periodically). Report generators are now generally incorporated in very high-level languages and database query languages.

Query languages are designed to enable the user to communicate easily with the computer mainly for retrieval of data from the database. Representative query languages are ADAM, CUPID, IQF, 24, QUEL, SEQUEL II, SQL, SQUARE, and System 2000. A special class of query languages is the natural language processor, which utilizes artificial intelligence (e.g., CLOUT, Q&A, and INTELLECT). This class is discussed in Chapter 6.

4.6 Fourth-generation Systems

A DBMS, when used as a development tool for DSS, is usually written in a 4GL and is integrated with several other elements.* Such an arrangement is an especially popular combination for mainframe computers and is called a complete **fourth-generation system.**

A complete fourth-generation system typically includes several features that make it easy for the user to communicate with the computer and for the builder to build a DSS (see Figure 4.1). The most common features are:

- Fourth-generation DBMS
- Nonprocedural report writer (or report generator)
- Nonprocedural language for data maintenance

*Based on Cobb [4].

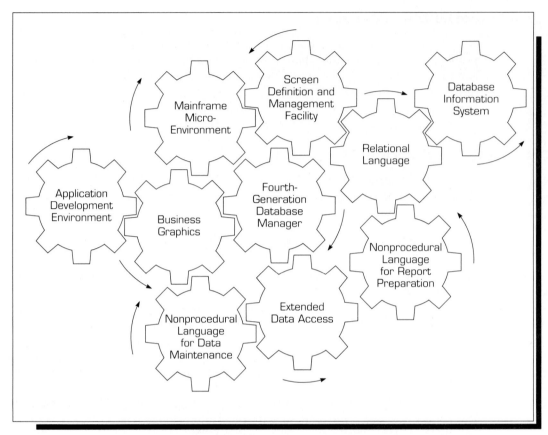

FIGURE 4.1   Integrated Fourth-generation System. (*Source:* Modified from Cobb [4].)

- Screen definition and management facility
- Graphic enhancement
- Query language
- Relational language
- Applications management
- Client/server management
- Extended data access
- Modeling language
- Environment for applications development
- Environment for information consumers
- Micro-to-mainframe environment.

A complete fourth-generation system is approaching a full-fledged DSS generator. This occurs when modeling capabilities are added (e.g., a spreadsheet).

Another way to look at the classification of fourth-generation systems is to distinguish between those that are used as DSS generators by end-users (or by

Information Center people) and those that are used as application generators (usually for non-DSS applications) by IS professionals. Examples of the first category are FOCUS, NOMAD 2, RAMIS II, and SAS. Examples of the second category are IDEAL, MANTIS, NATURAL, and ADS/ON-LINE.

There are two ways to acquire a complete fourth-generation system. One is to obtain each component separately and build bridges between the components. Although a feasible solution, it is difficult to implement because the separate components available are not designed to fit together.

The second solution is to acquire all the functions from one vendor in a single integrated system containing components designed and implemented specifically to work together. Representative fourth-generation products (mostly relational) are listed in Table 4.3.

TABLE 4.3 Representative Fourth-generation Systems.

Product	Vendor
ADS/ON-LINE	Cullinet (Westwood, MA)
Application System/400	IBM (Armonk, NJ)
CA-Datacom/DB	Comp. Associates (Garden City, NY)
Dataflex	Data Access Corp. (Miami, FL)
DB2	IBM (Armonk, NJ)
DB2-Xpert	XA Systems Corp. (Los Gatos, CA)
dBase III +, dBase IV	Ashton-Tate (Culver City, CA)
FOCUS	Information Builders, Inc. (New York, NY)
GDX	General Data System (Philadelphia, PA)
IDEAL	ADR (East Syracuse, NY)
Informix-SQL, STAR	Informix Software, Inc. (Menlo Park, CA)
Infoscope	Microstuf, Inc. (Roswell, GA)
INGRES	INGRES Div. Ask Computer (Alameda, CA)
Knowledge Man, MDBS	Micro Data Base Systems (Lafayette, IN)
MANTIS	CINCOM (Cincinnati, OH)
NATURAL	Software A & G (Reston, VA)
NOMAD	Must Software Int'l. (Norwalk, CT)
Oracle	Oracle, Inc. (Belmont, CA)
Present	Data General Corp. (Westboro, MA)
RAMIS	On-Line Software Int'l. (Fort Lee, NJ)
Rdb	Digital Equipment Corp. (Nashua, NH)
Reflex	Borland International (Scotts Valley, CA)
Revelation	COSMOS, Inc. (Seattle, WA)
R:Base	Microrim, Inc. (Bellevue, WA)
SQL Server	Microsoft (Redmond, WA)
Sybase	Sybase Corp. (Emerville, CA)

Not all DSS are constructed with 4GL. Some are being constructed with third-generation languages and many are being constructed with *both* third and fourth generations. One reason is that 4GLs are relatively new and many programmers are unfamiliar with the tools. In general, programs written in 4GL are considered less efficient than those written with 3GL (the computer run time is longer). This gap is being closed rapidly, however. Furthermore, 4GLs are starting to be integrated with artificial intelligence products, a fact that could make them *the* dominating tool in DSS construction. Of special interest is the combi-

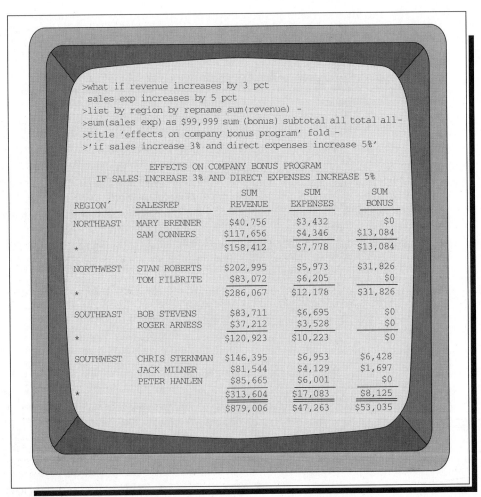

```
>what if revenue increases by 3 pct
 sales exp increases by 5 pct
>list by region by repname sum(revenue) -
>sum(sales exp) as $99,999 sum (bonus) subtotal all total all-
>title 'effects on company bonus program' fold -
>'if sales increase 3% and direct expenses increase 5%'
```

		SUM	SUM	SUM
REGION	SALESREP	REVENUE	EXPENSES	BONUS
NORTHEAST	MARY BRENNER	$40,756	$3,432	$0
	SAM CONNERS	$117,656	$4,346	$13,084
*		$158,412	$7,778	$13,084
NORTHWEST	STAN ROBERTS	$202,995	$5,973	$31,826
	TOM FILBRITE	$83,072	$6,205	$0
*		$286,067	$12,178	$31,826
SOUTHEAST	BOB STEVENS	$83,711	$6,695	$0
	ROGER ARNESS	$37,212	$3,528	$0
*		$120,923	$10,223	$0
SOUTHWEST	CHRIS STERNMAN	$146,395	$6,953	$6,428
	JACK MILNER	$81,544	$4,129	$1,697
	PETER HANLEN	$85,665	$6,001	$0
*		$313,604	$17,083	$8,125
		$879,006	$47,263	$53,035

EFFECTS ON COMPANY BONUS PROGRAM
IF SALES INCREASE 3% AND DIRECT EXPENSES INCREASE 5%

FIGURE 4.2 Example of "What-If" Analysis Done by NOMAD 2. The upper part of the figure shows the commands as programmed with NOMAD 2; the lower part shows the projections and their impacts. (*Source:* Courtesy of Must Software Int'l.)

nation of natural language processors and databases. A brief review of three products—CLOUT, PARADOX, and Q & A—is given in Chapter 6.

Two typical DSS capabilities provided by the NOMAD 2 generator are shown in Figure 4.2 (**"what-if" capability**) and Figure 4.3 (**goal seeking**).

Fourth-generation languages are popular not only for DSS databases; they are also used in several of the most powerful modeling tools.

4.7 Database Structures and SQL

The relationships between the many individual records stored in a database can be expressed by several logical structures. DBMS are designed to use these

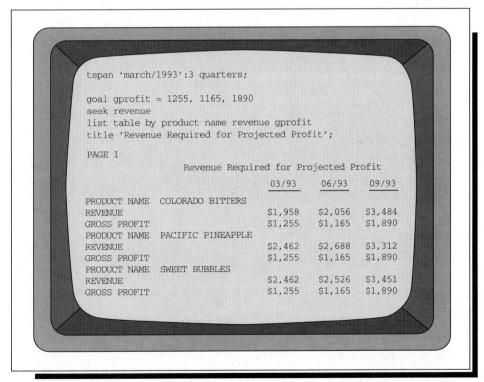

FIGURE 4.3 NOMAD 2: Goal Seek Analysis—Time Span. (*Source:* Courtesy of Must Software Int'l.)

structures to execute their functions. The three fundamental structures are relational, hierarchical, and network. They are shown in Figure 4.4.

Relational Database

This prominent form of database organization—described as tabular or flat—allows the user to think in the form of two-dimensional tables, which is the way many people see data reports. It takes its name from the mathematical theory of relations. This structure is most popular for DSS databases. Relational DBMS allows multiple access queries. It is fairly friendly software.

Thus, a data file consists of a number of columns proceeding down a page. These columns are considered individual fields. The rows on a page represent individual records made up of several fields. This is the very same design employed by spreadsheets. Several such data files may be "related" by means of a common data field found in the two (or more) data files. These common fields must be spelled exactly alike and must be the same size (number of bytes) and type (e.g., alphanumeric, dollar, etc.). For example, in Figure 4.4 the data field called customer name is found in both the customer and the product files, and they are thus related. The data field called product number is found in the product file and the usage file. It is through these common linkages that all three files are related and in combination form a relational database.

The advantage of this form of database is that it is simple for the user to learn, can be easily expanded or altered, and may be accessed in a number of formats not anticipated at the time of the initial design and development of the database.

Hierarchical

The hierarchical model orders the data items in a top-down fashion, creating logical links between related data items. It looks like a tree, or an organizational chart.

Network

This structure permits more complex links, including lateral connections between related items. This structure is also called the CODASYL model. It can save storage space owing to sharing of some items (e.g., Green and Brown are sharing S.1 and T.1).

SQL

SQL (Structured Query Language, a software package) is a data language that is becoming a standard for data access and manipulation in relational database management systems. It is an English-like language consisting of several "layers" of increasing complexity and capability.

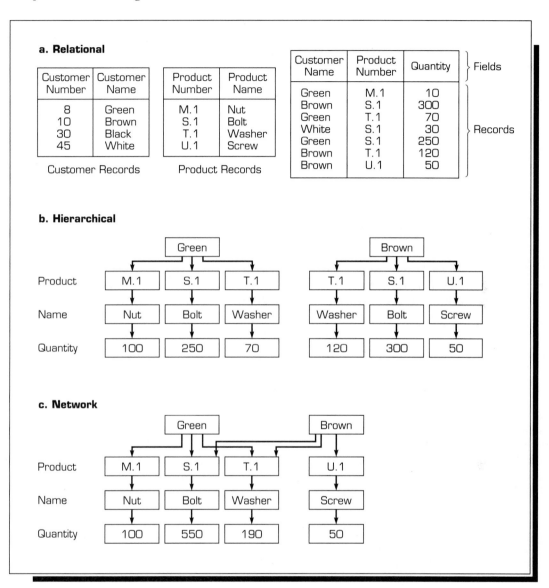

FIGURE 4.4 Database Structures.

SQL is used for online access to databases, for DBMS operations from programs, and for database administration functions. It is also used for data access and manipulation functions of some leading DBMS software products (such as ORACLE, DB2, Ingres, and Supra).

SQL is nonprocedural and very user friendly, so people can use it for their own queries and database operations. SQL can be used for programs written in all standard programming languages; thus it facilitates software integration.

SQL statements are free format. For example, "Alter Table Employees, ADD Bonus Number" is a command to change an existing table (called "employees") by adding a column called bonus.

A simple query to identify the employees whose monthly salary is greater than $2,000 is written as:

```
SELECT      Name, Salary
FROM        Employees
WHERE       Salary > 2000
```

Other examples of SQL programming are shown in Box 4.2.

4.8 Distributed DSS and Data Communication

The various components of the DSS and/or its users do not have to be in one location. They can be dispersed both geographically and organizationally throughout an organization and its environment. For example, the GLSC case in Chapter 3 illustrates a system of this kind where the DSS is used in many locations; data are purchased from online services (external databases) and one of the models is located outside the company. In such cases there is a need to communicate. This need is fulfilled by data communication systems.

Data communication systems (DCSs) provide for the transmission of data over communication links between one or more computer systems and a variety of input and/or output terminals. DCSs are part of the general area of telecommunications.

The DCSs are not generally considered to be a component of a DSS. However, almost any large DSS uses a DCS extensively. In addition, a DCS can greatly increase the power of micro-based DSS. Furthermore, DSS software contains the monitors and controls for accessing the DCS. (For more information, see Champine et al. [2], Fitzgerald and Eason [5], and Martin [10].)

The following related topics are discussed briefly:

- Micro-DSS
- Distributed DSS
- Local area networks (LANs)
- Client/server architecture.

Micro-DSS

During the last few years we have witnessed an increased number of DSS being constructed and operated on microcomputers. Many vendors have already created micro-versions of their mainframe DSS generators and tools. The rapid influx of microcomputers into the corporate environment is giving rise to a new concept, which is called the executive workstation. These stations support

Box 4.2: Sampler of SQL Statements

Natural Language	SQL
List of all purchases of L.B. University since January of 1992, in terms of products, prices, and quantities	SELECT PRODUCTS PURCH PRICE QUANTITY FROM PURCHASE-HIST WHERE CUST-NAME EQ L.B. UNIVERSITY AND PURCH-DATE GE 01/01/92
List the price of cotton shirts, medium size of short sleeves and white color	SELECT PRICE, AMOUNT-AVAIL FROM PRODUCT WHERE PROD-NAME EQ COTTON SHIRT AND SIZE EQ MEDIUM AND STYLE EQ SHORT SLEEVES AND COLOR EQ WHITE

not only decision making but also communications (via electronic mail) and calendaring, to mention a few. The micro-DSS is an important component in many client/server systems.

The success of the micro-DSS depends on its ability to integrate with the mainframe, to access data on a host (mainframe) computer, and on the capabilities provided by distributed systems and networks.

Distributed DSS

Distributed processing, also referred to as distributed data processing (DDP), is a form of information processing made possible by a network of computers "dispersed" throughout a single organization or over several organizations. Processing of user applications is accomplished by several computers (or workstations) interconnected by a network. For example, a distributed system may exist in a school or in a manufacturing plant.

Distributed processing permits users to work with their own microcomputers independently, yet communicate with other computers, and usually share a database and other resources. Therefore DDP is a movement *away* from a centralized processing approach, yet it is not a completely independent decentralized system either. It possesses five important characteristics:

- Computers are dispersed throughout an organization.
- Computers are connected by a DCS.
- A common database is shared by all (additional databases may exist).
- All computers are *centrally* coordinated with an information resource management plan.
- Input and output operations are done within user departments.

DDP permits centralized control over policies and processing while the system retains the flexibility of decentralization. The facilities at the sites are tailored to local needs and controlled by local management, avoiding the rigidity of centralized hardware and personnel, while integrating the sites and minimizing duplication of efforts. A typical distributed system is shown in Figure 4.5.

The DDP arrangement seems to offer the best of two worlds: the advantages of centralization and decentralization without the disadvantages of either. Distributed systems also enable the PC to be integrated with other computers and peripherals. One concept that helps in such integration is emulation.

DSS and Emulation. *Emulation* is the ability to imitate other machines. Usually, a microcomputer will emulate a (mainframe) terminal so that the user can

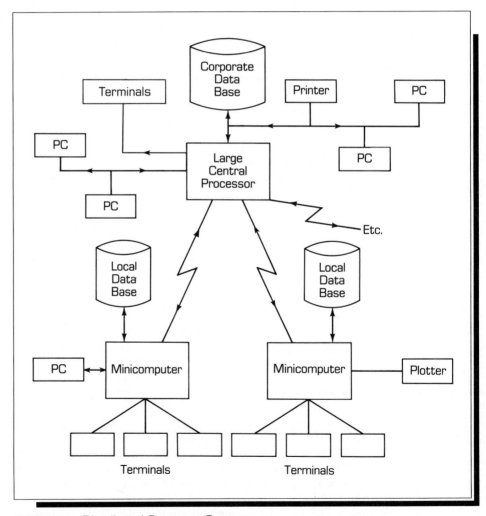

FIGURE 4.5 Distributed Computer System.

communicate with the company's central computer. Accessing the corporate database from a microcomputer is a tremendous benefit. Data files can be transferred from the mainframe and then used in the DSS. In effect, the microcomputer replaces a dumb terminal and is still used for generating spreadsheets, providing word processing support, and generating reports.

Local Area Networks (LANs)

A special case of distributed processing is the **local area network.** Computer networks consist of interconnected hardware, software, and communication channels that support several types of data communications activity for many users. **Local area networks** are *privately owned* networks that connect information processing devices within a *limited* physical area, such as an office building or a manufacturing plant or a university. The LANs are usually connected to larger external networks (private or public) by special communications interface devices. This connection enables, for example, communication between a PC and a mainframe computer (e.g., for downloading of data). It also allows a DBMS to extract data from an online service, and it permits electronic mail.

A possible problem in networks is ensuring compatibility of equipment served by the network. Several vendors offer complete systems including hardware, software, procedures, and protocols. Representative examples are:

- NetWare, from Novell Inc.
- Decnet, from Digital Equipment Corp.
- Wang-Net, from Wang Labs.
- Ethernet, from Xerox or from 3-Com (Ethernet is an open architecture).
- STARLAN, from AT&T.

Local area networks can be very useful for DSS because they can connect the internal parts of the DSS as well as the DSS with related computer-based systems. For example, a production DSS can be connected with numerically controlled machines, and a stock selection DSS may be connected with a brokerage house information and stock purchasing ordering system.

Because the LAN is owned by the using company, there is no need to pay for the use of the communication lines; in contrast, a DDP that does not use an LAN must pay for the communication (e.g., to a telephone company).

An LAN could provide the necessary access to external databases, primarily to commercial database (or data bank) services.

Client/Server Architecture

When computer terminals were "dumb," all processing was carried out by the central host computer to which the terminals were attached. With the advent of PCs the opportunity for the PC to act as a terminal as well as carrying out local processing became an option. Initially these two functions were mutually exclusive—either the PC carried out local processing or it acted like a dumb terminal. The advent of more sophisticated networks and software allowed the PC to process in cooperation with the host to which it was attached.

In "simple" client/server mode the PC carries out all the processing, but the data is held on the host (server) rather than the PC (i.e., there is a DBMS in each PC [the client]). Such an arrangement is called resource-sharing database processing. In another client/server mode the DBMS resides on the server. Application programs submit their requests for database service across LANs to the DBMS on the server. All database processing is done on the server. A more advanced client/server allows both host and PC to carry out processing, each carrying out the task most appropriate to it. In such a case there are DBMS both in the clients and in the server. This is described as "cooperative processing."

This approach is clearly of benefit to a management support system where the ease of use, graphics capability, and local processing of the PC can exist with the heavy-duty processing of large quantities of shared data of a typical host. In addition both host and PC based applications can be accessed from the management support system.

Client/server architecture plays a major role in MSS because it enables the most flexible distributed MSS.

4.9   Object-oriented Databases

Complex MSS applications such as those involving CIM (computer integrated manufacturing) require accessibility to complex data, which may include pictures and complex relationships. Neither hierarchical, nor network or even relational databases architecture can really handle complex databases. Even when SQL is used to create and access relational databases the solution may not be effective. All the above are alphanumerical databases. Sometimes it takes a graphic representation to achieve the best results.

Object-oriented data management is based on the principle of object-oriented programming. For an overview of object-oriented programming see Chapter 14. Object-oriented database systems combine the characteristics of an object-oriented programming language like Smalltalk or C++ with a mechanism for data storage and access. The object-oriented tools focus directly on the databases. An object-oriented database allows you to analyze data at a conceptual level that emphasizes the natural relationships between objects. Abstraction is used to establish inheritance hierarchies, and object encapsulation allows the database designer to store both conventional data and procedural code within the same objects.

Object-oriented database systems have the power to handle the complex data used in complex MSS applications (see Box 4.3).

The object-oriented data management system defines data as objects, and encapsulates data along with their relevant structure and behavior. The system uses a hierarchy of classes and subclasses (see Chapter 14) of objects. Structure, in terms of relationships, and behavior, in terms of methods and procedures, are contained within an object.

Representative object-oriented data managers are: GemStone (from Servio Logic Corp., Beaverton, OR), Vbase (from Ontalogic Inc., Billerica, MA), G-Base

Box 4.3: Object-oriented Database at Alcoa

Modern aluminum rolling mills are highly automated. Therefore a key factor for smooth operation is taking appropriate action to assure high quality and low downtime of equipment. The Tennessee rolling mill (in Alcoa, TN) has 1,500 sensors and 2,000 alarms. The relationship between alarms and sensors is often highly abstract. Troubleshooting requires fast access to an integrated body of data, information, and knowledge. Conversational DBMS as well as artificial intelligence were too slow. The solution: G-Base (from Graphael, Waltham, MA), an object-oriented database combined with relational DBMS, is used for retrieval of information. The system includes 4,000 objects. The G-Base stores information as objects and manipulates them independently of the data structure, allowing the structure to be modified at any time. The operator can locate information in seconds, instead of hours. The system is also equipped with hypertext (see Chapter 6) access to 30,000 pages of documentation. Last, but not least, the use of the system is very simple, requiring only minimal training.

(*Source:* Condensed from Tilghman, C. "An Object-Oriented Database at Alcoa." *Manufacturing Systems.* April 1989.)

(see Box 4.3), Express (from Empress Software, Greenbelt, MD), Ontos (from Ontologic, Burlington, MA) and Versant ODBMS (from Versant Object, Menlo Park, CA).

Object-oriented database managers are especially useful in distributed databases and DSS. In such case the applications are very complex and the new technology offers the best solutions. Object-oriented databases are related to another approach that is used to deal with database complexity, namely an expert system approach. This topic is described under the name intelligent databases in Chapter 18.

4.10   Database Applications versus Spreadsheets

The major role of DBMS is to manage the data. That is, to create, delete, change, and display the data. DBMS enables users to query the data as well as generate reports.

Spreadsheet programs deal with the modeling aspects of DSS, as will be shown in the next chapter. They help in creating and managing models, perform repetitive calculations on interrelated variables, and include extensive mathematical, statistical, and financial factors.

Unfortunately, there is confusion regarding the appropriate role of DBMS and spreadsheet programs. Most of the confusion is caused because many

DBMS offer capabilities similar to those available in a spreadsheet, enabling the DBMS user to perform spreadsheet work with a DBMS. Similarly, many spreadsheet programs offer a rudimentary set of DBMS capabilities. Although such a combination can be valuable in some cases, it may result in a lengthy process and frequently inferior results. The added on facilities are not robust enough, and they are cumbersome. Finally, a spreadsheet program assumes that the computer's RAM is large enough to hold the user's spreadsheet. Thus the user is restricted. The DBMS work with several databases and deal with much more data than a spreadsheet can.

For DSS application, it is frequently necessary to work both with data and modeling. Therefore, it is tempting to use only one enhanced tool. However, interfaces between DBMS and spreadsheets are fairly simple. These interfaces facilitate the exchange of data between independent programs.

DSS which integrate data and models can be built by either of the above approaches. That is, simple DSS can be built by either enhanced DBMS **or** by enhanced spreadsheets. Alternatively, they can be built with a DBMS and a spreadsheet. A third approach to the construction of DSS is to use a fully integrated DSS generator, as shown in Chapter 7. Finally, one can build the DSS from scratch and not use any of the available 4GLs.

4.11   IBM's Information Warehouse and Enterprise* Decision Support

The key to the successful use of MSS is the infrastructures that support access, retrieval, manipulation, analysis, presentation construction, graphical display methodologies, and communication (transfer) of the results of this series of activities. The most important issues include the availability of accurate, consistent, timely, and useable data. Managers and other knowledge workers who are the primary users of MSS have often in the past been denied proper access to important data because it was not in a form suitable for the MSS software in use, or because there was no guide to the availability and currency of the data required for use. Recognizing this situation, IBM created the concept of **Information Warehouse,** which is designed to allow enterprises to economically "unlock" the data that, until recently, has been unavailable to the user of MSS.

This framework brings together multiple vendor solutions, numerous MSS tools, relational databases, data categorizing and data modeling tools, and extensions to the informational databases for user access. (See Figure 4.6). The Information Warehouse can access data in multiple types of local or distributed heterogeneous (different formatted) data on an enterprise-wide basis via numerous enterprise data management, data delivery, data modeling, data analysis, and Decision Support software elements of the Information Warehouse. The Information Warehouse is centered around relational database architectures (DB2, SQL/DS, OS/2 Data Base Managers, AS/400 Relational DB, and over 30

---

*This section was contributed by Ronald S. Swift.

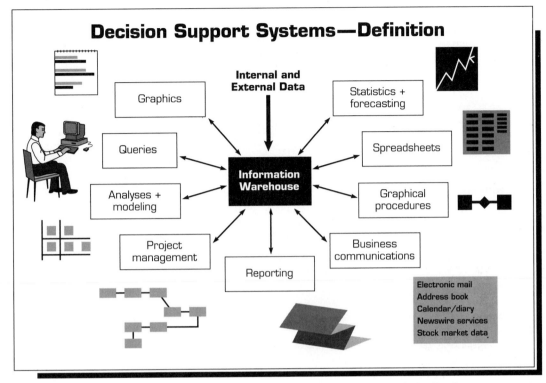

FIGURE 4.6 IBM's Information Warehouse. (*Source:* Charted by Ronald S. Swift, Consultant, IBM Corp., Dallas, TX. Used with permission.)

other types of data stored/managed on non-IBM database management subsystems). The true value of the Information Warehouse is that it provides access to the data while also maintaining security/protection/consistency within the operational data management systems that are vital to the enterprise's daily business operations. With the introduction of Distributed Database Architectures MSS will become a way of life in most organizations implementing a framework such as the Information Warehouse.

IBM Enterprise DSS Software. IBM provides a wide range of DSS and MSS tools that support various file systems and databases. They include:

- *Application System (AS).* A mainframe-based client/server integrated DSS tool for data access and retrieval, data manipulations, reporting, modeling (optimization, statistics), presentation (graphics), project management, business planning, and stored procedural applications. Easy interface to many IBM and other products.
- *SAA Personal Application System/2 (PAS/2).* A development tool for O/2 based user functions equivalent to the host based Application System product described earlier. With this, you can do on your PC what you can do on the mainframe or the mini-computer (with the Application System [AS]). See Figure 4.7.

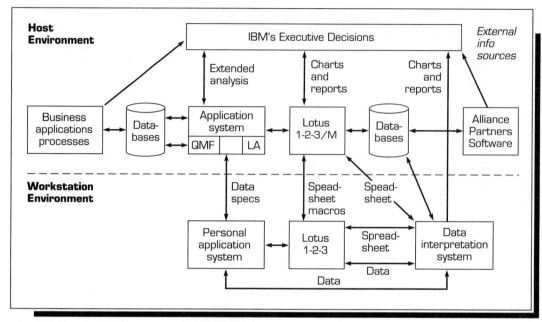

FIGURE 4.7   Interfaces Between IBM DSS Products. (*Source:* Charted by Ronald S. Swift, Consultant, IBM Corp., Dallas, Texas. Reproduced with permission.)

- *Query Management Facility (QMF).* A powerful and diversified query and report writer product for both end-user and IS professionals. It runs on an IBM System 370 or 390 architecture and provides extensive graphical reporting. Its primary database support is for S/370 relational databases (DB2 and SQL/DS).
- *Data Interpretation System (DIS).* This product is designed to analyze large amounts of data from local and remote databases. This LAN-based, relational database, iconic-interface system provides object-oriented module, modeling (spreadsheet) capabilities, masterful tool sets with complex algorithms, and multiple communication links.
- *SAA Structured Query Language (SQL/400).* This package interacts with the IBM AS/400 mid-range (mini- and work-group) computers and the powerful relational database system. It supports access to distributed databases through the Distributed Relational Database Architecture (DRDA).
- *Lotus 1-2-3/M.* This is a mainframe version (for MVS and VM systems) of Lotus 1-2-3. Its major purposes are to consolidate numerous PC spreadsheets and templates, therefore supporting major facilities for transferring data, spreadsheets, programs, files, macros, and templates between PC and mainframe users, databases, applications, and communications nodes.
- *IBM Executive Decisions.* This is IBM's Mainframe EIS package. It supports access to data from all of the tools listed here, relational databases through various IBM and non-IBM DSS tools, presentation of graphical, image,

video, voice, and online news and financial services. NewsEdge, Dow Jones News Retrieval, PRODIGY, and many other information providers can be attached.

- *IOC's TRACK-EIS.* A highly flexible and technologically advanced EIS and MSS solution to building applications through commands and an Iconic interface subsystem. The user can access data on most of the systems already described, as well as interfaces to Lotus's Notes groupware system, and to many other systems.

Chapter Highlights

- Data exist in internal, external, and personal sources.
- External data are available on thousands of online commercial databases, dictionaries, directories, reports, etc.
- Data for DSS need to be collected frequently in the field using one of several methods.
- Data for DSS may have problems such as: incorrect data, non-timely data, poorly measured and indexed data, too many data, or no data.
- Large online databases such as CompuServe and Dow Jones Information Service can be a major source of DSS data.
- DSS can be programmed with third-generation languages, but it is usually programmed with fourth-generation languages.
- Fourth-generation systems include many integrated features for data management.
- Data are organized in either relational, hierarchical, or network architectures. For many MSS, the relational type is preferable.
- SQL is a standard access to relational databases.
- There is a trend to have DSS (and other MSS) distributed via networks.
- Distributed DSS provide the benefits of a PC and the power of a mainframe.
- Many DSS are being offered on client/server systems.
- Object-oriented databases are especially suitable for complex DSS such as those in computer integrated manufacturing.
- Object-oriented databases are easy to use and very fast to access. They are especially useful in distributed DSS.
- Many companies are developing an enterprise-wide approach to data management. IBM's Information Warehouse is an example.

Key Words

client/server	fourth-generation	nonprocedural
database	systems	languages
distributed DSS	Information Warehouse	object-oriented
fourth-generation	local area networks	database
languages (4GLs)	(LANs)	

online (commercial)   query languages   SQL
    databases   relational database   "what-if" capability
procedural languages   report generators

Questions for Review

1. Define a procedural language and contrast it with a nonprocedural language.
2. Describe a complete fourth-generation system.
3. List some of the characteristics of distributed DSS.
4. What is SQL?
5. List the major categories of data sources for a DSS.
6. Describe the benefits of commercial databases.
7. Define a report generation and a query language.
8. Describe the role of LAN in a distributed DSS.
9. Describe client/server architecture.
10. Define object-oriented database management.

Questions for Discussion

1. Why are nonprocedural languages more suited to DSS? Be specific. Give an example if possible.
2. The most powerful DSS generators include both procedural and nonprocedural languages. What advantages may be derived from such a pairing?
3. Query languages and RPGs are extremely important in DSS construction. Explain why this is so. Use a managerial point of view.
4. Explain the relationship between SQL and a DBMS.
5. What is a database machine? Conduct some research to find the latest progress in this area and explain the potential impact on DSS.
6. Define and describe a commercial database (online) service. Name one or two that you are familiar with.
7. A university is installing a distributed DSS for budget preparation, expense monitoring, and financial planning. There are four schools at the university and eighteen departments. In addition there are two research institutions and many administrative services. Prepare a diagram that shows the distributed DSS. Suggest what decisions could be supported at each managerial level.
8. Review the list of data problems in Section 4.3. Alter [1] made some suggestions for handling these problems. Provide additional suggestions to each category.
9. Find a contact to a commercial database. Prepare a short paper that describes the services offered, the fees, and the process of obtaining the service.
10. It is said that relational database is the best for DSS (as compared to hierarchical and network structures). Explain why.

11. Many DSS are being built today on a client/server system. Explain the benefits of such a construction.
12. It is said the object-oriented DBMS are the best solutions to a complex (especially distributed) DSS. Explain.
13. Why is the spreadsheet included in a DBMS not as good as a stand-alone spreadsheet?
14. Many spreadsheet products have some DBMS capabilities. Why can't they have more capabilities? For example, why is dBaseIV better than the DBMS embedded in Lotus 1-2-3?
15. What is the concept of the "information warehouse" as envisioned by IBM?

References and Bibliography

1. Alter, S. L. *Decision Support Systems: Current Practices and Continuing Challenges.* Reading, MA: Addison-Wesley, 1980.
2. Champine, G. A., et al. *Distributed Computer Systems: Impact on Management Design and Analysis.* New York: Elsevier, 1980.
3. Courtney, J. F., and D. B. Paradice. *Database Systems for Management.* St. Louis: Times Mirror/Mosby College Printing, 1988.
4. Cobb, R. H. "In Praise of 4GLS." *Datamation,* July 15, 1985. See also *Computerworld,* October 14, 1985.
5. Fitzgerald, J., and T. S. Eason. *Fundamentals of Data Communications.* 2nd ed. New York: Wiley, 1984.
6. Furge, S., and D. H. Mau. "Fourth-generation Application Development." *Information Center,* June 1986.
7. Kroenke, D. M., and K. A. Dolan. *Database Processing.* 3rd ed. Chicago: SRA, 1988.
8. Madron, T. W. *Local Area Networks.* 2nd ed. New York: Wiley, 1990.
9. Martin, J. *Application Development Without Programmers.* Englewood Cliffs, NJ: Prentice-Hall, 1982.
10. Martin, J. *Telecommunication and the Computer.* 3rd ed. Englewood Cliffs, NJ: Prentice-Hall, 1983.
11. Martin, J. *Fourth-Generation Languages.* 3 vols. Englewood Cliffs, NJ: Prentice-Hall, 1985.
12. Neal, S., and K. L. Traunik. *Database Management System in Business.* Englewood Cliffs, NJ: Prentice-Hall, 1986.
13. Olson, D. L., and J. F. Courtney, Jr. *Decision Support Models and Expert Systems.* New York: Macmillan, 1992.
14. Schussel, G. "Distributed DBMS Decisions." *Computerworld,* May 6, 1991.
15. Seligman, D. "Life Will Be Different When We're All On-line." *Fortune,* February 4, 1985.
16. Swift, R. "DSS and the Information Warehouse." *GUIDE Proceedings,* March, 1992.
17. Swift, R. "EIS/DSS and the Information Warehouse." *The EIS Institute,* 1992.
18. Wilson, R. "The 4GL Evaluation Team." *Information Center,* February 1986.

APPENDIX A: COBOL vs. FOCUS

Without Focus (a)

```
IDENTIFICATION DIVISION.                    SORT SORT-FILE
PROGRAM-ID. SAMP1.                             ASCENDING KEY ACCOUNT-NUMBER
AUTHOR. K. MCKENNA.                         USING INPT-FILE
DATE-WRITTEN. AUG 17 1979.                  OUTPUT PROCEDURE SALES-RPT THRU SALES-
DATE-COMPILED. AUG 17 1979.              END.
SECURITY, NON-CLASSIFIED.                   CLOSE REPORT-FILE.
REMARKS. SAMPLE REPORT.                     STOP RUN.
ENVIRONMENT DIVISION.                    SALES-RPT SECTION.
CONFIGURATION SECTION.                      OPEN OUTPUT REPORT-FILE.
SPECIAL-NAMES.                              PERFORM HEAD-RTN THRU READ-EXIT.
   C01 IS TOP-OF-PAGE.                      PERFORM PROCESS-INPUT THRU PR-EXIT UNTIL
INPUT-OUTPUT SECTION.                    NO-MORE.
FILE-CONTROL.                               PERFORM FINAL-PROCESSING THRU FINAL-EXIT.
   SELECT INPT-FILE ASSIGN UT-S-INPT.    SALES-END. EXIT.
   SELECT SORT-FILE ASSIGN UT-S-SRT1.    PROCESS-INPUT.
   SELECT REPORT-FILE ASSIGN UT-S OUTPT.    IF ACCOUNT-NUMBER IS NOT EQUAL TO
DATA DIVISION.                           PREVIOUS-ACCOUNT
FILE SECTION.                                  PERFORM ACCOUNT-TOTAL-PROCESSING THRU
FD INPT-FILE                             ACCOUNT-EXIT.
   LABEL RECORDS OMITTED                     ADD ACCOUNT-DOLLARS TO ACCOUNT-TOTAL
   RECORD CONTAINS 60 CHARACTERS.         FINAL-TOTAL.
01 INPT-HEC          PIC X (80).             PERFORM READ-RTN THRU READ-EXIT.
SD SORT-FILE                             PR-EXIT. EXIT.
   RECORD CONTAINS 80 CHARACTERS.         READ-RTN.
01 SORT-REC.                                RETURN SORT-FILE AT END
   05 ACCOUNT-NUMBER   PIC X(5).              MOVE 'NO' TO FLAG-INPT.
   05 ACCOUNT-DOLLARS  PIC S9(5)V99.      READ-EXIT. EXIT.
   05 FILLER           PIC X(68).         FINAL-PROCESSING.
FD REPORT-FILE                              PERFORM ACCOUNT-TOTAL-PROCESSING THRU
   LABEL RECORDS ARE OMITTED.             ACCOUNT-EXIT.
01 REPORT-RECORD       PIC X (133).          MOVE SPACES TO DETAIL-LINE.
WORKING-STORAGE SECTION.                     MOVE FINAL-TOTAL TO ACCOUNT-TOT-OUT.
01 FLAGS.                                    MOVE 'TOTAL' TO ACCOUNT-TIT.
   05 FLAG-INPT        PIC XX VALUE ZEROS.   PERFORM LINE-OUT THRU LINE-EXIT.
      88 MORE-DATA     VLLUE 'YES'.       FINAL-EXIT. EXIT.
      88 NO-MORE       VALEE 'NO'.        ACCOUNT-TOTAL-PROCESSING.
      88 FIRST-TIME    VALEE ZEROS.          IF FIRST-TIME
01 COUNTS.                                      MOVE 'YES' TO FLAG-INPT
   05 LINE-NUMBER      PIC S99 VALUE +1.         MOVE ACCOUNT-NUMBER TO PREVIOUS
   05 PAGE-NUMBER      PIC S999 VALUE +1.  ACCOUNT
01 PREVIOUS-ACCOUNT    PIC S(5) VALUE         ELSE
SPACES.                                      MOVE SPACES TO DETAIL-LINE
01 TOTALS.                                   MOVE PREVIOUS-ACCOUNT TO ACCOUNT-NO-OUT
   05 ACCOUNT-TOTAL    PIC S9(6)V99 VALUE    MOVE ACCOUNT TOTAL TO ACCOUNT-TOT-OUT.
ZERO.                                        PERFORM LINE-OUT THRU LINE-EXIT
   05 FINAL-TOTAL      PIC S9(6)V99 VALUE    MOVE ACCOUNT-NUMBER TO PREVIOUS-ACCOUNT
ZERO.                                        MOVE ZERO TO ACCOUNT-TOTAL.
01 DETAIL-LINE.                          ACCOUNT-EXIT. EXIT.
   05 CARRIAGE-CONTROL PIC X.            LINE-OUT.
   05 ACCOUNT-NO-OUT   PIC ZZZZ9.           IF LINE-NUMBER = 1
   05 ACCOUNT-TIT-REDEFINES ACCOUNT-NO-OUT     MOVE PAGE-NUMBER TO PAG-NUMBER-OUT.
PIC X (5).                                   WRITE REPORT-RECORD FROM HEADING-LINE
   05 FILLER           PIC XXX.                 AFTER ADVANCING TOP-OF-PAGE
   05ACCOUNT-TOT-OUT   PIC $$$$, $$9.99.     MOVE SPACES TO REPORT-RECORD
   05 FILLER           PIC X(100).          WRITE REPORT-RECORD AFTER ADVANCING 2
01 HEADING-LINE.                         LINES
   05 CARRIAGE CONTROL PIC X.               MOVE 4 TO LINE-NUMBER
   05 FILLER           PIC X (41).          ADD 1 TO PAGE-NUMBER.
      VALUE 'ACCOUNT    TOTAL      PAGE'. WRITE REPORT-RECORD FROM DETAIL-LINE
   05 PAGE-NUMBER-OUT  PIC 29.              AFTER ADVANCING 1 LINES.
PROCEDURE DIVISION.                         IF LINE-NUMBER = 55
PREPARE SALES REPORT.                          MOVE 1 TO LINE-NUMBER
                                            ELSE
                                               ADD 1 TO LINE-NUMBER.
                                         LINE-EXIT. EXIT.
```

With Focus (b)

```
TABLE
> SUM SALES AND COLUMN-TOTAL
> BY ACCOUNT
> END
```

ACCOUNT	SALES
45452	$120.12
45453	$869.04
45632	$589.12
TOTAL	$1,578.28

Result

Chapter 5

Modeling and Model Management

In the previous chapter we introduced the first major component of DSS—the database and its management. In this chapter, the second major component—the model base and its management—are presented. The outline of this chapter is:

5.1   Modeling in MSS

Modeling in MSS can be executed in many ways.* In order to understand how modeling works in MSS, the case of Frazee Paint, Inc., in Student Project 1 (at the end of the book) gives an illustrative example. This DSS includes three types of models:

1. A statistical model (regression analysis), which is used for finding relationships among variables. This model is preprogrammed in the DSS development software tool.
2. A financial model for developing income statements and projecting financial data for several years. This model is semistructured and is written with a special DSS language called IFPS.
3. An optimization model is performed using a management science model called linear programming approach in order to determine media selection.

The Frazee case demonstrates that a DSS can be composed of *several models*, some *standard* and some *custom made*, which are used collectively to support the advertisement decisions in that company.

Other aspects of modeling must also be considered, such as the following:

Identification of the Problem and Environmental Analysis. This issue was discussed in Chapter 2. One aspect that was not discussed is the topic of **environmental scanning and analysis,** which refers to the monitoring, scanning, and interpretation of the collected information. It is frequently advisable to analyze the scope, the abstraction of the domain, and the forces and dynamics of the *environment*. It is necessary to identify the organizational culture and the corporate decision-making process (who makes decisions, degree of centralization, etc.). For further discussion see Ariav and Ginzberg [1], and Weber and Konsynski [27].

Identification of the Variables. The identification of the various variables is of utmost importance and so are their relationships. Influence diagrams, which are described in Section 5.7, can be very helpful in this process.

Forecasting. Forecasting is essential for the construction and manipulation of the models. Forecasting is described in Section 5.8.

Model. Decision support systems may include several models (sometimes dozens). Some of these models are fairly standard and they are built into the DSS

---

*Sections 5.4, 5.5, 5.6, and 5.8 are adapted from Turban and Meredith [25].

development software. Others are standard but are not available as built-in functions. Instead they are available as a free-standing software that can interface with the DSS. The nonstandard models need to be constructed from scratch.

The DSS builder is often faced with the dilemma of which models to include in the DSS. Then the decision must be made as to whether to build them, to use the ready-made ones, or to modify existing models.

Table 5.1 summarizes the categorization of models used in DSS into seven groups. It also lists several representative techniques in each category, and indicates the section number in which each category is discussed in this chapter.

Each of the techniques may appear in a form of either a static or a dynamic model (Section 5.2), and it may be constructed under assumed certainty, uncertainty, or risk (Section 5.3).

To expedite the construction of models one can use modeling languages (see Sections 5.10–5.12).

Model Management. Models, similarly to data, need to be managed. Such management is done with the aid of model base management software (Section 5.14).

TABLE 5.1 Types of Models.

Category	Process and Objective	Representative Techniques
Complete enumeration (Section 5.3)	Find the best solution from a relatively small number of alternatives	Decision tables, decision tree, decision analysis
Optimization via algorithm (Section 5.4)	Find the best solution from a large or an infinite number of alternatives, using a step-by-step improvement process	Linear and other mathematical programming models, network models
Optimization via analytical formula (Sections 5.4, 5.13)	Find the best solution, in one step, using a formula	Some inventory models
Simulation (Section 5.5)	Finding "good enough" solution, or the best among those alternatives checked using experimentation	Several types of simulation
Heuristics (Section 5.6)	Finding "good enough" solution using rules	Heuristic programming, expert systems
Other descriptive models (Section 5.9)	Finding "what-if" using a formula	Financial modeling, waiting lines
Predictive models (Section 5.8)	Predict future for a given scenario	Markov analysis, forecasting models

5.2   Static and Dynamic Models

DSS can be static or dynamic:

Static Analysis. Static models take a single snapshot of a situation. During this snapshot everything occurs in a single interval, which can be short or long in duration.

For example, a decision on whether to make or buy a product is static in nature. A quarterly or annual income statement is static and so is the investment decision shown in Section 5.3.

During a static analysis it is assumed that there is stability. There are no changes in the data.

Dynamic Analysis. Dynamic models are used to evaluate scenarios that change over time. A simple example would be a five-year profit projection, where the input data, such as costs, prices, and quantities are changed from year to year.

Dynamic models are time dependent. For example, in determining how many employees to have in the checkout points in a supermarket, it is necessary to consider the time of the day. This is because there are changes in the number of people that arrive at the supermarket at different hours.

Dynamic models are important because they show *trends* and patterns over time. They also show averages per period, moving averages, and comparative analysis (e.g., profit this quarter against the same quarter last year).

5.3   Treating Certainty, Uncertainty, and Risk

The concepts of certainty, uncertainty, and risk were introduced in Chapter 2. When we build models any of these conditions may occur. The following are some of the issues involved in each condition:

Certainty Models. Everyone loves certainty models because they are easy to work with and can yield optimal solutions. Of a special interest are problems that have an infinite (or a very large) number of feasible solutions. They are discussed in Sections 5.4 and 5.6. Many financial models are being constructed under assumed certainty. Unfortunately, very little is certain in this world.

Uncertainty. Managers attempt to avoid uncertainty as much as possible. Instead they attempt to acquire more information so that the problem can be treated under calculated risk. If you cannot acquire more information, you must treat the problem as an uncertain problem.

Risk. Most major business decisions are being made under assumed risk. Several techniques can be used to deal with risk analysis. They are discussed in this section and in Section 5.5.

Decision Analysis

Decision situations that involve a finite and usually not too large a number of alternatives are modeled by an approach called **decision analysis.** In this approach the alternatives are listed and their forecasted contributions to the goal(s) are assessed. Then, an evaluation takes place in order to select the best alternative.

Two cases are distinguished: single goal and multiple goals. Single goal situations are approached by the use of **decision tables** or **decision trees.** Multiple goals can be approached by several techniques (to be described later).

Decision Tables—Single Goal

Decision tables are a convenient way to organize information in a systematic manner.

Example: An investment company is considering investing in one of three alternatives: Bonds, stocks, or certificates of deposit (CDs).

The company is interested in one goal—maximizing the yield on the investment after one year. If it were interested in other goals such as safety or liquidity, then the problem would be classified as *multiple criteria decision analysis.*

The yield depends on the status of the economy, which can be either in solid growth, stagnation, or inflation. The following estimates of annual yield were solicited from the experts:

1. If there is solid growth in the economy, bonds will yield 12 percent; stocks, 15 percent; and time deposits, 6.5 percent.
2. If stagnation prevails, bonds will yield 6 percent; stocks, 3 percent; and time deposits, 6.5 percent.
3. If inflation prevails, bonds will yield 3 percent; the value of stocks will drop 2 percent from their current value; and time deposits will yield 6.5 percent.

The problem is to select the best investment alternative. Note: investing 50 percent in bonds and 50 percent in stocks is another alternative, and it can be added as a fourth alternative. Obviously, in reality the company may be faced with many other alternatives.

The investment problem can be organized in a table (see Table 5.2).

This is a mathematical model. According to our definition in Chapter 2, it includes: *decision variables* (the alternatives), *uncontrollable variables* (the states of the economy), and *result variables* (the projected yield; the numbers inside the table).

TABLE 5.2 Investment
Problem.

Alternative	Solid Growth	Stagnation	Inflation
Bonds	12.0%	6.0%	3.0%
Stocks	15.0%	3.0%	−2.0%
CDs	6.5%	6.5%	6.5%

Two cases can be distinguished: uncertainty and risk. In the case of uncertainty we do not know the probabilities of each state of nature. In the case of risk we assume we know the probabilities with which each state of nature will occur.

Treating Uncertainty. The intuitive reaction of any manager is not to make a decision under uncertainty until the chances of the economy can be assessed. However, if there is no information for assessing the chances (or if there is no time to collect such information), one can use one of several approaches to handle the uncertainty. For example, the *optimistic approach* involves considering the *best* possible outcome of each alternative and selecting the best of the bests (stocks). The *pessimistic (conservative) approach* involves considering the *worst* possible outcome for each alternative and selecting the *best* one (CDs).

For details on these and other approaches, see Turban and Meredith [25]. All the approaches of handling uncertainty have serious deficiencies. Therefore, any modeler should attempt to collect sufficient information so that the problem can be treated under assumed risk.

Treating Risk. Let us assume that the chance of solid growth is estimated to be 50 percent, that of stagnation 30 percent, and that of inflation 20 percent. In such a case the decision table is rewritten with the added information (see Table 5.3). The most common method for solving this **risk analysis** problem is to select the alternative with the largest expected value. An *expected value* is computed by multiplying the results (outcomes) by their respective probabilities and adding them. For example, for bonds we get: 12(0.5) + 6(0.3) + 3(0.2) = 8.4 (invest in bonds, for an average return of 8.4 percent).

Decision Trees

An alternative presentation of the decision table is a decision tree. A decision tree has two advantages: First, it shows graphically the relationships of the prob-

TABLE 5.3 Decision Under Risk and Its Solution.

Alternative	Solid Growth 0.50	Stagnation 0.30	Inflation 0.20	Expected Value
Bonds	12.0%	6.0%	3.0%	8.4% (Maximum)
Stocks	15.0%	3.0%	−2.0%	8.0%
CDs	6.5%	6.5%	6.5%	6.5%

TABLE 5.4   Multiple Goals.

Alternatives	Yield	Safety	Liquidity
Bonds	8.4%	High	High
Stocks	8.0%	Low	High
CDs	6.5%	Very High	High

lem and second, it can deal with more complex situations in a compact form (e.g., multiperiod investment problem).

Other Methods of Treating Risk. Several other methods of treating risk are discussed in this book. Specifically: simulation, certainty factors, and fuzzy logic.

Multiple Goals

A simplified case of **multiple goals** is shown in Table 5.4. Three goals (or criteria) are considered: yield, safety, and liquidity.

Notice that this situation is under assumed certainty, i.e., only one possible consequence is projected for each alternative. (Obviously, in the more complicated cases, a risk or uncertainty can be considered.) Notice also that some of the results are *not numerical* but symbolic (e.g., Low, High). For methods of dealing with multiple goals see Hwang and Yoon [11].

Extensive software is available for dealing with multiple criteria decision making (see section 5.13 and appendix 5-B).

5.4   Optimization via Mathematical Programming

The concept of optimization was introduced in Chapter 2 where an example of linear programming was developed. Linear programming is the most known technique in a family of tools called mathematical programming.

Mathematical Programming

Mathematical programming is the name for a family of tools designed to help solve managerial problems in which the decision maker must allocate scarce (or limited) resources among various activities to optimize a measurable goal. For example, distribution of machine time (the resource) among various products (the activities) is a typical allocation problem. Allocation problems usually display the following characteristics and necessitate making certain assumptions.

Characteristics.

1. A limited quantity of economic resources (such as labor, capital, machines, or water) is available for allocation.
2. The resources are used in the production of products or services.

3. There are two or more ways in which the resources can be used. Each is called a solution or a program.
4. Each activity (product or service) in which the resources are used yields a return in terms of the stated goal.
5. The allocation is usually restricted by several limitations and requirements called constraints.

Assumptions.

1. Returns from different allocations can be compared; that is, they can be measured by a common unit (such as dollars or utility).
2. The return from any allocation is independent of other allocations.
3. The total return is the sum of the returns yielded by the different activities.
4. All data are known with certainty.
5. The resources are to be used in the most economical manner.

The allocation problem can generally be stated as: Find the way of allocating the limited resources to various activities so the total reward will be maximized. Allocation problems, typically, have a large number of possible alternative solutions. Depending on the underlying assumptions, the number of solutions can be either infinite or finite. Usually, different solutions yield different rewards. Of the available solutions, one (sometimes more than one) is the *best*, in the sense that the degree of goal attainment associated with it is the highest (i.e., total reward is maximized). This is referred to as the optimal solution, which can be found by using a special algorithm.

A survey would find that many, or even most, problems in organizations are related to the allocation of resources (money, people, time, power, space, equipment). The reasons for this are that the resources are limited, there are many ways of allocation, it is difficult to measure the contribution of the allocation to the goals, and there is disagreement concerning the importance of the results. Mathematical programming provides a relatively unbiased approach to the allocation problem.

The field of mathematical programming is composed of several techniques:

Linear Programming (LP). Linear programming deals with allocation problems in which the goal (or objective) and all the requirements imposed on the problem are expressed by linear functions.

Integer Linear Programming. When the requirement that some or all of the decision variables must be integers (whole numbers) is added to a linear programming problem, it becomes one of integer (linear) programming.

Nonlinear Programming. Mathematical programming problems, where the goal and/or one or more of the requirements imposed on the problem are expressed by nonlinear functions, are referred to as nonlinear programming problems.

Goal Programming. This is a variant of linear programming that is used when multiple goals exist.

Distribution Problems. The *transportation* of a commodity from sources of supply to destinations, at minimum cost (or maximum profit), and the *assignment* of workers (or equipment) to jobs are examples of what are termed *distribution problems.*

The uses of mathematical programming, especially of linear programming, are so common that "canned" computer programs can be found today in just about any organization that has a computer.

DSS development tools, such as Lotus 1-2-3 or IFPS, can be used to model and solve linear programming situations, or have the capability to interface with a "canned" LP program (see descriptions in section 5.13).

Linear Programming

In Chapter 2 we presented a simple product-mix problem and formulated it as linear programming. Here we will introduce another typical LP problem called the blending problem.

Example: The Blending Problem (Minimization). In preparing Sungold paint, it is required that the paint have a brilliance rating of at least 300 degrees and a hue level of at least 250 degrees. Brilliance and hue levels are determined by two ingredients, Alpha and Beta. Both Alpha and Beta contribute equally to the brilliance rating, one ounce (dry weight) of either producing one degree of brilliance in one drum of paint. However, the hue is controlled entirely by the amount of Alpha, one ounce of it producing three degrees of hue in one drum of paint. The cost of Alpha is 45 cents per ounce, and the cost of Beta is 12 cents per ounce. Assuming that the objective is to minimize the cost of the resources, then the problem is to find the quantity of Alpha and Beta to be included in the preparation of each drum of paint.

Formulation of the Blending Problem. The *decision variables* are:

x_1 = Quantity of Alpha to be included, in ounces, in each drum of paint
x_2 = Quantity of Beta to be included, in ounces, in each drum of paint

The objective is to minimize the total cost of the ingredients required for one drum of paint. Since the cost of Alpha is 45 cents per ounce, and since x_1 ounces are going to be used in each drum, then the cost per drum is $45x_1$. Similarly, for Beta the cost is $12 x_2$. The total cost is, therefore, $45x_1 + 12x_2$, and as our objective function, it is to be *minimized* subject to the constraints of the following specifications:

1. To provide a brilliance rating of at least 300 degrees in each drum. Since each ounce of Alpha or Beta increases the brightness by one degree, the following relationship exists:

Supplied by Alpha   Supplied by Beta   Demand

$$1x_1 \qquad + \qquad 1x_2 \qquad \geq \qquad 300$$

2. To provide a hue level of at least 250 degrees, the effect of Alpha (alone) on hue can similarly be written as:

Supplied by Alpha   Supplied by Beta   Demand

$$3x_1 \qquad + \qquad 0x_2 \qquad \geq \qquad 250$$

In summary, the blending problem is formulated as follows: Find x_1 and x_2 that

minimize $z = 45x_1 + 12x_2$
subject to
$1x_1 + 1x_2 \geq 300$ (brightness specification)
$3x_1 + 0x_2 \geq 250$ (hue specification)

Solution. (derived by a computer)

$$x_1 = 83.333$$
$$x_2 = 216.667$$
$$\text{Total cost} = \$63.50$$

Note: The solution that is good for one drum will be correct for many drums as long as capacity or other constraints are not being violated.

General Formulation and Terminology

In the previous section, two classical managerial problems were formulated. Let us now generalize the formulation.

Every LP problem is composed of:

Decision Variables. The variables whose values are unknown and are searched for. Usually they are designated by x_1, x_2, and so on.

Objective Function. This is a mathematical expression, given as a linear function, that shows the relationship between the decision variables and a *single goal* (or objective) under consideration. The objective function is a measure of goal attainment. Examples of such goals are total profit, total cost, share of the market, and the like.

If the managerial problem involves multiple goals, one can use the following two-step approach:

1. Select a primary goal whose level is to be maximized or minimized.
2. Transform the other goals into constraints, which must only be satisfied.

For example, one may attempt to maximize profit (the primary goal) subject to a growth rate of at least 12 percent per year (a secondary goal).

Optimization. Linear programming attempts to either maximize or minimize the values of the objective function.

Coefficients of the Objective Function. The coefficients of the variables in the objective function (e.g., 45 and 12 in the blending problem) are called the profit (or cost) coefficients. They express the *rate* at which the value of the objective function increases or decreases by including in the solution one unit of each of the decision variables.

Constraints. The maximization (or minimization) is performed subject to a set of constraints. Therefore, linear programming can be defined as a *constrained optimization problem.* These constraints are expressed in the form of linear inequalities (or, sometimes, equalities). They reflect the fact that resources are limited or they specify some requirements.

Input-Output (Technology) Coefficients. The coefficients of the constraints' variables are called the *input-output* coefficients. They indicate the rate at which a given resource is depleted or utilized. They appear on the left-hand side of the constraints.

Capacities. The capacities (or availability) of the various resources, usually expressed as some upper or lower limit, are given on the *right-hand side* of the constraints. The right-hand side also expresses minimum requirements.

Example. These major components of a linear programming model are illustrated for the blending problem:

Find x_1 and x_2 (decision variables) that will minimize the value of the linear objective function:

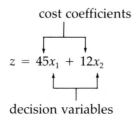

cost coefficients

$$z = 45x_1 + 12x_2$$

decision variables

subject to the linear constraints:

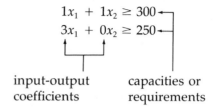

$$1x_1 + 1x_2 \geq 300$$
$$3x_1 + 0x_2 \geq 250$$

input-output   capacities or
coefficients   requirements

5.5 Simulation

Simulation has many meanings, depending on the area where it is being used. To *simulate*, according to the dictionary, means to assume the appearance of characteristics of reality. In MSS it generally refers to *a technique for conducting experiments (such as "what-if") with a digital computer on a model of a management system.*

Major Characteristics

To begin, simulation is not strictly a type of model; models in general *represent* reality, while simulation usually *imitates* it. In practical terms, this means that there are fewer simplifications of reality in simulation models than in other models.

Second, simulation is a technique for *conducting experiments*. Therefore, simulation involves the testing of specific values of the decision or uncontrollable variables in the model and observing the impact on the output variables.

Simulation is a *descriptive* rather than a normative tool; that is, there is no automatic search for an optimal solution. Instead, a simulation describes and/or predicts the characteristics of a given system under different circumstances. Once these characteristics are known, the best among several alternatives can be selected. The simulation process often consists of the repetition of an experiment many, many times to obtain an estimate of the overall effect of certain actions. It can be executed manually in some cases, but a computer is usually needed.

Finally, simulation is usually called for only when the problem under investigation is too complex to be treated by numerical optimization techniques (such as linear programming). Complexity here means that the problem either cannot be formulated for optimization (e.g., because the assumptions do not hold or the formulation is too complex).

Advantages and Disadvantages of Simulation

The increased acceptance of simulation is probably due to a number of factors:

1. Simulation theory is relatively straightforward.
2. The simulation model is simply the aggregate of many elementary re-

lationships and interdependencies, much of which is introduced slowly by request of the manager and in a patchwork manner.

3. Simulation is descriptive rather than normative. This allows the manager to ask "what-if" type questions. Thus, managers who employ a trial-and-error approach to problem solving can do it faster and cheaper with less risk, using the aid of simulation and computers (than to use a trial and error with a real system).

4. An accurate simulation model requires an *intimate* knowledge of the problem, thus forcing the MSS builder to constantly interface with the manager.

5. The model is built from the manager's perspective and in his or her decision structure.

6. The simulation model is built for one particular problem and, typically, will not solve any other problem. Thus, no generalized understanding is required of the manager; every component in the model corresponds one to one with a part of the real-life model.

7. Simulation can handle an extremely wide variation in problem types such as inventory and staffing, as well as higher managerial level functions like long-range planning. Thus, it is "always there" when the manager needs it.

8. The manager can experiment with different variables to determine which are important, and with different alternatives to determine which is the best.

9. Simulation, in general, allows for inclusion of the real-life complexities of problems; simplifications are not necessary. For example: simulation may utilize the real-life probability distributions rather than approximate theoretical distributions.

10. Due to the nature of simulation, a great amount of *time compression* can be attained, giving the manager some feel as to the long-term (1 to 10 years) effects of various policies, in a matter of minutes.

11. It is very easy to obtain a wide variety of performance measures directly from the simulation.

The primary disadvantages of simulation are:

1. An optimal solution cannot be guaranteed.
2. Constructing a simulation model is frequently a slow and costly process.
3. Solutions and inferences from a simulation study are usually not transferable to other problems. This is due to the incorporation in the model of the unique factors of the problem.
4. Simulation is sometimes so easy to sell to managers that analytical solutions that can yield optimal results are often overlooked.

The Methodology of Simulation

Simulation involves setting up a model of a real system and conducting repetitive experiments on it. The methodology consists of a number of steps (Figure 5.1). The following is a brief discussion of the process.

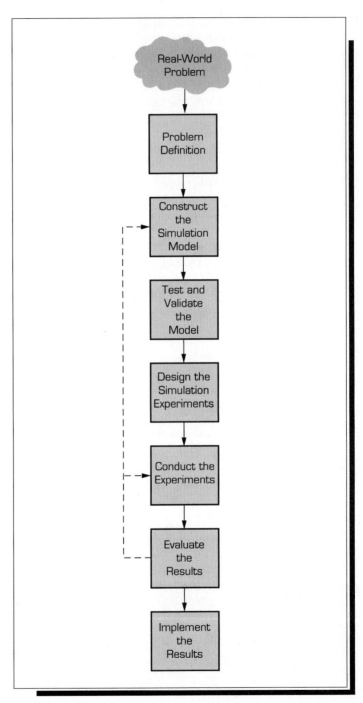

FIGURE 5.1 The Process of Simulation.

Problem Definition. The real-world problem is examined and classified. Here we should specify why simulation is necessary. The system's boundaries and other such aspects of problem clarification are attended to here.

Construction of the Simulation Model. This step involves gathering the necessary data. In many cases, a flowchart is used to describe the process. Then a computer program is to be written.

Testing and Validating the Model. The simulation model must properly imitate the system under study. This involves the process of validation, discussed later.

Design of the Experiments. Once the model has been proven valid, the experiment is designed. Included in this step is determining how long to run the simulation. This step deals with two important and contradictory objectives: accuracy and cost.

Conducting the Experiments. Conducting the experiment may involve issues such as random number generation, stopping rules, and presentation of the results.

Evaluating the Results. The final step is the evaluation of the results. Here, we deal with issues such as "What do the results mean?" In addition to statistical tools, we may use a sensitivity analysis (e.g., in the form of "what-if" questions).

Implementation. The implementation of simulation results involves the same issues as any other implementation. However, the chances of implementation are better since the manager is usually more involved in the simulation process than with analytical models.

Types of Simulation

There are several types of simulation. The major ones described in this book are:

Probabilistic Simulation. In this type of simulation one or more of the independent variables (e.g., the demand in an inventory problem) is probabilistic. That is, it follows a certain probability distribution. Two subcategories are recognized: discrete distributions and continuous distributions.

Discrete distributions involve a situation with a limited number of events (or variables) that can only take on a finite number of values. This situation is illustrated in the inventory example in this section.

Continuous distributions refer to a situation with an unlimited number of possible events that follow density functions such as the normal distribution. (See the IFPS example in Appendix A to this book.)

TABLE 5.5 Discrete and Continuous Distributions.

Discrete		Continuous
Daily Demand	Probability	
5	0.10	Daily demand is normally
6	0.15	distributed with a mean of 7 and
7	0.30	a standard deviation of 1.2
8	0.25	
9	0.20	

The two types of distributions are shown in Table 5.5.

Probabilistic simulation is conducted with the aid of a technique called Monte Carlo.

Time Dependent and Time Independent Simulation. *Time independent* refers to a situation where it is not important to know exactly when the event occurred. For example, we may know that the demand for a certain product is three units per day, but we do not care *when* during the day the item was demanded. Or in some situations, time may not be a factor in the simulation at all.

On the other hand, in waiting line problems, it is important to know the precise time of arrival (to know if the customer will have to wait or not). In this case, we are dealing with a *time dependent* situation.

Visual Simulation. This graphic display of computerized results is one of the more successful new developments in computer-human problem solving. It is described in Chapter 6.

Simulation Experimentation (Probabilistic)

The process of simulation experimentation involves eight steps:

1. Describe the system and obtain the probability distributions of the relevant probabilistic elements of the system.
2. Define the appropriate measure(s) of system performance. If necessary, write in equation form.
3. Construct cumulative probability distributions for each of the stochastic elements.
4. Assign representative numbers in correspondence with the cumulative probability distribution.
5. For each probabilistic element, take a random sample (generate a number at random or pick one from a table of random numbers).
6. Derive the measures of performance and their variances.
7. If stable results are desired, repeat steps 5 and 6 until the measures of system performance "stabilize."

8. Repeat steps 5–7 for various alternatives. Given the values of the performance measures and their confidence intervals, decide on the appropriate alternative.

The **Monte Carlo** procedure is not a simulation model per se, although it has become almost synonymous with probabilistic simulation. It basically includes steps 3 through 6 in the process. Namely, the procedure generates random observations of the variable(s) of interest.

The following example (which is a time-independent, discrete simulation) will illustrate the simulation experimentation of an inventory control situation.

The example is being worked manually. In real DSS, computers are being used.

Example. Marin's Service Station sells gasoline to boat owners. The demand for gasoline depends on weather conditions and fluctuates according to the following distribution.

Weekly Demand (gal)	Probability
2000	0.12
3000	0.23
4000	0.48
5000	0.17

Shipments arrive once a week. Since Marin's Service Station is located in a remote place, it must order and accept a fixed quantity of gasoline every week. Joe, the owner, faces the following problem: If he orders too small a quantity, he will lose, in terms of lost business and goodwill, 12 cents per gallon demanded and not provided. If he orders too large a quantity, he will have to pay 5 cents per gallon shipped back due to lack of storage. For each gallon sold he makes 10 cents profit. At the present time, Joe receives 3500 gallons at the beginning of each week before he opens for business. He feels that he should receive more, maybe 4000 or even 4500 gallons. The tank's capacity is 5500 gallons. The problem is to find the best order quantity.

This problem can be solved by trial and error. That is, the service station can actually order each quantity for, say, 10 weeks, then compare the results. However, simulation can give an answer in a few minutes. Furthermore, the results of the simulation will be much more accurate, since years of operations can be simulated rather than 10 weeks. Also, the losses are not real, they are on paper.

Solution by Simulation. To find the appropriate ordering quantity, it is necessary to compute the profit (loss) for the existing order quantity (3500 gallons) and for other possible order quantities. For example, 4000 and 4500 (as suggested by Joe) or any other desired figure (e.g., 3600, 3750, 3800, and so on) may be tried. Each quantity is a proposed solution, and steps 6 and 7 must be executed for each; the 8th step then concludes the analysis. Assume that today is the first day of the week, a shipment has just arrived, and there is now an inventory of 3800 gallons.

Before constructing a simulation, particularly if computerized, it is wise to construct a flow diagram of the tasks. A flow diagram is a schematic presentation of all computational activities used in the simulation. Its major objective is to help the computer programmer in writing the computer program. Figure 5.2 shows a flow diagram for the inventory problem. We will discuss the equations a bit later, but the logic flow for the simulation process is clear. Therefore, let us begin the eight steps for the simulation and then follow the steps in the diagram.

Step 1: Describe the system and determine the probability distributions. There is only one probability distribution in this case. It describes the demand for gasoline.

Step 2: Decide on the measures of performance. The primary measure of performance is the *average daily profit,* which is computed as (all quantities are in gallons)

$$\text{Average daily profit} = 10¢ \times (\text{Sales}) - 12¢ \times (\text{Unsatisfied demand}) - 5¢ \times (\text{Quantity shipped back})$$

Several less important measures such as the average shortage are discussed at the end of this example.

Step 3: Compute cumulative probabilities. The cumulative probabilities are computed in Table 5.6.

The cumulative probability column indicates the chance for a certain demand or less to occur. For example, there is a 0.35 chance for a demand of 3000 or less.

Step 4: Assign representative ranges of numbers. For each possible demand, a range of representative numbers is assigned in proportion to the probability distribution. For example, there is a chance of 0.12 for a demand of 2000 to occur. Therefore, out of 100 numbers (all two-digit numbers), 12 will be assigned to represent a demand of 2000*. An easy way of doing this is to assign the numbers 01, 02, 03, . . . , 12. (This information is entered in Table 5.6.) Next, the demand of 3000 is represented by 23 numbers, since it has a 0.23 chance of occurring. Since the numbers 01–12 have already been used, it is logical to use the next 23 two-digit numbers, 13–35.

*Step 5: Generate **random numbers** and compute the system's performance.* The first inventory system that will be considered is the current order policy of 3500 gallons per week. For purposes of demonstration, step 5 is repeated here only 10 times to simulate 10 weeks. In reality, it should continue until the measure of performance (average weekly profit) achieves *stability,* as will be explained later in step 7. The detailed computations are shown in Table 5.7 and are executed as follows:

---

*In this case, a two-digit random number is used. If the probability of demand were given by three-digit figures, for example, 0.115, then three-digit random numbers would have to be used.

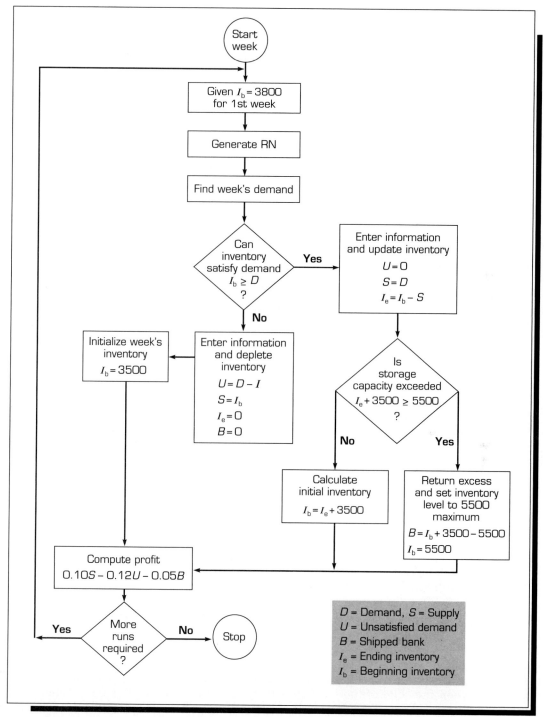

FIGURE 5.2 Flow Diagram for the Inventory Example (For a Shipment of 3500 Gallons).

TABLE 5.6 Assignment of
Representative Numbers.

(A) Weekly Demand (gal)	(B) Probability	(C) Cumulative Probability	(D) Representative Numbers (range)
2000	0.12	0.12	01–12
3000	0.23	0.35	13–35
4000	0.48	0.83	36–83
5000	0.17	1.00	84–00

Column 1 designates the simulated week. In this example, only 10 weeks are simulated.

Column 2 is a list of random numbers (RNs), taken from a table of random numbers. Here, we are interested in two-digit numbers, so the first and second of a four-digit random number are used, starting with 32, then the next two digits, 08, and so on.

Column 3 represents inventory at the beginning of each week (I_b). The column is computed by adding the 3500-gallon shipment to the inventory at the end of the previous week (I_e). The maximum inventory is 5500 gallons, due to limited storage capacity. Thus, $I_b = I_e + 3500$ (up to 5500 as an upper limit).

Column 4 represents the forecasted demand, D, based on the RN in column 2 and the range of RNs in Table 5.6. For example, the first RN, 32, falls in the representative range of 13–35, which is equivalent to a weekly demand of 3000. Once the second column (RN) is generated, the entire fourth column can be computed quickly.

Column 5 represents the amount sold. Two cases may occur.

1. The demand, D, is equal to or smaller than the inventory on hand, I_b. In this case, sales equal demand (i.e., $S = D$ as in weeks 1, 2, 3, and 4).
2. Demand is *larger* than the inventory on hand. In this case, sales are limited to the inventory on hand, I_b (i.e., $S = I_b$). The difference between the demand and the inventory on hand, $D - I_b$, is thus the unsatisfied demand, U (column 7). For example, in week 5 there is a demand of 4000, but an inventory of 3500. Therefore, the sales are 3500 and there is an unsatisfied demand of 500.

In *Column 6* the inventory at the end of each week, I_e, is listed. It is computed by subtracting the amount sold (column 5) from the beginning inventory (column 3), $I_e = I_b - S$.

Column 7 designates the unsatisfied demand, U. This column shows the difference between the demand and the beginning inventory whenever demand is larger (e.g., in week 5). Thus, $U = D - I_b$.

Column 8 designates the amount shipped back, B. Such a situation occurs when the "end-of-the-week inventory" plus the shipment (3500 gallons in the system under study) exceed the 5500-gallon tank capacity. In this case, the excess supply is shipped back and the beginning inventory is 5500. For example,

TABLE 5.7 The Simulation for 10 Weeks.

(1) Week Number	(2) RN	(3) Inventory at Beginning of Week $I_b = I_e + 3,500$	(4) Simulated Demand D	(5) Sold S	(6) Inventory at End of Week $I_e = I_b - S$	(7) Unsatisfied Demand $U = D - I_b$	(8) Shipped Back B	(9) Weekly Profit	(10) Average Weekly Profit
1	32	3,800	3,000	3,000	800			$ 300.00	$300.00
2	08	4,300	2,000	2,000	2,300		300	185.00	242.50
3	46	5,500	4,000	4,000	1,500			400.00	295.00
4	92	5,000	5,000	5,000	0			500.00	346.25
5	69	3,500	4,000	3,500	0	500		290.00	335.00
6	71	3,500	4,000	3,500	0	500		290.00	327.50
7	29	3,500	3,000	3,000	500			300.00	323.57
8	46	4,000	4,000	4,000	0			400.00	333.12
9	80	3,500	4,000	3,500	0	500		290.00	328.33
10	14	3,500	3,000	3,000	500			300.00	325.50
Total	—	40,100	36,000	34,500	5,600	1,500	300	$3,255.00	—
Average per week	—	4,010	3,600	3,450	560	150	30	325.50	325.50

in week 3, the shipment of 3500, added to the weekend inventory of week 2 of 2300, gives a total of 5800 gallons. Therefore, $5800 - 5500 = 300$ gallons are shipped back.

Column 9: The measure of performance in this problem is profit. The profit is calculated, every week, according to the formula

$$\text{profit} = 0.10S - 0.12U - 0.05B$$

For example, in week 1: $S = 3000$, $U = 0$, Profit $= 0.1(3000) = \$300$. In week 3: $S = 4000$, $U = 0$, $B = 300$. Profit $= 0.1(4000) - 0.05(300) = \$385$.

Column 10: The *average* weekly profit at any week is computed by totaling the weekly profits up to that week (cumulative profit) and dividing it by the number of weeks. For example, in week 3: Cumulative profit $= \$300 + \$200 + \$385 = \$885$. The weekly average: $\$885/3 = \$295$.

Step 6: Compute the measures of performance. Each simulation run is composed of multiple *trials*. The question of how many trials to have in one run (or finding the *length* of the run) involves statistical analysis. The longer the run, the more accurate are the results, but the higher the cost of running the simulation (true only with large-scale equation on a mainframe). This issue concerns what is labeled as *stopping rules*. The stopping rules are usually built into the simulation program. For example, the run could be terminated when a desired standard error in the measures of performance is attained. These measures are computed continuously during the simulation, since they determine stability and the stopping time.

The simulation performed thus far indicated an average weekly profit of $325.50. In addition to total profit, the following measures of performance can be computed:

1. *The probability of running short and the average shortage.* In 3 out of the 10 weeks there was an unsatisfied demand. Therefore, there is a $3/10 = 30$ percent chance of running out of stock. The average shortage, per week, is $1500/10 = 150$ gallons.
2. *The probability of shipping back and the average quantity shipped back.* In 1 out of the 10 weeks some gasoline was shipped back. On the average there is $1/10 = 10$ percent chance of shipping back; the average amount is $300/10 = 30$ gallons per week.
3. *The average demand.* The average weekly demand is computed as 3600 (from Table 5.6), which is close to the expected value of the demand of 3700. (In a stabilized process, these two numbers will be very close.)
4. *The average beginning inventory* is computed as 4010 gallons.
5. *The average weekly sales* is computed as 3450 gallons.
6. *The average ending inventory* is computed as 560 gallons.

Step 7: Stabilize the simulation process. Simulation begins to represent reality only after stabilization has been achieved. Examination of column 10 in Table 5.7 indicates that the process, although close to stabilizing, has not yet stabilized; that is, the *average* weekly profit is still fluctuating. Notice, however, that after six weeks, the differences are becoming very small.

Step 8: Find the best ordering policy. Steps 5, 6, and 7 are now repeated for other ordering policies in order to find the best. In the example just presented, the ordered quantity was 3500; other values (e.g., 3300, 3700, 4000) should next be considered. Each quantity constitutes an independent system for which the various measures of effectiveness such as average profit, average sales, and unsatisfied demand are computed. Each such experiment is called a *simulation run.* The best results seem to occur at about 4100 gallons.

Note: Simulation models can be constructed with Lotus 1-2-3 or any other modeling language or with special simulation building tools. Alternatively, the model can be written with COBOL or a similar language.

5.6   Heuristic Programming

The determination of optimal solutions to some complex decision problems could involve a prohibitive amount of time and cost, or it may even be an impossible task. Alternately, the simulation approach may be lengthy, complex and even inaccurate. In such situations, it is sometimes possible to arrive at *satisfactory* solutions more quickly and less expensively by using **heuristics.**

While heuristics are used primarily for solving ill-structured problems, they can also be used to provide satisfactory solutions to certain complex, well-structured problems much more quickly and cheaply than algorithms. The main difficulty in using heuristics is that they are not as general as algorithms. Therefore, they can normally be used only for the specific situation for which they were intended. Another problem with heuristics is that they may result in a poor solution.

Heuristic programming is the approach of employing heuristics to arrive at feasible and "good enough" solutions to some complex problems. "Good enough" is usually in the range of 90–99.9 percent of the true optimal solution.

In studying examples of applied heuristic programming, one can observe the attempt to reduce the amount of search for a satisfactory solution. In such a search, the computer is "taught" how to explore only relatively fertile paths and ignore relatively sterile ones. The computer choices are made by using heuristics that can be improved in the course of the search.

Methodology*

Heuristic thinking does not necessarily proceed in a direct manner. It involves searching, learning, evaluating, judging, and then again searching, relearning, and reappraisal as exploring and probing take place. The knowledge gained from success or failure at some point is fed back and modifies the search

---

*Based on Rowe [19].

process. More often than not, it is necessary either to redefine the objectives or the problem, or to solve related or simplified problems before the primary one can be solved.

Heuristic methods have been described by Pearl [18] based on intelligent search strategies for computer problem solving using several alternative approaches.

The heuristic procedure can also be described as finding rules that help to solve intermediate subproblems to discover how to set up these subproblems for final solution by finding the most promising paths in the search for solutions; finding ways to retrieve and interpret information on each experience; and then finding the methods that lead to a computational algorithm or general solution. The term heuristic has been used to include any or all of these steps.

A logical approach to heuristic rules incorporates:

1. A classification scheme that introduces structure into a problem.
2. Analysis of the characteristics of the problem elements.
3. Rules for selecting elements from each category to achieve efficient search strategies.
4. Rules for successive selections, where required.
5. An objective function that is used to test the adequacy of the solution at each stage of selection or search.

Problems in Using Heuristics

Geoffrion and Van Roy [6] identify the following shortcomings of heuristics:

1. Enumeration heuristics that consider all possible combinations in practical problems can seldom be achieved.
2. Sequential decision choices can fail to anticipate future consequences of each choice.
3. "Local improvement" can short-circuit the best solution because heuristics, similarly to simulation, lacks a global perspective.
4. Interdependencies of one part of a system can sometimes have a profound influence on the whole system.

The researchers maintain that common sense approaches and heuristics can fail because they are *arbitrary*. They are arbitrary in the choice of a starting point, in the sequence in which assignments or other decision choices are made, in the resolution of ties, in the choice of criteria for specifying the procedure, in the level of effort expended to demonstrate that the final solution is in fact best or very nearly so. The result is erratic and unpredictable behavior—good performance in some specific applications and bad in others.

Geoffrion and Van Roy also expressed concern about a more profound weakness of heuristics in the planning process. They see a critical need to *solve* planning problems under several alternative sets of assumptions. Consequently, the ability to ask "what-if" questions is more important than finding a so-called optimum plan.

When to Use Heuristics (per Zanakis and Evans [28])

The following are some scenarios where the use of heuristics (instead of optimization) is appropriate:

1. The input data are inexact or limited.
2. Reality is so complex that the optimization model is oversimplified.
3. A reliable, exact method is not available.
4. The computation time of optimization is too excessive.
5. It is possible to improve the efficiency of the optimization process (e.g., by producing good starting solutions using heuristics).
6. Problems that are being solved frequently (and repeatedly) and consume computer time.
7. Complex problems that are not economical for optimization or take too long a time and the heuristic can improve the noncomputerized solution.
8. When symbolic rather than numerical processing is involved.

Advantages of Heuristics

The major advantages of heuristics are that they:

1. Are simple to understand and therefore are easier to implement.
2. Help in training people to be creative and come up with heuristics for other problems.
3. Save formulation time.
4. Save programming and storage requirements on the computers.
5. Save computer running time (speed!).
6. Produce multiple solutions.

For a categorized survey with several hundred references see Zanakis et al. [29].

There is a tendency to use heuristics as an alternative to optimization methods. Heuristics can be fun to develop and use. What is required is an understanding of the nature of the problem and some ingenuity, as illustrated in the following example.

The Traveling Salesperson Problem (TSP)

The Problem. A traveling salesperson must visit N cities in a territory. The salesperson starts from a base and visits each city once, returning to his or her home city at the end. The TSP attempts to find out the best route (in terms of least cost, or least distance).

The Difficulty. The number of routes (counting only one-direction routes) is

$$R = 0.5(N - 1)!$$

For 10 cities there are 181,440 routes, for 11 cities there are about 2 million different routes, and for 20 cities there are approximately 6.1×10^{16} routes. This

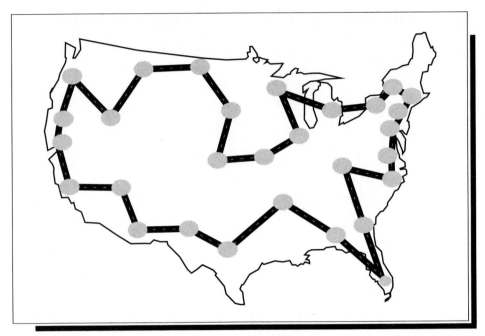

FIGURE 5.3 Heuristic Solution to the Traveling Salesperson Problem. (*Source:* Rowe [19])

is a typical combinatorial problem. With the addition of just a few more cities, the problem grows to an astronomical number of alternatives.

The Solutions. **Complete enumeration** and algorithms are inefficient or ineffective. Heuristic solutions provide good enough solutions, sometimes very quickly, as will be shown in the following examples. *Note:* Neural computing (Chapter 17) may be the best approach in the future.

Heuristic Solutions. "Start at any city and move to the closest city. Continue until the last city is visited, then return to the original city."

Another heuristic is shown in Figure 5.3. This time the solution has been derived by inspection, using trial and error. The heuristic is: "Start from any point, build up an *exterior* path, with no crossovers or backtracking, and return to the original city." (*Note:* there are several possible exterior paths. Figure 5.3 shows one of them.)

5.7   Influence Diagrams

An influence diagram provides a graphical presentation of a model. It provides a visual communication to the model builder. It also serves as a framework for expressing the exact nature of the relationship within the MSS model. The term *influence* refers to the dependency of a variable on the level of another variable. An influence diagram maps all the variables in a decision problem.

Influence diagrams appear in several shapes. We will use the following convention, suggested by Bodily [2]:

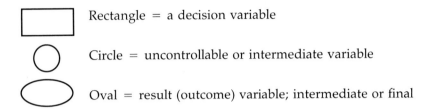

Rectangle = a decision variable

Circle = uncontrollable or intermediate variable

Oval = result (outcome) variable; intermediate or final

The variables are connected with arrows, which indicate the direction of the influence. The shape of the arrow also indicates the type of relationship. The following are typical relationships:

1. Certainty

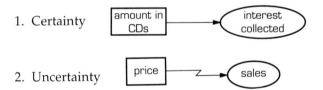

2. Uncertainty

3. Random variable: place ~ above the variable's name.

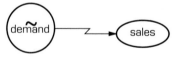

4. Preference (usually between outcome variables). This is shown as a double-line arrow.

Arrows can be one way or two-way (bidirectional).

Influence diagrams can be constructed at any degree of detail and sophistication. It enables the model builder to remember *all* the relationships in the model, as well as the direction of the influence.

Example. Given a model:

> Income = units sold × unit price
> Units sold = 0.5 × amount used in advertisement
> Expense = unit cost × units sold + fixed cost
> Profit = income − expense

An influence diagram of this simple model is shown in Figure 5.4.

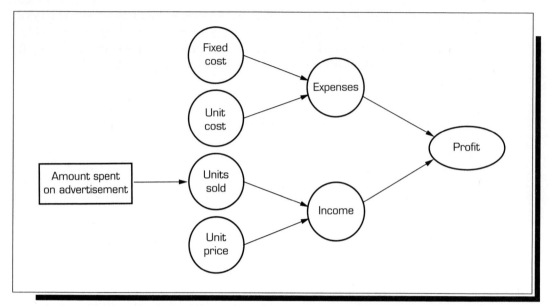

FIGURE 5.4   Influence Diagram.

Software. Several software products are available for the implementation of influence diagrams. The solution process of these products transforms the original problem into produced form. Representative products are:

- *DAVID* (from Duke University). This product helps the user to build, modify, and analyze models in an interactive graphical environment.
- *INDIA* (from Decision Focus, Inc., Palo Alto, CA). The solution process of this product transforms the original problem into a new reduced form in an attempt to determine optimal policy.
- *DPL* (from ADA Decision Analysis, Menlo Park, CA). This product provides a synthesis of influence diagrams and decision trees.

For comparative analysis see *Reliability Engineering and System Safety,* 30 (1990): 115–162.

Also, several computer graphic software and CASE packages can be used to draw influence diagrams.

5.8   Forecasting

As the reader may recall, decision making involves choosing an alternative course of action by evaluating the possible consequences of the alternatives. Although the choice is made today, the possible consequences will occur sometime in the future. Therefore, the quality of the decision largely depends on the quality of the forecast.

Forecasting models are an integral part of many DSS. One can build a forecast model or one may use preprogrammed software packages.

Many DSS development tools have some built-in forecasting capabilities.

The Uses of Forecasts

The major use of forecasting, as it relates to modeling, is to predict the value of the model variables, as well as the logical relationship of the model, at some time in the future. The future time of interest depends on "when" we want to evaluate the results. For example, in a regular investment decision we may be interested in prices and income a year from today, while in a capital investment decision we may be interested in projected prices and income during the next five years. Generally speaking, we distinguish between two types of forecasts: (a) short run (up to one year), where the forecast is used mainly in deterministic (certainty) models, and (b) long run (beyond one year), where the forecast is used in both deterministic and probabilistic models.

Forecasting Models and Methods

There exist many types of forecasting models because forecasting is an extremely difficult task. What is going to happen in the future depends, in many cases, on a multiplicity of factors, most of which are uncontrollable. Furthermore, data availability, accuracy, cost, and the time required to make the forecast also play an important role.

Forecasting methods can be grouped in several ways. One classification scheme distinguishes between formally recognized forecasting techniques (formal) and informal approaches such as intuition, spur-of-the-moment guesses, and seat-of-the-pants predictions. Our attention in this section is directed to the formal methods.

Formal methods can be divided into four categories: judgment methods, counting methods, time-series methods, and association or causal methods.

Each category is briefly discussed below. For a more detailed discussion see Georgoff and Murdick [7] and Makridakis and Wheelwright [16].

Judgment Methods. Judgment methods are those based on subjective estimates and expert opinion, rather than on hard data. They are often used for long-range forecasts, especially where external factors (e.g., technological or political developments) may play a significant role. They also are used where historical data are very limited or nonexistent, such as in new product/service introductions.

Counting Methods. Counting methods involve some kind of experimentations or surveys of a sample with an attempt to generalize about the entire market. These methods are primarily used for forecasting demand for products/services, a part of marketing research.

This type of forecasting methods is quantitative in nature. These methods are based on hard data and are thus generally considered more objective than the previous ones. They typically use historical data and are commonly divided between time-series and causal methods.

Time-series Analysis. A time series is a set of values of some business or economic variable, measured at successive (usually equal) intervals of time. For example, quarterly sales of a firm make up a time series, as does the population in a city (counted annually), the weekly demand for hospital beds, and so on. We undertake time-series analysis in decision making because we believe that knowledge of past behavior of the time series might help our understanding of (and therefore our ability to predict) the behavior of the series in the future. In some instances, such as the stock market, this assumption may be unjustified, but in managerial planning we assume that history will repeat itself and that past tendencies will continue. Time-series analysis efforts conclude with the development of a *time-series forecasting model* that can then be used to predict future events.

Association or Causal Methods. Association or causal methods include data analysis for finding data associations and, if possible, cause-effect relationships. They are more powerful than the time-series methods, but they are also more complex. Their complexity comes from two sources. First, they include more variables, some of which are external to the situation. Second, they use sophisticated statistical techniques for segregating the various types of variables. Causal approaches are most appropriate for midterm (between short- and long-term) forecasting.

Generally speaking, judgment and counting methods, which are subjective in nature, are used in those cases where quantitative methods are inappropriate or cannot be used. Time pressure, lack of data, or lack of money may prevent the use of quantitative models. Complexity of historical data (due to interactions or fluctuations, for example) may also inhibit the use of hard data.

Forecasting Model

The following is a list of representative forecasting packages.

Autobox, BOXX	Automatic Forecasting Systems, Inc. (Hatboro, PA)
Autocast	Levembach Assoc. Inc. (Morristown, NJ)
EXEC*U*STAT	EXEC*U*STAT Inc. (Princeton, NJ)
Forecast Master	Scientific Systems, Inc. (Cambridge, MA)
Forecast Plus	Stat Pac, Inc. (Minneapolis, MN)
Forecast Pro	Business Forecast Systems, Inc. (Belmart, MA)
Futurcast	Futurion Assoc., Inc. (Pittsburg, CA)
Micro TSP	McGraw-Hill (New York, NY)
Smart Forecast	Smart Software Inc. (Belmont, MA)
Soritec Econometrics	The Soritec Group (Springfield, VA)
SPSS/PC +	SPSS, Inc. (Chicago, IL)
Systat	Systat Inc. (Evanston, IL)
The Forecasting Edge	Human Edge Software (Palo Alto, CA)
1,2,3 Forecast	1,2,3 Forecast (Salem, OR)

5.9 Nonquantitative Modeling

The modeling approaches and issues discussed thus far have centered around quantitative models. However, modeling in MSS may involve nonquantitative models. In many cases nonquantitative modeling is presented in terms of rules. For example, the following can be viewed as a scheduling model:

a. If a job is not complex, and if it takes less than 15 minutes to complete, then schedule it early in the day.
b. If the job is complex and it takes a long time to complete, schedule it no later than 10 A.M.
c. If a job is complex, but it can be finished fast once started, schedule it in midday.
d. Assign short jobs to employees who are not so happy and long jobs to happy employees.

Nonquantitative modeling can be done separately from or in combination with quantitative modeling. In some cases it is possible to transform some qualitative measures to quantitative ones. For example, employee satisfaction can be measured on a scale that ranges from "very dissatisfied" to "highly satisfied." The two extreme points receive values of 1 and 10. Other values are placed in between.

5.10 Modeling Languages and Spreadsheets

Models can be written by a variety of programming languages. Relevant to this book are:

- Electronic spreadsheets (with their supplements), and
- Financial and planning modeling.

Electronic Spreadsheets

A very popular end user modeling tool for microcomputers is the electronic spreadsheet. This tool is the equivalent of an accounting spreadsheet, which is basically a column-and-row pad. The spreadsheet is represented electronically in the computer's memory. The intersections of the columns and rows are called *cells*. The user places numeric data or text in these cells. Then, the programmer can write a program to manipulate the data (e.g., "Multiply the content of cell C-5 by that of D-7"). Spreadsheets have many advantages over an accounting worksheet. Most notable is the modeling capability; users can write their own models and also conduct "what-if" analysis. In addition, reports can be consolidated, and data can be organized in alphabetical or numerical order. Other capabilities include setting up windows for viewing several parts of the spreadsheet simultaneously and executing mathematical manipulations. These enable the spreadsheet to become an important tool for analysis, planning, and

TABLE 5.8 Representative Spreadsheet and Spreadsheet-based Integrated Products for Micros.

Product	Vendor
Calcstar	Micro Pro Inter. (Comming, GA)
Excel	Microsoft (Redmond, WA)
Full Impact	Ashton-Tate (Torrance, CA)
Goldengate	Cullinet Software (Cranford, NJ)
Lotus 1-2-3	Lotus Development Co. (Cambridge, MA)
Multiplan	Microsoft Corp. (Bellview, WA)
Peachcalc	Peachware Co. (Atlanta, GA)
PlanPerfect	WordPerfect Corp. (Orem, UT)
Quattro Pro	Borland International (Scotts Valley, CA)
SuperCalc5	Computer Associates (New York, NY)
The Smart Spreadsheet	Innovative Software (Overland Park, KS)
20/20 and Trapeze	Access Technology (South Natick, MA)
Wingz	Informix Software (Lenexa, KS)

modeling. In addition to the ability of writing models with a spreadsheet, the software usually includes large numbers of built-in statistical, mathematical, and financial functions. The current trend is to integrate the spreadsheet with development and utility software, such as database management, communications, and graphics. Integrated micropackages like Lotus 1-2-3, Excel, and Quattro Pro are currently more popular than the stand-alone spreadsheets.

A major capability of spreadsheet programs is that formulas can be embedded using numbers in the spreadsheet; these numbers can be changed and the implications of these changes can immediately be observed and analyzed.

A spreadsheet can be used to build static or dynamic models. A static model does not include time as a variable. For example, spreadsheets are used to build balance sheets. A dynamic model, on the other hand, represents behavior over time (i.e., it *does* include a time element). For example, the balance sheet for a given year can be shown together with those of the five previous years.

Spreadsheets are used in almost every kind of organization in all functional areas.

An example of solving an inventory management problem with a spreadsheet (using Lotus 1-2-3) is given in Appendix 5-A to this chapter.

The models constructed with spreadsheets can be linked to each other (e.g., the output of the sales forecast can be used as an input to the inventory and cash flow models). Some of these applications are not strictly DSS; they are more in the nature of the traditional MIS. The point is that with a spreadsheet, users do not have to wait a long time anymore for the IS department to build a CBIS. They can build CBIS on their own (or with minimal help from the Information Center or the IS department) very quickly and inexpensively.

Spreadsheets were developed for micros, but they are also available for larger computers with increased capabilities. Spreadsheets are very popular modeling tools, but they have limitations. For example, several spreadsheets execute only modeling under certainty: they cannot handle risk (e.g., via Monte Carlo simulation). Other areas of deficiency are the lack of optimization capability and the two-dimensional constraints. Therefore, sometimes more powerful modeling tools are needed. Such tools are described in Section 5.12. A representative list of spreadsheet software is given in Table 5.8.

5.11 Templates, Macros, and Added-on Tools

The programming productivity of building DSS can be enhanced with the use of templates, macros, and other tools.

Templates. Templates are preprogrammed, reusable spreadsheet models with built-in titles and formulas, developed for specific applications. They are dataless files that contain formulas; the only task left to the user is to input the data. (See Exercise 5 at the end of this chapter.) For example, there are income tax preparation templates, real estate analysis templates, general financial planning templates, and budgeting templates. Users can build their own templates or buy prebuilt ones. Templates are available on diskettes and are used in conjunction with the spreadsheet programs.

For example, in preparing a budgeting template, the user can develop an overlay customized to a specific budgeting requirement. This "budgeting overlay" would be used as a shell to meet the budgeting application requirements and to keep the general budgeting categories and formats the same from year to year.

Templates provide a fast and flexible means for conducting calculations. Because the formulas are preprogrammed, the possibility of calculation errors is reduced. Finally, templates permit automatic transfer of entries among various tables or forms as required. The power of Lotus 1-2-3 (or a similar package), when used with templates, enables the user to review the result, ask "what-if" questions, and make quick changes and recalculations.

Templates can be fairly simple, containing financial, statistical, or mathematical models. Others are more advanced, allowing the manipulation of specified data items to show the impact of changes in one or more values on the dependent variables throughout the entire spreadsheet. Templates for micros are selling for about $100. Examples of popular templates are Multi-Tool Financial Statement, Multi-Tool Financial Budget, Investment Tax Analyst, Financial Projections, Business Forecasting Model, TK! Solver, and Loan Analyzer.

Macros. Suppose a marketing DSS includes a spreadsheet with information about the sales of various products in five regions, supported by bar charts. The marketing manager often tries out "what-if" scenarios by changing the variables that determine sales. The manager, using a spreadsheet, would have to make the changes in the spreadsheet and view each graph by typing in the many necessary commands to call up each graph. The commands would have to be *repeated* for all five graphs.

An alternative to this process is to use macros. Macros are collections of keystrokes representing commands, which are stored in the spreadsheet. To execute the commands, the user now has only to press the "alternate key" while typing the letter code for the macro.

The left side of Box 5.1 shows the commands that the marketing manager would have to type to create and view the five bar charts. The right side of the box shows what the manager would have to type to invoke a slide show of the graphs if a macro, named g (for graphs), had been created.

Lotus 1-2-3 would automatically display each graph, one at a time, on the screen and return to the ready mode so the manager could try out some new assumptions on the spreadsheet (performing "what-if" analysis). To view the effects of these changes, the manager would simply invoke the macro again.

Macros make spreadsheets easier and faster to use and they greatly enhance the "what-if" analysis.

Other Tools. Many tools can be added to a spreadsheet to increase its capabilities and/or ease of use. For example, the following tools can be easily combined with Lotus 1-2-3:

- What's Best (for spreadsheet optimization)
- What-if solver (for optimization, sensitivity analysis)
- Excel More (adds zoom, pan to Windows)
- Always (adds desktop publishing capabilities)
- Twist and Shout, and Sideways (prints spreadsheet files sideways)
- Tomorrow (financial forecasting)
- 4 Save (backs up spreadsheets)
- Spreadsheet optimization using What's Best
- Goal Seeking
- ORACLE for 1-2-3 Add On.

For a complete list, see *PC Magazine*, April 16, 1991.

Although templates and macros or other tools increase the modeling power of spreadsheets, the capabilities of the latter are fairly limited when compared with mainframe DSS generators that are based on financial planning software.

5.12   Financial and Planning Modeling

Many DSS applications deal with financial analysis and/or planning. Therefore it makes sense to develop DSS building tools to *rapidly* build such applications. While spreadsheet software can do the job, such tools can do it more efficiently or effectively. Such tools are being developed around financial and planning modeling software. Since the 1960s, planning models have advanced from an

Box 5.1: Spreadsheet Used by Manager in Marketing DSS

```
Lotus 1-2-3 spreadsheet for marketing example:
A                B           C          D          E         F
1              Region A Region B Region C Region D Region E
2 Sales:
3 Prod 1          100         400        900       1000      1500
4 Prod 2          200         500        800       1100      1400
5 Prod 3          300         600        700       1200      1300
   Lotus Commands:                     Macro:
  G (for graph)                        ``Alternate key''
  T (for type)                         and g
  B (for Bar chart)
  A (for data range)
  B3. . .B5
  X (for labeling)
  A3. . .A5
  O (for options)
  T (for title)
  F (for first line)
  Sales Report for
  T (for title)
  S (for second line)
  Region A
  T (for title)
  X (for X-axis)
  Products
  T (for title)
  Y (for Y-axis)
  Sales
  Q (for quitting options)
  N (for name)
  C (for create)
  Region A
  V (for view)
  Repeat for each region,
  substituting the appropriate
  information
```

obscure concept for large corporations to an appropriate tool for planning in almost any size company.

A major property of financial modeling is that their models are *algebraically* oriented. That is, the formulas are written in the manner that one would write equations. Spreadsheets, on the other hand, write their models with a computation or *calculation* orientation.*

Definition and Background of Planning Modeling

The definition of a planning model varies somewhat with the scope of its application. For instance, financial planning models may have a very short planning horizon and entail no more than a collection of accounting formulas for producing pro forma statements (i.e., a static model). On the other hand, corporate planning models often include complex quantitative and logical interrelationships among a corporation's financial, marketing, and production activities. In this sense, the model has great utility because any of the coordinated subroutines composing the comprehensive model may be isolated for narrower applications. Further on, most financial models are dynamic, multiyear models.

History of Planning Models

The rudiments of corporate modeling can be traced to the early 1960s with the large, expensive, cumbersome simulation models developed by major corporations (e.g., AT&T, Wells Fargo Bank, Dow Chemical, IBM, and Sun Oil). Most of the models were written in one of the third-generation general programming languages like FORTRAN, and were used for generating pro forma financial statements. Financial models were considered an untested concept suitable only for those corporations large enough to absorb the costs and risks of development.

Important advancements in computer technology in the early 1970s provided the means for greater diversity and affordability in corporate modeling.

According to several surveys, financial models were found to provide real support for upper management (see Box 5.2). The nature of the decisions made was clearly semistructured or unstructured. However, most of the models dealt only with deterministic situations.

Planning and modeling languages (PML) have been a major incentive in involving higher management in modeling. The PML are steadily edging out general programming languages. Models are built more easily and with shorter development time, are more easily understood by upper management, and are periodically updated with enhancements from the PML vendor. Most of the powerful PML are considered fourth-generation, nonprocedural languages.

A further convenience offered to companies looking into modeling is premade planning packages sold by software vendors. Included in this category are

---

*Much of the discussion in the first half of this section is based on Shim and McGlade [23].

Box 5.2: Typical Applications of Planning Models

Financial forecasting
Pro forma financial statements
Capital budgeting
Market decision making
Mergers and acquisitions
  analysis
Lease versus purchase decisions
Production scheduling
New venture evaluation
Manpower planning

Profit planning
Sales forecasting
Investment analysis
Construction scheduling
Tax planning
Energy requirements
Labor contract negotiation fees
Foreign currency analysis

templates for spreadsheets discussed earlier. These packages have often been criticized for their inflexibility, but the newer models allow for more user specificity. For example, analytical portfolio models tell an organization how to distribute resources across a portfolio of profit centers. Boston Consulting Group, Arthur D. Little, and McKinsey have developed models that categorize investments into a matrix of profit potentials and recommended strategies. A model for profit impact of market strategy (PIMS) is offered by the Strategic Planning Institute. The package uses a large, multiple regression-based model to identify the optimal strategy in a given business environment. In addition to generic DSS-based planning models, there are several industry-specific ones, notably for hospitals, banks, and universities. For example, Educom's Financial Planning Model (EFPM) is used by about 200 universities as a DSS construction tool for financial, long-range planning, and other university administration decisions (see Box 5.3). Similar packages are likely to proliferate in the future as more companies are forced to use DSS to remain competitive.

Today, there are about 100 PML on the market. They are available on time-sharing networks as well as packages for mainframe, mini- and microcomputers. For a representative list see Table 5.9.

The major differences between financial modeling-based generators and DBMS-based generators are shown in Table 5.10.

5.13   Ready-made Quantitative Models

Decision support systems offer several quantitative models in areas like statistics, financial analysis, accounting, and management science. These models can be called in the DSS generator by one command.

In addition, many DSS generators can easily interface with powerful quantitative methods stand-alone packages. Such packages are usually much more

Box 5.3: Educom's Financial Planning Model (EFPM)

EFPM is the best-known modeling system used in higher education. It has been used in about 200 universities and colleges. In contrast to a regular model that has predefined data definition and equations, this DSS generator is content free. Each institution can create models unique to its mission, structure, and decision-making styles. Thus, EFPM enables a wide range of administrative applications, a sample of which is shown as follows:

Area	University
Athletics	Stanford University
Buildings and Grounds	Harvard University
Business School	University of Pennsylvania
Cash Flow	Pepperdine University
Central Services Allocation	Claremont University Center
Computer Center Cost Recovery	Purdue University
Conference Center	Oregon State University
Continuing Education	University of Minnesota
Dental School	Tufts University
Dining Operations	Harvard University
Endowment Portfolio	Lexington Theological Seminary
Equipment Replacement	Purdue University
Faculty Tenure	Michigan State University
Formula Funding	San Jose State University
Graduate Student Apartments	Brite Divinity School
Fringe Benefits	Cornell University
Indirect Cost Allocations	Purdue University
Legislative Budget Requests	Purdue University
Medical School	University of Southern California
Music School	University of Rochester
Oil and Gas Capitalization	Texas Christian University
Off-Campus Operations	College of New Rochelle
Parking Facilities	Purdue University
Residence Hall Financing	Harvey Mudd College
Residence Hall Operations	University of Wisconsin
Wage and Salary Administration	Pepperdine University

TABLE 5.9 Representative DSS Generators with a Financial Modeling Base.

Product	Vendor
CONTROL STRATEGIST	Xerox Corp. Comp. Services (Los Angeles, CA)
EMPIRE	Applied Data Research (Princeton, NJ)
ENCORE	Ferox Microsystems (Arlington, VA)
EXPRESS, PC EXPRESS	Information Resources (Waltham, MA)
FAME	Fame Software, Citicorp (New York, NY)
FCS/EPS	THORN EMI Comp. Software (Chelmsford, MA)
FORESIGHT	Information Systems of America (Norcross, GA)
FINANCIAL PLANNER	Computer Associates (San Jose, CA)
IFPS, IFPS/Personal	Execucom Systems (Austin, TX)
INGOT	Pansophic Systems, Inc. (Oak Brook, IL)
Mapper	Unisys (Blue Bell, PA)
MODEL	Lloyd Bush & Assoc. (New York, NY)
PLANS+	IBM (Menlo Park, CA)
SIMPLAN	Simplan Systems (Chapel Hill, NC)
STRATAGEM	Integrated Planning (Boston, MA)
SYS/PLANNER	System Research Services (McLean, VA)
System W	Comshare (Ann Arbor, MI)
XSIM	Interactive Data Corp. (Lexington, MA)

powerful than the build-in routines. Another organization of preprogrammed quantitative models is via templates.

Preprogrammed models can be used to expedite the programming time of the DSS builder, especially when they are built-in or when an interface exists.

Some of these models are building blocks of other quantitative models. For example, a regression model can be a part of a forecasting model that supports a financial planning model. The *functions* in Lotus 1-2-3 provide examples of built-in models called by a short command.

SQRT: This function calculates the square root of a number that may be a part of an inventory model.

NPV: This function calculates the net present value of a collection of future cash flows for a given interest rate. It also may be a part of a make versus buy model.

Statistical Packages

Statistical functions are built into many DSS generators; for example:

- DSS/A (from Addison-Wesley) includes analysis of variance, chi-square cross tabulation, multiple linear regression, correlations, and frequency distributions; all are supported by graphics.

TABLE 5.10 Comparison of Financial Modeling Generators with Those Based Around DBMS.

	Major Advantages (Strong Points)	Major Disadvantages (Weak Points)
Financial Modeling-based Generators	Financial reporting (and consolidations with some systems)	Limited sorting with older two-dimensional packages
	Forecasting	Limited data entry
	Sensitivity analysis	Limited handling of text with data
	Usually easier to learn for financial people	Some systems are two-dimensional and require DBMS for consolidations
	Many built-in financial and statistical routines	
DMBS-based Generators	Data (record)-oriented	Cumbersome with time-series problems
	Best text handling	Cumbersome with multidimensional applications (multiple "passes" of the data required)
	Best sort/merge	
	Data integrity	
	Strong in ad hoc, unstructured queries and analysis	Cumbersome in sensitivity analysis applications

Source: Developed by Neil Dorf, Xerox Corporation, Los Angeles, CA.

■ NOMAD 2: mean, median, variance, standard deviation, kurtosis, *t* test, chi-square, regression (linear, polynomial, and stepwise).

An example of a regression analysis executed in NOMAD 2 is shown in Figure 5.5. Notice the following three features:

1. One-word command triggered the analysis ("multireg").
2. The equation for best-fit for the model is clearly identified.
3. The report is automatically formatted.

More power can be obtained from stand-alone statistical packages, some of which can be interfaced easily with Lotus 1-2-3 and other popular spreadsheets, a list of which is given in Table 5.11.

Management Science Packages

There are several hundred management science packages on the market for models ranging from inventory control to project management. Several DSS generators include optimization and simulation capabilities. For example, see Figure 5.6 on page 201 and the description of IFPS in Appendix A to this book. Table 5.12 on page 202 lists representative management science packages.

```
              1
              │
              ▼
        >multireg promotion accounts

        * NOMAD2 * Multiple Linear Regression

        Dependent variable (Y):     PROMOTION
        Independent variable (X):   ACCOUNTS

2 ──► The best fit for the model: Y = a + b1*(X1) + ... +  bk*(Xk) + e

        is:       PROMOTION       =      568.860 +     5.932 * (ACCOUNTS)
                                                                                3
        Number of observations used:    12

          No.     Variable name        Mean
        --------  ----------------   ----------
          1 (i)   ACCOUNTS             44.583
          2 (d)   PROMOTION           833.333

                                    Regression   Standard    Partial   F-Proba-
          No.     Variable name     coefficient    error     F-Value    bility
        --------  ----------------  -----------  ----------  --------- --------
          1       ACCOUNTS               5.932      1.500     15.634     0.003
        --------
        Intercept                      568.860     68.173

        Percent of variation explained by the model:     60.989
        Standard deviation of residuals:                  45.628

        Analysis of variance for the regression
        ----------------------------------------

        Variation   Degr of    Sum       Mean                   F-Pro-
         due to     freedom  of squares  square      F-Value    bability
        ----------  -------  ----------  ---------  ----------  --------
        Regression     1     32547.930   32547.930    15.634      0.003
        Residuals     10     20819.309    2081.931
                     -------  ----------
        Total         11     53367.238
```

FIGURE 5.5   Regression Analysis Performed by NOMAD 2. (*Source:* Courtesy of Must Software, Norwalk, CT.)

Financial Modeling

Financial functions (such as Net Present Value and Internal Rate of Return) are built into many spreadsheet and DSS generators. However, there is a large number of free-standing packages on the market. Some representative examples are:

Product	Vendor
FINAR	Finar Research Corp. (Denver, CO)
Micro-DSS/Finance	Addison-Wesley Pub. Co. (Reading, MA)
Peach Plan	Peachtree Software (Atlanta, GA)
PlanStar	MicroPro International (San Rafael, CA)
Target Financial	Comshare, Inc. (Ann Arbor, MI)
fisCAL	Halcyon Group (Charleston, SC)

TABLE 5.11 Representative Statistical Packages.

Product	Vendor
APL forecasting and time-series analysis	IBM (White Plains, NY)
BMDP	BMDP Statistical State, Inc.
Crosstab	Cambridge Comp. Assoc. (Cambridge, MA)
Forecast IV	Resource Software Intl. (Fords, NY)
Microstat	ECOSOFT, Inc. (Indianapolis, IN)
Minitab	Minitab Inc.
SAM	Decision Sciences Inc. (Sugar Land, TX)
SAS	SAS Institute, Inc. (Cary, NY)
SPSS and SPSS/PC+	SPSS, Inc. (Chicago, IL)
Systat	Systat, Inc. (Evanston, IL)

Decision Analysis and Multiple Criteria Decision-making Packages

Several software packages may be considered interesting decision aids. They can be incorporated into the DSS model base, or be used to supplement it either by providing input data (e.g., subjective judgments) or by "massaging" the output data of the DSS. Representative examples follow.

Expert Choice. Expert Choice (from Decision Support Software, McLean, VA) is a structured decision aid that allows users to graphically portray a complex decision analysis problem with multiple criteria for evaluation. See Box 5.4 on page 202 and Appendix 5-B at the end of this chapter.

Decision Master. Decision Master (from Generic Software, Inc., Bellevue, WA) helps the user to make decisions involving multiple choices and multiple criteria for each choice. It also allows each criterion to be separately weighted and each choice/criterion to be individually rated.

Decision Aid. Managerial problem-solving Decision Aid (from Computer Software Consultants, Inc., New York, NY) consists of several components: personnel selection, decision simulation, time-series analysis and projections, multiple regression, statistical hypothesis testing, financial planning, and project management.

Criterium. This is a very sophisticated package (from Sygenex, Redmond, WA) for decision analysis in general and multiple criteria decision making in particular.

Orion. This package (from Comshare, Inc., Ann Arbor, MI) provides a data analysis system for marketing and financial managers. It offers sales forecasting, market share analysis, cash flow projections, quality control charting, and production scheduling.

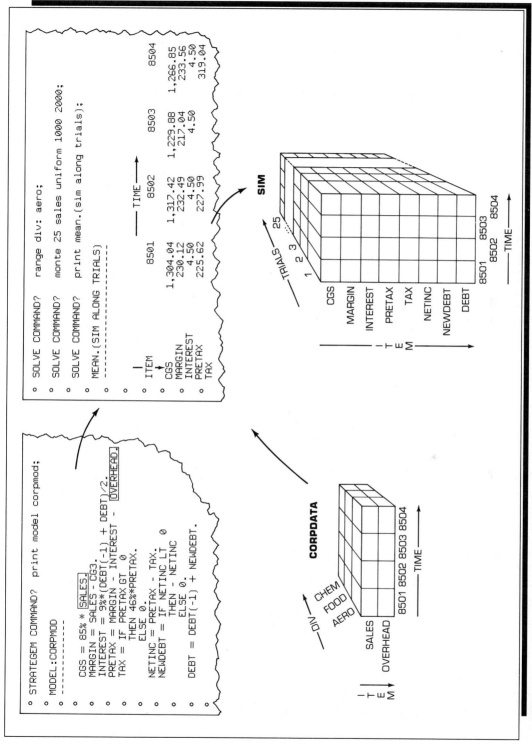

FIGURE 5.6 Monte Carlo Analysis Performed with Stratagem. (*Source:* Courtesy of Integrated Planning, Inc.)

TABLE 5.12   Representative Management Science Packages.

Topic	Product	Vendor
Simulation	STELLA	High Performance System Inc.
	Game Plan	Dean Meyer and Associates (Ridgefield, CT)
	GPSS/PC	Mainstream Software (Stow, MA)
	P C Simscript	CACI (La Jolla, CA)
	SLAM II/PC	Pritsker Assoc, Inc. (Lafayette, IN)
	PRISM Simulation	Tempus Development (Arlington, VA)
Decision Trees	Decision 1-2-Tree	Fast Decision Systems (Cambridge, MA)
	SUPERTREE	SDG Decision Systems (Menlo Park, CA)
Mathematical Programming	MP1-MP8	Eight programs for different mathematical programming models. SCI Computing (Wilmette, IL)
	LINDO, GINO, VINO	Lindo System Inc. (Chicago, IL)
	MPS III	Ketron, Inc. (Arlington, VA)
	MPSX	IBM (Armonk, NY)
	GAMS/MINOS	Stanford University (Stanford, CA)
	LP 83	Sunset Software (San Marino, CA)

Box 5.4: Use of **EXPERT CHOICE** in International Banking

EXPERT CHOICE is now being used by a leading bank to evaluate lending risks and opportunities in foreign countries. This bank had previously used studies to weigh economic, financial, and political considerations. Although the bank was satisified with the quality of the reports, both the bank and the consultant preparing the reports felt the information was not being put to best use. The complex data and decision-making process often resulted in "too much" or "too little" weight being placed on various aspects of the decision process. The bank's credit committee also had difficulty integrating the "expert information" into the deliberation process. Consequently, the bank's consultant prepared an EXPERT CHOICE model, enabling the credit committee to use the most recent information in making comparisons among factors. Without any prior exposure to microcomputers or EXPERT CHOICE, the bankers began using the software and evaluating the subject country within a matter of minutes.

(*Source:* Courtesy, Decision Support Software.)

Arborist. Arborist (from Texas Instruments, Dallas, TX) is a tool for solving decision situations under risk that are presented as decision trees. Using extensive graphics, the program allows one to view, over several windows, the entire decision tree, and/or portions of it. The probabilities of the states of nature are entered numerically (or the "probability wheel" can be used to graphically assist in estimating probabilities). With direct interface to Lotus 1-2-3, Arborist can be used for financial planning and for investment analysis.

Lightyear. Lightyear (from Lightyear, Santa Clara, CA) enables the user to weigh different factors in a decision-making process. The weighing is done numerically, or by using subjective ratings (such as "good" or "excellent"). The program, which uses graphics extensively, enables easy "what-if" sensitivity analysis.

Decision PAD. This package deals with multiple objective decision making (from Apian Software, Menlo Park, CA).

Decision AIDE II. Use of the vendor's methodology for multicriteria decision making (from Kepner-Trego, Inc., Princeton, NJ).

Other Representative DSS Products

Table 5.13 lists some other representative DSS products.

5.14 Model Base Management System Software

The concept of model base management calls for a software package with capabilities similar to that of the DBMS in the database. Unfortunately, although there are dozens of commercial DBMS packages, there are no comprehensive model base management packages currently on the market. Limited capabilities, which a model management package should exhibit, are provided by some spreadsheet programs and financial planning-based DSS generators (such as IFPS). One reason for this situation is that each company uses the models differently. Another reason is that some of the MBMS capabilities (e.g., selecting which model to use, deciding what values to insert, etc.) require expertise and reasoning capabilities. Thus, MBMS could be an interesting area for future application of expert systems. In the meantime most of the capabilities of the MBMS must be developed from scratch by systems analysts and programmers.

An effective model base management system (MBMS) will make the structural and algorithmic aspects of model organization and associated data pro-

TABLE 5.13 Representative DSS Products.

Product	Description	Vendor
Business-modular	Business modeling, forecasting, financial system	Business Model Systems (Westmont, IL)
Activator	Organizes, computes critical information	Control Data Corp. (Greenwich, CT)
Marksman	Supports sales and marketing decisions	Control Data Corp. (Greenwich, CT)
ICMS	Accesses summary level information from databases, links to network PCs	Cullinet (Westwood, MA)
BPCS DSS	Business modeling information retrieval, E-mail, interfaces	System Software Assoc. (Chicago, IL)
Direct Test	Evaluates direct marketing test activities	SPSS Inc. (Chicago, IL)
Simplan and Micro Simplan	Forecasting, risk analysis, modeling, simulation	Simplan Systems, Inc. (Chapel Hill, NC)
Planning Tool	Planning	ATR Inc. (Redondo Beach, CA)
MaxThink	60 different thought processing modules, helps creativity	MaxThink Inc.

cessing invisible to users of the MBMS.* Such tasks as specifying explicit relationships between models to indicate formats for models and which model outputs are input to other models are not placed directly on the user of an MBMS but handled directly by the system.

The following are desirable capabilities of MBMS:

1. *Control.* The DSS user should be provided with a spectrum of control. The system should support both fully automated as well as manual selection of models that seem most useful to the user for an intended application. This will enable the user to proceed at the problem-solving pace that is most comfortable for the user's experiential familiarity with the task at hand. It should be possible for the user to introduce subjective information without being required to provide full information.
2. *Flexibility.* The DSS user should be able to develop part of the solution to the task at hand using one approach and then be able to switch to another modeling approach, if this appears preferable. Any change or modification in the model base will be made available to all DSS users.
3. *Feedback.* The MBMS of the DSS should provide sufficient feedback to

---

*The material in the rest of this section was condensed from Sage [21].

enable the user to be aware of the state of the problem-solving process at any point in time.

4. *Interface.* The DSS user should feel comfortable with the specific model from the MBMS that is in use at any given time. The user should not have to laboriously supply inputs when he or she does not wish to do this.

5. *Redundancy Reduction.* This can be accomplished by use of shared models and associated elimination of redundant storage that would otherwise be needed.

6. *Increased Consistency.* This can be achieved through the ability of multiple decision makers to use the same model and the associated reduction of inconsistency that may result from use of different data or different versions of a model.

To provide these capabilities, it appears that an MBMS design must allow the DSS user to

1. *Access and retrieve existing models.*
2. *Exercise and manipulate existing models*—including model instantiation, model selection, and model synthesis, and the provision of suitable model outputs.
3. *Store existing models*—including model representation, model abstraction, and physical and logical model storage.
4. *Maintain existing models* as appropriate for changing conditions.
5. *Construct new models* with reasonable effort when they are needed, usually by building new models by using existing models as building blocks.

A number of auxiliary requirements must be achieved in order to provide these five capabilities. There must be, for example, appropriate communication and data changes among models that have been combined. It must also be possible to locate appropriate data from the DBMS and transmit it to the models that will use it.

In addition, it must be possible to analyze and interpret the results obtained from using a model. This can be accomplished in a number of ways. In this section, we will examine one of them: *relational MBMS.* Another way is the use of expert systems, which is discussed in Chapter 18.

Relational MBMS. As is the case with a relational view of data, a relational view of models is based on a *mathematical theory of relations.* Thus, a model is viewed as a *virtual file* or *virtual relation.* This virtual file is, in principle, created by exercising the model with a wide spectrum (theoretically all) of inputs.

Another issue of considerable significance relates to the contemporary need for usable *model base query languages,* and needs within such languages for relational completeness. Three operations are needed for relational completeness in model management: execution, optimization, and sensitivity analysis.

Chapter Highlights

- Models play a major role in DSS. They can be of several types.
- Model management is a concept analogous to data management.
- Models can be either static (single snapshot of a situation) or dynamic.
- Analysis is conducted either under assumed certainty (most desirable), risk, or uncertainty (least desirable).
- The major tool of optimization is mathematical programming.
- Linear programming is the simplest tool of mathematical programming. It attempts to find an optimal allocation of limited resources under organizational constraints.
- The major parts of linear programming are objective function, decision variables, and constraints.
- Simulation is a widely used DSS approach that involves experimentation with a model that assumes the appearance of reality.
- Simulation can deal with more complex situations than optimization, but it does not guarantee an optimal solution.
- Heuristic programming involves problem solving using rules of thumb.
- Influence diagrams show graphically the relationships within models.
- Most models require forecasting, but no one is a perfect forecaster.
- Electronic spreadsheets provide a programming language for modeling and computations.
- Spreadsheets can be enhanced by macros, templates, and many add-on tools.
- Special languages are available for financial modeling.
- Many DSS development tools include built-in quantitative models (financial, statistical) or can easily interface with such.
- Model base management systems perform tasks analogous to DBMS.

Key Words

blending problem	heuristics	random numbers
decision analysis	influence diagrams	ready-made models
decision trees	linear programming	simulation
dynamic models	Monte Carlo	spreadsheet (electronic)
enumeration	macros	static models
(complete)	model management	template
environmental analysis	modeling languages	time-series analysis
forecasting	multiple goals	risk analysis
heuristic programming	optimization	

Questions for Review

1. Distinguish between built-in models and models that need to be built.
2. What is environmental scanning and analysis of MSS?

3. What are the major types of models used in DSS?
4. What is the difference between built-in models and ready-made models that are not built-in?
5. What is complete enumeration?
6. Distinguish between a static and a dynamic model.
7. What is an expected value?
8. What is a decision tree?
9. What is an allocation problem?
10. List and briefly discuss the three major components of linear programming.
11. What is heuristic programming?
12. What is an influence diagram? What is it used for?
13. Describe judgmental forecasting methods.
14. What is a time-series analysis?
15. What are causal forecasting models?
16. Define electronic spreadsheet.
17. List the three components of Lotus 1-2-3.
18. Define templates and explain their use.
19. Define a planning model and compare it with a financial planning model.
20. What are the major advantages of a template?
21. What is the major benefit of a macro?
22. What is a nonquantitive model?

Questions for Discussion

1. What is the difference between environmental analysis and environmental scanning?
2. What is the difference between a decision analysis with a single goal and decision analysis with multiple goals (criteria)?
3. What is the difference between an optimistic approach and a pessimistic approach to decision making in uncertainty?
4. Why is an allocation problem so difficult to solve?
5. Describe the general process of simulation.
6. List some of the major advantages of simulation over optimization.
7. List some advantages of optimization over simulation.
8. Give examples of three heuristics that you are familiar with.
9. What type of language is Lotus 1-2-3?
10. Spreadsheet software is appearing now in three dimensions. Explain how this is possible.
11. Lotus 1-2-3 is probably the most popular PC software. Why? What can you do with this package that makes it so attractive?
12. Visit a computer store and review the latest capabilities of Lotus 1-2-3. Compare them with the capabilities of an ideal DSS generator as discussed in Chapters 3 and 7. How wide is the gap? Be specific.
13. Explain how templates are related to Lotus 1-2-3 (or to a similar package). Explain the advantages of using templates in DSS construction.

14. Templates can be purchased in a computer store or can be developed "in house." Explain the difference between the two types.
15. What is the role of a "planning and modeling language"? How does it differ from a general programming language? How does it relate to DSS?
16. The PIMS model discussed in the text uses "a large multiple regression model." Explain the connection between regression analysis and the role of PIMS.
17. There are over 100 DMBS packages on the market for micros and several dozen for mainframes. Why don't we have such packages for model base management systems (MBMS)?
18. Explain how linear programming is set up to solve allocation problems.

Exercises*

1. It has been suggested that DSS generators are English-like and have a variety of analysis capabilities. Even though you have no formal training in IFPS, see if you can identify the purpose and the analysis capabilities of the following IFPS program:

```
    MODEL RISK VERSION OF 05/08/89 13:11
1 COLUMNS 1-5
2 *
3 *       INCOME STATEMENT
4 *
5 VOLUME = VOLUME ESTIMATE, PREVIOUS VOLUME*VOLUME GROWTH
  RATE
6 SELLING PRICE = PRICE ESTIMATE, PREVIOUS SELLING PRICE*1.06
7 SALES = VOLUME*SELLING PRICE
8 UNIT COST = UNIRAND(.80,.95)
9 VARIABLE COST = VOLUME*UNIT COST
10 DIVISION OVERHEAD = 15%*VARIABLE COST
11 STLINE DEPR (INVESTMENT, SALVAGE, LIFE, DEPRECIATION)
12 COST OF GOODS SOLD = VARIABLE COST + DIVISION
   OVERHEAD + DEPRECIATION
13 GROSS MARGIN = SALES – COST OF GOODS SOLD
14 OPERATING EXPENSE = .02*SALES
15 INTEREST EXPENSE = 15742, 21522, 21147, 24905, 21311
16 *
17 NET BEFORE TAX = GROSS MARGIN – OPERATING EXPENSE – INTEREST
   EXPENSE 18 TAXES = TAX RATE*NET BEFORE TAX
19 NET AFTER TAX = NET BEFORE TAX – TAXES
20 *
21 INVESTMENT = 100000, 125000, 0, 100000, 0
22 *
23 RATE OF RETURN = IRR(NET AFTER TAX + DEPRECIATION, INVESTMENT)
```

---

*These exercises require a knowledge of spreadsheet or IFPS (Appendix A to this book). (Additional exercises are provided at the end of the same appendix.)

```
24 *
25 * DATA ESTIMATES
26 TAX RATE = .46
MONTE CARLO 200
SEED .4
COLUMNS 5
HIST RATE OF RETURN, NONE
```

Note: This question was borrowed from Kroeber and Watson [15]. The computer program was adapted from *IFPS Tutorial* (Austin, TX: Execucom Systems Corporation, 1979).

2. Prepare to hand in a printout of a spreadsheet program to analyze the following proposed new product investment. This exercise can use any popular microcomputer spreadsheet software, such as Lotus 1-2-3, Multiplan, Excel, or QUATTRO. It also could use the IFPS financial modeling software. Hand in a printout of the numerical analysis for each part of the exercise, along with a printout of the formulas used in the calculations (i.e., use PRINT Formulas in Lotus or Multiplan, or LIST in IFPS). Each printout must have a title heading that includes your name, your instructor's name, your course and section number, and the date prepared.

   Your client is considering an investment of $1000 in a new product venture that will cause an immediate increase of $400 in the client's annual gross sales. It is assumed the usefulness of this new product will end after 5 years, that its sales will increase by 15 percent per year for years 2 thru 4, and that sales in the final or fifth year will be half those of the fourth year. Although this illustrative exercise involves only a few trivial calculations, please use formulas throughout your model that could easily be extended over more time, with more complex relationships, thus showing the power of spreadsheets.

   The incremental variable costs for this new product are estimated at 40 percent of sales. The estimated incremental annual fixed costs begin at $30 for year 1, increase by $5 during each of the remaining 4 years of the new product's useful life, and then end. The initial investment, all during year 1, includes $400 of expenses that are immediately deductible from the firm's taxable profits. The remaining $600 of the investment is capitalized, and charged out as depreciation expense over several years, starting during year 1. The income tax rate applicable to the incremental net profit contribution of this new product is 28 percent for all years and all amounts. Because a reported accounting loss on this new product reduces other taxable profits, a cash savings of taxes payable of this same percentage will occur for years that show an accounting loss.

   Part 1. Develop a spreadsheet model for this proposed new product investment that shows each item of incremental investment, revenue, expenses, taxes, and net profit for each of the 5 years. Assume the $600 capitalized part of the investment is depreciated in equal amounts ($150 per year) over years 1 through 4.

Part 2. Now extend the spreadsheet model of Part 1 to include the incremental cash flow for each of the 5 years, and the cumulative cash flow for each year. Cash flow includes all investments, expenses, and taxes as outflows, and revenues as inflows.

Part 3. Extend Part 2 to show the net present value, at a 20 percent annual discount factor, of the incremental cash flow for this proposed 5-year investment venture. If possible, also show the internal rate of return, or yield, of this investment.

Part 4. The time period and calculation method for charging the depreciation expense of an investment against incremental taxable income can influence the cash flow pattern, and hence the attractiveness, of an investment. Please extend the spreadsheet of Part 3 to examine the impact on periodic net cash flow, and the total net present value and the internal rate of return, of the following different depreciation options:

a. Current option of equal allocation of the $600 total over 4 years—that is, a straight-line depreciation schedule over 4 years.
b. Then show straight-line over 5 years.
c. And, straight-line over 3 years.
d. Finally, use sum-of-years-digits method over 4 years. Notice that the digits 1, 2, 3, and 4 sum to 10; hence first-year depreciation is 4/10 of the total capitalized investment, and the following years are 3/10, 2/10, and 1/10, respectively.*

3. Finding a Seasonal Index. A seasonal index is an extremely important concept for both forecasting and analysis. Most government statistics are reported as "seasonally adjusted," meaning that the actual data were adjusted to reflect seasonal impacts. One method of finding a quarterly seasonal index is described as follows:

Step 1. List all historical data by quarter.
Step 2. Use a four-quarter moving average to smooth the data (take the sum of the first four quarters and divide it by 4, then sum quarters two through five and divide by 4, and so on).
Center the first average against quarter 3.
Step 3. Total the moving averages and find the simple average of the numbers. Call this SQA (smoothed quarterly average).
Step 4. Find the entry for every first quarter of the SQA and delete the highest and lowest numbers. Repeat this process for the second, third, and fourth quarters.
Step 5. Find the simple average for each quarter from the results of Step 4. Call it AQ1, AQ2, AQ3, and AQ4 respectively.
Step 6. Add the quarters' simple averages and divide by 4. Call this AQ.
Step 7. Compare the results of Step 6 to SQA. There should be a small

---

*This exercise was prepared by Dr. Warren Briggs of Suffolk University.

discrepancy. Divide SQA by QA. You should get a result that is close to 1 (e.g., 1.05).

Step 8. Multiply AQ1 by the result of Step 7. Repeat this step for AQ2, AQ3, and AQ4. This is the adjusted quarterly average.

Step 9. Add the result of Step 8. It should equal, or be very close to, SQA.

Step 10. Multiply each of the adjusted quarterly averages by 400 and divide the result by SQA. The final result is a seasonal index based on 100 = average season.

Note: This procedure assumes no trend. For simplicity, the moving average in Step 2 is placed against quarter 3 instead of between quarters 2 and 3, which would have required additional computation.

Use a spreadsheet or IFPS to build a DSS for this situation. In addition,

- Perform sensitivity analysis.
- Show the smoothed data over the original data on a graph.
- Show the four seasonal indices (found in Step 10) as bar and pie charts.

The input data are

	Quarter			
Year	1	2	3	4
1985	108	104	93	134
1986	110	100	90	125
1987	112	96	88	130
1988	106	93	85	142
1989	111	108	100	138
1990	98	112	94	155
1991	115	98	96	144
1992	104	102	91	150

4. Given a list of employees in a manufacturing company, use the DBMS functions and/or modeling to perform the following:
   a. Sort the employees by department
   b. Sort by salary in ascending order
   c. Sort by department and each department by ascending order of age
   d. Calculate average salary
   e. Calculate average salary of female employees
   f. Calculate the average age in department "A"
   g. Find the females who were hired after December 31, 1985
   h. Show graphically the age distribution (use a 5-year grouping) as a pie
   i. Compute the age to salary linear regression of all employees

Name	Sex	Age	Hired at	Dept.	Salary
Martin Dean	M	28	06-Jan-78	A	$22,000
Jane Hanson	F	35	15-Mar-86	D	$33,200
Daniel Smith	M	19	06-Dec-80	C	$18,500
Emily Brosmer	F	26	10-Jan-78	B	$27,000
Jessica Stone	F	45	26-May-73	A	$38,900
Tom Obudzinski	M	38	01-Dec-88	B	$29,800
Kathleen Braun	F	32	18-Apr-82	B	$35,600
Lisa Gregory	F	48	03-Sep-81	C	$32,400
Timothy Parker	M	29	03-Aug-83	A	$21,200
Jessica Hibscher	F	53	30-Jul-84	D	$38,900
Adam Handel	M	62	29-Nov-85	A	$40,250
Melissa Black	F	42	01-Dec-87	B	$26,400
Ray Ernster	M	29	02-Jul-79	C	$23,200
Daniel Baim	M	38	26-Feb-77	C	$31,000
Amy Melnikov	F	45	30-Apr-76	A	$36,400
Adrienne Cammizzo	F	30	15-Jun-76	A	$25,400
Steven Knowless	M	48	22-Oct-75	D	$33,200
Patricia Salisbury	F	56	26-Feb-74	B	$42,600
Matthew Broekhuizen	M	44	01-Jan-78	C	$45,400
Sarah Parent	F	64	03-Jan-89	A	$38,200

5. Given a Lotus template on the top and the formulas on the bottom, use Lotus to compute the values in rows 12–19. (*Source: Lotus,* February 1986)

	A	B
1	Selling Price of Order	$1200.00
2	Total Cost of Order	$1000.00
3	Discount for PV (1)	13.50%
4	Days to Payment	30
5	Probability of Payment	80.00%
6	Customer Will Reorder	
7	Yes (= 1) or No (=0)	1
8	Days to Reordering Date	30
9	Discount for PV (2)	13.75%
10	Probability of Payment (2)	95.00%
11		
12	Present Value of Order	
13	Present Value of Cost	
14	Expected Value of Order	
15		
16	Present Value of Reorder	
17	Present Value of Cost (2)	
18	Expected PV of Reorder	
19	Discounted EV of 2 Orders	

Formula Table

B12:	$+B1*(1+B3/365)^ - B4$
B13:	$+B2$
B14:	$+B5*(B12-B13)-(1-B5)*B13$
B16:	$+B1*(1+(@MAX(B3,B9)/365))^ - (B8+B4)*B7$
B17:	$+B2*(1+(@MAX(B3,B9)/365))^ - B8*B7$
B18:	$+B10*(B16-B17)-(1-B10)*B17$
B19:	$+B14+B5*B18/(1+@MAX(B3,B9))$

---

6. Many managers know that a small percent of the customers contribute to most of the sales. Similarly much of the wealth in the world is concentrated in the hands of a few. This phenomenon is called the 20–80, the A-B-C, and the value-volume and it is attributed to the famous economist, Pareto. How can this phenomenon be used in the modeling? What kind of approach is this: optimization, simulation, or heuristic?

7. Assume that you know that there is one irregular coin (either lighter or heavier) among 12. Using a two-pen scale you must find that coin (Is it lighter or heavier?) in no more than three tests.
    a. Solve this problem and explain the weighing strategy that you use.
    b. What approach to problem solving is used in this case?

8. Simulate the eight-step inventory problem of Section 5.5 for a demand of 3800.

9. Use the Expert Choice software to select your next car. Evaluate cars on price (actual $), comfort (from very comfortable to poor), performance (from outstanding to poor), looks (from attractive to ugly), and acceleration (seconds per first 50 yards).
    Consider three final cars on your list. Develop:
    a. problem hierarchy.
    b. comparison of the importance of the criteria against the goal.
    c. comparison of the alternative cars for each criterion.
    d. an overall ranking (synthesis of leaf nodes with respect to goal).
    e. a sensitivity analysis.
Maintain the inconsistency index lower than .1.

10. Identify the following in the model below:
    a. The decision variables
    b. The result variables
    c. The uncontrollable variables
    d. The mathematical relationships

```
10 COLUMNS 1991..1995
20\
30\            IFPS MODEL FOR COMPUTING DIVIDEND FORECAST
40\
50 DIVIDENDS = .50*NET PROFIT AFTER TAX
60 NET PROFIT AFTER TAX = SALES - COGS - TAXES
70 SALES = SELLING PRICE*QUANTITY SOLD
80 COGS = 0.8*SALES
90 TAXES = TAX RATE*(SALES-COGS)
100\
110\ ASSUMPTIONS
120\
130 SELLING PRICE = 5, PREVIOUS*1.05
140 TAX RATE = 28%
150 QUANTITY SOLD = 1000 FOR 2, 1250 FOR 2, 1450
```

References and Bibliography

1. Ariav, A., and M. J. Ginzberg. "DSS Design: A Systematic View of Decision Support." *Communications of the ACM*, October 1985.
2. Bodily, S. E. *Modern Decision Making*. New York: McGraw-Hill, 1985.
3. Courtney, J. E., Jr., et al. "A Knowledge-based DSS for Managerial Problem Diagnosis." *Decision Sciences*, Vol. 18, No. 3, 1987.
4. Davis, M. W. *Applied Decision Support*. Englewood Cliffs, NJ: Prentice-Hall, 1988.
5. Farnum, N. R., and L. W. Stanton. *Quantitative Forecasting Methods*. Boston, MA: PWS-Kent, 1989.
6. Geoffrion, A. M., and T. J. Van Roy. "Caution: Common Sense Planning Methods Can Be Hazardous to Your Corporate Health." *Sloan Management Review*, 1979.
7. Georgoff, D. M., and R. G. Murdick. "Manager's Guide to Forecasting." *Harvard Business Review*, January-February 1986.
8. Golden, B. L., et al. *The Analytical Hierarchy Process*. New York: Springer-Verlag, 1989.
9. Hertz, D. *Practical Risk Analysis*. New York: Wiley, 1983.

10. Horwitt, E. "Up from Spreadsheets." *Business Computer Systems*, June 1985.

11. Hwang, C. L., and K. Yoon. *Multiple Attribute Decision Making: Methods and Applications: A State of the Art Survey.* New York: Springer-Verlag, 1981.

12. Jeter, M. W. *Mathematical Programming—An Introduction to Optimization.* New York: Dekker, 1986.

13. Kimbrough, S. O., and R. M. Lee. "Logic Modeling: A Tool for Management Science." *Decision Support Systems*, Vol. 4, 1988.

14. Klein, R. "Computer-based Financial Modeling." *Journal of Systems Management*, May 1982.

15. Kroeber, D. W., and H. J. Watson. *Computer-based Information Systems*, 2nd ed. New York: Macmillan, 1988.

16. Makridakis, S., and S. C. Wheelwright. *The Handbook of Forecasting: A Manager's Guide.* New York: Wiley, 1982.

17. Mentzer, J. T., and R. Gomes. "Computer Systems that Help Decision Makers Utilize Data." *Industrial Marketing Management*, Vol. 18, 1990: 314.

18. Pearl, J. *Heuristics.* Reading, MA: Addison-Wesley, 1984.

19. Rowe, A. J. "The Meta Logic of Cognitively Based Heuristics." Special Report, University of Southern California, April 1988.

20. Saaty, T. S. *Decision Making: The Analytical Hierarchy Process.* Pittsburgh, PA: University of Pittsburgh Press, 1988.

21. Sage, A. P. *Decision Support Systems Engineering.* New York: John Wiley & Sons, 1989.

22. Shaw, M., et al. "Applying Machine Learning to Model Management in Decision Support Systems." *Decision Support Systems*, Vol. 4, 1988: 285–305.

23. Shim, J. K., and R. McGlade. "Current Trends in the Use of Corporate Planning Models." *Journal of Systems Management*, September 1984.

24. Tabucanon, M. T. *Multiple Criteria Decision Making in Industry.* New York: Elsevier, 1989.

25. Turban, E., and J. Meredith. *Fundamentals of Management Science*, 6th ed. Homewood, IL: Irwin, in press [1994].

26. Watson, H. J., and J. H. Blackstone, Jr. *Computer Simulation*, 2nd ed., New York: John Wiley & Sons, 1989.

27. Weber, E. Sue, and B. R. Konsynski. "Problem Management: Neglected Elements in Decision Support Systems." *JMIS*, Vol. No. 64–81, Winter 1987–1988.

28. Zanakis, S. H., and J. R. Evans. "Heuristic Optimization, Why, When, and How to Use It". *Interfaces* (October 1981).

29. Zanakis, S. H., et al. "Heuristic Methods and Applications: A Categorized Survey." *European Journal of Oper. Resc.*, June 1989.

APPENDIX 5-A: Spreadsheet Analysis for Quantity Discounts Using Lotus 1-2-3*

The Problem

Many vendors offer discount prices for products if purchased in large quantities. The buyers can save on the product price, but they have to pay for carrying large inventories. The formulas for determining whether to accept or reject a discount offer are not too complicated. However, they may not be found in many commercial application software packages. Writing these formulas with Lotus 1-2-3 takes only a few minutes. Furthermore, a "what-if" analysis can easily be performed. The decision is determined by the following variables:

- Annual usage (units per year)
- Unit price
- Cost per order (fixed)
- Holding cost (for each dollar value of inventory, in dollars per year)
- The minimum quantity that must be purchased in order to receive a discount
- The discounted price.

Example

In this example we show only one possibility of a discount (price break). However, our analysis can easily be extended to include several price breaks. The data for our case are:

Annual usage = 1000 units

Unit price = $50.00

Ordering cost = $25.00 per order

Holding cost = $0.35 per dollar value in inventory, per year (or $17.50 per unit).

The discount offer is $48.00 (a 4 percent discount per unit if a minimum of 500 units is purchased). The problem is whether to accept the offer or not.

Solution

The solution is based on the well-known economic order quantity (EOQ) formula, which states:

$$EOQ = \sqrt{\frac{2 \times \text{annual usage} \times \text{ordering costs}}{\text{unit price} \times \text{holding cost}}}$$

*Condensed from: Gardner, E. S. Jr. "Should You Take That Quantity Discount?" *Lotus,* June 1986.

The Lotus Model. (A minimum competence in Lotus 1-2-3 is assumed.) The Lotus 1-2-3 program enables the organization of the input and output information in a table (Table 5-A.1).

Developing this analysis involved the following steps:

Cell		Formula	Explanation
E12	EOQ	@SQRT((2*E5*E7/ (E6*E8))	This calculates the value of the EOQ according to the formula
E13	Actual order quantity	@Round(E12,0)	This command rounds the result of the EOQ formula to the nearest integer
E14	Number of orders	+E5/E13	The number of orders placed annually is computed by dividing the annual usage by EOQ
E15	Average inventory	+E13/2	The average inventory is computed to be equal to half of the EOQ
E17	Order costs	+E7*E14	Multiplies the cost per order by the number of orders per year
E18	Holding costs	+E15*E6*E8	Multiplies the average inventory times the unit cost times holding cost per unit
E19	Purchase costs	+E6*E5	Multiplies the unit cost by the annual usage
E20	Total costs	@SUM(E17..E19)	Totals the data in cells E17 through E19

Now, column G is to be completed for the discounted price. Some of the information and formulas can be copied from column E. Other information, such as the unit price in cell G6, must be entered directly or with a formula (+ E6*.96). The minimum amount required to be purchased in order to receive a discount (500) is also entered in cell G9.

The following formula should be entered into cell G13 to assure that the minimum quantity necessary for the discount is entered:

$$@IF(G12 >= G9,@ROUND(G12,0),G9)$$

This formula compares the new EOQ against the minimum order requirement and selects the appropriate one.

"What-If" Analysis. "What-if" analysis is easy to conduct with Lotus 1-2-3. Any of the input data can be changed and the entire output portion is recalculated instantly.

Extended Analysis. The same approach can be used to examine other discount offers; for example, the vendor may offer larger discounts (e.g., $47.00

TABLE 5-A.1 The Lotus 1-2-3 Screen.

	A	B	C	D	E	F	G
1			Quantity Discount Calculator				
2							
3					Standard Price		Discount Price
4	INPUT						
5	Annual usage (units)				1000		1000
6	Unit price				$50.00		$48.00
7	Cost per order				$25.00		$25.00
8	Holding cost per $				$0.35		$0.35
9	Minimum order quantity				0		500
10							
11	OUTPUT						
12	EOQ				53.45		54.55
13	Actual order quantity				53		500
14	Number of orders				18.87		2.00
15	Average inventory				26.50		250.00
16	Annual costs:						
17	Ordering				$471.70		$50.00
18	Holding				$463.75		$4,200.00
19	Purchasing				$50,000.00		$48,000.00
20	Total				$50,935.45		$52,250.00

and $46.00) for larger quantities (e.g., a minimum of 750 and 1000 units). These offers can be entered in columns H and I in a similar manner as the information in column G was entered. Such an extended analysis can aid in negotiating discounts with vendors.

Goal Seeking. Adding additional formulas can allow the user to conduct goal seeking. For example, the user may want to know the discounted unit price that will make the total cost $48,000. Execute this formula as a homework exercise. Other goal-seeking information requires additional formulas.

Graphic Support. The input and/or output data can easily be converted to bar charts, histograms, or any other presentation available in Lotus 1-2-3. For example, the costs in cells E19 and G19 can be shown as a bar graph. It is also possible to show how total cost relates to EOQ (both the theoretical and the actual).

Conclusion. The solution shown in Table 5-A.1 indicates that the discount offer should be rejected. Through trial-and-error or via goal seeking, one can find that the break-even discount unit price is $46.79 (for a 500 unit order size). This can be used as starting point for price negotiations.

APPENDIX 5-B: The Analytic Hierarchy Process (AHP) Using Expert Choice

The Analytic Hierarchy Process (AHP) developed by Saaty [20] helps the decision maker to arrive at the best decision in a case of multiple conflicting objectives (criteria). The AHP makes it possible to deal with both tangible and intangible factors. With it, one organizes thought and intuition in a logical fashion using a *hierarchy* and enters judgments according to understanding and experience. This approach tolerates uncertainty and allows for revision so that individuals and groups can grapple with all their concerns.

The answers can be tested for sensitivity to changes in judgment. Problems are broken down into smaller constituent parts so the decision maker makes only simple pairwise comparison judgments throughout the hierarchy to arrive at overall priorities for the alternatives of action. The decision problem may involve social, political, and technical factors; several parties; and many objectives, criteria, and alternatives; and may require negotiation. The process can be used to:

- Predict likely outcomes.
- Allocate resources.
- Plan projected and desired futures.
- Exercise control over changes in the decision-making system.
- Evaluate employees and allocate wage increases.
- Facilitate group decision-making processes.
- Select alternatives.
- Do cost/benefit comparisons.

Example:

Suppose you are looking for a house. You usually have many alternatives. The selection process is based on several (multiple) criteria, ranging from price to amount of down payment. A *simplified* selection situation is summarized in Table 5-B.1.

TABLE 5-B.1 A House Selection Decision.

Criteria / Alternatives	Cost	Number of bedrooms/ baths	Condition	Location	Financing	Structure	Down Payment
A	137,000	3/2	Average	Poor	Very good	All wood	None
B	108,000	2/1	Poor	Average	Excellent	Frame	10%
C	149,900	3/2	Good	Above average	Poor	Brick	20%
D	168,500	3/3	Excellent	Good	Good	Brick	10%
E	129,000	3/1.5	Poor	Poor	Good	Frame	15%

Developing the Hierarchy

The first step is developing the hierarchy, as shown in Figure 5-B.1

Comparing the Importance of the Criteria Against the Goal

The first step in the process is to *verbally* compare the criteria, two at a time (say, price and location). The user needs to specify which criterion is more important and by how much (moderately more important, strongly more important, etc.). Alternatively, a numerical comparison can be done (e.g., cost is 1.5 times more important than the number of bedrooms).

This information is sufficient for the program to calculate the relative importance of each criterion (given in fractions, total 1.00; for example, cost = 0.15, bedrooms = 0.11, etc.). The program also figures an inconsistency level; this level should be less than 0.10 or if you like more accuracy, use 0.05. If the inconsistency exceeds the threshold, you can adjust the proportion until a desired consistency is achieved.

Comparing Alternatives for Each Criterion

The process just described is now repeated for all alternatives against each criterion. We start with "cost" and compare two alternatives at a time. That is, we compare the cost of site A against that of B (equal ?, which one is more important, etc.).

Since cost is a numerical value, you can use a *numerical* comparison instead of the *verbal* one. For example, the cost of A is $137,000, that of B is $108,000, etc. The program can compute the *relative cost* on a scale totaling one (.198 for A, .156 for B, etc.). This was a linear calculation. Instead, the numerical comparison can be done on a nonlinear scale. (Such a comparison can also be done with verbal values.)

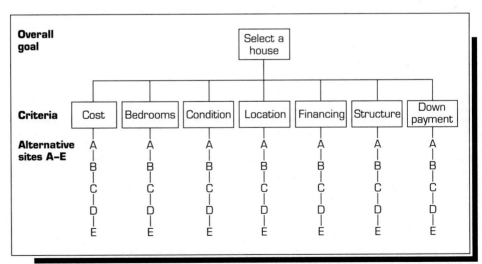

FIGURE 5-B.1 The Hierarchy.

TABLE 5-B.2 Priorities in Terms of Location.

	A	B	C	D	E
A	1	1/3	1/4	1/5	1
B	3	1	1/2	1/3	2
C	4	2	1	1/2	6
D	5	3	2	1	4
E	1	1/2	1/6	1/4	1

The comparison of the five sites with respect to "location" is shown in Table 5-B.2.

Overall Ranking. Using a "weighted average" approach, the overall ranking is obtained by multiplying the preferences in each criterion for each alternative by the relative importance of each criterion and totaling the weights for each alternative. The end product is a weighted average for each alternative. The alternatives then are ranked from the best to the worst.

An example of the overall ranking of the house selection problem, executed with Expert Choice, is shown in Figure 5-B.2. Note that a graphical view is also provided.

Rating Utility

For a large number of alternatives, the pairwise comparison of each two alternatives for all criteria can be very cumbersome. Therefore, a utility ap-

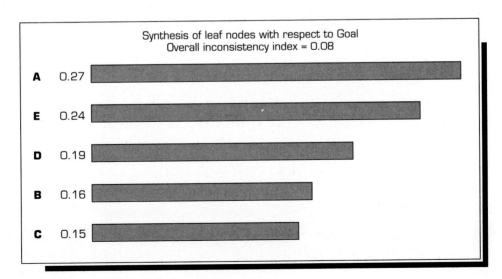

Synthesis of leaf nodes with respect to Goal
Overall inconsistency index = 0.08

A 0.27	
E 0.24	
D 0.19	
B 0.16	
C 0.15	

FIGURE 5-B.2 Printout of Final Results.

proach is used. To do so it is necessary to define intensities (or measures) for each criteria. For example, "cost" can be: very expensive, expensive, average, or cheap. "Condition" can be: excellent, very good, good, fair, and poor. The relative importance of these intensities is then assessed, using a numerical comparison similar to that shown in Table 5-B.1. Such an approach enables the use of a spreadsheet to calculate the weighted average of each alternative.

Sensitivity Analysis

Expert Choice enables the user to see how the final priorities will change if the user changes the relative importance of the criteria. This option is supported by graphics.

Chapter 6

User Interface

The key to successful use of any MSS is the user interface. The simpler the use of the computerized system the greater the chance that it will be utilized by managers. Unfortunately, most hardware and software are designed for computer literates. Even if the specific MSS is friendly, the operating system that drives it may not be simple to use. In this chapter we present the basics of user interface and the technologies that attempt to make it user friendly. Specifically, the following topics are covered:

6.1   User Interfaces: An Overview

Most MSS users have limited computer experience.* They are not prepared to learn the computer-oriented details typically required of experienced users. Often, they expect to walk up and use an MSS application as easily as they use the telephone or drive a car. But the operating systems and other software supporting MSS applications were developed for users accustomed to carrying out complicated tasks. The desire to meet the needs of users who demand power without complication has made the computer industry increasingly sensitive to the design of the user interface.

The user **interface** may be thought of as a surface through which data is passed back and forth between user and computer. Physical aspects of the user interface (Figure 6.1) include display devices, audio devices, and input devices such as tablet, joystick, mouse, microphone, or keyboard.

Data displayed on the workstation provides a context for interaction and it gives cues for action by the user (we assume the user knows how to interpret what is displayed). The user formulates a response and takes an action. Data then passes back to the computer through the interface. In this concept of an interface, all aspects of the system that are known to the user are defined at the interface. The quality of the interface, from the user's perspective, depends on what the user sees (or senses), what the user must know to understand what is sensed, and what actions the user can (or must) take to obtain needed results. The cyclical process shown in Figure 6.1 consists of these elements:

1. *Action language.* Using **action language,** user's action can take various shapes. He or she can select an item from the menu, answer a question, move a display window, or type in a command. He or she can use one or more input devices.
2. *Knowledge.* Knowledge is the information the user must know. The knowledge may be in the user's head, on a reference card, or in a series of "help" messages available on request. Knowledge determines the user's reaction.
3. *User's reaction.* The user interprets the display, processes the content, and plans an action.
4. *Presentation language.* **Presentation language** is the information displayed to the user. It can be shown as display menus, windows, or text. It can be static or dynamic, numeric or symbolic. It can appear on the CRT, as voice, or as print. A variety of studies have shown that the type of output provided has an impact on the quality of the decisions made and on the user's perception of the system. It is important to provide output that is appropriate for the users of the systems and for the decisions being supported.

---

*This section has been condensed from Bennett [3].

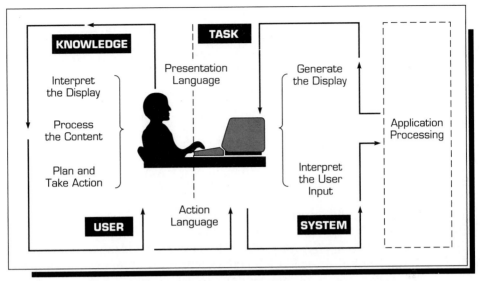

FIGURE 6.1 Two Sides of the User Interface (*Source:* J. L. Bennett, "Tools for Building Advanced User Interfaces," *IBM Systems Journal* [No. 3/4, 1986].)

5. *Computer.* The computer interprets the user's action (input), executes a task (e.g., computation), and generates a display that is basically the presentation language, or the output of the computer.
6. *Dialog.* **Dialog** is an observable series of interchanges or interactions between the human and the computer.
7. *User interface.* **User interface** is the hardware and software that enables a dialog. (The two terms are frequently used interchangeably.)

These elements can be designed and executed in different manners. The combination of presentation and action languages is referred to as an *interactive* (or dialog) *style. Dialog styles* determine how an MSS is directed, what the MSS requires as an input, and what is provided as outputs.

6.2   Interface Modes (Styles)

Interface modes refer to the interactive communication between the user and a computer. The interface mode determines how information is displayed on the monitor and how information is entered into the computer, as well as the ease and simplicity of learning the system and using it. The topic appears under several names, for example, dialog styles, dialog modes, and conversational formats. In this section we look at the following styles: menu interaction, command language, question and answer, form interaction, natural language, and object manipulation.

Menu Interaction. With the **menu interaction** interface, the user selects from a list of possible choices (the menu) the one he or she wants to perform, for example, what report to produce or what analysis to run. The choice is made by use of input devices ranging from a remote control infrared device to a keyboard. Menus appear in a logical order, starting with a main menu and going on to submenus. Menu items can include commands that appear in separate submenus or in the menus with noncommand items. Development tools such as EXSYS, Lotus 1-2-3, and Level5, as well as most MSS applications, involve extensive use of commands that are a part of a menu. Menus can become tedious and time consuming when complex situations are being analyzed, since it may take several menus to build or use a system and the user must shift back and forth among the menus.

Command Language. In the **command language** style, the user enters a command such as "run" or "plot." Many commands are composed of a verb-noun combination (e.g., "plot sales"). Some commands can be executed with the function keys (F1 through F10) on the keyboard. Another way to simplify commands (or even a series of commands) is to use macros.

Question and Answer. The *question and answer* interface mode is popular with ES. It begins with the computer asking the user a question. The user answers the question with a phrase or a sentence (or by selecting an item from a menu). The computer may prompt the user for clarification and/or additional input. Their dialog may involve a large number of questions, some of which result from previous answers. A question may involve the presentation of a menu from which the answer is to be selected. In certain MSS applications, the sequence of questioning may be reversed: the user asks a question and the computer gives an answer.

Form Interaction. In the interface style called **form interaction,** the user enters data or commands into designated spaces (fields) in forms. The headings of the form (or the report or the table) serve as a prompt for the input. The computer may produce some output as a result, and the user may be requested to continue the form interaction process. In some expert systems, instead of being asked to answer one question at a time, the user is asked to answer several questions at one time. The dialogue may involve a table or a form to fill in.

Natural Language. A human-computer dialog that is similar to a human-human dialogue is referred to as **natural language.** Such a dialogue will be conducted, in the future, using voice as input and output. Today, natural language dialogue is done with the keyboard. The problem of using natural language is essentially the inability of the computer to *understand* natural language (such as English or Japanese). However, as discussed later in this chapter, advances in AI enable limited natural language dialogue. For example, natural language processors are being used to access databases.

TABLE 6.1 Comparison of Interface Modes

Dimensions	Menu Interaction	Fill in the Blanks (Forms)	Command Languages	Object Manipulation	Questions and Answers
Speed	Slow at times	Moderate	Fast	Could be slow	Slow at times
Accuracy	Error free	Moderate	Many errors	Error free	Moderate
Training time	Short	Moderate	Long	Short	Short
Users' preference	Very high	Low	Prefer, if trained (only)	High	High
Power	Low	Low	Very high	Moderate-high	Moderate
Flexibility	Limited	Very limited	Very high	Moderate-high	High (if open ended)
Control	The system	The system	The user	The system and the user	The system

Source: Based, in part, on A. Majchrzak et al., *Human Aspects of Computer-Aided Design* (Philadelphia: Taylor and Francis, 1987).

Object Manipulation. In the **object manipulation** style, objects, usually represented as icons (or symbols), are directly manipulated by the user. For example, the user can point the mouse or the cursor at an icon and use a command to move it, enlarge it, or show the details behind it.

Several studies have been conducted to determine the efficiency and accuracy of the various interface styles. Majchrzak et al. [17] have summarized the research in this area and have evaluated the usability of four of the styles along four dimensions. Table 6.1 presents their research with the addition of the last three dimensions and the last two columns.

Several other interface modes are being developed (e.g., pen computers). Natural language processing complemented with voice recognition will probably be the style preferred by MSS users of the future.

6.3 Graphics

Many factors can affect a manager's decision-making capabilities. One of the most important factors is the way in which data are presented. If there are large volumes of data, the manager must reduce the volume to a manageable size and focus on those data points that are crucial. One approach in this case is to use *exception reporting*, where those data that do not meet certain standards are highlighted. Another way to handle large volumes of data is to summarize them by using statistics, tables, and graphs. Summarization provides, in a few chunks, the same information as a large number of data items would.

Graphics enable the presentation of information in a way that more clearly conveys to many managers the meaning of data and that permits managers to visualize relationships. The value of charts and graphs in the communication of numeric data has long been recognized (see the Wharton Experiment in Box 6.4).

Graphics can be produced by two methods, the traditional and the computerized. The traditional method employs graphic artists to produce visuals for meetings and formal presentations. The major deficiencies of this method are the long lead times and the significant cost. The second method, which is usually referred to as *computer graphics*, is gaining popularity (e.g., see Van Dam [35]). It makes it possible to generate graphics automatically from a computer-based information system. Computer graphics permit the user to quickly and inexpensively generate graphic information without the aid of a graphic artist. Furthermore, this information can even be presented in a dynamic (motion) mode.

Graphics Software

The primary purpose of graphics software is to present visual images of information on a computer monitor, a printer/plotter, or both. The information presented may be constructed from numeric data and shown as graphs or charts, or it may be generated from text and symbols and expressed as drawings or pictures. The boundaries between drawing-oriented applications and chart applications using numeric data are often hazy, and many software products support both.

The role of graphics in DSS is presented in Figure 6.2. As shown, the graphics present the output of various software components. The graphics software can be a stand-alone package, or it can be integrated with other software routines (e.g., with a database management system).

Integrated software packages allow managers to create graphic output directly from databases or spreadsheets in a nontechnical and user-friendly way. Therefore the user does not have to worry about the capability of transferring data from the spreadsheet or the database to the graphics modules. This transfer may be a problem in stand-alone graphics, plus it may be a time-consuming process.

Stand-alone graphics (like most other stand-alone packages) are usually more powerful than the integrated ones. They permit more graph styles. They often handle more data than the integrated graphics products can. Another capability of some stand-alone packages is that several graphs can be combined on one screen, compared with the one-graph-at-a-time capability of many of the integrated packages. Of course, with the integrated package, one does not have to buy the extra software. A list of representative software is given in Table 6.2.

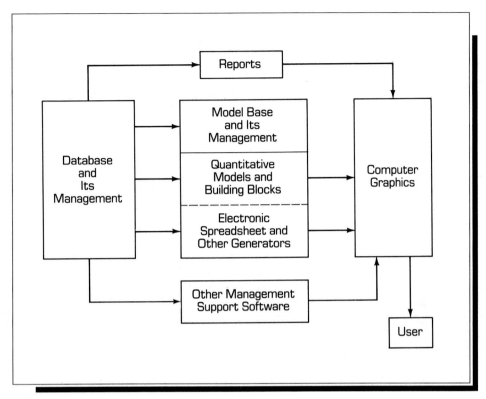

FIGURE 6.2 Computer Graphics in DSS.

TABLE 6.2 Representative Graphic Software.

Product	Vendor
Artpak	PalSoftware, Inc. (Stevens Point, WI)
Benchmark Graphics	Metasoft Corp. (Chandler, AZ)
Chart Start	Micropro Inter. (San Rafael, CA)
DISSPLA	Integ. Soft Syst. Corp. (ISSCO) (San Diego, CA)
Dr. Halo	Media Cybernetics, Inc. (Takoma Park, MD)
Harvard Graphics	Software Publishing Co. (Mountain View, CA)
GEM	Digital Research (Pacific Grove, CA)
GDSS	Data Business Vision, Inc. (San Diego, CA)
Giraph	IMRS Inc. (Stamford, CT)
Graftalk	Redding Group (Ridgefield, CT)
Graphic Assistant	IBM (Boca Raton, FL)
Graphic Environment Manager	Microsoft (Bellevue, WA)
Graph in the Box	New England Software (Greenwich, CT)
Mirage	Zenographics, Inc. (Irvine, CA)
SAS/Graph	SAS Institute, Inc. (Cray, NC)
Tell-A-Graf	ISSCO (San Diego, CA)

The Role of Computer Graphics in DSS

For almost two decades, supporters of computer graphics systems have been urging their use for business management purposes. The military has pioneered in the use of computer graphics for command and control. Graphics may be especially important for business problem solving and decision making because they help managers "visualize" data, relationships, and summaries.

Types of Graphics. A wide variety of graphics forms are in use today.* All can be generated by computers, many by microcomputers.

- *Text* plays a critical role in graphics—listing points that the speaker is discussing, showing subject titles, identifying components and values of a chart, and so on.
- *Time-series charts* show the value of one or more variables over time.
- *Bar and pie charts* can be used to show total values (by the size of the bar or pie), as well as component values, such as breakdowns of, say, "source of money received."
- *Scatter diagrams* show the relationship between two variables, such as the number of air travelers who fly on Mondays, on Tuesdays, and so on.
- *Maps* can be two- or three-dimensional. Two-dimensional maps are useful for showing spatial relationships, for example, the locations of customers and the locations of a company's customer service facilities. Three-dimensional maps show surface contours with a three-dimensional effect.
- *Layouts* of rooms, buildings, or shopping centers convey much information in relatively simple diagrams.
- *Hierarchy charts*, such as organizational, are widely used.
- *Sequence charts*, such as flowcharts, show the necessary sequence of events, and which activities can be done in parallel.
- *Motion graphics*, such as motion pictures and television, clearly will continue to perform vital functions.
- *Desktop publishing.* In-house computerized publishing systems that have extensive graphic capabilities (e.g., transferring a picture into the computer, laying it in a desirable position and then printing it) are gaining in popularity.

Use of Graphics in Decision Making

Here are some of the ways that people in business use these various types of graphics in decision making:**

---

*Based on Sprague and McNurlin [32]. *Information Systems Management in Practice.* © 1986, pp. 371–373. Reprinted by permission of Prentice-Hall, Inc., Englewood Cliffs, New Jersey.

**Based on Sprague and McNurlin [32]. *Information Systems Management in Practice.* © 1986. Reprinted by permission of Prentice-Hall, Inc., Englewood Cliffs, New Jersey.

Reports. Graphics are widely used in reports, such as those prepared for management. Perhaps the most common graphs are bar charts and time-series charts.

Presentations. Graphics are used in 35 mm slides and overhead transparencies for presentation of information at briefings, meetings, and conferences.

Management Tracking of Performance. "Management chart rooms" are common in business and industry, where the charts give reasonably up-to-date information on actual versus planned performance.

Analysis, Planning, and Scheduling. Certain types of graphics have proved to be very helpful for supporting management decisions. Maps, discussed above, are one type applicable to analysis, planning, and scheduling. Critical path charts (such as PERT and CPM) have been effective in vividly showing the critical activity path of (small) projects.

Command, Control, and Communication. Although not often found in business and industry, communication, command and control centers are widely used in the military. Some local governments also use them for controlling the operation of police, fire, and other vital public services. Maps and other graphics techniques play a key role in these centers.

Manufacturing Control Centers. Incorporating graphics with MSS and real time systems for production equipment experimentation and control is becoming very popular. This combination permits dynamic modeling and "what-if" analysis. The graphic outputs help visualize both the problem and the potential solutions.

Other Uses. One of the main uses of graphics is for providing design, engineering, and production drawings for the manufacture of products. Computer-aided design (CAD) and computer-aided manufacturing (CAM) systems are receiving a lot of attention these days. And graphics are being used in teleconferencing and videotex systems.

Graphics in Motion. Graphics can also be used in dynamic modeling. Of special interest are animation and visual interactive modeling which are presented later in this chapter.

Graphics in Action. The fact that some theoretical studies and limited experimentations indicate that tabular display is as good (or even better) than graphical aids* (e.g., see Remus [28]) does not seem to impress the buyers of graphics

---

*Note that these experiments were conducted several years ago with inferior graphics.

software. Sales of graphic products are increasing at a rate of 30 percent a year. (See Box 6.1.) In some cases computer graphics have become strategic tools. Companies that have realized high payoff applications are not broadcasting their successes for competitive reasons. For example, the August 13, 1985, issue of *Business Week* reports that General Motors considers its graphically supported financial DSS so competitive that it will not even discuss it. Table 6.3 includes some examples of successful graphical support for DSS. The list was extracted from Paller [23].

6.4   Graphical User Interface (GUI)

GUIs are direct manipulation systems in which the users have direct control of visible objects (such as icons), and actions replace complex command syntax.

Box 6.1: Some Facts About Graphics

A national study conducted at the University of Minnesota in 1984 regarding computer (business) graphics indicated (see Lehman et al. [15]):

- SAS/GRAPH—the most widely available mainframe package.
- Tell-A-Graf—a close second.
- Lotus 1-2-3 (contains a graphics component)—the most widely available micro package.
- User demand is the major factor influencing the decision to buy computer graphics.
- The heaviest users of graphics are finance, information systems, and marketing departments.
- About 34 percent of all professionals, 23 percent of managers, and 21 percent of all managerial assistants are the major interactors with software graphics to create graphs and charts. Only 9 percent of all executives work with these systems.
- Most useful applications of computer graphics are the support of written reports and oral presentations. Less frequent is the use for decision support and data analysis.
- Responsibility for computer graphics usually resides at the information systems department (or the Information Center).
- The major impediments to use are poor integration of graphics software with the database (and other MSS components) and insufficient user knowledge of graphics.
- The use of graphics will increase in the future.

TABLE 6.3 Graphics Applications.

Company	Hardware	Software	Graphical Application/Benefits
McDonald's	Xerox 9700 laser printer	DISSPLA, Tell-A-Graf	Proven monetary benefits. Charts of financial reports. Help store managers to monitor performance.
First National Bank of Chicago	Nicolet Zeta Plotters	Tell-A-Graf	Chartbook of 80 productivity measures. Used in marketing (best sales tool).
Electronic Data Systems	IBM 3287 and ISSCO slides service	DISSPLA, Tell-A-Graf	Monitor performance, revenue, and costs. Early warning system for clients. Data summaries.
"Chemco"	Plotters	DISSPLA, Tell-A-Graf	Support instant decision on buying raw materials. Convert results of mathematical programming to graphs.
Ford Motor Company	Dicomed film recorder	DISSPLA, Tell-A-Graf	Graph planning data. Large savings in transportation cost. Confidence in results.
"Epco"	Calcomp plotter	Tell-A-Graf	Proposal for rate increase, used during public hearings on rates.
"Foodco"	Xerox color laser printer	Tell-A-Graf	Sales data, including competition. Quick responses to competition. Visual analysis of alternatives.
Kodak	HP plotter, Nicolet Zeta plotters and Dicomed film recorders	DISSPLA, Tell-A-Graf	Feedback of data from service to manufacturing. Checking corrective alternatives. Improved quality.
Martin Marietta Energy Systems	III FR-80 and plotters	DISSPLA, Mapper, Tell-A-Graf, Tell-A-Plan	Save time on visual presentations. $2 million annual savings.
Monsanto	Matrix QCR film recorder	DISSPLA, Beauchart, Tell-A-Graf, SAS/Graph, FloChart	40,000 slides made directly from computer output. $1 million savings.
"Aerocorp"	Plotters, printers, laser printers, and film recorders	DISSPLA, Tell-A-Graf, Tell-A-Plan	Graphics for project management, for bidding, planning, monitoring, and control. Reports to clients.
New England Telephone	Xerox 6500 color laser printer and matrix QCR film recorder	Tell-A-Graf	Color printing. Investment recovered in three months.

Users just touch or aim at visual areas to interact with a computer. GUIs are predicted to be the interface for the 1990s. (See Figure 6.3.)

The GUI combined with object-oriented programming has been evolved from Xerox's Star and Apple's Lisa as a most powerful programming tool, especially for executive information systems and DSS. The major parts that the user touches or sees are: icons, pointing devices (e.g., mouse, light pen), menus, windows, intelligent icons, colors, and dialogue boxes. These parts create what is described as the WYSIWYG environment.

WYSIWYG Environment. In a What You See Is What You Get environment the user works with multiple overlapping windows and the other parts described earlier and is able to move text and graphics seamlessly across applications. The user can get an exact print of what he or she sees on the screen.

Many GUI products are available on the market, and they are used in the creation of the MSS interface (see Table 6.4).

The capabilities of GUIs are increasing constantly (see Reed [27]). Box 6.2 shows advanced features of GUI (existing or about to come). One of the most

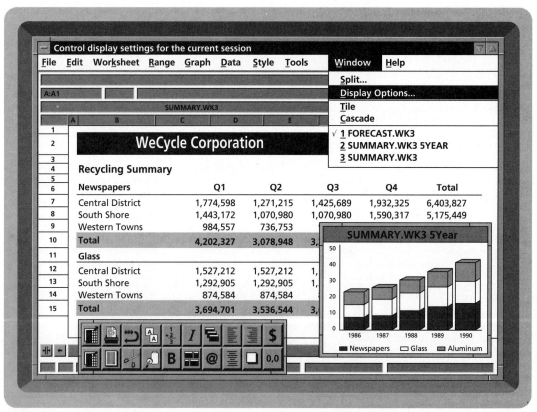

FIGURE 6.3   Example of GUI (Lotus 1-2-3 for Windows with "Smart Icons" at the Bottom)

TABLE 6.4 Representative
GUIs.

Product	Vendor
BTRON	Japan Inc.
DeskMate	Tandy Corp.
Desqview	Quarterdeck Software
DOS 5.0 and up	Microsoft Corp.
GeoWorks Ensemble	GeoWorks Corp.
Macintosh	Apple Computer
Motif (for UNIX)	Open Software
NewWave	Hewlett-Packard
NEXTStep GUI	NEXT Computer Corp.
Presentation Manager	IBM/Microsoft
Windows	Microsoft Corp.
X Window	A consortium of companies

interesting implementations of GUI is the visual interactive modeling described
next.

6.5 Visual Interactive Modeling (or Decision Making)

One of the most interesting developments in computer graphics is visual interactive modeling (VIM) (see Box 6.3). The technique has been used for DSS in

Box 6.2: Advanced Features of GUIs

- **Customized Interfaces.** Different colors and font sizes to select
  from, different icons (to match different cultures, maturation, train-
  ing, etc.), different levels and sequences of menu commands, and
  multiple hardware interfaces (input/output devices) to match the
  task and individual.
- **Multiple Screens and Wide Screen**
- **Animation** (e.g., moving messages to get the user's attention)
- **Blackout** of any information that needs to be secured.
- **Relaxation Displays** (e.g., of a beach or woods)
- **Color Shades.** The shades will replace full colors when too many are
  involved.
- **Aesthetic, Simple Displays**

(*Source:* Condensed from Neuman and Brock [22].)

Box 6.3: How Can Visual Interactive Decision Making Help a Manager?

The first exposure to VIM sets the manager on unfamiliar ground. A large color screen lights up with a graphic display that may include moving icons and blinking colors. The first response is usually a comparison with a video game and, indeed, the program creating the display has much in common with game software. The comparison is, however, short-lived. The power of the technique emerges in stages:

1. Managers recognize the screen display as a graphic representing a familiar process or situation.
2. Managers observe the screen carefully, perhaps also several other screen displays, and accept the picture(s) as a sufficiently detailed image of the real process, with any motion showing realistic process evolution.
3. Managers interact with the model, and observe that the screen image responds in accordance with their understanding of the real system.
4. Through experimentation and observation, managers gain confidence in the visual model and become convinced that the model producing the displays is a valid representation of the real system.
5. Once convinced of the validity of the visual model, managers can begin to ask "what-if," and the visual model becomes a powerful decision-making aid.

The power of VIM as a decision-making tool comes from the *confidence* in the model that grows as managers see the model confirm their understanding of the real system. Managerial validation of the model occurs because:

---

the area of operations management with unusual success (see Hurrion [13]). The technique appears under several names, such as visual interactive problem solving, visual interactive modeling, and visual interactive simulation.

Visual interactive modeling (VIM) uses computer graphic displays to present the impact of different management decisions. It differs from regular graphics in that the user can intervene in the decision-making process and can see the results of the intervention. A visual model is a graphic used as an integral part of decision making or problem solving and not just as a communication device. The VIM displays the effect of different decisions in graphic form on a computer screen.

- A picture is recognizable as a model of the real world more readily than a table of numbers; a street map of a city is easier to recognize as the city than a list of the coordinates of street intersections.
- A visual model is not a "black box." The interior workings of the model are in full view and nothing has to be taken on trust.
- Dynamic visual models show the same transient behavior of the process that the manager sees every day, rather than average behavior over a long period of time.
- VIM enables the manager to interact directly with the model rather than working with a mathematical model through an analyst.

Once confidence in the visual model is achieved, VIM provides the manager with a decision-making environment very much like that of a scientist working in a laboratory. The manager chooses experiments to be conducted, and evaluates them using results provided by the model. Explicit measures of the performance and the quality of alternative solutions can be incorporated into the model; for example, in a bus-routing problem it may be desirable to keep the routes as short as possible; after changing stops around, the total length of the routes can be computed and displayed. Optimizing procedures can also be built into the model: when a stop is moved from one route to another, the routes can be redrawn so that the distance traveled is a minimum.

VIM is particularly powerful when decision makers have multiple decision criteria, or where decision criteria are implicit or difficult to formalize. VIM allows decision makers to choose a best solution using whatever criteria they think appropriate. VIM is also a powerful *training* device, allowing exposure to operations that can be very like the real thing—a flight simulator, for example, is an advanced form of VIM application.

(*Source:* Bell et al. [2]. *Business Quarterly* published by School of Business, The University of Western Ontario, Canada)

VIM can represent a static or a dynamic system. Static models display a visual image of the result of one decision alternative at a time. (With computer windows, several results can be compared on one screen.) Dynamic models display systems that evolve over time. The evolution is represented by animation.

One of the most developed areas in dynamic VIM is **visual simulation.** It is a very important technique for DSS, because simulation is considered a major capability in DSS. Visual interactive simulation (VIS) is a decision simulation in which the end-user watches the progress of the simulation model in an animated form using graphics terminals. The user may interact with the simulation and try different decision strategies.

Conventional Simulation. Simulation has long been established as a useful method of giving insight into complex MSS problem situations. However, the technique of simulation does not usually allow decision makers to *see* how a solution to a complex problem is developing through time, nor does it give them the ability to interact with it. The simulation technique gives only statistical answers at the end of a set of particular experiments. As a result, decision makers are not an integral part of the simulation development, and their experience and judgment cannot be used to directly assist the study. Thus any conclusions obtained by the model must be taken on trust. If the conclusions do not agree with the intuition or practical judgment of the decision maker, a confidence gap will appear regarding the use of the model. The very nature of simulation studies means that a significant part of the analysis must appear as a "black box." For this reason a solution derived by simulation studies may not be implemented.

Visual Interactive Simulation. The basic philosophy of VIS is that decision makers will be able to watch a simulation model of their problem situation develop through time. This is achieved by using a visual display unit. Decision makers can also contribute to the validation of that model. They will have more confidence in its use because of their own participation. They are also in a position to use their knowledge and experience to interact with the model in order to explore alternative strategies.

Simulation can be interactive at the design stage, at the model running stage, or both. To gain insight into how systems operate under different conditions, it is important to be able to interact with the model while it is running so that alternative suggestions or directives can be tested.

Visual Interactive Models and DSS

VIM was used with DSS in several operations management decisions (see application case at the end of this chapter and Hurrion [13]). The method consists of priming a visual interactive model of a plant (or company) with its current status. The model is then rapidly run on a computer allowing management to observe how a plant is likely to operate in the future. A similar approach was used to assist in the consensus negotiations among senior managers for the development of their budget plans. A simple example of VIM is the area of waiting lines (queuing). A DSS in such a case usually computes several measures of performance (e.g., waiting time in the system) for the various decision alternatives.

Complex waiting line problems require simulation. The VIM can display the size of the waiting line or the value of the waiting time as it changes during the simulation runs. The VIM can also present graphically the answers to "what-if" questions regarding changes in input variables.

The VIM approach was also used in conjunction with artificial intelligence. The integration of the two techniques adds several capabilities that range from the ability to build systems graphically to learning about the dynamics of the system.

TABLE 6.5 Representative Interactive Simulation Packages with Animation

Product	Vendor
ADAS	Cadre Tech., Inc. (Providence, RI)
CADmotion, PC Model	SimSoft Inc. (Brookings, OR)
Cinema Animation System, SIMAN	Systems Modeling Corp. (Sewickley, PA)
COMNET, LANNET, MODSIM	CACI Products Co. (La Jolla, CA)
Extend	Imagine That, Inc. (San Jose, CA)
Factor, SLAM/TESS, XCELL	Pritsker Corp. (Indianapolis, IN)
Genetik	Insight International Ltd. (Ontario, Canada)
GPSS/H, Proof Animation	Wolverine Software Corp. (Annandale, VA)
GPSS/PC	Minuteman Software (Stow, MA)
Q+	AT & T Bell Labs (Holmdel, NJ)
SIMFactory, SIMSCRIPT	CACI Products Co. (La Jolla, CA)
SIMSOFT	Microsoft Corp. (Bellevue, WA)
SIMKIT	Intellicorp (Mountain View, CA)

General-purpose dynamic VIM software is commercially available for both mainframe and microcomputers. For a representative list of packages with **animation,** see Table 6.5.

6.6 Multimedia

User interface can be enriched with the use of multimedia. Management support systems employ several multimedia technologies both as presentation devices as well as an integral part of the decision-making system.

Multimedia. Multimedia refers to a pool of human-machine communication media, some of which can be combined in one application (Table 6.6). In information technology, the basic idea behind what is called an *interactive multimedia approach* is to use computers to improve human-machine communication by utilizing several items of the media pool with the computerized system as the center of the application. One new class in the multimedia collection is called hypermedia.

Hypermedia. Hypermedia is a term used to describe documents that could contain several types of media—text, graphics, audio, and video elements—which allow information to be linked by *association*. Hypermedia may contain several layers of information; here are some examples:

- A *menu-based natural language interface* to provide a simple and transparent way for users to run the system and query it

TABLE 6.6 Human-Machine Communication Media.		
	Computer	Projected still visuals
	CRT and terminals	Slide
	CD-ROM	Overhead projector
	Computer interactive	
	videodisc	Graphic materials
	Digital video interactive	Pictures
	Compact disc interactive	Printed job aids
	Computer simulation	Visual display
	Teletext/videotext	
	Intelligent tutoring system	Audio
	Hypertext	Tape/cassette/record
	Image digitizing	Teleconference/
	Scanners	audioconference
	Screen projection	Sound digitizing
	Object-oriented programming	Microphone
		Compact disc
		Music
	Motion image	
	Video disc (cassette)	Text
	Motion picture	
	Broadcast television	
	Teleconference/	
	videoconference	
	Animation	

Source: P. Chao, et al., "Using Expert Systems Approaches to Solve Media Selection Problem: Matrix Format," in *Proceedings of the Association of Computer Interface System,* © November 1990, IEEE.

- An *object-oriented database* that permits concurrent access to its data structures and operations
- A *relational query interface* that can efficiently support complex queries
- A *hypermedia abstract machine* that lets users link different types of information
- *Media editors* that provide ways to view and edit text, graphics, images, and voice
- A *change management virtual memory* to manage temporary versions, configurations, and transformations of design entities.

By adding control structures on top of hypermedia systems, it is possible to enhance MSS application ranging from GDSS to ES.

Work being done at Texas Instruments with hypermedia is aimed at producing widely applicable software tools for dealing with "semistructured" information. A hypermedia system is considered an authoring tool and an information organizer.

Hypermedia* are characterized by (1) having linked, different information structures in which links are explicit, (2) being in effect multimedia (e.g., text,

---

*This paragraph, and the next two, are condensed from Paul [24].

graphics, animation, voice), and (3) allowing information to be linked by association. They present an opportunity for delivering new services and products.

There are two classes of hypermedia. One is called presentation (or the *navigation* of the knowledge and of the data, and it is the common way of viewing hypermedia). The other is an active/generative component that records the process as it is going on. Hypermedia help capture the process and results—as you analyze data, interact with colleagues, and perform your tasks—and help to put the results into your presentation vehicle.

Figure 6.4 shows the typical view of hypermedia, that is, its use for knowledge navigation. Examples of commercial products include HyperCard and NoteCards. The idea here is that the context lengths are hard-wired into a multimedia information base, and it's up to the user to choose which way to go. What does the user want to see next? All of the links are built in by the developer, but the order in which they are processed can be affected by the *navigator*, the consumer of the products.

Figure 6.5 shows the role for hypermedia as suggested by the RAND Corp., that is, active participation in research to help record, organize, and integrate information and processes. The essence of the role is support of intelligent research management and information synthesis. The components include an active knowledge base, multilevel annotation, and multimedia integration. Hypermedia are valuable for a fast search of specific information; they have an open architecture and can be used with relative ease by nonprogrammers to rapidly build computer applications.

Hypertext. One of the most recent ingredients to the multimedia pool is **hypertext.** Hypertext is an approach for handling text and graphic information that allows the users to jump from a given topic, whenever they wish, to related

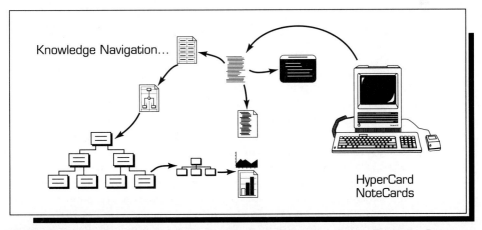

FIGURE 6.4 Hypermedia as a Presentation Tool (*Source:* J. Paul, "Toward a Strategy for Managing Computer-based Research," in *Proceedings, FAIM 90* [Alexandria, VA: Defense Systems Management College, 1990]. RAND Corp. Used with permission.)

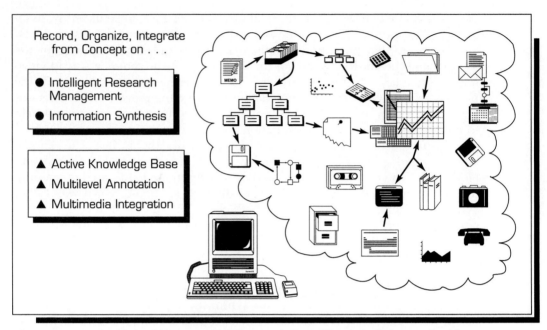

FIGURE 6.5   Active Role of Hypermedia (*Source:* J. Paul, "Toward a Strategy for Managing Computer-based Research," in *Proceedings, FAIM 90* [Alexandria, VA: Defense Systems Management College, 1990]. RAND Corp. Used with permission.)

ideas. Reading or viewing of information thus becomes open ended and controlled by the user. Hypertext allows users to access information in a nonlinear fashion by following a train of thought. It lets the reader control the level of details and the type of information displayed. It allows a quick search according to the reader's interest. For example, as you started reading this section the first word was *multimedia*. Using the hypertext approach, you can highlight the word *multimedia,* then press a button; the computer would show you a passage of text related to this topic. When you are finished, you can return to the beginning of the section or jump to any other related topic.

Hypertext is still in its developmental stages (for an overview and products see the entire October 1988 issue of *Byte*). The concept may contribute to improved user interfaces in MSS as well as to enhanced capabilities of the decision maker (e.g., by increasing the speed with which information is being retrieved). Hypertext is a natural companion to ES development tools. Both technologies deal with the *transfer of knowledge.* In hypertext, however, the user controls the tools, and he or she may not do it in the most efficient way. Expert systems can lead and direct users. For further information, see Shafer [31]. Several products perform such an integration. For example, KnowledgePro integrates hypertext and expert systems. Such integration enables a powerful knowledge representation including easy access to colors, windows, and mouse control. It lets communication take place between expert and novice, teacher and pupil, consultant and manager.

6.7 Virtual Reality

MSS application formerly had two dimensions. However, an increasing number of today's applications have 3-D user interfaces. Such presentation is especially important in the manufacturing and marketing environments. The 3-D user interface offers rich opportunities for powerful interactions that use the mind's natural experiences in spatial perception (per Marcus [18]). Furthermore, in 3-D environments, which are shown on flat 2-D screens, we see only 2-D projections of 3-D objects. The user, however, must use such views to deduce geometric properties and spatial relationships. Static images can be difficult to understand. Stereo viewing helps with depth perception, but to grasp a complex screen fully, it is best to let the user move freely about the objects by manipulating a virtual camera or eye. The implementation of 3-D user interface is, therefore, difficult and expensive. One of the most interesting implementations of 3-D user interface is virtual reality.

With virtual reality (VR), instead of looking at a flat computer screen, the user interacts with a 3-D computer-generated environment. To see and hear the environment, the user wears stereo goggles and a 3-D headset. To interact with the environment (control objects or move around), the user wears a computerized behavior transducing head-coupled display and hand position sensors ("gloves"). VR displays achieve the illusion of a surrounding medium by updating the display in real time. The user can grasp and move virtual objects. VR is available in some games and in limited (but expensive) commercial applications. However, it is expected that within a decade or so, there will be many commercial applications that will support decision making (e.g., make purchasing decisions by observing virtual products). For an overview, pictures, and extensive references see Ellis [7].

6.8 Research on User Interface in MSS

The issue of how to present data to decision makers occupied the minds of researchers for a long time. Recognizing that the presentation is important, researchers designed experiments attempting to find the most appropriate ways of presentation. The Wharton Experiment (Box 6.4) shows the power of ordinary overhead projectors. Its conclusions, however, can be generalized to computer graphics as well, because computer graphics can be projected on a screen much like the ordinary overhead transparencies.

Experiments regarding human-computer interface can be conducted along several dimensions due to the large number of variables involved. For example, Wang and Wu [36] identified the following variables:

Box 6.4: The Wharton Experiment

In a study conducted by the Wharton School, University of Pennsylvania, overhead projection was shown to significantly influence the decisions reached, how the presenter of information was perceived by meeting participants, and whether or not the meeting leader could quickly reach a consensus. The six-month study was conducted with masters in business administration candidates assuming the roles of corporate decision makers grappling with a major marketing decision.

Method. The students were divided into 36 groups of three or four and given the task of making a decision on whether to introduce a new product, "Crystal, a light beer." The groups were urged to reach a consensus decision on whether or not to market the beer—"go" or "no go."

The student presenters, playing the role of marketing experts, then gave opposing viewpoints for and against the product: one used overhead transparencies and the other used a white board to emphasize certain points. In one-third of the meetings the presenters in favor of a marketing decision used transparencies, in one-third those against used transparencies, and in one-third no transparencies were used.

Results. Regardless of which side they were favoring, the presenters were able to convince more people when they used the transparencies than when they did not. Sixty-seven percent agreed with the presenter promoting a "go" decision using visuals, and the same percent agreed when the presenter using visuals argued for a "no go" decision. When no overhead projector was used, deadlock at 50-50 occurred. In addition, the presenters who used transparencies were rated as "significantly better prepared, more professional, more persuasive, more credible, and more interesting" than those who did not use transparencies.

Finally, the study indicated that the leader of the group that was supported with graphics achieved consensus in a 28 percent shorter meeting time.

Note: A 28 percent reduction in meeting length could produce savings for American business equal to several billion dollars a year, or a time savings of up to 42 extra working days per year for average executives who spend half their time in business meetings.

(*Source:* L. Oppenheim, C. Kydd, V. P. Carroll, and G. Carroll, "A Study of the Effects of the Use of Overhead Transparencies on Business Meetings," Report of the Applied Research Center of the Wharton School, University of Pennsylvania, October 1981.)

Independent variables. Four variables were identified:

1. **Human user.** Here two measures were used:
   - Demographics (age, education, experience)
   - Psychological (cognitive style, intelligence, risk attitude)
2. **Decision environment.** Here the measures were:
   - Decision structure
   - Organizational level
   - Others (stability, time pressure, uncertainty)
3. **Task.** Here the measures were:
   - Decision support (e.g., complexity level)
   - Inquiry/information retrieval
   - Data entry
   - Word processing
   - Computer-aided instruction
4. **Interface characteristics.** Here the measures were:
   - Input/output media
   - Dialogue type
   - Presentation format (tabular, graphical, colors, animation)
   - Language characteristics (help facility, default options, other options)

Dependent variable.

Human/computer effectiveness. This variable was measured by:

- Performance (time, errors, task completion, profit)
- User attributes (satisfaction, confidence)
- Use of system option (high, low)

Results. The large number of variables led to inconclusive results or situational results in most of the studies. Of special interest to MSS are the following:

1. **Colors.** Generally speaking, empirical studies about colors (e.g., Hoadley [12]) indicated that color improves:
   - the performance in a recall task
   - the performance in a search-and-locate task
   - the performance in a retention task
   - the comprehension of instructional materials
   - the performance in a decision judgment
   - the ability to extract information.

   However, improvements were found to be situational.
2. **Graphic versus Tabular.** Generally speaking, the experiments that compared the impact of graphical presentation versus tabular presentation on decision making were found to be inconclusive (e.g., see Remus [28]).

Due to their newness there is little experimentation regarding GUIs. The results of one experiment are shown in Table 6.7.

TABLE 6.7 Comparing GUI to CUI.

Performance Attribute	Results*	
	Novices	Experienced Users
Work faster	GUI*	GUI*
Work better (quality)	GUI	GUI*
Higher productivity	GUI*	GUI*
Lower frustration	GUI*	GUI
Lower fatigue	GUI	GUI*
Better self-teaching	No difference	GUI
Better learning	GUI	Not measured

GUI means statistically significant GUI advantage over CUI; GUI (without the asterisk) means moderate GUI advantage.

Experiments on GUI. A comparative study on GUI versus character-based interface (CUI) was conducted by Temple, Barker, and Stone, Inc. [33] in 1989 and 1990.* Experiments were conducted with both experienced microcomputer users and novices. The users, both experienced and novices, were divided into two groups: those that worked with GUI and those that worked with CUI. The results of the laboratory tests are shown in Table 6.7. Seven performance attributes were checked. Overall, the GUI environment shows advantages over CUI.

6.9   Natural Language Processing—Overview

Natural language processing (NLP) is an applied AI technology (see Chapter 11). It refers to communicating with a computer in English or whatever language you may speak.** Today, to tell a computer what to do, we type commands by the keyboard or enter programs in a programming language. In responding to a user, the computer outputs symbols or short cryptic notes of information or direction.

To use a computer properly, you must learn the commands, languages, and jargon. This usually takes considerable time and practice. It is the main reason why computers have been called unfriendly. Menus and icons with pointing devices like light pens, mouse, and touch screens help, of course, but they are not perfectly natural.

Many problems could be minimized or even eliminated if we could communicate with the computer in our own language. We would simply type in directions, instructions, or information. The computer would be smart enough

---

Note: This experiment was commissioned by Microsoft and Zenith Data Systems.
**Major portions of Sections 6.9, 6.10 and 6.12 are taken from *Crash Course in Artificial Intelligence and Expert Systems*, by Louis E. Frenzel Jr.; Reproduced with the permission of the publisher, Howard W. Sams & Co., © 1987.

to interpret the input regardless of its format. An even better alternative would be to give the computer voice instructions.

NLP can be viewed as a special type of artificial intelligence (AI). To understand a natural language inquiry, a computer must have knowledge to analyze, then interpret the input. This knowledge may include linguistic knowledge about words, domain knowledge, common sense knowledge, and even knowledge about the users and their goals. NLP must understand grammar and the definitions of words. AI techniques are used to represent the internal knowledge and process the inputs. Once the computer understands the input, it can take the desired action.

In addition to *natural language understanding,* there is also *natural language generation.* Once the computer takes action, it will usually provide some output. In many cases it is desirable to provide that output in natural language. For that reason, the computer must be able to generate appropriate natural language, and the easiest way to do this is to provide "canned" sentences, phrases, paragraphs, or other outputs. More sophisticated techniques for generating natural language output are also available.

In this section we are going to talk about **natural language processing** software, the programs that understand and generate natural language inputs and outputs. We will also cover the practical applications of such software. Finally, we will consider **voice recognition** systems.

6.10   Natural Language Processing—Methods

NLP is an attempt to allow computers to interpret normal statements expressed in a natural human language, such as English or Japanese. The process of speech recognition, in contrast, attempts to translate the human voice into individual words and sentences understandable by the computer. Combining speech recognition and NLP will be required to realize the capability of the computer to converse in a manner normal to humans.

All prior computer languages (excluding 4GLs) have been sets of commands that had to be executed in a specified sequence or according to a procedure defined by the programmer. These are used for manipulating data in files, extracting information from a database, doing word processing, executing spreadsheet calculations, and performing other similar data processing activities. In other words, all those languages involve ways to "write a program" that give relatively explicit instructions and procedures on how to perform the operations.

With NLP, the computer's "understanding" of human statements may or may not be translated into a "program." It could just as easily be translated into another language. The most advanced fourth-generation languages today use the early results of NLP research, but their abilities are still quite limited compared with the ultimate goals of NLP.

Presently two major techniques are used in NLP programs: **Key word search** (pattern matching) and *language processing* **(syntactical and semantic anal-**

ysis). Other methods such as the use of neural computing and the method of conceptual dependency are in the research stage and will not be covered here.

Key Word Analysis (Pattern Matching)

In the **pattern matching** process, the NLP program searches through an input sentence looking for selected key words or phrases. Once a key word or phrase is recognized, the program responds with specific "canned" responses.

Alternately, the program may actually construct a response based on a partial reply coupled with the key word or selected phrases from the input. The program recognizes very specific inputs that it uses to construct an output response or initiate some other action.

Figure 6.6 shows a flow diagram of the basic procedures that a key word NLP program uses to understand input sentences. Let's work through the diagram to be sure you understand how key word processing works.

The program usually starts by displaying a message on the screen to elicit some input response from the user. The user's response is accepted by the program and stored in an input buffer.

Next, the program scans the input text searching for key words. The program can tell where one word ends and another begins by looking for spaces and punctuation marks. As each word is identified, it is used in a pattern-matching processing that compares it to a list of *prestored words* and phrases.

Since you want the program to be able to respond to random natural language input, a considerable number of words with their synonyms and variations will have to be stored if you wish to recognize the input text.

Each word in the input text string is matched against those in the key word directory stored in the program. The diamond element in the diagram labeled "key words found?" has two output paths, depending on the outcome of this search. The first possibility is that no key word is located. If that is the case, the program is set up to respond with one or more stock messages (e.g., "please rephrase your message"), then the process continues for all key words. This process may continue for several iterations until an appropriate word is recognized.

When a key word is located (the second possibility), it is flagged or marked so that it can be used to select an appropriate "canned" response or it can be used in an assembled response.

Example. Let's assume that a user requested the computer to *identify* all *employees* who *make* above *$50,000*. The *italicized* words are the key words. The following is a possible dialog between the computer (C) and the user (U).

c: By *identify* do you mean *list*?
u: Yes
c: By *make* do you mean model?
u: No
c: Please rephrase the word *make*
u: I mean whose salaries

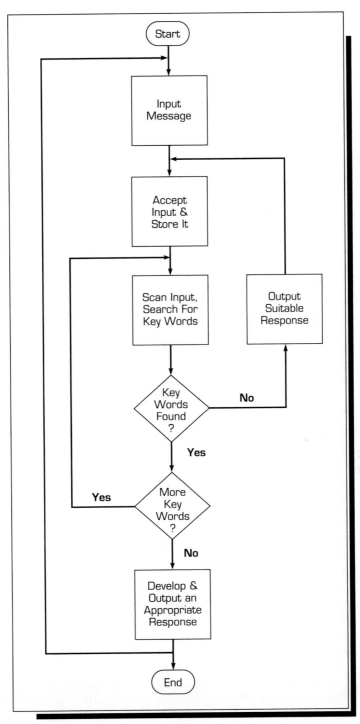

FIGURE 6.6 The Process of Key Word Analysis.

(*Note:* Now the word *salaries* has been identified as a key word.)
c: By *salaries* do you mean annual salaries?
u: Yes.
(*Note:* The NLP has now identified all the key words.)

Finally, an appropriate output response is selected or developed and sent to the user. An interesting key word matching program is ELIZA. Using ELIZA it is easy to see both the capabilities and the limitations of NLP (see Box 6.5).

Language Processing (Syntactic, Semantic, and Pragmatic Analysis)

Although key word pattern matching is a widely used natural language technique, its usefulness is restricted because it simply cannot deal with the large variations in language that naturally occur. For that reason, AI researchers have looked for and developed more sophisticated ways of analyzing an input sentence and extracting meaning from it.

The most obvious and straightforward approach to the problem is to perform a detailed analysis of the syntax and semantics of an input statement. In this way, the exact structure of an input sentence and its meaning can be determined. Of course, this is easier said than done. Even sophisticated systems for analyzing the syntax and semantics fall short of the job, because *there are too many words with multiple meanings* (such as "can," "will," and "class") and an enormous number of ways to put those together to form sentences.

Example: The following is one question rephrased in five different ways:

- How many nonstop flights are there from Phoenix to Boston?
- Do you have any nonstop flights from Phoenix to Boston?
- I would like to go from Phoenix to Boston without any layovers.
- What planes leave Phoenix and get to Boston without stopping?
- It's important that I find a nonstop Phoenix–Boston flight.

All the phrases just given request the same information, but they are syntactically dissimilar. A NLP can determine, through questions such as "do you mean to say . . ." exactly what the question is.

Definitions. First, the basic unit of the English language is the *sentence*. A sentence expresses a complete thought, asks a question, gives a command, or makes an exclamation. The sentence, of course, is made up of individual units known as *words*. The words have meaning and when they are linked together in various ways; their relationships represent ideas, thoughts, and visual images.

The individual words, besides having a meaning of their own, also fall into various categories known as parts of speech. As you recall from your English language classes, there are eight different parts of speech including: nouns, pronouns, verbs, adjectives, adverbs, prepositions, conjunctions, and interjections. Every word is classified as one of these parts of speech.

Box 6.5: Portion of a Real Conversation with the Key Word Matching Program Called ELIZA

HOW DO YOU DO.
PLEASE TELL ME YOUR PROBLEM.

My problem is artificial intelligence.
YOUR PROBLEM IS ARTIFICIAL INTELLIGENCE—THAT'S INTEREST-ING.

Well actually, the real problem is a subfield of artificial intelligence called natural language.
I AM NOT SURE I UNDERSTAND YOU FULLY.

That is the problem, getting a program to understand.
PLEASE GO ON.

How can I get a program to comprehend what I tell it in plain English?
WHY DO YOU ASK?

That is the source of my problem.
WHY DO YOU SAY YOUR PROBLEM?

Well, it is not my problem exclusively, but I still have it.
DOES THE FACT THAT IT IS YOUR PROBLEM EXCLUSIVELY SUG-GEST ANYTHING ELSE TO YOU?

Not at all.
DOES THAT HAVE ANYTHING TO DO WITH THE FACT THAT YOUR PROBLEM IS ARTIFICIAL INTELLIGENCE?

It sure does.
WHAT DOES THAT SUGGEST TO YOU?

If I understood AI well enough, I wouldn't have such a problem with natural language understanding.
DO YOU THINK IT'S LIKELY THAT YOU UNDERSTOOD AI WELL ENOUGH?

No.
WHY NOT?

It is a tough subject.
YOU SEEM TO HAVE AVOIDED SPEAKING OF YOUR PARENTS ALTOGETHER.

etc., etc., etc.

Syntax analysis looks at the way a sentence is built, the arrangement of its components and their relationships. Syntactic processes analyze and designate sentences to make the grammatical relationships between words in sentences clear. *Semantics* is concerned with assigning meaning to the various syntactic constituents. *Pragmatics* attempts to relate individual sentences to one another and to the surrounding context. The boundaries separating these levels are not distinct. In particular, sentences need not pass through these levels of interpretation sequentially. Research is continuing into how to integrate information from any level when it is needed.

How Natural Language Processing Works. In simple terms, a natural language system deciphers the parts of speech and action in a common sentence and then translates them into application commands, or into a compiled program language, so that the computer can respond.

Figure 6.7 shows a simplified block diagram of the major elements in a natural language processing program. The five major elements are: the parser, the lexicon, the understander, the knowledge base, and the generator. Let's look at each of these major elements in detail.

The parser. The key element in a natural language system is the parser. It is a piece of software that analyzes the input sentence syntactically. Each word is identified and its part of speech clarified. The parser then maps the words into a structure called a parse tree. The parse tree shows the meanings of all of the words and how they are assembled. This syntactical analysis is the first step toward trying to extract meaning from the sentence.

Recall that a sentence (S) is made up of a subject or noun phrase (NP) and a predicate or verb phrase (VP). We show this as:

$$S = NP + VP$$

The noun phrase could be a single noun, but it usually breaks down further into several additional parts of speech, such as an article (ART) or determiner (D) like "a", "this", or an adjective (ADJ) and the main noun (N). We show it like this:

$$NP = D + ADJ + N + ART$$

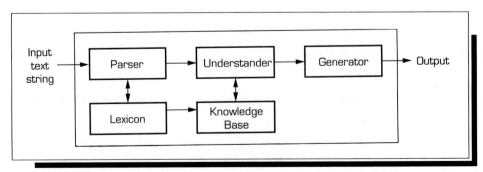

FIGURE 6.7 General Block Diagram of a Natural Language Understanding Program of the Syntax/Semantic Analysis Type.

The noun phrase may even have a prepositional phrase (PP) made up of a preposition (P) such as "of" or "with" and another determiner and a noun:

$$PP = P + D + N$$

The verb phrase (VP) is made up of the verb (V) and often the object of the verb, which is usually another noun and its determiner. A prepositional phrase may also be associated with the verb phrase. It might be represented as:

$$VP = V + D + N + PP$$

Of course, there are many other variations.

The lexicon. In order to perform the semantic analysis, the parser needs a dictionary. This dictionary is called the *lexicon*.

The lexicon contains all of the words that the program is capable of recognizing. The lexicon also contains the correct spelling of each word and its role in a sentence. For words that can have more than one meaning, the lexicon lists all of the various meanings permitted by the system.

The parser and the lexicon work together to pick apart a sentence and then create the parse tree, a new data structure that helps to get at the real meaning of the sentence. But even though the various parts of speech have been identified and the sentence has been fully analyzed syntactically, the computer still does not understand it. As a result, the need for semantic analysis becomes essential.

In operation, the parser is largely a pattern matcher. Once the individual word has been identified, the parser searches through the lexicon, comparing each input word with all of the words stored there. If a match is found, the word is put aside along with the other lexical information, such as part of speech and meaning. The parser then goes on to analyze additional words and ultimately builds the parse tree.

During this process, the parser can also take care of general housekeeping activities such as misspelled words.

Once the parse tree has been constructed, the system is ready for semantic analysis to obtain further meaning.

The understander *and knowledge base.* Semantic analysis is the function of the understander block in Figure 6.7. The understander works in conjunction with the knowledge base to determine what the sentence means.

In order to determine what is meant by an input sentence, the system must know things about words and how they are put together to form meaningful statements. The knowledge base is the primary means of understanding what has been said.

The purpose of the understander is to use the parse tree to reference the knowledge base. The understander can also draw inferences from the input statement. Many English sentences do not tell the whole story directly, but we are able to infer the meaning from our general knowledge.

The generator. The generator uses the understood input to create a usable output. The understander creates another data structure that represents the meaning and understanding of the sentence and stores it in memory. That data structure can be used to initiate additional action. If the NLP is part of an interface or a front-end, the data structure will be used to create special codes to control another piece of software. It may give the software commands needed to initiate some action. For example, in a DBMS, the generator would write a program in a query language to begin a search for specific information in the database.

In its simplest form, the natural language generator feeds standard prestored output responses to the user based on the meaning extracted from the input. However, more sophisticated generators will construct an original response from scratch.

6.11 Applications of Natural Language Processing and Software

Natural language processing programs have been applied in several areas. The most important are:

- NLP interfaces
- Abstracting and summarizing text
- Grammar analysis
- Translation of a natural language to another natural language (e.g., English to German)
- Translation of a computer language to another computer language
- Composing letters
- Speech understanding.

The first application is discussed in this section and the last one in the following section. For information on the other applications see Frenzel [8].

Natural Language Interfaces. By far the most predominant use of NLP is in interfaces, or "front-ends," for other software packages. Such **front-end interfaces** are used to simplify and improve the communications between the applications program and the user. Many programs are complex and difficult to use. They require learning a special language or set of commands. This takes a lot of time and effort and frequently puts off the user.

The natural language front-end allows the user to operate the applications programs with everyday language. Even the most inexperienced users can take advantage of the applications software.

The reason why NLP can be very helpful is demonstrated in Figure 6.8. The inverted triangle represents the number of people in each language category and their required training. The computer languages are listed on the right side. DSS languages are in the middle of the triangle, ranging from PL/1 and APL to RAMIS II and FOCUS (fourth-generation computer languages). The natural language interface is aimed at users who do not know (or do not want to know) formal computer languages but still want to be able to program the computer. Typical users in this category are managers, doctors, lawyers, and other profes-

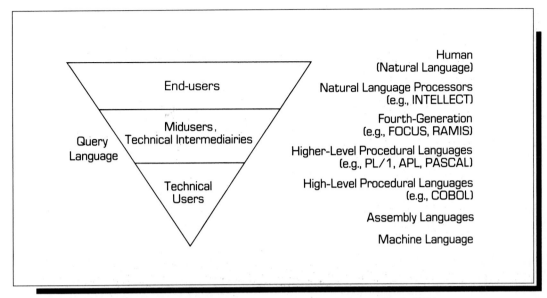

FIGURE 6.8   Market for Natural Language. (*Source:* Adapted from Harris [9].)

sionals usually referred to as knowledge workers. Because natural language front-end systems such as Intellect and Clout have been successfully applied to accessing complex databases, it seems reasonable to assume that they will become an integral part of many MSS.

Natural language front-ends make the software transparent to the user. Because users do not have to learn or worry about special languages or procedures, they can focus on the job, not on the process of getting it done. This will permit computer illiterate managers, executives, and other busy people to use the computer. Further, NLP will help open up the corporate mainframe database to users other than data processing programmers.

Although natural language front-ends are being created for a wide variety of applications programs, their most common use is with DBMS.

Natural Language Processing Software for Interfacing

Many NLP software packages are available on the market, both for mainframe and some for micros (for a representative list see Table 6.8). A brief description of some of these products follows:

Intellect (from AI Corp.). One of the oldest and most widely used natural language front-end interfaces is Intellect, which is a complete natural language interface for large mainframe computers. It is designed primarily to be used with DBMS that operate in the IBM operating systems environments.

In addition to being able to access data in a DBMS, Intellect allows the user to *create* databases using natural language. The built-in **lexicon** may be modified

TABLE 6.8 Representative Natural Language Processors.

Natural Language System	General Function	Specific Area
LADDER	Machine Translation/Interfacing	Ship Identification and Location
SAM	Machine Translation/Interfacing	Generic Story Understanding
ELLIE	Interfacing	Database Management System
SHRDLU	Interfacing	Location and Manipulation of Three-dimensional Figures
EXPLORER	Interfacing	Map Generation and Display, Mainframe
Intellect	Interfacing	Database Management, Mainframe
NATURALLINK	Interfacing	Dow Jones Data Retrieval and Display
TEAMS	Generic Interfacing	Database Management
MARKETEER	Interfacing	Market Analysis
POLITICS	Inference Making	Ideological Belief System Simulation
BROKER	Interfacing	Standard & Poor's Database Management System
STRAIGHT TALK	Interfacing	Word Processing/Microcomputer Workstations
THEMIS (Spock)	Interfacing	Database Management System, Minicomputers
Clout	Interfacing	R:Base 5000
K-CHAT	Integrating/Interfacing	Knowledge Man, GURU
RAMIS II English	Interfacing	RAMIS II
HAL	Interfacing	Spreadsheet (Lotus 1-2-3)

Source: Andriole, S.J., "The Promise of Artificial Intelligence," *Journal of Systems Management*, July, 1985. (Expanded.)

to fit a particular application. A lexicon editor allows the user to build and maintain special dictionaries for special uses. Unique words and their meanings or synonyms can be added to the lexicon. In this way, you can customize Intellect to the application. Intellect is available in a configuration that uses query languages (e.g., FOCUS) for large DBMS. Intellect allows the user to enter natural English statements and then converts them into the command structure of the query language which, in turn, accesses the desired data. (See Box 6.6.)

Clout (from Microrim, Inc., Bellevue, WA). Clout by Microrim is a front-end designed to be used with Microrim's popular R:Base 4000 and 5000 relational DBMS. It comes with a basic dictionary of 300 commonly used terms for accessing data and specifying relationships. The user can add up to 500 additional terms. Clout makes it extremely easy to tap the information in the database.

For instance, a user may want to look at some customer files. By using natural language, he can ask questions such as:

"How much does John F. Smith owe on his account?" "What was the date of the last purchase by Mary C. Jones?" "What did she buy?"

Box 6.6: Application of Intellect—British Gas

British Gas is a large natural gas provider; it serves 2 million customers in the United Kingdom. In less than three months, the company wrote twenty-five different management information systems with Intellect. The systems ranged from quality assurance customer inquiry handling for stores to accounting and legal systems. Of special interest is a system for the personnel director that allows a broad overview of staffing levels and requirements.

"It is as quick to use as any fourth-generation language on the market and is efficient in its use of machine resources," comments Dudley, the director of information systems. "We were also impressed by both the simplicity of the syntax and the privacy and access control aspects of the product."

The ultimate goal is for senior managers to be able to answer all their own inquiries using Intellect's capabilities themselves. New systems at British Gas are being designed to remove the need for regular printed reports and to enable users to produce their own information in the format they find most useful.

(*Source:* Publicly disclosed information of AI Corp.)

The natural language front-end can go into the database and find this information.

Clout is a very effective personal computer front-end. However, it works only with Microrim's DBMS. Further, it is strictly for use in retrieving data from the database. It cannot be used for creating new databases. Clout allows users to pose a question similarly to the way they would talk with an associate, rather than by formal commands. Thus a query using Clout could be posed as follows: "Give me the names of all persons with sales records of over $250,000 last year." Without Clout, the query would take this form: "SELECT Name, Sales from Annual Sales, WHERE Sales greater than 250,000 AND Year equals 1989."

An NLP software package has been programmed to look for key words in a sentence. In our query, these would be "names," "sales," "250,000," and "last year." The NLP stores predetermined key words and their synonyms. These will be used to determine the meaning of the query and to select appropriate relationships and data items. In our example, "names" could mean persons, people, executives, salespersons, and last names. The NLP builds a profile of common user terminology. If it cannot match a key word to a stored synonym, the NLP is programmed to ask the user to give another word, or to select from several choices that are probable synonyms. For example, the NLP will ask the user about "names": "Do you mean names of executives?" The user will answer: "No, I mean salespersons."

Although Clout and R:Base are two separate products, there are several packages that integrate NLP into DBMS. Two such products are Q & A and Paradox.

Q & A (from Symantec Corp., Cupertino, CA). Q&A is a basic file manager that contains modules for building files, accessing the files, and generating an output report in a specific format. It also contains a natural language front-end called "The Intelligent Assistant." The Intelligent Assistant parses common English input questions and converts them into queries that the file manager can understand. A built-in, 600-word vocabulary (more words are being added with every new version) provides the lexical information for understanding the input query.

A unique feature of Q&A is that it paraphrases your input request to ensure that it fully understands what you want. Using a sales example, you may request the following:

"Show the total 1992 sales for the Central Region"

Q&A's Intelligent Assistant may come back with an inquiry that looks like this:

SHALL I DO THE FOLLOWING?
CREATE A REPORT SHOWING THE AMOUNT OF SALES FOR THE
CENTRAL REGION IN 1992?
YES - CONTINUE   NO - CANCEL REQUEST

Paraphrasing verifies what you want to do. If it is correct, simply type Y for yes and the data access will be completed. A no answer will cancel the request, and then you may change it or rephrase it.

The primary disadvantage of the Q&A system is that it is not a relational database. For that reason, it cannot initiate queries for multiple information items that are contained in separate files. It can only access information in one file at a time. Relational databases, on the other hand, permit several files to be open at a time to access multiple data items. For example, if the sales for widgets is in a separate file from whizbangs, Q&A could not answer the question, "State the total sales of widgets and whizbangs." However, you can get the same information by asking for the sales in separate inquiries.

Paradox (from Borland International, Inc.). Paradox is a *relational* DBMS with an AI technology based on the "query by example" approach, developed by IBM. It does not have NLP capability but it has an inference capability that allows users to retrieve information from the database with only a most cursory knowledge of its inner details. Users are presented with a graphical representation of an empty record in the database called the "query table," which they fill in with data exemplary of the desired result of the search. By analyzing these entries, Paradox infers which information users are looking for, and takes appropriate action, creating an "answer table" on a screen to display its findings. Users may stipulate which fields should be included in the report and/or make changes in the query table. Paradox provides two major advantages: ease of use and correct interpretation of the user's request. The program uses a "heuristic query optimization" approach to improve the efficiency of the database search.

6.12   Speech (Voice) Recognition and Understanding

Speech or **voice recognition** is the process of having the computer recognize normal human speech. When a speech recognition system is combined with a natural language processing system, the result is an overall system that not only recognizes voice input but also *understands* it.

Speech recognition is a process that allows one to communicate with a computer by speaking to it. The term *speech recognition* is sometimes applied only to the first part of the process: recognizing the words that have been spoken without necessarily interpreting their meanings. The other part of the process, in which the meaning of the speech is ascertained, is called *speech understanding*. It may be possible to understand the meaning of a spoken sentence without actually recognizing every word and vice versa.

Advantages of Speech Recognition

The ultimate goal of speech recognition is to allow a computer to understand the natural speech of any human speaker at least as well as a human listener could understand it. In addition to being the most natural method of communication, speech recognition offers several advantages:

- *Ease of Access*—Many more people can speak than can type. As long as communication with a computer depends on developing typing skills, many people may not be able to use computers effectively.
- *Speed*—Even the most competent typists can speak more quickly than they can type. It is estimated that the average person can speak twice as fast as a proficient typist can type.
- *Manual Freedom*—Obviously, communicating with a computer by typing occupies your hands. There are, however, many situations in which computers might be useful to people whose hands are otherwise occupied, such as product assemblers, pilots of military aircraft, and busy executives.
- *Remote Access*—Many computers are set up to be accessed remotely by telephone. If a remote database includes speech recognition capabilities, you could retrieve information by issuing verbal commands into a telephone.
- *Accuracy*—In typing information one is prone to make mistakes, especially in spelling. These are minimized with voice input.

Classifying Speech Recognizers

Speech recognizers are classified in several different ways. First, there are systems that recognize individual words and others that recognize continuous speech. Second, the systems are further classified as either speaker dependent or speaker independent. Let's see what these terms mean.

Word Recognizers. A word recognizer, as its title implies, is a speech recognition system that identifies individual words. Such systems are capable of recognizing only a small vocabulary of single words or possibly simple phrases. To give commands or data to a computer using one of these systems, you must state the input information in clearly definable single words (with pauses in between) given one after another.

Continuous Speech Recognizers. These speech recognition units recognize a continuous flow of words. You can speak to them in complete sentences, and your input will be recognized and understood. **Continuous speech** recognizers are far more difficult to build. The difficulty lies in separating one word from another in a continuous phrase or sentence. When we speak, most of the words slur together in one continuous stream. It is difficult for such a system to know where one word ends and another begins. Far more sophisticated and complex techniques must be used to deal with continuous speech.

Today there are very few practical continuous speech systems in use. Most of them are research and experimental systems made on very large and expensive computers. Many of them do not even operate on real time. That is, the information spoken is not recognized instantly as it is with word recognition systems. It may take many minutes for only a few seconds of speech to be analyzed and understood.

Speaker Dependent. A speaker-dependent system means that the system has been customized to the voice of a particular individual. Because there are such wide variations in the way that people speak, it is difficult to build computer systems that will recognize anyone's voice. By limiting the system to the voice of specific people the system is not only simpler but also more reliable.

Speaker Independent. Speaker-independent systems mean that anyone can use the system. The speech recognizer is designed to be as versatile as possible so that even though voice characteristics may vary widely from one speaker to another, the system can recognize them. Most speaker-independent systems are incredibly complex and costly. They also have very limited vocabularies. Some of the most advanced systems in this area are Speech Recognition System (from Bell Labs) and a system developed at Carnegie-Mellon University. However, both systems can understand only limited vocabulary (a few thousand words). The Bell Labs system is used, for example, for airline reservations via human phone input.

How Speech Recognition Systems Work

All types of speech recognition systems use the same basic techniques. The voice input to the microphone produces an analog speech signal. This speech signal is then converted into binary words compatible with a digital computer by an analog-to-digital converter. The binary version of the input voice is then stored in the system and compared to previously stored binary representations of words and phrases. The computer searches through the previously stored speech patterns and compares them, one at a time, to the current speech input. When a match occurs, recognition is achieved. Once recognition is achieved, the spoken word in binary form is written on a video screen or passed along to a natural language understanding processor for additional analysis.

A Typical Word Recognizer

A typical speaker-dependent word recognizer is shown in Figure 6.9. The voice input is applied to a microphone. The electrical analog signal from the microphone is fed to an amplifier where it is increased in level. The amplifier will contain some kind of automatic gain control (AGC) to provide an output signal in a specific voltage range.

The analog signal representing a spoken word is a complex waveform that contains many individual frequencies. The way to recognize the spoken word is to break that complex input signal into its component parts. This is usually done with a set of filters. A filter is an electronic circuit that passes or rejects frequencies in a certain range. In speech recognition equipment, bandpass filters (BPF) are used. These filters pass frequencies only in a certain frequency range.

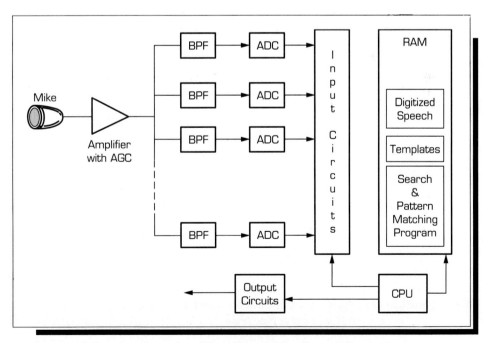

FIGURE 6.9   A Speaker-dependent Word Recognition Speech Recognizer.

The filter output is then fed to analog-to-digital converters (ADC) that translate the output into digital words. The ADCs feed input circuits controlled by a CPU. The digital values are stored in a large memory (RAM).

The computer must first be taught to recognize the input of a particular user. The user speaks all the words in the vocabulary. These words are digitized and stored as templates in the memory.

When the user activates the system, the computer, through a search routine, matches each spoken word against the templates. Once a word is identified a binary or ASCII version is displayed or used in some other manner.

Voice Synthesis

This refers to the technology by which computers "speak." The synthesis of voice by computer differs from a simple playback of a prerecorded voice by either analog or digital means. As the term "synthesis" implies, the sounds that make up words and phrases are constructed electronically from basic sound components and can be made to form any desired voice pattern.

Voice synthesis has already come of age. There are several good, commercially available voice synthesis packages that work on limited domains and encompass phonetic rules.

The quality of synthesized voice is currently very good, but the technology remains somewhat expensive. The anticipated lower cost and improved performance of synthetic voice in the near future will encourage more widespread commercial applications. The opportunities for its use will encompass almost all applications that can provide an automated response to a user, such as inquiries by employees pertaining to payroll and benefits. Several banks already offer a voice service to their customers, informing them about their balance, about which checks were cashed, and so on. Another example is the answer provided for requests for telephone numbers. For an overview of the topic see Lee et al. [14] and Schutzer [29].

6.13   The User Interface Management System

The **user interface management system** (UIMS, also referred to as the dialog generation and management software) is that DSS component which accommodates the various *information representations* identified during the requirements specification portion of the DSS design phase. The DGMS also accommodates the **action languages** that enable the user to manage the DSS outputs and inputs in the form of dialogues or processes. The DGMS provides an interface between the system user and the rest of the DSS. There is much interest in the subject of human-computer interfaces at this time and an emerging literature on this subject (see Harrison and Hix [10]). Some of this literature deals with such physiological issues as clearances under work surfaces for legs, illumination, noise, and humidity. Other research is concerned more with cognitive and perceptive abilities. The UIMS are interactive tools that support the interface management activities that were outlined in Chapter 3.

For further discussion regarding the design of UIMS see Harrison and Hix [10] and Seacord [30].

Chapter Highlights

- User interface is critical to the success of any MSS.
- Interface is the hardware, software, and procedures that provide a human-machine dialog.
- An interface is composed of action and presentation languages, computer hardware and software, and procedures.
- The major interface (dialog) styles are: menu interaction, command language, questions and answers, form interactions, object manipulation, and natural language processing.
- Graphics play a major role in MSS, both as a presentation language and lately for active user interface.
- There are many types of graphics and software.
- Graphical user interface (GUI) enables the user to control visible objects and actions. This replaces the use of commands.
- Visual interactive modeling is an implementation of GUI, which is usually combined with simulation and animation.
- Multimedia is actively combined with managerial decision making both for presentation and for actions such as expediting search using a hypertext.
- Virtual reality is the implementation of GUI in three dimensions. It also includes audio, sensors, and other features which take the user into a realistic environment.
- Considerable research has been conducted (and is still going on) on the potential benefits of graphics and colors. Results regarding GUI and colors are very positive; others are inconclusive.
- Natural language processing (NLP) provides an opportunity for a user to communicate with a computer in day-to-day spoken language.
- NLP uses either key word analysis or complex language analysis (syntactic, semantic, pragmatic).
- NLP is mainly used as a front-end to databases and DBMS.
- Speech recognition enables people to communicate with the computer by voice. There are many benefits to this emerging technology.
- Voice synthesis is the transformation of computerized output to voice.
- Like DBMS and MBMS, the interface system is managed by a user interface management system.

Key Words

action language	menu interaction	speech understanding
animation	multimedia	syntactic analysis
command language	natural language	understander
continuous speech	interface	user-interface
dialog	natural language	management system
form interaction	processing	virtual reality
front-end interface	object manipulation	visual interactive
GUI	parser	modeling
hypermedia	pattern matching	visual simulation
hypertext	pragmatic analysis	voice recognition
interface	presentation language	word recognizer
key word search	semantic analysis	WYSIWYG
lexicon		

Questions for Review

1. List the various modes of interface.
2. List the major types of graphics.
3. Define graphical user interface (GUI).
4. Explain what WYSIWYG is.
5. Define a user interface management system.
6. Describe how hypertext works. What is its major advantage?
7. It is said that voice synthesis is not AI technology. Why?
8. Define user interface.
9. Define a natural language and natural language processing.
10. What are the major advantages of NLP?
11. Distinguish between NLP and natural language generation.
12. Explain how language processing works (use Figure 6.7).
13. Give an example of how the parser segregates a sentence.
14. Describe the functions of the lexicon.
15. What is the role of the understander and the knowledge base in NLP?
16. The use of NLP as an interface to DBMS is gaining popularity. Explain how NLP increases the accessibility to databases.
17. Obtain an NLP/DBMS software (e.g., Clout and R:Base, Q&A). Try to use it on the database of Chapter 5, Exercise 4. Compare the use of a regular DBMS to the one supported by NLP.
18. List the major advantages of voice recognition.
19. Describe the difference between word and continuous speech recognizers.
20. Define visual simulation and compare it to conventional simulation.
21. Define visual interactive modeling (VIM).

Questions for Discussion

1. Results of research indicate that graphical presentation is not more effective than tabular presentation. Practitioners disagree. They claim that graphics are superior. Explain why such differences may occur. For extra credit, read Remus's paper [28] (*Management Science*, May 1984) and discuss it.
2. Discuss the role of graphics in DSS. How can graphics support decisions?
3. Discuss the major benefits of GUI.
4. Discuss the major research areas on graphics (per Wang and Wu [36]). Find a current research paper and discuss it.
5. Compare the role of UIMS to that of DBMS.
6. It is said that the interface is the most important component of an MSS. Explain why.
7. Explain the *process* of user-computer interaction (per Figure 6.1).
8. Define presentation and action languages.
9. Menu interaction is probably the most liked interface style. Explain why.
10. Why is a command language the preferred style of experienced users?
11. Which interface style is used mostly in expert systems and which in DSS? Why?
12. Describe a combination of menus and commands from your own experience.
13. Explain how key word search works. What are its major limitations?
14. Obtain an access to ELIZA and run a conversation with it. After about 12–15 questions and answers, stop. What are the major limitations of ELIZA?
15. It is said that language processing is far more effective than key word search. Why?
16. Compare Paradox to Q&A. List the major differences.
17. What is the difference between voice recognition and voice understanding?
18. Give five examples where voice recognition can be applied today and list the benefit(s) in each case. Be specific.
19. Why is a speaker-independent system preferred over a speaker-dependent one? Why is it so difficult to build it?
20. Several computer games, such as Flight Simulation II and GATO, can be considered visual simulation. Explain why.
21. It is said that VIM is particularly helpful in implementing recommendations derived by computers. Explain why.

References and Bibliography

1. Allen, J. *Natural Language Understanding*. Menlo Park, CA: Benjamin-Cummings, 1987.
2. Bell, P. C., et al. "Visual Interactive Problem Solving—A New Look at Management Problems." *Business Quarterly*, Spring 1984.

3. Bennett, J. L. "Tools for Building Advanced User Interfaces." *IBM System Journal*, No. 3/4, 1986.

4. Booth, P. *An Introduction to Human-Computer Interaction*, New York: Lawrence Erlbaum Associates, 1989.

5. DeSanctis, G. "Computer Graphics as Decision Aids: Direction for Research." *Decision Sciences*, Vol. 15, 1984.

6. Dos Santos, B. L., and M. L. Bariff. "A Study of User Interface Aids for Decision Support Systems." *Management Science*, 1988.

7. Ellis, S. R. "Nature and Origins of Virtual Environments: A Bibliographical Essay." *Computing Systems in Engineering* (April 1991).

8. Frenzel, L. *Crash Course in AI and Expert Systems*. Indianapolis: Howard W. Sams & Co., 1987.

9. Harris, L. R. "Natural Language Front Ends." In Winston, P. H., and K. A. Prendergast, eds. *The AI Business*. Cambridge, MA: MIT Press, 1984.

10. Harrison, H. R., and D. Hix. "Human-Computer Interface Development: Concepts and Systems for Its Management." *ACM Computing Surveys*, Vol. 21, No. 1, March 1989: 5-92.

11. Hartson, H. R., and D. Hix. "Human-Computer Interface Development: Concepts and Systems for Its Management." *ACM Computing Surveys*, Vol. 21, No. 1, 1989.

12. Hoadley, E. D. "Investigating the Effects of Color." *Communications of the ACM*, February 1990.

13. Hurrion, R. D. "Implementation of Consensus Decision Support Systems." *European Journal of Operations Research*, Vol. 20, 1985.

14. Lee, S. M., et al. "Voice Recognition: An Examination of an Evolving Technology and Its Use in Organizations." *Computers and Operations Research*, Vol. 14, No. 6, 1987.

15. Lehman, J. A., et al. "Business Computer Graphics." *Datamation*, November 15, 1984.

16. Lembersky, M. R., and U. H. Chi. "Decision Simulators Speed Implementation and Improve Operations." *Interfaces*, July-August 1984 (see also January-February 1986).

17. Majchrzak, A., et al. *Human Aspects of Computer-Aided Design*. Philadelphia: Taylor and Francis, 1987.

18. Marcus, A. "User-Interface Developments for the Nineties." *Computer*, September 1991.

19. Marcus, A. "Color in User Interface Design: Functionality and Aesthetics." *Proceedings ACM/SIGCHI*, May 1989.

20. Molich, R., and J. Nielson. "Improving a Human-Computer Dialog." *Communications of the ACM*, Vol. 33, No. 3, March 1990: 338–349.

21. Myers, B. *Creating User Interfaces by Demonstration*. Boston: Academic Press, 1988.

22. Neuman, W. A., and F. J. Brock. "Graphical User Interfaces in the 90's." *Information Executive* (Winter 1991).

23. Paller, A. "Million-dollar Applications." *Information Center* (February 1986).

24. Paul, J. "Toward a Strategy for Managing Computer-based Research," in

Proceedings, FAIM 90 (Alexandria, VA: Defense Systems Management College, 1990) RAND Corp.

25. Pracht, W. E. "Model Visualization: Graphical Support for DSS Problems Structuring and Knowledge Organization." *Decision Support Systems,* Vol. 6, 1990: 18–26.
26. Ravden, S., and G. Johnson. *Evaluating Usability of Human-Computer Interfaces: A Practical Method.* New York: Wiley, 1989.
27. Reed, S. "GUI Face-off." *PC/Computing* (December 1991).
28. Remus, W. "An Empirical Investigation of the Impact of Graphical and Tabular Data Presentations on Decision Making." *Management Science,* May 1984.
29. Schutzer, D. *AI—An Applications Oriented Approach,* New York: Van Nostrand Reinhold, 1987.
30. Seacord, R. C. "User Interface Management Systems and Application Portability." *IEEE Computer,* Vol. 23, No. 10, October 1990: 73–75.
31. Shafer, D. "Hypermedia and Expert Systems: A Marriage Made in Hyper Heaven." *Hyperage,* May-June 1988.
32. Sprague, R. H., Jr., and B. McNurlin. *Information Systems Management in Practice.* Englewood Cliffs, NJ: Prentice-Hall, 1986.
33. Temple, Barker and Stone, Inc. *The Benefits of the Graphical User Interface,* Special Report. Lexington, MA, Spring 1990.
34. Thimbleby, H. *User Interface Design.* Reading, MA: Addison-Wesley, 1990.
35. Van Dam, A. "Computer Graphics Comes of Age." *Communications of the ACM,* July 1984.
36. Wang, M. I. H., and B. J. P. Wu. "The Effectiveness of Computer Graphics for Decision Support: A Meta Analytical Integration of Research Findings," *Database,* Fall 1990.
37. Watt, A. *Fundamentals of Three-Dimensional Computer Graphics.* Boston: Addison-Wesley, 1990.

CASE STUDY: Visual Simulation at Weyerhaeuser Co.

Weyerhaeuser Co. (of Tacoma, WA) is a large timber processor. The company developed several applications of VIM (one of which is described here). The company estimates the annual increase in profit contribution to top $7 million, owing to the introduction of VIM.

Log-cutting Decisions*

Timber processing involves harvesting trees that are delimbed and topped. The resulting "stems" are crosscut into logs of various lengths. These logs are allocated among different mills, each of which makes a different end product

---

*Abstracted by permission of Mark R. Lembersky and Uli H. Chi [16].

(e.g., plywood, lumber, paper). For each tree there may be hundreds of reasonable cutting and allocating combinations. The cutting and allocation decisions are the *major* determinant of revenues of the company and its profitability. The decisions are made on a stem-by-stem basis, because each tree is physically different from every other tree. Many variables determine the manner in which a stem is cut. Because costs are not affected much by these decisions, the larger the revenue generated, the larger the profit.

Management scientists have developed a theoretical optimization model for the cutting and allocating decisions, using the technique of dynamic programming. However, the employees in the field were reluctant to use solutions that resulted from an unfamiliar, somewhat intimidating, "black box" algorithm. Furthermore, like any other mathematical models, this model too is based on several assumptions that do not always capture reality. Thus, the operators have had a legitimate reason for not following the computer's recommendations. Visual decision simulator allows the operators to deal with the proposed solutions

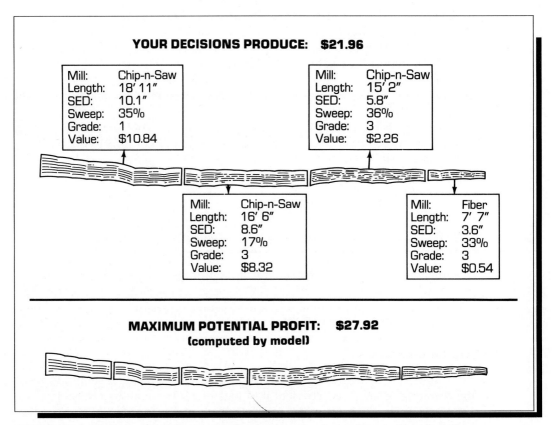

FIGURE 6.10 Display of the Economic Consequences of the User's Decision Compared with the Model's Maximization Results. Log information (shown in boxes in the upper part) is available, but not shown, in the lower part.

on their own terms. This is done by allowing the operators to simulate on a video display a realistic representation of each stem. The simulator allows the operator to roll, rotate, cut, and allocate each representation of each stem. The simulator allows the operator to roll, rotate, cut, and allocate each stem the way he or she wants on the computer screen, of course. One can *see* the end product and the resultant profit contribution of the suggested solution (see Figure 6.10). He or she then can compare it with the profit resulting from the recommendation of the dynamic programming model. If not satisfied, the operator can recut the same stem repeatedly (on the computer screen, of course) to explore alternate decisions. The final decision, how to cut, is always made by the operator; therefore the system is nonthreatening. Furthermore, the repeated cutting experimentations on the screen have been documented to improve decision-making skills in the field. The system is used also by management to evaluate alternative stem-processing strategies.

Questions

1. Why is log cutting such a complex problem?
2. Why were the employees reluctant to use the dynamic programming optimization technique?
3. How does visual simulation overcome the deficiencies of the regular optimization model?

Chapter 7

Constructing a Decision Support System

The previous chapters presented the essentials of DSS, stressing capabilities of DSS and giving sample cases. The first question that may enter a manager's mind is what must be done to acquire a DSS? Unfortunately DSS are designed to deal with complex situations and therefore they cannot simply be acquired. Rather they must be custom tailored to the specific use. This chapter deals with the DSS construction process, and includes the following sections:

7.1   Introduction

The construction of a DSS, especially a large one, is a complicated process. It involves issues ranging from the technical, such as hardware selection, to the behavioral, such as person-machine interfaces and the potential impact of DSS on individuals and groups. This chapter concentrates mainly on construction issues involving DSS software.

Because there are several types and categories of DSS, there is no single best approach to the construction of a DSS. There are also variations because of the differences in organizations, individual decision makers, and the DSS problem area. For example, the Houston Minerals DSS (Box 1.4) was constructed to support a one-time decision, whereas the GLSC DSS (Chapter 3) was developed for repetitive use. The Houston case was constructed in only a few days with the help of a specialized **planning language.** In contrast, the GLSC DSS was developed over a four-year period. Why was one DSS developed so quickly, yet the other took so long? What is a "specialized planning language"? What are some of the managerial aspects of DSS construction? These questions and several others are addressed in this and the forthcoming chapters.

7.2   The System Development Life Cycle (SDLC)

The development of a computerized information system can be an event of major consequence to an organization. It usually follows a lengthy process termed a **system development life cycle.** Although there are many versions of this process, it can be generalized into six basic phases. (For details, see Dickson and Wetherbe [7], Lucas [14], and Zmud [26].)

The process, described in Figure 7.1, is appropriate for most transaction processing systems, traditional MIS, and for some DSS. However, building most DSS is quite a different proposition. Specifically, the design, implementation, and evaluation of DSS tend to proceed concurrently. These processes are evolutionary in that the DSS is likely to be incomplete when put to work for the first time. Because of the semistructured or unstructured nature of problems addressed by decision support systems, managers' perceived needs for information will change and so the DSS must also change. Therefore most DSS are developed by a process that is different from the SDLC.

7.3   The DSS Development Process

The development process described in this section includes all the activities that could go into a complex DSS development. However, not all the activities are performed for every DSS. For example, a simple ad hoc DSS goes through a shorter process, and a user-developed DSS may involve both a shorter process

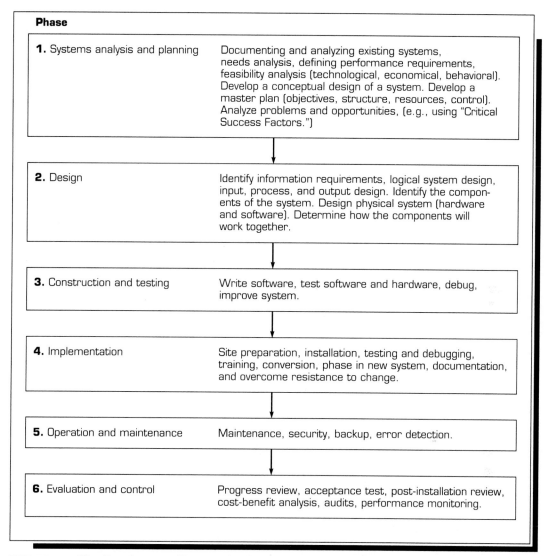

Phase	
1. Systems analysis and planning	Documenting and analyzing existing systems, needs analysis, defining performance requirements, feasibility analysis (technological, economical, behavioral). Develop a conceptual design of a system. Develop a master plan (objectives, structure, resources, control). Analyze problems and opportunities, (e.g., using "Critical Success Factors.")
2. Design	Identify information requirements, logical system design, input, process, and output design. Identify the components of the system. Design physical system (hardware and software). Determine how the components will work together.
3. Construction and testing	Write software, test software and hardware, debug, improve system.
4. Implementation	Site preparation, installation, testing and debugging, training, conversion, phase in new system, documentation, and overcome resistance to change.
5. Operation and maintenance	Maintenance, security, backup, error detection.
6. Evaluation and control	Progress review, acceptance test, post-installation review, cost-benefit analysis, audits, performance monitoring.

FIGURE 7.1   The Development Phases of a Computerized Information System.

and a different development orientation. The illustrated process is based on an integration of the work of Keen and Scott-Morton [12] and Meador et al. [16]. The process is summarized in Figure 7.2. The various phases are described below.

Phase A: Planning

Planning deals mainly with need assessment and problem diagnosis. Here the objectives and goals of the decision support effort are defined. A crucial step

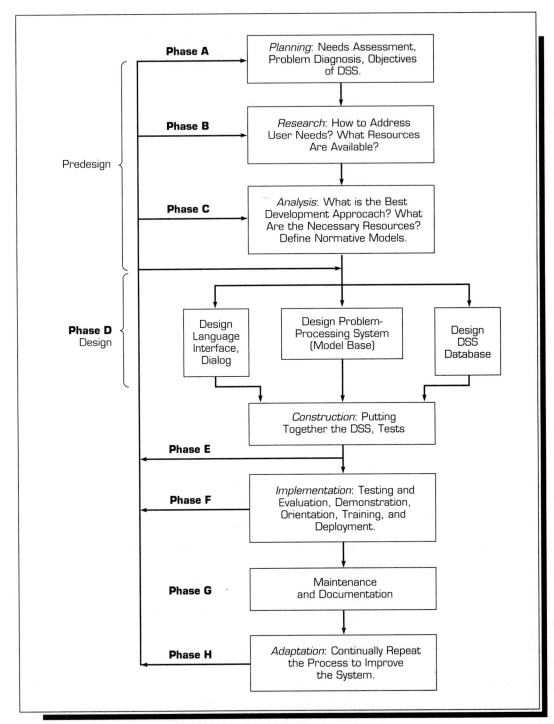

FIGURE 7.2 Phases in Building a Decision Support System.

in the planning effort is determining the key decisions of the DSS. For example, in a portfolio management system, a key decision might be selecting the correct stocks for a particular customer's needs. It could be difficult to provide information that would advise a portfolio manager which stocks to select because of the many factors involved. Some customers might be very conservative and desire low-risk stocks only. Others might prefer higher-risk situations because of the greater potential returns. Two points should be emphasized relative to the key decisions. First, the DSS is only a tool providing information to the manager. The portfolio manager, not the DSS, makes the final decision on which stocks to select. Second, though we may find it difficult to provide relevant information for a decision, it is still crucial to identify the key decisions. The method of critical success factors (CSF) is recommended for this stage (see Shank et al. [22]) to help with this identification.

Phase B: Research

This phase involves the identification of a relevant approach for addressing user needs and available resources (hardware, software, vendors, systems, studies or related experiences in other organizations, and review of relevant research).

Phase C: Analysis

This phase includes the determination of the best approach and specific resources required to implement it, including technical, staff, financial, and organizational resources. It is basically a *conceptual* design followed by a **feasibility study.**

A normative approach is suggested here (by Keen and Scott-Morton [12]) to define the ideal models that can provide information for key decisions. Such models are likely to be theoretical. In the actual implementation of the DSS it is unlikely that we will attain the level of the normative model. But it represents a goal we should try to attain in a real-world situation. Even though it may not be practical or advisable to implement the normative model, we should keep it in mind when designing the actual DSS. Such normative models are a major part of our design objectives, because the models tell us the ideal level of performance.

Phase D: Design

The detailed specifications of the system components, structure, and features are determined here. The design can be divided into three parts corresponding to the three major components of a DSS: database and its management, model base and its management (the problem-solving part of the DSS), and the dialog subsystems. Here one selects appropriate software tools and generators (such as database manager and a spreadsheet) or writes them. A major issue in the design effort is deciding what commercially available software to use. This issue is discussed later on in this chapter.

Phase E: Construction

A DSS can be constructed in different ways depending on the design philosophy and the tools being used. The construction is the technical implementation of the design. The system is being tested continuously and improvements are being made.

Phase F: Implementation

At the end of the construction phase, the system is ready to be implemented. The implementation phase consists of the following tasks: testing, evaluation, demonstration, orientation, training, and deployment. Several of these tasks happen simultaneously and are conducted in the field.

Testing. In this phase, data on the system's performance are collected and compared against the design specifications.

Evaluation. During this phase, the implemented system is evaluated to see how well it meets users' needs. Technical and organizational loose ends are also identified. Evaluation is particularly difficult with a DSS because the system is continuously being modified or expanded, and therefore does not have neatly defined completion dates or standards for comparison. The testing and evaluation usually result in changes in the design and in construction. The process is cyclical, and it repeats itself several times.

Demonstration. Demonstration of the fully operational system capabilities to the user community is an important phase. Viewers can become believers. As a result they accept the system with less or no resistance.

Orientation. This involves instruction of managerial users in the basic capabilities of the system.

Training. Operational users are trained in system structure and functions. Users are also trained how to maintain the system.

Deployment. The full system is operationally deployed for all members of the user community.

The development effort ends with two additional phases: maintenance and adaptation.

Phase G: Maintenance and Documentation

Maintenance involves planning for ongoing support of the system and its user community. Proper documentation for using and maintaining the system is also developed.

Phase H: Adaptation

Adaptation requires recycling through the steps above on a regular basis to respond to changing user needs. As mentioned earlier, these steps are not linear (i.e., there are loops and cycles, see Figure 7.2).

Summary. The preceding process has many variations (owing to the many variations of DSS), two of which are presented in Sections 7.9 and 7.10.

Next, to enhance the understanding of specific design processes, we explore the following conceptual foundations, which are unique to DSS:

- Development strategies
- Participants in the process
- Approaches to DSS construction
- Iterative nature of the process
- Team-developed versus user-developed DSS.

7.4   Development Strategies

Five basic development strategies for DSS exist. They are:

1. *Write a customized DSS in general-purpose programming language, such as COBOL or PASCAL.* Although this strategy was viable in the 1970s, very few organizations use it in the 1990s. Usually very large-scale DSS, where lots of interfaces with other CBIS are required, are built from scratch.

2. *Use a fourth-generation language.* Several classes of 4GL were described in Chapters 4 and 5—for example, data-oriented languages (such as Focus, NOMAD, or Oracle), spreadsheet (such as Multiplan), and financial-oriented languages (such as IFPS). These tools can boost productivity by a magnitude of 10 to 1 or even more over general-purpose languages.

3. *Use a DSS generator.* These packages eliminate the need to use several 4GLs by integrating several tools into one package. A simple generator is Lotus 1-2-3; a more sophisticated generator is Express. Generators are more efficient than individual 4GLs, but they are subject to more constraints (less flexibility).

4. *Use a domain-specific DSS generator.* Domain-specific DSS generators are designed to build a highly structured system, usually in a functional area. For example, there are several packages for building strategic management systems (see Mockler [18]). BPCS/Budgets and modeling (from System Software Associates, Inc., Chicago, IL) is used for budgeting and financial analysis, and EFPM is used for building DSS for universities (see Appendix 7-D).

5. *Develop the DSS under the rigors of CASE methodology* (see Box 7.1).

The development strategy is dependent on many factors, but most of all on the participants.

Box 7.1: DSS at Columbia Gas—Use of CASE

Columbia Gas (of Columbus, Ohio) is using CASE as a corporate strategy for application development. The corporation built a mainframe DSS residing in IBM's DB2 relational DBMS, using the CASE approach. The DSS is designed to track natural gas that, for reasons such as transmission line loss, cannot be accounted for. It reduces the volume of gas lost.

   The DSS was constructed with significant users' involvement. The CASE methodology assures quality (nothing is missed); the system capabilities were found in an audit to be a very precise match of the users' requirements.

7.5   The Participants

Several types of participants play major roles in the construction and operation of DSS. The number of participants involved in developing a DSS vary. In some cases, the user is the sole participant; in other cases, several parties participate, each with a different degree of involvement.

The User. The user is the manager, the analyst, or a committee—the individual(s) responsible for making the decision, conducting some analysis, or solving a problem.

The Intermediary. Sometimes called the *chauffeur,* this individual, who is usually a staff analyst, helps the manager to use the DSS. Because most early DSS were not very "user-friendly," they generally required an intermediary.

The DSS Builder (or Facilitator). This individual is responsible for technical decisions like what tools and/or generators to use, and whether to use a micro-, a mini-, or a mainframe computer. The builder must possess an understanding of both the problem area and DSS technology. During the 1970s (and today for large DSS), this role was carried on by a special DSS group. Currently, especially for smaller DSS, the functions of a DSS builder are most likely to be provided by a member of the **information center.** (See Box 7.2.)

The Technical Support Person. This participant develops additional information system capabilities or components as needed and may also provide technical assistance to the DSS builder. This individual is a computer scientist and/or programmer who participates mainly in large-scale DSS development. He or she does the necessary programming to "glue" together the DSS and to connect it with other CBIS if needed.

Box 7.2: The Information Center (IC)

The information center concept was conceived in an attempt to reduce the growing number of requests for computer applications and to alleviate the "backlog" problem. It is a user-oriented organizational unit that provides service to end-users. The concept means different things to different people, and it appears under different structures and names.

The information center provides the end-user with appropriate education, technical support, usable tools, consulting (e.g., selection of DSS software), accessibility to databases, and convenient access to other computer systems. It is designed to improve turnaround time to users' requests for information, and to facilitate data analysis, special reports, and other one-shot, brief information needs. It is staffed mainly by user-oriented people experienced in the functional business areas who are specifically trained in the use of DBMS (particularly query language and report writing) and in modeling languages. It is designed mainly for PC users but can serve other end-users. It also protects the IS staff from being "bogged down" by users' requests for assistance.

The Toolsmith. Although the trend is to use existing tools, it is possible that some large-scale DSS will be enriched by new hardware, software, or even programming languages. The toolsmith's responsibility is to research and develop tools that improve the efficiency and/or effectiveness of the DSS package.

Note: One individual may assume several of the above roles or several individuals may fill one role.

The typical participation in many personal DSS consists of a manager (user) with some help from the information center. There is less involvement of the technical people from the information systems (IS) department in building DSS, especially in micro-DSS. The technical support and toolsmithing in such cases can be provided by vendors. Thus the role that the information center plays in DSS (and in ES) construction is expanding rapidly. Some organizational implications of this situation are discussed in Chapters 19 and 20.

7.6   Approaches to DSS Construction

There are several approaches to DSS construction. These can be classified into three categories: quick-hit, staged development, and development of a complete DSS (Sprague and Carlson [24]).

Quick-hit

According to this approach, a specific DSS is constructed when there is a recognized need and a high potential payoff, or a difficult problem exists. The Houston Minerals DSS was constructed in this manner. Many micro-DSS are being constructed this way, using an available generator. In the quick-hit approach, costs and risks are low, the latest technology can be utilized, and the DSS can be constructed relatively quickly. A major advantage is that it uses commercially available generators. Thus much of the software tool updating and maintenance is done by vendors rather than by the user's organization. The disadvantages are that quick-hit DSS are usually constructed for one person or for one purpose, they do not relate to other DSS, and there is usually limited carryover of experience to the next DSS. They are also inefficient in computing time as compared with the complete DSS. However, this approach is appropriate in many cases. (See Box 7.3.)

Staged Development

According to this approach, a specific DSS is constructed with some advanced planning, so that part of the effort in developing the first system can be reused in future DSS. Such an approach can lead to the development of an in-house DSS generator. The staged development approach takes more time than the quick-hit, yet it can yield similar success and visibility.

Box 7.3: When Is a Quick-hit Appropriate?

- *Clear-cut goals*—The goals of the project should be both settable and set at the outset; no research should be needed to define them.
- *Clear-cut procedure*—The DSS should be based on existing types of well-understood procedures and calculations; again, no research should be needed to define them.
- *Available data*—The needed data should be readily available.
- *Few users*—The DSS should be for the benefit of one or a few highly motivated users with common goals and concerns. The DSS should not cross organizational boundaries, nor should major selling or educational efforts be required.
- *Independent system*—Although the DSS may use input data prepared by other systems, it should operate independently of all other systems once those data have been received.

(*Source:* Condensed and adapted from S. Alter, in D. Young and P. G. W. Keen, eds., *DSS-81 Transactions*, Austin, TX: Execucom System Corp., 1981.)

Complete DSS

This approach requires the development of a full-service, large-scale, DSS generator; large-scale, specific DSS; and an organizational unit to manage such a project. An example of such an approach is the development of the GADS (Geodata Analysis and Display System) by IBM, one of the first DSS generators, which included a generator and several specific DSS. It is a lengthy process that is likely to result in an efficient generator with excellent integration of basic tools. It may take several years to develop such a system; therefore, success and visibility are delayed. Furthermore, there is a high risk of technological obsolescence.

The approach to be selected will depend on the specific situation (i.e., the organization, purpose of the DSS, users, tasks, available tools, and builder). In some companies a combination approach is used—namely, there is a large-scale, companywide DSS and several unrelated quick-hit DSS. With the development of more commercial DSS generators and increased capabilities of microcomputers, the quick-hit will probably become the most frequently used approach.

7.7   The Development Process: Iterative and Adaptive

DSS construction can be executed in several different ways. We will differentiate between the *life cycle approach* and the **iterative process.**

The Life Cycle Approach

This design strategy involves the fundamental assumption that the **information requirements** of a system can be predetermined. Therefore there has been a keen interest in the last decade in information requirements definition (IRD) as a formalized approach to systems analysis. Traditionally, IRDs are determined by combining logical analysis with investigation of user information processing behavior. For example, the requirements of an accounts receivable information system can be determined by examining accounting procedures and by speaking with experienced accountants. The concept of **critical success factors (CSF)** can also be used to determine IRD.

But where does the life cycle approach leave us with decision support systems? DSS are designed to enhance the decision processes of managers faced with poorly structured problems. By definition, we do not, perhaps cannot, completely understand the user's needs. As a result, we must explicitly acknowledge the role of learning in our design strategy or process. That is, it is expected that as part of the design and implementation effort, users will "learn" more about their problem or environment and therefore will identify new and unanticipated information needs.

Generally, DSS designers have recognized a need for a departure from the traditional design process. The process suggested as most appropriate is called the **evolutionary process** (Keen [11]), *iterative* process (Sprague and Carlson

[24]), or *prototyping* (Henderson and Ingraham [9]). Other names are middle-out process, adaptive design, and incremental design.

The Iterative Approach

The iterative approach aims at building a DSS in a series of short steps with immediate feedback from users to ensure that development is proceeding correctly. DSS tools and generators must, therefore, permit changes to be made quickly and easily.

The iterative design process combines four major phases of the traditional SDLC (analysis, design, construction, and implementation) into a single step that is repeated. The iterative process includes the following four activities (per Courbon et al. [6]):

1. Select an important subproblem (or a segment of the future system). The user and the builder jointly identify a subproblem for which the initial DSS is constructed. This early joint effort sets up initial working relationships between the participants and opens the lines of communication. The subproblem should be small enough so that the nature of the problem, the need for computer-based support, and the nature of that support are clear. It should have high interest value to the decision maker even if that interest may be short-lived.

2. Develop a small but usable system to assist the decision maker. No major system analysis or feasibility analysis is involved. In fact, the builder and the user go through all the steps of the system development process quickly, though on a small scale. The system should, out of necessity, be simple.

3. Evaluate the system constantly. At the end of each cycle the system is evaluated by the user and the builder. Evaluation is an integral part of the development process, and it is the control mechanism for the entire iterative design process. The evaluation mechanism is what keeps the cost and effort of developing a DSS consistent with its value.

4. Refine, expand, and modify the system in cycles. Subsequent cycles expand and improve the original version of the DSS. All the analysis-design-construction-implementation-evaluation steps are repeated in each successive refinement.

This process is repeated several times until a relatively stable and comprehensive system evolves. The interaction between the user, the builder, and the technology are extremely important in this process (Keen [11]). Note that user involvement is very high. There is a balance of effort and cooperation between the user and the builder: the user takes the lead in the utilization and evaluation activities, while the builder is stronger in the design and implementation phases. The user plays a joint and active role in contrast to conventional systems development, where the user frequently operates in a reactive or passive role.

The iterative design approach produces a specific DSS. The process is fairly straightforward for a DSS designed for personal support. The process becomes more complicated, although not invalidated, for a DSS that provides group support or organizational support. Specifically, there is a greater need for mechanisms to support communication among users and builders. There is also a need for mechanisms to accommodate personal variations while maintaining a common core system that is standard for all users. This is not a completely new concept; mechanisms that provide personal, group, and public data files have been a standard part of time-sharing systems for years.

As the number of users for a given system increases, the communication links required to operate the iterative design process must become more formal and structured. It may be necessary to establish checkpoints to define the beginning of each usage-evaluation cycle. When a DSS has many users and is designed for organizational support, it must be integrated into the organization by formalizing some of the stages in the systems development process.

The iterative process can be summarized as follows. It begins with a model of a part of the problem or with a simplified version of the entire problem. This gives end-users something concrete to react to. End-users then offer suggestions that may be incorporated into the DSS and they are then given a new version of the DSS. The process continues until the end-user is satisfied (at least temporarily) with the model. This process is necessary because in complex decisions the users often do not know what they want and the DSS builder does not understand what end-users need or will accept. The iterative process permits mutual learning to occur.

The iterative process is often referred to as **prototyping.** However, there is a difference between conventional prototyping and the iterative process. It is only lately that prototyping has been modified and is now similar to the iterative process. This issue is presented in Appendix 7-A.

DSS and the Iterative Approach—Summary

DSS are constructed in several different ways. Some are constructed by following the system development life cycle approach; the majority, however, are built by using the evolutionary prototyping approach.

Such iterative processes have three main advantages:

- Short development time
- Short user reaction time (feedback from user)
- Improved users' understanding of the system, its information needs, and its capabilities.

There is also a disadvantage to the iterative process. When such an approach is used, the gains obtained from cautiously stepping through each of the system's life-cycle stages might be lost. These gains include a thorough understanding of the information system's benefits and costs, a detailed description of the business's information needs, an information system design that is easy to maintain, a well-tested information system, and a well-prepared group of users.

The construction method that the DSS builder will use depends, in many cases, on whether the DSS is built by the end-user or by a DSS team.

7.8   Team-developed versus User-developed DSS

Many of the DSS developed in the 1970s and early 1980s were large-scale, complex systems designed primarily to provide organizational support. Such systems are still being developed for complex problems and for companywide applications. These systems are constructed by a team composed of users, intermediaries, DSS builders, technical support experts, and toolsmiths. Because there can be several individuals in each category, these teams are often large and their composition may change over time. Constructing a DSS with a team is a complex, lengthy, and costly process.

Another approach to the construction of a DSS is a user-developed system. This approach gained momentum in the 1980s owing to the development of microcomputers, computer communication networks, and micro-mainframe communication. In addition, the spread of user-developed DSS was fueled by the increasing amount of friendly development software for microcomputers, the reduced cost of both software and hardware, and the increased capabilities of microcomputers. Finally, the establishment of information centers contributed to an even greater proliferation of DSS constructed by users.

Often a mixture between these two extremes is developed. For example, a team can develop the basic DSS and a specific user can then develop additional applications. In addition, one can find other approaches to development such as that of Security Pacific Bank (Los Angeles), which has a DSS unit within its financial services division. This unit is completely separated from the IS department, and it is the major contributor to financial DSS construction in the bank. In the forthcoming sections we outline the process involved in each of the two extreme approaches.

7.9   Team-developed DSS

A team-developed DSS requires a substantial effort. Therefore it needs extensive planning and organization. The planning and organization depends on the specific DSS, the organization where it will be used, and so on. However, certain activities are generic and can be executed by any team. The planning and organizing activities discussed here include the following:*

- Forming the DSS group.
- An action plan.
- Planning for a DSS generator and the specific DSS.

---

*The material in this section has been condensed, with permission, from Sprague and Carlson [24]. (Ralph H. Sprague, Jr./Hugh J. Watson, *Decision Support Systems: Putting Theory into Practice*, © 1986, pp. 3–4. Reprinted by permission of Prentice-Hall, Inc., Englewood Cliffs, New Jersey.) Other team-developed DSS procedures are used by many organizations, but they are not documented in the literature.

- Representations, operations, memory aids, and mechanism control (ROMC).
- Flexibility in DSS.

Forming the DSS Group

A complex DSS requires a group of people to build and to manage it. The number of people in the group will depend on the size of the effort and the tactical development option used (e.g., prototyping versus SDLC). Some companies have initiated a DSS effort with as few as two or three people; others have used as many as twelve to fifteen people.

In general, the responsibilities of the DSS group include the following:

1. To develop a good understanding of the DSS philosophy and formulate a group mission based on that philosophy
2. To become familiar with the procedures for building and implementing DSS
3. To manage the DSS generator(s) and the collection of tools used to provide DSS building services to users
4. To play the role of a facilitator helping users bring the technology to bear on their problems.

The builder's role is needed to bridge the gap between the technology and the user. This is the same role that applications-oriented systems analysts have occupied in building traditional systems. Sometimes the builder must act as the intermediary and counsel the user, while at other times the builder must play the role of technical support when working with the toolsmith.

The DSS group can be formed by redefining and extending the charter of an existing group, or it can be newly initiated. In either case, the group or individuals can come from several sources.

1. A special-purpose team of systems analysts
2. A reoriented software tools group
3. A management science or industrial engineering group
4. The planning department
5. A staff analysis group from one of the functional areas such as a market research group, or a budget analysis group from accounting/finance.

The organizational placement of the DSS group varies. Here are some typical locations:

1. Within the information services (IS) department
2. As a highly placed executive staff group
3. Within the finance or other functional area
4. Within the industrial engineering department
5. Within the management science group
6. Within the information center group.

Regardless of the organizational location, the DSS group will have to confront the issue of centralization versus decentralization. In a centralized organization, the DSS group is more likely to have the full responsibility for the DSS generators and tools, and for handling all users. In a decentralized organization, the group may provide the technical expertise to manage the generators and tools while supporting work done by or with users in each division or geographic region. In the past there was reluctance by the IS staff to participate in the DSS team whenever it was constructed with a non-SDLS approach. This situation is changing and there is more willingness by the IS staff to participate in the DSS team. Once the group is formed, an action plan is developed.

Action Plan

The **action plan** comprises four phases.

Phase 1. Preliminary study and feasibility assessment. This phase includes needs assessment (present and future) and review of all requests for DSS. Conduct a few pilot projects.

Phase 2. Developing the DSS environment. Activate the DSS group, acquire the tools, and find the necessary data. Plan the development process (e.g., what to make and what to buy).

Phase 3. Developing the initial DSS. Use the iterative process. Improve and redesign until the DSS is in full working condition.

Phase 4. Developing a subsequent DSS. Search for a second DSS that can "fit into" the first. For example, if the first DSS deals with budget planning, the second can be expense analysis (to be compared with the budget). However, in many cases one may not find a fit, or the second related DSS is of a low priority. In such a case, the best way is to look at applications needs.

Planning for a DSS Generator

The staged development approach discussed earlier leads to the development (or purchase) of a DSS generator(s). What would an ideal **DSS generator** look like, and what should it do? Identifying the necessary and desirable characteristics of a DSS generator is a crucial step in phase 2 of the plan. A typical but inappropriate approach to this task would be to list all possible features a DSS generator should have, then prepare a checklist to see which existing software system provides the most features. Such an approach may be inappropriate for two reasons. First, because there is little rationale for choosing items on the initial list, it could be difficult to assess the importance of their presence or absence in a given DSS generator. Second, there is no ideal "full-service" generator currently available, either in the software market or in a user organization, against which existing software may be compared.

The construction approach suggested by Sprague and Carlson is in a form of "top-down" analysis at four levels (see Figure 7.3):

1. Identify the *overall objectives* for a DSS generator.
2. Infer from level 1 the *general capabilities* that a DSS generator must have to respond to the objectives. Segregate the general objectives into those related to the data, models, and dialog components of the DSS.
3. Infer from level 2 a set of *specific capabilities* that are required to accomplish the general capabilities.
4. Infer from levels 2 and 3 *specific devices, strategies,* and *hardware/software* features necessary to implement the specific capabilities.

The general objectives, capabilities, and features of DSS generators are described as follows:

Level 1—Overall Objectives. There are two basic objectives of a DSS generator:

1. To permit quick and easy development of a wide variety of specific DSS.

2. To be flexible and adaptive enough to facilitate the iterative design process. This allows specific DSS to respond quickly to changes in the organiza-

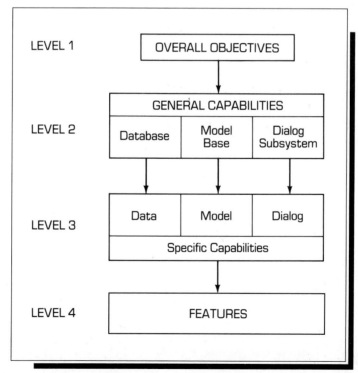

FIGURE 7.3 A Top-down Criterion for a DSS Generator. (*Source:* Adapted from Sprague and Carlson [24], pp. 70–72.) Details are shown in Fig. 3.10.

tional or physical environment, in the style of the user, or in the nature of the task. The generator must also facilitate communication and interaction between the user and the builder.

Level 2—General Capabilities.

1. The generator should be easy to use. Specifically,
   a. The generator should be able to create a specific DSS that is easy and convenient for nontechnical people to use.
   b. The generator should be easy and convenient for a builder to use for developing and modifying a specific DSS.
2. A DSS generator should provide access to a wide variety of data sources.
3. A DSS generator should provide access to analytical capabilities. This capability is related to the model base.

Levels 3 and 4—Capabilities and Features.
The specific capabilities and features in the dialog (user interface), data management, and model management subsystems were presented in Chapter 3.

The Representations, Operations, Memory Aids, and Control Mechanisms Approach (ROMC Approach)

The **ROMC approach** is a framework for DSS systems analysis and design that was developed by Sprague and Carlson [24]. The major objective of this approach is to identify the characteristics and capabilities that a specific DSS needs to have.

The major difficulty in building a DSS is that the information requirements, which are the starting point for systems design, are usually poorly specified (owing to the unstructured nature of the problems solved by a DSS). The ROMC approach helps overcome this difficulty. It is composed of a set of four user-oriented entities:

- Representations. The ability to provide representations, if possible visual, to help conceptualize and communicate the problem. This is the context in which users interpret output and invoke operations.
- Operations. The ability to provide operations to analyze and manipulate those representations (the ways in which users manipulate objects in the given context).
- Memory Aids. To assist the user in linking representations and operations, a set of memory aids is used. These are fundamental learning aids in making decisions.
- Control Mechanisms. Those mechanisms used to control and operate the entire system—the framework for integrating the three entities into a useful decision-making system.

Note: For a detailed list of items included in ROMC, see Appendix 7-B.

The ROMC approach, which is process-independent, is based on five observed characteristics regarding decision making:

1. Decision makers have difficulties describing situations. They prefer to use graphical conceptualizations whenever possible.
2. The decision-making phases of intelligence, design, and choice can be applied to DSS analysis.
3. Memory aids (such as reports, "split screen" displays, data files, indexes, mental rules, and analogies) are extremely useful in decision making and should be provided by a DSS.
4. Decision makers differ in style, skills, and knowledge. Therefore the DSS should help decision makers use and develop their own styles, skills, and knowledge.
5. The decision maker expects to exercise direct, personal control over the support system. This observation does not suggest that users must work without an intermediary; it does suggest, however, that they must understand the DSS capabilities and be able to analyze the inputs and interpret the outputs of the DSS.

Examples based on these five observations are summarized in Table 7.1 (left column) and are compared with the corresponding ROMC components (right column). The closer the match between the left and right columns (and this is precisely what the ROMC approach aims to do), the better the DSS will be.

The ROMC components are identified and integrated during the actual system analysis (i.e., the DSS is designed as a set of representations with associated operations).

Flexibility in DSS

The Case for Flexibility. Some observations on the characteristics of DSS users, tasks, and environment that illustrate the need for flexibility include the following, according to Keen [11]:

- Neither the user nor the builder is able to specify functional requirements in advance.
- Users do not know, or cannot articulate, what they want and need. Therefore they need an initial system to react to and improve on.
- The users' concept of the task, and perception of the nature of the problem, change as the system is used.
- Actual uses of DSS are almost always different from those originally intended.
- Solutions derived through a DSS are subjective.
- There are wide variations among individuals in how they use DSS.

In summary, there are two basic reasons for the importance of flexibility in DSS:

TABLE 7.1 Decision Requirements versus DSS Capabilities

Decision Makers Use	DSS Provides
1. Conceptualizations: A city map Relationship between assets and liabilities	1. Representations: A map outline A scatterplot of assets versus liabilities
2. Different decision-making processes and decision types, all involving activities, for intelligence, design, and choice Gather data on customers Create alternative customer assignments for salespeople Compare alternatives	2. Operations for intelligence, design, and choice: Query the database Update lists to show assignments Print summary statistics on each alternative
3. A variety of memory aids: List of customers Summary sheets on customers Table showing salespeople and their customer assignments File drawers with old tables Scratch paper Staff reminders Rolodex	3. Automated memory aids: Extracted data on customers Views of customer data Workspace for developing assignment tables Library for saving tables Temporary storage DSS messages Computerized addresses
4. A variety of styles, skills, and knowledge, applied via direct, personal control: Accepted conventions for interpersonal communication Orders to staff Standard operating procedures Revise orders or procedures	4. Aid to direct personal control conventions for user-computer communication: Training and explanation in how to give orders to the DSS Procedures formed from DSS operations Ability to override DSS defaults or procedures

Source: Carlson [5]. Used with permission.

1. A DSS must evolve or grow to reach an operational design because no one can completely predict or anticipate in advance what is required.
2. The system can seldom be final; it must change frequently to adjust to changes in the problem, user, and environment because these factors are inherently volatile. Changes must be easy to execute.

Let us now consider the nature of this flexibility. Sprague and Carlson [24] distinguish four levels of flexibility:

1. The flexibility to *solve*. The first level of flexibility gives the user of a specific DSS the ability to confront a problem in a flexible, personal way. It is the flexibility to perform intelligence, design, and choice activities

and to explore alternative ways of viewing or solving a problem. Such flexibility is provided, for example, by the "what-if" capability.

2. The flexibility to *modify*. The second level of flexibility is the ability to modify the configuration of a specific DSS so that it can handle somewhat different problems, or an expanded set of problems. This flexibility is exercised by the user and/or the builder.

3. The flexibility to *adapt*. The third level of flexibility is the ability to adapt to changes that are extensive enough to require a completely different specific DSS. This flexibility is exercised by the DSS builder.

4. The flexibility to *evolve*. The fourth level of flexibility is the ability of the DSS and the DSS generator to evolve in response to changes in the basic nature of the technology on which DSS are based. This level may require a change in the tools and the generator for better efficiency.

7.10   End-user Computing and User-developed DSS

End-user Computing

A user-developed DSS is directly related to a trend in information systems called end-user computing. Broadly defined, **end-user computing** is the development and use of computer-based information systems by people outside the formal information systems areas. This definition includes managers and professionals using personal computers, word processing done by secretaries, electronic mail used by the CEO, and time-sharing systems used by scientists and researchers. Relevant to DSS is a more narrow definition, which includes decision makers and professionals (such as financial or tax analysts and engineers) *building* and/or *using* computers directly to solve problems or enhance their productivity mainly through personal computers, although they may also use terminals connected to a large computer or a time-sharing network. (See Box 7.4.)

The end-user can be on any level of the organization, or in any functional area. Their levels of computer skill can also vary substantially. End-user computing can be classified according to the extent and method of use, type of application, training requirements, and required support. The number of end-users is growing at a rate of 50 to 100 percent annually (Rockart and Flannery [20]).

It is only natural that many end-users will attempt to construct their own DSS. Although we do not have much empirical evidence, it seems from discussions with users in small and large organizations that many DSS are being constructed today by information centers with the active participation of end-users, or by end-users themselves. Furthermore, a study conducted by Mittman and Moore [17] indicated that even some top executives like to build their own DSS (using Lotus 1-2-3, for example).

Box 7.4: An End-User's Story

The vice president for management services at Florida Power and Light, D. L. Dady, a major user of an end-user facility, cites an experience to demonstrate the value of the system to him.

"I had a telephone call about a quarter of five on a Tuesday afternoon relative to some information I was going to need at a meeting the next morning. The staff had just left for the evening. I was able to go to the terminal and compare some payroll information from Florida Power and Light with several other companies. From the COMPUSTAT database I had access to 20 years of payroll data from all utilities. I was able to put in parameters on what I wanted to look at. In a few seconds I had a list of 23 utility companies. There was one other company I also wanted to include, so I keyed that company in.

"I asked the terminal to do a calculation: I wanted to know what the average payroll was per employee among those utility companies. I got back the figures for as many years as COMPUSTAT had data from the companies. I had the information in my hands in 20 minutes and was able to go home and look it over quietly that evening. There I added the numbers together and produced some averages, which took me another 30 minutes.

"The next morning it took me 25 minutes to produce a new graph of the data. On one graph I was able to show Florida Power and Light compared with the average of 24 selected companies, with the average of 8 selected companies, as well as with the high and low companies.

"Developing this kind of information would have taken weeks without the system. Moreover, it allowed me to refine my own thinking as I proceeded, depending on the significance of the numbers I generated."

(*Source:* Condensed from "Graphic Systems Aid Executive Fact Finding." *IBM Information Processing*, Vol. 1, No. 3, June–July 1982, pp. 5–6.)

User-developed DSS: Advantages and Risks

There are several advantages for users building their own DSS:

1. Short delivery time. You do not have to wait in line for the information services (IS) people to come. A backlog of two to three years is rather common in IS (e.g., see Rockart and Flannery [20]).
2. The prerequisites of extensive and formal user requirements specifications, which are part of system analysis in a conventional system development life cycle, are eliminated. These specifications (Zmud [26]) are

often incomplete or incorrect owing to such issues as the users' inability to specify the requirement, or the communication difficulties between analyst and user. They also take a long time to develop.

3. Some DSS implementation problems could be greatly reduced by transferring the implementation process to the users.
4. The cost is very low.

The risks of user-developed DSS are listed as follows:

1. User-developed DSS could be of poor quality (e.g., see Alavi [1]). Lack of practical DSS design experience and the tendency of end-users to ignore conventional controls, testing procedures, and documentation standards can lead to low-quality systems. (See Box 7.5.)
2. Potential quality risks may be classified in three categories: (a) substandard tools and facilities used in DSS development, (b) risks associated with the development process (e.g., inability to develop workable systems, or developing of systems that generate erroneous results), and (c) data management risks (e.g., loss of data).

To reduce these risks and enhance the quality of the DSS, Alavi suggested four general approaches and eight specific tactics (see Appendix 7-C). In addition, cooperation with an information center may be sufficient to assure quality DSS.

The Construction Process

The construction of user-developed DSS varies from situation to situation. It depends on the user's skill level, the availability of organizational resources (see Zmud [26]), the nature of the DSS, and the type of software used, to mention a few. A typical process may be composed of the following phases (see Figure 7.4).

Box 7.5: Example Risk of User-Developed DSS

Using a spreadsheet package, in 1984 a California executive predicted $55 million in sales over the first two years for a computer his company planned to introduce. Based on this projection, other managers began making plans for hiring additional staff and expanding inventories. Unfortunately the sales projections were wrong because the executive had forgotten to include a price discount planned for a key component. On closer examination of the model, he discovered the sales estimates were inflated by $8 million because of an error in the pricing formula. Had the executive's mistake not been detected, the actual profit margins would have been considerably lower than the projection.

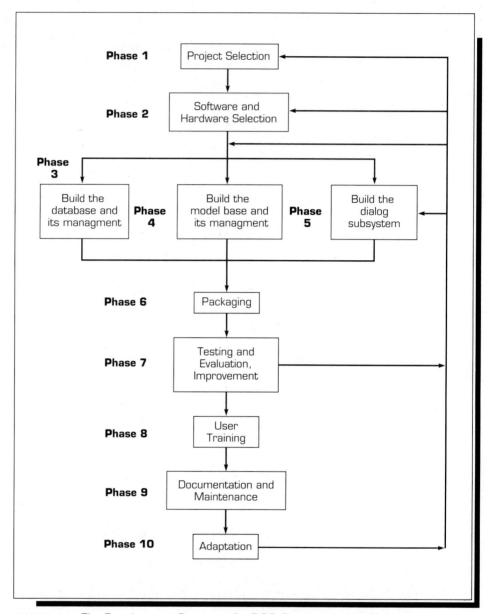

FIGURE 7.4 The Development Process of a DSS Constructed by End-users.

Phase 1. *Deciding on the project (or problem to be solved)*. Execution of this phase may involve a formal cost-benefit analysis. Such analysis is not usually needed because the cost of a user-developed DSS is fairly small, especially when the software and hardware are already available. Selection of the project by the user will contribute to an increased likelihood of successful implementation. Sometimes the information center staff will look for DSS opportunities.

Phase 2. *Selecting software and hardware*. An end-user DSS is usually constructed using a commercial software package and existing hardware. The selection of hardware and software are interrelated issues. Some companies already have a variety of software. The less sophisticated end user will need help in the selection.

Phase 3. *Data acquisition and management*. The DSS may require data that are available in external and/or internal databases. Several questions will have to be answered: what data to use, how to ensure the quality of the data, where the data are available, how to transfer the data to the user (e.g., how to download the data from the mainframe to the micro), how these data can be kept secure, and how the data are incorporated into the DSS. A DBMS can be a part of the DSS generator or a package of its own that interfaces with the DSS.

Phase 4. *Model subsystem acquisition and management*. Users can write their own models and reports, and they may use standard models at times. Standard models may be part of the DSS generator, or they could be acquired separately to supplement the DSS generators. For example, a forecasting template can be used in conjunction with Lotus 1-2-3, and an SAS statistical package can supplement a DSS generator.

Phase 5. *Dialog subsystem and its management*. Several hardware and software components make up the dialog subsystem. They range from a natural language processor to a graphics software package.

Phase 6. *Packaging*. Once the components have been acquired and the data identified, the DSS can be put together. The packaging can be executed by end-users if they have experience and basic computer skills. Otherwise, help will be required from the information center or the IS department. The programming is usually done in procedural languages (such as COBOL or C) to bond together the various software components of the DSS.

Phase 7. *Testing, evaluation, and improvement*. The user should test the DSS on sample problems, improve it if necessary, and analyze the results provided by the DSS to make sure they are reliable and valid.

Phase 8. *Training*. End-user training is very important. It can be provided by various sources ranging from the information center to the vendor who provides the DSS generator. (For a discussion, see *EDP Analyzer* [8].)

Phase 9. *Documentation and maintenance*. Most end-users do not like to write documentation for their personal DSS nor to develop formal maintenance plans. However, both activities should be carried out by the user. A formal documentation approach can eliminate potential problems that arise, for example, when the DSS builder-user leaves the organization.

Phase 10. *Adaptation*. This should be the easiest part of the process, because the developer is also the user. If the DSS is effective and easy to use, it will be used whenever relevant problems occur.

As indicated earlier, this development process is a typical one; however, variations can be found. For example, some end-users could use extensive planning, which is usually associated with the team-developed approach.

7.11   Some Constructive Comments

Use of System Development Life Cycle. Sometimes the traditional system development life cycle (SDLC), or some variation of it, is used to build a DSS. This may happen when a complex companywide DSS is being developed from scratch (without generators, using only tools). If IS people control the development of the DSS, they tend to use the SDLC. Obviously, if the information requirements are clear (a rare but possible situation), there may be less need for the iterative approach. The SDLC approach was found to be useful for building DSS that support operational control decisions while the iterative approach was more often used in support of strategic planning systems (see Hogue and Watson [10]).

Organizational Decision-making Style. For a DSS to be effective, its design should take into consideration the organization's attitudes and approaches toward decision making; for example, the degree of participative management, the amount of reliance on quantitative methods, and the decision-making processes used. For further details, see Taylor [25].

Make-or-Buy Considerations. Most companies will buy some software for the DSS rather than write it. But even the best packages may require supplemental programming and tool integration, especially for large DSS. Several questions may be considered when the make-versus-buy issue surfaces:

1. Which alternative is more economical?
2. Which alternative is faster?
3. Should time-sharing be considered?
4. Should a mainframe and/or micro version be acquired?
5. Should a consultant be hired to build the DSS?
6. What networking is needed?

Building a New DSS from an Old One. Some companies are facing decision situations that are similar in nature yet differ on specific details. For example, a commercial loan requested by a certain company in a particular industry may be similar to a loan request of another company in the same or a related industry. In such cases management faces a series of ad hoc decisions. There is no need, however, to develop a DSS from scratch for each loan request. Morgan Guaranty Trust (of New York City) uses the following approach:

The company is using a mainframe DSS generator (called IFPS) to build a specific DSS for each loan requested. A team composed of the experts on the industry, the finance people, and an analyst are assigned to each loan. The DSS is constructed by the company analyst, who is the only one interacting directly with the computer for loan analysis.

Once a DSS is completed, it is used to help decide whether to approve or reject the loan request. The computer program is then stored. For example, Loan

L-13 was granted to a company in the chemical industry; a few weeks or months later, when a similar request for a loan arises, the DSS for L-13 can be modified to a new ad hoc DSS in only a few days.

Construction of the DSS in a day or a few days illustrates another important point. As in many quantitative analyses, a major difficulty may not be the model construction or computing the solution but getting the required data. It usually takes Morgan Guaranty Trust several weeks to acquire the data for a DSS, which is constructed in days and may be used for only a few minutes.

Project Selection and Approval. In small-scale DSS the problem area, or the project, is selected by the user. In most cases, the existing hardware and software provide an environment that enables building the DSS at a very low cost. Therefore there is no need for a formal process for project selection and approval. However, large systems may be fairly expensive, and in addition may involve people from several departments. In the latter case, a formal selection is desirable.

According to Meador et al. [16], the construction of a DSS is usually quite well done. However, this effort could be merely a waste if the DSS does not appropriately address the *right* problem. Several factors must be considered when deciding whether a project should be approved. They are listed in order of importance in Table 7.2.

DSS Architecture. The integration (or "gluing") of the basic components of DSS into one system can be done in different ways. Four different arrangements or architectures have been proposed by Sprague and Carlson [24]: DSS *network*, DSS *bridge*, DSS *sandwich*, and DSS *tower*. The details of the four configurations, as well as alternative configurations, are beyond the scope of this book.

TABLE 7.2 Average Rated Importance of Factors in DSS Project Approval Process.

Factor	Average Rated Importance
Top management emphasis	5.91
Return on investment (cost/benefit)	5.04
Technically do-able	4.87
DSS development costs	4.76
Impact on data processing resources	4.70
Degree of user commitment	4.70
Increase in user effectiveness	4.67
DSS operating costs	4.64
Increase in user efficiency	4.61
Adaptability of organization to change	4.52
Urgency of user needs	4.49
Uncertainty of objectives for DSS design	4.27
Qualitative or "soft" benefits	4.11
Company politics	4.09

Scale: 1, Low; 7, High.
Source: Meador et al. [16], reprinted by special permission of the *MIS Quarterly*, © 1984.

Incorrect integration of the DSS components will result in an incorrect DSS, even when all the components are properly designed. Incorrect integration can affect many of the DSS capabilities, thus causing the DSS to fail.

7.12 DSS Generators

DSS generators combine the ability to do several general-purpose applications in one program. It is an alternative to the use of several separate, single-function (stand-alone) packages (see Figure 7.5). In the latter case, it is necessary to load each package and the same data files into the computer each time a

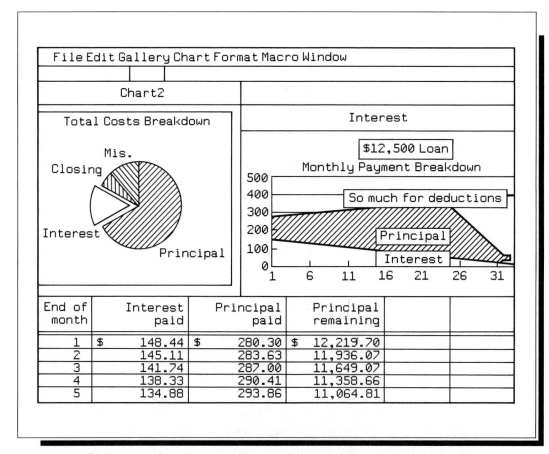

FIGURE 7.5 An integrated package provides graphics, modeling, and other capabilities. This example is provided by an integrated package based on an expanded spreadsheet, Excel (from Microsoft Corp.). The program enables the user to change or edit individual chart components (e.g., text or arrow, or resize the legend). These strong graphics capabilities are performed on Apple's Macintosh.

package is used. Sometimes stand-alone packages "refuse" to work with data files created by other programs. Integrated packages have solved these problems by allowing the user to work with a variety of tools that use standardized commands and allow shifting among various applications (in a manner similar to a "call waiting" in a telephone). Thus, for example, data can pass from one function to another rather easily. The integration of several programs into one allows a user to follow a natural thought process.

The following programs are typical "raw materials" for integrated packages:

- Spreadsheet
- Data management
- Word processing
- Communication
- Business graphics
- Calendar (time management)
- Desk management
- Project management.

Note: When determining these parts one should consider the objectives of the DSS as discussed in Section 7.9, Phase 1 of action plan.

The most popular integrated package, Lotus 1-2-3, includes three components: spreadsheet, graphics, and database management. More recent packages include five or more components. The integrated micropackages exhibit many of the ideal DSS generator capabilities described earlier.

Integrated products are continuously improving, but most of them, especially the micro based, are still no match for a group of stand-alone packages. An integrated package may have an excellent word processor but only a good spreadsheet and mediocre graphics. None of the database managers in integrated programs is powerful enough for heavy data handling. The more programs integrated into one package, the more difficult the learning and operation of the package becomes. For example, Lotus 1-2-3 has several customized features that make it easy to use by a novice. Lotus's Symphony, which includes more programs, does not have some of these features. Furthermore, Symphony requires more diskettes arranged in a manner that may baffle many novices. Another possible deficiency of integrated packages is that they require vast amounts of memory. This can slow many PCs to a frustrating crawl (or it may require additional memory purchases).

Recognizing these deficiencies, some software vendors offer both integrated packages and individual tools. For example, the IFPS family includes DATA-SPAN, GRAPHICS, OPTIMUM, and SENTRY, as well as the IFPS integrated package.

Modularly Integrated Systems

A relatively new approach to software integration is the "modularly integrated" systems of stand-alone products that function as one by using the same commands. For example, a spreadsheet user can pass the data disk *directly* to the word processing user. Two representative examples of this approach are ENABLE and SMART. SMART includes several stand-alone systems: spreadsheet, word processing, graphics, communications, time manager, and data manager. All systems use the same commands for easy data interchange. The modularly integrated systems are much more powerful than the fully integrated systems (such as Lotus 1-2-3), because stand-alone packages are usually more powerful than components in an integrated system; however, they cost more money.

Modular integration can also be achieved by software packages called *task managers* (such as DESQVIEW and TOPVIEW).

7.13   Selection of a DSS Generator and Other Software Tools

A large number of DSS generators and other tools are commercially available at price tags that vary from hundreds to hundreds of thousands of dollars. Some of the software has been created for personal computers, whereas other software programs are available only for minicomputers or mainframes.

Two interrelated questions must be answered by an organization that would like to use a DSS generator. (1) Which generator(s) should be used, and (2) which hardware should it run on—mainframe, mini, micro, or time-sharing?

Mainframe DSS Software. Mainframe DSS software costs between $30,000 and $300,000 and has several powerful capabilities. For example, Metafact (from Integrated Data Architects, Northridge, CA) and System W (from Comshare, Inc., Ann Arbor, MI) sell for over $200,000 (mainframe versions).

Micro DSS Software. Several vendors offer a microversion of their mainframe product at a considerably lower price. With the increased capabilities of micros and the improvement of the micro to mainframe connection, it is likely that more micro-DSS will be used in the future. Table 7.3 lists several representative micro-DSS generators.

Software Selection. The basic software tools to be considered are:

- Relational database facilities with powerful report generation and ad hoc inquiry facilities
- Graphics generation languages
- Modeling languages
- General-purpose statistical data analysis languages
- Other special languages (e.g., for building a simulation)
- Programming languages (third generation).

In building a DSS, the builder must select these tools and/or a comprehensive DSS generator that is a set of all (or some) of the above.

TABLE 7.3 Representative Micro-DSS Generators.

Product	Company
DSM	Decision System Support Inc. (San Juan Capistrano, CA)
Econometric Software	Alpha Software Co. (Burlington, MA)
Enable	The Software Group (Ballston Lake, NY)
Encore	Ferox Microsystems (Arlington, VA)
Focus/PC	Information Builders, Inc. (New York, NY)
GSA/GSM	Prediction Systems, Inc. (Manasquan, NJ)
Horizon 370	Chase Decision Systems (Waltham, VA)
IFPS/Personal	Execucom Systems, Inc. (Austin, TX)
Informix	Relational Database Systems, Inc. (Menlo Park, CA)
Ingres/ABF	Relational Technology, Inc. (Almeda, CA)
MAPS/PRO	Ross Systems, Inc. (Palo Alto, CA)
Micro-FCS	Thorn EMI Computer Software (Chelmsford, MA)
MicroPROphit	Via Computer, Inc. (San Diego, CA)
Micro SIM	Simplan Systems (Chapel Hill, NC)
Micro W	Comshare, Inc. (Ann Arbor, MI)
Nomad 2 PC	D&B Computing Services (Wilton, CT)
One-up	Comshare, Inc. (Ann Arbor, MI)
Open Access	Software Products, Int'l. (San Diego, CA)
PC Analect	Dialogue, Inc. (New York, NY)
PC Express	Information Resource, Inc. (Manhasset, NY)
PC/SIBYL	Applied Decision System (Lexington, MA)
Plans +	IBM (Menlo Park, CA)
SMART	Innovative Software, Inc. (Overland Park, KS)
SPSS/PC	SPSS, Inc. (Chicago, IL)
TM/1	Sinper Corp. (North Bergen, NJ)
20/20	Access Technology (South Natick, MA)
Works	Microsoft (Bellevue, WA)

Source: Horwitt [10].

Selecting the tools and/or generator is a complex process for the following reasons:

1. At the time of the selection, DSS information requirement and outputs are not completely known.
2. There are hundreds of software packages on the market.
3. The software packages are being changed (usually improved) very rapidly (especially for micros).
4. Price changes are frequent.
5. Several people may be involved in the evaluating team.

6. One language may be used in the construction of several DSS. Thus the required capabilities of the tools may change from one application to another.
7. The selection decision involves dozens of criteria against which competing packages are compared.
8. Technical, functional, end-user, and managerial issues are all considered.
9. Commercially available evaluations by companies such as Data Decisions, Data Pro, and Software Digest, Inc., and the buyer's guides of journals, such as *PC Week* and *Infosystems,* are frequently superficial. They can be used as one source of information.

The Selection Process of a DSS Generator. When an organization has a DSS generator or has access to one on a time-sharing network, it is likely that this generator will be the one used for DSS applications. However, firms do not necessarily use only one generator. Some DSS generators are better for certain types of applications than others. Thus, organizations may need to purchase a new DSS generator at times.

A Proposed Methodology for DSS Generator Selection. Procedures for selecting DSS software are shown in Figure 7.6. The procedure is participative (i.e., it involves users). A similar process has been proposed by Meador and Mezger [15]. This goes beyond the traditional software selection approach in three basic ways. First, end-users are extensively involved in the evaluation from beginning to end. Second, the technical features to be evaluated are listed in detail and given in terms that end-users can understand. Third, the traditional role of the data processing department as the leader in software selection is abandoned in favor of end-user control.

The proposed selection process consists of a number of steps, as illustrated in Figure 7.6. First comes the initial organization of the selection team, or task force. The next step is the development of a set of user-oriented evaluation criteria, based on a survey of user needs and a survey of vendor product capabilities. Then comes a series of increasingly demanding and thorough screenings of the candidate products. The first three screens should eliminate all but one or two "finalists." These would then be brought in house (one at a time, or in parallel) for the development of a "prototype" application. This approach should enable the selection team to choose a generator that will satisfy most of the intended users' needs.

The proposed process, which is applicable mainly to mainframe and minicomputer DSS generators, can be used (with modifications) for selecting microsoftware or any DSS tool.

Putting the System Together. Development tools increase the productivity of builders and help them produce, at a moderate cost, a DSS responsive to the true needs of users. The philosophy of the development tools and generators is based on two simple, yet very important, concepts: (1) the use of highly auto-

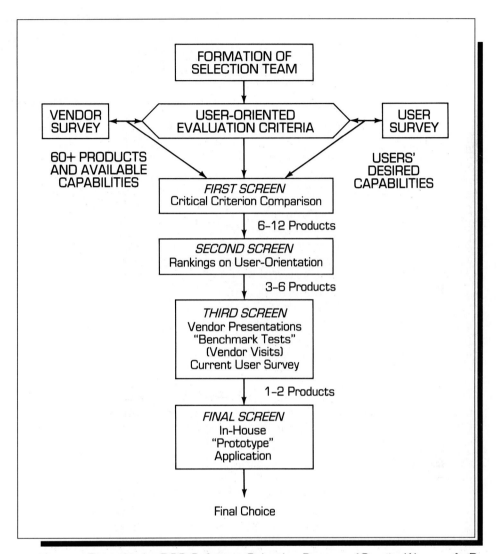

**FORMATION OF
SELECTION TEAM**

**VENDOR
SURVEY**

**USER-ORIENTED
EVALUATION CRITERIA**

**USER
SURVEY**

**60+ PRODUCTS
AND AVAILABLE
CAPABILITIES**

**USERS'
DESIRED
CAPABILITIES**

FIRST SCREEN
Critical Criterion Comparison

6–12 Products

SECOND SCREEN
Rankings on User-Orientation

3–6 Products

THIRD SCREEN
Vendor Presentations
"Benchmark Tests"
(Vendor Visits)
Current User Survey

1–2 Products

FINAL SCREEN
In-House
"Prototype"
Application

Final Choice

FIGURE 7.6 Steps in the DSS Software Selection Process. (*Source:* Warren, A. D. and B. Reimann. "Selecting a DSS Generator: A Participative Process." *International Journal on Policy and Information*, Dec. 1985. Used with permission.)

mated tools and/or a generator throughout the development process, and (2) the use of prefabricated pieces in the manufacturing of a whole system, whenever possible. The first concept increases the productivity of the builder in the same way an electric saw improves the productivity of a carpenter formerly using a hand saw. The second concept increases productivity analogous to the way a prefabricated wall increases the productivity of the carpenter building a house.

A DSS development system can be thought of as a workshop with several tools and components. Such a system includes the major components discussed earlier:

- Request (query) handler (obtains information from database)
- System analysis and design facility (editing, interpreting, etc.)
- Dialog management system (user interface)
- Report generator (formats output reports)
- Graphics generator
- Source code manager (stores and accesses built-in and user-developed models)
- Model base management system.

Some of these components may be integrated into a DSS generator. Other components may be added as needed. These components and tools can be used to build a new DSS, or upgrade or repair an existing one. The core of the system includes a development language or a DSS generator. The construction is done by combining programming modules. (A *programming module* is a set of executable lines of code that has a name and is written to do a certain job.)

Modules can be written in command languages, which are available in all DSS generators, or in other programming languages (e.g., COBOL or PASCAL). A module can be used independently, or it can be used in conjunction with other modules to build a more complex module. A module can perform computations, read and write operations, transform data, or perform any other computer operation to achieve a certain objective. A DSS generator may include several preprogrammed modules.

Chapter Highlights

- DSS are developed by a unique development process based on prototyping.
- The major steps are: planning, research, analysis, design, construction, implementation, maintenance, and adaptation.
- Several development strategies are available. They range from using CASE tools to programming with general-purpose (3GL) languages.
- The participants in the construction process are: the user, the intermediary, the builder, the technical support person, and the toolsmith.
- Most DSS can be built by a quick-hit approach.
- The iterative (prototyping) approach is most common in DSS since the information requirements are not known precisely.
- DSS can be built by teams or by individuals.
- Building a DSS by a team needs to follow a structure process, including planning, appropriate selection of software (generator if needed) and hardware.

- ROMC is an approach for a systematic support to the construction process of DSS.
- Four types of flexibility exist in DSS: to solve, modify, adapt, and evolve.
- A major portion of end-user computing is building DSS for personal support by individuals.
- The major benefits of people building their own DSS are: short delivery time, users' familiarity with their need, low cost, and easier implementation.
- User-developed DSS could be of a poor quality. Appropriate control can improve this situation.
- Most DSS are constructed with DSS development generators or with non-integrated development tools.
- There are many tools and generators on the market. The selection of the appropriate ones for building a specific DSS must be carefully designed.

Key Words

action plan	flexibility in DSS	prototyping
complete DSS	generators	quick-hit
critical success factors (CSF)	information center	ROMC (representation, operations, memory
DSS builder	information requirements	aids, mechanism control)
DSS generators	intermediary	staged development
end-user computing	iterative process	system development
evolutionary process	make-or-buy	life cycle (SDLC)
feasibility study	planning language	

Questions for Review

1. List the six phases of the traditional life cycle development process.
2. List some activities that are included in systems analysis.
3. List some activities that are included in the design phase of SDLC.
4. List all the phases of the DSS development process.
5. List and discuss the various development strategies of DSS.
6. Define "DSS generators" and discuss their objectives.
7. List the participants in the DSS construction.
8. What is an information center?
9. What does a quick-hit, a staged development, and a complete DSS strategy imply?
10. What is the major difference between the iterative design process and the SDLC?
11. List the major steps of the iterative process (per Courbon et al. [6]).
12. List the five features of prototyping. (See Appendix 7-A.)
13. Summarize the process of forming a DSS group.

14. To whom may a DSS team report?
15. List the four phases of a DSS action plan.
16. Describe the "top-down" criteria-setting and steps for a DSS generator.
17. List the potential quality risk areas in user-developed DSS.
18. List the four types of flexibility in DSS.
19. Define "end-user" and "end-user computing."
20. List the major advantages of user-developed DSS.
21. List the steps in the construction process of a user-developed DSS.

Questions for Discussion

1. Why is the classical SDLC not appropriate for most DSS?
2. Explain how the critical success factor methodology can help the DSS development process. (See Shank [22].)
3. Explain how the classification to technology levels can improve the understanding of the DSS development process.
4. Why do managers use intermediaries? Will they continue to use them in the future? Why or why not?
5. Discuss under what conditions people will tend to select each of the following strategies: quick-hit, staged development, and a complete DSS.
6. Explain the relationship between prototyping and CSF (see Figure 7.7).
7. Explain how the iterative approach bypasses the life cycle step of information requirements definition.
8. Explain how the establishment of information centers contributed to user-developed DSS.
9. How would you choose the participants in a DSS group?

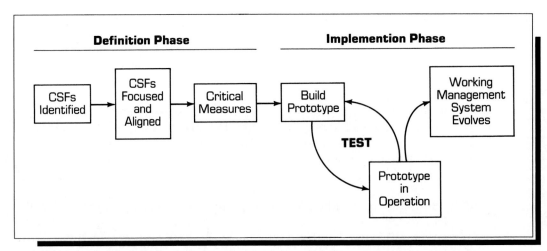

FIGURE 7.7 Combining CSF and Prototyping. (*Source:* A. D. Crescenzi and R. H. Reck. "CSF Helping as Managers Pinpoint Information Needs." Reprinted from *Infosystems*, July 1985. © Hitchcock Publishing Company. Used with permission.)

10. Can a DSS group that completed its job be assigned to another DSS? Why or why not?

11. Why is the "top-down" approach for setting up the DSS objectives, capabilities, and features better than a "bottom-up" approach?

12. Discuss the five observations used to support the idea of ROMC. Do you agree with these observations?

13. Explain why flexibility is essential to DSS.

14. Discuss the reasons why user-developed DSS can be of poor quality. What can be done to improve the situation (per Alavi [2], Appendix 7-C)? Do you agree with her suggestions?

15. Why is building a DSS from an old one desirable? Under what conditions will it work?

16. Compare Figures 7.2 (phases in building a DSS) and 7.4 (end-user construction of a DSS) and comment on their major differences.

17. How does the iterative process secure more user input than the conventional approaches?

18. What are the disadvantages of *not* having complete specifications for a CBIS, but instead letting it grow from a small prototype?

19. How does prototyping relate to nonprocedural languages? (See Appendix 7-A.)

20. Given the relative ease of using nonprocedural languages, why do users need support from the information center?

21. Explain why the user is considered a component of the DSS.

22. Give two examples each, not mentioned in this text, of specific DSS, DSS generators, and DSS tools.

23. Why are most micro-based DSS being developed with the quick-hit approach?

24. Compare the process described in Figure 7.2 (building a DSS) with that proposed in Section 7.9 (team-developed DSS). Comment on the differences.

Exercise

a. Think of a decision problem that is relevant to you that you believe could be aided by the development of a small end-user DSS. A problem that is currently real to you is best, although hypothetical problems, either in the past or anticipated for the future, are acceptable. The problem can be either a "one-shot" decision or recurring. Describe this decision problem.

b. How would you normally make this decision(s) without the aid of DSS? Specifically, what information would you need to gather? With whom would you need to consult? Would you need to make any "back of the envelope" calculations? If so, what would they be? Why do you think that a DSS will be helpful?

c. Use the ROMC approach to sketch a mini-DSS for aiding your decision problem. Without making reference to specific software, discuss possible representations, operations, memory aids, and control mechanisms for such a DSS.

CASE STUDY: An Iterative Decision Support System for Energy Policy Analysis (EPLAN)

Background

The National Audubon Society is involved in an ongoing project to develop an interactive computer system that models the impacts of various public policies on U.S. energy demand. The system (EPLAN, or Energy Plan) uses a decision support system framework that assists the user by managing a large amount of engineering and economic data, performing calculations, permitting the evaluation of different energy-use scenarios, and keeping track of various constraints.

In 1981 the National Audubon Society published its first energy plan based on an energy-demand model that projected the amount of energy needed in various U.S. energy-demand sectors. At that time the process was manual and limited in scope by the volume and complexity of the information involved. The consequence was that only one scenario could have been examined and a number of approximations had to be made; it was clear that computer assistance was needed.

Database

EPLAN has a number of stored data sets for use in displays and calculations. The user can choose from among the sets of stored values and, in some cases, modify the data. The model base contains formulas that calculate yearly values of energy demand for each fuel type in each energy sector. The initial values used in the computations are the actual data for 1980, and those quantities are subsequently updated.

Auxiliary data are stored for use in the calculations as well. For example, projected oil prices are stored for each future year through 2010. Another structure in the database contains data on industrial energy use each year, starting in 1979, recorded by industry type and fuel type. The auxiliary data in the database can be modified during the session so that the user can test different scenarios ("what-if" and goal seeking analyses).

The Audubon model for U.S. energy demand focuses on how and why people use energy and how energy demand can be reduced. The underlying assumption of the model is that reduced energy production and use, especially for nonrenewable resources, is beneficial to wildlife and the environment.

This energy model is used to evaluate present and planned governmental actions that could affect energy consumption. The impacts of development of alternative energy technologies are examined also. The model incorporates target levels of energy efficiencies for a variety of technologies that are consistent with realistic engineering and economic considerations. Policy options are examined in terms of their efficiency in relation to the target levels in various sectors of the economy, and energy use is broken down by the particular fuel types in each sector. At the end, policy recommendations are made by the society.

One of the goals of the computerization effort has been to stimulate the analysis carried out by energy experts who devised the original model and, at the same time, to advance the model's policy analysis capabilities.

Software and Hardware

A Wang VS minicomputer was used, with the Wang VS Basic high-level scientific language. The Wang text editor was found especially useful in developing the EPLAN software.

Issues in Implementation

In implementing the system, first the skeleton of the whole system was set up with a module for the initialization phase for each of the five energy-demand sectors. After testing to verify structural accuracy, subroutines were added to each sector to represent calculations of energy consumption for each of the fuel types. The systematic, top-down testing assured that each phase of the implementation was error-free before the next layer of complexity was added. The rest of the project involved adding the details for each sector, providing constraints and dependencies among competing fuel uses, and creating the many displays.

Implementation enabled programmers to work on modules in parallel, and periodic testing of their enhancements and checks on performance of the whole system allowed manageable growth in complexity without introducing untraceable bugs.

Hints for Successful Implementation

The following DSS features and capabilities were highlighted as being important for creating a successful system like EPLAN:

1. *Adaptive filtering.* The system should enable users to filter information so that only relevant data will be highlighted for a given issue and information overload can be avoided.
2. *System memory.* Information processed at one stage should be available at another stage without having to be reanalyzed.
3. *Processing facilities.* Users should have access to a variety of capabilities including the ability to combine, weigh, alter, and otherwise put information into usable, convenient forms.

CASE STUDY: DSS at LS&B—An Application in a Small Business

Introduction

Lox, Stock & Bagel (LS&B) is a small independent food service company in Champaign, Illinois.* The company operates a restaurant and a bakery. The DSS was developed to support short-term (daily, weekly) planning and control decisions essential to small business operations. This DSS is typical of small businesses, but similar DSS are used for personal support in large organizations.

The Decision Supported

The planning and control model is shown schematically in Figure 7.8. The decisions are structured and semistructured and of the operation control nature. The major objective of the system is to monitor actual performance of labor and material, compare it with the budget, generate variance reports, and perform a standard variance analysis. Management then can reschedule, rebudget, and so forth.

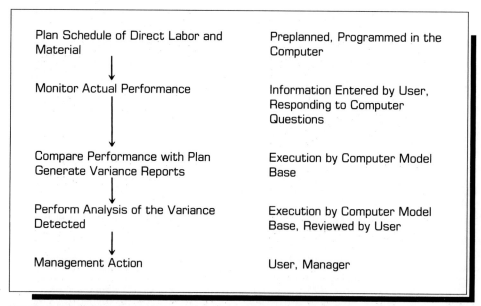

FIGURE 7.8   Planning and Control Model at LS&B.

Components of the DSS

There is no database per se in this small DSS. The necessary data are input whenever needed. When actual quantities are entered, the computer figures theoretical labor needed and compares it with the actual. Built into the formulas are reasonable variances (broken down into periods and/or food types). This arrangement allows the computer to flag exceptions. Daily data are saved in interim storage for weekly summaries. These weekly summaries can be organized in a database if further analysis is desired. The model base includes all necessary formulas.

The dialog is conducted in plain English. It permits changes to be made interactively in the formulas' parameters. An example of a report is given in Table 7.4.

Characteristics of the DSS

1. This DSS is limited to simple periodic reports. However, today with the capabilities of a spreadsheet or a DBMS, the user can quickly generate ad hoc reports as well.
2. This DSS has detection mechanisms on the reasonableness and accuracy of the data entered, which are provided by built-in limits and tests.
3. Help and explanatory material are provided on request (e.g., presentation of the formula used).
4. The system reduced weekly labor variances from about 22 percent to about 6 percent, because managers were able to change schedules quickly and achieve fairly accurate results. In addition, managers improved their forecasting and planning capabilities. Being more accurate on required labor resulted in an improved schedule, which is translated

TABLE 7.4 Direct Labor Variance Analysis (Sample Daily Results Page).

Prod 1	Prod 2	Serv 1	Serv 2	Serv 3	Serv 4	Serv 5
Friday						
Budgeted hours						
18.0	10.0	8.0	55.0	14.0	54.0	14.0
Actual hours						
18.0	10.0	10.0	58.0	20.0	57.0	16.0
Man-hour variance						
0.0	0.0	2.0	3.0	6.0	3.0	2.0
Expected variance						
1.1	0.6	0.5	3.5	0.9	3.4	0.9

	Budgeted	Variance	Actual	Expected variance
Man-hours	173.0	16.0	189.0	11.0
Dollar pool	656.25	62.95	718.20	41.62
Sales	4375.00	277.50	4652.50	200.00

into a savings of over $10,000 a year. This savings easily recouped the initial investment the company made in the DSS.

APPENDIX 7-A: Prototyping

Prototyping refers to a process of building a "quick and dirty" version of information systems. Two kinds of prototyping are recognized: the throwaway and the evolutionary.

The *throwaway* concept is based on traditional prototyping centered around a pilot test program, which was developed to achieve a better understanding of the system performance and user's requirements. Once the pilot test is done, the prototype is discarded and a preliminary design takes place. After that, the final system is completed (see Figure 7-A.1).

The *evolutionary* approach, on the other hand, starts with a minisystem that is refined iteratively, over a long trial period. The process, which is shown in Figure 7-A.1, includes the following steps (per Dickson and Wetherbe [7]):

1. Identify user's information and operating requirements in a "quick and dirty" manner.
2. Develop a working prototype that performs only the most important function (e.g., using a sample database).
3. Test and evaluate (done by user and builder).
4. Redefine information needs and improve the system.

The last two steps are repeated several times. This new concept of prototyping is gaining popularity as an approach to developing computerized systems in general. Actually, "new prototyping" and the iterative DSS development process are very similar to each other. For further details, see Henderson and Ingraham [9].

The Primary Features of Prototyping

There are five distinct features of prototyping.

First, learning is explicitly integrated into the design process. This is normally accomplished by designing systems in an iterative fashion. A prototyped system is built and placed in the hands of the user. The user evaluates the system, determines necessary enhancements, and returns it to the analyst. The analyst updates the prototype and returns it to the users for more "commercial" testing. In other words, the designer expects to err but attempts to learn as much as possible from such errors. This learning aspect of prototyping can be contrasted with the traditional design approach, which is based on a single, sequential iteration of the design life cycle. Recycling or looping back to early stages implies that the initial analysis was incomplete. The key to success in the traditional approach is to do it right the first time. Obviously this greatly reduces the opportunity to apply lessons learned during later stages.

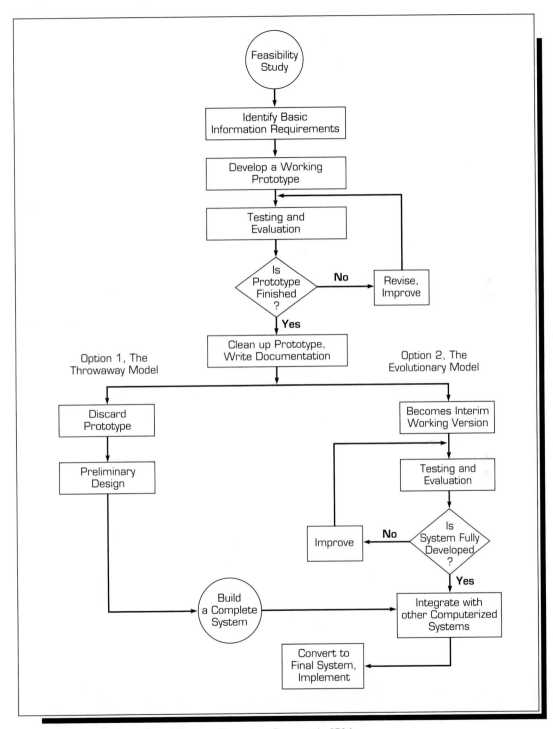

FIGURE 7-A.1   Prototyping. (*Source:* Based on Bernstein [2].)

314 Part 2: Decision Support Systems

Second, a key criterion associated with prototyping is the short intervals between iterations. The feedback must be relatively fast. This criterion results from the required learning process; good and timely feedback is a prerequisite to effective learning.

Third, involvement of users is a very important feature. Prototyping assumes that the user may actively participate in and direct the design. This requirement stems from a need for user expertise in the design effort, and also recognizes that successful implementation will be more easily achieved with active involvement.

Fourth, the initial prototype must be "low cost." It must fall below the minimum threshold of capital outlays requiring special justification. The development of a prototype may be a risky decision, particularly for a DSS. However, because the benefits of a DSS are often intangible, relating to such issues as "improved decision making" or "better understanding," a high initial investment may result in a decision *not* to proceed.

Fifth, prototyping essentially bypasses the life-cycle stage of information requirements definition. Rather, it allows requirements to evolve as experience is gained. This strategy assumes that the requirements can be known only partially at the beginning of the system development, and it attempts to clarify users' needs by actively involving them in a low-cost, fast-feedback development process.

The association between prototyping and DSS is significant. First, many DSS go through the iterative process, which is basically prototyping. Second, prototyping of non-DSS is executed with the same software packages that the DSS is constructed with, including DSS generators and DSS tools like report generators, CRT screen generators, and electronic spreadsheets. As a matter of fact, the "application generator" mentioned earlier is a collection of prototyping tools that enables a full range of systems development activities, and as such it is very similar to a DSS generator.

DSS may take on some of the characteristics of prototyping. As a matter of fact, not all DSS are constructed using the evolutionary approach. Several companies are using the concept of throwaway DSS, that is, the building of a "quick and dirty" DSS in a process similar to that of throwaway prototyping. Instead of refining the DSS after some use, they discard it and build a completely new one. This approach is made economically feasible by the availability of DSS generators.

APPENDIX 7-B: Items in the ROMC Approach*

Representations. Lists, graphs, cross-tabulation, economic curves, scatterplot, icons, pie charts, reports, windows, maps, spreadsheets, organizational charts, and animation.

*Source: Carlson [5].

Operations. Examples of general decision-making operations classified as intelligence, design, and choice:

Intelligence	Design
▪ Gather data.	▪ Gather data.
▪ Identify objectives.	▪ Manipulate data.
▪ Diagnose problem.	▪ Quantify objectives.
▪ Validate data.	▪ Generate reports.
▪ Structure problem.	▪ Generate alternatives.
▪ Plot data, analyze.	▪ Assign risks or values to
▪ Perform windowing.	alternatives.
	▪ Superimpose partitions.

Choice

- ▪ Generate statistics on alternatives.
- ▪ Simulate results of alternatives.
- ▪ Explain alternatives.
- ▪ Choose among alternatives.
- ▪ Explain choice.
- ▪ Rank.
- ▪ Generate and weigh criteria.

Memory Aids. Several types of memory aids can be provided in a DSS to support the use of representations and operations. The following are examples:

- ▪ A database from sources internal and external to the organization
- ▪ Views (aggregations and subsets) of the database
- ▪ Work spaces for displaying the representations and for preserving intermediate results as they are produced by the operations
- ▪ Libraries for saving work space contents for later use
- ▪ Links for remembering data from one work space or library that is needed as a reference when operating on the contents of another work space
- ▪ Triggers to remind a decision maker that certain operations may need to be performed
- ▪ Profiles to store default and status data
- ▪ Directory for quick reference
- ▪ Rolodex card file
- ▪ Note pad.

Control Mechanisms. Examples: menus, function keys for operation selections, repeated procedures, windows, error messages, help comments, exception reporting, tutoring, editing, and devices for correcting errors and making changes.

APPENDIX 7-C: Specific Tactics Within Different Quality-control Approaches Aimed at Controlling the Risks of User-developed DSS

Quality-control Approaches	Specific Tactics	User-developed DSS Risks
■ Analyst reviews and audits	■ Formation of quality assurance teams	■ Incorrect problem specifications ■ Piecemeal and incremental development approach ■ Modeling errors
■ Organizational and management policies	■ Data management policies ■ Hardware/software standards ■ Formal justification policies	■ Threats to data security and integrity ■ Device/software incompatibility ■ Misconceived investment of organizational resources
■ Support and training	■ Organizational consultants	■ Incorrect problem specifications ■ Insufficient search for solution ■ Modeling errors ■ Piecemeal development approach ■ Threats to data integrity and security
	■ Training in end-user computing and DP concepts	■ Incorrect problem specifications ■ Modeling errors ■ Piecemeal development approach ■ Threats to data integrity and security
■ Hardware/software techniques	■ Software for spreadsheet audits ■ Software/hardware for access and monitoring	■ Poor data integrity ■ Calculation errors ■ Poor data security

Source: Alavi [1]. Used with permission.

APPENDIX 7-D: DSS Illustrative Application: Wesleyan University—A DSS for Student Financial Aid

The annual rate of increase in financial aid provided by Wesleyan University was in the 20 to 30 percent range in the late 1970s.* This rate was much faster

---

*Condensed from Hopkins, S. P., et al. "Financial Modeling: Four Success Stories." Adapted with permission from the EDUCOM Bulletin, Fall 1982.

than the university's income increase, and the situation was greatly exacerbated by the reduction in federal grants and student loan programs, as well as by declining enrollment.

The increased competition among universities for the very best students, coupled with the budgetary strains mentioned previously, forced many universities to rethink their policies and procedures regarding financial aid.

Wesleyan University used an aid-blind admission policy during the 1970s. Under this policy, students were admitted without regard to financial need. Financial aid was provided later to all those admitted who requested it. Thus over 40 percent of the students received scholarships, whereas over 50 percent received loans, job assistance, or grants.

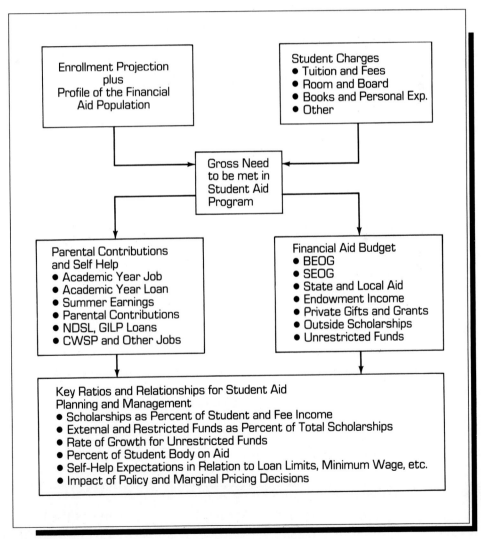

FIGURE 7-D.1   Wesleyan's Student Aid Planning Model.

A five-year budget forecast predicted a potential financial crisis if this policy were to have continued. As a result, a detailed financial aid model was developed using a DSS to assess alternative strategies that could prevent the crisis. The DSS was constructed in 1979 to solve the problem. A DSS generator specifically designed for use in universities, called EFPM, was used.

The financial aid model is shown schematically in Figure 7-D.1.

The model brings together the multitude of policy and planning variables that affect financial aid. The model is particularly useful in computing "what-if" questions relating to the input variables. For example, what if inflation remains high and there is a reduction in federal support? What if self-help expectations bump up against legislated limits in student loans? What is the budgetary impact of admitting more students? What policy changes are required to contain the program within certain limits? The model reaffirmed the projected financial crisis, and Wesleyan's president appointed a faculty/student/administration advisory committee to deal with the situation. The committee used another EFPM-based model—the budgetary model (the two are linked) to examine alternative policies. As a result, budget limits were set on financial aid. The board of trustees adopted the recommendations and the crisis was averted. The model is being continuously used to monitor the financial aid situation.

References and Bibliography

1. Alavi, M. "End-User Developed DSS: Steps Towards Quality Control." *Proceedings: Managers, Micros and Mainframe,* NYU Symposium, New York, May 1985.
2. Bernstein, A. "Shortcut to System Design (Fourth-Generation Prototyping)." *Business Computer System,* June 1985.
3. Blanc, L. A., "An Assessment of DSS Performance," *Information and Management,* Vol. 20, 1991: 137–148.
4. Chrisman, C., and B. Beccue. "Training for Users as a Management Issue," *Jour. of Info. Syst. Mgt.,* Summer 1990.
5. Carlson, E. D. "An Approach for Designing Decision Support Systems." *Data Base,* Winter 1979.
6. Courbon, J. C., J. Grajew, and J. Tolovi, Jr. "Design and Implementation of Decision Support Systems by an Evolution Approach." Unpublished working paper, 1980.
7. Dickson, G. W., and J. C. Wetherbe. *The Management of Information Systems.* New York: McGraw-Hill, 1985.
8. *EDP Analyzer* (now *IS Analyzer*), "Computer-Based Training For End-Users," Vol. 12, No. 12, 1983.
9. Henderson, J.C., and R. S. Ingraham. "Prototyping for DSS: A Critical Appraisal." In *Decision Support Systems,* M. J. Ginzberg et al., eds. New York: North-Holland, 1982.
10. Hogue, J. T., and H. J. Watson. "Current Practices in the Development of Decision Support Systems." *Proceedings, 5th International Conference of Information Systems,* Tucson, AZ, November 1984.

11. Keen, P. G. W. "Adaptive Design for Decision Support Systems." *Data Base*, Vol. 12, Nos. 1 and 2. Fall 1980.

12. Keen, P. G. W., and M. S. Scott-Morton. *Decision Support Systems: An Organizational Perspective*. Reading, MA: Addison-Wesley, 1978.

13. Keen, P. G. W., and R. D. Hackathorn. "Decision Support Systems and Personal Computing." *MIS Quarterly*, Vol. 5, No. 1, March 1981.

14. Lucas, H. C., Jr. *The Analysis, Design and Implementation of Information Systems*, 3rd ed. New York: McGraw-Hill, 1985.

15. Meador, C. L., and R. A. Mezger. "Selecting an End-user Programming Language for DSS Development." *MIS Quarterly*, December 1984.

16. Meador, C. L., et al. "Setting Priorities for DSS Development." *MIS Quarterly*, June 1984.

17. Mittman, B. S., and J. H. Moore. "Senior Management Computer Use: Implications for DSS Design and Goals." Paper presented at DSS-84, Dallas, TX, April 1984.

18. Mockler, R.J. *Computer Software to Support Strategic Management Decision Making*. New York: Macmillan, 1992.

19. Robinson, M., "Measuring the Bottom Line Impact of Decision Support Systems." *Information Executive*, Spring 1991.

20. Rockart, J. F., and L. S. Flannery. "The Management of End-User Computing." *Communications of the ACM 26*, Vol. 10, 1983.

21. Sauter, V. L., and J. L. Schofer. "Evolutionary Development of DSS." *JMIS*, Spring 1988.

22. Shank, M. E., et al. "Critical Success Factor Analysis as a Methodology for MIS Planning." *MIS Quarterly*, June 1985.

23. Sprague, R. H., Jr. "A Framework for the Development of Decision Support Systems. *MIS Quarterly*, December 1980.

24. Sprague, R. H., Jr., and E. D. Carlson. *Building Effective Decision Support Systems*. Englewood Cliffs, NJ: Prentice-Hall, 1982.

25. Taylor, S. P. "Organizational Decision Making and DSS Design." *Systems Development Management*. Pennsauken, NJ: Auerbach Publishers, 1984.

26. Zmud, R. W. *Information Systems in Organizations*. Glenview, IL: Scott, Foresman, 1983.

Part 3

Advanced and Unique DSS

The concepts outlined in Chapters 3–7 are used successfully by millions of individuals worldwide for personal support, or by small fairly homogeneous groups (e.g., salespeople, accountants) for support of certain aspects in the functional organizational areas. However, decision support can be provided in more complex settings, potentially yielding large benefits. This part of the book covers the following topics: First, organizational DSS and some other advanced applications are presented in Chapter 8. The use of computers to support collaborative work, especially when a group is engaged in decision making, is the topic of Chapter 9. Finally, the specialized support given to executives and top managers is described in Chapter 10.

Chapter 8

Organizational DSS and Advanced Topics

In the previous chapters we described the philosophy of DSS, the major components, and the development process. In this chapter the concept of DSS is expanded to include organizational DSS and several types of "intelligent" DSS. The chapter also describes some research issues in DSS and its future directions. The specific topics are:

323

8.1   Case: DSS in the Egyptian Cabinet*

The Egyptian Cabinet is the highest executive body in the country. It is composed of thirty-two ministries, each responsible for one department (e.g., labor, energy, education). The cabinet is headed by the prime minister and, as a body, deals with the country-wide policies and strategic issues. The cabinet also includes four sectored ministerial committees assisted by staff. The cabinet makes extremely important decisions in areas such as national socioeconomic and infrastructure. Most difficult are the decisions regarding the allocation of scarce resources. Depending on the scope, urgency, and criticality of an issue, it is addressed by the entire cabinet or by a committee. Many of the issues are complex and require considerable preparation and analysis. Furthermore, due to conflicting interests, there is considerable disagreement among the ministries.

The cabinet must work with the parliament and with many governmental agencies (the "bureaucracy"). There are many other links between the cabinet and external agencies ranging from universities to international bodies. Information is essential for effective decision making. It makes sense to support decision making in the Egyptian Cabinet with some computer-based information system, but it is difficult to do it. The reason is that many decisions are being made by many people (individually or in groups). The composition of the decision makers is frequently changing. Decisions are made at various locations. Finally, the participants use different methodologies and styles.

The Cabinet Information and Decision Support Center (IDSC). To properly support the information needs of the cabinet, a special center was developed. The IDSC was guided by three strategic objectives:

1. Develop information and support systems for the cabinet.
2. Support the establishment of end-user managed information and decision support centers in the thirty-two ministries.
3. Encourage, support, and initiate IS projects that would accelerate the development of the Egyptian government ministries and agencies.

To achieve these objectives, a tri-level architecture was conceived: at the IDSC level, at the national level, and at the international level. A schematic view of the system is shown in Figure 8.1. Obviously extensive national and international telecommunication support is required for such a system. The center started in 1985 and grew to about 200 employees by 1989. Dozens of specific

---

*This section is based on material from: El Sherif, H., "Managing Institutionalization of Strategic Decision Making for the Egyptian Cabinet," *Interfaces,* Vol. 20, No. 1, 1990, and El Sherif, H., and O. A. El Sawy, "Issue-Based Decision Support Systems for the Egyptian Cabinet." *MIS Quarterly,* Vol. 12, No. 4, December 1988.

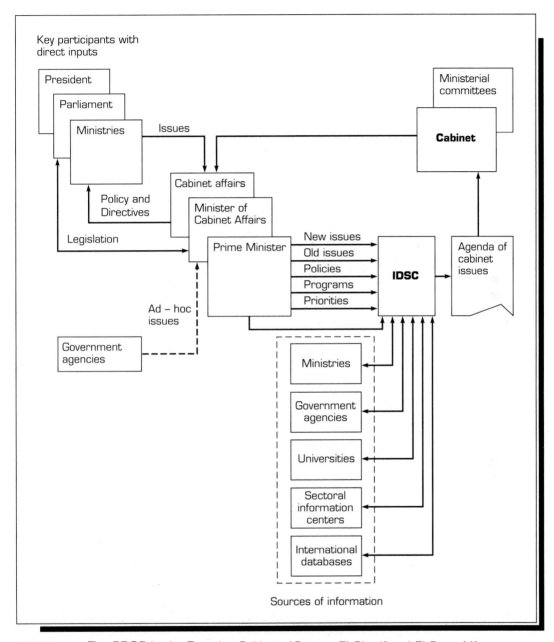

FIGURE 8.1 The ODSS in the Egyptian Cabinet. (*Source:* El Sherif and El Sawy [4]. Reprinted by special permission from the *MIS Quarterly*, Volume 12, Number 4, December 1988. Copyright 1988 by the Society for Information Management and the Management Information Systems Research Center at the University of Minnesota.)

DSS were constructed; several of them were highly interrelated. Examples of specific DSS are:

1. *Customs tariff policy formulation DSS.* This area involved six ministries, so coordination was difficult and diversity of opinions played a major role in any decision. The DSS helped to achieve consistent tariff structure and increased government revenue (yet minimized the burden on low income families).

2. *Debt management DSS.* Egypt relies on foreign debt (about 5000 loans, over $33 billion in the late 1980s). The purpose of the DSS was to manage the debt. For example, to best schedule payments, to decide on appropriate refinancing, and to simulate how the debt is going to look in the future.

Conclusion. The use of DSS has significantly leveraged the strategic decision-making process in Egypt. However, the system that was supported by the DSS was very complex. The system provided for DSS analysis throughout a complex organization, used by several people, at several organizational units. The system is used for both ad hoc and for repetitive decisions. This type of system is an example of organizational DSS (ODSS).

8.2   The Conceptualization of Organizational DSS (ODSS)*

The case just presented shows a system that provides decision support throughout large and complex organizations. The major benefit of the system was that many organization members became familiar with computers, analytical techniques, and DSS. This large-scale DSS was highly integrated with an extensive data management system.

Organizational decision support was first defined in 1981 by Hackathorn and Keen [12], who distinguished between three types of decision support: individual, group, and organization. They maintain that computer-based systems can be developed to provide decision support for each of these levels. They perceived an organization decision support as one that focuses on an organization task or activity involving a sequence of operations and actors (e.g., developing a divisional marketing plan, capital budgeting). Furthermore, they said that each individual's activities must mesh closely with other people's work. The computer support was seen primarily as a vehicle for improving communication and coordination in addition to that of problem solving.

Not much was done with the concept of providing organization support with DSS for the next seven or so years. Then, beginning in 1988, the idea began

---

*This section is based in part on the work of George [11].

to be the focus of work for several different researchers. The rest of this section provides several conceptualizations of ODSS, developed from 1988 to 1992. As these conceptualizations vary, the end of the section represents an attempt to find some common ground in them.

The definitions of ODSS are:

- Watson [33] defined an ODSS as "a combination of computer and communication technology designed to coordinate and disseminate decision-making across functional areas and hierarchical layers in order that decisions are congruent with organizational goals and management's shared interpretation of the competitive environment."
- Carter, et al., [2] defined ODSS as: "a DSS that is used by individuals or groups at several workstations in more than one organizational unit who make varied (interrelated but autonomous) decisions using a common set of tools."
- Swanson (see Swanson and Zmud [31]) call ODSS a distributed decision support system (DDSS). He stated that an organizational DSS should not be thought of as a manager's DSS. Rather it should be viewed as supporting the organization's division of labor in decision making. He defined a DDSS as a DSS that supports distributed decision making.
- King and Star [17] provide a different perspective. They believe that the concept of ODSS in principle is simple: apply the technologies of computers and communications to enhance the organizational decision-making process. In principle, ODSS takes the vision of technological support for group processes to the higher level of organizations, in much the same way that group DSS (Chapter 9) extended the vision of technological support for individual action to group process.

Fedorowicz and Konsynski [10] distinguish four types of ODSS:

- *Type 0: Structure Enforcing ODSS.* Any basic computer-based support system that reenforces traditional norms.
- *Type 1: Structure Preserving ODSS.* Information technology (IT) used at the organizational level for organization-wide purposes. An example is an EIS used to analyze organization-wide data.
- *Type 2: Structure Independent ODSS.* IT that spans the organization, used by individuals outside of functional or hierarchical boundaries.
- *Type 3: Structure Transforming ODSS.* Any IT that changes existing or enables new organizational structures.

Based on the above definitions, George [11] found the following common characteristics of ODSS:

- The focus of an ODSS is an organizational task or activity or a decision that affects several organization units or corporate problems.
- An ODSS cuts across organizational functions or hierarchical layers.
- An ODSS almost necessarily involves computer-based technologies, and may also involve communication technologies.

8.3   The Architecture of ODSS*

In the previous section we examined several definitions of ODSS. Obviously, each different type of ODSS may have a different structure.

A general structure for ODSS has been proposed by Carter, et al. [2]. This structure is shown in Figure 8.2. Notice that there are two major differences between this structure and the structure described in Chapter 3, for the traditional DSS. First, a case management component is attached. Second, the DSS is accessible to several users, in several locations, via LANs and Wide Area Networks.

Case Management (per Carter, et al. [2])

A single user of an ODSS will often run a model many times, each time with inputs that are only slightly different from the previous run. He will generally create large amounts of output and many computer files. In the past, the effort to create input data files, to keep track of runs made, and to catalog output data files overwhelmed the user. As a result, his use of the DSS gradually decreased. It has recently been recognized by builders of DSSs that the user needs help in all of these areas. So, just as DBMSs were developed to manage large databases and MBMSs are being developed to manage systems containing large numbers of models, case management systems (CMSs) are being developed to help the user who wants to make large numbers of runs of similar decisions.

We define a case to be a specific run of a computer model. A case includes a specification of all the input data used in the run (names of data files, parameters supplied by the user), the names of the output files generated, and (optionally) a brief description of the run.

A CMS performs three main functions:

1. It acts as an accounting system for the runs made by a user, facilitating the creation, delegation, copying, documenting, and cataloging of model cases.
2. It provides the user with simple ways to modify the input data for a given model from one run to the next (by specifying changes only), and keeps track of the differences. As a result, it can also report on the differences in inputs between two runs.
3. It facilitates the comparison of outputs from various runs of the model.

A good CMS can provide the user with clarity and control of what he is doing. An example of a CMS is found in a DSS package called MathPro from

---

*Note: Sections 8.3-8.6 are based on the work of Walker [32] (© 1990 IEEE) and Carter et al. [2] (Reprinted by permission of the publisher.).

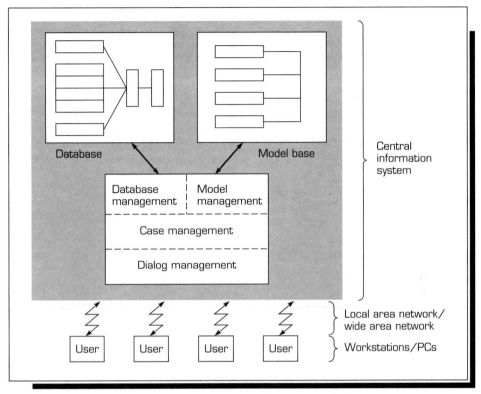

FIGURE 8.2 Components of an Organizational Decision Support System. (*Source:* Carter et al. [2]. Reprinted by permission of the publisher.)

MathPro, Inc. (Washington, DC). In MathPro, whose objective is to solve mathematical programming problems. The case manager establishes a hierarchical (tree-structured) case bank for each distinct model/user combination. In this hierarchy, each case is subordinate to a parent case, logically "inherits" all elements from its parents, and physically contains only elements that differ from those of its parent. Each case is named, time stamped, and documented.

Relationship to Group DSS and Executive Information Systems

Because of its complexity, ODSS may be connected with a GDSS and/or with an EIS. For example, the Egyptian Cabinet system includes an EIS. In many other cases, a GDSS can be used to prioritize items and resolve conflicts. If this is the case, the structure of ODSS can be related to (or even centered around) GDSS. Figure 8.3 shows conceptual design of such architecture. The relationship between ODSS and EIS is discussed by Philippakis and Green [25].

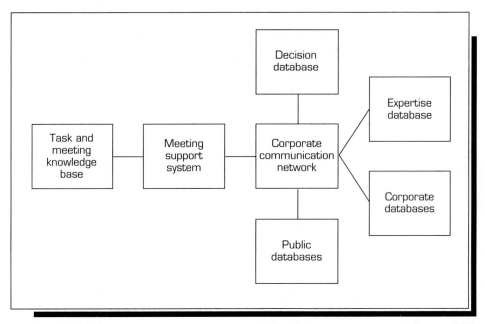

FIGURE 8.3 An ODSS Structured around GDSS. (*Source:* Watson [33] © 1990 IEEE.)

8.4   **Constructing an ODSS**

The development of an ODSS requires a formal, structured approach, since we are talking about a large, complex, system programming effort. But this does not mean that it should be developed using a traditional system development life cycle (SDLC) approach.

The approach for building an ODSS recommended by Carter, et al. [2] is a combination of the SDLC and iterative approaches. It divides the process into four phases. The first two phases of the process are structured, and provide a framework for the development of the system. The third phase is iterative, involving prototyping for the development of the system's modules. And the fourth phase uses both approaches. These phases are:

1. *Getting started.* This is the organizational phase. It includes activities such as:
   - *Needs assessment.* What is wrong with the existing system and what would it take to solve it? What would be the objectives and goals of the ODSS? Does building an ODSS for these purposes make sense?
   - *Getting management support.* One must sell the idea to top management, and obtain a commitment (and resources) to build the system.
   - *Getting organized.* This involves setting up a steering committee and identifying the members of the project team.

- *Getting a plan of action.* This involves laying out the plan for the development process. What steps must be carried out? What specific problems would the ODSS address? In what order should the problems be addressed? How will team members communicate with each other? How will work get documented? How will decisions get made?

2. *Developing the conceptual design.* This is the most important phase in developing an ODSS, and it is not iterated. This phase produces a blueprint for the system, which serves to guide subsequent decisions made by the system's builders.

3. *Developing the system.* This phase includes two types of activities:
   - *Designing the physical system.* This activity includes choosing the DSS generator and other software, choosing the hardware, and designing the database.
   - *Developing the system's models and database.* Models are usually an important factor in an ODSS.

4. *Implementing and maintaining the system.* This phase includes:
   - Installing the physical system.
   - Programming and updating the system's modules. (For clarity, the computer programs are referred to as modules and their mathematical specifications as models.)
   - Creating and updating the database.
   - Documenting the modules and database.
   - Training users.

8.5 The Enlisted Force Management System (EFMS)

One of the best documented ODSS is the United States Air Force Enlisted Management System (EFMS).

The EFMS is a computer-based system whose purpose is to improve the effectiveness and efficiency of the efforts of Air Force staff members engaged in managing the enlisted force in carrying out their decision-making and information-processing responsibilities. The objective in managing the enlisted force is to provide a group of airmen that is best able to support the missions and operational programs that the Air Force must execute. This is an iterative, continuous task, for the Air Force's needs and resources change in response to Congressional, Presidential, and Department of Defense decisions, decisions by the Air Force, and exogenous labor market forces. The task is becoming increasingly difficult as the technology of weapons systems becomes more sophisticated and as budget pressures force the Air Force to make more effective use of its resources.

The EFMS is designed to support many of the functions related to the enlisted force that are carried out by three different units (PRM, DPX, and DPP). There are data exchanges between the EFMS and the computer systems used by several Air Force units that permit the EFMS to obtain inputs from these systems and to supply information to them.

Management of the enlisted force means making decisions about force structure, promotion policies, and the procurement, assignment, training, compensation, separation, and retirement of personnel. These functions (and their support activities) are spread among five major, somewhat independent organizational units, led by four different two-star generals. The five organizations reside in three geographically dispersed locations: three are in the Pentagon; one is at Bolling Air Force Base, about 20 miles away; and one is at Randolph Air Force Base in San Antonio, Texas. The EFMS was designed and developed jointly by a team of Air Force personnel and analysts from the RAND Corporation. The project (called the Enlisted Force Management Project, or EFMP) was begun in 1981. Implementation began in 1986. By 1990, the critical components of EFMS were in place and had been validated against 1990 data. Building the EFMS absorbed more than 125 person-years. As of the end of 1991 there were 21 person-years allocated to the development, operation, and maintenance of the system.

The Elements of EFMS. The major elements of EFMS are shown in Figure 8.4.

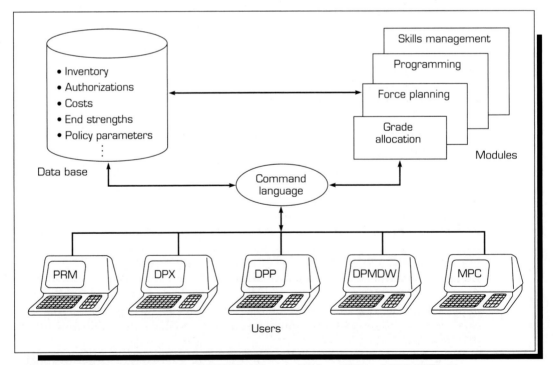

FIGURE 8.4 Major Elements of the EFMS. (*Source:* Walker [31] © 1990 IEEE. Note: PRM = Manpower Directorate; DPX = Personnel Planning Unit; DPP = Directorate Personnel Program; DPMDW = Systems Management Office; MPC = Mailing Personnel Center.)

Model Base. The system includes four major sets of models. The sets are:

- Authorization projection
- Grade allocation
- Aggregate planning, programming, and oversight
- Skills management.

The models in the EFMS can be divided into two categories: screening and impact assessment. Screening models are generally designed for rapid comparison of many alternative plans or programs using summary or approximate measures of performance. Impact assessment models are used when more detailed or more accurate calculations are required.

Hardware and Databases. Most of the above models and their databases reside on the EFMS's mainframe computer and are programmed in the system's DSS generator language EXPRESS. Users at microcomputer workstations have access to these models and their databases, but most of them are run on the mainframe. That is, a client/server architecture is useful. Output reports are displayed at the user's workstation. The databases are centrally updated and maintained by the Systems Management Office at Bolling Air Force Base.

Most of the screening models are microcomputer models that are installed on the microcomputer workstations of their users. They do not reside on the mainframe computer and are not programmed in EXPRESS.

The databases for the models include three types of data:

- Output from another EFMS model
- Data supplied by other branches of the Air Force (e.g., information on the current airman inventory comes from the Air Force Military Personnel Center (AFMPC)
- External data (e.g., projected unemployment rates).

End-users, in geographically dispersed sites, utilize microcomputer workstations. Through EXPRESS each user interacts with both the integrated database and the interlinked system of modules, both of which reside mainly on a mainframe computer. The system's detailed hardware configuration is shown in Figure 8.5.

8.6 Issues in ODSS

From the example, definitions, and cases presented so far it is possible to infer that ODSS is indeed a unique system. The major differences between ODSS and regular DSS are summarized in Table 8.1.

Some issues of interest in ODSS are:

1. *Steering Committee.* A committee of the top- and middle-level managers from all organizational units that are related to the ODSS must provide direction and control.

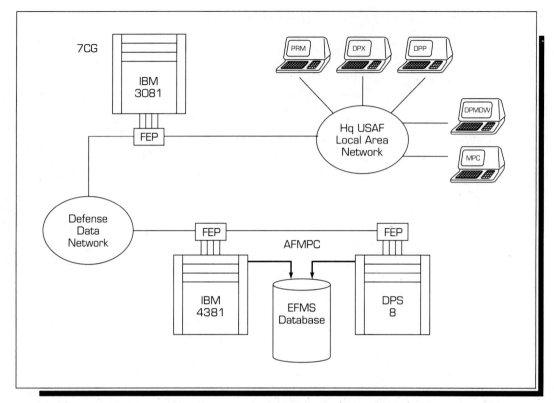

FIGURE 8.5 Enlisted Force Management System Architecture. (*Source:* Walker [31]
© 1990 IEEE. Note: FEP is a technical name for a hardware link connector.)

2. *Project Team.* The builders work as a team. Members can be from several
   units, including outsiders. Although the team is composed on an ad hoc
   basis, it also includes members from a permanent ODSS unit called the
   System Management Office (SMO).
3. *The SMO.* This technically oriented unit participates in the development
   of the ODSS from its inception. The SMO plays a major role in the development and implementation. Once a certain module of the ODSS is
   implemented, the attention of the SMO shifts to maintenance and updating.
4. *Conceptual Design.* Once it has been decided that an ODSS will be built,
   but before any work is done on specifying hardware, software, or
   models, it is necessary to produce a conceptual design. The design must
   include at least the following elements:
   - Design principles, which will guide all decisions for the remainder of
     the project
   - Functions to be supported

TABLE 8.1 Differences between Regular DSS and ODSS.

	Regular (Traditional) DSS	**ODSS**
Purpose	Improve performance of an individual decision maker.	Improve the efficiency and effectiveness of organizational decision making.
Policies	Must "sell" the system to an individual.	The system must be sold to the organization.
Construction	Usually an informal process (except in large DSS).	Significant undertaking; requires structured approach.
Focus	On the individual and to his (her) objectives.	Focus on the *functions* to be performed and not on the individual users.
Support	Support is usually provided to one individual, or one unit, in one location.	Disseminate and coordinate decision making across functional areas, hierarchical levels, and geographically dispersed units.

Source: Based on Walker [32] (© 1990 IEEE).

- Models to provide the support, how the models would work (including inputs and outputs), and the relationship among the models (e.g., a flowchart showing interconnections)
- Data requirements (generic data; no file names or database layouts)
- Hardware and software considerations (hardware configuration and software capabilities, not specific equipment and languages)
- Approach to implementation (structure of SMO, priorities, prototyping strategy, documentation rules, responsibilities of participating organizational units).

Modelbase. The desire for flexibility, adaptability and easy maintainability suggested the use of an interlinked system of many small models, each designed for one specific purpose. A module (or a model) can be used by itself to study the impacts of a proposed decision on a specific portion of the organization, or interactively with other modules to study wider impacts.

Database. The desire for coordination and integration leads the specification of a common, consistent, easily accessed, centralized database for the system. The database provides input to the modules, retains output from the modules for management reports, and is available for direct inquiry by users. Information generated by one module would be automatically (and instantaneously) available to other modules. Data both internal and external to the organization would be included. (For example, the EFMS database includes information on the inventory of airmen and data on the U.S. economy.) The system need not have a single, unified, integrated database. In the EFMS, many modules have their own database. But database administration should be centralized.

User Interface. The primary implication of the design principles for the user interface is that the system has a common interface for all of its elements; that is, that dialogs be managed in a uniform fashion regardless of the particular module being run. Of course, each module would have different specific input and output screens. But each would enable the user to do the same types of things in the same ways.

Since the users of ODSS are not programmers, the interface should be menu driven, easy to learn, and easy to use. The user (without the help of a programmer) should be able to

- request information from the database
- make temporary or permanent changes to data in the database
- specify parameters and input data for a module
- run a module
- tailor output reports (scope, aggregation, time periods).

Data. An ODSS has much more demanding needs for data than does a regular DSS, and more attention has to be given to this aspect of the system. In general, there are four different types of data that are used during the course of building an ODSS. These are data:

- To understand or define the problem situation being addressed
- To estimate the models
- To validate the models
- To run the models (input data)

Note: The database construction and data "cleaning" consumed about 25 to 30 percent of all time invested in this project. This is a very important and usually neglected issue in ODSS.

8.7 Intelligent DSS (Active, Symbiotic)

In presenting the structure of DSS we alluded to the possible existence of an intelligent component in the DSS. There are several ways in which we can make a DSS smarter. Some of the specific structures are discussed in Chapter 18 on integration. Intelligent components can be used for many purposes. In the not-so-distant future we will see many DSS with intelligent components. Intelligent components will be economically feasible for generic process tasks (e.g., problem formulation), which are transportable across different DSS. Intelligent components will also be economically feasible for repetitive decisions made by the same DSS. The intelligent agent will probably be embedded in future DSS. Some examples of DSS structures involving intelligent agents follow.

Active (Symbiotic) DSS. Regular DSS plays a passive role in a human-machine interaction. The DSS will execute computations, will present data in a tabular form, and will respond to many commands. But it will not play the role of an intelligent assistant to the decision maker. This restricts the use of DSS to well-defined and unambiguous tasks.

However, certain tasks in problem solving are ambiguous and complex. In such a case we need a DSS that can play an *active* role. For example, the DSS should be able to take the initiative without getting specific orders. This type of DSS is called **active or symbiotic DSS** (Manheim [21]).

According to Mili [22], an active DSS is needed for the following tasks:

1. *Understanding the domain* (terminology, parameters, interactions). Here the active DSS could provide explanations.
2. *Problem formulation*. Here an active DSS can help in determining assumptions, abstract reality, deciding what is relevant, etc.
3. *Relating a problem to solver*. Here the active DSS can assist with proper problem-solver interaction, advise what procedures to use, what solution techniques to follow, etc.
4. *Interpreting results*.
5. *Explaining results and decisions*.

For executing these tasks one needs an intelligent component(s) in the DSS. In Chapter 12 we describe how expert systems can provide such intelligent components.

Most intelligent DSS include only one agent. For example, several expert systems were designed for problem formulation, and many DSS have an expert system component that conducts interpretation of results. The intelligence is provided by a knowledge base and an inference mechanism (Chapter 12).

Most important is the human-DSS interaction. To play an active role, the interaction between the user and the machine must be close and frequently in real time. The DSS must (1) have a perception of the user's need; (2) maintain an image of the user and of the user's problem-solving processes; and (3) have a mechanism for finding and scheduling actions.

Problem Management. Most DSS are centered around the design and choice phases of decision making. The intelligence phase, which includes problem finding, problem representation, and information surveillance, is neglected by most DSS. Furthermore, several activities in the design and choice, such as model management, are being executed manually. To make DSS more effective, it is necessary to automate as many tasks as possible. Weber and Konsynski [33] suggested dividing the decision-making process into five steps and proposed architecture support to the functional requirements of these steps (see Table 8.2).

TABLE 8.2   Problem Management, Functional Requirements, and Architectural Support

Problem Management Stage	Functional Requirements	Architectural Support
Problem finding	Perceptual filters, knowledge management	Flexible knowledge management; intelligent filters
Problem representation	Model and pattern management, suspension of judgment	Flexible dialog and knowledge management; reason maintenance system; pattern search strategies
Information surveillance	Knowledge and model management	Demons; intelligent lenses; scanners; evaluators; interpreters
Solution generation	Knowledge management, idea generation	Idea and solution model management; heuristic and analytic drivers
Solution evaluation	Meta-level dialog and knowledge management	Flexible knowledge management; analytic and symbolic processors

Source: Weber and Konsynski [34].

They termed their approach as **problem management.** As can be seen, the suggested support involves several intelligent agents.

8.8   Self-Evolving DSS

A **self-evolving DSS** is an approach to DSS design (see Liang and Jones [20]) whose basic premise is that a DSS should be aware of how it is being used, and then it should automatically adapt to the evolution of its users. This capability is achieved by adding an extra component: an intelligent self-evolving mechanism. The purpose of this approach is to build a DSS, in a special manner, such that the specific DSS will be able to adapt to the evolution of user requirements automatically. To do so one needs capabilities such as:

- A dynamic menu that provides different hierarchies to fulfill different user requirements
- A dynamic user interface that provides different output representation for different users
- An intelligent model base management system that can select appropriate models to satisfy different preferences.

The purposes of a self-evolving DSS are: (1) increasing the flexibility of the DSS; (2) reducing the effort required to use the system (make it more user friendly); (3) enhancing control over the organization's information resource; and (4) encouraging system sharing.

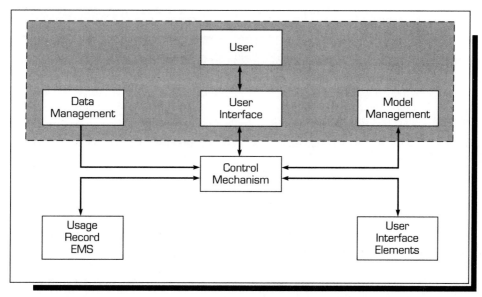

FIGURE 8.6 The Architecture of a Self-evolving DSS. The shaded area surrounded by broken lines is a basic DSS. (*Source:* Adapted from Liang and Jones [20].)

Structure. The structure of such DSS is shown in Figure 8.6. The major components are:

1. *Data management, model management, and a user interface,* which are the basic components of any DSS.
2. *A usage record* that contains system usage data pertinent to the evolution of the system and its management (EMS = Evolution Management System).
3. *The user interface elements* are those elements that are needed for creating a very user-friendly interface.
4. *The central control mechanism* coordinates all the operations of the DSS. This is an intelligent control that contains a knowledge base.

The control mechanism collects the user's usage data and stores them in the usage record base. Then the control mechanism analyzes these data and as a result a new version of the DSS is created. This process is repetitive and will continue as long as necessary. The control can work on each component of the DSS independently. That is, it can provide an intelligent interface, intelligent model management, and intelligent data management. Finally, the system is an online real time system.

8.9   Idea Generation and Creativity*

Many decision theory models assume that the alternative courses of action are known to the decision makers or are very easy to generate. Although this assumption is probably correct in many structured decisions, there are many semi-structured and unstructured situations for which the alternative courses of action are not given. DSS deals with such situations and, therefore, it is frequently necessary to generate ideas that are processed and evaluated by the DSS. To generate good ideas people need to be creative. (See Young [35].)

In the past it was believed that an individual's creative ability stemmed primarily from personality traits such as inventiveness, independence, individuality, enthusiasm, and flexibility. However, several studies have indicated that individual creativity can be learned and improved and is not as strong a function of individual traits as once believed. This has led innovative companies to recognize that the key to fostering creativity may not necessarily come from genius as much as from the development of an idea-nurturing work environment. Idea generation methods and techniques are consequently being developed, to be used by either individuals or in groups. Many of these approaches focus on listing attributes, reviewing lists, and helping to realize relationships linked to the problem at hand. Techniques for evaluation and choice are available that use weighing and scoring alternatives. Implementation techniques assist in the development of an action plan and strategies.

Manual methods of **idea generation** (such as **brainstorming**) can be very successful in some settings. However, there are circumstances where such an approach is either not economically feasible or not possible. For example, manual methods will not work or will not be effective in the following situations:

1. There is a single decision maker.
2. There is a poor facilitator (or there is no facilitator).
3. There is not time to conduct a proper idea generation session.
4. It is too expensive to conduct an idea generation session.
5. The subject is too sensitive for a face-to-face idea generation session.
6. There are not enough participants, the mix of the participants is not optimal, or there is no climate for idea generation.

In such cases it makes sense to electronically induce idea generation (**electronic brainstorming**).

Brainstorming Software. Idea generation software is designed to help stimulate a single user or group with new ideas, options, and choices. It is an electronic brainstorming tool based on the principle of synergy (and/or association). The user does all the work, but the software encourages and pushes just like a

---

*Much of this section was written by Suzanne Schoij, an MBA student at California State University at Long Beach.

personal trainer. Although idea generation software is still relatively new, there are several packages on the market. The prices range from $100 to $600 per package, making it affordable for almost any business today. A representative sample of the software is provided in Table 8.3.

The key feature in idea-generating software is the bombardment of the user with many ideas. This is critical because it helps the user move away from an analytical mode and into a creative mode. Psychological research indicates that people tend to "anchor" their thoughts early in their problem solving endeavors, using their first ideas as springboards for others. The drawback is that subsequent ideas may not be significantly new but simply variations of the original idea. Because brainstorming software is free from human subjectivity, it can help to broaden the thinking platform to encourage truly unique ideas to emerge. For the relationship between software and creativity see Elam and Mead [6].

Various approaches are used by the idea-generating software to increase the flow of ideas to the user. One package (IdeaFisher) is unique in that it has an associative lexicon of the English language that cross-references words and phrases. These associative links make it easy for the user to be fed words related on some level to a given theme based on analogies and metaphors.

These nonlinear associations can be absurd, but absurdity can often trigger new and useful ideas. Personal associations may also be added to the database to broaden its creative application base.

TABLE 8.3 Creativity Software Tools

Product	Vendor
Brainstorm	Mustang Software, Inc.
Brainstormer	Soft Path Systems
Calliope	Innovision
Circles of Creativity	New Product Development Corp.
Consultant	ODS, Inc.
Creative Whack Pack	Creative Think
Genesis	Macintosh
IdeaFisher	Fisher Idea Systems, Inc.
Idea Tree	Mountain House Publishing, Inc.
Inspiration	Ceres Software
MacFlow	Mainstay
Meta Design	Meta Software
Mind Link	Mindlink Software
Pocket Innovator	Creative Learning International
The Idea Generator	Experience in Software, Inc.
Think Tank	Living Videotext
TopDown	Kaetron Software

Most brainstorming software packages use questions to prompt the user into taking new, unexplored directions of thought patterns (see Box 8.1). This is especially useful to help users break out of cyclical thinking patterns or when users have mental blocks or are victims of procrastination. One software package uses a 64-card deck that provides techniques to "whack" the user out of habitual thought patterns. Another program designed to unblock writers prompts the user to write for a timed interval. If the user stops before the interval is over, the program prompts him to keep writing. The feature of prompting the user for input via a questioning session makes the tool very interactive, which can take the frustration out of staring at a blank page and makes the user feel as though he has an ally in his quest for a solution.

Box 8.1: IdeaFisher Uses Associations

Using its large database, the program generates lists of related words (or phrases) related to a topic. Many of these words make little sense (like in a regular brainstorming). The participant(s) can then eliminate them. Any selected word can be a subject to further association by the program. The figure below shows a partial list of words generated once the word "Native American" was selected by the user.

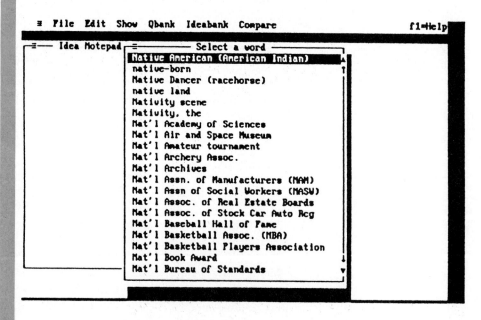

(*Source:* Courtesy of Fisher Idea Systems, Inc.)

Because brainstorming software is self-paced, it facilitates the unique creative style and pace of its user. Most packages allow for random thoughts to be recorded automatically and are organized into flowcharts. This feature frees the user from worrying about cataloging his ideas, leaving him undisturbed and more focused in the creative mode.

Many idea-generating software packages make it easier to visualize the options and make decisions by allowing the user to organize thoughts and ideas into flowcharts. "Idea trees" can help the user keep track of his train of thought and can assist him in pruning his ideas.

The benefits from creativity enhancement afforded by idea-generating software are numerous. The competitive advantage of the tool is realized across all industry spectrums because of the many new ideas and approaches that result from its use. This means greater product differentiation. It also acts as a catalyst to generate alternative solutions to help operations run more efficiently. When fresh ideas are infused into the operation and in dealing with clients, improved sales effectiveness will result.

8.10 DSS Research Directions

A group of leading DSS researchers and practitioners have defined a vision for DSS, and delineated a set of research questions.* The following points are based on their research:

1. Currently DSS are passively responding to "what-if" questions when posed. But as discussed earlier, the DSS/ES combination can add a proactive flavor. More active tools can encourage deeper thinking about problem situations.
2. Today's DSS are not creative, but future DSS should be, providing new ways of defining models, structuring problems, managing ambiguity and complexity, and solving new classes of decisions in new contexts of decision making. ES can make a major contribution in this direction.
3. DSS has been decision-centered but not decision-paced. Future DSS should also deal with the reasons for selecting particular decision classes for support.
4. Management science, the DSS model source, should play a much larger DSS role by improving the thought quality in decision making. Similar contributions should be forthcoming from cognitive psychology, behavioral theory, information economics, computer science, and political science.

*Source: J. J. Elam, J. C. Henderson, P. G. W. Keen, and B. Konsynski, *A Vision for Decision Support Systems*, Special Report, University of Texas at Austin, 1986.

5. The latest advances in computer technology, in particular telecommunications, client/server architecture, knowledge-based systems, and advanced data management tools, should be used to build improved DSS.

6. These improved DSS should deal with the more unstructured problems, such as those that impact overall organizational efficiency and effectiveness. Neural computing can be added to deal with ambiguities.

7. The DSS of the future must be able to create alternative courses of action on its own, in addition to judging those alternatives supplied by the decision maker.

8. DSS research must take a much longer-range perspective, dealing with organization effectiveness and strategic planning. This new perspective will be supported by the addition of creativity and innovation capabilities, resulting in a DSS that is proactive in creating change rather than just reactive.

9. Research should be conducted on interactions between individuals and among groups. In particular, social and ethical problems should be addressed.

10. The human component of DSS should be examined in terms of the impact of DSS on learning.

11. The integration of DSS with ES and with other CBIS and different computer technologies (e.g., telecommunications) will be a major research area.

12. The model management concept should be expanded, both theoretically and in software development. Again, ES can make a valuable contribution in such areas as model selection by providing the judgmental elements needed in model construction. (See Kandt [14].)

13. DSS theory should be enhanced. Theories must be developed on topics such as decision quality measurement, learning, and effectiveness.

14. Theories must also be developed for the areas of organizational decision making and group decision making.

15. DSS applications could be enhanced by the inclusion of values, ethics, and aesthetics. But the problem is how to do it. This will require a broader range of variables, which are difficult to measure or even to define.

16. Human-machine interfaces and their impacts on creativity and learning should be a major thrust of DSS research.

17. Exploration is needed to find the appropriate architectures that enable the decision maker to use ES to improve decision-making capabilities.

18. The organizational impacts of MSS could be significant. Considerable research should be conducted in this area.

Extensive research on DSS has been done on many of these issues (e.g., see summaries of research in [1] and [5]). One way to summarize the research effort was suggested by Evans and Riha [9]. The basic idea is outlined in Figure 8.7. Five categories of variables are identified: Environment, task, user behavior (and characteristics) (dependent variables), and quality of decisions made (indepen-

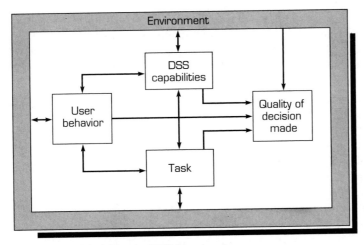

FIGURE 8.7   Variables in DSS Research.

dent variable). The relationship among these variables can be explored. For example, top management support is considered an environmental variable. One may check its impact on either another independent variable (e.g., "user behavior"), or on the dependent variable (quality of decision made).

8.11   The DSS of the Future

The intersection of the continued progress in DSS and the developments cited earlier resulted in some important trends in DSS. The following six short-term DSS trends are forecast by Sprague and McNurlin [28]:

1. Personal computer-based DSS will continue to grow mainly for personal support. Integrated micropackages containing spreadsheets will take on more and more functions, eventually encompassing some of the functions previously performed by DSS generators. Newer packages for "creativity support" will become more popular as extensions of analysis and decision making.
2. For institutional DSS that support sequential and interdependent decision making, the trend is toward distributed DSS—close linkages between mainframe DSS languages and generators and the PC-based facilities. Vendors of both mainframe and PC products are now offering DSS generator versions that run on, and link with, each other.
3. For pooled interdependent decision support, group DSS will become much more prevalent in the next few years. The growing availability of local area networks and group communication services like electronic mail will make this type of DSS increasingly available.

4. Decision support system products will begin to incorporate, and eventually include, the tools and techniques of artificial intelligence work. Many of the self-contained, stand-alone products in AI will prove to be like the stand-alone statistical and management science models of a decade ago—they will need to be embedded in a "delivery system" that facilitates their use. DSS will provide the system for the assimilation of ES knowledge representation, natural language query, voice and pattern recognition, and so on. The result will be "intelligent DSS" that can "suggest," "learn," and "understand" in dealing with managerial tasks and problems. The first area of such integration is adding natural language processors as a front-end to database management systems and to DSS generators. See Kandt [14] for discussion.

5. DSS groups will become less like special project "commando teams" and more a part of the support team for a variety of other end-user support, perhaps as a part of an information center.

6. Cutting across all the trends previously given is the continued development of user-friendly capabilities. This, more than any other feature, is what put DSS on the map and promises to put "a computer on every manager's desk." The development of dialog support hardware, such as light pens, mouse devices, touch screens, and high-resolution graphics, will be further advanced by speech recognition and voice synthesis. Dialog support software such as menus, windows, and "help" functions will also continue to advance. The "virtual desktop" dialog pioneered by the Xerox Star, and currently used by both Apple's Macintosh computers and IBMs and compatibles, embodies many user-friendly features and has set the pace for other personal computers. Users appreciate the ability to quickly move the cursor (via a "mouse"), call up a menu, select an item on the menu, and obtain the results—all in two to three seconds. Selecting spreadsheet commands, storing files, initiating data communications—all can be handled in this manner. Features like these will help support the growing use of DSS by both new and experienced users. For further discussion see Er [8] and Keen [16].

Chapter Highlights

- Organizational DSS deals with decision making across functional areas and hierarchical organizational layers.
- ODSS is used by individuals and groups and it operates in a distributed environment.
- ODSS deals with organizational tasks.
- ODSS for similar, repetitive situations involves a case management component.
- ODSS is frequently connected to EIS and/or GDSS.

- Because of its complexity, ODSS is built using both traditional SDLC and prototyping.
- The four major phases of ODSS are: getting started (organized), conceptual design, system development, and system implementation and maintenance.
- ODSS requires attention from the end-users' IS steering committee.
- Data and databases are critical to the success of ODSS.
- ODSS usually use several models.
- There are several types of intelligent DSS.
- An intelligent DSS must play an active role to deal with ambiguous and complex problem-solving tasks.
- Intelligence is added to DSS by embedding knowledge bases in DSS software.
- Intelligence is especially needed in problem management (including model management).
- Active, symbiotic, and self-evolving DSS are different configurations of intelligent DSS.
- Creativity for idea generation is an important activity in decision making.
- Idea generation can be enhanced by electronic software.
- Electronic brainstorming is one way of supporting idea generation.
- Electronic software uses associations, identification of patterns, and other well-known techniques to support idea generation.
- The three major areas in DSS are: user behavior, nature of the task, and the DSS capabilities as impacting the quality of decisions made.

Key Words

active DSS	idea generation	self-evolving DSS
brainstorming	intelligent DSS	steering committee
case management	organizational DSS	symbiotic DSS
electronic	problem management	
brainstorming		

Questions for Review

1. Define ODSS (at least two definitions).
2. Define "case management" in ODSS.
3. List the major components (element) in a ODSS.
4. List the four phases used in constructing ODSS.
5. Define self-evolving DSS.
6. Define an intelligent DSS.
7. Define symbiotic DSS.
8. Define idea generation.
9. Define brainstorming.

Question for Discussion

1. Discuss the differences between ODSS and DSS.
2. Why are there several definitions of ODSS?
3. Explain how ODSS can interface with an EIS (give an example).
4. Review the construction phases suggested by Carter et al. How do they relate to the phases of system development life cycle (SDLS) discussed in Chapter 7?
5. Why is it necessary to have a steering committee in ODSS?
6. How does the model base of ODSS differ from a model base of a regular DSS?
7. Networking plays a major role in ODSS. Explain why.
8. Describe the importance of conceptual design in ODSS.
9. It is said that a self-evolving DSS is an intelligent DSS. Explain why.
10. Explain how a self-evolving DSS works and how it relates to the regular DSS components.
11. What is common in the many ODSS definitions?
12. Describe the role of problem management in DSS. How is it related to model management?
13. Describe how computer software can enhance creativity and idea generation.

References and Bibliography

1. Benbasat, I., and B. R. Nault. "An Evolution of Empirical Research in Management Support Systems." *Decision Support Systems,* August 1990.
2. Carter, G. M., et al. *Building Organizational Decision Support Systems.* Cambridge, MA: Academic Press, 1992.
3. Chen, Y. S. "Organizational Strategies for Decision Support and Expert Systems." *Journal of Information Science,* Vol. 15, 1989: 27–34.
4. El Sherif, H., and O. A. El Sawy. "Issue-Based Decision Support Systems for the Egyptian Cabinet." *MIS Quarterly,* Vol. 12, No. 4, 1988.
5. Elam, J., G. Huber, and M. Hurt. "An Examination of the DSS Literature (1975-1985)." *Decision Support Systems: A Decade in Perspective,* Amsterdam, New Holland: H. Sol, (ed.), 1987.
6. Elam, J., and A. Mead. "Can Software Influence Creativity?" *Information Systems Research,* January-March 1990.
7. Eon, H. B. "The Emergence of Global Decision Support Systems." *OR/MS Today,* Vol. 17, No. 5, 1990: 12–13.
8. Er, M. C. "DSS: A Summary of Problems and Future Trends." *Decision Support Systems,* Vol. 4, 1988.
9. Evans, C. E., and J. R. Riha. "Assessing DSS Effectiveness Using Evaluation Research Methods." *Information and Management,* April 1989.
10. Fedorowicz, J., and B. Konsynski. "Organizational Support Systems." *Proceedings, The Information Systems and Decision Processes Workshop,* University of Arizona, Tucson, AZ, October 1989.

11. George, J. F. "The Conceptualizations and Development of Organizational Decision Support Systems." Working paper, Department of MIS, University of Arizona, 1990.

12. Hackathorn, R. D., and P. G. W. Keen. "Organizational Strategies for Personal Computing in Decision Support Systems." *MIS Quarterly*, Vol. 5, No. 3, 1981.

13. Iyer, R. K., and M. K. Raja. "Toward an Organizational DSS: A Process-Oriented Approach." *Human Systems Management*, Vol. 7, No. 1, 1987: 21–30.

14. Kandt, K. "On Building Future Decision Support Systems." *Proceedings of the Twenty-first Annual Hawaii International Conference on System Sciences*. Los Alamitos, CA: IEEE Computer Society Press, January 1988.

15. Kaula, R., and U. R. Dumdum, Jr. "Towards an Organization DSS Architecture: An Open-Systems Perspective." *DSS-91 Transactions*, Providence, RI: The Institute of Management Sciences, 1991: 168–176.

16. Keen, P. G. W. "Decision Support Systems: The Next Decade." *Decision Support Systems*, Vol. 4, 1988.

17. King, J. L., and S. L. Star. "Conceptual Foundations for the Development of Organizational Support Systems." *Proceedings of the Twenty-third Annual Hawaii International Conference on System Sciences*. Los Alamitos, CA: IEEE Computer Society Press, 1990.

18. King, J. L., and S. L. Star, "Conceptual Foundations for the Development of Organizational Decision Support Systems." *Proceedings of the Twenty-Third Annual Hawaii International Conference on System Sciences*, Vol. III. Los Alamitos, CA: IEEE Computer Society Press, January 1990: 143–151.

19. Lee, R. M., et al. (eds.) *Organizational Decision Support Systems*, Amsterdam: North-Holland, 1988.

20. Liang, T. P., and C. V. Jones. "Design of a Self-Evolving Decision Support System." *Journal of Management Information Systems*. Summer 1987.

21. Manheim, M. L., "Issues in the Design of Symbiotic DSS." *Proceedings of the Twenty-second Annual Hawaii International Conference on System Sciences*. Los Alamitos, CA: IEEE Computer Society Press, 1989.

22. Mili, F. "Active DSS: Issues and Challenges." Paper presented at TIMS/ORSA National Conference, Las Vegas, May 1990.

23. Monahan, G. E., and T. L. Smunt. "Multilevel DSS for the Financial Justification of Automated Flexible Manufacturing Systems." *Interfaces*. November/December 1987.

24. O'Keefe, R. M. "The Evaluation of Decision-Aiding Systems: Guidelines and Methods." *Information and Management*, November 1989.

25. Philippakis, A., and Green. "Research Issues in Organizational DSS." *Proceedings of the Ninth International Conference on Information Systems* (J.I. DeGross and M.H. Olson, editors). Minneapolis, November 30, 1988.

26. Silver, M. S. *Systems that Support Decision Makers: Description and Analysis.* New York: J. Wiley & Sons, 1991.

27. Sol, H. (ed.) *Decision Support Systems: A Decade in Perspective.* Amsterdam, New Holland, 1987.

28. Sprague, R. H., Jr., and H. Watson, eds. *Information Systems in Practice,* 2nd ed. Englewood Cliffs, NJ: Prentice-Hall, 1989.

29. Stohr, E., and B. R. Konsynski. (eds.) *Information Systems and Decision Processes.* IEEE Computer Society Press, 1992.

30. Silver, M. S. "Decisional Guidance for Computer-Based Decision Support." *MIS Quarterly,* March 1991.

31. Swanson, E. B. and R. Zmud. "Distributed Decision Support Systems: A Perspective." *Proceedings of the Twenty-Third Annual Hawaii International Conference on System Sciences,* Vol. III. Los Alamitos, CA: IEEE Computer Society Press, January 1990: 129–136.

32. Walker, W. E. "Differences Between Building a Traditional DSS and an ODSS: Lessons from the Air Force's Enlisted Force Management System." *Proceedings of the Twenty-Third Annual Hawaii International Conference on System Sciences,* Vol. III. Los Alamitos, CA: IEEE Computer Society Press, January 1990.

33. Watson, R. T. "A Design for and Infrastructure to Support Organizational Decision Making." *Proceedings of the Twenty-third Annual Hawaii International Conference on System Sciences.* Los Alamitos, CA: IEEE Computer Society Press, 1990.

34. Weber, E. S., and B. R. Konsynski. "Problem Management: Neglected Elements in Decision Support Systems." *Journal of Management Information Systems,* Winter 1987–88.

35. Young, L. F. *Decision Support and Idea Processing Systems.* Dubuque, IA: William C. Brown, 1988.

Chapter 9

Group Decision Support Systems

Most complex decisions in organizations are made by groups of people. As complexity of organizational decision making increases, the need for meetings and for working in groups increases. Such decisions are supported by a technology called group decision support systems (GDSS), whose major mission is supporting *group processes.* The specific sections of this chapter are:

9.1   Case: Quality Improvement Teams*

Many organizations, private and public, are placing increased emphasis on changes in management, use of technology, and introduction of quality improvement programs as means to increase productivity and to better cope with increased competition, customer demands, decreased budgets, and the emergence of global markets. In Manhattan, the management and employees of the Internal Revenue Service (IRS), with the help of the University of Minnesota, implemented a quality improvement program based on participative management (quality teams), which is supported by a group decision support system (GDSS).

A major part of any quality improvement program is the *quality team* structure, which is similar to the Japanese *quality circles* concept. Groups, composed of managers and employees, meet as small units (of three to twelve people) to chart out methods for solving problems and for using opportunities to improve quality.

The Problem

Participants in quality teams often come from different functional areas or supervisory levels, and bring a variety of perspectives to the team. Although such variety can enrich the meetings, it can slow work as well. In addition, groups are subject to generic phenomena that inhibit the success of teamwork. These phenomena include domination by one or a few members, poor interpersonal communication, and fear to express innovative ideas. To reduce such negative effects, the IRS introduced extensive training and professional facilitation. However, as the number of teams increases, the budget becomes a problem and it also becomes difficult to find high-quality facilitators.

The Solution

GDSS is a new technology that could support the various activities carried out by the members of the group, the leader, and the facilitator (see Table 9.1). GDSS offers teams the potential to reduce their effort in applying quality improvement methods by providing automated means to enter, record, and operate on team members' ideas during face-to-face meetings. Specifically, support is provided to idea generation (brainstorming), issue prioritization, problem analysis, strategy selection, and so on. In addition, GDSS helps to reduce many of the negative phenomena of teamwork (e.g., fear to express ideas). Finally, the technology provides extensive documentation on team meetings and decision procedures.

---

*Condensed from DeSanctis, et al. [12].

TABLE 9.1 The Decision Support Needs of the Quality Teams.

Quality Team Roles and Responsibilities	Decision Support Needs
Members: ■ Identify problems ■ Generate and evaluate ideas ■ Develop and implement solutions Leader: ■ Plans meetings ■ Coordinates team activities ■ Monitors and reports team progress Facilitator: ■ Promotes use of problem-solving techniques ■ Encourages consensus building ■ Serves as a liaison between team and quality steering committee	Access to group problem-solving techniques Methods for encouraging open participation by all members Efficient use of team meeting time (for example, agenda management) Documentation of team decision-making processes and outputs

Implementation

GDSS started as research projects in some universities. Special laboratories were built during the late 1980s in several universities, including the University of Minnesota. The IRS case started in 1988. At that time there was no commercially available hardware and software on the market. Therefore, it was necessary to bring the participating team members to the GDSS facility at the University of Minnesota. (Called SAMM for Software-aided Meeting Management [see Figure 9.1]; the details of some of the seven modules of this or similar software will be described later.) Team leaders and members were trained to use the software, and were shown how to enhance the quality improvement process by using several features of SAMM (see Figure 9.2).

Results

During the period of September 1989–January 1991, SAMM was used for several hundred meetings. The SAMM was used by members for:

- Idea generation and evaluation (in 19.4 percent of the meetings)
- Use of sophisticated decision aid tools (in 59.4 percent of the meetings)
- Creating and managing the agenda (in 36.5 percent of the meetings)
- Group writing and record keeping (15.3 percent of the meetings)

On a scale of 1 to 7 (1 low, 7 high), team members expressed a satisfaction level of about 5.5 in these areas: "Being comfortable with the technology," "improvement of the teamwork," "GDSS was *easy* for the group to use," and "GDSS played a major role in meetings." Almost no negative effects were reported. Overall, the GDSS had a tremendous positive impact on the work of the groups (see Table 9.2).

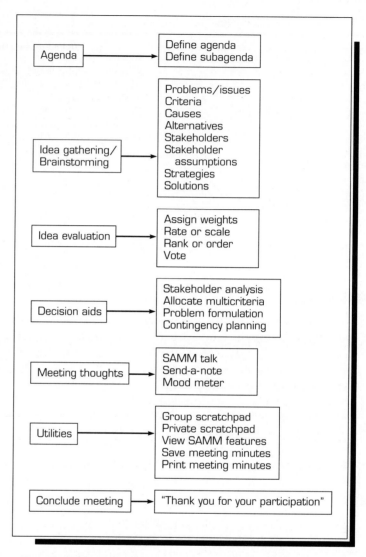

FIGURE 9.1 The Main Menu of Software-Aided Meeting Management (SAMM). Reprinted by permission of G. DeSanctis et al. [12]. Copyright 1991 The Institute of Management Sciences.

Epilogue

The GDSS in the IRS case was so successful that its capabilities are being enhanced. Expansions will enable team members to access the system modules at different times and from different locations. In addition, the GDSS will be able to support more emotional aspects of quality teamwork (e.g., social exchanges, negotiation).

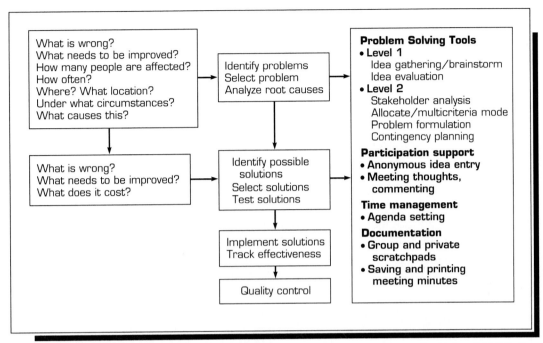

FIGURE 9.2 Enhancement of the Quality Improvement Process by Using SAMM. Reprinted by permission of G. DeSanctis et al. [12]. Copyright 1991 The Institute of Management Sciences.

9.2   Fundamentals of GDSS

The case of the quality improvement teams introduces some of the features of group decision making and GDSS. Specifically:

1. *Groups.* The term "group" (or work group) refers to two or more (usually up to about twenty-five) individuals whose mission is to perform some task and who act as one unit. The group can be permanent or temporary. The group can be in one location or in several locations, and it can meet concurrently or at

TABLE 9.2   Impacts on the Work of Quality Teams (as Reported by IRS Participants)

- GDSS enables teams to gather and explore multiple viewpoints.
- It provides structure when teams confront complex, unstructured decision tasks.
- It helps move the group forward when progress has stagnated.
- It enhances meeting efficiency as compared to using something like a flip chart.
- It facilitates full participation and conflict management
- GDSS was used differently by different teams (voluntary use). Thus, it permitted a great deal of flexibility.

Reprinted by permission of G. DeSanctis et al. [12]. Copyright 1991 The Institute of Management Sciences.

different times. A group can be a committee, a review panel, a task force, an executive board, a team, or a permanent unit.

2. *The Nature of Group Decision Making*. Although most business organizations are hierarchical, decision making is usually a shared process. Face-to-face meetings among groups of managers are an essential element of reaching a consensus. The group may be involved in a decision or in a decision-related task like creating a short list of acceptable alternatives or deciding on criteria for accepting an alternative. These group meetings are characterized by the following activities and processes:

- Meetings are a joint activity, engaged in by a group of people, usually of equal or near equal status, typically involving five to twenty-five individuals.
- The outcome of the meeting depends partly on the knowledge, opinions, and judgments of its participants.
- The outcome of the meeting also depends on the composition of the groups and on the decision-making process used by the groups.
- Differences in opinion are settled either by the ranking person present or, more often, by negotiation or arbitration.

3. *Group Decision Support Systems—Definitions*. Here are some typical definitions of GDSS: "A GDSS consists of a set of software, hardware, language components, and procedures that support a group of people engaged in a decision-related meeting" (Huber [23]).

"A GDSS is an interactive, computer-based system that facilitates the solution of unstructured problems by a set of decision makers working together as a group" (DeSanctis and Gallupe [11]).

A GDSS mainly supports the *process* of decision making rather than the solution of a specific problem.

4. *Electronic Meeting Systems*. Group DSS is considered a subset of a broader field titled **electronic meeting systems** (EMS) or **Group Support Systems.** EMS is defined by Dennis et al., [9] as:

> An information technology (IT)-based environment that supports group meetings, which may be distributed geographically and temporally. The IT *environment* includes, but is not limited to, distributed facilities, computer hardware and software, audio and video technology, procedures, methodologies, facilitation, and applicable group data. Group *tasks* include, but are not limited to, communication, planning, idea generation, problem solving, issue discussion, negotiation, conflict resolution, system analysis and design, and collaborative group activities such as document preparation and sharing (page 593).

EMSs support more tasks than just decision making; they focus on *communication*, moving beyond the GDSS decision room. The EMS concept is presented in detail in several publications from the University of Arizona (e.g., Dennis et al., [8] and [9]).

5. *Computer-Supported Cooperative Work (CSCW)*. This concept describes computerized systems that intend to support effective communication for small

groups, and it is not necessarily related to decision making of a specific task. For example, CSCW is ideal for working jointly on a document, participating in training, exchanging opinions or preparing for a meeting. In contrast with GDSS, such software can support people at different locations and at different times. In some cases people mix CSCW with GDSS, and indeed there is a trend to blend CSCW with GDSS.

6. *Asynchronous GDSS.* An **asynchronous GDSS** is one where simultaneous communication is not facilitated (e.g., as in E-Mail). *Synchronous systems*, on the other hand, allow interactive two-way communication among group members. If such a system is one where face-to-face communication is possible, then it is called an EMS.

9.3.   Decision Making in Groups

As stated earlier, most major decisions in most organizations are being made by groups. The advantages of participative management have long been recognized. On the other hand, there are many cases where groups are unable to make decisions, or make poor decisions, due to the presence of several dysfunctions that result from the process used by the group. In this section we briefly describe the benefits and dysfunctions of making decisions in a group, as well as some of the noncomputerized efforts to deal with the dysfunctions.

The Benefits of Decision Making by Groups

In theory, there are many potential benefits for making decisions in groups. A representative list is provided in Table 9.3.

The Dysfunctions of Groups

Although there are many potential benefits to working in groups, there are also many dysfunctions. As a result, many decisions that are made by groups are considered ineffective and/or inefficient. A representative list of dysfunctions of process losses is provided in Table 9.4.

Improving the Work of Groups

For many years there were attempts to improve the work of groups. If we can eliminate or lessen some of the phenomena that cause the dysfunctions, then the benefits can greatly be enhanced. Behavioral scientists, personnel experts, efficiency experts, and others have developed many approaches to the solution of the problems (some of which appear under the label "group dynamics"). Two representative methods are:

1. *The Nominal Group Technique.* The **nominal group technique** (NGT), a method developed by Delbecq and Van de Ven (see Lindstone and Turoff [29]), includes a sequence of activities: (1) silent generation of ideas in writing, (2)

TABLE 9.3   The Benefits of Working in a Group

- Groups are better at understanding problems.
- People are accountable for decisions that they participate in.
- Groups are better at catching errors.
- A group has more information (knowledge) than any one member and as a result, more alternatives for problem solving.
- Synergy may be produced.
- Working in a group may stimulate the participants and the process.
- Group members will have their ego embedded in the decision, so they will be committed to the implementation.
- The *participation* of the members in a decision means less likelihood to resist implementation.

round-robin listing of ideas on a flip chart, (3) serial discussion of ideas, (4) silent listing and ranking of priorities, (5) discussion of priorities, and (6) silent re-ranking and rating of the priorities. The nominal group process is based on social-psychological research indicating that this procedure is clearly superior to conventional discussion groups in terms of generating higher quality, quantity, and distribution of information on fact-finding tasks.

The success of the nominal group technique (and similar methods) is heavily dependent on the quality of the facilitator (all group dynamic approaches require a facilitator), and on the training given to the participants. Also, the approach does not solve several of the problems (e.g., fear to speak, poor planning and organization of the meeting, compromises, and lack of appropriate analysis).

TABLE 9.4   The Dysfunctions of Group Process

- Social pressure of conformity ("groupthink").
- Time-consuming, slow process.
- Lack of coordination of the work done by the group.
- Inappropriate influence of group dynamics (e.g., domination of time, topic, or opinion by one or few individuals; fear to speak; rigidity).
- Tendency of group members to rely on others to do most of the work.
- Tendency toward compromise solutions of poor quality.
- Incomplete task analysis.
- Nonproductive time (socializing, getting ready, waiting for people).
- Tendency to repeat what already was said.
- Larger cost of making decision (many hours of participation, travel expenses, etc.).
- Incomplete or inappropriate use of information.

2. *The Delphi Method.* The Delphi method was developed by the RAND Corporation as a technique for groups of experts making decisions that would eliminate the undesirable effects of interaction between members of the group. The experts need not meet face-to-face, nor even know who the other experts are. The method generally begins by having each expert provide an individual written assessment or opinion (e.g., a forecast), along with any supporting arguments and assumptions. These forecasts are submitted to the Delphi coordinator, who edits, clarifies, and summarizes the data. These data are then provided as anonymous feedback to the experts along with a *second round* of questions. Questions and feedback continue in writing for several rounds, becoming increasingly more specific, until consensus among the panel members is reached, or until the experts do not change their assessments any more.

The Delphi method benefits from multiple opinions and communication among group members of diverse opinions and assumptions. At the same time it avoids the negative effects of dominant behavior, "groupthink," and stubbornness to change one's mind that are often associated with committee solutions. For more details on the Delphi method, see Lindstone and Turroff [29].

Although the Delphi method provides anonymity, and may encourage some original ideas, it has several limitations. It is slow, expensive, and usually limited to one issue (e.g., technological forecasting, "go" or "no go" of a program).

The manual methods just described (as well as similar manual methods) are beneficial. But they may be expensive, slow, and not so effective. Therefore attempts are being made to use information technologies to support the work of groups.

The Use of Information Technology—Groupware

The importance of making decisions in groups, the many dysfunctions that appear in face-to-face meetings, and the limited success of methods such as Nominal Groups and Delphi, led to attempts to use information technology for supporting groups. Such support appears under many configurations (see Box 9.1) and it is commonly known as groupware. An emerging name that covers the same areas is Group Support Systems (GSS) (see [26]).

Groupware

The term **groupware** refers to software products that support groups of people engaged in a common task or goal, and provide an interface to share environment (per Ellis et al. [14]). The term groupware is known in the computer industry to be very ambiguous. It seems that every vendor tries to manipulate the term to its own advantage, and indeed there are dozens of products on the market (e.g., see Briere [4]), some of which may not be true groupware. Johansen [27] has identified seventeen different approaches for computer support in groups. Our interest in this chapter is in that segment of groupware that directly supports decision making.

Box 9.1: Computer Support to Groups

- Conferencing services (computerized plus video and audio)
- Electronic mail
- Electronic meeting systems and support tools
- Negotiation support systems
- Intelligent agents
- Coordination systems
- Workgroup project management
- Message systems
- Computerized bulletin boards
- Document interchange services
- Collaboration services
- Information analysis services
- Group decision support systems.

Source: Based on McNurlin and Sprague [30] and Ellis et al., [14].

9.4   What Is a GDSS?*

A group decision support system (GDSS) is an interactive computer-based system that facilitates the solution of unstructured problems by a set of decision makers working together as a group. Components of a GDSS include hardware, software, people, and procedures. These components are arranged to support a group of people, usually in the context of a decision-related meeting. Important characteristics of a GDSS can be summarized as follows:

1. The GDSS is a specially designed information system, not merely a configuration of already existing system components.
2. A GDSS is designed with the goal of supporting groups of decision makers in their work. As such, the GDSS should improve the decision-making process and/or the decision outcomes of groups over outcomes that would occur if the GDSS were not present.
3. A GDSS is easy to learn and easy to use. It accommodates users with varying levels of knowledge regarding computing and decision support.
4. The GDSS may be specific (designed for one type of problem) or general (designed for a variety of group-level organizational decisions).
5. The GDSS contains built-in mechanisms that discourage development of negative group behaviors, such as destructive conflict, miscommunication, or "**groupthink**."

*This section is based on DeSanctis and Gallupe [11].

Appropriate settings for a GDSS range from an executive group meeting that occurs in a single location for the purpose of considering a specific problem (such as a merger/acquisition decision) to a sales manager's meeting held via telecommunications channels for the purpose of considering a variety of problems (such as hiring of sales representatives, product offerings, and sales call schedules). Because the contexts of group decision making vary so greatly, it is useful to think of a GDSS in terms of the common "group" activities that, therefore, are in need of computer-based support. They are information retrieval, which includes selection of data values from an existing database as well as simple retrieval of information (including attitudes, opinions, and informal observations) from other group members; information sharing, which refers to the display of data to the total group on a viewing screen or sending of data to selected group members' terminal sites for viewing; and information use, which involves the application of software technology (such as modeling packages or specific application programs), procedures, and group problem-solving techniques for reaching a group decision.

Setting for GDSS

There are four possible GDSS settings:

1. *Same-Time/Same-Place.* This is the decision room where participants meet face to face, in one place and at the same time.
2. *Same-Time/Different-Place.* This setting refers to a meeting where the participants are in different places, but they communicate at the same time. A telephone conference call and teleconferencing are examples.
3. *Different-Time/Same-Place.* This setting can materialize when people work in shifts. The first shift leaves work to a second shift. For example, processing of international currency trading occurs around the clock.
4. *Different-Time/Different-Place.* Imagine a company in Los Angeles with a subsidiary in Japan. It is nighttime in Japan when it is daytime in Los Angeles. People can leave messages and receive answers later. Electronic mail is an example of such a setting. *Note:* VisionQuest is a software product (see Section 9.13) that aims at supporting this type of GDSS.

9.5   The Goal of GDSS and Its Levels

The goal of GDSS is to improve productivity of the decision-making meetings, either by speeding up the decision-making process or by improving the quality of the resulting decisions. This is done by providing support to the exchange of ideas, opinions, and preferences within the group (Finholt and Sproull [15]).

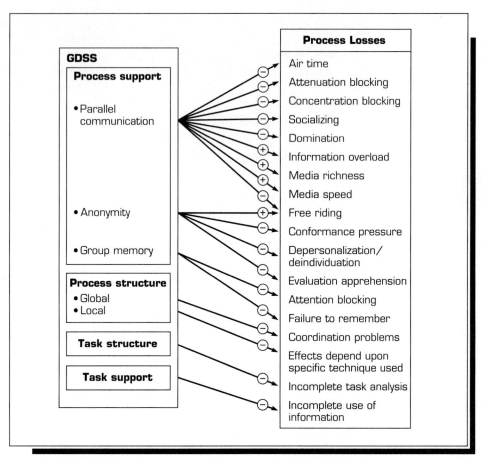

FIGURE 9.3 Reduction of Process Losses through GDSS. (*Source:* Nanamaker et al. [34]. Used by permission. Note: a plus sign (+) indicates an increase in process losses; a minus sign (−) indicates a decrease in process losses.)

This goal can be achieved due to the potential benefits of GDSS. GDSS can reduce the process losses (see Figure 9.3) and can increase process gains (see Table 9.5). This was shown in experiments conducted with the support of IBM by the University of Arizona. For example, one study reported a person-hour savings of more than 50 percent, and a 92 percent reduction in the time required to complete a project by the team using the Arizona GDSS room. More than 150 corporations have used the Arizona room in the past few years and have reported equally dramatic results (DeSanctis and Gallupe [10]).

DeSanctis and Gallupe [10] divide the GDSS technologies into three levels:

- Level 1: Process Support
- Level 2: Decision-Making Support
- Level 3: Rules of Order

TABLE 9.5 Process Gains from GDSS

- Supports parallel processing by the partipants
- Enables larger groups with more complete information, knowledge, and skills to participate in the same meeting
- Permits the group to use structured or even unstructured techniques and methods to perform the task
- Offers access to external information
- Supports the development of an organization memory from meeting to meeting
- Allows nonsequential computer discussion (unlike verbal discussions, computer discussions do not have to be serial or sequential)
- Helps participants deal with the larger picture
- Produces instant anonymous voting results (summaries)
- Provides structure to planning process, which keeps the group on track
- Enables several users to interact simultaneously
- Provides easy access to external data
- All information that passes through the system is automatically recorded for future analysis.

Level 1: Process Support. This is basically what the IRS system, presented earlier, provides. Items that are supported by such a system are:

- Electronic messaging between group members
- Networks linking each member's personal computer terminals to those of the other group members, to the facilitator, and to the public screen, database, or any other common CBIS
- A public screen available at each group member's terminal or visible to all members in a central place
- Anonymous input of ideas and votes, to enhance participation of group members who prefer anonymity
- Active solicitation of ideas or votes from each group member to encourage participation and induce creativity
- Summary and display of ideas and opinions, including statistical summaries and vote displays (on the public screen)
- A format for an agenda that can be completed by the group to aid organization of meetings
- Continuous display of the agenda, as well as other information, to keep meetings on schedule.

Level 2: Decision-Making Support. At this level the software adds capabilities for modeling and decision analysis (see Figure 9.4). Features in this category include:

- Planning and financial models
- Decision trees
- Probability assessment models

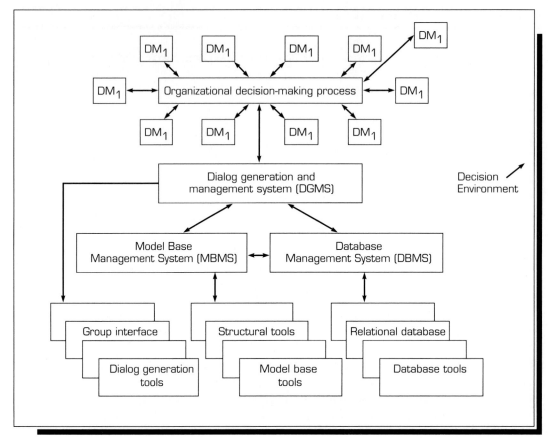

FIGURE 9.4 A Structure of GDSS at Level 2. (*Source:* Sage [38] Copyright © 1981 Reprinted by permission of John Wiley & Sons, Inc.)

- Resource allocation models
- Social judgment models.

Such models may exist in regular DSS packages and can be added on to Level 1 software. In addition, one can add idea generation software or software support to Delphi or to the nominal group technique.

Level 3: Rules of Order. At this level a special software containing rules of order is added. For example, some rules could determine the sequence of speaking, the appropriate response, or voting rules.

9.6   The Technology of GDSS

A typical GDSS configuration, and a rather basic one, includes a group of decision makers with access to a database, a model base, and GDSS application

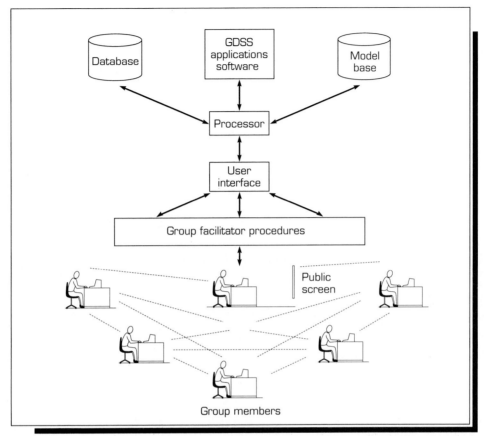

FIGURE 9.5   A Model of GDSS. (*Source:* Modified from DeSanctis and Gallupe [11].)

software during the course of a decision-related meeting. A group facilitator coordinates the group's use of the technology, and there is a flexible, friendly, user-interface language available for use by the facilitator and each group member.

DeSanctis and Gallupe [11] define the components of GDSS as being *hardware, software, people,* and *procedures.* (See Figure 9.5.)

Hardware. Three basic types of hardware configurations can be used by a group:

1. *Single PC.* In such a case, participants gather around a single PC, while one person enters data. The screen leads the groups to a series of questions, prioritizing and consolidating answers. Finally a decision is indicated. Such a system has very few benefits.
2. *PCs and Keypads.* This is basically a workstation with keypads for voting. The machines can be portable so they travel easily. They are simple to

operate but very limited in their capabilities. Such PCs can be connected via E-mail or a network.

3. *A Decision Room.* This is a GDSS facility dedicated for electronic meetings and designed as such. A detailed description of such a system is given in Section 9.7.

Software. The software component of the GDSS includes a database, a model base, specialized application program(s) to be used by the group, and an easy-to-use, flexible, user interface. GDSS software includes packages to support the *individual, the group, the process,* and *specific tasks.* For a detailed discussion see Section 9.8. It allows each individual to do private work; the usual collection of text and file creation, graphics, spreadsheet, database, and help routines are provided at the individual workstations. Typical *group* features include:

1. Numerical and graphical summarization of group members, ideas, and votes
2. Programs for calculation of weights for decision alternatives; anonymous recording of ideas; formal selection of a group leader; progressive rounds of voting toward consensus building; or elimination of redundant input during brainstorming
3. Text and data transmission among the group members, between the group members and the facilitator, and between the members and a central computer processor. See Box 9.2.

People. The people component of the GDSS includes the group members and a facilitator who is responsible for the smooth operation of the GDSS technology. The facilitator is usually present at all group meetings and serves as the group's "chauffeur," operating the GDSS hardware and software and displaying requested information to the group as needed.

Procedures. The final component of the GDSS consists of procedures that enable ease of operation and effective use of the technology by group members. These procedures may apply only to the operation of the hardware and software, or they may extend to include rules regarding verbal discussion among members and the flow of events during a group meeting.

Box 9.2: How to Represent Expressions without Face-to-Face Interaction

Making "faces" during an electronic meeting is not a problem. All you have to do is to agree on a set of symbols like this:

:) = smile	;) = wink	:O = bored
:D = laughter	:(= frown	:X = angry

9.7   The Decision (Electronic Meeting) Room

Electronic meeting rooms consist of a large, usually U-shaped table equipped with twelve to thirty networked microcomputers recessed into a table to facilitate interaction among participants. A microcomputer attached to a large-screen projection system is connected to the network and permits the display of work done at individual workstations and aggregated information from the total group. Breakout rooms are equipped with microcomputers that are networked to the microcomputers at the main conference table. The output from these small group sessions can also be displayed on the large "public" screen projector (Barco) for group presentations and can be updated and integrated with planning session results.

A well known example is PlexCenter (Planning and Decision Support Laboratory) at the University of Arizona. It is equipped with IBM PS/2 Model 50 workstations running in MS-DOS, one for each participant, up to a total of twenty-four; a local area network; an IBM PS/2 Model 80 server and PS/2 Model 70 "facilitator station" driving a Barco large-screen projection system. (See Figure 9.6.) The concept can be scaled up or down depending upon a specific user's requirement. The room is the result of a multiyear program exploring how information technology can be used to complement face-to-face meetings. IBM has installed similar systems in several dozen locations across the U.S. and Canada, and has sponsored thousands of research and practical sessions in these rooms.

An electronic decision room requires a trained facilitator. The success of any GDSS is largely dependent on the quality of such facilitator.

9.8   The GDSS Software

Several software packages were developed at research universities (e.g., University of Arizona and University of Minnesota). They usually can be segregated into the following categories:

- *Idea Generation (Electronic Brainstorming)* tool allows participants to simultaneously and anonymously share comments on a specific question with other participants. For example, members enter a comment to a question on their individual computer screen and send it out onto the network to be received by other participants who review previous comments, append an additional comment, and return the response to the network (see Figure 9.7 for an example). Comments from all participant screens are consolidated after the session and systematic analysis support is used to identify common issues or concerns, associated attributes, and relationships between categories. This interchange of ideas was found to increase creativity and generate alternative possible courses of action.
- *Issue Analyzer* tool helps group members identify and consolidate key fo-

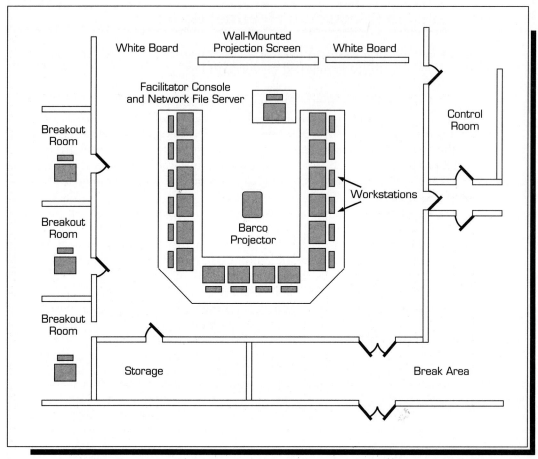

FIGURE 9.6 University of Arizona GDSS Facility Group Systems. (*Source:* Nunamaker et al. [34] Used by permission.)

cus items resulting from idea generation. Information from external sources can be integrated as well.

- *The Stakeholder Identification and Analysis* (SIAS) tool is used to identify stakeholders pertinent to a proposed plan, record assumptions or expectations of those stakeholders, and rate the stakeholder assumptions in terms of importance to the stakeholder as well as importance to the proposed plan. Assumption ratings are captured, consolidated, and displayed graphically for review and consideration by the group.
- *Topic Commentor* tool supports idea solicitation and provision of additional detail in conjunction with lists of topics. Each topic may have subtopics.
- *Session Director* tool guides the facilitator in selecting the tools to be used in a session.
- The *Voting* tool can be used to consolidate group sentiments at any stage of the planning process, using several different formats including

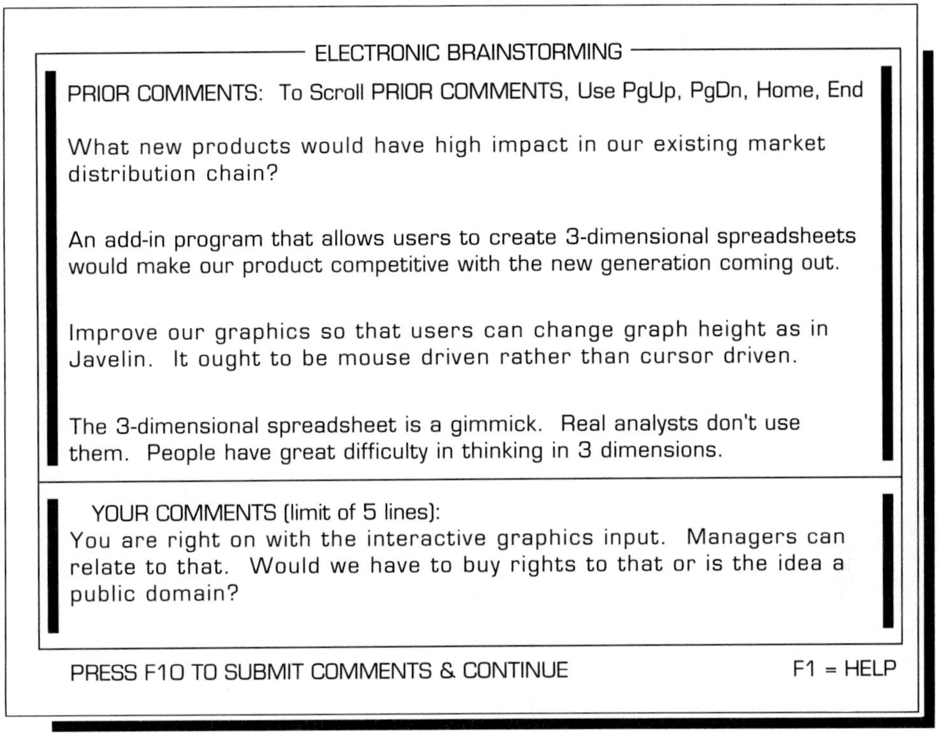

```
┌─────────────────────────────────────────────────────────────┐
│  ┌──────────────────── ELECTRONIC BRAINSTORMING ──────────┐  │
│  │ PRIOR COMMENTS:  To Scroll PRIOR COMMENTS, Use PgUp, PgDn, Home, End │
│  │                                                         │  │
│  │ What new products would have high impact in our existing market │
│  │ distribution chain?                                     │  │
│  │                                                         │  │
│  │ An add-in program that allows users to create 3-dimensional spreadsheets │
│  │ would make our product competitive with the new generation coming out. │
│  │                                                         │  │
│  │ Improve our graphics so that users can change graph height as in │
│  │ Javelin.  It ought to be mouse driven rather than cursor driven. │
│  │                                                         │  │
│  │ The 3-dimensional spreadsheet is a gimmick.  Real analysts don't use │
│  │ them.  People have great difficulty in thinking in 3 dimensions. │
│  └─────────────────────────────────────────────────────────┘  │
│  ┌─────────────────────────────────────────────────────────┐  │
│  │   YOUR COMMENTS (limit of 5 lines):                     │  │
│  │ You are right on with the interactive graphics input.  Managers can │
│  │ relate to that.  Would we have to buy rights to that or is the idea a │
│  │ public domain?                                          │  │
│  └─────────────────────────────────────────────────────────┘  │
│     PRESS F10 TO SUBMIT COMMENTS & CONTINUE          F1 = HELP  │
└─────────────────────────────────────────────────────────────┘
```

FIGURE 9.7 Electronic Brainstorming Screen as Seen by Participant after Several Rounds; Arizona GDSS Interface. (*Source:* Gray [19]. Used by permission.)

agree/disagree, multiple choice, 10-point scale ranking, or ranking in order.

- The *Policy Formulation* tool enables group members to develop policy (or mission) statements, based on the issues identified. The facilitator enters the initial wording of a proposed policy on the group's verbal direction. This policy is then sent to individual participants who edit it and send it back for group comments until a group consensus is reached.
- The *Enterprise Analyzer* is the means through which an organization can be represented in the knowledge base. It is conceptually similar to IBM's Business Systems Planning (BSP) methodology, but it is a computerized version updated to reflect a user-friendly approach to the definition of organization structure and resources.
- *Negotiation Support Systems* (NSS) can be a portion of GDSS, or it can be an independent package. Its major function is to support conflict resolution via negotiations among members of the group.

An example of the software module at the University of Arizona is shown in Figure 9.8.

Additional tools and models provide support for session initialization, agenda generation, issue prioritizing, statistical analysis, interface, and display.

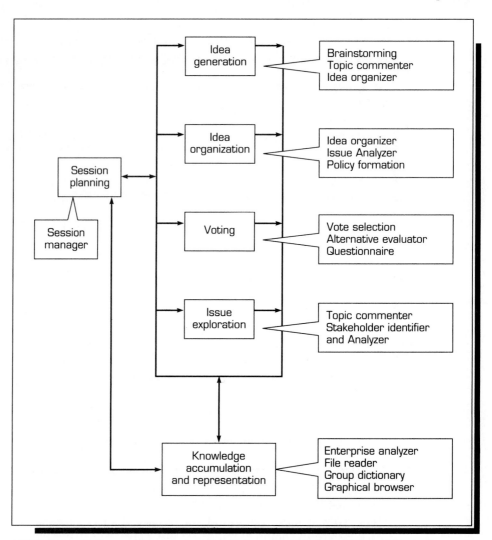

FIGURE 9.8 Software Structure at the University of Arizona (Also of GroupSystems, from Ventana Corp.) (*Source:* Nunamaker [34]. Used by permission.)

Several of the software tools are integrated in one product. Others are available as stand-alone packages. For details on representative commercial packages see Section 9.13.

9.9   Idea Generation

Idea generation software helps to generate a free flow of turbulent creative thinking: ideas, words, pictures, and concepts set loose with fearless enthusiasm by intelligent people (Gallupe and DeSanctis [17]). Some packages are designed to mimic the creative thought process of the human mind and can be used to create new product ideas, marketing strategies, promotional campaigns, names, titles, slogans, stories, or just brainstorming in general.

By definition, idea generation in GDSS is a collaborative effort. One person's idea triggers the other's ideas, which triggers even more ideas. With electronic tools, the individual does all the thinking, but the software encourages the individual and pushes him along. Joanne Gallitano, Personal Systems director at the Decision Support Center at the US Marketing and Services Business Systems facility in Southbury, Connecticut, says that electronic brainstorming is for most people a very exhilarating experience. This is because the technology is an anonymous, safe way to get out ideas that have been lurking in the back of people's minds but which they were reluctant to express in a more conventional setting. Then, by building on each other's ideas, individuals get creative insights they didn't have before (Gray [18]).

The results of each idea generation session can be electronically stored so they can be carried over from one meeting to another to enhance the creativity of more people.

Research on how a group should organize itself to generate ideas clearly shows that, in contrast to findings from non-computer-mediated idea generation, one single EMS-supported group generates more ideas with higher quality than the same number of participants working as individuals or in several smaller groups (Bostrom, et al. [2]). Group DSS participants probably use the idea generation software more frequently than they use any other software (e.g., see the opening case in Section 9.1).

9.10   Negotiation Support Systems (NSS)

Conflict resolution mechanisms form an important aspect of GDSS design. When a conflict is present, finding compromised solutions is a key support activity of NSS.

Conflicts among decision makers can arise from differences in interest or in objectives and from cognitive limitations.

The need for negotiations arises from different types of disputes (Greif [20]):

1. Negotiators' interests are fundamentally opposed (e.g., contract negotiations—labor dispute).
2. Negotiators share basic objectives but they differ in their assessment of the priorities of the objectives, (e.g., resource allocation—budgeting problems).

Intragroup conflict has been studied extensively in game-theory, social, psychological, and political science frameworks. Common to most of these studies is the belief that conflicts arise primarily because of differences in interests among individuals. However, conflicts often arise simply because group members differ in their understanding (or misunderstanding) of the problem, even when their respective interests converge. Such conflicts are a routine feature in group decision making and, consequently, even if differences in motives among group members are eliminated, conflict in a group may persist. In the presence of cognitive conflict, groups behave inconsistently and, as a result, arrive at low quality decisions (Grohowski and McGoff [21]). Therefore, it is important to develop decision aids that can help the facilitator to diagnose cognitive conflicts and reduce them.

Decision Aids for Negotiations

MEDIATOR, Co-op, and NEGO are examples of systems that span from modeling individual interests to seeking negotiated solutions. They assist in situations where conflicts arise from interest differentials. However, there is little research on building systems to support group decision making in situations involving cognitive conflict.

NSS should help emerge as common ground for people to accept recommendations, instead of blindly accepting proposals sponsored by interested parties. Concession-making procedures may lead to a compromising solution or a break-off (at which point the negotiation conceivably could be restructured). Here, redefining the negotiation problem is the key approach.

Two methods that could provide knowledge for restructuring are:

1. *AI restructuring methods.* Such methods involve case-based reasoning, situational assessment packets, persuasive argumentation, and goal graph procedures.
2. *Rule-based approaches* (utilization of expert systems). On the whole, much more research is needed validating NSS software and assessing its impact on negotiations.

9.11   How a GDSS Runs

Electronic meetings generally follow a superficially similar formula, independent of the topics, which can vary widely: *First,* the group leader meets with the facilitator to plan the meeting, select the software tools to be used, and develop an agenda. *Second,* the leader poses a question or problem to the group.

Third, the participants type their comments, so the results can be publicly displayed. Since the participants can see what others are saying, they can provide comments (e.g. positive or negative). *Fourth,* the facilitator, using the idea organization software, searches for common themes, topics, and ideas and organizes them into rough categories (key ideas) with appropriate comments. The results are publicly displayed. *Fifth,* the leader starts a discussion, either vocal or electronic. At that point the participants *prioritize* the ideas. (Software can be of great help at this step.) *Sixth,* the top five or ten topics are routed to idea generation, after being discussed. *Finally,* the process can repeat itself (idea generation, idea organization, prioritization) or a final vote takes place. A topic commenter software can be used to support this step. The major activities of this process are shown in Figure 9.9 on page 374.

9.12 Constructing a GDSS and the Determinants of Its Success

Constructing a GDSS

Developing a GDSS differs considerably from developing an application of DSS or an expert system. GDSS is a facility that implies constructing a decision room, developing (or acquiring) the software, developing the procedures, training a facilitator, and putting it all together. Many organizations prefer to use someone else's facility. Unless you have a constant use for the facility, why not rent one? However, GDSS is becoming more and more attractive to organizations. Several GDSS vendors offer extensive consulting services on how to build such a facility, how to install the software, and how to operate the facility.

Having a facility is of course necessary but not sufficient for the success of GDSS. Some helpful suggestions for successful implementation are offered next.

Determinants of GDSS Success

The experience gained from almost two years of experimentations at the University of Arizona Planning and Decision Laboratory has been analyzed. Of special interest are the detected determinants of GDSS success. This analysis focuses on the effectiveness and efficiency of GDSS in facilitating the decision-making process, and the degree of satisfaction of the group members. According to Vogel et al. [45], these experiments suggest the following attributes of successful GDSS:

- The setting should be multipurpose and flexible to better meet the needs of different group sizes and task environments. Aesthetics should provide a measure of executive appeal in terms of comfort and familiarity to allow decision makers to better focus on issues at hand.
- The provision of an electronic interface for each group member encourages all group members to participate and enhances the efficiency of that participation. Each workstation should have a high degree of local intelligence and in-residence software options. As such, each participant can maintain some independence while contributing to the group as a whole through an interface that is flexible and individually supportive.
- The software should not be merely user-friendly but *user seductive*, to present a professional image and encourage end-user involvement in group decision-making sessions. The software should not impose on or frustrate

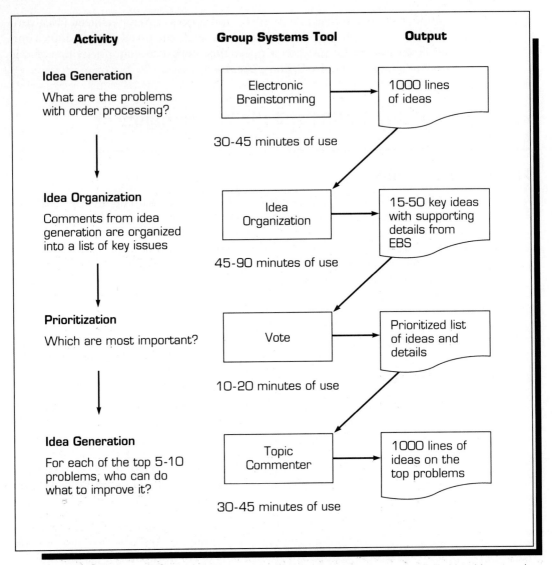

FIGURE 9.9 One Sequence of Use. (*Source:* Nunamaker et al. [34]. Used by permission.)

users, but encourage user interaction through effective use of color, over-
lays, windowing, and other features.

- Anonymity is important to groups especially when sensitive issues are
being discussed. For groups of differing organizational levels, anonymity
provides a sense of equality and encouragement for participation by all
members in the group independent of perceived status. Problems of
groupthink, pressures for conformity, and dominance of the group by
strong personalities of particularly forceful speakers are minimized. Members can contribute without the personal attention and anxiety associated
with singularly gaining the floor and being the focus of attention.

- Tasks that involve generating ideas or plans, solving problems with or
without optimal solutions, and resolving conflicts of different viewpoints
or interests are particularly good candidates for effective GDSS utilization.
Those that involve resolving conflicts of power or group leadership, and
those that are more related to actual detail execution, which more often
resides with individuals, are less effectively addressed by a GDSS.

- The use of a GDSS, however, tends to heighten conflict within a group as
members tend to become more blunt and assertive in their comments.
Members tend to express themselves more forcefully and are often not as
polite when interfacing through the system rather than in person.

- Efficiency considerations (measured by the time it takes to reach a decision) of group decision support systems become increasingly apparent as
group size increases. It is difficult to demonstrate that GDSS promotes
group efficiency for small groups (e.g., of three to five people). For larger
groups (e.g., of eight or more people), the GDSS enhances group efficiency by facilitating input from all group members in a relatively simultaneous fashion.

- Group effectiveness (measured by the quality of the decisions) when using
GDSS is also enhanced as group size increases. For groups of six to eight
or more, the effectiveness of GDSS becomes particularly apparent in the
facilitation and coordination of large numbers of issues associated with a
complex question. Small groups, by contrast, often find that although the
GDSS is interesting, it is difficult to suggest that any striking measure of
increased effectiveness has been attained.

- Member satisfaction with the group process is also better when groups are
larger. Larger groups appreciate the structuring inherent with the GDSS
to keep the group from becoming bogged down or subject to domination
by member personalities. Small groups are more frustrated by GDSS constraints, and are less likely to conclude that the GDSS is more effective or
efficient than an unstructured face-to-face meeting for the relatively less
complex questions typically addressed by small groups.

Conclusions from University of Arizona GDSS Research. The University
of Arizona's experience confirms that the key to success rests in an appreciation
of the need for:

1. Facilities that provide a professional setting in which sophisticated software and hardware are well organized and effectively supported.
2. Ability to accommodate groups of sufficient size that may vary considerably in composition and experience and which address tasks that are real and complex by nature.
3. Facilitation that demonstrates technical competence in combination with an appreciation for group dynamics that encompasses a multidisciplinary approach.

For a list of factors found critical to the success of GDSS, see Box 9.3.

More on Critical Success Factors for GDSS

Buckley and Yen studied the critical success factors for GDSS [5] and categorized them into three major groups: design, implementation, and management.

Box 9.3: Critical Success Factors of Electronic Meeting Systems (EMS)*

1. Organizational commitment—a must
2. Executive sponsor who is committed and informed
3. Operating sponsor to provide quick feedback
4. Dedicated facilities with attention to aesthetics and user comfort
5. Reciprocal site visits that recognize the need for informed personnel who understand the EMS environment
6. Communication and liaison extending beyond site visits—important in maintaining responsiveness to questions arising
7. Fast iteration of software changes—critical to meet the evolving needs
8. Training for site personnel at technical, facilitation, and end-user levels
9. Transfer of control to site personnel
10. Cost/benefit evaluation—crucial to expansion of EMS beyond initial trials
11. Software usage flexibility—essential for meeting the evolving needs of groups
12. Facilitation support—an important aspect of quickly getting new users to be productive in an EMS environment
13. Meeting managerial expectations—the ultimate indicator of successful EMS implementation.

---

*Based on IBM's experience (Grohowski and McGoff [21]).

1. *Design.* Four factors are included:
   - Enhance the structuredness of unstructured decisions (e.g. by providing database access for added information).
   - Preserve anonymity of the participant as needed.
   - Provide organizational involvement (from all affected individuals and groups), mainly by top management, end-users, and the IS department.
   - Include ergonomic considerations that create a comfortable and productive environment.
2. *Implementation.* Four factors are included:
   - Provide extensive and proper user training.
   - Assure the support of top management (not just their involvement).
   - Provide a qualified facilitator.
   - Execute trial runs by conducting experiments to assure appropriate operations.
3. *Management.* Three factors are considered:
   - The system must be reliable. Appropriate maintenance, smooth operation, and quality support are a must.
   - The system must be incrementally improved. Using feedback of the participants and hardware and software innovations, the GDSS facility needs to be enhanced constantly.
   - To implement the previous factor, it is necessary for the GDSS staff to keep up with the state of the art of the technology.

9.13   Commercial GDSS Software

Several software products are available on the market to support GDSS. They can be divided into two categories: comprehensive products that are fully integrated tool kits, and functional tools, which include only one or a few tools.

Comprehensive Products.

1. *TeamFocus* (IBM Corp.)
2. *GroupSystems* (Ventana Corp., Tucson, AZ). This product is an enhanced version of IBM's TeamFocus. It enables a company to create and use a decision room.
3. *VisionQuest* (from Collaborative Technologies Corporation, Austin, TX). This product supports a wide range of interactive team functions such as control over agenda, prioritizing, idea generation, and documentation of activities. It also supports meetings in which the participants are in different locations and can communicate at different times.

Functional Tools. Functional tools are intended to support some of the functions of GDSS. Representative examples are:

1. *Idea Generation.* These products were discussed in Chapter 8.
2. *Managing Sessions.* Two expert system products were developed for managing group sessions: Expert Session Manager and Expert System Planner. (For details contact Robert Mockler at St. John's University, New York.)
3. *Multiple Criteria Products.* These are listed in Chapter 5.
4. *Strategic Planning Planner.* (From Ronin Development Corporation of Princeton, NJ; see Mockler [32] for details.) A simple stand-alone brainstorming tool (from Experience in Software Inc., Berkeley, CA) guides users through three levels of problem solving.
5. *Innovator.* This meeting-enhancement keypad system polls an audience and provides feedback (from Wilson Learning Corp., Eden Prairie, MN); it is specifically geared toward idea generation, consensus building, and focus research for strategic planning.
6. *One Touch.* This multimedia-based package (from One Touch System, Santa Clara, CA) is designed to support remote teaching and conferencing. It has voting keypads, one-way satellite-relayed video, and two-way audio.
7. *OptionFinder.* This "X-Y Window"-based package (from Option Technology, Mendota Heights, MN) allows groups to brainstorm, weigh alternatives, identify priorities, vote, and work toward consensus in a non-decision room setting.
8. *Higgins.* This is basically a group scheduler software (from Enable Software Higgins Group, Ballston Lake, NY). To do its job, the software interacts with personal calendars of the participants. It works via E-mail to confirm schedules.
9. *Lotus Notes.* This distributed database, which resides on E-mail (from Lotus Development Corporation, Cambridge, MA), helps users to prepare for a meeting (e.g., post ideas, print an agenda, and write up minutes). It is basically a server-based document and task management application software. (See Box 9.4.)
10. *Consensus Builder.* This product has a knowledge base for supporting decision making in a group (from Magic 7 Software, Los Altos, CA). It helps in resolving conflicts and taking prompt action. The product weights each participant's judgment in accordance with his or her own personal standards, capabilities, and biases. It points to similarities among the participants, as well as to differences.
11. *For Comment.* This server-based software (from Access Technology Inc., Natick, MA) manages all the documents related to group meetings and conferences.
12. *Together.* This is an application integrator that enables multiple users to access multiple applications through a windowed desktop screen (from Coordination Technology, Inc., Trumbell, CT). It enables users to work with each other on one task (at the same time or at different times).

Box 9.4: Lotus Notes

This software consists of six folders that organize its database. By click-ing on an icon (see Figure) one can get up-to-the-minute news reports, peruse activity in a different department, or participate in a discussion with colleagues around the world.

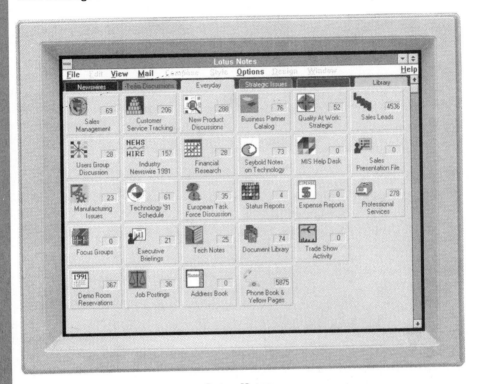

Lotus Notes.

9.14   GDSS Research Challenges

GDSS is a state-of-the-art technology. Unlike other technologies in MIS research, such as end-user computing or system development techniques, it cannot yet be widely investigated for its use in the hands of practitioners. Few organiza-tions use GDSS technology as researchers know it today. Findings from GDSS lab experimentations have been distinctly different from those of GDSS field studies. (For example, see Jessup and Valacich [26].) The first step toward clos-ing the gap between the laboratory experiments and field studies is to embark on multimethodological research programs that provide individual researchers with first-hand understanding of the key GDSS issues from both the experimental and field research perspectives. The absence of either experiments or field studies in a research program reduces the strength within which conclusions can be drawn, and the applicability of those conclusions to actual organizations. A second challenge would be to understand the effects that these differences have on the process and outcome of group meetings, and to use this understanding in interpreting and applying the conclusions of experiments to the use of GDSS by business organizations. From this understanding, we can develop new research designs: field studies with greater rigor (internal validity) and experiments with greater relevancy to the organizational use of GDSS (external validity).

Research Models. GDSS research is one of the most fertile areas for academic research. Several reseachers proposed a framework for organizing the increasing number of studies. Two approaches were used: (1) outline all the variables in the study of GDSS, and (2) list research topics.

1. *GDSS Variables.* This approach divides the variables into three groups: inputs, processes, and outcome. The initial work was done by DeSanctis and Gallupe. Their work was summarized by Gray (see Figure 9.10). A slightly different research model was proposed by Dennis et al. [8]

2. *GDSS Research Topic.* A proposal for specific research topics made by DeSanctis and Gallupe is summarized in Table 9.6.

Additional suggestions were provided by Dickson [13]. He suggests topics such as: (1) tradeoffs on advanced features versus simplicity, (2) interface studies, (3) supporting groups with difficulties, (4) research on anytime/anyplace configuration, (5) GDSS benefit identification, (6) the level of support required, (7) embedded knowledge bases (intelligent GDSS), and (8) training issues.

Chapter Highlights

- Electronic meeting systems, computer-supported cooperative work, groupware, and other names designate various types of computer support to groups.
- Computers can support the work of groups in many ways. Here the interest is in supporting decisions made by groups.
- There are many benefits to the work of groups ("two heads are better than one"), but there are many dysfunctions due to process loss.
- There are several noncomputerized methods that attempt to improve the process of group decision making. Such methods depend heavily on a facilitator and can be lengthy and expensive.
- GDSS attempts to reduce process losses and increase the process gains.
- The Delphi method is a non-face-to-face, nonelectronic method that as-

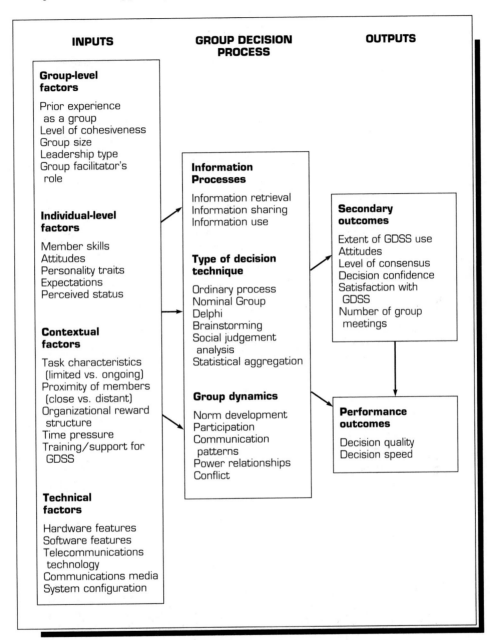

FIGURE 9.10 Variables in the Study of Group Decision Support. (*Source:* Gray, P., "Group Decision Support Systems," in *Decision Support Systems*, Vol. 3 (1987), p. 239.)

TABLE 9.6 Research Issues in GDSS.

I. GDSS DESIGN
  - Human factors design (e.g., spatial arrangement, public screens, informal communications channels)
  - Database design
  - User interface design
  - Interface with DSS
  - Design methodologies

II. APPROPRIATENESS OF GDSS
  - When should a GDSS be used and when should it not be used?
  - When is a GDSS preferred to a DSS?
  - Selecting the right GDSS design

III. GDSS SUCCESS FACTORS
  - Measures of success (e.g., reduction in group conflict, degree of consensus, group norms)
  - Effects of hardware, software, user motivation, and top management support on GDSS's success

IV. IMPACT OF GDSS
  - Communication patterns
  - Confidence in decision
  - Costs
  - Level of consensus
  - User satisfaction

V. MANAGING THE GDSS
  - Responsibility for GDSS in organization
  - Planning requirements for GDSS
  - Training, maintenance, and other support needed

Source: Based on G. DeSanctis and R. B. Gallupe, "Information System Support for Group Decision Making," unnumbered working paper, Dept. of Management Science, University of Minnesota (undated).

- sures anonymity of the participants and provides equal chances to participate.
- There are four settings for GDSS: same-time/same-place, same-time/different place, different-time/same-place, and different-time/different-place.
- High level GDSS can support decision making in addition to process support. A very high level GDSS utilizes knowledge in terms of rules.
- A group DSS is usually structured on a LAN and is conducted in a decision room environment.
- A GDSS software includes the following modules: idea generation, idea organization, stakeholder identification, topic commentor, voting tool, policy formulation, enterprise analyzer, and negotiation support system.
- Idea generation is achieved by allowing participants to generate ideas simultaneously and to share them (yet keeping anonymity).
- Resolving conflicts in groups is an essential task. The software supports negotiation for conflict resolution.
- GDSS software is generic. You normally buy it. Several packages with different capabilities exist on the market.
- GDSS can easily fail. There are many important determinants of its success.

- GDSS research is very diversified. Areas of interest range from individual-level characteristics (of the participants) to types of decision techniques used.

Key Words

asynchronous GDSS	group support systems (GSS)	nominal group technique (NGT)
brainstorming		
Delphi method	groupthink	
electronic meeting systems (EMS)	groupware	
	idea generation	
group decision support systems (GDSS)	negotiation support systems (NSS)	

Questions for Review

1. List the major characteristics of GDSS.
2. List three benefits of GDSS.
3. Describe a decision room and contrast it with other GDSS scenarios.
4. Define GDSS.
5. List some of the dysfunctions (or losses) when working in groups.
6. What are the benefits of making decisions in a group?
7. Describe the nominal group technique approach.
8. Describe the Delphi method.
9. Define groupware.
10. List methods, other than GDSS, that support groups.
11. Describe an electronic meeting room.
12. Describe the major software components (modules) in a GDSS.
13. What is meant by electronic brainstorming?
14. Describe the role of negotiation support systems.
15. Describe the process of building GDSS.

Questions for Discussion

1. Compare GDSS to noncomputerized group decision making.
2. It is said that GDSS supports the process while DSS supports the task. Comment.
3. How can GDSS support creativity?
4. Relate GDSS to EMS to CSCW.
5. Describe the deficiencies of NGT and Delphi.
6. Describe the differences between the three levels of GDSS technologies.
7. Describe the following GDSS components: hardware, software, people, and procedures.
8. Explain how the various software modules support the work of a group.
9. Compare the idea generation activities here with that of IdeaFisher (see Chapter 8).

10. Discuss the major role of a negotiated software.
11. Many factors are necessary to the success of GDSS. Review all of them. Which, in your opinion, are the most important ones (list three)?
12. Distinguish between comprehensive GDSS and functional tools.
13. It is said that TeamFocus and GroupSystems are conceptually similar to CASE (Computer Aided Software Engineering) tools. Why?
14. If you were to do research on GDSS, what would you do and why?

Case Study: GDSS in City Government*

Problem

In Louisville, Kentucky, one volunteer group called Third Century is working to define a future for the inner city. Nearly 500 community members from all neighborhoods, public and private sector business organizations, and education meet regularly to identify the major issues confronting the city. Their activities include open forums to discuss critical issues, gathering data to understand the opportunities and problems facing the city, and sponsoring meetings and festivals to help revitalize the downtown as a viable place to live, work, and shop. Third Century's major goal is to develop a set of policy priorities for the future of the community.

The University of Louisville developed a limited GDSS to help the large, dispersed, heterogeneous group to arrive at consensus goals.

Most GDSS operate in laboratory conditions. Very few GDSS involve actual decision makers, usually in the private sector where there is a less conflicting environment.

The problem, common to every community, is to provide an arena in which each agenda can be dealt with openly while sharing realistic expectations regarding what is possible, given existing resources and competing agendas.

Third Century first identified a list of critical community concerns, which included a wide variety of issues. From their data gathering they found education was at the top of the list in terms of community interest. Third Century planners then refined a list of ten specific education-related items most often cited in the community survey. They identified executives, neighborhood and community leaders, and key government people who were the opinion leaders and invited them to participate in a consensus-building exercise. The task was to rank the ten issues. This ranking can then be used for planning and resource allocation purposes.

---

*Condensed from Taylor and Beauclair [42]. Used with permission of the authors and the Institute of Management Sciences. © 1990 the Institute of Management Sciences.

Design and Implementation

The first step was to design the GDSS to assure that all of the leaders had an opportunity to make a case for the educational priorities they felt appropriate.

A flow chart was developed to clarify the GDSS process to technical and nontechnical users (see Figure 9.11). A programmer then translated the chart into usable code. Because of excessive costs and the unavailability of commercial software (this was in 1989), university faculty developed the GDSS application to support the process.

Representatives from Third Century visited each group leader (representatives from the local school board, teachers, parents, parochial and private school heads, business people, political leaders, and individuals from higher education). From these interviews, a list of the ten most frequently cited educational concerns was identified and each was rephrased as an action item. The action items were short statements clarifying each main concern. The cost to fully implement all ten action items far exceeded the available resources of the community; furthermore, some actions had to be taken before others could be accomplished. Priorities had to be established.

The Third Century representatives were invited to discuss the list in the GDSS research room, which included seven networked microcomputers in a comfortable discussion setting. They participated in a pilot exercise to determine whether consensus could be achieved and whether the GDSS configuration was "user-friendly." From the testing, the action items and software were revised.

Group Process

Fifty individuals were identified by Third Century to participate. They included the U.S. senator from Louisville, school superintendents from public and private schools, university administrators, outstanding teachers, principals, community leaders, neighborhood advocates, minority leaders, and citizen activists. They were invited to participate in one of four GDSS sessions. Because of scheduling constraints, the number of participants was reduced to 28.

Four sessions of seven participants each were conducted. After a brief orientation to the GDSS process, each of the ten issues was discussed. Participants often advocated their position during this discussion but, more importantly, everyone seemed to achieve a common understanding about the nature and scope of the issues. The ten specific issues were:

1. Corporate and Community Involvement
2. Curriculum
3. Early Childhood Education
4. Funding
5. Higher Education
6. Holding Power (reducing dropout rate)
7. Literacy

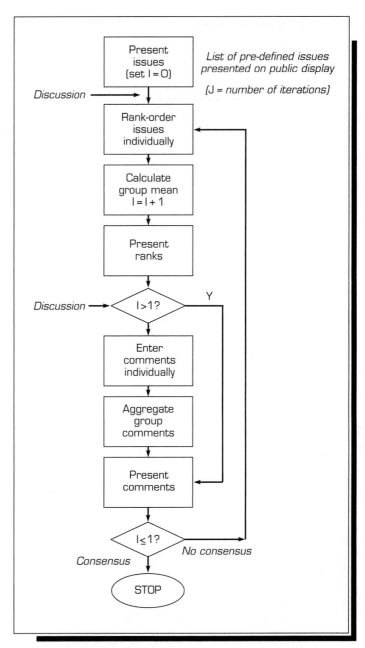

FIGURE 9.11 System Flowchart.

8. Research and Technology
9. Responsiveness to Student Needs
10. Professional Teaching Issues

Each session was scheduled for three hours. The orientation and discussion took about an hour, and then the first iteration of the GDSS process began.

The university provided facilitators and technical assistants so that the process would go smoothly and the participants could overcome any fears they might have about using a computer or an unfamiliar program. Deliberations were tape recorded to provide a record of the session and for researchers to analyze the process. An electronic log of each session was compiled by the system.

In the first iteration, participants were asked to rank order the issues, assigning a value of 10 to the most important and 1 to the least important. The system collected this information and calculated mean ranks for the group. A consensus list was displayed to the group in order of ranking. Group members were then asked to enter comments about their rankings relative to the group ranking for each of the ten issues. The system collected these comments and then presented them *by issue* back to the group. Lively discussion followed. In general, the first iteration took approximately one hour.

Substantive arguments were made for each of the issues. It was found that the participants spent more time listening than they did advocating their own points of view. There seemed to be a greater degree of understanding about others' points of view and a willingness to rethink initial positions. Although the artificiality of the process seemed to encourage participants to be on their best behavior, it is unlikely that this accounts for all of the activity expressed by group members; the GDSS also appeared to have a positive effect. Much of the discussion in this first iteration centered on what could realistically be done given limited resources.

A second iteration was then initiated, and participants reprioritized the issues on the basis of prior discussion. There was a greater degree of consensus the second time around. A brief discussion was then held, but comments were not collected electronically. This second iteration took no more than thirty minutes.

A final iteration allowed participants to prioritize the issues once more. In each case, there was a surprising degree of consensus, and participants felt they had accomplished something significant. A wrap-up discussion was then held to talk about the list and highlight the importance of advocating this priority list to implement change.

Case Questions

1. Why is this a "limited GDSS"?
2. The decision room accommodates the participants in shifts, due to the small size of the facility. What could be the impact of such a restriction?
3. Compare this case to a Delphi process.

4. What are some of the major advantages of this GDSS?
5. How would a GDSS for public policy compare with one in a for-profit organization?

References and Bibliography

1. Applegate, L. M. "Technology Support for Cooperative Work: A Framework for Studying Introduction and Assimilation in Organization." *Journal of Organizational Computing*, Vol. 1, No. 1, 1991.

2. Bostrom, R. et al. *Computer Augmented Teamwork: A Guided Tour.* New York: Van Nostrand Reinhold, 1992.

3. Bratimo, J. "An Electronic Encounter." *"Corporate Planner" Business Week*, June 1990.

4. Briere, D. "Groupware: A Spectrum of Productivity Boosters." *Network World*, September 16, 1991.

5. Buckley, S. R., and D. Yen. "Group Decision Support Systems: Concerns for Success." *The Information Society*, Vol. 7 (1990): 109–123.

6. Canning-McNurlin, B. "Experiences with Work Group Computing." *I/S Analyzer*, July 1989.

7. Connolly, T., et al. "Effects of Anonymity and Evaluative Tone on Idea Generation in Computer-Mediated Groups." *Management Science*, Vol. 36, No. 6, 1990.

8. Dennis, A., et al. "Group, Sub-Group and Nominal Group Idea Generation in an Electronic Meeting Environment." *System Sciences*, Vol. 3 (1991): 573–579.

9. Dennis, A., et al. "Information Technology to Support Electronic Meetings." *MIS Quarterly*, December 1988.

10. DeSanctis, G., and B. Gallupe. "A Foundation for the Study of Group Decision Support Systems." *Management Science*, Vol. 33, No. 5 (1987): 589–609.

11. DeSanctis, G., and B. Gallupe. "Group Decision Support Systems: A New Frontier." *Data Base*, Winter 1985. Also see *Management Science*, May 1987.

12. DeSanctis, G., et al. "Using Computing to Facilitate the Quality Improvement Process: The IRS-Minnesota." *Interfaces*, November-December, 1991.

13. Dickson, G. W. "Futures in Computer Supported Collaborative Work: A Look at GDSS Practice & Research," *DSS-91 Transactions*, The Institute of Management Science, June 1991.

14. Ellis, C. A., et al. "Groupware: Some Issues and Experiences (Using Computer to Facilitate Human Interaction)." *Communication of the ACM*, Vol. 34, January 1991.

15. Finholt, T., and L. S. Sproull. "Electronic Groups at Work." *Organization Science*, Vol. 1, No. 1, 1990.

16. Finley, M. "Welcome to the Electronic Meeting." *Training*, July 1991.

17. Gallupe, B., and G. DeSanctis. "Computer-Based Support for Group Problem-Finding: An Experimental Investigation." *MIS Quarterly*, June 1988.

18. Gray, P. "Group Decision Support Systems." *Transactions DSS 86,* Washington, DC, April 21–23, 1986.
19. Gray, P., and L. Olfman. "The User Interface in Group Decision Support Systems." *Decision Support Systems,* Vol. 5, No. 2, 1989.
20. Greif, I. *Computer Supported Cooperative Work: A Book of Readings.* San Mateo, CA: Morgan-Kaufman, 1988.
21. Grohowski, R., and C. McGoff. "Implementing Electronic Meeting Systems at IBM: Lessons Learned and Success Factors." *MIS Quarterly,* December 1990.
22. Hiltz, S. R., and K. Johnson. "User Satisfaction with Computer-Mediated Communication Systems." *Management Science,* June 1990.
23. Huber, G. P. "Issues in the Design of Group Decision Support Systems." *MIS Quarterly,* September 1984.
24. Jelassi, M., and A. Foroughi. "Negotiation Support Systems: An Overview of Design Issues and Existing Software." *Decision Support Systems,* Vol. 5 (1989): 167–81.
25. Jessup, L. M., et al. "The Effects of Anonymity on GDSS Group Process with an Idea-Generating Task." *MIS Quarterly,* Vol. 14, No. 3, 1990.
26. Jessup L. M., and J. Valacich (eds.). *Group Support Systems: New Perspectives.* New York: Macmillan, 1993.
27. Johansen, R. *Groupware: Computer Support for Business Teams.* New York: Free Press, 1988.
28. Kraemer, K. L., and J. L. King. "Computer-Based System for Cooperative and Group Decision Making." *ACM Computing Surveys,* Vol. 20, No. 2, 1988.
29. Lindstone, H., and M. Turroff. *The Delphi Method: Technology and Applications.* Reading, MA: Addison-Wesley, 1975.
30. McNurlin, B., and R. Sprague, Jr. *Information Systems Management.* 2nd ed. Englewood Cliffs, NJ: Prentice-Hall, 1989.
31. Mockler, R. J. *Computer Software to Support Strategic Management Decision Making.* New York: Macmillan, 1992.
32. Mockler, R. J., and D. G. Dologite. "Using Computer Software to Improve Group Decision Making." *Long Range Planning,* Vol. 24, No. 4, 1991.
33. Mumpower, J. and F. Darling. "Modeling Resource Allocation Negotiations." *Systems Sciences,* Vol. 3, 1991.
34. Nunamaker, J. F., Jr., D. Chappel, D. Vogel, and C. McGoff. "Electronic Meeting System: A Tutorial." University of Arizona, January 2, 1990.
35. Nunamaker, J. F., Jr., et al. "Electronic Meeting Systems to Support Group Work: Theory and Practice at Arizona." Working paper, College of Business, University of Arizona, March 27, 1990.
36. Nunamaker, J. F., Jr., et al. "Electronic Meeting Systems to Support Group Work." *Communication of the ACM,* July 1991.
37. Pastrick, G. "Brainstorming Software: A Free Flow of Ideas." *PC Magazine,* April 30, 1991.
38. Sage, P. A., *Decision Support Systems Engineering.* New York: John Wiley & Sons, 1991.

39. Sengupta, K., and D. Te'eni, "Reducing Cognitive Conflict Through Feedback in GDSS." *System Sciences,* Vol. 3, 1991.

40. Southworth, M. "How to Have an Electronic Brainstorm." *Think Magazine,* No. 1, 1990.

41. Straub, D. W., Jr., and R. A. Beauclair. "Current and Future Uses of Group Decision Support System Technology: Report of A Recent Empirical Study." *Journal of Management Information Systems,* Vol. 5, No. 1, Summer 1988.

42. Taylor, R. L., and R. A. Beauclair, "GDSS as a Tool in Public Policy: The Louisville Experience," *DSS 89 Transactions,* Institute of Management Sciences, 1990.

43. Turoff, M. "Computer-Mediated Communication Requirements for Group Support." *Journal of Organizational Computing,* March 1991.

44. Valacich, J. S., et al. "Electronic Meeting Support: The Group Systems Concept." *International Journal of Man-Machine Studies,* February 1991.

45. Vogel, D., et al. "Group Decision Support Systems: Determinants of Success." *Transactions DSS 87,* San Francisco, June 1987.

Chapter 10

Executive Information and Support Systems

Most existing DSS users are professionals (e.g., financial analysts, loan officers, auditors, or production schedulers) or middle managers. Very seldom, however, do these systems directly support top executives. Why is this so? What are the needs of top executives and what is needed in computer-based information systems to make them more appropriate for the upper managerial levels? For answers let us examine a new development in managerial support, the executive information and support system. This chapter is divided into the following sections:

391

10.1   Executive Information System at Hertz Corporation*

The Problem

The car rental industry is characterized by cut-throat competition and fast-shifting opportunities. Hertz, the largest company in the industry, competes against dozens of competitors in hundreds of locations. The key to success is marketing. Several marketing decisions must be made almost instantaneously (e.g., whether to follow a competitor's price discount or not). These decisions are decentralized, and are based on information about cities, climates, holidays, business cycles, tourist activities, past promotions and competitors' and customers' behavior. The amount of such information is huge, and the only way to process it is to use a large mainframe computer. The problem faced by Hertz was how to provide accessibility to this information and use it properly.

The Initial Solution—A DSS

A DSS was developed in 1987 to allow fast analysis by executives and managers. The system was constructed on the corporate mainframe with System W (from Comshare Inc.). The DSS was very helpful in analyzing information, but when a marketing manager had a question he or she had to go to a staff assistant, tell that person what was needed, and then wait for the result. There were some problems with this method: the staff assistant was not always available, sometimes there were problems of misunderstanding, and quite often managers needed answers to additional questions—all of which made the process lengthy and cumbersome. When time is of essence, late information is useless to the manager. The need for a better system was obvious.

The EIS

In 1988 Hertz decided to add an EIS—a PC-based system that is used as a front-end to the DSS. The EIS was built with Commander EIS (also from Comshare Inc.). The combined system gave executives tools to analyze the mountains of stored information and make real-time decisions without the help of assistants. Now marketing executives can answer their own questions and plug in their own variables. The system is extremely user-friendly and is maintained by the marketing staff, who continuously upgrade and improve it. Since its assimilation into the corporate culture conformed to the way Hertz executives work, implementation was no problem. The system allows Hertz to better use its information and IS resources.

Executives can manipulate and refine data to be more meaningful and stra-

---

*Condensed from M. O'Leary, "Putting Hertz Executives in the Driver's Seat," *CIO Magazine,* February, 1990.

tegically significant to them. Further, the work load on the mainframe programming resources has been reduced, since the EIS allows executives to draw information from the mainframe, store the needed data on their own PCs, and perform a DSS-type analysis on their own PCs without tying up valuable mainframe time. The people at Hertz feel that the EIS creates synergy in decision making. It triggers questions, a greater influx of creative ideas, and more cost-effective marketing decisions.

10.2 Concepts and Definitions

Hertz's case indicated that neither MIS nor the addition of DSS were sufficient in supporting executives. What is needed is a tool that can handle the many needs for timely information. (See Box 10.1.) The published information about DSS shows that the majority of personal DSS support the work of professionals and middle-level managers. Institutional DSS provide support primarily to planners, analysts, and researchers. Rarely do we see a DSS used directly by top executives. In many cases DSS tools are employed by analysts in finding answers to managers' questions.

Executive information systems (EIS), also known as executive support systems (ESS) (see Rockart and Treacy [29]), is a new technology emerging in re-

---

Box 10.1: Why EIS?

The following factors were identified by Watson et al. [37] (arranged in descending order of importance).

External:

- Increased competition
- Rapidly changing environment
- Need to be more proactive
- Need to access external databases
- Increasing government regulations.

Internal:

- Need for timely information
- Need for improved communications
- Need for access to operational data
- Need for rapid status updates on different activities
- Need for increased effectiveness
- Need to be able to identify historical trends
- Need for access to corporate databases
- Need for more accurate information.

sponse to the situation just described. In a survey conducted by the Center for Information Systems Research (CISR) at MIT, it was found that more than half of the EIS systems were used by people with titles of CEO, CFO, and COO.

The growth of EIS was evident in a study released in 1986 by MIT's CISR. This study showed that about one-third of large U.S. corporations have had EIS programs installed or were developing programs. This figure had grown to more than 50 percent in 1989 (*Computerworld*, February 27, 1989).

Definitions. The terms **executive information systems** and **executive support systems** mean different things to different people. In many cases, the terms are being used interchangeably. The following definitions, based on Rockart and DeLong [30], distinguish between EIS and ESS.

- *Executive Information System (EIS).* An EIS is a computer-based system that serves the information needs of top executives. It provides rapid access to timely information and direct access to management reports. EIS is very user-friendly, supported by graphics, and provides exceptions reporting and "drill-down" capabilities. It is also easily connected with online information services and electronic mail. *Note:* **Drill down** is an important capability that enables the user to break down data to details. For example, a report on daily corporate rates can be drilled down to find the daily sales in a region, or by product, or by salesperson. A drill down helps the user to identify problems (opportunities).
- *Executive Support System (ESS).* An ESS is a comprehensive support system that goes beyond EIS to include communications, office automation, analysis support, and intelligence. (See Box 10.2.)

Box 10.2: ESS in the Persian Gulf War

The Second Marine Aircraft Wing had to plan its activities in a fast-changing political and military environment. The commanding general and his staff of about 100 needed large amounts of information, such as personnel availability, logistics status, and aviation weather conditions and forecasts. Getting all this information via telephones and paper reports was a slow and possibly inaccurate task.

Using RediMaster (from American Information Systems), a local area network, and information downloaded from a mainframe or PCs, an ESS was constructed that could provide the commanders with the needed information in seconds. The ESS included: E-mail, calendar, word processing, spreadsheet, graphics software, and anything else that could be used to support the commanders.

By mid-January, 1991, when the war started, the system was up and running and the Marine's commanding general was able to receive online, real-time reports on subjects ranging from target lists to casualty reports. Indeed, computer technology such as ESS contributed to the success of Desert Storm.

10.3   The Nature of the Executive's Work

In order to build an information system for an executive it is first necessary to understand the nature of the executive's work. A classical study on this topic was conducted by Mintzberg [24], who divided the manager's roles into three categories:

1. *Interpersonal Roles.* Figurehead, leader, liaison
2. *Informational Roles.* Monitor, disseminator, spokesperson
3. *Decisional Roles.* Entrepreneur, disturbance handler, resource allocator, negotiator.

Early EIS mainly supported some of the informational roles, while the purpose of the second generation EIS is to support as many roles as possible.

To determine the information needs of executives, it is necessary to specify the activities that are performed in each role. Table 10.1 presents the findings of a study conducted by McLeod and Jones [21]. Notice that the table provides the percentage of information transactions that were used to support the specific activities (decision roles). The table indicates that most information is used in two roles: Handling disturbances and entrepreneurial activities.

We divide the executive work, as it is related to decisional roles, into two phases. Phase I is the identification of problems and/or opportunities. Phase II

TABLE 10.1   Executive Activities and Information Support

Nature of Activity (Decision Role)	Percentage of Support
Handling disturbances. A disturbance is something that happens unexpectedly and demands immediate attention, but it might take weeks or months to resolve.	42
Entrepreneural activity. Such an activity is intended to make improvements that will increase performance levels. They are strategic and long-term in nature.	32
Resource allocation. Managers allocate resources within the framework of the annual and monthly budgets. Resource allocation is tied with budget and activity planning tasks.	17
Negotiations. The manager attempts to resolve conflicts and disputes, either internal or external to the organization. Such attempts usually involve some negotiations.	3
Other.	6

Source: McLeod and Jones [21].

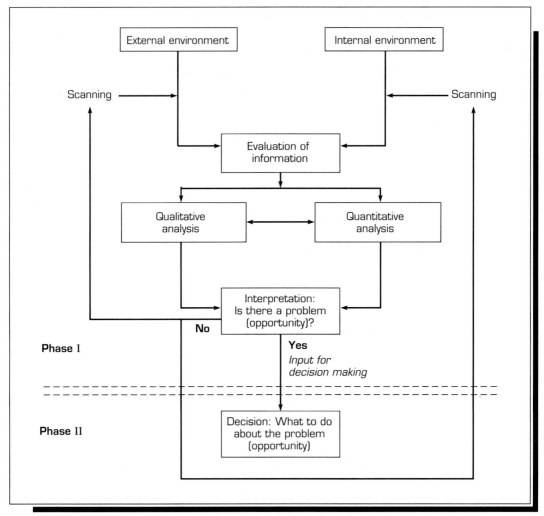

FIGURE 10.1   The Decisional Role of Process Executive Work

is the decision of what to do about it. Figure 10.1 provides a flow chart of this process and the flow of information in it.

10.4   Executives' Information Needs

As shown in Figure 10.1, information flows to the executive from the external and the internal environment. Internal information is generated from the functional units (finance, marketing, production, accounting, personnel, etc.). The external information comes from sources such as online databases, newspapers, industry newsletters, government reports, personal contacts, etc. It is clear that the combined information is extremely valuable; it is an important organizational resource needed for successful competition and survival. Due to the large amount of information available, it is necessary to **scan the environment** and data sources to find the relevant pieces. Scanning can be done by the executives themselves, by staff, and/or by machine. The collected information is then evaluated and channeled to quantitative and qualitative analysis (which is carried out by experts whenever needed). Then, a decision (by the executive or by a team) is made on whether a problem or opportunity exists. This is basically an *interpretation* of the information. If it is decided that there is a problem, then this interpretation is an input to the next step: a decision made by the executive, or by a group, on what to do about the problem. Not shown in the figure is the extensive communication that may take place among executives, managers, and staff. The basic purpose of EIS is to support the process of Figure 10.1, as well as to support the specific roles described earlier.

Methods for Finding Information Needs

There are many methods for finding executives' information needs (see Box 10.3). Three approaches are of special interest.

Box 10.3: How to Find Executives' Information Needs

1. Ask senior executives what questions they would ask upon their return from a three-week vacation.
2. Use the critical success factor methodology (discussed in Section 10.4).
3. Interview all senior managers to determine what data they think is most important.
4. List the major objectives in the short- and long-term plans and identify their information requirements.
5. Ask the executives what information they would least like for their competition to see.
6. Either through an interview or observation process, determine what information from current management reports is actually being used by the executive.
7. Provide more immediate, online access to their current management reports, and then ask them how you can better tailor the system to their needs. (Executives are much better at telling you what is wrong with what you have given them than telling you what they need.)
8. Use prototyping (show, criticize, improve). (This approach will be described later.)

---

a. Wetherbe's Approach [42]. This approach consists of a two-phase process (see Figure 10.2). In the Phase I a *structured interview* is conducted to determine the executives' perceived information needs. Wetherbe suggested three methods for conducting the structured interviews. They are: IBM's Business System Planning (BSP), Critical Success Factors (CSF), and Ends/Means (E/M) Analysis. Table 10.2 illustrates sample questions raised in each method.

In Phase II (see Figure 10.2) a **prototyping** is used. Based on the conceptual information requirements found in Phase I, a prototype of the EIS is quickly constructed (in a couple of days or weeks). The prototyped system is shown to the executives who then make suggestions for improvements. The system is modified and shown again to the executives. The testing and modification goes through several rounds of trial-and-error until the detailed requirements are established. The best sources of information are then determined and the EIS can be finished.

b. Watson and Frolick's Approach [40]. This approach is based on the following basic strategies for determining information requirements:

1. Asking (the interview approach presented earlier)
2. Deriving the needs from an existing information system
3. Synthesis from characteristics of the systems
4. Discovering from experimentation with evolving systems that are utilized (prototyping).

Based on these approaches, the authors suggested ten specific methods that are organized along two dimensions: (1) the source of information (either direct

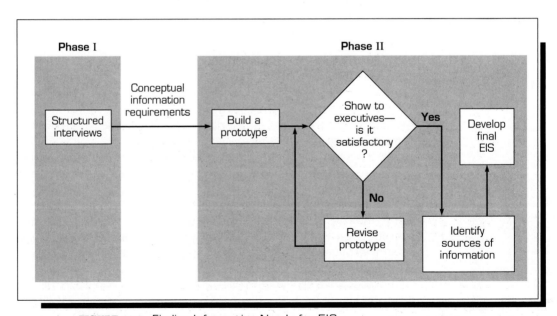

FIGURE 10.2 Finding Information Needs for EIS

TABLE 10.2 Methods and Sample Questions for Structured Interviews

Method	Sample Interview Questions
1. *The executive interview portion of IBM's Business System Planning (BSP):* Specify problems and decisions	a. What are the major problems encountered in accomplishing the purposes of the organizational unit you manage? b. What are good solutions to those problems? c. How can information play a role in any of those solutions? d. What are the major decisions associated with your management responsibilities? e. What improvements in information could result in better decisions?
2. *Critical Success Factors (CSF):* Specify critical factors	a. What are the critical success factors of the organizational unit you manage? Most managers have four to eight of these. b. What information is needed to ensure that critical success factors are under control? c. How do you measure the specific CSFs? For example: Prompt shipment of orders (a CSF) is measured by delivery time.
3. *End/Means (E/M) Analysis:* Specify effectiveness criteria or outputs and efficiency criteria for processes used to generate outputs	a. What is the end: goods or services provided by the business process? b. What makes these goods or services effective to recipients or customers? c. What information is needed to evaluate that effectiveness? d. What are the key means or processes used to generate or provide goods or services? e. What constitutes efficiency in the providing of these goods or services? f. What information is needed to evaluate that efficiency?

or indirect interaction with the executive) and (2) the primary method of determining requirements (computerized vs. noncomputerized). The ten methods are shown in Table 10.3.

c. Volonino and Watson's Approach [35]. This approach takes a company-wide perspective for EIS development. A six-step process is proposed:

1. Identify strategic business objectives.
2. Identify critical business processes.
3. Prioritize the above.
4. Define the information needed for the above.
5. Identify links among business processes.
6. Plan a modular EIS development, implementation, and evaluation.

TABLE 10.3 Methods for Assessing Information Requirements.

Interaction	Noncomputer Related	Computer Related
Direct Executive Interaction	▪ Participation in strategic planning sessions ▪ Formal CSF sessions ▪ Informal discussions of information needs ▪ Tracking executive activity	▪ Collaborative work system sessions
Indirect Executive Interaction	▪ Discussions with support personnel ▪ Examination of noncomputer-generated information ▪ Attendance at meetings	▪ Software tracking of EIS usage ▪ Examinations of computer-generated information

Source: Watson and Frolick [40]. *Reprinted from Journal of Information Systems Management* (New York: Auerbach Publications). © 1992 Research Institute of America Inc. Used with permission.

10.5   The Characteristics of EIS

The desired characteristics of EIS as well as its benefits are presented in Table 10.4. Not all implemented systems possess all of these characteristics.

Discussion of Important Terms Related to the Characteristics

a. Drill Down. One of the most useful capabilities of an EIS is to provide details of any given information. For example, an executive may notice a decline in corporate sales in a daily (or weekly) report. To find the reason, the executive may like to see sales in each region. If a problematic region is identified, the executive may like to see further details (e.g., by product or by salesperson). In certain cases, this "drill down" process may continue into several levels of detail. To provide such capability, the EIS may include several thousand menus and submenus.

b. Critical Success Factors (CSF). Critical factors that must be considered in attaining the organization's goals are called CSFs. Such factors can be strategic or operational, and are derived mainly from three sources: organizational factors, industry factors, and environmental factors. Success factors can be at the corporate level as well as other levels (division, plant, department). Sometimes it is necessary to consider the CSF of individuals.

Critical success factors, once identified, can be monitored by five types of information (per Kogan [17]). They are: key problems narratives, highlight charts, top-level financials, key factors, and detailed responsibility reports. A brief description of each follows on page 402.

TABLE 10.4 The Characteristics and Benefits of EIS.

Quality of information:
- Is flexible
- Produces correct information
- Produces timely information
- Produces relevant information
- Produces complete information
- Produces validated information.

User interface:
- Includes sophisticated graphic user interface (e.g., GUI)
- Includes a user-friendly interface
- Allows secure and confidential access to information
- Has a short response time (timely information)
- Is accessible from many places
- Includes a reliable access procedure
- Minimizes keyboard use; alternatively uses infrared controllers, mouse, touch pads, and touch screen
- Provides quick retrieval of desired information
- Is tailored to management styles of individual executives
- Contains self-help menu.

Technical capability provided:
- Access to aggregate (global) information
- Extensive use of external data
- Written interpretations
- Highlights problem indicators
- Hypertext and hypermedia
- Ad hoc analysis
- Information presented in hierarchical form
- Incorporates graphic and text in the same display
- Provides management by exception reports
- Shows trends, ratios, and deviations
- Provides access to historical and most current data
- Organized around critical success factors
- Provides forecasting capability
- Produces information at various levels of details ("drill down")
- Filters, compresses, and tracks critical data
- Supports open-ended problem explanation.

Benefits:
- Facilitates the attainment of organizational objectives
- Facilitates access to information
- Allows the user to be more productive
- Increases the quality of decision making
- Provides a competitve advantage
- Saves time for the user
- Increases communication capacity
- Increases communication quality
- Provides better control in the organization
- Allows the anticipation of problems/opportunities
- Allows planning
- Allows finding the cause of a problem
- Meets the needs of executives.

Source: Based on Bergerson et al. [2]

1. *Key Problems Narratives.* These reports highlight overall performance, key problems, and the possible reasons for the problems within an organization. Explanations are often combined with tables, graphs, or tabular information.
2. *Highlight Charts.* These summary displays show high-level information based on the user's own judgment or preference. Because they are designed from the user's perspective, these displays quickly highlight areas of concern, visually signaling the state of organizational performance against CSF.
3. *Top-level Financials.* These displays provide information on the overall financial health of the company in the form of absolute numbers and comparative performance ratios.
4. *Key Factors.* These factors provide specific measures of CSF, called key performance indicators (KPI), at the corporate level. The displays are often used on an exceptional basis to examine specific measures of CSF that are flagged as problems on the highlight charts (see Box 10.4).
5. *Detailed KPI Responsibility Reports.* These reports indicate the detailed performance of individuals or business units in those areas critical to the success of the company.

c. Status Access. In this mode the *latest data* or reports on the status of key variables can be accessed at any time, by using telecommunications. The *relevance* of information is important here. Emphasis is placed on the latest data.

Box 10.4: Typical Key Performance Indicators

Profitability	Profitability measures for each department, product, region, etc. Comparisons among departments and products and with competitors.
Financial	Financial ratios, balance sheet analysis, reserve position, rate of return on investment
Marketing	Market share, advertisement analysis, product pricing, weekly (daily) sales results, customer sales potential
Human Resources	Turnover rate
Planning	Corporate partnership ventures, growth/share analysis
Economic Analysis	Market trends, foreign exchange, industry trends, labor cost trends
Consumer Trend	Consumer confidence level, purchasing habits, demographical data

This may require daily or even hourly operational tracking and reporting. In extreme cases, real-time reporting may be required. Although status access allows executives to pursue the information requested (e.g., to conduct a drill down), it is not geared to *data manipulation*.

d. Personalized Analysis. Analytical capabilities are available in executive support systems (ESS). Instead of merely having access to the data, executives can use the ESS to do creative analysis on their own. This analysis is personalized. The executives select the contents of the databases, the programming tools to be used (e.g., Lotus 1-2-3, Excel, IFPS), the outputs (information requirements), and the desired presentation of information.

e. Exception Reporting. **Exception reporting** is based on the concept of *management by exception*. According to this concept, attention should be given by the executive to exceptions from the standards. Thus, in exception reporting the executive's attention will be called only to cases of very bad (or very good) performance. This approach saves considerable time for the producers and readers of reports.

10.6   Comparing EIS and MIS

In examining several of the EIS characteristics in the previous section one may come to the conclusion that an EIS is nothing but a fancy MIS. However, as indicated by Millet et al. [23], this is really not the case; their view of the relationship between MIS and EIS is shown in Figure 10.3.

According to their view, MIS provides managers with detailed and summarized information from operational databases, which are created by the various functional transaction processes (TPS) activities in the various business areas (e.g., accounting, finance, marketing). Therefore, the capabilities of MIS are constrained by the limitations of TPS, which are relatively inflexible. For example, transactions may be updated only once a month. Also, MIS are basically geared to *internal* data. MIS is usually geared to one functional area (accounting information systems, marketing information systems). Thus, MIS lacks data integration across functional areas. This may result in a serious limitation when attempting to satisfy the needs of top management for comprehensive organization-wide information. Millet et al. summarized the differences between MIS and EIS in a tabular form (see Table 10.5 on p. 405).

In addition, several EIS capabilities, such as making presentations that fit the decision styles of specific users, are simply too expensive to be designed in an MIS system that serves hundreds or thousands of users, of whose population changes continuously. Another deficiency of a traditional MIS is slow response time. This is mainly due to the fact that the information they process is not oriented to the format, content, or organization of the executive's need. Furthermore, executive decision making, especially that of a strategic nature, is complex and multidimensional. Conventional MIS are usually designed to deal

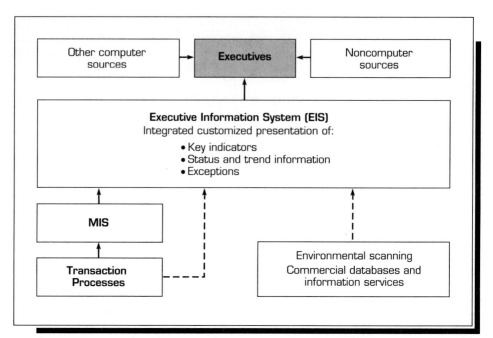

FIGURE 10.3   The EIS Role (*Source:* Reprinted with permission, Millet et al. [23], DSS-91 Transactions, Eleventh International Conference on Decision Support Systems, Ilze Zigurs (Ed.), The Institute of Management Sciences, 290 Westminster Street, Providence, Rhode Island 02903.)

with fairly structured and much simpler configurations. Finally, conventional MIS are *not* usually designed to combine data from different sources.

10.7   Comparing and Integrating EIS and DSS

The above characteristics and capabilities are unique to EIS primarily because an EIS is designed to support top executives, helping them to discover problems and opportunities. A DSS, on the other hand, supports an analysis that aims at giving an answer to the question of what to do with a problem (or an opportunity). Tables 10.6 and 10.7 compare the two systems. Table 10.6 contains portions of typical DSS definitions as they relate to EIS. Table 10.7 compares EIS and DSS along several dimensions (which are derived from the characteristics and capabilities of EIS).

Examination of the two tables points out that in a general sense, EIS is really part of the decision support field. That is, it is designed to support some tasks of the top management decision process. However, in a functional sense, EIS and DSS are two different, although complementary, applications. The differences are simple but profound. Fundamentally, EIS is a structured, automated tracking system that operates continuously to keep management abreast of what is happening in all important areas both inside and outside the corporation. EIS

TABLE 10.5 MIS and EIS: A Comparison

System	Primary Purpose	Primary Users	Primary Output	Primary Operations	Time Orientation	Example
MIS	Internal monitoring	Managers and executives	Pre-defined periodic reports	Summarize information	Past	Sales report
EIS	Internal and external monitoring	Executives	Pre-defined customized periodic or ad-hoc reports, presentations and queries	Integrate present, track CSF	Past and present	Market share tracking

Source: Reprinted with permission, Millet et al. [23], DSS-91 Transactions, Eleventh International Conference on Decision Support Systems, Ilze Zigurs (Ed.), The Institute of Management Sciences, 290 Westminster Street, Providence, Rhode Island 02903.)

is designed to support the complex and multidimensional nature of top-level decision making. Furthermore, the major role of EIS is to provide *communication*.

EIS delivers information that managers need in their day-to-day job responsibilities. The information is typically presented in a structured, easy-to-access manner with only limited capability for *direct* ad hoc analysis. If there are analytical capabilities in EIS, they tend to be of a repetitive nature (e.g., trend analysis), as opposed to the unique ad hoc analysis of DSS. Although this is the usual case, both DSS and EIS may center on the investigation and understanding of problems that are not necessarily predictable, structured, or repetitive.

TABLE 10.6 Definitions of DSS as They Relate to EIS

Relevant Portion of DSS Definition	Comparison to EIS	Author
"CBIS consisting of three subsystems: a problem-solving subsystem . . ."	No problem-solving subsystem exists in an EIS.	Bonczek et al. [3]
"DSS can be developed *only* through an adaptive process . . ."	EIS is not usually developed through an adaptive process.	Keen [16]
"Model-based set of procedures . . ."	EIS is not model based.	Little [19]
"Extendable system . . . , supporting decision modeling . . . , used at irregular intervals."	EIS is not extendable, does not have modeling capabilities, and it is used at regular intervals.	Moore and Chang [25]
"Utilizes data and models . . ."	EIS does not utilize models.	Scott-Morton [33]

TABLE 10.7   A Comparison of EIS and DSS

Dimension	EIS	DSS
Focus	Status access	Analysis, decision support
Typical users served	Senior executives	Analysts, professionals, managers (via intermediaries)
Impetus	Expediency	Effectiveness
Application	Environmental scanning, performance evaluation, identification of problems and opportunities	Diversified areas where managerial decisions are made
Decision support	Indirect support, mainly high-level and unstructured decisions and policies	Supports semistructured and unstructured decision making, and ad hoc, but some repetitive, decisions
Type of information	News items, external information on customers, competitors, and the environment; scheduled and demand reports on internal operations	Information to support specific situations
Principle use	Tracking and control	Planning, organizing, staffing, and control
Adaptability to individual users	Tailored to the decision-making style of each individual executive, offers several options of outputs	Permits individuals' judgment, what-if capabilities, some choice of dialog style
Graphics	A must	Important part of many DSS
User-friendliness	A must	A must if no intermediaries are used
Treatment of information	Filters and compresses information, tracks critical data and information	Information that is provided by the EIS is used as an input to the DSS
Supporting detailed information	Instant access to the supporting details of any summary ("drill down")	Can be programmed into the DSS, but usually not
Model base	Can be added, usually included or limited in nature	The core of the DSS
Construction	By vendors or IS specialists	By users, either alone or in combination with specialists from the IC or the IS department
Hardware	Distributed systems. Some run on micros	Mainframe, micros, or distributed
Nature of software packages	Interactive, easy access to multiple databases, online access, sophisticated DBMS capabilities, complex linkages	Large computational capabilities, modeling languages and simulation, application and DSS generators

EIS is designed very differently from DSS. For example, a good EIS must offer a high-speed, nontechnical method for managers to investigate business dynamics (i.e., to understand where and why things are happening, so tactical changes and course corrections can be made). This is also a major area that distinguishes EIS from a standard MIS reporting system. Any summary coming up on an EIS screen must offer instant access to the supporting detail; otherwise, it is just a glorified slide show. In addition, the supporting details must be meaningful (e.g., time-series orientation with graphic and numerical content or written narratives from those "in the know"). In this fashion, a simple analysis or investigation can be quickly and easily accomplished by the nontechnical manager.

DSS overlaps this process when more complex analysis is required to understand *why* things are happening the way they are or to investigate alternative solutions to a problem or a prospective opportunity. These appraisals are done as needed, usually require evaluation of much raw data, consume more time, and almost always require an analyst who is technically proficient with the tools at hand.

Integrating EIS and DSS—An Executive Support System (ESS)

Previously, we concluded that EIS differs from DSS. And indeed, they are being used as two independent products by many organizations. However, in some cases it makes sense to integrate the two technologies. It is especially common for EIS to be used as a source of data for PC-based DSS modeling applications. For example, at a large drug company, product (brand) managers download from Pilot's Command Center (an EIS) the previous day's orders of their products. The download creates a Lotus-readable file on their PC disk. They then exit to a PC and run a Lotus DSS model against the data to predict where they will be at the end of the month. The results of this model are then uploaded to the EIS. So, by 11 A.M. every morning, senior managers can get on their EIS and see where each brand manager thinks he or she is going to be at the end of the month. This is a good example of the complementary nature of EIS and DSS.

The integration of EIS and DSS can be accomplished in several ways. The most likely is that the output of the EIS is being used as an input to the DSS. For instance, executives at GE's Major Appliance Division decided that an immediate marketing response was needed to a competitor's action reported by the EIS. Exactly what that response would be, however, might well have been determined by DSS models and simulation tools. More sophisticated systems include feedback from the DSS to the EIS and even an explanation capability. An integrated EIS/DSS is often called an executive support system (ESS) and, if an intelligent module with explanation and interpretation capabilities is added, then the system can be defined as an "intelligent ESS." (See Chapter 18.)

Another dimension along which EIS and DSS can be compared is the users' roles. Executive roles differ substantially from the roles of the typical users of DSS, namely middle line and functional supervisory levels and functional analysts, such as financial and marketing analysts. Although lower level managers focus much of their time on pursuing predetermined strategies, executives are faced with developing these strategies. Ambiguity and uncertainty characterize an executive's environment, resulting in a need for "what-if" and "goal-seeking" analyses that are provided by most DSS. Yet, studies have shown that many senior executives leave this technical analysis to lower level, functional managers and staff analysts. It is possible that this occurrence results because functional managers have less of a need for status updates, due to their proximity to the functional areas of business. Top level executives, on the other hand, are more isolated from functional operations, and need to be informed of these activities on a timely basis. It is only with these reports that senior executives can pursue planning functions and set corporate strategy.

Another point is that although much of this information is internal, the demand for external data exists as well. Whatever the needed information is about, be it industry, competitors, or general environmental scanning, executives need systems that can provide external information. To address such divergent needs of the executive, an ESS must be able to provide not only an MIS reporting capability, but a user-friendly, less complex DSS component as well.

The integration of EIS and DSS is reflected in the tools offered by the major vendors as seen in Box 10.5.

Integrating EIS and GDSS

As shown in Figure 10.1, the information generated in phase I flows to phase II, where determination is made on what to do about the problem. A DSS supports the quantitative analysis of phase I and can support phase II as well. Therefore, it makes sense to integrate an EIS (which supports most of the tasks in phase I) with DSS. In phase II, however, the decision may be made by a group. Therefore, it is likely that the EIS will be integrated with some GDSS applications. For example, an EIS can be used to provide information in a decision room setting.

10.8   Hardware

There are at least four options for hardware configurations for an EIS. The simplest option is to support executives from mainframe computers using graphics terminals. In general, this approach is difficult to implement successfully, because the options for implementing the user interface are much more limited than is acceptable for executive users. A second configuration is to have personal computers connected to a mainframe or a minicomputer. In this situation, the PCs handle the interface and some of the data reduction functions, while the large system handles the data management and the bulk of the analysis. The third option involves PCs only. In this case, information is downloaded onto stand-alone LANs, and then it is delivered to PCs. See Davis [6]. In the fourth configuration, which seems to be the configuration of the future, workstations are used in a network, so that the interface is handled on high-speed graphics display devices, and so that the data management and analysis can be distributed over the network. This environment offers the potential of providing maximum performance and flexibility.

The key to an effective hardware decision is to try to match the actual delivery of the system with the computational philosophy of the organization. This

Box 10.5: ESS Integrated Products

1. *Commander EIS.* This system is designed for easy interface with System W, a DSS generator. (Both products are from Comshare Inc.)

2. *EIS Toolkit.* This PC-based product (from Ferox Microsystems Inc.) works with Encore Plus, a financial modeling DSS from the same vendor. The EIS/DSS combination is designed primarily to support financial and accounting planning.

3. *Redi Master.* This is an application generator (from American Information System) for building a custom-made EIS and/or ESS. It can be used to build easy interfaces to databases, DSS generators (such as Lotus 1-2-3), and graphics. It provides for fast prototyping and quick alternation of existing systems.

4. *Command Center EIS.* This product (from Pilot Executive Software) is linked with a back-end software called Advantage/G. It is designed to help executives retrieve and *analyze* several types of corporate data.

5. *Express/EIS.* This product (from Information Resources Inc.) is an enterprise-wide system that integrates the powerful Express DSS generator with EIS II. This product is based on a multidimensional relational data model and it provides single, unifying, and flexible architecture.

6. *EIS-EPIC.* This LAN- and UNIX-based product (from EPIC Software Inc.) integrates, at the PC level, DSS capabilities with EIS.

7. *Holos.* This product (from Holistic Systems) combines EIS and DSS activities into one system, together with dynamic links to operational data.

8. *The Executive Edge.* The Executive Edge (from Execucom Systems Corp.) is an example of an integrated ESS development tool with limited artificial intelligence capabilities.

9. *IBM's Executive Decisions.* Interfaces with several DSS tools (see Section 4.11) and with TRACK-EIS (from Intelligent Office Co., of London, U.K.).

ensures that the support of whichever system is installed will be within the capabilities of the organization itself. It also makes it easier to implement an ESS that will match with the corporate culture of the implementing organization.

Organizations that go with a PC-only EIS are typically smaller than organizations that use a distributed micro/mainframe solution. They have fewer executives to serve, and manage smaller EIS information bases. Therefore they can deliver acceptable levels of performance via smaller personal computers. Larger organizations tend to prefer the micro/mainframe products such as Express-EIS, Command Center, or Commander EIS, because these tools leverage their existing investment in minicomputer/mainframe technology and databases. Larger organizations require the additional horsepower and connectivity of a shared computer to deliver acceptable response time for complex queries and analyses, to permit shared access to large information bases, and to connect executives in a geographically distributed E-mail network.

The usefulness of PC-only systems will increase with the increased desktop horsepower. These systems will also benefit from the transparent connectivity that will be available through advances in communications and database technology. The growth in distributed database software, peer-to-peer communications, and standardized network protocols should eventually permit a LAN-based or PC-based EIS solution to offer all of the capabilities of today's micro-/mainframe architectures.

An example of different architectures available with Express/EIS (from Information Resources) is shown in Box 10.6.

Box 10.6: Hardware Configuration for Express/EIS

Express/EIS supports the most cost-effective architecture. It can run on a PC LAN or on a stand-alone PC. It can also act as a front-end to a mainframe or minicomputer, and it is flexible enough to accommodate any combination of these configurations.

Standard Architecture. Express/EIS supports two standard architectures that can be extended to provide greater configuration flexibility. The two standard architectures are:

- PC workstations interactively connected to a shared database on a LAN server. In many situations, a PC/LAN alternative is best, and Express/EIS provides a powerful PC/LAN solution. Given the continually increasing power of PCs, the low hardware and support costs of LANs, and the ready user access to familiar PC packages (such as Lotus 1-2-3), the PC/LAN solution is becoming an increasingly attractive EIS alternative. This is especially true in light of the fact that the PC version of Express has the power of a mainframe product, with the ability to handle hundreds of megabytes of data.
- PC workstations operating locally, using data downloaded from a mainframe, minicomputer, or LAN server. In some situations, downloading data to individual PCs is preferable. This alternative gives you portability, reduced communications costs, independence from com-

(*Source:* Publicly advertised material from Information Resources, Inc.)

10.9   Software

Software Products. Commercially available software products typically address one or more of the following functional areas: office automation, electronic mail, information management, remote information access, and information analysis. No single product currently offers extensive features in all of these areas, although some of the more open-ended products permit ESS applications to directly incorporate additional software tools that specialize in some of these areas, such as office automation and E-mail. A representative list of EIS software products is given in Table 10.8. One of these systems, the Command Center, is described next.

The Command Center. The Command Center includes sophisticated communications software on both the mainframe and PCs. Consequently, perfor-

munications interruptions, and significant response time improvements over many mini/mainframe alternatives.

Extended Architectures. Sometimes running Express/EIS as a front-end to a mainframe or minicomputer is the most desirable configuration. This alternative makes sense if you have a large, frequently updated EIS database. Here, the PC offloads the interface processing from the host and uses the host only for the data selection and retrieval for which it is optimized.

Express/EIS can be dynamically linked to host systems in two common configurations:

- PC workstations (perhaps on a LAN) acting as dynamic front-ends to a shared Express database on a mainframe or minicomputer. This architecture takes advantage of the dictionary and syntax compatibility of Express across all platforms, in order to act in a distributed file-server mode. The Express/EIS product and catalog databases reside on the PC workstations, while the shared data variables reside on a mainframe or minicomputer. This configuration uses the Express/EIS DBA tools in a manner consistent with the two standard architectures.
- PC workstations (perhaps on a LAN) acting as dynamic front-ends to other database systems. This architecture takes advantage of Express's underlying dialog management capabilities and embedded SQL supports to manage an interactive dialog with an SQL database or any system that supports a query facility (e.g., ADABAS).

TABLE 10.8   Representative EIS Products

Product	Vendor	Architecture
Access Executive	Dialogue	All
AMIS	Interactive Software Services	Host
CIO-Vision	Computer Associates	LAN
Command Center	Pilot Executive Software	Host
Commander EIS	Comshare Inc.	All
Compete	Manageware	LAN
EIS	CompuServe/Collier Jackson	LAN
EIS/Cor.Per.Ana.	Cogent Information Systems	PC
EIS-Track	Intelligent Office Co.	LAN
Encore EIS Toolkit	Xerox Microsystems	LAN
Epic	Epic Software	LAN
Exec. Info. System	Meta Media	All
Exec. Man. System	Softouch Software	LAN
Execumate II	Southware Innovations	All
Executive Edge	Execucom Systems Corp.	Host
Executive Decisions	IBM Corp.	Host
Express/EIS	Information Resources	LAN
Focus/EIS	Information Builders	LAN
Forest & Trees	Channel Computing	LAN
Framework IV	Ashton-Tate	LAN
Global Info Manager	Global Software	Host
Harry	Adviseurs	Host
Holos	Holistic Systems	All
IBM Data Interp Sys	Metaphor Computer Systems	LAN
IMRS Ontrack	IMRS Inc.	LAN
Interactive Query	New Generation Software	Host
LightShip	Pilot Executive Software	LAN
Manager's Portfolio	Easel Corp.	LAN
Metafact	Integrated Data Architects	All
Optimal Manager	Transpower Corp.	LAN
Probus EIS	Decision Technologies	PC
Redimaster	American Information Systems	LAN
Resolve 2000	Metapraxis	LAN
Smartview	Dun & Bradstreet Software	All
The SAS Application System	SAS Institute	All
Vital Signs 2000	Software 2000	Host

mance is exceptionally fast even over lower-speed communications links. The structure of the Command Center is shown in Figure 10.4 on page 414. Notice that the Command Center does not have a model base. However, it does have an interface that allows it to receive and transmit data to and from DSS, free-standing model(s), or other CBIS.

Note: For a complete EIS software review, see *Computer World,* July 22, 1991.

The EIS software products are designed to provide the extensive capabilities discussed earlier. They are usually structured in a modular fashion. An example of five EIS screens representing five modules is provided in Box 10.7 on page 415, as explained below:

Screen A   Status report (with possibility of drill down and exception re-
            porting): textual explanation and trend graph
Screen B   Reminder: notes, calendar, tracking information about messages
Screen C   Investigation: comparisons, calculations, drill down, personal-
            ized analysis, graphics
Screen D   Electronic mail: alerts if mail is pending, monitoring mail, can
            transmit any screen of the other modules
Screen E   News service: both external and internal with capability to drill
            down for details. Hypertext capabilities are available

Note: Several other EIS products are structured in a modular fashion. Notable is IBM's Executive Decisions and Pilot's The Command Center.

EIS on LAN: The LightShip Example. An interesting EIS product specifically designed both for LAN and an easy GUI (using Windows) is LightShip (from Pilot Executive Software). This is a product that can be classified as a client/server EIS, which is designed to provide enterprise-wide open system solutions. LightShip can be used to build simple EIS by end-users. It also can be used as a client working with Pilot's Command Center as a server. In such a case the user may have all the power of Command Center plus the capabilities of LightShip (GUI, open architecture, object-oriented programming environment and accessibility to many LAN data servers, such as dBase files and Lotus files). With its Dynamic Data Exchange capability (DDE), it is possible to access thousands of programs via the LAN and Windows. Several screens from LightShip are shown in Box 10.8.

10.10 System Development

Like any other system, EIS can be developed in-house, or it can be purchased. If developed in-house it can be programmed from scratch, or it can be developed with special productivity tools. For example, Interactive Images (Woburn, MA) sells an EIS generator called EASEL.

Another approach is an attempt to modify an existing information system to serve EIS goals. Several companies attempted to turn their DSS into a dual

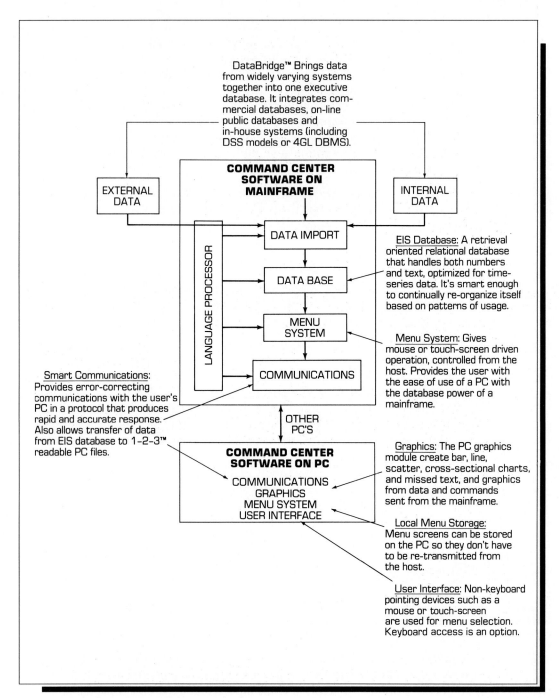

FIGURE 10.4   Command Center. (*Source:* Courtesy of Pilot Executive Software, Boston, MA. Used with permission.)

Box 10.7: Sample Screens from Commander EIS

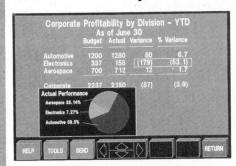

Screen A: Status report (Briefing Book
Module)

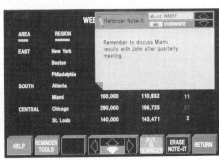

Screen B: Reminder note, attached in
appropriate place (Reminder
Module)

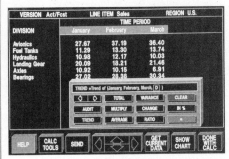

Screen C: Investigation, analysis, exceptions
(Execu-View Module)

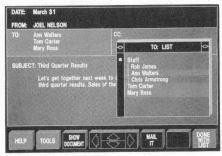

Screen D: Electronic mail (Redi-Mail Module)

Screen E: News service, external and internal
(Newswire Module)

(*Source:* Courtesy of Comshare Inc. [One screen from each major module.])

Box 10.8: Screens from LightShip

Screen (a) shows the visual programming environment. Various EIS routines are activated once icons are defined. Appropriate reports or presentations appear as a result. For example, (b) and (c) are generated. Queries are answered with scrolled bars (c).

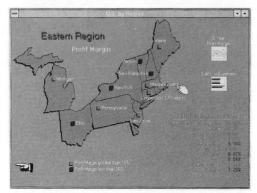

(a)

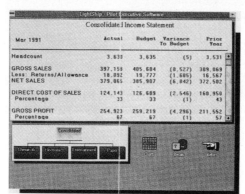

(b)

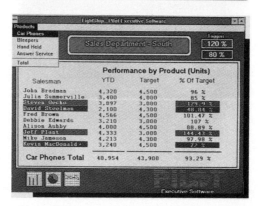

(c)

purpose (DSS/EIS) system. This usually does not work. The reason is that a DSS that is productive for an analyst may be counterproductive for the executive. All the design criteria and the capabilities are completely different as well. These systems are designed differently and they perform different functions.

Another interesting issue is who is going to be the EIS developer. In contrast with DSS, which can be built by the information system people and even by end-users, EIS and ESS are usually constructed by vendors or information system consultants. The following are some explanations to this situation: *First* of all, it typically takes more personnel to create an EIS than to maintain it over time. Temporary consultants can make up this difference. *Second,* outside consultants bring a level of objectivity that might be required to identify the real needs of executives in the organization. Insiders often have too many preconceptions and too much historical perspective to correctly identify the critical success factors affecting the organization today. Executives may also be more reluctant to open up and discuss their real information problems with a member of the in-house MIS staff than with an outside consultant. *Third,* and perhaps most important, is that the area of computer-based executive support is too new for any established application paradigms or—probably—any extensive in-house expertise. The chances of being successful will go up appreciably if one works with experienced outside consultants who have already developed several successful executive support applications for other organizations. Experienced consultants will know the pitfalls to avoid, such as how to properly condition the expectations of the executive users. They can also ensure that the first prototype shown to the executives is both immediately useful and delivered in a reasonably short time period. *Fourth,* the executive user generally has many other tasks to perform and cannot take much time out of his/her already busy schedule to do the development, whereas the DSS developer's tasks are primarily oriented around the analysis of data, and so the development of the DSS is a normal part of the job. *Fifth,* the data requirements of an EIS typically span multiple parts of an organization, and the data itself may reside on different computer systems. The procedural difficulties that this raises can only be solved by a trained technical analyst. *Sixth,* the analytical underpinnings to a good EIS are sometimes quite detailed and complex. Once again, although this may be something the executives could do, it is not something they should be doing given the competing demands on their time. *Seventh,* the interface issues and the presentation techniques on which the system is based require the attention of professionals skilled in the communication of information. Anything less might result in information displays that could mislead. *Finally,* the organizational impacts of EIS can be significant. If these issues are not handled well, the EIS can easily be destroyed by political problems.

The Process. The process of building an ESS can be very complex and lengthy. The general phases are similar to those that are used in other management support systems (see Chapters 7 and 16). The complexity of the process can be seen in Table 10.9, which summarizes an EIS development framework. The framework is divided into three modules—first, structural perspective (see

TABLE 10.9 Aspects of the
EIS Development Framework.

STRUCTURAL

Personnel

    EIS Initiator
    Executive Sponsor
    Operating Sponsor
    EIS Builder/Support Staff
    EIS Users
    Functional Area Personnel
    IS Personnel

Data

    Internal
    External

DEVELOPMENT PROCESS

External and Internal Pressures
Cost/Benefit Analysis
Costs
    Development Costs
    Annual Operating Costs
Development Time
Development Methodology
Hardware
Software
Spread
Evolution
Information Provided
EIS Capabilities

USER-SYSTEM DIALOG

Knowledge Base
    Training
    User Documentation
    System User

Action Language
    User-System Interface
    System Response Time

Presentation Language
    Multiple Information Formats
    Color

Source: Watson et al. [41]. Used with permission.

Figure 10.5), then a development process, and finally a user-system dialog development, which is extremely important (a good EIS interface is said to be "seductive" to attract users). The complexity of building an EIS is demonstrated in Figure 10.6. This is an example of an EIS at Rockwell International Corporation (see Armstrong [1]). Notice that building the system is a team effort, so coordination is needed.

The developer needs to consider the issues discussed earlier and especially

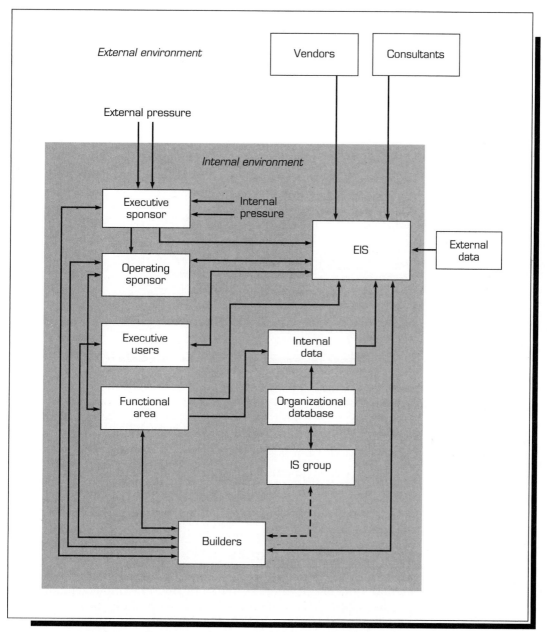

FIGURE 10.5 Structural Perspective of the EIS Development Framework (*Source:* Watson et al. [41]. Used with permission.)

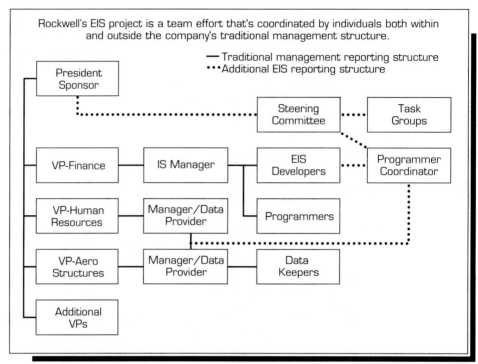

Rockwell's EIS project is a team effort that's coordinated by individuals both within and outside the company's traditional management structure.

— Traditional management reporting structure
••• Additional EIS reporting structure

FIGURE 10.6 Rockwell's EIS Executive Framework (*Source:* Armstrong, "The People Factor in EIS Success." Reprinted with permission of *DATAMATION* Magaine, April 1, 1990 © 1990 by Cahners Publishing Company).

the establishment of information needs (see Section 10.4 and the Lockheed Corp. debate in Appendix B to this book).

The appropriate development of EIS requires attention to EIS implementation factors. These are presented in the next section.

10.11 EIS Implementation: Success or Failure

The implementation of an EIS could be different from the implementation of a DSS or any other CBIS, since it involves executives. DeLong and Rockart [7] offer the following list of factors that they feel are critical for the successful implementation of EIS:

1. *A committed and informed executive sponsor.* There must be an executive who has both a realistic understanding of the capabilities (and limitations) of EIS, and who really wants the system so badly that he or she is willing to put considerable time and energy into seeing that a system

gets developed. There should also be commitment of company resources for a long period.

2. *An operating sponsor.* Because the executive sponsor usually lacks sufficient time to devote to the project, it appears very worthwhile to have an "operating sponsor" designated to manage the details of implementation from the user's side.

3. *Clear link to business objective(s).* The EIS must help in solving business problems or meet a need that is addressed most effectively with information systems (IS) technology. There should be a clear benefit to using the technology. It must provide something that would not otherwise be available, such as very rapid access to external databases, superb graphical displays, or data with textual annotations.

4. *Appropriate IS resources.* The quality of the EIS project manager on the IS side is most critical. This person should have not only technical knowledge, but also business knowledge and the ability to communicate effectively with senior management.

5. *Appropriate technology.* The choice of hardware and software has a major bearing on the acceptance or rejection of a system. One of the early barriers to executive support systems has been the lack of hardware and software that could meet the demands of highly variable executive work styles and environments. Things are improving, however, as more and more products are being designed specifically for the EIS market.

6. *Management of data problems.* The physical and technical ability to provide reliable access to data can be a major issue in EIS development. Aggregating, accessing, and managing databases in a corporation with multiple divisions can be the biggest physical roadblock to the EIS implementation.

7. *Management of organizational resistance.* Political resistance to EIS is one of the most common causes of implementation failure. An EIS alters information flows, and this always has the potential to significantly shift power relationships in a company.

8. *Management of spread and system evaluation.* An installation that is successful and used regularly by the executive sponsor will almost inevitably produce demand by peers or subordinates for access to a similar system.

Other suggestions for successful implementation are:

- Develop a small, but significant, prototype and plan its evaluation properly.
- Communicate to overcome resistance (change management).
- Use MIS experts.
- Correctly define executives' information requirements.

For further discussion of EIS implementation see Raths, D., "The Politics of EIS," *Infoworld*, May 15, 1989.

10.12   The Future of EIS and Research Issues*

From a technological standpoint, the capabilities of the current generation of EIS/ESS are achieved by dividing the labor between a PC and a mainframe. Under this division, the mainframe houses both the corporate data and the DSS or DBMS used to produce the summary results, which are then shipped to the PC. This division of labor capitalizes on the strengths and minimizes the weaknesses of both systems. But, the division also places limitations that can be overcome only by newer hardware platforms.

Executives place substantial requirements on EIS. *First,* they often ask questions that require complex, real-time analyses for their answers. This is why many EIS/ESS are being built on top of mainframe DSS systems, which provide the necessary analytical tools for performing these requisite analyses. But even these systems often lack the ability to respond in real time. Delay in the delivery of information can mean loss of competitive position, loss of sales, and loss of profits. *Second,* like other infrequent, untrained, or uncooperative users, executives require systems that are "easy to use," "easy to learn," and "easy to navigate." Current EIS/ESS systems generally possess these qualities. However, "ease of use" can also mean that the system has enough intelligence to automatically determine which tasks need to be performed and either performs the tasks directly or guides the user through the tasks. Although current systems provide executives with the capabilities to monitor the present state of affairs, the systems typically lack the ability to automate the processes of interpreting or explaining information. The automation of these tasks requires the integration of current EIS/ESS capabilities with those of an expert system. *Third,* executives tend to have highly individualized workstyles. Although the current generation of EIS/ESS can be molded to the needs of the executive, it is very difficult to alter the "look-and-feel" of the system or to alter the basic way in which the user interacts with the system. *Finally,* any information system is essentially a social system. One of the key elements of an EIS/ESS is the E-mail capabilities that it provides for members of the executive team. In the current generation of systems, however, these capabilities are again limited.

Therefore, the EIS/ESS of the future will look substantially different from today's systems. Like most other systems, EIS/ESS will migrate to the networked world of the technical workstation. Within 5 years, these will have at least 10 times the speed and memory of today's PCs; will have at least 4–8 times the disk capacity; will possess a very high resolution, bitmapped screen; will be multitasking; and will be connected with other workstations over a high-speed network (e.g., Ethernet). The advantages of such a configuration are that data and programs can be distributed and shared as needed. Individual workstations will have the ability to house and run mainframe versions of most DSS and DBMS

---

*This section was condensed from an unpublished work of D. King of Execucom Systems Corp. (courtesy of D. King), 1991.

software. In fact, because of their multitasking capabilities, these programs can run simultaneously (in separate windows), if need be.

The following list briefly describes some of the features that are likely to appear in the next generation on EIS/ESS:

- *A toolbox for building customized systems.* In order to quickly configure a system for an executive, the builder of the system needs a toolbox of graphic and analytical objects that can be easily linked together to produce the system. In the future EIS/ESS systems are likely to provide toolkits like HyperCard for building visual and graphic front-ends.

- *Multimedia support.* The requirement that an EIS/ESS be configurable also requires support of multiple modes of input and output. The current generation basically provides text and graphic output with touch screen, mouse, or keyboard input. The rapid proliferation of databases supporting image data and the slow, but sure, appearance of video as well as voice I/O, will probably mean that future EIS/ESS will be multimedia in nature. For example, in the next generation of systems an executive may be sitting in front of a high-resolution map of the company's sales regions. By touching one of these regions the executive might be presented with an animated display of the region's revenue and expense figures over the past few years along with a voice summary of the results mailed by the regional sales directors. Not only does this mean that the workstation will have to support the storage and display of multimedia objects but also that the network will support the transfer of these objects.

- *Merging of analytical systems with desktop publishing.* Many of the reports prepared for executives contain tables, graphs, and text. To support the preparation of these reports, some software companies are now beginning to merge desktop publishing capabilities with various analytical capabilities. Examples are the Wingz product from Informix and the Trapeze program for the Macintosh. In keeping with the multimedia features, coming EIS/ESS are likely to have the capability to at least cut and paste data and graphs from various windows into a document, and to ship that document via E-mail to other executives.

- *Automated support and intelligent assistance.* Expert systems and other AI technologies (e.g., natural language) are currently being embedded or integrated with existing DSS or DBMS systems. This will clearly add more automated support and assistance to the analytical engines underlying EIS/ESS. However, we are also likely to see other forms of intelligent or automated assistance. One such form is the "agent." We might think of an "agent" as a small, individualized, knowledge-based system designed to carry out a few rudimentary tasks. For example, we might have a mail "agent" that monitors incoming E-mail, and, based on various built-in rules, places the mail in appropriate slots. Thus, instead of thinking of an EIS/ESS as a single program or system, we might think of the system as a society of cooperating agents whose actions need to be coordinated. Although the concept of an agent may appear a bit foreign, it is currently being touted as the foundation for Apple's Knowledge Navigator—the ultimate ESS of the future.

- *Client/server architecture.* This approach, described in Chapter 4, could be extremely important for small scale EIS.

Research Issues. The following research issues were suggested by Watson et al. [41]:

- Is the organizational position and level of commitment of the executive sponsor related to EIS success?
- What considerations are most important when selecting an operating sponsor?
- How can the benefits of an EIS be assessed in advance?
- How does the software used in building an EIS affect the development process and system success?
- What level of staffing and organizational structure are best for the EIS builder/support staff?
- What methods can be most effectively used to identify executives' information requirements?
- What are the major EIS data management problems and their solutions?
- What impact does the inclusion of soft data have on EIS success?
- What are the major problems associated with EIS "spread" and its evolution?
- How can EIS functionality be increased while maintaining ease of use?
- What emerging technologies (e.g., voice, optical disc) can be effectively used with EIS?
- What are the most effective screen presentation formats for an EIS?

Research activities will help in creating more effective and efficient executive information systems.

Chapter Highlights

- Many internal and external factors create the need for EIS.
- EIS serves the information needs of top executives.
- EIS provides rapid access to timely information at various levels of details. It is very user friendly.
- ESS is basically an EIS with analysis capabilities.
- Executives play three major roles: interpersonal, informational, and decisional.
- Executives' work can be divided into two major phases: finding problems (opportunities) and deciding what to do about them.
- Finding information needs of executives is a very difficult process. Methods such as CSF and BSP (Business System Planning) are effective, especially if they are followed by prototyping.

- If properly designed and operated, EIS has many benefits, but most of them are intangible.
- Drill down is an important capability of EIS. It allows the executive to look at details (and details of details).
- EIS uses a management by exception approach. It centers around CSF, key performance indicators, and highlight charts.
- In contrast with MIS, EIS has an overall organizational perspective and it uses external data extensively.
- There is a trend to integrate EIS and DSS tools.
- EIS requires either a mainframe or it can run on a LAN.
- Constructing an EIS is a difficult task. Using vendors or consultants is a viable approach.
- EIS success depends on many factors ranging from appropriate technology to managing organizational resistance.

Key Words

critical success factors	highlight charts	prototyping
drill down	information	scanning the
exception reporting	requirements (needs)	environment
executive information	key problems	status access
system (EIS)	narratives	
executive support		
system (ESS)		

Questions for Review

1. Define EIS.
2. Define ESS.
3. List the pressures for the creation of EIS.
4. Define the executive's interpersonal, informational, and decisional roles.
5. List a few methods of soliciting executives' information needs.
6. Describe the interviewing approach to information discovery.
7. List the major characteristics and capabilities of EIS in the following categories: quality of information, user-interface, and technical capabilities.
8. List the major benefits of EIS.
9. Define "drill down" and list its advantages.
10. Define status access.
11. Define exception reporting.
12. List the major differences between MIS and EIS.
13. List the major differences between EIS and DSS.
14. List the major hardware configuration for EIS.

Questions for Discussion

1. If a DSS is employed in finding answers to management questions, what is the EIS used for?
2. Explain how the CSF approach is used in an interviewing approach for finding information needs.
3. Discuss the concept of status access and contrast it with ad hoc analysis.
4. Review the five types of information essential to senior management. Relate these to a fast-food company and to a hospital. (Be specific and imaginative in your response.)
5. Prepare a table that shows the differences between a traditional reporting system and an EIS.
6. American Can Company announced in early 1986 that it was interested in acquiring a company in the health maintenance organization (HMO) field. Two decisions are involved in this act: (1) the decision to acquire an HMO, and (2) the decision of which one to acquire. How can a DSS and EIS be used in such a situation?
7. Why is a typical office automation system insufficient for providing executives' needs?
8. Compare the structure of EIS with that of a typical DSS and comment on the differences.
9. Why is it advantageous to include both a mainframe and PCs in an EIS?
10. It is said that EIS supports unstructured decisions. It is also said that EIS is used to perform structured, somewhat repetitive analyses. Use Simon's phases of the decision-making process, described in Chapter 2, to reconcile these statements.
11. What is the difference between EIS and ESS?
12. Why can't a conventional MIS fulfill the information needs of executives?
13. Why is it advisable to use vendors or consultants to build an EIS?
14. List a few approaches that can be used to discover the information needs of executives.
15. Describe the logic of Wetherbe's two-phase information discovery approach.
16. Why is it so difficult to find the information needs of executives?
17. Explain how CSF are monitored.
18. Relate CSF to key performance indicators.
19. What are the major benefits of integrating EIS and DSS?
20. What are the relationships between EIS and GDSS?
21. Why is it difficult to build an EIS in-house?
22. Why is it desirable to use a vendor or a consultant to build an EIS?

CASE STUDY: Whose Fault Is It?—The Lockheed Corp. Debate*

Developed in house in the late 1970s and early 1980s, Lockheed's EIS is considered one of the first successful EIS (e.g., see Houdeshel and Watson in Watson et al. [37]). Lockheed believed that its EIS tracked all critical factors, until a critical error was discovered. The weight of the P-7 aircraft that Lockheed was building for the U.S. Navy was never programmed into the EIS. This omission cost the company millions of dollars (possibly $300 million). The designers of the EIS claim that the system works fine. However, the information requirements were established improperly. Decisions about what was to be included in the EIS involved both the executives and information systems staff. Such decisions are complicated by the fact that the potentially critical information is not obvious. Did the problem occur because the information system professional did not understand the business side of Lockheed? Or was it because the executives failed to mention weight as being a critical factor?

The builders blamed the executives, the executives blamed the builders. Whose fault is it anyway? Note: The Lockheed case is presented in Appendix B to this book.

References and Bibliography

1. Armstrong, D. A. "The People Factor in EIS Success." *Datamation*, April 1, 1990.
2. Bergerson, F., et al. "Top Managers Evaluate the Attributes of EIS," *DSS 91 Transactions*, Manhattan Beach, CA, 1991.
3. Bonczek, R. H., C. W. Holsapple, and A B. Whinston. "The Evolving Role of Models in Decision Support Systems." *Decision Sciences*, Vol. 11, No. 2 (1980).
4. Brandel, M. "Executive Information Systems (LAN-based vs. Host-based EISs)." *Computerworld*, July 22, 1991.
5. Burkan, W. C. *Executive Information Systems.* New York: Van Nostrand Reinhold, 1991.
6. Davis, S. G., "Can Stand-Alone EIS's Stand Up?" *Datamation*, July, 1, 1989.
7. DeLong, D. W., and J. F. Rockart. "Identifying the Attributes of Successful Executive Support System Implementation." In Fedorowicz [9].
8. Emery, C. C., Jr. "Implementing an Executive Information System at Samaritan Health Services." *Transactions, DSS 91 Information Technology for Executives and Managers*, The Institute of Management Sciences, 1991.
9. Fedorowicz, J., ed. *DSS 86 Transactions.* 6th Annual Conference on DSS. Washington, DC: Institute of Management Sciences, April 1986.

*Based on material published in *PC Week,* January 29 and February 5, 1990.

10. Fleck, R. A., and R. Kuehn. "Implementing an EIS in a Large Insurance Corporation." *Journal of Systems Management,* January 1991, pp. 6–11, 17.
11. Fried, L. "Decision-Making Prowess." *Computerworld,* March 1991, pp. 59–60.
12. Friend, D. "Executive Information Systems: Successes, Failures, Insights, and Misconceptions." In Fedorowicz [9].
13. Guimaraes, T., and J. V. Saraph. "The Role of Prototyping in Executive Decision Systems." *Information and Management,* December 1991.
14. "Implementing an EIS: Two Stories," *Information Center,* February, 1988.
15. Jones, J. W., and R. McLeod. "The Structure of Executive Information Systems: An Exploratory Analysis." *Decision Sciences,* Spring 1986.
16. Keen, P. G. W. "Adaptive Design for Decision Support Systems." *Data Base,* Vol. 12, Nos. 1, 2 (Fall 1980).
17. Kogan, J. M. "Information for Motivation: A Key to Executive Information Systems That Translate Strategy Into Results for Management." In Fedorowicz [9].
18. Leinweber, D. "Finance." In *Expert Systems and AI: Applications and Management.* T. C. Bartee, ed. Indianapolis: H. W. Sams, 1988.
19. Little, J. D. C. "Models and Managers: The Concept of a Decision Calculus." *Management Science,* Vol. 16, No. 2 (April 1970).
20. McCartney, L. "How ESS Keeps Hertz Managers Out In Front." *Business Month,* July, 1989.
21. McLeod, R., Jr., and J. W. Jones. "Making Executive Information Systems More Effective." *Business Horizons,* September-October, 1986.
22. McNurlin, B. "Executive Information Systems." *EDP Analyzer,* April, 1987.
23. Millet, I., et al. "Alternative Paths to EIS." *Transactions, DSS 91 Information Technology for Executives and Managers,* The Institute of Management Sciences, 1991.
24. Mintzberg, H. "The Manager's Job: Folklore and Fact." *Harvard Business Review,* July-August 1975.
25. Moore, J. H., and M. G. Chang, "Design of Decision Support Systems." *Data Base,* Vol. 12, Nos. 1, 2, Fall, 1980.
26. Nelson, R. "Culture Clash at the Top." *Personal Computing,* April 27, 1990.
27. Paller, A. *The EIS Book.* Homewood, IL: Dow Jones-Irwin, 1990.
28. Pinella, P. "An EIS for the Desktop." *Datamation,* May 1991, pp. 26–30.
29. Rockart, J. F., and M. E. Treacy. "The CEO Goes On-Line." *Harvard Business Review,* January-February, 1982.
30. Rockart, J. F., and D. DeLong. *Executive Support Systems.* Homewood, IL: Dow Jones-Irwin, 1988.
31. Rockart, J. F. "Chief Executives Define Their Own Data Needs?" *Harvard Business Review,* January-February, 1982.
32. Rowe, C., and B. Herbert. "Information Technology in the Boardroom: The Growth of Computer Awareness Among Chief Executives." *Journal of General Management,* Summer 1990.
33. Scott-Morton, M. S. *Management Decision Systems: Computer Based Support for Decision Making.* Cambridge, MA: Harvard Univ., Div. of Research (1971).

34. Shafer, D. "Making EIS Intelligent." *PC AI*, July-August, 1990.

35. Volonino, L., and H. J. Watson. "The Strategic Business Objectives Method for Guiding Executive Information Systems Development." *Journal of Management Information Systems*, Winter, 1990–91.

36. Wallis, L. "Power Computing at the Top." *Across the Board*, January-February, 1989.

37. Watson, H. J., et al. "Executive Information Systems: A Framework for Development and a Survey of Current Practices." *MIS Quarterly*, March 1991.

38. Watson, H. J., et al. *Executive Information Systems.* New York: Wiley, 1992.

39. Watson, H. J., and H. Glover. "Common and Avoidable Causes of EIS Failure." *Computerworld*, December 4, 1989.

40. Watson, H. J., and M. Frolick. "Determining Information Requirements for an Executive Information System." *Information System Management*, Spring 1992.

41. Watson, H. J., et al. *Executive Information Systems: A Framework for Development and Survey of Current Practices*, working paper 41, Dept. of Management, Univ. of Georiga, Athens, GA (1991).

42. Wetherbe, J. C. "Executive Information Requirements: Getting it Right." *MIS Quarterly*, March 1991.

Part 4

Fundamentals of Artificial Intelligence and Expert Systems

Artificial intelligence is a dynamic and varied field. Its applied technologies range from expert systems to computer vision. In this part we present two topics. First, AI is defined, its major characteristics and benefits are described, and its major technologies are outlined (Chapter 11). Second, an overview of expert systems is provided (Chapter 12).

Chapter 11

Applied Artificial Intelligence: An Overview

Artificial intelligence (AI) is a subdivision of computer science devoted to creating computer software and hardware that attempt to produce results such as those produced by people.

The concept of artificial intelligence and the commercial applications that result from research in this area may change the way some organizations operate and are managed. This chapter introduces you to AI and its applications in the following sections:

11.1   Introduction

The past few years have witnessed an increased interest in applied AI. The topic is enjoying tremendous publicity. Many major periodicals have published cover stories on AI or have dedicated special issues to it. Dozens of books on AI have appeared on the market. Many AI newsletters are being published regularly, and conferences and conventions on this topic are being held worldwide. To a certain extent, AI has become a sensation.

The commercial applications of AI are projected to reach several billion dollars annually. Major management consulting firms (e.g., Arthur D. Little, Inc. and Andersen Consulting) are deeply involved in applied AI. Many research institutions in the United States and all over the world are also heavily involved in AI research projects.

These developments may have a significant impact on many organizations, both private and public, and on the manner in which organizations are being managed. The fundamentals of AI and its major technologies are described in the remainder of this chapter. Some of the discussion in this chapter was adopted from Frenzel [11].

11.2   Definitions

Artificial intelligence is a term that encompasses many definitions (see Turban [26]). Most experts agree that AI is concerned with two basic ideas. First, it involves studying the thought processes of humans (to understand what intelligence is); second, it deals with representing those processes via machines (computers, robots, etc.).

One well-publicized definition of AI is as follows: Artificial intelligence is behavior by a machine that, if performed by a human being, would be called intelligent. A thought-provoking definition is provided by Rich and Knight [22]: "Artificial Intelligence is the study of how to make computers do things at which, at the moment, people are better." Mark Fox of Carnegie-Mellon University often says that AI is basically a theory of how the human mind works. Winston and Prendergast [29] list three objectives of artificial intelligence:

1. Make machines smarter (primary goal)
2. Understand what intelligence is (the Noble laureate purpose)
3. Make machines more useful (the entrepreneurial purpose).

Let us explore the meaning of the term *intelligent behavior*. Several abilities are considered signs of intelligence:

- Learn or understand from experience.
- Make sense out of ambiguous or contradictory messages.
- Respond quickly and successfully to a new situation (different responses, flexibility).

- Use reason in solving problems and directing conduct effectively.
- Deal with perplexing situations.
- Understand and infer in ordinary, rational ways.
- Apply knowledge to manipulate the environment.
- Acquire and apply knowledge.
- Think and reason.
- Recognize the relative importance of different elements in a situation.

Although AI's ultimate goal is to build machines that will mimic human intelligence, the capabilities of current commercial AI products are far from exhibiting any significant success when compared with the abilities just listed. Nevertheless, AI programs are getting better all the time, and they are currently useful in conducting several tasks that require some human intelligence.

An interesting test designed to determine if a computer exhibits intelligent behavior was designed by Alan Turing and is called the **Turing Test.** According to this test, a computer could be considered to be smart only when a human interviewer, conversing with both an unseen human being and an unseen computer, could not determine which is which. The idea of the Turing Test has been challenged by John Searle; see Bourbaki [4] and exercise 4.

The definitions of AI presented to this point concentrated on the notion of intelligence. The following definitions and characteristics of AI focus on decision making and problem solving.

Symbolic Processing

When human experts solve problems (see Appendix 11-A), particularly the type that are considered appropriate for AI, they do not do it by solving sets of equations or performing other laborious mathematical computations. Instead, they choose symbols to represent the problem concepts and apply various strategies and rules to manipulate these concepts. According to Waterman [28], the AI approach represents knowledge as sets of symbols that stand for problem concepts. In AI jargon a **symbol** is a string of characters that stands for some real-world concept. Here are some examples of symbols:

- Product
- Defendant
- 0.8

These symbols can be combined to express meaningful relationships. When these relationships are represented in an AI program, they are called **symbol structures.** The following are examples of symbol structures:

- (DEFECTIVE product)
- (LEASED-BY product defendant)
- (EQUAL (LIABILITY defendant) 0.8)

These structures can be interpreted to mean "the product is defective," "the product is leased by the defendant," and "the liability of the defendant is 0.8."

They may, however, be interpreted differently. This is one of the problems we encounter in building AI systems.

To solve a problem, an AI program manipulates these symbols. The consequence of this approach is that knowledge representation—the choice, form, and interpretation of the symbols used—becomes very important.

Symbolic processing is an essential characteristic of artificial intelligence as reflected in the following definition: Artificial intelligence is that branch of computer science dealing with symbolic, nonalgorithmic methods of problem solving. This definition focuses on two characteristics of computer programs:

1. Numeric versus symbolic: Computers were originally designed specifically to process numbers (**numeric processing**). People, however, tend to think symbolically; our intelligence seems to be based, in part, on our mental ability to manipulate symbols rather than just numbers. Although symbolic processing is at the core of AI, this does not mean that AI does not involve math; rather, the emphasis in AI is on manipulation of symbols.

2. Algorithmic versus nonalgorithmic: An **algorithm** is a step-by-step procedure that has well-defined starting and ending points and that is guaranteed to reach a solution to a specific problem. Computer architecture readily lends itself to this step-by-step approach. Many human reasoning processes, however, tend to be nonalgorithmic; in other words, our mental activities consist of more than just following logical, step-by-step procedures.

Heuristics

Heuristics (rules of thumb) are included as a key element of AI in the following definition: "Artificial intelligence is the branch of computer science that deals with ways of representing knowledge using symbols rather than numbers and with rules-of-thumb, or heuristics, methods for processing information" (*Encyclopaedia Britannica*).

People frequently use heuristics, consciously or otherwise, to make decisions. By using heuristics one does not have to rethink completely what to do every time a similar problem is encountered.

Inferencing

Artificial intelligence involves an attempt by machines to exhibit *reasoning* capabilities. The reasoning consists of **inferencing** from facts and rules using heuristics or other search approaches. Artificial intelligence is unique in that it makes inferences by employing the pattern-matching (or recognition) approach.

Pattern Matching

The following definition of AI focuses on **pattern-matching** techniques: Artificial intelligence works with pattern-matching methods which attempt to describe objects, events, or processes in terms of their qualitative features and logical and computational relationships.

11.3   Artificial Versus Natural Intelligence

The potential value of artificial intelligence can be better understood by contrasting it with natural, or human, intelligence. According to Kaplan [16], AI has several important commercial advantages:

- AI is more *permanent*. Natural intelligence is perishable from a commercial standpoint in that workers can change their place of employment or forget information. AI, however, is permanent as long as the computer systems and programs remain unchanged.
- AI offers *ease of duplication and dissemination.* Transferring a body of knowledge from one person to another usually requires a lengthy process of apprenticeship; even so, expertise can never be duplicated completely. However, when knowledge is embodied in a computer system, it can be copied from that computer and easily moved to another computer, sometimes across the globe.
- AI can be *less expensive* than natural intelligence. There are many circumstances in which buying computer services costs less than having corresponding human power carry out the same tasks (over the long run).
- AI, being a computer technology, is *consistent and thorough.* Natural intelligence is erratic because people are erratic; they do not perform consistently.
- AI can be *documented*. Decisions made by a computer can be easily documented by tracing the activities of the system. Natural intelligence is difficult to reproduce; for example, a person may reach a conclusion but at some later date may be unable to re-create the reasoning process that led to that conclusion or to even recall the assumptions that were a part of the decision.

Natural intelligence does have several advantages over AI:

- Natural intelligence is *creative,* whereas AI is rather uninspired. The ability to acquire knowledge is inherent in human beings, but with AI, tailored knowledge must be built into a carefully constructed system.
- Natural intelligence enables people to benefit from and *use sensory experience* directly, whereas most AI systems must work with symbolic input.
- Perhaps most important, human reasoning is able to make use at all times of a wide *context of experience* and bring that to bear on individual problems; in contrast, AI systems typically gain their power by having a very narrow focus.

The advantages of natural intelligence over AI result in the many limitations of expert systems, which are discussed in detail in the next chapter.

Computers can be used to collect information about objects, events, or processes; and, of course, computers can process large amounts of information more efficiently than people can. People, however, instinctively do some things that have been very difficult to program into a computer: they recognize relationships between things; they sense qualities; and they spot patterns that explain how various items relate to each other.

Newspaper photographs are nothing more than collections of minute dots, yet without any conscious effort, people discover the patterns that reveal faces and other objects in those photos. Similarly, one of the ways that humans make sense of the world is by recognizing the relationships and patterns that help give meaning to the objects and events that they encounter.

If computers are to become more intelligent, they must be able to make the same kinds of associations among the qualities of objects, events, and processes that come so naturally to people.

11.4   Knowledge in AI

Definitions

In the field of information systems it is customary to distinguish between data, information, and knowledge.

Data. The term *data* refers to numeric (or alphanumeric) strings that by themselves do not have a meaning. They can be facts or figures to be processed.

Information. Information is data organized so that it is meaningful to the person receiving it.

Knowledge. **Knowledge** has several definitions. For example, according to the *Webster's New World Dictionary of the American Language*, knowledge is:

- a clear and certain perception of something.
- understanding.
- learning.
- all that has been perceived or grasped by the mind.
- practical experience, skill.
- acquaintance or familiarity.
- cognizance; recognition.
- organized information applicable to problem solving.

Data, information, and knowledge can be classified by their degree of abstraction and by their quantity (Figure 11.1). Knowledge is the most abstract and exists in the smallest quantity.

Another definition of knowledge is that given by Sowa [25]: "Knowledge encompasses the implicit and explicit restrictions placed upon objects (entities),

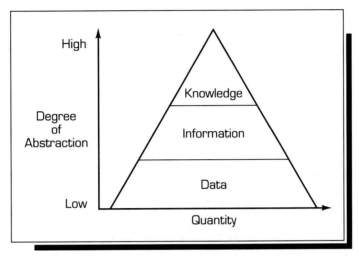

FIGURE 11.1 Abstraction and Quantity of Data, Knowledge, and Information

operations, and relationships along with general and specific heuristics and inference procedures involved in the situation being modeled."

Uses

Although a computer cannot have (as yet) experiences or study and learn
as the human mind can, it can use knowledge given to it by human experts.
Such knowledge consists of facts, concepts, theories, heuristic methods, procedures, and relationships. Knowledge is also information that has been organized
and analyzed to make it understandable and applicable to problem solving or
decision making. The collection of knowledge related to a problem (or an opportunity) to be used in an AI system is called a **knowledge base.** Most knowledge bases are limited in that they typically focus on some specific subject area
or domain.

Once a knowledge base is built, artificial intelligence techniques are used
to give the computer inference capability. The computer will then be able to
make inferences and judgments based on the facts and relationships contained
in the knowledge base.

Knowledge Bases and Knowledge-based Organizations

With a knowledge base and the ability to draw inferences from it, the computer can now be put to some practical use as a problem solver and decision
maker. Figure 11.2 illustrates the concept of a computer using AI in an application. By searching the knowledge base for relevant facts and relationships, the
computer can reach one or more alternative solutions to the given problem.
The computer's knowledge base and inferencing capability augment those of
the user.

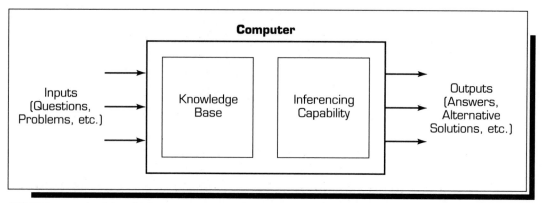

FIGURE 11.2 Applying AI Concepts with a Computer

The importance of AI and knowledge bases is rapidly increasing. Therefore, many people believe that we are moving from the information age into the *knowledge age*, and some even talk about knowledge-based organizations and societies.

11.5   How AI Differs from Conventional Computing

Conventional Computing

Conventional computer programs are based on an algorithm, which is a clearly defined, step-by-step procedure for solving a problem. It may be a mathematical formula or a sequential procedure that will lead to a solution. The algorithm is converted into a computer program (sequential list of instructions or commands) that tells the computer exactly what operations to carry out. The algorithm then uses data such as numbers, letters, or words to solve the problem (a typical example is the preparation of a payroll in an organization).

Table 11.1 summarizes some of the ways traditional computers process data. This process is limited to very structured applications.

AI Computing

AI software is based on symbolic representation and manipulation. (See Appendix 11-B and 11-C.) In AI, a symbol is a letter, word, or number that is used to represent objects, processes, and their relationships. Objects can be people, things, ideas, concepts, events, or statements of fact. By using symbols, it is possible to create a knowledge base that states facts, concepts, and the relationships among them. Then various processes are used to manipulate the symbols to generate advice or a recommendation for solving problems.

TABLE 11.1 How Computers
Process Data

Process	Manipulation
Calculate	Perform mathematical operations such as add, subtract, multiply, divide, find a square root, etc. Solve formulas
Perform logic	Perform logic operations such as "and," "or," "invert," etc.
Store	Remember facts and figures in files
Retrieve	Access data stored in files as required
Translate	Convert data from one form to another
Sort	Examine data and put it into some desired order or format
Edit	Make changes, additions, and deletions to data and change its sequence
Make decisions	Reach simple conclusions based on internal or external conditions
Monitor	Observe external or internal events and take action if certain conditions are met
Control	Take charge of or operate external devices

Once a knowledge base is built, some means of using it to solve problems must be developed. How does the AI software reason or infer with this knowledge base? The basic techniques are **search** and **pattern matching.** Given some initial start-up information, the AI software searches the knowledge base looking for specific conditions or patterns. It looks for matchups that satisfy the criteria set up to solve the problem. The computer literally hunts around until it finds the best answer it can give based on the knowledge it has.

Even though AI problem solving does not take place directly by algorithmic processes, algorithms, of course, are used to implement the search process.

A word of caution! Some people believe that AI is magic. It is not. AI is basically a different approach to programming computers, and it should be treated as such. We may use different terminology, but an AI system is a computer-based information system (CBIS), although it has some different characteristics (Table 11.2).

11.6   Does a Computer Really Think?

Knowledge bases and search techniques certainly make computers more useful, but can they really make computers more intelligent? AI specialists, computer

TABLE 11.2 Artificial Intelligence Versus Conventional Programming

Dimension	Artificial Intelligence	Conventional Programming
Processing	Mainly symbolic	Primarily computing
Nature of input	Can be incomplete	Must be complete
Search	Heuristic (mostly)	Algorithms
Explanation	Provided	Usually not provided
Major interest	Knowledge	Data, information
Structure	Separation of control from knowledge	Control integrated with information (data)
Nature of output	Can be incomplete	Must be correct
Maintenance and update	Relatively easy, due to modularity	Usually difficult
Hardware	Mainly workstations and personal computers	All types
Reasoning capability	Yes	No

scientists, and others regularly debate this question. The fact that most AI programs are implemented by search and pattern-matching techniques leads to the conclusion that computers are not really intelligent. You can give the computer a lot of information and some guidelines about how to use this information. Using that information and those criteria, the computer can come up with a solution. All it does is test the various alternatives and attempt to find some combination that meets the designated criteria. When that is done, typically a solution is achieved. So the computer appears to be "thinking" and often gives a satisfactory solution.

Let's face it. Although AI is making computers smarter and more powerful, the dream of building a machine that can fully duplicate the human brain will probably not be realized in our lifetime. Despite major advances in all areas of computer science, many question whether we will ever be able to create a computer that will accurately emulate the function of a human mind. Dreyfus and Dreyfus [8] feel that the public is being misled about AI—its usefulness is overblown and its goals are impossible. They say we will never be able to establish rules for all the ways we think. The human mind is just too complex to duplicate.

Nevertheless, despite criticisms, AI methods are valuable. They are showing us how we think and how to better apply our intelligence. AI techniques will make computers easier to use and make greater knowledge available to the masses. Perhaps it does not matter if we do not fully duplicate the human brain. Even when we simulate parts of it, the resulting hardware and software are very useful.

11.7   Advantages and Disadvantages of AI

AI is sure to be a big hit with computer users once it becomes more widely known and firmly established. But there is also a downside. Let's examine some of the pros and cons of AI software.

The Good News

For openers, AI software will make any computer more user-friendly than any of these machines are now. Users will be able to communicate with the computer in their own natural language. With AI, an untrained user will be able to approach the machine and accomplish useful work. Computers will be no more difficult to use than the telephone.

Special natural language interfaces will have to be written to achieve these ambitious results, and already many commercial natural language interfaces are available for popular computers and software packages. The database management system (DBMS) is one of the first types of conventional software to take advantage of natural language interfaces. These interfaces permit fast, easy access to data without tricky programming.

Another major benefit is that computers will be far more useful. It has been said that computers are a solution looking for a problem. However, not all problems yield to an algorithmic or data processing solution, which are the core of the conventional CBIS. Not all problems require calculation or data storage and retrieval. There are many problems to be solved that do not fit the capabilities usually associated with a conventional computer.

Artificial intelligence can change all that. With AI techniques, a whole new realm of opportunities opens up. New kinds of problems can be solved. The same computers that do data processing can now address problems associated with acquiring and accessing knowledge, making decisions, and otherwise performing some functions heretofore reserved only for humans. AI is great for "messy" problems in which the data are unknown or incomplete or in which there are no known algorithms. Such capabilities, combined with users' expertise, can lead to improved performance and productivity. AI techniques as used in expert systems have the potential to make problem solving and decision making in specific domains faster and easier.

Most of us are still in **information overload;** there is simply too much information to deal with. Furthermore, we do not always know that it exists or how to obtain it once we know that we need it. And while the information glut is real, we need that information desperately. We need it to do our jobs competently, and we want information so that we can live an informed, intelligent life.

Artificial intelligence will help relieve our information overload. It will provide new means of finding and accessing the information we need. In addition, natural language interfaces will make computer databases easier to tap.

But perhaps the most important aspect of AI is that it will force, or encourage, the conversion of information into knowledge. Typically, you have to analyze the information, organize it, sift through it, and extract from it what is important to you. At the point information becomes knowledge, it can be applied to solving a problem or making a decision.

The Bad News

Surely, as with everything, AI offers advantages and benefits, but not without a price. Medium- or large-scale AI applications usually require very powerful computers with fast CPUs and lots of memory. Most AI research and many AI applications until 1990 were implemented on mainframes and big minicomputers such as Digital Equipment Corp.'s (DEC) VAX series.

On the other hand, microcomputers are getting faster and more powerful. Sixteen-bit and 32-bit machines are commonplace. Memory chips are getting denser and cheaper. The 386 chips are common and inexpensive, the 486 chip is becoming affordable, and the 586 chip will be affordable soon. As a result, many AI applications can be readily implemented on workstations and on faster personal computers. Thus, the cost disadvantage is slowly going away.

Another disadvantage is the difficulty of AI software development. AI programs are incredibly complex. As a result, they take more time to develop and they are far more expensive. Software development tools such as improved AI programming languages and expert system shells help speed up and simplify software development, but they, too, are expensive and require some talent to use.

11.8   The AI Field

The development of machines that exhibit intelligent characteristics involves many different sciences and technologies, such as linguistics, psychology, philosophy, computer hardware and software, mechanics, hydraulics, and optics. The intersection between psychology and AI centers on the areas known as cognition and psycholinguistics. Philosophy and AI come together in the areas of logic, philosophy of language, and philosophy of mind. Intersections with linguistics include computational linguistics, psycholinguistics, and sociolinguistics. Mutual interactions between electrical engineering and AI include image processing, control theory, pattern recognition, and robotics.

Lately there have been contributions from management and organization theory (e.g., decision making, implementation), statistics, mathematics, management science (heuristic programming, cost-effectiveness), and management information systems (MIS).

The various disciplines that participate in the AI field overlap and interact. Thus, it is difficult to classify the AI field according to these disciplines. A much more practical classification scheme is achieved by considering the outputs, that is, the applied areas of *commercial applications*.

Artificial intelligence is not in itself a commercial field; it is a science and a technology. It is a collection of concepts and ideas that are appropriate for research but that cannot be marketed. However, AI provides the scientific foundation for several growing commercial technologies. (See Davis [6].) The major areas are expert systems, natural language processing, speech understanding, robotics and sensory systems, computer vision and scene recognition, and intelligent computer-aided instruction. These are illustrated in Figure 11.3, together with the major disciplines of AI, and are discussed next.

Expert Systems

Expert systems are computerized advisory programs that attempt to imitate the reasoning processes and knowledge of experts in solving specific types of problems. They are used more than any other applied AI technology. Expert systems are of great interest to organizations because of their potential to enhance productivity and to augment work forces in many specialty areas where human experts are becoming increasingly difficult to find and retain. Current applications are restricted to relatively limited and narrowly defined areas of expertise (called *domains*).

Human experts tend to specialize in relatively narrow problem-solving areas or tasks. Typically, human experts possess these characteristics: they solve problems quickly and fairly accurately, explain what (and sometimes how) they do, judge the reliability of their own conclusions, know when they are stumped, and communicate with other experts. They can also learn from experience, change their points of view to suit a problem, and transfer knowledge from one domain to another. Finally, they use tools, such as rules of thumb, mathematical models, and detailed simulations to support their decisions.

Knowledge is a major resource, and it often lies with only a few experts. It is important to capture that knowledge so others can use it. Experts get sick or become unavailable and knowledge is thus not always available when needed. Books and manuals can capture some knowledge, but they leave the problem of a particular application up to the reader. Expert systems can provide a direct means of applying expertise. An expert system permits the knowledge and experience of one or more experts to be captured and stored in a computer. This knowledge can then be used by anyone who requires it. The purpose of an expert system is not to replace the experts, but simply to make their knowledge and experience more widely available. Typically, there are more problems to solve than there are experts available to handle them. An expert system permits others to increase their productivity, improve the quality of their decisions, and solve problems when an expert is not available.

Natural Language Processing

Natural language technology gives computer users the ability to communicate with the computer in their native language. This technology allows for a conversational type of interface, in contrast to using the **programming language**

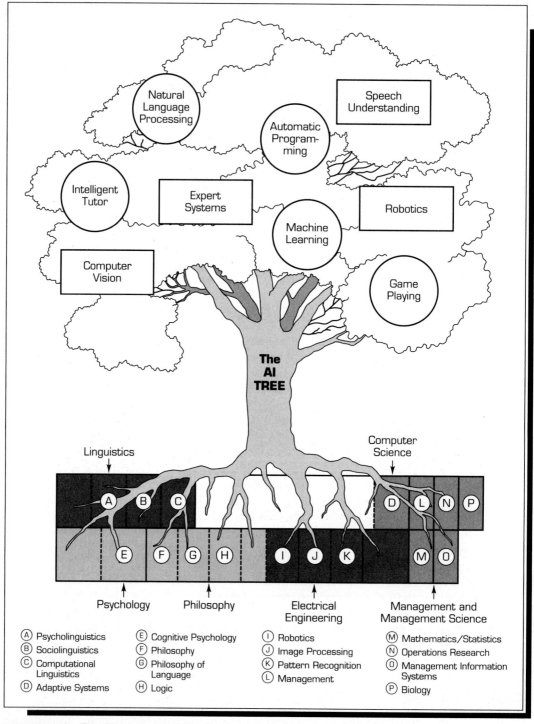

FIGURE 11.3 The Disciplines of AI (the Roots) and the Applications. (*Source:* Adapted from N. Cercone and G. McCalba, "Artificial Intelligence: Underlying Assumptions and Basic Objectives," *Journal of the American Society for Information Science* [September 1984] and from G. S. Tuthill, *Knowledge Engineering* [Blue Ridge Summit, PA: TAB Books, 1990].)

of computer jargon, syntax, and commands. Limited success in this area is typified by current systems that can recognize and interpret written sentences relating to very restricted topics. Although this ability can be used to great advantage with some applications, a general **natural language processing** (NLP) system is not yet possible.

The field of natural language processing is divided into two subfields:

- Natural language *understanding* investigates methods of allowing the computer to comprehend instructions given in ordinary English so that computers can understand people more easily.
- Natural language *generation* strives to have computers produce ordinary English language so that people can understand computers more easily.

These topics were briefly discussed in Chapter 6.

Speech (Voice) Understanding

Speech understanding is the recognition and understanding by a computer of spoken language.

Speech understanding is a process that allows one to communicate with a computer by speaking to it. The term **speech recognition** is sometimes applied only to the first part of the process: recognizing the words that have been spoken without necessarily interpreting their meanings. The other part of the process, in which the meaning of the speech is ascertained, is called **speech understanding.** It may be possible to understand the meaning of a spoken sentence without actually recognizing every word.

Natural language processing is an attempt to allow computers to interpret normal statements expressed in a natural human language, such as English or Japanese. The process of speech understanding, in contrast, attempts to translate the human voice into individual words and sentences understandable by the computer. A combination of speech understanding and NLP will be required to realize the capability of the computer to converse in a manner normal to humans.

Robotics and Sensory Systems

Sensory systems, such as vision systems, tactile systems, and signal processing systems, when combined with AI define a broad category of systems generally referred to as **robotics.** A robot is an electromechanical device that can be programmed to perform manual tasks. The Robotic Institute of America formally defines a robot as "a reprogrammable multifunctional manipulator designed to move materials, parts, tools, or specialized devices through variable programmed motions for the performance of a variety of tasks."

Not all of robotics is considered to be part of AI. A robot that performs only the actions that it has been preprogrammed to perform is considered to be a "dumb" robot, possessing no more intelligence than, say, a dishwasher. An "intelligent" robot includes some kind of sensory apparatus, such as a camera, that collects information about the robot's operation and its environment. The intelligent part of the robot allows it to interpret the collected information and to *respond* and adapt to changes in its environment, rather than just to follow instructions "mindlessly."

Robots combine sensory systems with mechanical motion to produce machines of widely varying intelligence and abilities. The research and application areas under the sensory systems umbrella include machines that sense, move, and manipulate their environment. Assembly line operations, particularly those that are highly repetitive or hazardous, are beginning to be performed by robots.

Computer Vision and Scene Recognition

Visual recognition has been defined as the addition of some form of computer intelligence and decision making to digitized visual information received from a machine sensor. The combined information is then used to perform, or control, such operations as robotic movement, conveyor speeds, and production-line quality. The basic objective of computer vision is to interpret scenarios rather than generate pictures (which preoccupies computer graphics). What "interpreting scenarios" means differs depending on the application. For example, in interpreting pictures taken by satellite, it may be sufficient to roughly identify regions of crop damage. On the other hand, robot vision systems may find it necessary to precisely identify assembly components to correctly affix the components to the item being assembled.

Research in machine vision may enhance the abilities of automated systems to handle the manipulation of unlike objects in multiple orientations, such as forms lying on a table or parts moving on a conveyor belt. Optical recognition systems, for example, can retrieve handwritten or typed data from a form and reformat it for storage.

Intelligent Computer-aided Instruction

Intelligent computer-aided instruction (ICAI) refers to machines that can tutor humans. To a certain extent, such a machine can be viewed as an expert system. However, the major objective of an expert system is to render advice, whereas the purpose of ICAI is to teach.

Computer-assisted instruction, which has been in use for many years, brings the power of the computer to bear on the educational process. Now AI methods are being applied to the development of *intelligent* computer-assisted instruction systems in an attempt to create computerized "tutors" that shape their teaching techniques to fit the learning patterns of individual students.

ICAI applications are not limited to schools; as a matter of fact, they have found a sizable niche in the military and corporate sectors. ICAI systems are being used today for various tasks such as problem solving, simulation, discovery, learning, drill and practice, games, and testing. Such systems are also being used to support impaired people.

Even though ICAI programs are user interactive, use knowledge bases, and employ some AI technologies (like natural language interfaces), there is some debate about whether the programs themselves are really examples of AI. Often these programs are databases structured to respond to specific inputs with specific answers within a predetermined structure.

Other Applications

AI has been developed in several other commercial areas (see Winston and Prendergast [29]). Some interesting examples are discussed next.

Automatic Programming. In simple terms, programming is the process of telling the computer exactly what you want it to do. Developing a computer program frequently requires a good deal of time. A program or a system (a group of interrelated programs) must be designed, written, tested, debugged, and evaluated—all as part of an information system development process.

The goal of automatic programming is to create special programs that act as "intelligent" tools to assist programmers and expedite each phase of the programming process. The ultimate aim of automatic programming is a computer system that could develop programs by itself, in response to and in accordance with the specifications of a program developer.

Summarizing News. Some computer programs "read" stories in newspapers or other documents and make summaries in English or several other languages. This helps in handling the information overload problem.

Translation from One Language to Another. Computer programs are able to translate words and simple sentences from one language to another. For example, a package called LOGOS is used for translating from English to German (and German to English).

11.9   The Future of AI

So what does the future hold? Plenty. First, AI research and development will continue, and all of the various subfields will evolve and improve. New software techniques will be discovered. Improved software development tools will be created for easier development of expert systems and other AI applications.

Advances will also occur in hardware. In addition to the usual ongoing developments in semiconductor technology that will bring us larger and faster microprocessors and RAM chips, entirely new devices will be created. Special search, pattern-matching, and symbolic computing chips are being developed. The new parallel computing and especially neural computing architectures, with multiple CPUs operating simultaneously, will bring a whole new dimension to AI.

For the immediate future, you can expect to see AI added to existing software. Natural language interfaces will become a common feature on many applications programs, and intelligent databases are being developed. Internally, programs will use segments of AI to make some performance improvements. Expert systems that advise on many important topics will become widely available.

Generally speaking, however, there will be relatively few stand-alone AI application products. Expert systems are the exception. Predictions are that AI software will, in most applications, be combined with conventional algorithmic software; that is, AI subroutines, including expert systems, will be embedded in traditional software. AI will be virtually transparent to the user. (See Box 11.1.)

Although AI is an excellent technology, it is not the panacea we might like it to be. Look at it for what it really is: some special software techniques now developed to the point that they can be practical and useful. Where possible, consider AI another computer-based information system that can expand the

Box 11.1: The Fifth-generation Project

Artificial intelligence is often referred to as the fifth generation of computer technology. The Japanese plan to create a fifth-generation computer to leapfrog the leaders in this field. If successful, it will represent a highly significant event in human history. The Japanese are determined to shed their imitator image and make a revolutionary push. They plan to create a computer that can talk, listen, learn, and make sophisticated decisions. That means an extensive utilization of AI techniques.

Some of the objectives of this fifth-generation computer are as follows:

- Provide a high intelligence level to cooperate with people.
- Assist people to discover and develop unknown fields.
- Offer vast knowledge bases.
- Aid in management.
- Solve social problems.
- Acquire new perceptions by simulating unknown situations.
- Offer significant software productivity improvement.
- Reduce time and cost to develop computerized systems by a factor of ten.

Ultimately, the computer is to have the capability to recognize continuous speech, possess super vision, make intelligent decisions, perform self-repair, and augment the decision maker in general.

For a detailed discussion of Japan's Fifth-generation Project, see Feigenbaum and McCorduck [10] and Chapter 20 in this text.

applicability of computers and increase productivity and compatibility. Look for ways to use it, but do not expect miracles.

So far you have been introduced to the highlights of AI. In subsequent chapters, you will be exposed to its most applied technology—expert systems.

Chapter Highlights

- Artificial intelligence is an interdisciplinary field that can be defined many ways.
- The primary objective of AI is to build computers that will perform tasks that can be characterized as intelligent.
- The major characteristics of AI are symbolic processing, use of heuristics instead of algorithms, and application of inference techniques.
- AI has several major advantages over people: it is permanent, it can be easily duplicated and disseminated, it can be less expensive than human intelligence, it is consistent and thorough, and it can be documented.
- Natural (human) intelligence has advantages over AI: it is creative, it uses sensory experiences directly, and it reasons from a wide context of experiences.
- Knowledge rather than data or information is the key concept of AI.
- A knowledge base is the collection of knowledge related to a specific issue (problem or opportunity).
- We are moving into an era of knowledge-based organizations.
- AI applications can be programmed in conventional computer languages as well as in special AI languages (e.g., LISP, PROLOG).
- In conventional computing we tell the computer how to solve the problem. In AI we tell the computer what the problem is and give it the knowledge needed to solve similar problems and the necessary procedures to use the knowledge.
- All digital computers are algorithmic in their operation, but they can be programmed for symbolic manipulation.
- The basic techniques of reasoning are search and pattern matching (recognition).
- Despite the fact that AI computers cannot think, they can be very valuable by increasing the ways computers can be used.
- The major application areas of AI are expert systems, natural language processing, speech understanding, intelligent robotics, computer vision, and intelligent computer-aided instruction.
- Expert systems, the most applied AI technology, attempt to imitate the work of experts. They apply expertise to problem solving.
- Natural language processing is an attempt to allow users to communicate with computers in a natural language. Currently, conversation is done via the keyboard; in the future, it will be carried out by voice.

- Speech understanding will enable people to communicate with the computer by voice.
- An intelligent robot is one that can respond to changes in its environment. Most of today's robots do not have the capability.
- Computer vision allows the interpretation of pictures or other visible objects.
- Computers can be used as tutors. If they are supported by AI, they can improve training and teaching.
- The various AI technologies can be integrated among themselves and with other computer-based technologies.

Key Words

algorithm	knowledge base	search
artificial intelligence	natural language	speech recognition
expert system	natural language	speech understanding
inferencing	processing	symbol
information overload	numeric processing	symbol structure
intelligent computer-	pattern matching	symbolic processing
aided instruction	programming language	Turing Test
knowledge	robotics	visual recognition

Questions for Review

1. Define artificial intelligence.
2. What is the Turing Test?
3. What do we mean by inferencing?
4. What is the fifth-generation computer?
5. List the major advantages artificial intelligence has over natural intelligence.
6. List the major disadvantages of artificial compared with natural intelligence.
7. Distinguish between data, information, and knowledge.
8. Define a knowledge base.
9. How does the computer use the knowledge base?
10. What are the major differences between traditional computing and AI?
11. Explain why AI is beneficial even though computers cannot really think.
12. List the major AI technologies.
13. Define expert system.
14. Distinguish between a natural language and a programming language.
15. Define natural language processing.
16. Define speech recognition and understanding.
17. What is a robot? How does it relate to AI?
18. What is the difference between an automatic machine and an intelligent robot?
19. Define visual recognition as it applies to computer technology.
20. List the major benefits of intelligent computer-aided instruction.

Questions for Discussion

1. Inflated expectations were a major problem with AI in the past. Why? Is this a problem today? Why or why not?
2. What are the major factors that can help push AI from the lab to the real world?
3. Compare and contrast numeric and symbolic processing techniques.
4. Compare and contrast conventional processing from artificial intelligence processing.
5. "Speech understanding or even recognition could increase the number of managers using the computer directly tenfold." Do you agree? Why or why not?
6. List and discuss the steps involved in processing of data by computers.

Exercises

1. Interview an information systems manager in a company. Determine the extent to which the company is using AI technology. Also, ask what the company plans for the next three to five years. Are there any problems? (List and discuss.) Prepare a two-page report on your visit.
2. Debate 1: Computers are programmed to play chess. They are getting better and better and soon may beat the world champion. Do such computers exhibit intelligence? Why or why not?
3. Debate 2: Prepare a table showing all the arrangements you can think of that justify the position that computers cannot think. Then prepare arguments that show the opposite.
4. Debate 3: Bourbaki [4] describes Searle's argument against the use of the Turing Test. Summarize all the important issues in this debate.

References and Bibliography

1. Alexander, I., and P. Burnett. *Thinking Machines.* New York: A. Knopf, 1987.
2. Bloomfield, B. P., ed. *The Question of Artificial Intelligence: Philosophical and Sociological Perspectives.* London: Croom Helm, 1988.
3. Browing, J. "Artificial Intelligence." *The Economist* (March 1992).
4. Bourbaki, N. "Turing, Searle and Thought." *AI Expert* (July 1990).
5. Cohen, P. R., and E. A. Feigenbaum. *The Handbook of Artificial Intelligence.* Vol. 3. Los Altos, Calif.: William Kaufmann, 1982.
6. Davis, D. B. "Artificial Intelligence Goes to Work." *High Technology Business* (April 1987).
7. de Garis, H. "What If AI Succeeds? The Rise of the Twenty-First Century Artilect." *AI Magazine* 10 (Summer 1989):16–22.
8. Dreyfus, H., and S. Dreyfus. *Mind Over Machine.* New York: Free Press, 1988.

9. *Environmental Scan Report on Artificial Intelligence.* Washington, DC: U.S. Dept. of the Treasury, IRS, December 1983.

10. Feigenbaum, E. A., and P. McCorduck. *The Fifth Generation Computer.* Reading, MA: Addison-Wesley, 1983.

11. Frenzel, L. *Crash Course in Artificial Intelligence and Expert Systems.* New York: Howard W. Sams and Co., 1987.

12. Gill, K. S., ed. *Artificial Intelligence for Society.* New York: John Wiley & Sons, 1986.

13. Guha, R. V., and D. B. Lenat. "CYC A Midterm Report." *AI Magazine* (Fall 1990).

14. Hill, W. C. "The Mind at AI: Horseless Carriage to Clock." *AI Magazine* 10 (Summer 1989):29–41.

15. Johnson-Laird, P. N. *The Computer and the Mind.* Cambridge, MA: Harvard University Press, 1988.

16. Kaplan, S. J. "The Industrialization of Artificial Intelligence: From By-Line to Bottom-Line." *AI Magazine* (Summer 1984).

17. Lugar, G. F. *Artificial Intelligence and the Design of Expert Systems.* Reading, MA: Addison-Wesley, 1989.

18. Mongar, R. F. "AI Applications: What's Their Competitive Potential?" *Journal of Information Systems Management* (Summer 1988).

19. Narasimhan, R. "Human Intelligence and AI: How Close Are We to Bridging the Gap?" *AI Expert* (April 1990).

20. Newell, A., and H. A. Simon. *Human Problem Solving.* Englewood Cliffs, NJ: Prentice-Hall, 1972.

21. Patterson, D. W., *Introduction to AI and Expert Systems.* Englewood Cliffs, NJ: Prentice-Hall, 1990.

22. Rich, E., and K. Knight. *Artificial Intelligence,* 2nd ed. New York: McGraw-Hill, 1991.

23. Rubinger, B. *Applied Artificial Intelligence in Japan.* New York: Hemisphere Publishing, 1989.

24. Shapiro, S. U., ed. *Encyclopedia of Artificial Intelligence.* New York: John Wiley & Sons, 1987.

25. Sowa, J. F. *Conceptual Structures.* Reading, MA: Addison-Wesley, 1984.

26. Turban, E. *Expert Systems and Applied Artificial Intelligence.* New York: Macmillan, 1992.

27. Unger, J. M. *The Fifth Generation Fallacy: Why Japan Is Betting Its Future on Artificial Intelligence.* New York: Oxford University Press, 1987.

28. Waterman, D. *A Guide to Expert Systems.* Reading, MA: Addison-Wesley, 1986.

29. Winston, P. H., and K. A. Prendergast, eds. *The AI Business.* Cambridge, MA: MIT Press, 1984.

APPENDIX 11-A: Human Problem Solving—An Information Processing Approach (The Newell-Simon Model)

In applying AI, we consider a special approach to problem solving and decision making. This approach is based on the belief that problem solving can be understood as information processing; it is based on a cognitive approach that uses a qualitative description of the ways in which people are similar and of the manner in which people think. Of special interest to AI is the Newell-Simon model of human information processing.

Newell-Simon Model

Allen Newell and Herbert A. Simon [20] proposed a model of human problem solving that makes use of the analogy between computer processing and human information processing. This model can help us understand how AI works and what its limitations are. The human information processing system consists of the following subsystems: a perceptual subsystem, a cognitive subsystem, a motor subsystem, and external memory. (See Fig. 11-A.1.)

Perceptual Subsystem. External stimuli are the input for the human information processing system. These stimuli enter through sensors like our eyes and ears. The *perceptual subsystem* consists of these sensors along with buffer memories that briefly store incoming information while it waits processing by the cognitive subsystem.

Cognitive Subsystem. Human senses are constantly placing a huge amount of information in the buffer memories. Whenever there is a need to make a decision, the *cognitive subsystem* selects the appropriate information. Like a central processing unit in a computer, the elementary processor obtains the information necessary to make this decision from the sensory buffers and transfers it to the *short-term memory*. The processor works in cycles, which are analogous to the "fetch-execute" cycles of the computer. During each cycle the processor obtains information from a memory, evaluates it, and then stores the information in another memory.

The cognitive system contains three parts: the elementary processor; the short-term memory; and the interpreter, which interprets part or all of the program of instructions for problem solving. This problem will depend on a number of variables such as the task and the intelligence of the problem solver.

In the simplest tasks, the cognitive system merely serves as a point for transferring information from sensory inputs to motor outputs. Habitual tasks, such as reaching to turn off a light switch, are like that. The performer needs to coordinate the action, but there is little or no "deep thought" involved. In fact, the "thinking" that occurs during such behavior is impossible to recover.

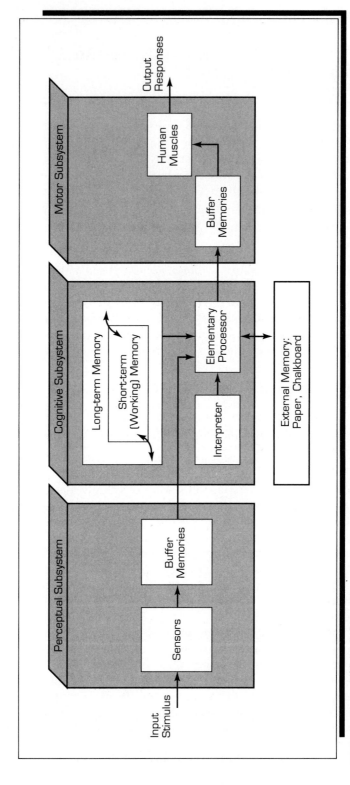

FIGURE 11-A.1 Newell-Simon Model of Human Information Processing. (*Source:* Adapted from P. Harron and D. King. *Expert Systems*, New York: John Wiley & Sons, 1985.)

More complex tasks involve more information. That, in turn, calls for more elaborate processing. To accomplish these tasks, the cognitive processor will draw on a second memory system: long-term memory.

Long-term memory consists of a large number of stored symbols with a complex indexing system. There are competing hypotheses about what the elementary symbols are and how they arrange themselves. In the simplest memory model, related symbols are associated with one another. In a more elaborate model, symbols are organized into temporal scripts. Another view is that memory consists of clusters of symbols called "chunks." A chunk is a unit of stored information—it can be a digit, a symbol, or a word associated with a set or pattern of stimuli. Chunks are hierarchically organized collections of still smaller chunks. In this conception, memory is a vast network of chunks. It requires only a few hundred milliseconds to read (recall) from long-term memory, but the write time (commitment to memory) is fairly long (say, $5N$ to $10N$ seconds, for N symbols, where N = number of symbols involved).

Human beings can support the decision-making process with another memory, the external one. The external memory consists of external media like a pad of paper or a chalkboard. The processing, retrieval, and storage of data by computers can be thousands and millions of times faster than that of humans. Humans are also limited in their ability to generate, integrate, and interpret probabilistic data.

The long-term memory has essentially unlimited capacity. The short-term memory is quite small. It holds only five to seven chunks. However, only about two chunks can be retained while another task is being performed. This suggests that part of the short-term memory is used for input and output processing. This is one of the major limitations of the human as compared with a computer. The limits of the short-term memory can be expanded, for example, through analogies, associations, or the use of graphics. A graph may provide, in a few chunks, the same information as a large number of data items would. And so graphics play an important role in the support of managerial decision making.

The human operates according to this model in serial rather than parallel fashion. This means that a human can perform only one information processing task at a time, whereas a computer may operate in either serial or parallel designs.

Motor Subsystem. After scanning and searching memories, the processor sends information to the *motor subsystem.* Motor processors initiate actions of muscles and other internal human systems. This, in turn, results in some observable activity, for example, talking.

APPENDIX 11-B: Problem Representation in AI

To understand how the blind and the heuristic searches work, it is necessary first to illustrate how problems are represented in AI.

State-Space Representation

The general process of solving any problem using AI involves three major elements: problem states, a goal, and operators. Problem states define the problem situation and existing conditions.

States are snapshots of varying conditions in the environment. For example, a state can be "you cannot start your car," or "there is an oil leak." States can also be potential alternative solutions to problems. All states are unique. The goal is the objective to be achieved, a final answer, or a solution; for example, your goal is finding what is wrong with your car. There may be more than one goal. *Operators* are procedures used for changing from one state to another. An operator describes a process whereby some action is taken to change the initial state into another state that more closely approaches the goal. Operators move the problem from one state to the next, following the guidance of a master control strategy, until a goal is reached. An operator could be an algorithmic subroutine.

Figure 11-B.1 shows the relationship between the initial state, procedures, and goal. The initial conditions provide the states that are manipulated by procedures to achieve the goal. A *control strategy* selects or guides the procedures.

It is important to point out that even though we may treat search as being separate from the knowledge representation scheme, the two are very much interrelated. The selection of a particular knowledge representation method will greatly affect the type of search and control strategy used.

A *state space* represents the set of all attainable states for a given problem. It is often useful to express the problem graphically because graphics illustrate not only the state space, but also the search process. The most common graphic presentations are described next.

Graphic Presentations

Directed State Graph. Figure 11-B.2 is a *state graph* for a simple problem: attempting to find the best path from one city, the source (S), to another city, the destination, or goal (G). This state graph is a map showing the various intermediate towns and cities that would be passed through in reaching the de-

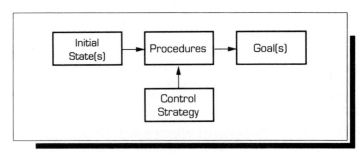

FIGURE 11-B.1 Relationship between Initial State(s), Procedures, and Goal(s) in the Search Process.

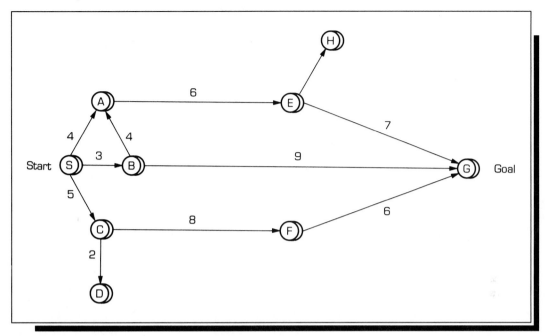

FIGURE 11-B.2   State Graph Showing Alternate Routes from the Start (S) to the Goal (G).

sired destination. In such a problem, there often will be several alternative routes. The problem is to reach the destination in the least amount of time, or using the shortest route.

The nodes in a state graph are interconnected by arcs, or links, which usually have arrows showing the direction from one state to the next. The arcs represent the application of an operator to a node. The numbers above the arcs represent the distance (or travel time) between nodes.

In practice, it is difficult to represent a state graph in a software form. For example, some of the paths through the state graph can be retraced repeatedly. The path "S to node B to node A back to node S" could be repeated over and over again. Such endless loops cannot be tolerated in a computer program and, therefore, some procedures must be followed to eliminate undesired cyclical conditions such as this. This is done by converting the state graph into a search tree.

Search Tree. A *search tree* based on the state graph in Figure 11-B.2 is illustrated in Figure 11-B.3. The new tree diagram states the same problem but in a slightly different format. The network thus formed is more like a hierarchy. Note that some of the nodes are repeated to eliminate the cyclical loop problem described earlier.

A special language has been developed to describe a search tree. For example, the initial state node is called the *root node.* It usually describes the object

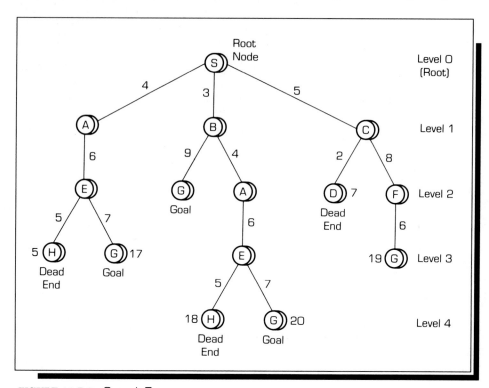

FIGURE 11-B.3 Search Tree.

(or topic). Other nodes branch out from the root. These successor, or descendant, nodes are also sometimes referred to as children. They are intermediate nodes. Working backwards through the tree, nodes are said to have predecessors, ancestors, or parents. Nodes with no children or successors are called *leaf nodes*. They designate the end of the search, either by arriving at a goal or by being at a dead end. The interconnecting arcs are referred to as branches. Note in Figure 11-B.3 that a search tree is divided into various levels that are a function of the hierarchy. These levels describe the *depth* of the tree. The root node is usually designated level 0, and successively deeper levels are designated sequentially from numbers 1 through the highest level required to represent the state space.

AND/OR branches are another aspect of search trees. The branches from a node to its successors can represent two or more alternative paths to subgoals. One path or another could lead to the goal. We call these OR nodes because one branch, OR another, OR another could be the path to the goal.

In some problems, however, the successor nodes might represent problem states that must all be achieved or traversed before the goal is reached. These are referred to as AND nodes. One subgoal AND another subgoal (AND possibly others) must be achieved to solve the problem.

APPENDIX 11-C: Blind Search Methods

A blind search is a collection of procedures used arbitrarily to search a state space. Blind search methods can be classified as exhaustive or partial, and the two partial methods are distinguished as breadth-first and depth-first methods.

Exhaustive Search

In an *exhaustive search* operators are used to generate successor states. Beginning at the root node, the search continues until a solution is found. The idea behind an exhaustive search is to examine the *entire* tree in an orderly manner, using all the operators and generating as many successor nodes as possible to find the desired solution.

Starting with the root node, several procedures are possible for proceeding through the tree; but the approaches are usually inefficient. In very large problems, a huge number of new states are generated and many alternatives are considered. As a result, it takes a considerable amount of time and effort to find the solution. Very-high-speed computers make blind search acceptable for some problems; however, others are too large for an exhaustive search.

Consider the possible number of moves in a chess game—estimated to be 10 to the 120th power. For such cases, a heuristic search is more appropriate. However, for many other cases the following two partial blind search methods can be effective.

Partial Search

Breadth-first Search. A *breadth-first search* examines all of the nodes (states) in a search tree, beginning with the root node. The nodes in each level are examined completely before moving on to the next level. A simple breadth-first search is illustrated in Figure 11-C.1. The numbers inside the node circles designate the sequence in which the nodes are examined. In this instance, the search (follow the broken line) would actually end at node 7, as that is the goal state.

The process usually starts at the initial state node and works one level at a time from left to right. A terminal node is not necessarily a goal node; it can be a dead-end node. Breadth-first procedures are good when the number of paths emanating from each goal is relatively small and where the number of levels in each branch is of a different depth (number of levels).

Depth-first Search. A *depth-first search* begins at the root node and works downward to successively deeper levels. An operator is applied to the node to generate the next deeper node in sequence. This process continues until a solution is found or backtracking is forced by reaching a dead end.

A simple depth-first search is illustrated in Figure 11-C.2. This process con-

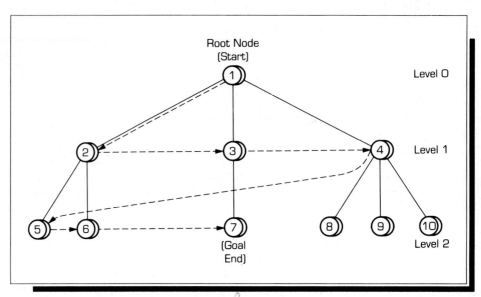

FIGURE 11-C.1 Breadth-first Search

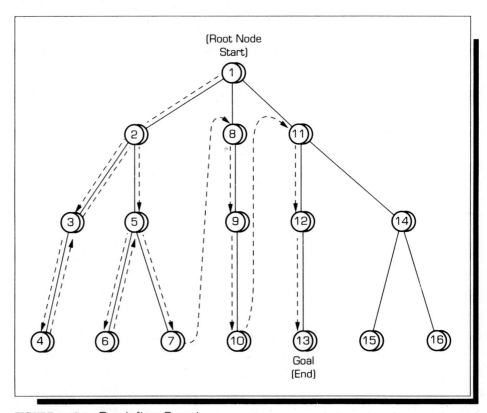

FIGURE 11-C.2 Depth-first Search

tinues downward and in a left-to-right direction until the state goal is discovered. Here, the search would actually end at node 13.

When a dead-end node is discovered, such as node 4, the search process *backtracks* so that any additional branching alternative at the next higher node level is attempted. The search backs up to node 3. It has no alternate paths, so the search backtracks to node 2. Here, another path through node 5 is available. The path through node 6 is explored until its depth is exhausted. The backtracking continues until the goal is reached.

The depth-first search guarantees a solution, but the search may be a long one. Many different branches will have to be considered to a maximum depth before a solution is reached. (By setting a "depth bound," it is frequently possible to reduce the search.) The method is especially attractive in cases where short paths exist and where there are no lengthy sub-branches.

Chapter 12

Fundamentals of Expert Systems

Of all applied AI areas, expert systems is the most managerially challenging. In the forthcoming chapters we attempt to show why. This chapter constitutes an overview of the field; the following specific topics are discussed:

465

12.1   Introduction

The name *expert systems* was derived from the term *knowledge-based expert systems.* An **expert system** is a system that employs human knowledge captured in a computer to solve problems that ordinarily require human expertise. Well-designed systems imitate the reasoning processes experts use to solve specific problems. Such systems can be used by nonexperts to improve their problem-solving capabilities. Expert systems (ES)* can also be used by experts as knowledgeable assistants. ES are used to propagate scarce knowledge resources for improved, consistent results. Ultimately, such systems could function better than any single human expert in making judgments in a specific, usually narrow, area of expertise (referred to as a **domain**). This possibility may have a significant impact both on advisory professionals (financial analysts, lawyers, tax advisors, etc.) and on organizations and their management.

The purpose of this chapter is to introduce the fundamentals of expert systems. A brief history is followed by an actual case. The case leads to a presentation of the basic ideas of ES as well as to its capabilities and structure. Finally, various types of ES, their benefits, and their limitations are discussed.

12.2   History of Expert Systems

Expert systems were developed by the AI community as early as the mid-1960s. This period of AI research was dominated by a belief that a few laws of reasoning coupled with powerful computers would produce expert or even superhuman performance. One attempt in this direction was the General-purpose Problem Solver.

General-purpose Problem Solver

The **General-purpose Problem Solver** (GPS), a procedure developed by Newell and Simon [11] from their Logic Theory Machine, was an attempt to create an "intelligent" computer. Thus, it can be viewed as a predecessor to ES. GPS tries to work out the steps needed to change a certain initial situation into a desired goal. For each problem to be solved, GPS is given (1) a set of operators that can change a situation in various ways, (2) a statement of what preconditions each operator needs to be true before it can be applied, and (3) a list of postconditions that will be true after the operator has been used. It also has an optional set of heuristics for operators to try first. In ES terms, these form a rule base.

GPS attempts to find operators that reduce the difference between a goal and current states. Sometimes the operators cannot operate on the current states

---

*ES is both a singular and plural abbreviation (expert system or expert systems).

(their preconditions are not suitable). In such cases, GPS sets itself a subgoal: to change the current state into one that is suitable for the operators. Many such subgoals may have to be set before GPS can solve a problem.

GPS, like several other similar programs, did not fulfill its inventors' dreams. Nevertheless, such programs did produce extremely important side benefits.

Early Expert Systems

The shift from general-purpose to special-purpose programs occurred in the mid-1960s with the development of DENDRAL* by E. Feigenbaum at Stanford University, followed up by the development of MYCIN (see Appendix 12-B). At that time researchers also recognized that the problem-solving mechanism is only a small part of a complete, intelligent computer system.

The construction of DENDRAL led to the following conclusions:

- General problem solvers are too weak to be used as the basis for building high-performance ES.
- Human problem solvers are good only if they operate in a very narrow domain.
- Expert systems need to be constantly updated with new information. Such updating can be done efficiently with rule-based representation.
- The complexity of problems requires a considerable amount of knowledge about the problem area.

By the mid-1970s, several expert systems had begun to emerge. Recognizing the central role of knowledge in these systems, AI scientists worked to develop comprehensive knowledge representation theories and associated general-purpose decision-making procedures and inferences. Within a few years it became apparent that these efforts had limited success for reasons similar to those that doomed the first general problem solvers. "Knowledge," as a target of study, is too broad and diverse; efforts to solve knowledge-based problems in general were premature. On the other hand, several different approaches to knowledge representation proved sufficient for the expert systems that employed them. A key insight was learned at that time: *The power of an ES is derived from the specific knowledge it possesses, not from the particular formalisms and inference schemes it employs.*

By the beginning of the 1980s, ES technology, first limited to the academic scene, began to appear as commercial applications. Notable were XCON and XSEL (see Appendix 12-B) and CATS-1 (see Section 12.3).

In addition to building ES, a substantial effort was made to develop tools for speeding up the construction of ES. These tools included programming tools like EMYCIN and AGE, knowledge acquisition tools like EXPERT and KAS, and tools for learning from experience such as META-DENDRAL and EURISKO.

---

*Systems referred to in this chapter are described in Appendix 12-A.

Such tools became commercially available starting in 1983. Most of the early development tools required special hardware (e.g., LISP machines), but since the late 1980s, development software can run on regular computers including microcomputers.

The following list indicates the latest developments in the expert system area:

- Availability of many tools that are designed to expedite the construction of ES at a reduced cost
- Dissemination of ES in thousands of organizations, some of which use hundreds or even thousands of specific systems
- Extensive integration of ES with other computer-based information systems, especially integration with databases and decision support systems
- Increased use of expert systems in many tasks, ranging from help desks to complex military and space shuttle applications
- Use of ES technology as a methodology for expediting the construction of regular information systems
- Increased use of the object-oriented programming approach in knowledge representation
- Development of complex systems with multiple sources of knowledge, multiple lines of reasoning, and fuzzy information
- Use of multiple knowledge bases.

12.3   The Case of CATS-1 (DELTA)

Problem

General Electric's (GE) top locomotive field service engineer, David I. Smith, had been with the company for more than forty years. He was the top expert in troubleshooting diesel electric locomotive engines. Smith was traveling throughout the country to places where locomotives were in need of repair to determine what was wrong and to advise young engineers about what to do. The company was very dependent on Smith. The problem was that he was nearing retirement.

Traditional Solution: Apprenticeship

GE's traditional approach to such a situation was to create teams that paired senior and junior engineers. The pairs worked together for several months or years, and by the time the older engineers finally did retire, the younger engineers had absorbed enough of their seniors' expertise to carry on troubleshooting or other tasks. This practice proved to be a good short-term solution, but GE still wanted a more effective and dependable way of disseminating expertise among its engineers, and preventing valuable knowledge from retiring with David Smith. Furthermore, having railroad service shops throughout the country requires extensive travel by an expert or moving the locomotives to an expert, because it is not economically feasible to have an expert in each shop.

Expert System

In 1980, GE decided to build an ES by modeling the way a human trouble-shooter works. The system builders spent several months interviewing Smith and transferring his knowledge to a computer. The computer programming was prototyped over a three-year period, slowly increasing the information and the number of decision rules stored in the computer. The new diagnostic technology enables a novice engineer or a technician to uncover a fault by spending only a few minutes at the computer terminal. The system can also *explain* to the user the logic of its advice, thus serving as a teacher. Furthermore, the system can lead users through the required repair procedures, presenting a detailed, computer-aided drawing of parts and subsystems and providing specific how-to instructional demonstrations.

The system is based on a flexible, humanlike thought process, rather than rigid procedures expressed in flowcharts or decision trees.

The system, which was developed on a minicomputer but operates on a microcomputer, is currently installed at every railroad repair shop served by GE, thus eliminating delays and boosting maintenance productivity. For further information, see Bonissone and Johnson [2].

12.4 Basic Concepts of Expert Systems

The CATS-1 example introduces the basic concepts of expert systems: expertise, experts, transferring expertise, inferencing rules, and explanation capability. These concepts are defined in this section; the remainder of the chapter is then devoted to a more detailed description and discussion of them and their role in ES.

Expertise

Expertise is the extensive, task-specific knowledge acquired from training, reading, and experience. The following types of knowledge are examples of what expertise includes:

- Facts about the problem area
- Theories about the problem area
- Hard-and-fast rules and procedures regarding the general problem area
- Rules (heuristics) of what to do in a given problem situation (i.e., rules regarding problem solving)
- Global strategies for solving these types of problems
- Meta-knowledge (knowledge about knowledge).

These types of knowledge enable experts to make better and faster decisions than nonexperts in solving complex problems. It takes a long time (usually several years) to become an expert, and novices become experts only incrementally. (See Box 12.1.)

Box 12.1: Some Facts about Expertise

- Expertise is usually associated with a high degree of intelligence but it is not always connected to the smartest person.
- Expertise is usually associated with quantity of knowledge.
- Experts learn from past successes and mistakes.
- Experts' knowledge is well-stored, organized, and retrievable quickly.
- Experts can call up patterns from their experience (excellent recall).

Experts

It is difficult to define what an **expert** is because we actually talk about degrees or levels of expertise. (The question is how much expertise should a person possess before qualifying as an expert.) Nevertheless, it has been said that nonexperts outnumber experts in many fields by a ratio of 100 to 1. Distribution of expertise appears to be of the same shape regardless of the type of knowledge being evaluated. Figure 12.1 represents a typical distribution of expertise. The top tenth (decile) performs three times better than the average, and thirty times better than the lowest tenth. This distribution suggests that the overall effectiveness of human expertise can be significantly increased (up to 200 percent) if we can somehow make top-level expertise available to other decision makers.

Typically, human expertise includes a constellation of behavior that involves the following activities:

- Recognizing and formulating the problem
- Solving the problem quickly and properly
- Explaining the solution
- Learning from experience
- Restructuring knowledge
- Breaking rules
- Determining relevance
- Degrading gracefully (awareness of limitation).

Experts can take a problem stated in some arbitrary manner and convert it to a form that lends itself to a rapid and effective solution. Problem-solving ability is necessary, but not sufficient by itself. Experts should be able to explain the results, learn new things about the domain, restructure knowledge whenever needed, break rules whenever necessary (i.e., know the exceptions to the rules), and determine whether their expertise is relevant. Finally, experts "degrade gracefully," meaning that as they get close to the boundaries of their knowledge, they gradually become less proficient at solving problems. All these activities must be done efficiently (quickly and at low cost) and effectively (with high-quality results).

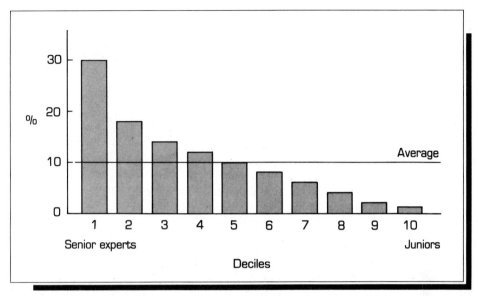

FIGURE 12.1 Distribution of Expertise: Percent Successes Achieved per Decile. (*Source:* Adapted from N. R. Augustine, "Distribution of Expertise," *Defense Systems Management* [Spring 1979].)

To mimic the human expert, it is necessary to build a computer that exhibits all these characteristics. To date (1993), work in ES has primarily explored the second and third of these activities (solving problems and explaining the solutions).

Transferring Expertise

The objective of an expert system is to transfer expertise from an expert to a computer and then on to other humans (nonexperts). This process involves four activities: knowledge acquisition (from experts or other sources), knowledge representation (in the computer), knowledge inferencing, and knowledge transfer to the user. The knowledge is stored in the computer in a component called a knowledge base. Two types of knowledge are distinguished: *facts* and *procedures* (usually rules) regarding the problem domain.

Inferencing

A unique feature of an expert system is its ability to reason. Given that all the expertise is stored in the knowledge base and that the program has accessibility to databases, the computer is programmed so that it can make inferences. The inferencing is performed in a component called the **inference engine,** which includes procedures regarding problem solving.

Rules

Most commercial ES are **rule-based systems;** that is, the knowledge is stored mainly in the form of rules, as are the problem-solving procedures. A rule in the CATS-1 example may look like this: "*IF,* the engine is idle, and the fuel pressure is less than 38 psi, and the gauge is accurate, *THEN,* there is a fuel system fault." There are about 600 such rules in the CATS-1 system. Recently, a frame representation is complementing the rule representation (in some applications).

Explanation Capability

Another unique feature of an ES is its ability to explain its advice or recommendations. The explanation and justification is done in a subsystem called the **justifier,** or the **explanation subsystem.** It enables the system to examine its own reasoning and to explain its operation.

The characteristics and capabilities of ES make them different from conventional systems. For a comparison, see Table 12.1.

TABLE 12.1   Comparison of Conventinal Systems and Expert Systems

Conventional Systems	Expert Systems
Information and its processing are usually combined in one sequential program.	Knowledge base is clearly separated from the processing (inference) mechanism (i.e., knowledge rules separated from the control).
Program does not make mistakes (programmers do).	Program may make mistakes.
Do not (usually) explain why input data are needed or how conclusions were drawn.	Explanation is a part of most ES.
Changes in the program are tedious.	Changes in the rules are easy to accomplish.
The system operates only when it is completed.	The system can operate with only a few rules (as the first prototype).
Execution is done on a step-by-step (algorithmic) basis.	Execution is done by using heuristics and logic.
Effective manipulation of large databases	Effective manipulation of large knowledge bases
Representation and use of data	Representation and use of knowledge
Efficiency is a major goal.	Effectiveness is the major goal.
Easily deal with quantitative data.	Easily deal with qualitative data.
Capture, magnify, and distribute access to numeric data or to information.	Capture, magnify, and distribute access to judgment and knowledge.

12.5   Structure of Expert Systems

Expert systems are composed of two major parts: the **development environment** and the **consultation** (runtime) **environment** (Figure 12.2). The development environment is used by the ES builder to build the components and to introduce knowledge into the knowledge base. The consultation environment is used by a nonexpert to obtain expert knowledge and advice.

The following components may exist in an expert system:

- Knowledge acquisition subsystem
- Knowledge base
- Inference engine
- Blackboard (workplace)

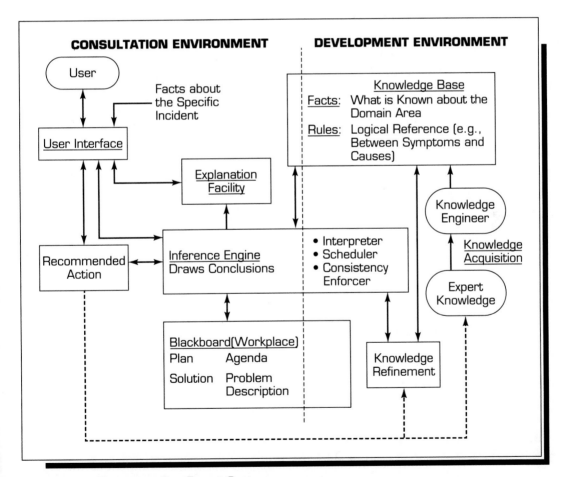

FIGURE 12.2   Structure of an Expert System

- User
- User interface
- Explanation subsystem (justifier)
- Knowledge refining system

Most existing expert systems do not contain the knowledge refinement component. There are also large variations in the content and capabilities of each component. These components are underlined in Figure 12.2, which also shows the relationships among the components. A brief description of each component follows.

Knowledge Acquisition Subsystem

Knowledge acquisition is the accumulation, transfer, and transformation of problem-solving expertise from some knowledge source to a computer program for constructing or expanding the knowledge base (see Chapter 13). Potential sources of knowledge include human experts, textbooks, databases, special research reports, and pictures.

Acquiring knowledge from experts is a complex task that frequently creates a bottleneck in ES construction. The state of the art today requires a **knowledge engineer** to interact with one or more human experts in building the knowledge base. Typically, the knowledge engineer helps the expert structure the problem area by interpreting and integrating human answers to questions, drawing analogies, posing counterexamples, and bringing to light conceptual difficulties.

Knowledge Base

The knowledge base contains knowledge necessary for understanding, formulating, and solving problems. It includes two basic elements: (1) facts, such as the problem situation and theory of the problem area and (2) special heuristics, or rules that direct the use of knowledge to solve specific problems in a particular domain. (In addition, the inference engine includes *standard* problem-solving and decision-making rules.) The heuristics express the informal judgmental knowledge in an application area. Global strategies, which can be both heuristics and a part of the theory of the problem area, are usually included in the knowledge base. Knowledge, not mere facts, is the primary material of expert systems. The information in the knowledge base is incorporated into a computer program by a process called **knowledge representation,** which will be discussed in Chapter 14.

Inference Engine

The "brain" of the ES is the inference engine, also known as the *control* structure or the rule interpreter (in rule-based ES). This component is essentially a computer program that provides a methodology for reasoning about information in the knowledge base and in the "blackboard," and for formulating conclusions. This component provides directions about how to use the system's knowledge by developing the agenda that organizes and controls the steps taken to solve problems whenever consultation is performed.

The inference engine has three major elements:

- An *interpreter* (rule interpreter in most systems), which executes the chosen agenda items by applying the corresponding knowledge base rules.
- A *scheduler*, which maintains control over the agenda. It estimates the effects of applying inference rules in light of item priorities or other criteria on the agenda.
- A *consistency enforcer*, which attempts to maintain a consistent representation of the emerging solution.

Blackboard (Workplace)

The **blackboard** is an area of working memory set aside for the description of a current problem, as specified by the input data; it is also used for recording intermediate results. The blackboard records intermediate hypotheses and decisions. Three types of decisions can be recorded on the blackboard: (1) *plan*—how to attack the problem, (2) *agenda*—potential actions awaiting execution, and (3) *solution*—candidate hypotheses and alternative courses of action that the system has generated thus far.

Blackboards exist only in some systems. The use of the blackboard approach is especially popular when several experts team up in solving one problem.

Let's consider an example. When your car fails, you enter the symptoms of the failure into the computer for storage in the blackboard. As the result of an intermediate hypothesis developed in the blackboard, the computer may then suggest that you do some additional checks (e.g., see if your battery is connected properly) and ask you to report the results. Again, this information is recorded in the blackboard.

User Interface

Expert systems contain a language processor for friendly, problem-oriented communication between the user and the computer. This communication could best be carried out in a natural language, and in some cases it is supplemented by menus and graphics.

Explanation Subsystem (Justifier)

The ability to trace responsibility for conclusions to their sources is crucial both in the transfer of expertise and in problem solving. The explanation subsystem can trace such responsibility and explain the ES behavior by interactively answering questions such as the following:

- *Why* was a certain question asked by the expert system?
- *How* was a certain conclusion reached?

- *Why* was a certain alternative rejected?
- *What* is the plan to reach the solution? For example, what remains to be established before a final diagnosis can be determined?

Knowledge Refining System

Human experts have a **knowledge refining** system; that is, they can analyze their own performance, learn from it, and improve it for future consultations. Similarly, such evaluation is necessary in computerized learning so that the program will be able to analyze the reasons for its success or failure. This could lead to improvements that result in a better knowledge base and more effective reasoning. Such a component is not available in commercial expert systems at the moment, but it is being developed in experimental ES in several universities and research institutions.

12.6   The Human Element in Expert Systems

At least two humans, and possibly more, participate in the development and use of an expert system. At a minimum there is an expert and a user. Frequently, there is also a knowledge engineer and a system builder. Each has a role to play.

The Expert

The expert, commonly referred to as the domain expert, is a person who has the special knowledge, judgment, experience, and methods along with the ability to apply these talents to give advice and solve problems. It is the domain expert's job to provide knowledge about how he or she performs the task that the knowledge system will perform. The expert knows which facts are important and understands the meaning of the relationships among facts. In diagnosing a problem with an automobile's electrical system, for example, an expert mechanic knows that fan belts can break and cause the battery to discharge. Directing a novice to check the fan belts and interpreting the meaning of a loose or missing belt are examples of expertise. When more than one expert is used, situations can become difficult if the experts disagree.

Usually, the initial body of knowledge, including terms and basic concepts, is documented in textbooks, reference manuals, sets of policies, or a catalog of products. However, this is not sufficient for a powerful ES. Not all expertise can be documented because most experts are unaware of the exact mental process by which they diagnose or solve a problem. Therefore, an interactive procedure is needed to acquire additional information from the expert to expand the basic knowledge. This process is fairly complex and usually requires the intervention of a knowledge engineer.

The Knowledge Engineer

The **knowledge engineer** helps the expert(s) structure the problem area by interpreting and integrating human answers to questions, drawing analogies, posing counterexamples, and bringing to light conceptual difficulties. He or she is usually also the system builder. The shortage of experienced knowledge engineers is a major bottleneck in ES construction. To overcome this bottleneck, ES designers are using productivity tools (e.g., special editors), and research is being conducted on building systems that will bypass the need for knowledge engineers.

The User

Most computer-based systems have evolved in a single-user mode. In contrast, an ES has several possible types of users:

- A nonexpert client seeking direct advice. In such a case the ES acts as a *consultant* or *advisor*.
- A student who wants to learn. In such a case the ES acts as an *instructor*.
- An ES builder who wants to improve or increase the knowledge base. In such a case the ES acts as a *partner*.
- An expert. In such a case the ES acts as a *colleague* or as an *assistant*. For example, an ES can provide a "second opinion," so the expert can validate his or her judgment. An expert can also use the system as an assistant to carry on routine analysis or computations or to search for and classify information.

Users may not be familiar with computers and may lack in-depth knowledge in the problem domain. Many, however, have an interest in making better and possibly cheaper and faster decisions by using expert systems. The domain expert and the knowledge engineer should anticipate users' needs and limitations when designing ES.

Other Participants

Several other participants may be involved in ES. For example, a *system builder* may assist in integrating the expert system with other computerized systems. A *tool builder* may provide or build specific tools. *Vendors* may provide tools and advice, and *support staff* may provide clerical and technical help. The various participants and their roles are demonstrated in Figure 12.3. Notice that several roles can be executed by one person. For example, some systems include only an expert and a user while others include only a system builder, an expert, and a user.

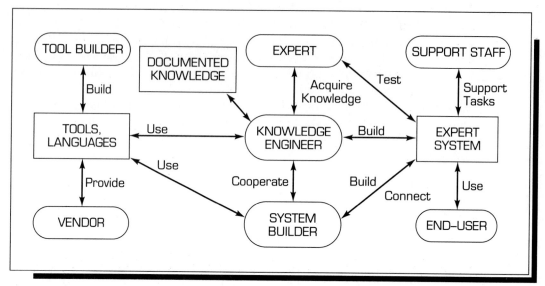

FIGURE 12.3 Participants in Building Expert Systems and Their Roles. (*Source:* Modified from D. A. Waterman, *A Guide to Expert Systems* [Reading, MA: Addison-Wesley, 1985]. Reprinted by permission of Addison-Wesley Publishing Co., Inc., Reading, MA.)

12.7   How Expert Systems Work

Three major activities are part of ES construction and use: development, consultation, and improvement.

Development

The development of an expert system involves the construction of the knowledge base by acquiring knowledge from experts and/or from documented sources. The knowledge is separated into *declarative* (factual) and *procedural* aspects. Development activity also includes the construction (or acquisition) of an inference engine, a blackboard, an explanation facility, and any other required software, such as interfaces. The major participants in this activity are the domain expert, the knowledge engineer, and possibly information system programmers (especially if there is a need to interface with other computer programs). The knowledge is represented in the knowledge base in such a way that the system can draw conclusions by emulating the reasoning process of human experts.

The process of developing ES can be lengthy (see Chapter 16). A tool that is frequently used to expedite development is called the *ES shell*. ES shells include all the generic components of an ES, but they do *not* include the knowledge. EMYCIN is a shell constructed by taking MYCIN minus its knowledge. (The letter *E* in EMYCIN stands for empty, that is, MYCIN without its knowledge.)

Consultation

Once the system is developed and validated, it is transferred to the users. When users want advice, they come to the ES. The ES conducts a bidirectional dialog with the user, asking her or him to provide facts about a specific incident. After accepting the user's answers, the ES attempts to reach a conclusion. This effort is made by the inference engine, which "decides" which heuristic search techniques should be used to determine how the rules in the knowledge base are to be applied to the problem. The user can ask for explanations. The quality of the inference capability is determined by the knowledge representation method used and by the power of the inference engine.

Because the user is usually a computer novice, the ES must be very easy to use. At the present state of the technology, the user must sit by the computer terminal and type in the description of the problem (future ES will use voice input). The ES asks questions and the user answers them; more questions may be asked and answered; and, finally, a conclusion is reached. The consultation environment is also used by the builder during the development phase to test the system. At that time, the interface and the explanation facility may be tested.

Improvement

Expert systems are improved several times through a process called **rapid prototyping** during their development (see Chapter 16).

12.8   An Expert System at Work

Let's look at a simple rule-based expert system programmed with EXSYS, the development shell. This is a typical consultation with a system called *Select Auto*. The opening statement follows:

Select Auto is an expert system designed to assist a user
to make a right decision of buying a new car. It will review
prospective cars that match with the users' needs and
preference.

Now the consultation continues. User's answers are in boldface characters.

The car is made in
1   the United States
2   foreign countries
3   don't know
1

In this menu-driven consultation the user selected answer number 1.

Quality is
1   the highest concern
2   of high concern

```
3      of moderate concern
4      don't know
1
```

The computer keeps asking questions. The user may want to know *why* specific information is needed by the computer.

```
Price of the car is
1      important
2      unimportant
3      don't know
WHY
```

In a reply to the user question the computer will display the rule(s) in which price is a factor. This is part of the explanation capability. Rules can be presented either in plain English or in the way they are programmed. For example, EXSYS will show rule 5 (and possibly other related rules).

```
RULE NUMBER: 5
IF:
(1) Price of a car is important
and
(2) The payment is in installments
THEN:
The monthly payment is determined.
```

Now, the user answers the question.

```
Price of a car is
1      important
2      unimportant
3      don't know
1
```

The computer will ask more questions. Later on we will explain why and when questions are being asked. Here are some typical questions with a user's selection shown.

```
The monthly payment is no more than
1      $100
2      $150
3      $200
4      $250
5      $300
4

Front seat is
1      important
2      unimportant
1
```

Acceleration is
1   strong
2   moderate
3   don't know
2

Engine is
1   between 1000–1500 cc
2   between 1501–2000 cc
3   over 2000 cc
4   don't know
2

Notice that "don't know" is an option. Expert systems can work with fuzzy or incomplete information just as human experts do.

Reliability of a car is
1   of high concern
2   of concern
3   of less concern
4   not sure
4

The computer will ask some more questions.

The most considered factor in making a
decision to buy a car is
1   price
2   fuel economy
3   comfort and convenience
4   performance of a car
5   safety
6   reliability
7   quality
8   don't know
1, 7

Here again, the user gave an indirect answer, stating that *both* price and quality are most important.

Once all questions are answered the computer will make a statement like this:

The following are the automobiles most likely to suit your
stated needs. If no selection has been made, it is most
likely the result of the fact that there does not exist an
automobile with all the attributes you desire. Should this
occur readjust your criteria and try again.

In our case this is exactly what happened. Therefore, the computer allowed the user to *change* the answers to the questions. This is done by displaying the questions and answers.

1	The car is made in the United States
2	Quality is the highest concern
3	The price of the car is important
4	The monthly payment is no more than $250.00
5	The front seat is important
6	Acceleration is moderate
7	Engine is between 1501–2000 cc
8	Reliability is not sure
9	The most considered factors are price and quality

We changed the first answer from a car made in the United States to one made in a foreign country. This time we were advised that two cars are recommended.

Values based on – 100 to + 100 systems		VALUE
1	Toyota Corolla	51
2	Renault Alliance	23

Since 100 points can be considered as the highest possible recommendation, neither car is really highly recommended. (We will explain later how the "value" is computed.) So we can now change our requirement again.

The user may ask *how* a certain recommendation has been derived. The computer will display all the rules that were used in deriving the recommendation.

12.9   Problem Areas Addressed by Expert Systems

Expert systems can be classified in several ways. One way is a generic categorization that uses the general problem areas they address. For example, diagnosis can be defined as "inferring system malfunctions from observations." Diagnosis is a generic activity executed in medicine, organizational studies, computer operations, and so on. The generic categories of expert systems are listed in Table 12.2. Some ES belong to two or more of these categories. A brief description of each category follows.

Interpretation systems infer situation descriptions from observations. This category includes surveillance, speech understanding, image analysis, signal interpretation, and many kinds of intelligence analysis. An interpretation system explains observed data by assigning them symbolic meanings describing the situation.

Prediction systems include weather forecasting, demographic predictions, economic forecasting, traffic predictions, crop estimates, and military, marketing, or financial forecasting.

Diagnostic systems include medical, electronic, mechanical, and software diagnosis. Diagnostic systems typically relate observed behavioral irregularities to underlying causes.

TABLE 12.2 Generic Categories of Expert Systems

Category	Problem Addressed
Interpretation	Inferring situation descriptions from observations
Prediction	Inferring likely consequences of given situations
Diagnosis	Inferring system malfunctions from observations
Design	Configuring objects under constraints
Planning	Developing plans to achieve goal(s)
Monitoring	Comparing observations to plans, flagging exceptions
Debugging	Prescribing remedies for malfunctions
Repair	Executing a plan to administer a prescribed remedy
Instruction	Diagnosing, debugging, and correcting student performance
Control	Interpreting, predicting, repairing, and monitoring system behaviors

Design systems develop configurations of objects that satisfy the constraints of the design problem. Such problems include circuit layout, building design, and plant layout. Design systems construct descriptions of objects in various relationships with one another and verify that these configurations conform to stated constraints.

Planning systems specialize in problems of planning like automatic programming. They also deal with short- and long-term planning in areas such as project management, routing, communications, product development, military applications, and financial planning.

Monitoring systems compare observations of system behavior with standards that seem crucial for successful goal attainment. These crucial features correspond to potential flaws in the plan. Many computer-aided monitoring systems exist for topics ranging from air traffic to fiscal management tasks.

Debugging systems rely on planning, design, and prediction capabilities to create specifications or recommendations for correcting a diagnosed problem.

Repair systems develop and execute plans to administer a remedy for some diagnosed problems. Such systems incorporate debugging, planning, and execution capabilities.

Instruction systems incorporate diagnosis and debugging subsystems that specifically address the student as the focus of interest. Typically, these systems begin by constructing a hypothetical description of the student's knowledge that interprets his or her behavior. They then diagnose weaknesses in the student's knowledge and identify appropriate remedies to overcome the deficiencies. Finally, they plan a tutorial interaction intended to deliver remedial knowledge to the student.

Control systems adaptively govern the overall behavior of a system. To do this, the control system must repeatedly interpret the current situation, predict the future, diagnose the causes of anticipated problems, formulate a remedial plan, and monitor its execution to ensure success.

Not all the tasks that are usually found within each of the preceding ten categories are suitable for expert systems.

12.10   Benefits of Expert Systems

ES can provide major benefits to users. Some of the *potential* benefits are discussed next.

Increased Output and Productivity. ES can work faster than humans. For example, XCON (see Appendix 12-B) has enabled DEC to increase fourfold the throughput of VAX configurating orders. Increased output means fewer workers needed and reduced costs.

Increased Quality. ES can increase quality by providing consistent advice and reducing error rate. For example, XCON reduced the error rate of configurating computer orders from 35 to 2 percent.

Reduced Downtime. Many operational ES (e.g., the CATS-1 system described earlier) are used for diagnosing malfunctions and prescribing repairs. By using ES it is possible to reduce downtime significantly. For example, one day of lost time on an oil rig can cost as much as $250,000. A system called Drilling Advisor was developed to detect malfunctions in oil rigs. This system saved a considerable amount of money for the company involved by cutting down the downtime.

Capture of Scarce Expertise. The scarcity of expertise becomes evident in situations where there are not enough experts for a task, the expert is about to retire or leave a job, or expertise is required over a broad geographic location. Typical systems that capture scarce expertise are CATS-1 and TARA (see Box 12.2).

Flexibility. ES can offer flexibility in both services and in manufacturing industries. For example, DEC tries to make each VAX order fit the customer's needs as closely as possible. Before XCON, DEC found it increasingly difficult to do this because of the variety of customer requests.

Easier Equipment Operation. ES makes complex equipment easier to operate. For example, STEAMER is an ES intended to train inexperienced workers to operate complex ship engines. Another example is an ES developed for Shell Oil Co. (by Intelligent Terminal Ltd.) to train people to use complex FORTRAN routines.

Box 12.2: Innovative Expert Systems—A Sampling

Of the many innovative expert systems on the market, the following are of particular interest.

TARA: An Intelligent Assistant for Foreign Traders. Foreign exchange currency traders cannot afford to think over multimillion dollar situations for long. In real time, they must examine large quantities of data; consider historical trends; determine what is relevant; and, many times in the course of a day, make the ever-critical decision to buy or sell. It is a high-risk, high-reward job of prediction where even the best traders are pleased with being right 60 percent of the time. At Manufacturers Hanover Trust an expert system called the Technical Analysis and Reasoning Assistant (TARA) was built to assist foreign currency traders. *Source:* Schorr and Rappaport [17].

Soviet Union Trade Adviser. This system provides advice about doing business and marketing in the former Soviet Union. The advice ranges from assessing the probability of obtaining an export license (in the United States) to information about demand and products in Russia. (See the second case study at the end of this chapter for details.)

Managing Toxicological Studies. This system helps in identifying computing resources (and their costs) that support toxicological research programs for assessing the risks posed by toxic chemicals in an effort to reduce human health hazards. *Source:* H. Berghel, et al., "An Expert System for Managing Toxicological Studies," *Expert Systems: Planning, Implementation, Integration* (Spring 1991).

Analyst: An Advisor for Financial Analysis for Automobile Dealerships. One of the services General Motors (GM) offers to approximately 12,000 domestic GM dealerships (and affiliates) is inventory financing. This service is also known as wholesale, or "floor-plan," financing. In exchange for funds, dealers must adhere to a set of rules, the most important of which is to promptly pay GM as vehicles are sold. Adherence is analyzed at least annually. The process of analyzing a dealership is, in essence, financial risk analysis. An expert system was developed to expedite analysis, specifically to predict a dealership's likely performance until the next scheduled review. The system also recommends credit lines and suggests ways to reduce risk. *Source:* Schorr and Rappaport [17].

Elimination of the Need for Expensive Equipment. In many cases a human must rely on expensive instruments for monitoring and control. ES can perform the same tasks with lower-cost instruments because of their ability to investigate more thoroughly and quickly the information provided by instruments. DENDRAL is an example of such an ES.

Operation in Hazardous Environments. Many tasks require humans to operate in hazardous environments (see Box 12.2 on page 485). The ES may enable humans to avoid such environments. It enables workers to avoid hot, humid, or toxic environments, such as a nuclear power plant that has malfunctioned. This characteristic is extremely important in military conflicts.

Accessibility to Knowledge and Help Desks. Expert systems make knowledge (and information) accessible. People can query systems and receive advice. One area of applicability is support of help desks. Another is the support of any advisory service (see Box 12.3).

Reliability. ES are reliable. They do not become tired or bored, call in sick, or go on strike; and they do not talk back to the boss. ES also consistently pay attention to all details and so do not overlook relevant information and potential solutions.

Increased Capabilities of Other Computerized Systems. Integration of ES with other systems makes the other systems more effective: they cover more applications, work faster, and produce higher quality results.

Integration of Several Experts' Opinions. In certain cases, ES forces us to integrate the opinions of several experts and thus may increase the quality of the advice.

Ability to Work with Incomplete or Uncertain Information. In contrast to conventional computer systems, ES can, like human experts, work with incomplete information. The user can respond with a "don't know" or "not sure" answer to one or more of the system's questions during a consultation, and the expert system will still be able to produce an answer, although it may not be a certain one.

Provision of Training. ES can provide training. Novices who work with ES become more and more experienced. The explanation facility can also serve as a teaching device, and so can notes that may be inserted in the knowledge base.

Enhancement of Problem Solving. ES enhance problem solving by allowing the integration of top experts' judgment into analysis. For example, an ES called Statistical Navigator was developed to help novices use complex statistical computer packages.

Box 12.3: Expert System Advises Students

From semester to semester, students are plagued with decisions about which courses to take, and even what to do after graduation. This semester's no different.

But Eastern Illinois University's students may find those decisions a little bit easier to handle with the Siggi-Plus computer system at Eastern's Counseling Center. This program's main function is to help students with undecided majors choose what will best suit their own personal needs by having them enter information about themselves. The computer asks what work experience the student has had thus far, what the student values most about a job, and what extracurricular activities and interests the student enjoys. Then it produces a printout of careers to consider based on all of these factors.

The biggest benefit of this system is that is gives the student a much broader outlook than did the old program (called Discover). In the past, all students had to do to get a career listing from Discover was take an interest test. The information provided, however, did not take into account the student's actual job abilities.

"I sang in a choir as a boy, and had much interest in music," counselor Bud Sanders said. "With Discover I would most likely be told to pursue a career in music. Unfortunately, I do not have the abilities to do this. Siggi-Plus would recognize both of these factors, and give me a more accurate listing."

Siggi-Plus is not only aimed at students with undecided majors, though. It is also beneficial to students on academic probation or to those who believe they are in the wrong major.

Ability to Solve Complex Problems. Expert systems may, one day, solve problems whose complexity exceeds human ability. Already some ES are able to solve problems where the required scope of knowledge exceeds that of any one individual.

Knowledge Transfer to Remote Locations. One of the greatest potential benefits of ES is its ease of transfer across international boundaries. An example of such a transfer is an eye-care ES (for diagnosis and recommended treatment) developed at Rutgers University in conjunction with the World Health Organization. The program has been implemented in Egypt and Algeria, where serious eye diseases are prevalent but eye specialists are rare. The program is rule based, runs on a micro, and can be operated by a nurse, a physician's assistant, or a general practitioner.

12.11   Problems and Limitations of Expert Systems

Available ES methodologies are not straightforward and effective, even for applications in the generic categories (see Table 12.2). Here are some problems that have slowed down the commercial spread of ES:

- Knowledge is not always readily available.
- Expertise is hard to extract from humans.
- The approach of each expert to situation assessment may be different, yet correct.
- It is hard, even for a highly skilled expert, to abstract good situational assessments when he or she is under time pressure.
- Users of expert systems have natural cognitive limits.
- ES work well only in a narrow domain.
- Most experts have no independent means of checking whether their conclusions are reasonable.
- The vocabulary, or jargon, that experts use for expressing facts and relations is frequently limited and not understood by others.
- Help is frequently required from knowledge engineers who are rare and expensive—a fact that could make ES construction rather costly.
- Lack of trust by end-users may be a barrier to ES use.
- Knowledge transfer is subject to a host of perceptual and judgmental biases.

Last, but not least, is the fact that expert systems may not be able to arrive at conclusions (especially in early stages of system development). For example, even the fully developed XCON cannot fulfill about 2 percent of the orders presented to it. Finally, expert systems, like human experts, sometimes produce incorrect recommendations.

These limitations clearly indicate that today's ES fall short of generally intelligent human behavior. Several of these limitations will diminish or disappear with technological improvements over time.

12.12   Types of Expert Systems

Expert systems appear in many varieties. The following classifications of ES are not exclusive, that is, one ES can appear in several categories.

Expert Systems Versus Knowledge-based Systems. According to this classification, an ES is one whose behavior is so sophisticated that we would call a person who performed in a similar manner an expert. MYCIN and XCON are good examples. Highly trained professionals diagnose blood diseases (MYCIN) and configure complex computing equipment (XCON). These systems truly attempt to emulate the best human experts.

In the commercial world, however, systems are emerging that can perform effectively and efficiently tasks for whose execution you really do not need an expert. Such systems are referred to as **knowledge-based systems*** (also known as advisory systems, knowledge systems, intelligent job aid systems, or operational systems). As an example, let us look at a system that gives advice on immunizations recommended for travel abroad. The advice depends on many attributes such as the age, sex, and health of the traveler and the country of destination. One needs to be knowledgeable to give such advice, but one need not be an expert. In this case, practically *all* the knowledge that relates to this advice is documented in a manual available at most public health departments (in only 1 or 2 percent of the cases it is necessary to consult a physician). Another example is supporting help desks.

The distinction between the two types may not be so sharp when it comes to reality. Many systems involve both documented knowledge and undocumented expertise. Basically it is a matter of *how much* expertise is included in the systems that classifies them in one category or the other.

Knowledge systems can be constructed more quickly and cheaply than expert systems, as will be demonstrated in Chapters 13 and 15.

Rule-based Expert Systems. Many commercial ES are rule based, because the technology of rule-based systems is relatively well developed. In such systems the knowledge is represented as a series of production rules. The classic example of a rule-based ES is MYCIN.

Frame-based Systems. In these systems, the knowledge is represented as frames, a representation of the object-oriented programming approach (see Chapter 14).

Hybrid Systems. These systems include several knowledge representation approaches, at minimum frames and rules, but usually more.

Model-based Systems. Model-based systems are structured around a model that simulates the structure and function of the system under study. The model is used to compute values which are compared to observed ones. The comparison triggers action (if needed) or further diagnosis.

Systems Classified by Their Nature. Buchanan and Shortliffe [4] distinguish several types of ES. One type deals with *evidence gathering*.

A second type is a *stepwise refinement* system. It deals with a large number of possible outcomes by means of successive levels of detail.

A third type of system is *stepwise assembly*, where the subject domain can have an extremely large number of possible outcomes. A special case of this type

---

*This terminology is not widely accepted as yet. Therefore the terms *expert systems* and *knowledge-based systems* are frequently used interchangeably.

is called a *catalog selection*. This system deals with problems like choosing the right chemical, steel, or auto parts from a catalog of choices.

Ready-made (Turnkey) Systems. ES can be developed to meet the particular needs of a user (custom-made), or they can be purchased as ready-made packages for any user. **Ready-made systems** are similar to application packages like an accounting general ledger or project management in operations management. Ready-made systems enjoy the economy of mass production and therefore are considerably less expensive than customized systems. They also can be used as soon as they are purchased. Unfortunately, ready-made systems are very general in nature, and the advice they render may not be of value to a user involved in a complex situation.

Real-Time Expert Systems. **Real-time systems** are systems in which there is a strict time limit on the system's response time, which must be *fast enough* for use to control the process being computerized. In other words, the system *always* produces a response by the time it is needed.

To learn about other classification schemes refer to Coursey and Shangraw [5] and Meyer and Curley [9].

Chapter Highlights

- Expert systems imitate the reasoning process of experts for solving difficult problems.
- A predecessor of ES was the General-purpose Problem Solver (GPS). The GPS (and similar programs) failed because they attempted to cover too much and ignored the importance of the specific knowledge required.
- The power of an ES is derived from the specific knowledge it possesses, and not from the particular knowledge representation and inference schemes it employs.
- Expertise is a task-specific knowledge acquired from training, reading, and experience.
- Experts can make fast and good decisions regarding complex situations.
- Most of the knowledge in organizations is possessed by a few experts.
- Expert system technology attempts to transfer knowledge from experts and documented sources to the computer and make it available for use by nonexperts.
- The reasoning capability in expert systems is provided by an inference engine.
- The knowledge in ES is separated from the inferencing (processing).
- Expert systems provide limited explanation capabilities.
- A distinction is made between a development environment (building an ES) and a consultation environment (using an ES).

- The major components of an ES are the knowledge acquisition subsystem, knowledge base, inference engine, blackboard, user interface, and explanation subsystem.
- The knowledge engineer captures the knowledge from the expert and programs it into the computer.
- Although the major user of the ES is a nonexpert, other users (such as students, ES builders, and even experts) may utilize ES.
- Knowledge can be declarative (facts) or procedural.
- Expert systems are being improved in an iterative manner using a process called rapid prototyping.
- The ten generic categories of ES are: interpretation, prediction, diagnosis, design, planning, monitoring, debugging, repair, instruction, and control.
- Expert systems can provide many benefits. The most important are improvement in productivity and/or quality, preservation of scarce expertise, enhancing other systems, coping with incomplete information, and providing training.
- Although there are several limitations to the use of expert systems, some of them will disappear with improved technology.
- Expert systems, just as human experts, can make mistakes.
- Some make a distinction between expert systems, where most of the knowledge comes from experts, and knowledge systems, where the majority of the knowledge comes from documented sources.
- Some ES are available as ready-made systems; they render generic advice for standard situations.
- Expert systems can also be provided in a real-time mode.

Key Words

blackboard	General-purpose	knowledge-based
consultation	Problem Solver	system
environment	inference engine	model-based system
development	justifier	rapid prototyping
environment	knowledge acquisition	ready-made system
domain	knowledge engineer	real-time system
expert	knowledge refining	rule-based system
expertise	knowledge	
expert system	representation	
explanation subsystem		

Questions for Review

1. List three capabilities of ES.
2. Why did the General-purpose Problem Solver fail?
3. Explain this statement: "The power of an ES is derived from the specific

knowledge it possesses, not from the particular formulas and inference schemes it employs."

4. Explain how ES can distribute (or redistribute) the available knowledge in an organization.
5. List the types of knowledge included in expertise.
6. From Figure 12.1, estimate the percentage of knowledge possessed by the top 30 percent of experts (percent success achieved by deciles 1, 2, and 3).
7. List and describe the eight activities that human experts perform. Which activities are performed well by current expert systems?
8. Define the ES development environment and contrast it with the consultation environment.
9. List and define the major components of an ES.
10. What is the difference between knowledge acquisition and knowledge representation?
11. What is the role of a knowledge engineer?
12. A knowledge base includes facts and rules. Explain the difference between the two.
13. Which component of ES is mostly responsible for the reasoning capability?
14. List the major components of the inference engine.
15. What are the major activities performed in the ES blackboard (workplace)?
16. What is the function of the justifier?
17. List four types of potential users of ES.
18. List the ten generic categories of ES.
19. Describe some of the limitations of ES.
20. What is a ready-made ES?

Questions for Discussion

1. It is said that reasoning ability, powerful computers, inference capabilities, and heuristics are necessary but not sufficient for solving real problems. Why?
2. Comprehensive knowledge representation theories and associated general-purpose systems added to the capabilities listed in question 1 were helpful but still not sufficient. Why?
3. Review the CATS-1 case. What are the major lessons learned? What kind of ES is CATS-1 (according to Table 12.2)? What are the major advantages of this system?
4. A major difference between a conventional decision support system and ES is that the former can explain a "how" question whereas the latter can also explain a "why" question. Discuss.
5. Explain how the major components of the inference engine relate to the major components of the blackboard.
6. Why is it so difficult to build a component that will automatically refine knowledge?
7. Explain the relationship between development environment and consultation (runtime) environment.

8. What kind of mistakes do ES make and why? Why is it easier to correct mistakes in ES than in conventional programs?

9. Table 12.2 provides a list of ten categories of ES. Compile a list of twenty examples, two in each category, from the various functional areas in an organization (accounting, finance, production, marketing, personnel, etc.).

10. Review the limitations of ES discussed in the chapter. From what you know, which of these limitations are the most likely to remain as limitations in the year 2100? Why?

11. A ready-made ES is selling for $10,000. Developing one will cost you $50,000. A ready-made suit costs you $100; a tailored one will cost you $500. Develop an analogy between the two situations and describe the markets for the ready-made and the customized products.

12. Which generic category of ES best fits the following statements?
    a. Computer-controlled fuel injection system in a satellite
    b. Advice to farmers on what fertilizer to use
    c. Instructions on how to handle a computer with problems.

Exercise

Can an ES enhance the image of a bank? First, a reporter's opinion regarding an ES used by a bank for loan approval is given. A counterargument follows. Read the arguments of both sides and express your opinion. Can you reconcile the different arguments?

Against ES*. If you saw the classic science fiction film *2001: A Space Odyssey*, you might remember the astronaut saying, "Open the pod bay door, HAL." That was the computer's name, the HAL 2000. HAL replies, "I'm sorry, Dave, I can't do that."

HAL could say things like that. He had artificial intelligence. Well, there's a computer in your future. When you go into the bank to ask for a loan, it might just say to you, "I'm sorry, Dave, I can't do that." The First National Bank of Chicago is experimenting with a special artificial intelligence software program that supposedly is able to reason and make decisions just like a human banker.

That's how the bank AI programs are supposed to work. Experienced bankers feed all their knowledge and criteria for making loans into a computer. They program the computer with the various criteria they use to make lending decisions. The AI program then has about 150 rules on how to make lending decisions.

When you come in for a loan, the less experienced lending officer types your information into the system. Then the computer asks some questions to clarify a few points. Then it recommends whether you get the loan.

---

*Condensed from *The Orange County Register*, Feb. 17, 1986.

Using AI to diagnose illnesses, locate petroleum deposits, or play chess (as many of the programs are designed to do) seems like a sensible thing. But making a loan is based on a list of criteria, such as that the bank wants to "reduce its exposure to risk."

That strikes me as pretty cold, but it's exactly the reason I take a dim view of AI computers in banking. Banks have been trying to shake that cold, impersonal image they had for years by taking out the steel bars at the teller windows and developing a business style that is more sensitive to customers. Now, along comes this cold, calculating computer that will never understand, or be able to take into account, somebody's personal situation. A couple with a new child on the way won't get a home improvement loan for a room addition because the computer says the bank wants to "reduce its exposure" to those kinds of loans.

Computers can't think, they can't feel, and so far, they cannot reason. Don't get me wrong; I like computers, and I use them every day. But it's how they're used that's important. AI programs could be used to find reasons to say "yes" when people want a loan. They could be used to help people solve complex personal financial planning problems. I'd like to see the bankers realize that their AI programs ought to be designed to say, "Sure, Dave, I'd be happy to open the pod bay door."

For ES*. Many banks are busily developing ES that capture the experience of their top loan officers in sizing up loan applicants. These capture not just the formulas loan officers use to analyze the applicant's financial statements and the condition of the applicant's industry, but also all the subjective factors—the loan officers' "sixth sense"—which lead them to grant a loan to an applicant who looks questionable on paper, or to turn down an applicant who looks good. These allow junior loan officers to draw on the expertise of the most successful lenders as advisory systems.

Furthermore, loan officers must have at their fingertips an enormous amount of constantly changing data—on industry conditions, interest rates, tax law, credit ratings of the applicant's customers, and so on. Systems that make available the latest data, coupled with heuristic rules, are providing a service that easily pays for itself and provides better service to the clients.

There is a concern that lenders would put too much reliance on the dumb system and lose the human element. But from experience so far, the reality seems the opposite. Bankers who are unsure of their ability to make good decisions tend to be too conservative and to turn down potentially good loans. This costs the bank just as much as granting poor loans. So these expert loan advisers allow more people to make better decisions. As a result, banks keep their clients happy and improve their own profitability.

---

*Per Van Horn [22], p. 194.

CASE STUDY: Expert System in Building Construction (EXSOFS)*

Problem

Construction costs in Singapore are escalating. Builders are attempting various cost-reduction approaches. Because many of the buildings are underpinned by concrete structures, the selection of an appropriate formwork is especially important. A selection can be made from six possible methods. The problem is to find the most appropriate method for the construction of concrete slabs of each individual building. Both building conditions and site conditions influence the selection of the appropriate method. Their relationships are complex, including both qualitative and quantitative factors. Thus, considerable expertise is needed.

Solution

A system, called EXSOFS, was constructed with an expert system shell named Xi Plus (from Inference Corp.). Knowledge was acquired from experts in industry and academia. The knowledge is contained in eleven different knowledge bases. The system interfaces with a database that is managed by dBase IV and is supported by a spreadsheet. There, calculations are performed and reports are generated.

Structure of the System. The system is composed of the following modules:

- The formwork selection module—selects one of the six methods
- The cost-calculation module (using the BASIC program)—calculates the ownership cost
- Cost calculation for a rented formwork system
- Cost of using a conventional formwork system
- Graphic presentation (extensive)
- Database management module.

Several of the modules include more than one knowledge base. The system, which is really a combination of a decision support system and an expert system, allows DSS analysis (e.g., what-if). It has been successfully validated against recommendations provided by human experts.

Application. The system, which runs on a personal computer, is used by relatively inexperienced construction engineers. Experienced engineers can run quick consultations to validate their judgments. Also, the experienced engineers saved time in executing support calculations.

---

*Condensed from Tiong and Koo [20].

CASE STUDY: Soviet Union Trade Advisor*

Problem

The economic and political changes in what used to be the Soviet Union may provide an opportunity for many companies to trade with the new countries. However, there is little expertise in Western countries on what is really going on in Russia and other countries of the old Soviet Union. So while there are opportunities, there are also risks. The situation is clouded by a stream of incomplete and frequently contradictory and even incorrect data. Businesspeople want quick and reliable advice, but it is rarely available. (The U.S. Department of Commerce is flooded with such requests.)

Solution

An expert system called Soviet Union Trade Advisor (SUTA) was developed by Deloitte and Touche, a large management consulting (and CPA) company. The major objective of the system is to provide advice on trade opportunities and licensing requirements for medium- to high-technology products. The system started as an advisory service to the company's employees (consultants, auditors). Now it is being further developed so it can be marketed (for a fee) to potential traders.

System Development. SUTA contains many knowledge bases and since the domain is very complex, subdivision is essential. The builder prepared a list of preliminary questions most frequently asked (e.g., what products are needed, what is the competition, and what are the export and import controls). In addition, traders like to find the prospective buyers. The first module of SUTA was developed to provide this kind of information.

Knowledge was difficult to accumulate. Therefore, a small prototype was constructed first with the Crystal shell (from Intelligent Environments, Inc.). Russian experts were identified and the knowledge was validated. Also, the ES had to interface with several databases (some of which are online). The system was expanded to deal with export licensing requirements and provides a facsimile of an application for export license (displayed on the screen with instructions on how to complete it). The system is supported by hypertext that navigates through the complex forms.

Use. The system is very user-friendly; it is based on simple sets of menus. The market is divided into twelve sectors with which potential products are matched. The system assesses the opportunities for general classes of products

---

*Condensed from Szuprowicz [19].

and then for specific ones. Then, potential buyers are identified together with procedures for making contacts. Explanations are provided on request. Several other types of valuable information are provided by the system. The system is being improved in cooperation with Russian sources.

CASE STUDY: Ticket Auditing at Northwest Airlines*

Problem

When Northwest Airlines (NWA) acquired Republic Airlines, its volume of operations increased to 50,000 tickets per day. These tickets needed to be audited by comparing a carbon of each ticket against fare information. The fare information includes commission. There are about 40,000 separate agreements between NWA and particular travel agents. The travel agents report the commission, but not how it was computed. The manual comparison was slow and expensive. Therefore only samples of the tickets (about 1 percent) were audited. The sample indicated an error rate of about 10 percent (usually a loss to the airline).

Solution

A ticket auditing system was built in 1990–1991. All tickets are scanned electronically and stored in a database. Another database stores all the fares and commission agreements. Then an expert system goes to work. The system is written in ART IM (from Inference Corporation). The system first determines the correct fare (least possible fare), using 250 rules. Then the most favorable commission to the agent is determined. Any discrepancy results in a report to the agent, with a debit or credit and an appropriate explanation. The system can handle most of the tickets, and because sometimes scanned images cannot be interpreted, the exceptions are handled by an accountant who views the tickets on screen (no paper, no mess). The system also provides information for marketing, contract management, planning, and control.

Results

The system can process, overnight, 70,000 tickets on a SUN workstation. Thus, all tickets are being audited. Furthermore future growth will be easily handled. The reduction in agent errors (estimated to be 2 percent, down from 10 percent) saves NWA about $10 million annually.

---

*Condensed from R. Smith and C. Scott, *Innovative Applications of Artificial Intelligence*, Vol. III. Menlo Park, CA: AAAI Press, 1991.

CASE STUDY: Credit Clearinghouse—Dun & Bradstreet Corp.*

Problem

The credit clearinghouse provides risk analysis to manufacturers, wholesalers, jobbers, and marketers in the apparel industry. Credit rating and specific dollar amounts are recommended for each of about 4,000 retail customers. Dun & Bradstreet maintains and updates a database of credit ratings on approximately 200,000 businesses. The apparel industry is only a portion of it. Dun & Bradstreet customers used to complain about inaccuracies (it is difficult to constantly update the material in time), inconsistencies (different interpretations by different risk analysis people), and slow response time.

Solution

An expert system was developed (using ART IM from Inference Corporation). Using its close to 1,000 rules and the corporate databases, the system is capable of handling more than 90 percent of all requests.

Results

Response time was reduced from about three days to several seconds. The recommendations generated are very consistent. Also, as soon as there are changes in the retailers' data, the expert system reevaluates the implications on creditworthiness and informs its clients if needed. Similar systems are under development for other business units at Dun & Bradstreet.

CASE STUDY: DustPro—Environmental Control in Mines**

Problem

The majority of the 2,000 active mines in the United States are medium or small, so they cannot afford a full-time dust control engineer whose major job is to reevaluate and reassign facilities each time operating conditions change. If a dust control engineer is not readily available, the mine must be shut off until an expert arrives. This can be very costly since experts are expensive and so is downtime. Operating without appropriate testing and interpretation of results is a violation of federal regulations.

---

*Condensed from: Harvey P. Newquist III, "No Summer Returns." *AI Expert* (Oct. 1990).
**Courtesy of Information Builders, Inc., corporate publication, 1988.

Solution

DustPro is a small rule-based system developed by the U.S. Bureau of Mines. It includes about 200 rules and was developed with a Level5 shell (from Information Builders, Inc.) on a microcomputer. It took 500 hours to develop the system. The system is now in operation in more than 200 mines. It is so successful that more than ten countries have requested permission to use the system in their mines.

System Characteristics. DustPro advises in three areas: control of methane gas emission, ventilation in continuous operations, and dust control for the mine's machines. The system is completely independent. Data on air quality is entered manually. The user interface is very friendly. The system is composed of thirteen subareas of expertise, and the average consultation time is ten to fifteen minutes.

System Use. DustPro, through a series of questions, determines what types of ventilations are used, what the dust standard is, and which group of mines is most affected by the dust. Thus, the system can advise the operators about what to do. The system and its variants are used at the U.S. Bureau of Mines (Pittsburgh Research Center) to diagnose problems telephoned in by operators of mines. This saves bureau staff time and travel expense. Also, the staff can respond more quickly and can devote more time to research and development.

References and Bibliography

1. Augustine, N. R. "Distribution of Expertise." *Defense Systems Management* (Spring 1979).
2. Bonissone, P. P., and H. E. Johnson, Jr. "Expert System for Diesel Electric Locomotive Repair." *Human Systems Management* 4 (1985).
3. Bowerman, R. G., and D. Glover. *Putting Expert Systems into Practice.* New York: Van Nostrand Reinhold Co., 1988.
4. Buchanan, B. G., and E. H. Shortliffe, eds. *Rule-Based Expert Systems.* Reading, MA: Addison-Wesley, 1984.
5. Coursey, D. H., and R. G. Shangraw. "Expert System Technology for Managerial Applications: A Typology." *Public Productivity Review* 12 (Spring 1989).
6. Feigenbaum, E., et al. *The Rise of the Expert Company.* New York: Times Books, 1988.
7. Hertz, D. B. *The Expert Executive.* New York: John Wiley & Sons, 1988.
8. Holsapple, C. W., and A. B. Whinston. *Business Expert Systems.* Homewood, IL: Richard D. Irwin, 1987.
9. Meyer, M. H., and K. F. Curley. "Expert System Success Models." *Datamation* (September 1, 1989).
10. Monger, R. F. "AI Applications: What's Their Competitive Advantage?" *Journal of Information Systems Management* (Summer 1988).

11. Newell, A., and H. Simon. *Human Problem Solving*. Englewood Cliffs, NJ: Prentice-Hall, 1973.
12. Parsaye, K., and M. Chignell. *Expert Systems for Experts*. New York: John Wiley & Sons, 1988.
13. Prietula, M. J., and H. A. Simon. "The Experts in Your Midst." *Harvard Business Review* (Jan.-Feb. 1989).
14. Robinson, J. A. "The Generalization Resolution Principle." In *Machine Intelligence*, vol. 3, D. Michie, ed. New York: Elsevier, 1986.
15. Rubinger, B. *Applied AI in Japan*. New York: Hemisphere Publishing, 1989.
16. Samual, R. L., III, and W. T. Jones. "A Method for the Strategic Assessment of Expert Systems Applications." *Expert Systems: Planning, Implementation, Integration* (Fall, 1990).
17. Schorr, A., and A. Rappaport. *Innovative Applications of Artificial Intelligence*. Menlo Park, Calif.: AAAI Press, 1989.
18. Sviokla, J. J. "An Examination of the Impact of Expert Systems on the Firm: The Case of XCON." *MIS Quarterly* (June 1990).
19. Szuprowicz, B. O. "The Soviet Union Trade Advisor." *Expert Systems* (Spring 1991).
20. Tiong, R., and T. K. Koo, "Selecting Construction Formwork: An Expert System Adds Economy." *Expert Systems* (Spring 1991).
21. Turban, E., and P. Watkins, eds. *Applied Expert Systems*. Amsterdam: North Holland, 1988.
22. Van Horn, M. *Understanding Expert Systems*. Toronto: Bantam Books, 1986.
23. Waterman, D. A. *A Guide to Expert Systems*. Reading, MA: Addison-Wesley, 1985.
24. Waterman, D. A. "How Do Expert Systems Differ from Conventional Programs?" *Expert Systems* (January 1986).

APPENDIX 12-A: Systems Cited in Chapter

System	Vendor (Developer)	Description
AGE	Stanford University (Stanford, CA)	It is an ES development tool that helps the builder to select a framework, design a rule language, and assemble parts into a system (different architectures, including a blackboard).
DENDRAL	Stanford University (Stanford, CA)	It infers the molecular structure of unknown compounds from mass spectral and nuclear magnetic response data. The system uses a special algorithm to systematically enumerate all possible molecular structures; it uses chemical expertise to prune this list of possibilities to a manageable size. Knowledge in DENDRAL is represented as a procedural code.

System	Vendor (Developer)	Description
EURISKO	Stanford University (Stanford, CA)	It learns new heuristics and new domain-specific definitions of concepts in a problem domain. The system can learn by discovery in a number of different problem domains, including VLSI design. EURISKO operates by generating a device configuration, computing its input/output behavior, assessing its functionality, and then evaluating it against other comparable devices.
META-DENDRAL	Stanford University (Stanford, CA)	It helps chemists determine the dependence of mass spectrometric fragmentation on substructural features. It does this by discovering fragmentation rules for given classes of molecules. META-DENDRAL first generates a set of highly specific rules that account for a single fragmentation process in a particular molecule. Then it uses the training examples to generalize these rules. Finally, the system reexamines the rules to remove redundant or incorrect rules.
STEAMER	U.S. Navy in cooperation with Bolt, Beranek, and Newman (Cambridge, MA)	It is an intelligent CAI that instructs Navy personnel in the operation and maintenance of the propulsion plant for a 1078-class frigate. The system can monitor the student executing the boiler light-off procedure for the plant, acknowledge appropriate student actions, and correct inappropriate ones. The system works by tying a simulation of the propulsion plant to a sophisticated graphic interface program that displays animated color diagrams of plant subsystems. The student can manipulate simulated components like valves, switches, and pumps, and observe the effects on plant parameters, such as changes in pressure, temperature, and flow. STEAMER uses an object-oriented representation scheme.
XSEL	Digital Equipment Corp.	See description in Appendix 12-B.

APPENDIX 12-B: Classic Expert Systems

1. MYCIN

Each year 2 million people get sick while in hospitals recovering from something else; and perhaps 50,000 of them die. The cause is hospital-borne infections. These may develop unnoticed, and when discovered they need to be diagnosed quickly. MYCIN, which is considered the granddaddy of ES, was developed to aid physicians in diagnosing meningitis and other bacterial infections of the blood and to prescribe treatment. Specifically, the system's objective is to aid physicians during a critical 24–48-hour period after the detection of symptoms, a time when much of the decision making is imprecise because all the relevant information is not yet available. Early diagnosis and treatment can save a patient from brain damage or even from death.

MYCIN was developed at Stanford Medical School in the 1970s by Dr. Edward H. Shortliffe. The program's record of correct diagnoses and prescribed treatments has equaled the performance of top human experts.

MYCIN introduced several features that have become the hallmarks of ES:

- *Rule-based knowledge representation.* The knowledge base consists of about 500 IF-THEN inference rules. For example:

    IF   1. The infection that requires therapy is meningitis, and
           2. The patient has evidence of serious skin or soft tissue infection, and
           3. Organisms were not seen on the stain of the culture, and
           4. The type of infection is bacterial

    THEN   There is evidence that the organism (other than those seen on cultures or smears) that might be causing the infection is *Staphylococcus coagpos* (0.75), or *Streptococcus* (0.5).

- *Probabilistic rules.* Many of the rules include a *chance* option that allows the system to reach plausible conclusions from uncertain evidence. The chance figures in the rules are expressed as certainty factors. (See Chapter 15 of this text.)

- *Backward chaining method.* The program executes an exhaustive *backward chaining* search (see Chapter 15) for a diagnosis, augmented by a numeric heuristic function.

- *Explanation.* MYCIN can explain its reasoning. The user (a physician) can interrogate it in various ways—by inquiring *why* the ES asked a particular question or *how* it reached an intermediate or final conclusion. Because each rule is a semi-independent package of knowledge, the user can easily trace the rules that led to a certain question or conclusion.

- *User-friendly system.* MYCIN is very easy to use. The required training is minimal. The entire dialog is conducted in plain English.

In a typical consultation session, the physician conducts an interactive dialog with MYCIN about a particular patient. He or she provides information (e.g., symptoms, patient's characteristics) and responds to questions generated by the ES. The user can also apply *certainty factors* to qualify the answers. MYCIN examines approximately a hundred potential diagnoses. Once the diagnosis is completed, a drug treatment is prescribed.

Because physicians have the final responsibility for treatment, transparency in the system is essential. By typing "RULE," the user obtains an English-language explanation of the last rule executed. Typing "WHY" triggers a backtrace of the inference process that fired the system's last question. Repeated use of RULE and WHY activates further backtracing. A sample consultation with MYCIN is shown next:

> MYCIN: What is the infection?
> Physician: Endarteritis [an inflammation of the inner layer of an artery that can be caused by a number of agents].
> MYCIN: Is organism-1 a rod or a coccus? [This question will narrow the range of possible agents for the disease.]
> Physician: Rod.

MYCIN then asks additional questions about laboratory test results to help determine what organisms might be causing the disease. When it has reached its conclusion, it will recommend a particular drug therapy to combat the organism or organisms involved. So that the physician will trust MYCIN's conclusions, the program is designed to answer questions about its reasoning. For example:

> Physician: How did you decide that organism-1 is *E. coli?*
> MYCIN: I used rule 084 to conclude that organism-1 is *E. coli.* This gave a cumulative certainty factor of 0.51. [The physician can question further, either by looking at the text of the rule involved, or by questioning its antecedents.]

2. XCON (Expert VAX System Configuration)

Digital Equipment Corp. (DEC) has always offered its customers a wide range of custom-made minicomputers. It is not uncommon to have thousands of customer orders on hand, each one involving different needs and specifications. This wide range of combinations creates a complex business environment involving many interdependent decisions and tasks for processing the orders, scheduling the necessary manufacturing and other operations, and distributing computer system orders to the customer in a timely manner.

Until XCON became available, the computer system configuration task was accomplished manually. Technical editors in manufacturing reviewed all customer orders for technical correctness and order completeness. This was an extremely difficult task that required many knowledgeable people. Traditional work methods did not yield the accurate, cost-effective, fast response that XCON provides.

Most of the computer system orders that customers send to DEC have unique specifications (many line items per order). The development of XCON represented a very significant tool for managing the complexity of DEC's business. A dramatic increase in productivity of the technical editors has occurred as a result of the effective use of XCON in the manufacturing environment. XCON is a rule-based system with many thousand rules, implemented in OPS5, a general-purpose, rule-based language.

When XCON was first installed for the configuration of the VAX 11/750 and 11/780 computers, the system had limited capability and knowledge. Therefore, much interaction was required with the technical editors to increase the system's expertise. The results, however, were astonishing. Traditionally trained manufacturing technical editors required twenty to thirty minutes to configure each system order. In contrast, XCON can configure extremely complex system orders in less than a minute. It also provides additional functions and capabilities not formerly performed by the traditional technical editors, such as (1) defining the exact cable length for all cables required between each system component, and (2) providing the vector addresses calculation for the computer bus options.

By 1985 all VAX family system orders in U.S. and European plant operations were configured by XCON. As the workload increased in the system manufacturing plants, no additional technical editors were hired because of the increase in productivity and capacity provided by XCON.

In the past, a large portion of the system orders scheduled for the factory floor had numerous configuration errors and lacked completeness; with XCON, VAX orders have accurate configurations 98 percent of the time (compared with 65 percent in the manual system). Manufacturing operation benefits from accurate system configurations include (1) an increased throughput order rate, (2) fewer shipments delayed because of system configuration errors, and (3) better use of materials on hand.

When numerous line item changes occur on customer orders already scheduled in the manufacturing process, XCON provides a tool to save time, increase output per person, and lower manufacturing costs.

Redeployment of DEC's highly skilled senior technicians has occurred, allowing them to address more technically difficult tasks. Cost savings to DEC are estimated at about $15 million each year. Plant management, extremely satisfied with the emerging artificial intelligence methodologies, is participating in this pioneering effort with great enthusiasm.

The company is developing related ES. Figure 12-B.1 shows the expansion to XSEL, XSITE, and several other related systems. XSEL is a system that checks orders for consistency, such as making sure that power supplies match the equipment being shipped. XSITE provides a site plan for the customer's machine room and lists the equipment needed. Other systems are ISA, to aid scheduling; XFL, which helps in diagramming a computer room floor layout for the configurations; IMACS, to aid manufacturing; ILRPS, to aid long-range planning; IPMS, to aid in project management; and ICSR, to aid in customer service.

DEC's experience provides a good argument for the use of expert systems. Without the flexibility and modular organization inherent in the rule-based ES

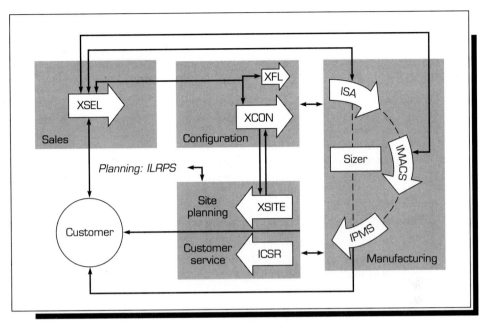

FIGURE 12-B.1   ES Network at Digital Equipment Corp.

approach, developers would have been hard-pressed to maintain the incremental growth needed to support DEC's changing product lines.

For more information about XCON see V. Barker and D. O'Connor, "Expert Systems for Configuration at Digital, XCON and Beyond," *Communications of ACM* (March 1989) and J. J. Sviokla, "An Examination of the Impact of Expert Systems on the Firm: The Case of XCON," *MIS Quarterly* (June 1990).

APPENDIX 12-C: Typical Expert Systems Applications*

- Verification, validation, and authorization of warranty or medical insurance claims
- Analyzing consumer loan applications, recommending actions
- Identifying anomalies in foreign exchange trading
- Scheduling auditing of several hundred business units
- Underwriting insurance policies
- Financial planning
- Analysis of whether a company is creditworthy and how much credit should be extended
- Identification of possible safety problem in air-traffic control

*Developed from a list provided by Inference Corp.

- Radar signals analysis
- Analysis of problems in computer networks and telecommunications
- Control and management of water system in a state
- Diagnosis of problems and suggestion of repairs in space stations
- Monitoring a nuclear power plant's systems; diagnosis of problems and suggestions for repairs
- Airport photo interpretations
- Nuclear test ban treaty verification (seismological analysis)
- Retirement planning for employees
- Planning of complex manufacturing processes
- Checking compliance with fire codes
- Debugging FORTRAN code prior to compilation
- Performance of time-and-motion analysis to support labor allocations
- Determination of the amount of water and fertilizers in agriculture
- Advisory system for change management
- A tactical resource planning for military systems
- Managing inventory and purchasing in complex environment

Part 5

Knowledge Engineering

The theoretical fundamentals of knowledge processing, which is also called knowledge engineering, are described in Part 5. The result of the process is a knowledge base—an essential part of most AI applications.

Knowledge engineering involves several tasks. First, knowledge is collected (from people or from documented sources) in a process called knowledge acquisition (Chapter 13). Acquisition can be done manually and with some degree of automation. Then the acquired knowledge is organized into a knowledge base. In many systems knowledge representation (Chapter 14) involves IF-THEN rules, but other representations are available (e.g., frames).

Making use of the represented knowledge is done through reasoning, or inferencing, procedures (Chapter 15). This can be done under assumed certainty or uncertainty.

Finally, the knowledge engineering construction process is described in Chapter 16.

Chapter 13

Knowledge Acquisition and Validation

Knowledge acquisition is the process of extracting, structuring, and organizing knowledge from one or more sources. This process has been identified by many researchers and practitioners as a (or even as *the*) bottleneck that currently constrains the development of expert systems and other AI systems. This chapter, which attempts to present the most important issues and topics in knowledge acquisition, is divided into the following sections:

13.1   Knowledge Engineering

The activity of **knowledge engineering** has been defined by Feigenbaum and McCorduck [14] as:

> the art of bringing the principles and tools of AI research to bear on difficult applications problems requiring experts' knowledge for their solutions. The technical issues of acquiring this knowledge, representing it, and using it appropriately to construct and explain lines-of-reasoning are important problems in the design of knowledge-based systems. The art of constructing intelligent agents is both part of and an extension of the programming art. It is the art of building complex computer programs that represent and reason with knowledge of the world.

Knowledge engineering can be viewed from two perspectives: narrow and wide. According to the narrow perspective, knowledge engineering deals with knowledge acquisition, representation, validation, inferencing, explanation, and maintenance. Alternatively, according to the wide perspective the term describes the *entire process* of developing and maintaining AI systems. In this book the narrow definition is being used.

Knowledge engineering involves the cooperation of human experts in the domain who work with the knowledge engineer to codify and make explicit the rules (or other procedures) that a human expert uses to solve real problems.

Knowledge engineering usually has a synergistic effect. The knowledge possessed by human experts is often unstructured and not explicitly expressed. The construction of a knowledge base aids the expert to articulate what he or she knows. It can also pinpoint variances from one expert to another (if several experts are being used).

A major goal in knowledge engineering is to construct programs that are modular in nature, so that additions and changes can be made in one module without affecting the workings of other modules.

The Knowledge Engineering Process

The knowledge engineering process includes five activities:

Knowledge Acquisition. **Knowledge acquisition** involves the acquisition of knowledge from human experts, books, documents, sensors, or computer files. The knowledge may be specific to the problem domain and the problem-solving procedures, or it may be general knowledge (e.g., knowledge about business), or it may be **metaknowledge** (knowledge about knowledge). By the latter, we mean information about how experts use their knowledge to solve problems.

Knowledge Validation. The knowledge is validated and verified (e.g., by using test cases) until its quality is acceptable.

Knowledge Representation. The acquired knowledge is organized in an activity called knowledge representation. This activity involves preparation of a "knowledge map" and encoding the knowledge in the knowledge base.

Inference. This activity involves the design of software that will enable the computer to make inferences based on the knowledge, and then provide advice to the user on specific issues.

Explanation and Justification. This activity involves the design and programming of an explanation capability; for example, programming the ability to answer questions like *why* a specific piece of information is needed by the computer or *how* a certain conclusion was derived by the computer.

The process of knowledge engineering and the interrelationships among these activities is shown in Figure 13.1. The topics of knowledge acquisition and validation are discussed in this chapter. The other activities are presented in subsequent chapters.

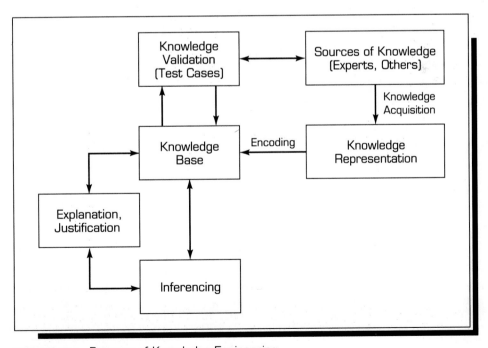

FIGURE 13.1 Process of Knowledge Engineering

13.2 Scope of Knowledge

Knowledge acquisition is the extraction of knowledge from sources of expertise and its transfer to the knowledge base, and sometimes to the inference engine. Acquisition is actually done throughout the entire development process.

Knowledge is a collection of specialized facts, procedures, and judgment rules. Some types of knowledge used in AI are shown in Figure 13.2. These types of knowledge may come from one source or from several sources.

Sources of Knowledge

Knowledge may be collected from many sources. A representative list of sources includes books, films, computer databases, pictures, maps, flow diagrams, stories, songs, or observed behavior. These sources can be divided into two types: **documented** and *undocumented*. The latter resides in people's minds.

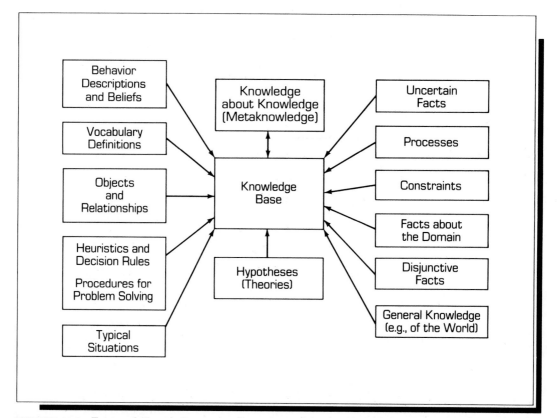

FIGURE 13.2 Types of Knowledge to be Represented in the Knowledge Base. (*Source:* Adapted from R. Fikes and T. Kehler, "The Role of Frame-Based Representation in Reasoning," *Communications of ACM* [September 1985]. Copyright 1985, Association for Computing Machinery, Inc., reprinted by permission.)

Knowledge can be identified and collected by using any of the human senses. Knowledge can also be identified and collected by machines.

The multiplicity of sources and types of knowledge contribute to the complexity of knowledge acquisition. This complexity is only one reason why it is difficult to acquire knowledge.

Levels of Knowledge

Knowledge can be represented at different levels. The two extremes are **shallow knowledge** (surface) and **deep knowledge.**

Shallow Knowledge. Shallow knowledge refers to representation of only surface level information that can be used to deal with very specific situations. For example, if you don't have gasoline in your car, the car won't start. This knowledge can be shown as a rule:

> If gasoline tank is empty → then car will not start.

The shallow version represents basically the input-output relationship of a system. As such, it can be ideally presented in terms of IF-THEN types of rules.

Shallow representation is limited. A set of rules by itself may have little meaning to the user. It may have little to do with the manner in which experts view the domain and solve problems. This may limit the ability of the system, for example, to provide appropriate explanations to the user. Shallow knowledge may also be insufficient in describing complex situations. Therefore, a deeper presentation is frequently required.

Deep Knowledge. Human problem solving is based on deep knowledge of a situation. Deep knowledge refers to the internal and causal structure of a system and considers the interactions among the system's components. Deep knowledge can be applied to different tasks and different situations. It is based on a completely integrated, cohesive body of human consciousness that includes emotions, common sense, intuition, etc. This type of knowledge is difficult to computerize. The system builder must have a perfect understanding of the basic elements and their interactions as produced by nature. To date, such a task has been found to be impossible. We may never be able to computerize deep knowledge, at its extreme.

It is possible, however, to implement a computerized representation that is *deeper* than shallow knowledge. To explain how this is done, let us return to the gasoline example. If we want to investigate at a deeper level the relationship between lack of gasoline and a car that won't start, we need to know the various components of the gas system (for example, pipes, pump, filters, and starter). Such a system is shown schematically in Figure 13.3.

To represent this system and knowledge of its operation, we use special knowledge representation methods such as semantic networks and frames (see Chapter 14). They allow the implementation of deeper-level reasoning such as abstraction and analogy. Reasoning by abstraction and analogy is an important

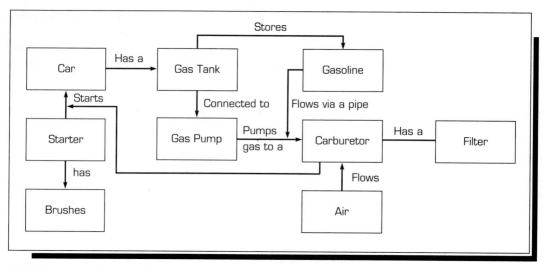

FIGURE 13.3   Schematic Representation of a Deep Knowledge

expert activity. We can also represent the objects and processes of the domain of expertise at this level; the relations among objects are important.

One type of expertise that has been represented with a deep-level approach is tutoring. The goal of tutoring is to convey to students a domain knowledge that is best represented at the deep level: concepts, abstractions, analogies, and problem-solving strategies.

Major Categories of Knowledge

Knowledge appears in various categories. The major ones are described next.

Declarative Knowledge. Declarative knowledge is a descriptive representation of knowledge. It tells us facts—*what* things are. It is expressed in a factual statement: "There is a positive association between smoking and cancer." Domain experts tell us about truths and associations. This type of knowledge is considered shallow, or surface-level, information that experts can verbalize. Declarative knowledge is especially important in the initial stage of knowledge acquisition.

Procedural Knowledge. Procedural knowledge considers the manner in which things work under different sets of circumstances. For example, "Compute the ratio between a price of a share and the earnings per share. If this ratio is larger than twelve, stop your investigation. Your investment is too risky. If the ratio is less than twelve, check the balance sheet." Thus, procedural knowledge includes step-by-step sequences and how-to types of instructions; it may also include explanations. Procedural knowledge involves automatic response to stimuli. It also may tell us how to use declarative knowledge and how to make inferences. *Descriptive knowledge* relates to a specific object. It includes information about the meaning, roles, environment, resources, activities, associations, and outcomes of the object. *Procedural knowledge* relates to the procedures employed in the problem-solving process (e.g., information about problem definition, data gathering, the solution process, and evaluation criteria).

Metaknowledge. Metaknowledge means knowledge about knowledge. In ES, metaknowledge refers to knowledge about the operation of knowledge-based systems, that is, about its reasoning capabilities.

13.3   Difficulties in Knowledge Acquisition

In general, transferring information from one person to another is difficult. Several mechanisms can be used to conduct such a transfer—written words, voice, pictures, music—and not one of them is perfect.

Problems also exist in transferring any knowledge, even simple messages. Transferring knowledge in ES is even more difficult, and now we'll see why.

Problems in Transferring Knowledge

Expressing the Knowledge. To solve a problem a human expert executes a two-step process. First, the expert inputs information about the external world into the brain. This information is collected via sensors or is retrieved from memory. Second, the expert uses an inductive, deductive, or other problem-solving approaches on the information. The result (output) is a recommendation on how to solve the problem.

This process is *internal*. The knowledge engineer, when collecting knowledge from an expert, must ask the expert to be introspective about his or her (the expert's) decision-making process and about the inner experiences that are involved in it. It may be very difficult for the expert to express his or her experiences about this process, especially when the experiences are made up of sensations, thoughts, sense memories, and feelings. The expert is often unaware of the detailed process that he or she uses to arrive at a conclusion. Therefore, the expert may actually use different rules to solve real-life problems than he or she states in an interview.

Transfer to a Machine. Knowledge is transferred to a machine where it must be organized in a particular manner. The machine requires the knowledge to be expressed explicitly at a lower, *more detailed* level than humans use. Human knowledge exists in a compiled format. A human simply does not remember all the intermediate steps used by his or her brain in transferring or processing knowledge. Thus, there is a mismatch between computers and experts.

Number of Participants. In a regular transfer of knowledge there are two participants (a sender and a receiver). In ES there could be as many as four participants (plus a computer): the expert, the knowledge engineer, the system designer (builder), and the user. Sometimes there are even more participants (e.g., programmers and vendors). These participants have different backgrounds, use different terminology, and possess different skills and knowledge. The experts, for example, may know very little about computers, while the knowledge engineer may know very little about the problem area.

Structuring the Knowledge. In ES it is necessary to elicit not only the knowledge, but also its structure. We have to *represent* the knowledge in a structured way (e.g., as rules).

Other Reasons. Several other reasons add to the complexity of transferring the knowledge:

- Experts may lack time or may be unwilling to cooperate.
- Testing and refining knowledge is complicated.
- Methods for knowledge elicitation may be poorly defined.
- System builders have a tendency to collect knowledge from one source, but the relevant knowledge may be scattered across several sources.
- Builders may attempt to collect documented knowledge rather than use experts. The knowledge collected may be incomplete.
- It is difficult to recognize specific knowledge when it is mixed up with irrelevant data.
- Experts may change their behavior when they are being observed and/or interviewed.
- Problematic interpersonal communication factors may exist between the knowledge engineer and the expert.

Overcoming the Difficulties

Many efforts have been made to overcome some of these problems (for a comprehensive survey, see Boose [4]). For example, research on knowledge acquisition tools has begun to focus on ways to decrease the representation mismatch between the human expert and the program under development. One form of this research might be characterized as research on learning by being told. The attempt here is to develop programs capable of accepting advice as it would often be given to a human novice. Several ES development software packages such as EXSYS, Level5 and VP Expert greatly simplify the syntax of the rules (in a rule-based system) to make them easier for an ES builder to create and understand without special training. Also, a natural language processor can be used to translate knowledge to a specific knowledge representation structure.

Finally, some of the difficulties may be lessened or eliminated with computer-aided knowledge acquisition tools and with extensive integration of the acquisition efforts (see Boose [4]).

Required Skills of Knowledge Engineers

The use of computers and special methods to overcome the difficulties requires qualified knowledge engineers. Listed here are some of the skills and characteristics that are desirable in knowledge engineers:

- Computer skills (hardware, programming, software)
- Tolerance and ambivalence
- Effective communication abilities—sensitivity, tact, and diplomacy
- Broad education
- Advanced, socially sophisticated verbal skills
- Fast-learning capabilities (of different domains)
- Understanding of organizations and individuals
- Wide experience in knowledge engineering
- Intelligence
- Empathy and patience
- Persistence
- Logical thinking
- Versatility and inventiveness
- Self-confidence.

These requirements make knowledge engineers in *short supply* (and costly because of high salaries). Some of the automation developments described later attempt to overcome the short supply problem.

13.4   Process of Knowledge Acquisition

The general process of knowledge acquisition can be viewed as being composed of five stages (Hayes-Roth et al. [17]). These stages are explained here and shown in Figure 13.4.

1. *Identification.* During this stage the problem and its major characteristics are identified. The problem is broken into subproblems (if necessary), the participants (experts, users, etc.) are identified, and the resources are outlined. The knowledge engineer learns about the situation, and all agree on the purpose of the ES application.
2. *Conceptualization.* The knowledge relevant to the decision situation can be quite diversified. Therefore, it is necessary to determine the concepts and relationships used. These and several other questions are answered during conceptualization such as: Which information is used and how can it be represented in the knowledge base? Are rules a good representation medium? How is certain knowledge to be extracted?
3. *Formalization.* Knowledge is acquired for representation in the knowledge base. The manner in which knowledge is organized and represented could determine the acquisition methodology. For example, in

rule-based systems the knowledge must be organized in terms of rules. In this stage knowledge acquisition is actually mixed with knowledge representation. Here, the various software and hardware pieces are also examined. This stage is very difficult because it includes the extraction of knowledge from experts.

4. *Implementation.* This stage involves the programming of knowledge into the computer. However, refinements of the knowledge are made with additional acquisitions or changes. A prototype ES is developed at this stage.

5. *Testing.* In the final stage, the knowledge engineer tests the system by subjecting it to examples. The results are shown to the expert and the rules or the frames are revised if necessary. In other words, the validity of the knowledge is examined.

As you can see in Figure 13.4, each stage involves a circular procedure of iteration and reiteration (i.e., the knowledge engineer reformulates, redesigns, and refines the system constantly). In addition, rules (or other representations of knowledge) are added and deleted periodically. During the entire time, the knowledge engineer works closely with the domain expert.

13.5   Methods of Knowledge Acquisition: An Overview

The basic model of knowledge engineering portrays teamwork in which a knowledge engineer mediates between the expert and the knowledge base. The knowledge engineer elicits knowledge from the expert, refines it with the expert, and represents it in the knowledge base. The **elicitation of knowledge** from the expert can be done manually or with the aid of computers. Most of the manual elicitation techniques have been borrowed (but frequently modified) from psychology or from system analysis. These elicitation methods are classified in different ways and appear under different names.

The methods described in this book are classified in three categories: manual, semiautomatic, and automatic.

Manual methods are basically structured around some kind of interview. The knowledge engineer elicits knowledge from the expert and/or other sources and then codes it in the knowledge base. The process is shown in Figure 13.5. The three major manual methods are interviewing (structured, semistructured, unstructured), tracking the reasoning process, and observing. Manual methods are slow, expensive, and sometimes inaccurate. Therefore, there is a trend to automate the process as much as possible.

Semiautomatic methods are divided into two categories: (1) those that are intended to support the experts by allowing them to build knowledge bases with little or no help from knowledge engineers (Figure 13.6), and (2) those that are intended to help the knowledge engineers by allowing them to execute the necessary tasks in a more efficient and/or effective manner (sometimes with only minimal participation by an expert).

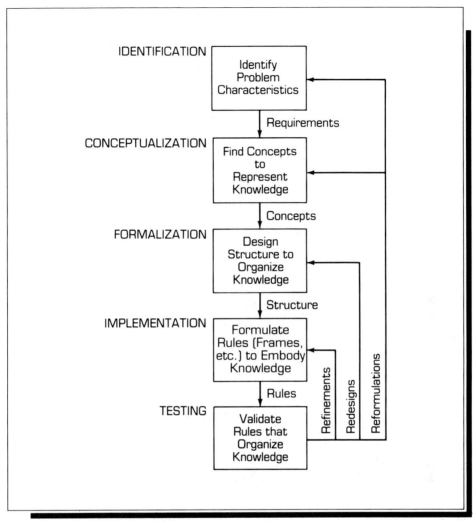

FIGURE 13.4 Stages of Knowledge Acquisition. (*Source:* F. Hayes-Roth, "The Knowledge-Based Expert System: A Tutorial," *Computer* [September 1984], © 1984, IEEE.)

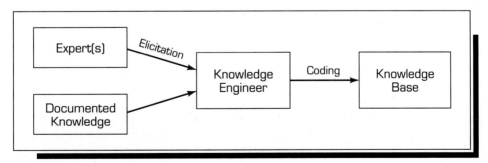

FIGURE 13.5 Manual Methods of Knowledge Acquisition

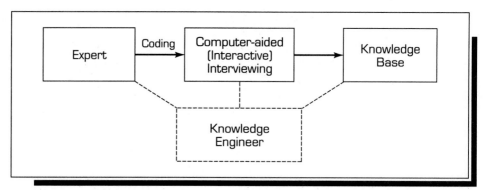

FIGURE 13.6 Expert-driven Knowledge Acquisition; broken lines designate optional interactions.

In *automatic methods* the role of both the expert and/or the knowledge engineer is minimized or even eliminated. For example, the **induction** method of Figure 13.7 can be administered by any builder (e.g., a system analyst). The role of the expert is minimal and there is no need for a knowledge engineer. The term *automatic* may be misleading. There is always going to be a human builder, but there may be little or no need for a knowledge engineer and an expert.

13.6   Interviews

The most commonly used form of knowledge acquisition is face-to-face **interview analysis.** It is an explicit technique and it appears in several variations. It involves a direct dialog between the expert and the knowledge engineer. Information is collected with the aid of conventional instruments (such as tape recorders or questionnaires), and it is subsequently transcribed, analyzed, and coded.

In the interview, the expert is presented with a simulated case, or if possible, with an actual problem of the sort that the ES will be expected to solve. The expert is asked to "talk" the knowledge engineer through the solution. Sometimes this method is referred to as the **walkthrough** method. One variant of the interview approach begins with no information at all being given to the expert. Any facts that the expert requires must be asked for explicitly. By doing this,

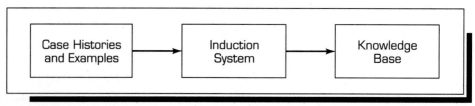

FIGURE 13.7 Induction

the expert's path through the domain may be made more evident, especially in terms of defining the input an ES would require.

The interview process can be tedious. It places great demands on the domain expert, who must be able not only to demonstrate expertise but also to express it. On the other hand, it requires little equipment, it is highly flexible and portable, and it can yield a considerable amount of information. Two basic types of interviews can be distinguished: unstructured (informal) and structured.

Unstructured Interviews

Many knowledge acquisition interviews are conducted informally, usually as a starting point. Starting informally saves time; it helps to get quickly to the basic structure of the domain. Usually it is followed by a formal technique. In contrast to what many people believe, unstructured interviews are not this simple. In fact, they may present the knowledge engineer with some very problematic aftereffects.

Unstructured interviewing, according to McGraw and Harbison-Briggs [23], seldom provides complete or well-organized descriptions of cognitive processes. The following are the reasons: (a) The domains are generally complex. (b) The experts usually find it very difficult to express some of the more important elements of their knowledge. (c) Domain experts may interpret the lack of structure as requiring little preparation on their part prior to the interview. (d) Data acquired from an unstructured interview are often unrelated, exist at varying levels of complexity, and are difficult for the knowledge engineer to review, interpret, and integrate. (e) Because of a lack of training and experience, few knowledge engineers can conduct an efficient unstructured interview.

Example. Here is a simple example (provided by D. King of Teknowledge, Inc.) of knowledge acquisition for the topic of helping novices use the Statistical Analysis System (SAS) computer package. The dialog between the expert and the knowledge engineer (KE) may look like this:

EXPERT: Yesterday I talked with a typical novice. He couldn't get started because he didn't understand the DATA step. That's generally a first step and people often forget it.

KE: What did this novice need in the DATA step?

EXPERT: Well, he needed one and it was missing. There are about five different kinds of DATA steps. I recommended a simple fixed-field input and suggested he put the data in the deck rather than in a separate file. By doing that, it cuts down on the complexity of the JCL.

KE: JCL?

EXPERT: JCL is job control language, a nasty set of instructions mostly for file handling. If the data are elsewhere, then a line of JCL must be prepared that says where the data file is and how it is formatted.

KE: We may need to talk more about JCL, but for now, let's return to the man yesterday and his need for a DATA step. Why did you suggest a fixed-format DATA step?

EXPERT: Mostly because his data set was simple. Fixed-format requires the person to refine his data and organize them neatly in rows and columns. Free-field input in the DATA step seems easier to novices, but the possibility of error is greater and finding mistakes in a free-field data set is difficult.

KE: When you say that this man's data set was simple, what do you mean?

EXPERT: There were fewer than a hundred records and only about fifteen variables. There also were no missing data and no complexity in the cases. Last week I talked with a woman who couldn't decide what a record was. She had scores for people who were in classrooms that were nested in schools. She wanted to study school differences. That's not a simple data set.

By interviewing the expert, the knowledge engineer slowly, step by step, learns what is going on. Then he or she builds a representation of the knowledge in the expert's terms.

The process of knowledge acquisition involves uncovering the attributes of the problem to which the expert pays attention (e.g., the DATA step, fixed-field input) and making explicit the thought process (usually expressed as rules) that the expert uses to interpret these attributes.

The unstructured interview is most common. It appears in several variations. In addition to the "talkthrough" one can ask the expert to "teachthrough" or "readthrough." In a teachthrough the expert acts as an instructor and the knowledge engineer as a student. The expert not only tells *what* he or she does, but also explains *why* and, in addition, instructs the knowledge engineer in the skills and strategies needed to perform the task. In a readthrough approach the expert is asked to instruct the knowledge engineer *how* to read and interpret the documents that are used for the task.

Structured Interviews

The **structured interview** is a systematic goal-oriented process. It forces an organized communication between the knowledge engineer and the expert. The structure reduces the interpretation problems inherent in unstructured interviews, and it allows the knowledge engineer to prevent the distortion caused by the subjectivity of the domain expert. Structuring an interview requires attention to a number of procedural issues, which are summarized in Table 13.1.

Because of the specific nature of each interview, it is difficult to provide good guidelines for the entire interview process. Therefore, interpersonal communication and analytical skills are important. There are, however, several guidelines, checklists, and instruments that are fairly generic in nature (see McGraw and Harbison-Briggs [23]).

TABLE 13.1 Procedures for Structured Interviews.

- The knowledge engineer studies available material on the domain to identify major demarcations of the relevant knowledge.

- The knowledge engineer reviews the planned expert system capabilities. He or she identifies targets for the questions to be asked during the knowledge acquisition session.

- The knowledge engineer formally schedules and plans (using a form) the structured interviews. Planning includes attending to physical arrangements, defining knowledge acquisition session goals and agendas, and identifying or refining major areas of questioning.

- The knowledge engineer may write sample questions, focusing on question type, level, and questioning techniques.

- The knowledge engineer ensures that the domain expert understands the purpose and goals of the session and encourages the expert to prepare prior to the interview.

- During the interview the knowledge engineer follows guidelines for conducting interviews.

- During the interview the knowledge engineer uses *directional control* to retain the interview's structure.

Source: Condensed from K. L. McGraw and B. K. Harbison-Briggs, *Knowledge Acquisition, Principles and Guidelines* (Englewood Cliffs, NJ: Prentice-Hall, 1989).

Interviewing techniques, though very popular, do have many disadvantages. They range from inaccuracies in collecting information to biases introduced by the interviewer (see references 23, 24, and 26).

In summary, interviews are important techniques, but they must be planned carefully, and the interview results *must* be subjected to thorough verification and validation methodologies. Interviews are sometimes replaced by tracking methods. Alternatively, they can be used to supplement tracking or other knowledge acquisition methods.

13.7   Tracking Methods

Process tracking refers to a set of techniques that attempt to *track* the reasoning process of an expert. It is a popular approach among cognitive psychologists who are interested in discovering the expert's "train of thought" while he or she reaches a conclusion.

The knowledge engineer can use the tracking process to find what information is being used and how it is being used. Tracking methods can be informal or formal. The most common formal method is protocol analysis.

Protocol analysis, particularly a set of techniques known as verbal protocol analysis, is a common method by which the knowledge engineer acquires detailed knowledge from the expert. A protocol is a record or documentation of the expert's step-by-step information processing and decision-making behavior.

In this method, which is similar to interviewing but more formal and systematic, the expert is asked to perform a real task and to verbalize his or her thought process. The expert is asked by the knowledge engineer to "think aloud" while performing the task or solving the problem under observation. Usually, a recording is made as the expert thinks aloud; it describes every aspect of the information processing and decision-making behavior. This recording then becomes a record, or protocol, of the expert's ongoing behavior. Later, the recording is transcribed for further analysis (e.g., to deduce the decision process) and coded by the knowledge engineer. For further details see Ericsson and Simon [13] and Wolfgram et al. [31].

In contrast with interactive interview methods, a protocol analysis involves mainly a one-way communication. The knowledge engineer prepares the scenario and plans the process. During the session the expert does most of the talking as he or she interacts with data to solve the problem. Concurrently, the knowledge engineer *listens* and records the process. Later, he or she must be able to analyze, interpret, and structure the protocol into knowledge representation for a review by the expert.

The process of protocol analysis is summarized in Table 13.2 and its advantages and limitations are presented in Table 13.3.

13.8   Observations and Other Manual Methods

Observations

In some cases it may be possible to observe the expert at work in the field. In many ways this is the most obvious and straightforward approach to knowledge acquisition. The difficulties involved should not, however, be underestimated. For example, most experts advise several people, and possibly work in several domains, simultaneously. The observations being made thus cover all other activities as well. Therefore, large quantities of data are being collected from which only a little is useful. In particular, if recordings and/or videotapings

TABLE 13.2   Procedure of Protocol Analysis

Provide the expert with a full range of information normally associated with a task.

Ask the expert to verbalize the task in the same manner as would be done normally while verbalizing his or her decision process and record the verbalization on tape.

Make statements by transcribing the verbal protocols.

Gather the statements that seem to have high information content.

Simplify and rewrite the collected statements and construct a table of production rules out of the collected statements.

Produce a series of models by using the production rules.

Source: Organized from J. Kim and J. F. Courtney, "A Survey of Knowledge Acquisition Techniques and Their Relevance to Managerial Problem Domains," *Decision Support Systems* 4 (October 1988), p. 273.

TABLE 13.3 Advantages and Limitations of Protocol Analysis

Advantages	Limitations
Expert consciously considers decision-making heuristics	Requires that expert be aware of why he or she makes a decision
Expert consciously considers decision alternatives, attributes, values	Requires that expert be able to categorize major decision alternatives
Knowledge engineer can observe and analyze decision-making behavior	Requires that expert be able to verbalize the attributes and values of a decision alternative
Knowledge engineer can record, and later analyze with the expert, key decision points	Requires that expert be able to reason about the selection of a given alternative
	Subjective view of decision making Explanations may not track with reasoning

Source: K. L. McGraw and B. K. Harbison-Briggs, *Knowledge Acquisition, Principles and Guidelines* (Englewood Cliffs, NJ: Prentice-Hall, 1989), p. 217.

are made, the cost of transcribing from large quantities of tape or video should be carefully considered.

Observations, which can be viewed as a special case of protocols, are of two types: motor and eye movement. In the first type the expert's *physical* performance of the task (e.g., walking, reaching, talking) is documented. In the second type a record of where the expert fixes his or her gaze is being made. Observations are used primarily as a way of supporting verbal protocols. They are generally expensive and time consuming.

Other Manual Methods

Many other manual methods can be used to elicit knowledge from experts. A representative list is given here; for complete discussion see Diaper [9].

- *Case analysis.* Experts are asked how they handled specific cases in the past. Usually this method involves analyzing documentation. In addition to the experts, other people (e.g., managers, users) may be questioned.
- *Critical incident analysis.* In this approach only selected cases are investigated, usually those that are memorable, difficult, or of a special interest. Both experts and others may be questioned.
- *Commentaries.* In this method the knowledge engineer asks experts to give a running commentary on what they are doing. This method can be supported by videotaping the experts in action or by asking an observer to do the commentary.
- *Conceptual graphs.* Diagrams and other graphic methods can be instrumental in supporting other acquisition methods.

- *Brainstorming*. This method can be used to solicit the opinion of multiple experts. The method helps to generate ideas.
- *Prototyping*. Working with a prototype of the system is a powerful approach to induce experts to contribute their knowledge. Experts like to criticize systems. Changes may be made instantly.
- *Multidimensional scaling*. The complex technique of **multidimensional scaling** identifies various dimensions of knowledge and then places the knowledge in a form of a distance matrix. By using least-squares fitting regression, the various dimensions are analyzed, interpreted, and integrated.
- *Johnson's hierarchical clustering*. This is another scaling method, but it is much simpler to implement and therefore is used more. It combines related knowledge elements into clusters (two elements at a time).

13.9   Expert-driven Methods

In the previous methods the major role of knowledge acquisition was played by the knowledge engineer. However, knowledge engineers typically lack knowledge about the domain, their services are expensive, and they may have problems communicating with experts. As a result knowledge acquisition may be a slow process with many iterations (for verification and learning purposes). The process, then, is expensive, and even unreliable because the experts may find it difficult to contribute their knowledge via the knowledge engineer.

Perhaps experts should be their own knowledge engineers, encoding their own expertise into computers. Such expert-driven arrangements could solve some of the difficulties described earlier as well as result in less "noise" being introduced into the knowledge base. The role of knowledge engineers will be reduced and the acquisition process will be drastically expedited.

Two approaches to expert-driven systems are available: manual and computer aided (semiautomatic).

Manual Method: Expert's Self-reports

Sometimes it is possible to elicit knowledge from experts manually by using a self-administered questionnaire or an organized report. Open-ended questionnaires are appropriate for knowledge discovery in which high-level concepts are usually the result. Close-ended (or forced-answer) questionnaires are more structured and easy to fill in, but the knowledge collected is limited. In addition to questionnaires, experts may be asked to log their activities, prepare a one-hour introductory lecture, or produce reports about their problem-solving activities.

Experts' reports and questionnaires exhibit a number of problems according to Wolfgram et al. [31].

1. They essentially require the expert to act as a knowledge engineer, without a knowledge engineer's training.
2. The reports tend to have a high degree of bias; they typically reflect the expert's opinion concerning how the task "should be done" rather than "how it is really done."
3. Experts will often describe new and untested ideas and strategies they have been contemplating but still have not included in their decision-making behavior. Thus, there is a mixture of past experience, actual behavior, and "ideal future" behavior.
4. Experts' reports are time-consuming efforts, and the experts lose interest rapidly. The quality of information attained will rapidly decrease as the report progresses.
5. Experts must be proficient in flowcharting or other process-documenting techniques.
6. Experts may forget to specify certain pieces of knowledge (which may result in ambiguity).
7. Experts are likely to be fairly vague about the nature of associations among events (which may result in an indeterminate bias).

Given these caveats, under certain conditions such as the inaccessibility of an expert to the knowledge engineer, expert reports and self-questionnaires may provide useful preliminary knowledge discovery and acquisition.

Some of the limitations of the manual approach can be removed if a computer is used to support the process.

Computer-aided Approaches

The purpose of computerized support to the expert is to reduce or eliminate the potential problems discussed, especially those of indeterminate bias and ambiguity (see Kim and Courtney [21]). These problems dominate the gathering of information for the initial knowledge base and the interactive refinements of this knowledge. A smart knowledge acquisition tool needs to be able to add knowledge incrementally to the knowledge base and refine or even correct existing knowledge.

Visual modeling techniques are often used to construct the initial domain model. The objective of the visual modeling approach is to give the user the ability to visualize real-world problems and to manipulate elements of it through the use of graphics. Kearney [20] indicates that diagrams and drawings are useful in representing problems; they serve as a set of external memory aids and can reveal inconsistencies in an individual's knowledge.

Several other tools can be used by experts (for a survey see Boose and Gaines [6]). Of a special interest are those methods that are based on repertory grid analysis, a topic presented next.

13.10   Repertory Grid Analysis

Experience is often based on perception, insight, and intuition. Therefore, many experts have difficulties in expressing their line of reasoning. Experts may also be confused between facts and factors that actually influence decision making. To overcome these and other limitations of knowledge acquisition by gaining insight into the expert's mental model of the problem domain, a number of elicitation techniques have been developed. These techniques, derived from psychology, use an approach called the *classification interview.* Since they are fairly structured, when applied to technologies, these methods are usually aided by a computer. The primary method is **repertory grid analysis** (RGA).

Basis for the Grid

The RGA is based on Kelly's model of human thinking called Personal Construct Theory (see [16]). According to this theory each person is viewed as a "personal scientist" who seeks to predict and control events by forming theories, testing hypotheses, and analyzing results of experiments. Knowledge and perceptions about the world (or about a domain or a problem) are classified and categorized by each individual as a personal, perceptual model. Based on the model developed, each individual is able to anticipate and then act on the basis of these anticipations.

This personal model matches our view of an expert at work; it is a description of the development and use of the expert's knowledge, and therefore it is suitable for expert systems as suggested by Hart [16]. The RGA is a method of investigating such a model.

How the RGA Works

The RGA employs several processes. First, the expert identifies the *important objects* in the domain of expertise. For example, computer languages (LISP, C, COBOL) are objects in the case of a need to select a computer language. This identification is done in an interview.

Second, the expert identifies the important attributes that are considered in making decisions in the domain. For example, availability of commercial packages and ease of programming are important in the case of selecting a computer language.

Third, for each attribute the expert is asked to establish a bipolar scale with distinguishable characteristics (traits) and their opposites. For example, in the case of selecting computer languages the information shown in Table 13.4 may be included.

Fourth, the interviewer picks any three of the objects and asks: What attributes and traits distinguish any two of these objects from the third? For example, if a set includes LISP, PROLOG, and COBOL, the expert may point to "orientation." Then the expert will tell that LISP and PROLOG are symbolic in nature, while COBOL is numeric. These answers are translated to points on a

TABLE 13.4 RGA Input for Selecting a Computer Language

Attributes	Trait	Opposite
Availability	Widely available	Not available
Ease of programming	High	Low
Training time	Low	High
Orientation	Symbolic	Numeric

scale of 1-3 (or 1-5). This step continues for several triplets of objects. The answers are recorded in a grid as shown in Table 13.5. The numbers inside the grid designate the points assigned to each attribute for each object.

Once the grid is completed, the expert may change the ratings inside the box. The grid can be used afterward to make recommendations in situations where the importance of the attributes is known. For example, in a simplistic manner, it can be said that if numeric orientation is very important, then COBOL is the recommended language.

Use of RGA in Expert Systems

A number of knowledge acquisition tools have been developed based on the RGA. These tools are aimed at helping in the conceptualization of the domain. Three representative tools are ETS, KRITON, and AQUINAS.

Expertise Transfer System. Expertise Transfer System (ETS) is a computer program that interviews experts and helps them build expert systems. ETS interviews experts to uncover vocabulary conclusions, problem-solving traits, trait structures, trait weights, and inconsistencies. It has been utilized to construct prototypes rapidly (often in less than two hours for very small ES), to aid the expert in determining if there is sufficient knowledge to solve the problem, and to create knowledge bases for a variety of different ES shells from its own internal representation. An improved version of ETS called NeoETS has been developed to expand the capabilities of ETS. The method is limited to classification-type problems. For details see Boose [3].

TABLE 13.5 Example of a Grid

Attribute	Orientation	Ease of Programming	Training Time	Availability
Trait Opposite	Symbolic (3) Numeric (1)	High (3) Low (1)	High (1) Low (3)	High (3) Low (1)
LISP	3	3	1	1
PROLOG	3	2	2	1
C	2	3	2	2
COBOL	1	2	1	3

AQUINAS. AQUINAS is a very complex tool (see Boose and Bradshaw [5]) that extends the problem solving and knowledge representation of ETS by allowing experts to structure knowledge in hierarchies. A set of heuristics has been defined and incorporated in the Dialog Manager, a subsystem of AQUINAS, to provide guidance in the knowledge acquisition process to domain experts and knowledge engineers.

KRITON. KRITON is a system that attempts to automate the use of the repertory grid approach. First it conducts interviews with experts; then it analyzes protocols and documents by interacting with the experts. The expert, based on key word statistics, selects portions of texts for propositional analysis using the same tools used in protocol analysis. Since documents are normally not as problem-oriented as protocols, the expert adds goal information to the results of the analysis. Should experiments with this system be successful, it can in some cases replace a knowledge engineer, resulting in a true breakthrough in applications. For further details see Diederich et al. [10].

Finally, the Auto-Intelligence tool (see Section 13.12) is based on the RGA. It was the first commercial tool to combine the repertory grid approach with rule induction.

13.11   Supporting the Knowledge Engineer

A number of acquisition and encoding tools greatly reduce the need for the time (and/or skill level) of the knowledge engineer. Nevertheless, the knowledge engineer in such a case still plays an important role in the process, as shown in Figure 13.8. The figure depicts the major tasks of the knowledge engineer:

- Advise the expert on the process of interactive knowledge elicitation
- Manage the interactive knowledge acquisition tools, setting them up appropriately
- Edit the unencoded and coded knowledge base in collaboration with the expert
- Manage the knowledge encoding tools, setting them up appropriately
- Validate the application of the knowledge base in collaboration with the expert
- Train the clients in the effective use of the knowledge base in collaboration with the expert by developing operational and training procedures.

This use of interactive elicitation can be combined with manual elicitation and with the use of the interactive tools by the knowledge engineer. The knowledge engineer can (1) directly elicit knowledge from the expert and (2) use interactive elicitation tools to enter knowledge into the knowledge base.

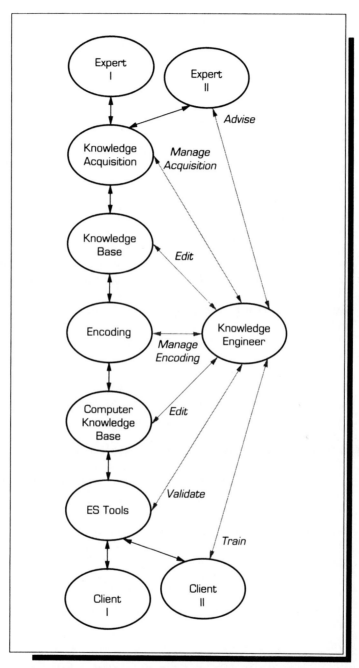

FIGURE 13.8 Knowledge Engineers' Roles in Interactive Knowledge Acquisition. (*Source:* Adapted from B. R. Gaines, University of Calgary, with permission.)

Knowledge Acquisition Aids

Several types of tools have been developed for supporting knowledge acquisition. Some representative examples follow.

Editors and Interfaces. Use of a text editor or a special knowledge-base editor can facilitate the task of entering knowledge into the system and decrease the chance of errors. A good editor provides smooth user interfaces that facilitate instruction and display information conveniently. The editor checks, for example, syntax and semantics for completeness and consistency. The rule editor of EXSYS is an example of one that simplifies rule input and testing. A spelling and a grammar checker can also be used to detect errors.

Explanation Facility. The explanation subsystem serves not only the user but also the knowledge engineer and the expert in refining and improving the knowledge base. In addition to general-purpose devices (such as debugging and trace mechanisms), there are specially constructed explanation facilities, which can trace, for example, the chain of reasoning after it has been completed.

Revision of the Knowledge Base. Changes in the knowledge base can be made by selecting an appropriate revision from a set of possibilities. To avoid introducing new bugs or inconsistencies with the existing knowledge base, aids such as a semantic consistency checker or automated testing can be used.

Pictorial Knowledge Acquisition (PIKA). PIKA is a graphics editor whose output is a collection of structured graphic objects that can be combined to support a multilevel interface (see Freiling et al. [15]).

Example of a Knowledge Acquisition Aid. TEIRESIAS (see Hayes-Roth et al. [17]) is a classic program that was developed to assist knowledge engineers in the creation (or revision) of rules for a specific ES while working with the EMYCIN shell. The program uses a natural language interface to assist the knowledge engineer in testing and debugging new knowledge. It provides an expanded explanation capability. For example, if system builders find that a set of knowledge rules leads to an inadequate conclusion, they can have TEIRESIAS show all the rules used to reach that conclusion. With the rule editor, adjustments can easily be made. To expedite the process, TEIRESIAS translates each new rule, which is entered in natural language, into LISP. Then it retranslates the rule into natural language. The program thus can point out inconsistencies, rule conflicts, and inadequacies.

Integrated Knowledge Acquisition Aids

Most of the preceding tools and many others were designed as stand-alone tools on the assumption that they will be used by a specific ES participant (e.g., the expert) for the execution of a specific task. In reality, however, participants may play multiple roles or even exchange roles. Therefore, there is a trend to integrate the acquisition aids. For an overview of such integration tools see Boose and Gaines [6]. Examples of such tools are Auto-Intelligence, described in Section 13.12, and KADS, which is described next.

Knowledge Acquisition and Documentation System (KADS). The purpose of these techniques, which were developed at the University of Amsterdam, is to aid the knowledge engineer in acquiring, structuring, analyzing, and documenting expert knowledge. KADS is known to be very successful in increasing the knowledge engineer's productivity.

Front-end Tools

Knowledge needs to be coded in a specific manner in various knowledge-based tools. In an attempt to automate the coding, various tools have been developed. For example, Knowledge Analysis Tool (KAT) converts knowledge to a specific rule format for a tool called Level5. NEXTRA is a similar tool that helps the knowledge engineer to code rules in Nexpert Object.

13.12 Induction

The elicitation methods presented so far in this chapter are labor intensive. The two major participants are the knowledge engineer, who is difficult to get and is highly paid, and the domain expert, who is usually busy and sometimes uncooperative. Therefore, manual and even the semiautomatic elicitation methods are both slow and expensive. In addition, they exhibit some other deficiencies:

- It is difficult to validate the acquired knowledge.
- There is frequently weak correlation between verbal reports and mental behavior.
- In certain situations experts are unable to provide an overall account of how their decisions are made.
- The quality of the system depends too much on the quality of the expert and the knowledge engineer.
- The expert does not understand the ES technology.
- The knowledge engineer does not understand, in many cases, the nature of the business.

Thus it makes sense to develop knowledge acquisition methods that will reduce or even eliminate the need for these two participants. These methods, which are described as *computer-aided* knowledge acquisition, or automated knowledge acquisition, vary in their objectives, some of which are listed here:

- Increase the productivity of knowledge engineering (reduce the cost)
- Reduce the skill level required from the knowledge engineer

- Eliminate (or drastically reduce) the need for an expert
- Eliminate (or drastically reduce) the need for a knowledge engineer
- Increase the quality of the acquired knowledge.

Two major topics are frequently covered under automated knowledge acquisition: machine learning (discussed in Chapter 17) and **rule induction,** which is presented next.

Automated Rule Induction

Induction means a process of reasoning from the specific to the general. In ES terminology it refers to the process in which rules are generated by a computer program from example cases.

A rule-induction system is given examples of a problem (called a *training set*) where the outcome is known. After it has been given enough examples, the rule induction system can create rules that fit the example cases. The rules can then be used to assess other cases where the outcome is not known. The heart of a rule-induction system is an algorithm, which is used to induce the rules from the examples (see Box 13.1).

An example of a simplified rule induction can be seen in the work of a loan officer in a bank. Requests for loans include information about the applicants such as income level, assets, age, and the number of dependents. These are the *attributes,* or characteristics, of the applicants. If we log several example cases, each with its final decision, we will find a situation that resembles the data in Table 13.6.

From these cases it is easy to infer the following three rules:

1. If income is $70,000 or more, approve the loan.
2. If income is $30,000 or more, age is at least forty, assets are above $249,000, and there are no dependents, approve the loan.
3. If income is between $30,000 and $50,000 and assets are at least $100,000, approve the loan.

Box 13.1: Induction Algorithms

Induction methods use various algorithms to convert a knowledge matrix of attributes, values, and selections to rules. Such algorithms vary from statistical methods to neural computing.

A popular induction algorithm is ID3. ID3 first converts the knowledge matrix into a decision tree. Irrelevant attributes are eliminated and the relevant attributes are organized in an efficient manner. For more information on ID3 consult pages 406—410 of Cohen and Feigenbaum [8].

TABLE 13.6 Cases for Induction.

	Attributes				
Applicant	Annual Income ($)	Assets ($)	Age	Number of Dependents	Decision
Mr. White	50,000	100,000	30	3	Yes
Ms. Green	70,000	None	35	1	Yes
Mr. Smith	40,000	None	33	2	No
Ms. Rich	30,000	250,000	42	0	Yes

Advantages of Rule Induction. One of the leading researchers in the field, Donald Michie, has pointed out that only certain types of knowledge can be properly acquired using manual knowledge acquisition methods like interviews and observations. These are cases in which the domain of knowledge is certain, small, loosely coupled, or modular. As the domain gets bigger and more complex, experts become unable to explain how they operate. They can, however, still supply the knowledge engineer with suitable examples of problems and solutions. Using rule induction allows ES to be used in more complicated, and more commercially rewarding, fields (see Michie [26]).

Another advantage is that the builder does not have to be a knowledge engineer. He or she can be the expert or a system analyst. This not only saves time and money, but it also solves the difficulties of dealing with the knowledge engineer who is an outsider unfamiliar with the "business."

Machine induction also offers the possibility of deducing new knowledge. It may be possible to list all the factors that influence a decision, without understanding their impacts, and to induce a rule that works successfully.

Once rules are generated they are reviewed by the expert and modified if necessary. A big advantage of rule induction is that it enhances the thinking process of the expert.

Difficulties in Implementation. Despite the advantages, several difficulties exist with the implementation of rule induction:

- Some induction programs may generate rules that are not easy for a human to understand, because the way in which the program classifies a problem's attributes and properties may not be in accordance with the way that a human would do it.
- Rule-induction programs do not select the attributes. An expert still has to be available to specify which attributes are significant; for example, the important factors in approving a loan.
- The search process in rule induction is based on special algorithms that generate efficient decision trees, which reduce the number of questions

that must be asked before a conclusion is reached. Several alternative algorithms are available and they vary in their processes and capabilities.

- The method is good only for rule-based, classification-type problems, especially of the yes-or-no types. (However, many problems can be rephrased or split so that they fall into the classification category.)
- The number of attributes must be fairly small. With more than fifteen attributes there may be a need for a mainframe computer. The upper limit on the number of attributes is approached very quickly.
- The number of "sufficient" examples that is needed can be very large.
- The set of examples must be "sanitized"; for example, cases that are exceptions to rules must be removed. (Such exceptions can be determined by observing inconsistent rules.)
- The method is limited to situations under certainty (deterministic).
- A major problem with the method, according to Hart [16], is that the builder does not know in advance whether the number of examples is sufficient and whether the algorithm is good enough. To be sure of this would presuppose that the builder had some idea of the "solution"; the reason for using induction in the first instance is that the builder *does not know* the solution, but wants to discover it by using the rules.

Because of these limitations, the induction method is used to provide a first prototype; then it is translated into something more robust and handcrafted into an improved system.

Software Packages. Several induction software packages are available on the market both for personal computers and for larger computers. Here are some representative packages:

- 1st-CLASS (personal computer)
- TIMM (larger computer)
- Rule Master (personal computer and larger)
- EX-Tran 7 (personal computer and larger)
- Knowledgeshaper (workstation and mainframe)
- BEAGLE (personal computer and larger)
- Level5 (personal computer)
- VP Expert (personal computer)

Most of these programs not only generate rules, but also check them for possible logical conflict. Furthermore, some of them can be used as ES shells; that is, they can be used to generate the rules and then to construct an ES that uses this knowledge.

Interactive Induction

The combination of an expert supported by a computer is labeled **interactive induction.** One interesting attempt that combines induction and interactive acquisition can be found in a tool called Auto-Intelligence (IntelligenceWare, Inc., Los Angeles).

Auto-Intelligence captures the knowledge of an expert through interactive interviews, distills the knowledge, and then automatically generates a rule-based knowledge base. An important part of the interaction with Auto-Intelligence is a "structure discovery," during which the *system* interviews the expert prior to classifying the information and distilling knowledge by induction.

Structure is discovered by utilizing special deductive question-generation techniques based on repertory grids, multidimensional scaling, and data classification. These techniques help experts think about problems locally and piece by piece, thus gradually revealing their expertise.

Auto-Intelligence builds ES for structured selection or heuristic classification tasks in which an expert makes decisions and selects among a number of choices based on available criteria. Examples of heuristic classification tasks include diagnosis, investment selection, situation assessment, and so forth. Auto-Intelligence interacts with experts (without knowledge engineers); it helps them bypass their cognitive defenses and biases and identify the important criteria and constructs used in decision making. For details, see Parsaye [28].

13.13   Selecting an Appropriate Method

Several years ago the objectives of an ideal knowledge acquisition system were outlined by Hill et al. [18]:

- Direct interaction with the expert without intervention by a knowledge engineer
- Applicability to unlimited, or at least a broad class of, problem domains
- Tutorial capabilities to eliminate the need for prior training of the expert
- Ability to analyze work in progress to detect inconsistencies and gaps in knowledge
- Ability to incorporate multiple sources of knowledge
- A human interface (i.e., a natural conversation) that will make the use of the system enjoyable and attractive
- Ability to interface easily with different expert system tools as appropriate to the problem domain.

To attain these objectives it is necessary to automate the process. However, automatic knowledge acquisition methods, known also as *machine learning*, are presently limited in their capabilities. Nevertheless, diligent efforts on the part of researchers, vendors, and system builders are helping to slowly approach these objectives. Best results can be achieved in acquisition of knowledge that is difficult to acquire manually (e.g., large databases). In the interim, acquisition will continue to be done manually in most cases, but it will be supported by productivity improvement aids.

13.14   Knowledge Acquisition from Multiple Experts

An important element in the development of an ES is the identification of experts. This is a complicated task in the real-world environment, perhaps because often so many support mechanisms are used by practitioners for certain tasks (questionnaires, informal and formal consultations, texts, etc.). Together these support mechanisms contribute to the high quality of professional output. They may also, however, tend to make it difficult to identify a knowledge "czar" whose estimates, process, or knowledge are clearly superior to what the system and mix of staff, support tools, and consulting skills produce in the rendering of normal client service.

The usual approach to this problem is to build ES for a very narrow domain in which expertise is clearly defined. In such a case it is easy to find one expert. However, even though many ES have been constructed with one expert—an approach that is advocated as a good strategy for ES construction—there could be a need for **multiple experts,** especially when more serious ES are being constructed or when expertise is not particularly well defined.

The major purposes of using multiple experts are (1) to broaden the coverage of proposed solutions (i.e., the solutions complement each other) and (2) to combine the strengths of different approaches of reasoning. Table 13.7 lists benefits and problems with multiple experts.

When multiple experts are used, there are often differences of opinion and conflicts that have to be resolved. This is especially true when developing knowledge bases from multiple sources, where these systems address problems that involve the use of subjective reasoning and heuristics. Conflicts can arise due to a lack of knowledge of a certain aspect of the problem or as a result of statistical uncertainty (e.g., different experts may assign different event outcome probabilities while observing the same evidence). Experts may also follow different lines of reasoning derived from their background and experience, which could lead to conflicting solutions.

TABLE 13.7   Benefits of and Problems with Participation of Multiple Experts

Benefits	Problems
On the average, fewer mistakes by a group of experts than by a single expert	Groupthink phenomena
Several experts in group eliminate need for using a world-class expert (who is difficult to get and expensive)	Fear on the part of some domain experts of senior experts or a supervisor (lack of confidentiality)
Wider domain than a single expert's	Compromising solutions generated by a group with conflicting opinions
Synthesis of expertise	Waste of time in group meetings
Enhanced quality from synergy among experts	Difficulties in scheduling the experts
	Dominating experts (controlling, not letting others speak)

Other related issues are identifying different aspects of the problem and matching them with different experts, integrating knowledge from various experts, assimilating conflicting strategies, personalizing community knowledge bases, and developing programming technologies to support these issues.

Multiple Expert Scenarios

Four possible scenarios, or configurations, of multiple experts exist (see McGraw and Harbison-Briggs [23]): individual experts, primary and secondary experts, small groups, and panels.

Individual Experts. In this case several experts contribute knowledge individually. Using multiple experts in this manner relieves the knowledge engineer from the stress associated with multiple expert teams. However, this approach requires that the knowledge engineer have a means of resolving conflicts and handling multiple lines of reasoning.

Primary and Secondary Experts. In this case a primary expert is responsible for validating information retrieved from other domain experts. Knowledge engineers may consult the primary expert at the beginning of the program for guidance in domain familiarization, refinement of knowledge acquisition plans, and the identification of individuals who may be asked to serve as secondary experts. The primary expert is consulted periodically to review the results of knowledge acquisition sessions.

Small Groups. In this case several experts are consulted, together, and asked to provide agreed-upon information. Working with small groups of experts allows the knowledge engineer to observe (1) alternate approaches to the solution of a problem and (2) the key points made in solution-oriented discussions among experts.

Panels. To meet goals for verification and validation of ongoing development efforts, some programs choose to establish a council of experts. These individuals typically meet together at times scheduled by the developer for the purpose of reviewing knowledge base efforts, content, and plans. In many cases, the functionality of the expert system itself is tested against the expertise of such a panel.

These scenarios determine, in part, the method to be used for handling multiple expertise.

Methods of Handling Multiple Expertise

Several major approaches to the issue of integrating experts' opinions have been defined by Alexander and Evans [1]:

- Blend several lines of reasoning through consensus methods.
- Use an analytical approach.
- Keep the lines of reasoning distinct and select a specific line of reasoning based on the situation.
- Automate the process.
- Decompose the knowledge acquired into specialized knowledge sources (blackboard systems).

Now a brief description of each method follows.

Consensus Methods. Consensus in small groups can be reached in several ways using methodologies borrowed from behavioral sciences such as group dynamics. Each expert is provided information on the judgment of the other experts within the group and is provided an opportunity to revise his or her judgment based on this information. The interaction could include a face-to-face meeting of the experts, or the experts' identities might be concealed from each other to avoid personality influences. The following activities are some acceptable techniques for achieving consensus: the nominal-group technique, brainstorming, Delphi, consensus decision making, and computer-supported cooperative work. For further discussion and references see McGraw and Harbison-Briggs [23].

Generic consensus methods may not be effective in knowledge acquisition because experts are very much opinionated, and because the process may be too expensive for implementation.

Analytical Approaches. An analytical approach can be appropriate when the expertise involves numeric values (such as assessment of probabilities). Methods borrowed from the literature on multiple-criteria decision making can be used. Several attempts have been made to develop a "group probability" as a weighted aggregation of individual probability assessments. For details, see Alexander and Evans [1].

Specific Lines of Reasoning. According to this procedure, which was developed by LeClair [22], multiple lines of reasoning are allowed to coexist without unwanted interactions that could compromise an expert's advice.

Once multiple lines of reasoning are accommodated in the expert system, the system should attempt to select a line of reasoning based on the characteristics of each situation. The goal is not to achieve a consensus solution, but to select the most appropriate solution. LeClair achieves this by introducing information specific to the decision situation; the expert system then *automatically* selects a line of reasoning using this information. The basis for this approach is that each expert's line of reasoning is founded on his or her unique experiences in the problem domain and therefore represents a distinct philosophy regarding the problem domain.

Automated Processes. The previous method uses an automated approach for selecting a line of reasoning. Once multiple lines of reasoning are programmed and accommodated in the knowledge base, however, an attempt can also be made to automate the *entire process.* Expert Ease (an early ES shell, which currently sells under the name Expert One) allows for the input of multiple lines of reasoning. Once the multiple lines of reasoning have been input, the system determines the most efficient way (using the theory of entropy, or uncertainty reduction) to reach the solution.

Blackboard Systems. Blackboard systems maximize independence among knowledge sources by appropriately dividing the problem domain. In this approach expertise is divided among subdomains. Then, one knowledge base is constructed for each subdomain, and the experts in each subdomain cooperate to solve the problem. Any interaction among knowledge sources can be handled in several ways. For example, conclusions of the different knowledge sources can be posted on a "blackboard" available to all knowledge sources. The knowledge sources have a condition and an action part. The condition component specifies the situations under which a particular knowledge source could contribute to an activity. A scheduler, or an event manager, controls the progress toward a solution in blackboard systems by determining which knowledge source to schedule next or which problem subdomain to focus on. For further details see Englemore and Morgan [12].

13.15 Validation and Verification of the Knowledge Base

Knowledge acquisition involves quality control aspects that appear under the terms *evaluation, validation,* and *verification.* These terms are frequently confused, mixed up, or used interchangeably. We use the definitions provided by O'Keefe et al. [27].

Evaluation is a broad concept. Its objective is to assess an expert system's *overall value.* In addition to assessing acceptable performance levels, it analyzes whether the system would be usable, efficient, and cost-effective. This topic is revisited in Chapter 19 on implementation.

Validation is the part of evaluation that deals with the *performance* of the system (e.g., as it compares to the expert's). Simply stated, validation refers to building the "right" system, that is, substantiating that a system performs with an acceptable level of accuracy.

Verification refers to building the system "right," that is, substantiating that the system correctly implements its specifications.

In the realm of ES these activities are dynamic, since they must be repeated each time that the prototype is changed. Benbasat and Dhaliwal [2] have developed a framework for such validation.

In terms of the knowledge base, it is necessary to assure that we have the *right* knowledge base, that is, that the knowledge is valid. It is also essential to assure that the knowledge base was constructed properly (verification).

In executing these quality control tasks, we are dealing with several activities and concepts. These are listed in Table 13.8.

Automated verification of knowledge is offered in the Auto-Intelligence product described earlier. Verification is conducted by measuring the system's performance, and it is limited to classification cases with probabilities. It works as follows: When an ES is presented with a new case to classify, it assigns a confidence factor to each selection. By comparing these confidence factors with those provided by an expert, one can measure the *accuracy* of the ES as it is reflected in each case. By performing comparisons on many cases one can arrive at an overall measure of performance of the ES. For details see Parsaye [28].

13.16 Analyzing, Coding, Documenting, and Diagramming

The collected knowledge must be analyzed, coded, and documented. The manner in which these activities take place depends on the methods of acquisition and representation. The following example (based on Wolfgram et al. [31]) illustrates some of the steps in this process. It deals with knowledge acquired with the use of verbal protocols and includes four steps.

Transcription. First, a complete transcription of the verbal report is made, including not only the expert's utterances, but also those of the knowledge engineer and any other distractions or interferences that may have occurred during the session.

Phrase Indexing. Second, a phrase index is compiled by breaking up the transcription into short phrases, each identified by an index number. Each phrase should correspond to the knowledge engineer's assessment of what constitutes a piece of knowledge, that is, a single task, assertion, or data collection process by the expert.

Knowledge Coding. Third, knowledge is coded. This activity attempts to classify the knowledge. One useful classification is to distinguish between descriptive and procedural knowledge.

Documentation. Fourth, the knowledge should be properly organized and documented. One way of organizing the documentation is to divide it into four parts: comprehensive domain listing, descriptive knowledge, procedural knowledge, and glossary. Certainly, the documented knowledge should be maintained and updated properly. The documentation should be done in a consistent manner. Forms can be used, and some vendors of ES provide their clients with necessary forms.

TABLE 13.8 Measures of Validation

Measure (Criteria)	Description
Accuracy	How well the system reflects reality; how correct the knowledge is in the knowledge base
Adaptability	Possibilities for future development, changes
Adequacy (or Completeness)	Portion of the necessary knowledge that is included in the knowledge base
Appeal	How well the knowledge base matches intuition and stimulates thought and practicability
Breadth	How well the domain is covered
Depth	Degree of the detailed knowledge
Face validity	Credibility of knowledge
Generality	Capability of a knowledge base to be used with a broad range of similar problems
Precision	Capability of the system to replicate particular system parameters; consistency of advice; coverage of variables in knowledge base
Realism	Accounting for relevant variables and relations; similarity to reality
Reliability	Fraction of the ES predictions that are empirically correct
Robustness	Sensitivity of conclusions to model structure
Sensitivity	Impact of changes in the knowledge base on quality of outputs
Technical and operational validity	Goodness of the assumed assumptions, context, constraints, and conditions, and their impact on other measures
Turing Test	Ability of a human evaluator to identify if a given conclusion is made by an ES or by a human expert
Usefulness	How adequate the knowledge is (in terms of parameters and relationships) for solving correctly
Validity	Knowledge base's capability of producing empirically correct predictions

Source: Adapted from B. Marcot, "Testing Your Knowledge Base," *AI Expert* (August 1987).

Knowledge Diagramming. **Knowledge diagramming** is a graphic approach to improving the process of knowledge acquisition. It consists of hierarchical, top-down descriptions of the major types of knowledge used to describe facts and reasoning strategies for problem-solving in expert systems. These types are objects, events, performance, and metaknowledge. Diagramming also describes the linkages and interactions among the various types of knowledge. As knowledge is acquired, the diagrams support the analysis and planning of subsequent acquisitions. The process is similar to diagramming in system analysis; by acting as a high-level representation of knowledge, the *productivity* of the builders and the *quality* of the system can be increased.

Hierarchical diagramming ends with a primitive level that cannot be decomposed. The decomposition in all levels is diagrammed to provide a partitioned view of events and objects. A special knowledge representation language called KRL (Knowledge Representation Language) is used in the process. Graphic techniques augment the scope, understanding, and modularity of knowledge.

Knowledge diagramming can be used to manage acquisition very effectively when it is tied to the five-stage model of knowledge acquisition (see Figure 13.4). A special expert system called INQUEST has been developed using this approach. For information about this system and knowledge diagramming in general, see Hillman [19].

13.17   Numeric and Documented Knowledge Acquisition

Acquisition of Numeric Knowledge

Traditional knowledge acquisition methods are designed to deal mainly with symbolic representation of knowledge. Drake and Hess [11] claim that a special approach is needed to capture numeric knowledge. They suggest complementing symbolic knowledge acquisition with a numeric one. Drake and Hess present a methodology called *abduction*, which handles numeric, complex, and uncertain relationships.

The methodology is implemented in a hybrid knowledge acquisition process (Figure 13.9). A special tool to support the numeric process is AIM Problem Solver (from AbTech Corp.).

Acquisition of Documented Knowledge

In many cases knowledge can be acquired from other sources in addition to, or instead of, human experts. The major advantage of this approach is that there is no need to use an expert. The approach is used in knowledge-based systems where the concern is to handle a large or complex amount of information rather than world-class expertise. Searching through corporate policy manuals or catalogs is an example of such a situation.

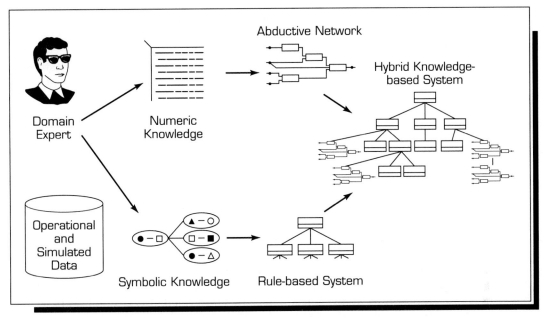

FIGURE 13.9 Hybrid Development Process for Knowledge-based Systems. (*Source:* K. C. Drake and P. Hess. "Abduction." *PC AI.* 1990. p. 61. Courtesy of AbTech Corp., Charlottesville, VA)

At present, very few methodologies deal with knowledge acquisition from documented sources. The approach has, however, a great potential for automation. Documented knowledge of almost any type can be easily (and inexpensively) scanned and transferred to a computer's database. The analysis of the knowledge can then be done manually, but it can also be done with the use of AI technologies (perhaps a combination of a speech understanding and expert systems). Thus, expert systems may be used to build other expert systems.

Expert systems can scan databases and digitize books, journals, and magazines, and this capability is increasing. Data stored in another computer system could be retrieved electronically to create or update the knowledge base of the expert system, all without the intervention of a knowledge engineer or an expert.

Chapter Highlights

- ■ Knowledge engineering involves acquisition, representation, reasoning (inference), and explanation of knowledge.
- ■ Knowledge is available from many sources, including those that are documented and those that are undocumented (experts).
- ■ Knowledge can be shallow, describing a narrow input-output relationship, or deep, describing complex interactions and a system's operation.

- Knowledge acquisition, especially from human experts, is a difficult task due to several communication and information processing problems.
- The process of knowledge acquisition is composed of five stages: identification, conceptualization, formalization, implementation, and testing.
- The methods of knowledge acquisition can be divided into manual, semiautomated, and automated.
- The primary manual approach is interviewing. Interviewing methods range from completely unstructured to highly structured.
- The reasoning process of experts can be tracked by several methods. Protocol analysis is the primary method used in AI.
- Although it is possible to observe experts in action, this observation is limited in scope.
- Attempts are being made to reduce or even eliminate the role of the knowledge engineer by providing experts with manual and/or computerized tools for knowledge acquisition.
- The repertory grid analysis (RGA) is the most applied method of semiautomated interviews used in AI. Several software packages that use RGA improve the knowledge acquisition process.
- Many productivity tools are available for knowledge acquisition (e.g., editors, interfaces, diagramming).
- Rule induction examines historical cases and generates the rules that were used to arrive at certain recommendations.
- Rule induction can be used by a system engineer, an expert, or any other system builder.
- Several procedures are available for selecting an appropriate method of knowledge acquisition for any special situation.
- There are benefits as well as limitations and problems in using several experts to build a knowledge base.
- The four possible scenarios for use of multiple expertise are individual experts, primary and secondary experts, small groups, and panels.
- The major methods of dealing with multiple experts are consensus methods, analytical approaches, selection of an appropriate line of reasoning, automation of the process, and a blackboard system.
- Validation and verification of the knowledge base are critical success factors in ES implementation.
- More than a dozen specific measures are available to determine the validity of knowledge.
- Automated knowledge acquisition methods are easier to validate and verify.
- Knowledge collected must be analyzed and coded prior to its representation in the computer.

Key Words

deep knowledge	interactive induction	multiple experts
documented	interview analysis	protocol analysis
knowledge	knowledge acquisition	repertory grid analysis
elicitation of	knowledge	rule induction
knowledge	diagramming	shallow knowledge
evaluation	knowledge engineering	structured interview
Expertise Transfer	metaknowledge	walkthrough
System	multidimensional	validation
induction	scaling	verification

Questions for Review

1. Define knowledge engineering.
2. What are the steps in the knowledge engineering process?
3. What is metaknowledge?
4. Define knowledge acquisition and contrast it with knowledge representation.
5. List several sources of knowledge.
6. What is the difference between documented and undocumented knowledge?
7. Compare declarative and procedural knowledge.
8. Give four reasons why knowledge acquisition is difficult.
9. What are the major desired skills of a knowledge engineer?
10. Name the five stages in the knowledge acquisition process.
11. Describe the process of protocol analysis.
12. What is repertory grid analysis?
13. Describe the process of observing an expert at work.
14. What is the major advantage of using documented knowledge?
15. Briefly discuss three deficiencies of manual knowledge acquisition.
16. Describe the process of automated rule induction.
17. List the major difficulties of knowledge acquisition from multiple experts.
18. Briefly discuss the five major approaches to knowledge acquisition from multiple experts.
19. Describe the four possible scenarios of multiple experts.
20. Define evaluation, validation, and verification of knowledge.

Questions for Discussion

1. Discuss the major tasks performed by knowledge engineers.
2. Define and contrast shallow and deep knowledge.
3. Assume that you are to collect knowledge for one of the following systems:
   a. Advisory system on equal opportunity hiring situations in your organization

b. Advisory system on investment in residential real estate

c. Advisory system on how to prepare your federal tax return (Form 1040) What sources of knowledge would you consider? (Consult Figure 13.2.)

4. Why is knowledge acquisition considered by many as the most difficult step in knowledge engineering?

5. Discuss the major advantage of rule induction. Give an example that illustrates the method and point to a situation where you think it will be most appropriate.

6. Discuss the difficulties of knowledge acquisition from several experts. Describe a situation that you are familiar with where there could be a need for several experts.

7. Transfer of knowledge from a human to a machine to a human is said to be a more difficult task than a transfer from a human to a human. Why?

8. Explain the importance of conceptualization and list some of the detailed issues that are involved.

9. What are the major advantages and disadvantages of interviews based on example problems?

10. Compare and contrast protocol analysis to interviews based on example cases.

11. What are the major advantages and disadvantages of working with a prototype system for knowledge acquisition?

12. Why is repertory grid analysis so popular? What are its major weaknesses?

13. What are the major advantages and disadvantages of the observation method?

14. Discuss some of the problems of knowledge acquisition through the use of expert reports.

15. What are the present and future benefits of knowledge acquisition through an analysis of documented knowledge? What are its limitations?

16. Why are manual elicitation methods so slow and expensive?

17. Why can the case analysis method be used as a basis for knowledge acquisition?

18. What are the advantages of rule induction as an approach to knowledge acquisition?

19. What are the major benefits of Auto-Intelligence (or similar products) over a conventional rule induction package?

20. Discuss how some productivity improvement tools can expedite the work of the knowledge engineer.

21. Give an example for which an automated approach to knowledge acquisition from multiple experts would be feasible.

22. Explain why it is necessary to both verify and validate the content of the knowledge base. Who should do it?

23. Why is it important to have the knowledge analyzed, coded, and documented in a systematic way?

24. What are the major advantages of acquiring knowledge through a knowledge engineer?

25. Compare and contrast semantic and episodic knowledge.
26. Knowledge engineers are compared to system analysts. Why?
27. Discuss the conditions that are necessary to assure success when an expert is his or her own knowledge engineer.

Exercises

1. Fill in Table 13.9 with regard to the type of communication between the expert and the knowledge engineer. Use the following symbols: Y = yes, N = no, H = high, M = medium, L = low.
2. Evaluate the current success of automated rule induction and interactive methods in knowledge acquisition. Use Table 13.10. Then, comment on the major limitation of each method.
3. Read the following knowledge acquisition session and complete exercises a and b:
   a. List the heuristics cited in this interview.
   b. List the algorithms mentioned.

> KNOWLEDGE
> ENGINEER (KE): You have the reputation for finding the best real estate properties for your clients. How do you do it?
> EXPERT: Well, first I learn about the clients' objectives.
> KE: What do you mean by that?
> EXPERT: Some people are interested in income, others in price appreciation. There are some speculators, too.

TABLE 13.9 Communication between Expert and Knowledge Engineer

Method	Type of Communication				
	Face-to Face Contact	Written Communications	Continuing for a Long Time	Time Spent by Expert	Time Spent by Knowledge Engineer
Interview analysis					
Observations of experts					
Questionnaires and expert report					
Analysis of documented knowledge					

TABLE 13.10 Comparisons of Automated Rule Induction and Interactive Methods

Method/Tool	Time of Expert	Time of Knowledge Engineer	Skill of Knowledge Engineer
Rule induction			
Auto-Intelligence			
Smart editors			
Expertise Transfer System			

KE: Assume that somebody is interested in price appreciation. What would your advice be?

EXPERT: Well, I will find first how much money the investor can put down and to what degree he or she can subsidize the property.

KE: Why?

EXPERT: The more cash you put as downpayment, the less subsidy you will need. Properties with high potential for price appreciation need to be subsidized for about two years.

KE: What else?

EXPERT: Location is very important. As a general rule I recommend looking for the lowest-price property in an expensive area.

KE: What else?

EXPERT: I compute the cash flow and consider the tax impact by using built-in formulas in my calculator.

4. Examination of admission records of Pacifica University showed the admission cases listed in Table 13-11.
   a. Assume that admission decisions are based only on the scores of GMAT and GPA. Find, by induction, the rules used. Subject all five cases to the rules generated; make sure they are consistent with the rules.
   b. Assume that only *two* rules were used. Can you identify these rules?
5. Give an example of shallow and deep knowledge in an area of your interest.

TABLE 13.11 Admission Cases

Case #	GMAT	GPA	Decision
1	510	3.5	Yes
2	620	3.0	Yes
3	580	3.0	No
4	450	3.5	No
5	655	2.5	Yes

References and Bibliography

1. Alexander, S. M., and G. W. Evans. "The Integration of Multiple Experts: A Review of Methodologies." In *Applied Expert Systems*, E. Turban and P. Watkins, eds. Amsterdam: North Holland, 1988.
2. Benbasat, I., and J. S. Dhaliwal. "A Framework for the Validation of Knowledge Acquisition." *Knowledge Acquisition* 1 (1989).
3. Boose, J. H. *Expertise Transfer for Expert Systems Design*. New York: Elsevier, 1986.
4. Boose, J. H. "A Survey of Knowledge Acquisition Techniques and Tools." *Knowledge Acquisition* 1 (March 1989).
5. Boose, J. H., and J. M. Bradshaw. "A Knowledge Acquisition Workbench for Eliciting Decision Knowledge." In *Proceedings, 20th HICSS*. Hawaii, January 1987.
6. Boose, J. H., and B. R. Gaines, eds. *The Foundations of Knowledge Acquisition*. New York: Academic Press, 1990.
7. Brule, J. F., and A. Blount. *Knowledge Acquisition*. New York: McGraw-Hill, 1989.
8. Cohen, P. R., and E. A. Feigenbaum. *The Handbook of Artificial Intelligence*, vol. 3. Reading, MA: Addison-Wesley, 1982.
9. Diaper, D., ed. *Knowledge Elicitation*. New York: Ellis Horwood, 1989.
10. Diederich, J., et al. "KRITON: A Knowledge Acquisition Tool for Expert Systems." *International Journal of Man-Machine Studies* (January 1987).
11. Drake, K. C., and P. Hess. "Abduction, A Numeric Knowledge Acquisition Approach." *PC AI* (September/October 1990).
12. Englemore, R., and T. Morgan, eds. *Blackboard Systems*. Reading, MA: Addison-Wesley, 1989.
13. Ericsson, K. A., and H. A. Simon. *Protocol Analysis, Verbal Reports and Data*. Cambridge, MA: MIT Press, 1984.
14. Feigenbaum, E., and P. McCorduck. *The Fifth Generation*. Reading, MA: Addison-Wesley, 1983.
15. Freiling, M., et al. "Starting a Knowledge Engineering Project: A Step by Step Approach." *AI Magazine* (Fall 1985).
16. Hart, A. *Knowledge Acquisition for Expert Systems*. New York: McGraw-Hill, 1986.
17. Hayes-Roth, F., et al. *Building Expert Systems*. Reading, MA: Addison-Wesley, 1983.
18. Hill, R. B., D. C. Wolfgram, and D. E. Broadbent. "Expert Systems and the Man Machine Interface." *Expert Systems* (October 1986).
19. Hillman, D. "Bridging Acquisition and Representation." *AI Expert* (November 1988).
20. Kearney, M. "Making Knowledge Engineering Productive." *AI Expert* (July 1990).
21. Kim, J., and J. F. Courtney. "A Survey of Knowledge Acquisition Techniques and Their Relevance to Managerial Problem Domains." *Decision Support Systems* 4 (October 1988).

22. LeClair, S. R. "A Multiple-Expert Knowledge System Architecture for Manufacturing Decision Analysis," Ph.D. diss., Arizona State Univ., 1985.
23. McGraw, K. L., and B. K. Harbison-Briggs. *Knowledge Acquisition, Principles and Guidelines.* Englewood Cliffs, N.J.: Prentice-Hall, 1989.
24. McGraw, K. L., and C. R. Westphal, eds. *Readings in Knowledge Acquisition.* New York: Ellis Horwood, 1990.
25. Marcot, B. "Testing Your Knowledge Base." *AI Expert* (August 1987).
26. Michie, D., ed. *Introductory Readings in Expert Systems.* New York: Gordon & Breach, 1984.
27. O'Keefe, R. M., et al. "Validating Expert System Performance." *IE Expert* (Winter 1987).
28. Parsaye, K. "Acquiring and Verifying Knowledge Automatically." *AI Expert* (May 1988).
29. Prerau, D. S. "Knowledge Acquisition in the Development of a Large Expert System." *AI Magazine* (November 1988).
30. Tuthill, G. S. *Knowledge Engineering.* Blue Ridge Summit, PA: TAB Books, 1990.
31. Wolfgram, D. D., et al. *Expert Systems.* New York: John Wiley & Sons, 1987.

Chapter 14

Knowledge Representation

Once knowledge is acquired it needs to be organized. The software program that hosts the knowledge is called a knowledge base. A knowledge base can be organized in several different configurations to facilitate fast inferencing (or reasoning) from the knowledge. The topics in this chapter are divided into these sections:

14.1   Introduction

Most artificial intelligence systems are made up of two basic parts: a knowledge base and an inference mechanism (engine). The knowledge base contains facts about objects in the chosen domain and their relationships. It can also contain concepts, theories, practical procedures, and their associations. The knowledge base forms the system's source of intelligence and is used by the inference mechanism to reason and draw conclusions.

The inference mechanism is a set of procedures that are used to examine the knowledge base in an orderly manner to answer questions, solve problems, or make decisions within the domain. Much of the inference knowledge is generic and it can be used to solve many different problems, especially if they have a similar structure. For example, in diagnosing malfunctions in a human, a machine, or an organization, we may use the same problem-solving procedures, and all can be constructed with the same inference engine.

Knowledge can be organized in one or more configurations or networks. Furthermore, the knowledge in the knowledge base may be organized differently from that in the inference engine.

A variety of **knowledge representation** schemes have been developed over the years. They share two common characteristics. First, they can be programmed with existing computer languages and stored in memory. Second, they are designed so that the facts and other knowledge contained within them can be used in reasoning. That is, the knowledge base contains a data structure that can be manipulated by an inference system that uses search and pattern-matching techniques on the knowledge base to answer questions, draw conclusions, or otherwise perform an intelligent function.

The representation methods discussed in this chapter are: logic, semantic networks, scripts, lists, tables, trees, "O-A-V triplets," production rules and frames.

14.2   Representation in Logic

The general form of any logical process is illustrated in Figure 14.1. First, information is given, statements are made, or observations are noted. These form the inputs to the logical process and are called *premises*. The premises are used by the logical process to create the output which consists of conclusions called *inferences*. With this process, facts that are known to be true can be used to derive new facts that also must be true.

For a computer to perform reasoning using logic, some method must be used to convert statements and the reasoning process into a form suitable for manipulation by a computer. The result is what is known as *symbolic logic*. It is a system of rules and procedures that permit the drawing of inferences from various premises using a variety of logical techniques.

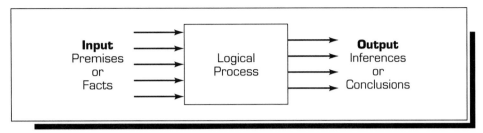

FIGURE 14.1 Using Logic to Reason

The two basic forms of computational logic are **propositional logic** (or propositional calculus) and **predicate logic** (or **predicate calculus**). The term *calculus* here does not refer to the differential and integral calculus which we ordinarily associate with the term. Instead, calculus simply refers to a system for computing.

Propositional Logic

A proposition is nothing more than a statement that is either true or false. Once we know what it is, it becomes a premise that can be used to derive new propositions or inferences. Rules are used to determine the truth (T) or falsity (F) of the new proposition.

In propositional logic we use symbols such as letters of the alphabet to represent various propositions, premises, or conclusions. For example, consider the propositions used as follows in this simple deductive process:

> Statement: A = The mail carrier comes Monday through Saturday.
> Statement: B = Today is Sunday.
> Conclusion: C = The mail carrier will not come today.

Single, simple propositions like these are not very interesting or useful. Real-world problems involve many interrelated propositions. To form more complex premises, two or more propositions can be combined using logical connectives. These connectives or operators are designated as AND, OR, NOT, IMPLIES, and EQUIVALENT.

By using symbols for the various propositions and relating them with connectives, a complete set of premises with resulting conclusions can be expressed. The resulting symbolic expression looks very much like a math formula. It can then be manipulated using the rules of propositional logic to infer new conclusions.

Predicate Calculus

Although propositional logic is a knowledge representation alternative, it is not very useful in artificial intelligence. Since propositional logic deals primarily with complete statements and whether they are true or false, its ability to represent real-world knowledge is limited. (It cannot make assertions about the individual elements that make up the statements.) Consequently, AI uses *predicate logic* instead.

Predicate logic is a more sophisticated form of logic that uses all the same concepts and rules of propositional logic. It gives added ability to represent knowledge in finer detail. Predicate logic permits you to *break a statement down into component parts, namely an object, a characteristic of the object, or some assertion about the object.* In addition, predicate calculus lets you use variables and functions of variables in a symbolic logic statement. Predicate calculus is the basis for the AI language called PROLOG (programming in logic).

In predicate calculus, a proposition is divided into two parts, the arguments (or objects) and the predicate (or assertion). The arguments are the individuals or objects about which an assertion is made. The predicate is the assertion made about them. In a common English language sentence, objects and individuals are nouns that serve as subjects and objects of the sentence. For further details refer to Winston [12]. Once knowledge is organized as either propositional or predicate logic, it is ready for inferencing.

14.3   Semantic Networks

Semantic networks are basically graphic depictions of knowledge composed of *nodes* and *links* that show hierarchical relationships between objects.

A simple semantic network is shown in Figure 14.2. It is made up of a number of circles, or nodes, which represent objects and descriptive information about those objects. Objects can be any physical item such as a book, car, desk, or even a person. Nodes can also be concepts, events, or actions. A concept might be the relationship of supply and demand in economics, an event such as a picnic or an election, or an action such as building a house or writing a book. Attributes of an object can also be used as nodes. These might represent size, color, class, age, origin, or other characteristics. In this way, detailed information about objects can be presented.

The nodes are interconnected by links, or arcs. These arcs show the *relationships* between the various objects and descriptive factors. Some of the most common arcs are of the is-a or has-a type. Is-a is used to show class relationship, that is, that an object belongs to a larger class or category of objects. Has-a links are used to identify characteristics or attributes of the object nodes. Other arcs are used for definitional purposes.

Now refer to the example in Figure 14.2. As you can see, the central figure in the domain of knowledge is a person called Sam. One link shows that Sam is a man and that man is a human being or is part of a class called humans. Another arc from Sam shows that he is married to Kay. Additional arcs show that Kay is a woman and that a woman is, in turn, a human being. Other links show that Sam and Kay have a child, Joe, who is a boy and goes to school.

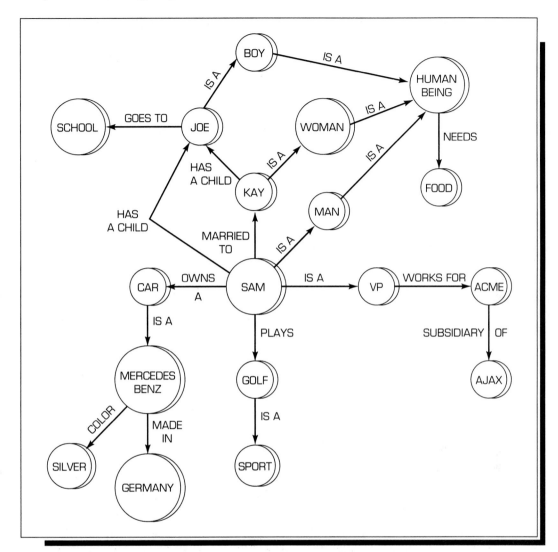

FIGURE 14.2 Representation of Knowledge in a Semantic Network

Some nodes and arcs show other characteristics about Sam. For example, he is a vice president for Acme, a company that is a subsidiary of Ajax, a large corporation. We also see that Sam plays golf, which is a sport. Further, Sam owns a Mercedes Benz whose color is silver. We also see that Mercedes Benz is a type of car that is made in Germany.

One of the most interesting and useful facts about a semantic network is that it can show **inheritance.** Since the semantic network is basically a hierarchy, the various characteristics of some nodes actually inherit the characteristics of others. As an example, consider the links showing that Sam is a man and a man is, in turn, a human being. Here, Sam inherits the property of human being. We can ask the question, "Does Sam need food?" Because of the inheritance links, we can say that he needs food if human beings need food.

Although the semantic network is graphic in nature, it does not appear this way in a computer. Instead, the various objects and their relationships are stated in verbal terms, and these are programmed into the computer using one of several different kinds of languages. Searching semantic networks (especially large ones) may be difficult. Therefore, the technique is used mainly for analysis purposes. Then, a transformation to rules or frames is executed. Semantic nets are used basically as a visual representation of relationships, and they can be combined with other representation methods. Their major advantages and limitations are summarized in Table 14.1.

14.4   Scripts, Lists, Tables, and Trees

Scripts

A **script** is a knowledge representation scheme describing a *sequence of events*. Some of the elements of a typical script include entry conditions, props, roles, tracks, and scenes. The *entry conditions* describe situations that must be

TABLE 14.1 Advantages and Limitations of Semantic Networks

Advantages

The semantic net offers flexibility in adding new nodes and links to a definition as needed. The visual representation is easy to understand.

The semantic net offers economy of effort since a node can inherit characteristics from other nodes to which it has an is-a relationship.

The semantic net functions in a manner similar to that of human information storage.

Since nodes in semantic nets have the ability to inherit relationships from other nodes, a net can support the ability to reason and create definition statements between nonlinked nodes.

Limitations

No standards exist for the definition of nodes or relationships between and among nodes.

The power of inheriting characteristics from one node to another offers potential difficulties with exceptions.

The perception of the situation by the domain expert can place relevant facts at inappropriate points in the network.

Procedural knowledge is difficult to represent in a semantic net, since sequence and time are not explicitly represented.

Source: G. S. Tuthill, *Knowledge Engineering: Concepts and Practices for Knowledge-based Systems* (Blue Ridge Summit, PA.: TAB Books, 1989).

satisfied before events in this script can occur or be valid. *Props* refer to objects that are used in the sequence of events that occur. *Roles* refer to the people involved in the script. The result is conditions that exist after the events in the script have occurred. *Track* refers to variations that might occur in a particular script. And finally, *scenes* describe the actual sequence of events that occur.

A script is useful in predicting what will happen in a specific situation. Even though certain events have not been observed, the script permits the computer to predict what will happen to whom and when. If the computer triggers a script, questions can be asked and accurate answers derived with little or no original input knowledge. Scripts are a particularly useful form of knowledge representation because there are so many stereotypical situations and events that people use every day. Knowledge like this is generally taken for granted, but in computer problem-solving situations, such knowledge must often be simulated to solve a particular problem using artificial intelligence.

Lists

A **list** is a written series of related items. It can be a list of names of people you know, things to buy at the grocery store, things to do this week, or products in a catalog.

Lists are normally used to represent hierarchical knowledge where objects are grouped, categorized, or graded according to rank or relationship. Objects are first divided into groups or classes of similar items. Then, their relationships are shown by linking them together. The simplest form is one list, but a hierarchy is created when two or more related lists are combined.

Another way to look at related lists is as an outline. An outline is nothing more than a hierarchical summary of some subject. The various segments of the outline are lists.

Decision Tables

In a **decision table,** knowledge is organized in a spreadsheet format, using columns and rows. The table is divided into two parts. First, a list of attributes is developed, and for each attribute all possible values are listed. Then, a list of conclusions is developed. Finally, the different configurations of attributes are matched against the conclusion.

Knowledge for the table is collected in knowledge acquisition sessions. Once constructed, the knowledge in the table can be used as input to other knowledge representation methods. It is not possible to make inferences with the domain tables by themselves, except when rule induction is used.

Decision tables are easy to understand and program. For further discussion see Carrico et al. [3].

Decision Trees

Decision trees are related to tables and are used frequently in system analysis (in non-AI systems). According to Carrico et al. [3], a decision tree may be thought of as a hierarchical semantic network bound by a series of rules. It couples search strategy with knowledge relationships. The trees are similar to the decision trees used in decision theory. They are composed of nodes representing goals and links representing decisions. The root of the tree is on the left and the leaves are on the right. All terminal nodes except the root node are instances of a primary goal.

Decision trees, like rules, depict a strong sense of cause and effect. Their major advantage is that they can simplify the knowledge acquisition process. Knowledge diagramming is frequently more natural to experts than formal representation methods (such as rules or frames). For further discussion see Gruber and Cohen [5]. Decision trees can easily be converted to rules. The conversion can be executed by a computer program.

14.5   Objects, Attributes, and Values

A common way to represent knowledge is to use objects, attributes, and values, the **O-A-V triplet**. *Objects* may be physical or conceptual. *Attributes* are the characteristics of the objects. *Values* are the specific measures of the attributes in a given situation. Table 14.2 presents several O-A-V triplets. An object may have several attributes. An attribute itself may be considered as a new object with its own attributes. For example, in Table 14.2 a bedroom is an attribute of a house but also an object of its own. O-A-V triplets are used both in frame and semantic network representations.

The O-A-V triplet can be viewed as a variation of either frames or semantic networks. For example, the semantic representation of Figure 14.2 includes a segment that is shown in Figure 14.3. We added to this segment the O-A-V triplet. Thus, objects and values are designated as nodes, while attributes are designated as arcs. The O-A-V triplet can be used in both static and dynamic presentations (in dynamic presentations the object value portions can change). O-A-V triplets can be used to show order and relationships by using a tree structure. For example, they can show inheritance, causal relationships, or part-to-subpart links.

TABLE 14.2   Representative O-A-V Items

Object	Attributes	Values
House	Bedrooms	2, 3, 4, etc.
House	Color	Green, white, brown
Admission to a university	Grade-point average	3.0, 3.5, 3.7, etc.
Inventory control	Level of inventory	15, 20, 30, etc.
Bedroom	Size	$9' \times 10'$, $10' \times 12'$, etc.

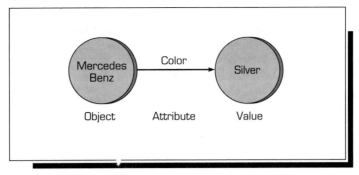

FIGURE 14.3   O-A-V Triplet Representation

14.6   Production Rules

Production systems were developed by Newell and Simon for their model of human cognition (see Chapter 11 and [20]). The basic idea of these systems is that knowledge is presented as **production rules** in the form of condition-action pairs: "IF this *condition* (or premise or antecedent) occurs, THEN some action (or result, or conclusion, or consequence) will (or should) occur." Consider these two examples:

1. IF the stop light is red AND you have stopped, THEN a right turn is okay.
2. (This example from an internal control procedure includes a probability.) IF the client uses purchase requisition forms AND the purchase orders are approved and purchasing is segregated from receiving, accounts payable, AND inventory records, THEN there is strongly suggestive evidence (90 percent probability) that controls to prevent unauthorized purchases are adequate.

Each production rule in a knowledge base implements an autonomous chunk of expertise that can be developed and modified independently of other rules. When combined and fed to the inference engine, the set of rules behaves synergistically, yielding better results than that of the sum of the results of the individual rules. In reality, knowledge-based rules are not independent. They quickly become highly interdependent. For example, adding a new rule may conflict with an existing rule, or it may require a revision of attributes and/or rules.

Production systems are composed of production rules, working memory, and a control. Such systems are useful as mechanisms for controlling the interaction between statements of declarative and procedural knowledge. Production systems have been used in many ES, as well as in many commercially available ES development tools.

Finally, rules can be viewed, in some sense, as a simulation of the cognitive behavior of human experts. According to this view, rules are not just a neat formalism to represent knowledge in a computer; rather, they represent a model of actual human behavior.

Rules may appear in different forms. Some examples follow:

- *IF premise, THEN conclusion.*
  IF your income is high, THEN your chance of being audited by the IRS is high.
- *Conclusion, IF premise.*
  Your chance of being audited is high, IF your income is high.
- *Inclusion of ELSE.*
  IF your income is high OR your deductions are unusual, THEN your chance of being audited by the IRS is high, ELSE your chance of being audited is low.
- *More complex rules.*
  IF credit rating is high AND salary is more than $30,000, OR assets are more than $75,000, AND pay history is not "poor," THEN approve a loan up to $10,000, and list the loan in category "B." The action part may include additional information: THEN "approve the loan" and "refer to an agent."

The IF side of a rule may include dozens of IFs. The THEN side may include several parts as well.

Knowledge and Inference Rules

Two types of rules are common in AI: knowledge and inference. Knowledge rules, or **declarative rules,** state all the facts and relationships about a problem. Inference rules or **procedural rules,** on the other hand, advise on how to solve a problem, given that certain facts are known.

For example, assume you are in the business of buying and selling gold. Knowledge rules may look like this:

- RULE 1: IF international conflict begins
  THEN the price of gold goes up.
- RULE 2: IF inflation rate declines
  THEN the price of gold goes down.
- RULE 3: IF the international conflict lasts more than seven days and IF it is in the Middle East
  THEN buy gold.

Inference (procedural) rules may look like this:

- RULE 1: IF the data needed is not in the system
  THEN request it from the user.
- RULE 2: IF more than one rule applies
  THEN deactivate any rules that add no new data.

Inference rules contain rules about rules. These types of rules are also called **metarules.** They pertain to other rules (or even to themselves).

The knowledge engineer separates the two types of rules: *knowledge rules* go to the knowledge base, whereas *inference rules* become part of the inference engine.

Advantages and Limitations of Rules

Rule representation is especially applicable when there is a need to recommend a course of action based on observable events. It has several major advantages:

- Rules are easy to understand. They are communicable because they are a natural form of knowledge.
- Inference and explanations are easily derived.
- Modifications and maintenance are relatively easy.
- Uncertainty is easily combined with rules.
- Each rule is usually independent of all others.

The major limitations of rule representation are as follows:

- Complex knowledge requires many, many (thousands of) rules. This may create problems in both using the system and maintaining it.
- Builders like rules; therefore they try to enforce all knowledge into rules rather than looking for more appropriate representations.
- Systems with many rules may have a search limitation in the control program. Some programs have difficulty in evaluating rule-based systems and making inferences.

The major characteristics of rules are summarized in Table 14.3.

TABLE 14.3   Characteristics of Rule Representation

	First Part	**Second Part**
Names	Premise ⟶ Antecedent ⟶ Situation ⟶ IF ⟶	Conclusion Consequence Action THEN
Nature	Conditions, similar to declarative knowledge	Resolutions, similar to procedural knowledge
Size	Can have many IFs	Usually one conclusion
Statements	AND statements	All conditions must be true for a conclusion to be true
	OR statements	If any of the OR statement is true, the conclusion is true

14.7 Frames*

Definitions and Overview

A frame is a data structure that includes all the knowledge about a particular object. This knowledge is organized in a special hierarchical structure that permits a diagnosis of knowledge independence. Frames are basically an application of **object-oriented programming** for AI and ES. (For an overview of object-oriented programming, see Appendix 14-A.)

Each **frame** describes one *object*. To describe what frames are and how the knowledge is organized in a frame we need to use a special terminology, which is presented in Table 14.4. The specific terms will be defined as we encounter them.

Frames, as in frames of reference, provide a concise, structural representation of knowledge in a natural manner. In contrast to other representation methods, the values that describe one object are grouped together into a single unit called a frame. Thus, a frame encompasses complex objects, entire situations, or a management problem as a single entity. The knowledge is partitioned in a frame into slots. A slot can describe declarative knowledge (such as the color of a car) or procedural knowledge (such as "activate a certain rule if a value exceeds a given level"). The major capabilities of frames are summarized in Table 14.5.

A frame is a relatively large block or chunk of knowledge about a particular object, event, location, situation, or other element. The frame describes that object in great detail. The detail is given in the form of slots that describe the various attributes and characteristics of the object or situation.

Frames are normally used to represent stereotyped knowledge or knowledge built on well-known characteristics and experiences. We all have a great deal of commonsense knowledge and experiences stored away in our brains that we call on to analyze a new object or experience to solve a problem. Frames can be used to represent that kind of knowledge.

TABLE 14.4 Terminology for Frames

Default	Instantiation
Demon	Master frame
Facet	Object
Hierarchy of frames	Slot
If needed	Value (entry)
Instance of	

*Section 14.7 is based, in part, on Arcidiancono [1].

TABLE 14.5 Capabilities of Frames

Ability to clearly document information about a domain model, for example, a plant's machines and their associated attributes

Related ability to constrain the allowable values that an attribute can take on

Modularity of information, permitting ease of system expansion and maintenance

More readable and consistent syntax for referencing domain objects in the rules

Platform for building a graphic interface with object graphics

Mechanism that will allow us to restrict the scope of facts considered during forward or backward chaining

Access to a mechanism that supports the inheritance of information down a class hierarchy

Source: R. A. Edmonds, *The Prentice-Hall Guide to Expert Systems* (Englewood Cliffs, NJ: Prentice-Hall, 1988), p. 102.

A frame provides a means of organizing knowledge in slots that contain characteristics and attributes. In physical form, a frame is somewhat like an outline with categories and subcategories. A typical frame describing an automobile is shown in Figure 14.4 on page 566. Note the slots describing attributes such as name of manufacturer, model, origin of manufacturer, type of car, number of doors, engine, and other characteristics.

Content of a Frame

A frame includes two basic elements: slots and facets.

A **slot** is a set of attributes that describe the object represented by the frame. For example, in the automobile frame, there are weight and engine slots.

Each slot contains one or more **facets.** The facets (sometimes called subslots) describe some knowledge or procedures about the attribute in the slot. Facets may take many forms:

- *Values.* These describe the attributes such as blue, red, and yellow for a color slot.
- *Default.* This facet is used if the slot is empty, that is, without any description. For example, in the car frame one default value is that the number of wheels on the car is four. It means that we can assume the car has four wheels unless otherwise indicated.
- *Range.* Range indicates what kind of information can appear in a slot (e.g., integer numbers only, two decimal points, 0 to 100).
- *If added.* This facet contains procedural information or attachments. It specifies an *action* to be taken when a value in the slot is *added* (or modified). Such procedural attachments are called **demons.**
- *If needed.* This facet is used in a case when no slot value is given. It triggers, much like the if-added situation, a procedure that goes out and gets or computes a value.
- *Other.* Slots may contain frames, rules, semantic networks, or any type of information.

> **Automobile Frame**
>
> Class of: Transportation
> Name of Manufacturer: Audi
> Origin of manufacturer: Germany
> Model: 5000 Turbo
> Type of car: Sedan
> Weight: 3300 lb.
> Wheelbase: 105.8 inches
> Number of doors: 4 (default)
> Transmission: 3-speed automatic
> Number of wheels: 4 (default)
> Engine: (Reference Engine Frame)
> • Type: In-line, overhead cam
> • Number of cylinders: 5
> Acceleration (procedural attachment)
> • 0–60: 10.4 seconds
> • Quarter mile: 17.1 seconds, 85 mph
> Gas mileage: 22 mpg average (procedural attachment)
>
> **Engine Frame**
>
> Cylinder bore: 3.19 inches
> Cylinder stroke: 3.4 inches
> Compression ratio: 7.8 to 1
> Fuel system: Injection with turbocharger
> Horsepower: 140 hp
> Torque: 160 ft/LB

FIGURE 14.4 Frame Describing an Automobile

Certain procedures can be attached to slots and used to derive slot values. For example, slot-specific heuristics are procedures for deriving slot values in a particular context. An important aspect of such procedures is that they can be used to direct the reasoning process. In addition to filling in slots, they can be triggered when a slot is filled.

In Figure 14.4, both acceleration and gas mileage are procedural attachments. They refer to a step-by-step procedure that would define how to acquire this information. For example, to determine acceleration, time needed to go from 0 to 60 mph and quarter-mile elapsed time would be described. A procedural attachment to determine gas mileage would state a procedure for filling the gas tank, driving a certain number of miles, determining the amount of gasoline used, and then computing the gas mileage in terms of miles per gallon.

Hierarchy of Frames

Most AI systems use a collection of frames that are linked together in a certain manner. For example, Figure 14.5 illustrates five frames. Frame A is connected in a slot named is-a to frame B. The same frame also has a capacity slot

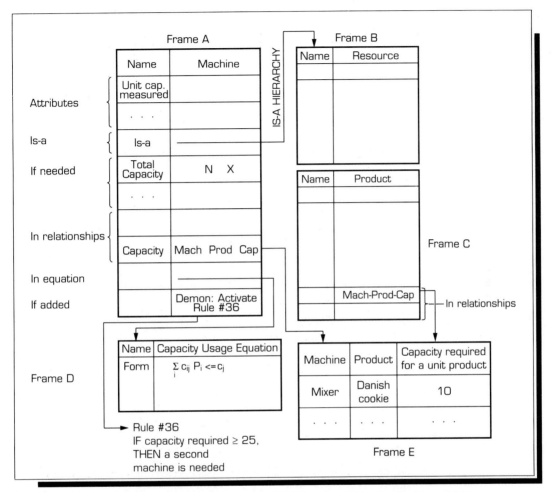

FIGURE 14.5 Hierarchy of Frames (*Source:* R. W. Blanning, "The Application of AI to Model Management," working paper, Owen Graduate School of Management, Vanderbilt Univ., 1988.)

that refers to a mixer (frame E) and a procedure (demon) which activates rule #36 when a second machine is added. Notice that these relationships create a hierarchy of frames. This hierarchy is not necessarily on a one-to-one basis. For example, frame A is formed from slots in frames A and C. Also, frame A is related to frames B, D, and E and to an independent rule.

Inheritance. The hierarchical arrangement of frames permits inheritance frames. Figure 14.6 shows a set of vehicles that are organized in a tree. The root of the tree is at the top, where the highest level of abstraction is represented. Frames at the bottom are called leaves of the tree. The hierarchy permits inheritance of characteristics. Each frame usually inherits the characteristics of all related frames of *higher levels*. For example, a passenger car has the *general prop-*

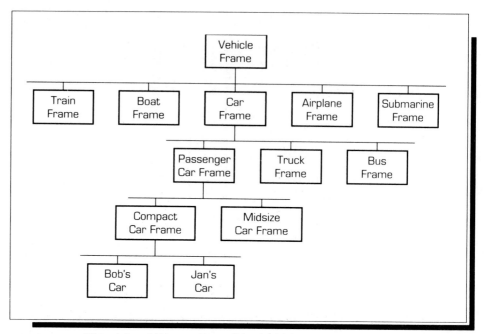

FIGURE 14.6 Hierarchy of Frames Describing Vehicles

erties of a car (e.g., engine, carburetor). These characteristics are expressed in the internal structure of the frame. **Inheritance** is the mechanism for passing such knowledge, which is provided in the value of the slots, from frame to frame.

Parent frames provide a more general description of the entities. The higher one is in the hierarchy, the more general is the description. Parent frames contain the attribute definitions. When we describe actual, physical objects, we **instantiate** the child's frame. The instances (child frames) contain actual values of the attributes. An example is shown in Figure 14.7.

Note that every parent is a child of a higher-level parent. In building a frame it is possible to have a frame where different slots are related to different parents. The only frame without a parent is the one at the top of the hierarchy. This frame is called a master frame. It is the *root frame* and it has the most general characteristics. The use of frame-based tools to build expert systems is demonstrated in Level5 Object.

14.8 Multiple Knowledge Representation

Knowledge representation should be able to support the tasks of acquiring and retrieving knowledge as well as subsequent reasoning. Several factors must be

Name: Compact Car			Name: Jan's Car Instance of: compact car frame	
Slots	**Facets**		**Slots**	**Facets**
Owner	Check registration list		Owner	Jan
Color	List, per manufacturer			
No. of cylinders			Color	Blue
Range	4 or 6			
If needed	Ask owner		No. of cylinders	6
Make			Make	Honda
Range	List of all manufacturers			
If needed	Ask owner			
Model	Use frame corresponding		Model	Accord
	to make			
Vintage (year)			Vintage (year)	1992
Range	1950–1992			
If needed	Ask owner			
(a) Parent frame			(b) Child frame	

FIGURE 14.7   Parent and Child Frames

taken into account in evaluating knowledge representations for these three tasks:

- Naturalness, uniformity, and understandability of the representation
- Degree to which knowledge is explicit (declarative) or embedded in procedural code
- Modularity and flexibility of the knowledge base
- Efficiency of knowledge retrieval and the heuristic power of the inference procedure. (Heuristic power is the reduction of the search space achieved by a heuristic mechanism.)

No single knowledge representation method is ideally suited by itself for all tasks (Table 14.6). When using several sources of knowledge simultaneously, the goal of uniformity may have to be sacrificed in favor of exploiting the benefits of **multiple knowledge representations,** each tailored to a different subtask. The necessity of translating among knowledge representations becomes a problem in such cases. Nevertheless, some recent ES shells use two or more knowledge representation schemes.

A rather successful combination of knowledge representation methods is that of production rules and frames. By themselves, production rules do not provide a totally effective representation facility for many ES applications. In

TABLE 14.6   Advantages and Disadvantages of Different Knowledge Representations

Scheme	Advantages	Disadvantages
Production rules	Simple syntax, easy to understand, simple interpreter, highly modular, flexible (easy to add to or modify)	Hard to follow hierarchies, inefficient for large systems, not all knowledge can be expressed as rules, poor at representing structured descriptive knowledge
Semantic networks	Easy to follow hierarchy, easy to trace associations, flexible	Meaning attached to nodes might be ambiguous, exception handling is difficult, difficult to program
Frames	Expressive power, easy to set up slots for new properties and relations, easy to create specialized procedures, easy to include default information and detect missing values	Difficult to program, difficult for inference, lack of inexpensive software
Formal logic	Facts asserted independently of use, assurance that all and only valid consequences are asserted (precision), completeness	Separation of representation and processing, inefficient with large data sets, very slow with large knowledge bases

particular, their expressive power is inadequate for defining terms and for describing domain objects and static relationships among objects.

The major inadequacies of production rules are in areas that are effectively handled by frames. A great deal of success, in fact, has been achieved by integrating frame and production-rule languages to form hybrid representation facilities that combine the advantages of both components. The frames provide a rich structural language for describing the objects referred to in the rules and a supporting layer of generic deductive capability about those objects that does not need to be explicitly dealt with in the rules. Frame taxonomies can also be used to partition, index, and organize a system's production rules. This capability makes it easier for the domain expert to construct and understand rules, and for the system designer to control when and for what purpose particular collections of rules are used by the system. For a detailed overview of frames and rule integration see Thuraisingham [10].

14.9   Representing Uncertainty—An Overview

One of the basic assumptions previously made was that any rule can have only one of two truth values (i.e., it is either true or false). In this sense, our previous discussion forced us to be exact about the truth of statements.

However, human knowledge is often inexact. Sometimes we are only partially sure about the truth of a statement and still have to make educated guesses to solve problems. Some concepts or words are inherently inexact. For instance, how can we exactly determine if someone is tall? The concept *tall* has a built-in form of inexactness. Moreover, we sometimes have to make decisions based on partial or incomplete data.

One source of uncertainty occurs when a user cannot provide a definite answer when prompted for a response. For example, when asked to provide a choice between responses B or C, the user may respond that he or she is 30 percent sure of B and 70 percent sure of C.

Another source of uncertainty stems from imprecise knowledge. In many situations, a set of symptoms can help indicate a particular diagnosis without being conclusive.

Yet another source of uncertainty is incomplete information. The information (or some parts of it) is simply not available or is too expensive or time consuming to obtain.

To deal with inexact knowledge in knowledge-based systems, it is necessary to understand how people process uncertain knowledge. In addition, in AI there is a need for inexact inference methods because we often have many inexact pieces of data and knowledge that need to be combined.

Several approaches are available to deal with uncertainty; none is clearly superior in all cases to all others. Most of the approaches are related to mathematical and statistical theories such as Bayesian statistics, Dempster and Shafer's belief functions, and fuzzy sets. Other approaches such as the use of neural computing (Chapter 17) are extremely promising but are still in a research stage.

14.10   Issues and Approaches in Uncertainty

The term **uncertainty** has several meanings. According to *Webster's New World Dictionary of the American Language,* uncertainty connotes doubtful, dubious, questionable, not sure, or problematical. Uncertainty ranges in implication from a mere lack of absolute sureness to such vagueness as to preclude anything more than guesswork.

Uncertainty in AI

In AI, the term *uncertainty* (also referred to as *approximate reasoning* or *inexact reasoning*) refers to a wide range of situations where the relevant information is deficient in one or more of the following ways:

- Information is partial.
- Information is not fully reliable (e.g., unreliable observation of evidence).
- Representation language is inherently imprecise.
- Information comes from multiple sources and it is conflicting.
- Information is approximate.
- Non-absolute cause-effect relationships exist.

In numeric context, uncertainty can be viewed as a value with a known error margin. When the possible range of values for a variable is *symbolic* rather than *numeric*, uncertainty can be represented in terms of qualitative expressions or by using fuzzy sets with a corresponding membership function.

Chapter Highlights

- The two main parts of any AI system are a knowledge base and an inferencing system.
- The knowledge base is made up of facts, concepts, theories, procedures, and relationships representing real-world knowledge about objects, places, events, people, and so on.
- The inference engine, or thinking mechanism, is a method of using the knowledge base, that is, reasoning with it to solve problems.
- To build the knowledge base, a variety of knowledge representation schemes are used including logic, lists, semantic networks, frames, scripts, and production rules.
- Propositional logic is a system of using symbols to represent and manipulate premises, prove or disprove propositions, and draw conclusions.
- Predicate calculus is a type of logic used to represent knowledge in the form of statements that assert information about objects or events and apply them in reasoning.
- Semantic networks are graphic depictions of knowledge that show relationships (arcs) between objects (nodes); common relationships are is-a, has-a, owns, made from, etc.
- A major property of networks is the inheritance of properties through the hierarchy.
- Scripts describe an anticipated sequence of events (like a story); they indicate the participants, the actions, and the setting.
- Decision trees and tables are frequently used in conjunction with other representation methods. They help to organize the knowledge acquired before it is coded.
- Production rules take the form of an IF-THEN statement such as: IF you drink too much, THEN you should not drive.
- There are two types of rules: declarative (describing facts) and procedural (inference).
- Rules are easy to understand and inferences can be easily derived from them.
- Complex knowledge may require tens of thousands of rules, which may create problems in both search and maintenance. Also, some knowledge cannot be represented in rules.
- A frame is a holistic data structure based on object-oriented programming technology.

- Frames are composed of slots that may contain different types of knowledge representation (e.g., rules, scripts, formulas).
- Frames can show complex relationships, graphic information, and inheritance in a concise manner. Their modular structure helps in inferences and maintenance.
- Integrating several knowledge representation methods is gaining popularity due to decreasing software costs and increasing capabilities.
- Knowledge may be inexact and experts may be uncertain at a given time.
- Uncertainty can be caused by several factors ranging from incomplete to unreliable information.

Key Words

decision table	instantiation	predicate logic
decision tree	knowledge	(calculus)
declarative rule	representation	procedural rule
demon	list	production rule
facet	metarule	propositional logic
frame	multiple knowledge	script
inexact (approximate)	representation	semantic network
reasoning	object-oriented	slot
inheritance	programming	uncertainty
inheritance methods	O-A-V triplet	

Questions for Review

1. What do we mean by knowledge representation?
2. What are some of the benefits of pictorial representation?
3. List the major knowledge representation methods.
4. What is propositional logic? Give an example.
5. Describe the sources of uncertainty and provide examples.
6. Define a semantic network.
7. List two advantages and two limitations of semantic networks.
8. Define O-A-V.
9. Define a "list" and give an example.
10. What is a production rule? Give an example.
11. What are the basic parts of a production rule? List several names for each part.
12. Define and contrast declarative and procedural knowledge.
13. What is an inference rule?
14. List two advantages and two disadvantages of rule representation.
15. Describe a frame. Give an example of a frame for sailboat or for kitchen.
16. What is an instantiation of a frame?
17. List three types of facets of a frame and explain their meaning.

18. What is a demon and what is its role in frames?
19. What is a slot in a frame?
20. Describe inheritance using an example.

Questions for Discussion

1. Give an example that illustrates the difference between propositional logic and predicate calculus.
2. Give examples of production rules in three different functional areas (e.g., marketing, accounting).
3. Why is frame representation considered more complex than production-rule representation? What are the advantages of the former over the latter?
4. It is said that multiple knowledge representation can be very advantageous. Why?
5. Compare knowledge representation to data representation in a database.
6. Provide an example that shows how a semantic network can depict inheritance.
7. Give an example that will show inheritance in a banking system or in a hospital.
8. Compare and contrast a knowledge and a procedural rule.
9. Review the benefits of frames over rules. In what cases would you use frames? (Give two examples.)
10. Explain this statement: Every parent is a child of a higher-level parent.
11. What are the major advantages of combining rules and frames?

Exercises

1. Construct a semantic network for the following situation: Mini is a robin; it lives in a nest which is on a pine tree in Ms. Wang's backyard. Robins are birds; they can fly and they have wings. They are an endangered species and they are protected by government regulations.
2. Write a frame that will describe the object robin, as described in the previous question.
3. Prepare a set of frames of an organization, given the following information:

   - Company: 1,050 employees, $130 million annual sales, Yuki Sunny is the president.
   - Departments: accounting, finance, marketing, production, personnel
   - Production department: five lines of production
   - Product: computers
   - Annual budget: $50,000 + $12,000 × number of computers produced
   - Materials: $6,000 per unit produced
   - Working days: 250 per year
   - Number of supervisors: one for each twelve employees
   - Range of number of employees: 400–500 per shift (two shifts per day). Overtime or part-time on a third shift is possible.

4. Write a narrative of Figure 14.2.
5. List attributes and values in the following objects: a lake, a stock market, a bridge, a car's engine. Use O-A-V representation.
6. Prepare a frame of a university that you know. Show two levels of hierarchies. Fill some slots, use a demon, and show at least one rule as it relates to a slot.
7. The following is a typical instruction set found in most cars' shop manuals (this one is based on Nissan's shop manual):

   ■ Topic: starter system troubles
   ■ Procedures: Try to crank the starter. If it is dead or cranks slowly, turn on the headlights. If the headlights are bright (or dim only slightly), the trouble is either in the starter itself, the solenoid, or in the wiring. To find the trouble, short the two large solenoid terminals together (not to ground). If the starter cranks normally, the problem is in the wiring or in the solenoid; check them up to the ignition switch. If the starter does not work normally check the bushings (see section 7-3 of the car manual for instructions). If the bushings are good send the starter to a test station or replace it. If the headlights are out or very dim, check the battery (see section 7-4 for instructions). If the battery is okay, check the wiring for breaks, shorts, and dirty connections. If the battery and connecting wires are not at fault, turn the headlights on and try to crank the starter. If the lights dim drastically, it is probably because the starter is shorted to ground. Have the starter tested or replace it. (Based on Carrico et al. [3].)

   Now translate the information into rules. (Can you do it in only six rules?)

8. Given a rule: IF animal lays eggs and animal has feathers THEN animal is bird. Prepare an O-A-V diagram of this rule. Hint: it is necessary to add an assumption to solve this problem.

References and Bibliography

1. Arcidiancono, T. "Computerized Reasoning," *PC Tech Journal* (May 1988).
2. Bench-Capon, T. *Knowledge Representation.* New York: Academic Press, 1990.
3. Carrico, M. A., et al. *Building Knowledge Systems: Developing and Managing Rule-based Applications.* New York: McGraw-Hill, 1989.
4. Fikes, R., and T. Kehler. "The Role of Frame-Based Representation in Reasoning." *Communications of ACM* 28 (September 1985).
5. Gruber, T. R., and P. R. Cohen. "Design for Acquisition Principles of Knowledge System Design to Facilitate Knowledge Acquisitions." *International Journal of Man-Machine Studies* (no. 2, 1987).
6. Khoshafian, S., and R. Abnous. *Object Orientation: Concepts, Languages, Databases, User Interface.* New York: John Wiley & Sons, 1990.
7. Owen, S. *Analogy for Automated Reasoning.* New York: Academic Press, 1990.

8. Ringland, G. A., and D. A. Duce. *Approaches to Knowledge Representation: An Introduction.* New York: John Wiley & Sons, 1988.

9. Stefik, M. J., et al. "Integrated Access-Oriented Programming into a Multiparadigm Environment." *IEEE Software* (January 1986).

10. Thuraisingham, B. "Rules to Frames and Frames to Rules." *AI Expert* (October 1989).

11. Tuthill, G. S. *Knowledge Engineering: Concepts and Practices for Knowledge-based Systems.* Blue Ridge Summit, PA: TAB Books, 1989.

12. Winston, P. H. *Artificial Intelligence,* 2nd ed. Reading, MA: Addison-Wesley, 1984.

APPENDIX 14-A: Object-oriented Programming*

Object-oriented programming (OOP) is a novel way of thinking about data, procedures, and relationships among them. Some people view OOP as a unique programming language; others claim that it is *not* a programming language at all. OOP is a design principle that views descriptive and procedural attributes of an object as being associated with each individual object. Thus, each object can receive and send its own messages and perform independent actions (e.g., modify itself).

OOP features can be added to most existing programming languages for the purpose of increasing programmers' productivity as well as for making these languages more flexible. A comparison between traditional and OOP programming approaches is shown in Table 14-A.1.

TABLE 14-A.1 Comparison of Traditional and Object-oriented Programming Approaches

Traditional	Object-oriented
Procedures (routines)	Methods
Data	Instances (objects)
Procedure/invocation	Messages (events)
Data types	Classes
No inheritance	Inheritance
Programmer decides what to call when	System decides what to call when

Source: K. Hinsch et al., "Object-oriented Programming: Its Role in Computing," *Library Software Review* (January–February 1990).

---

*This appendix is based, in part, on P. Harmon, et al. *Expert Systems Tools and Applications* (New York: John Wiley & Sons, 1988) and on G. S. Howard, "Object-Oriented Programming Explained," *Journal of Systems Management* (July 1988).

Benefits

OOP eliminates data dependency problems that exist in conventional programming. Thus, the complexity of information systems is dramatically reduced. Programmers' productivity can also be increased.

Frames

When AI programmers develop OOP environments, they tend to refer to objects as *frames*. Thus, when we talk about frame representation we essentially talk about using OOP in building knowledge bases.

Key Concepts

Several key concepts underlie OOP.

Objects. An object can be physical or it can be a concept or an event. It can be anything that we want to describe. For example, an object can be a car, a university, a course that you take, or a computer program. Objects are described by a modular software program; that is, an object software is composed of several independent software units.

Encapsulation. Data (and other representations) are packaged inseparably in capsules that describe an object (Figure 14-A.1).

Reusability. An object can be made sufficiently general and self-contained so it can be a component or a module that is "plugged in" when a system is programmed.

Inheritance. Objects inherit properties from other objects.

Multiple Inheritance. Inheritance can be singular or multiple.

Execution. In contrast to other programming languages that execute programming in a procedural, nonprocedural, functional (such as LISP), or logical (such as PROLOG) manner, in OOP a program execution is regarded as a physical

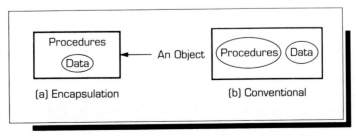

FIGURE 14-A.1 Encapsulation Versus Conventional Organization

model. Such a model simulates the behavior of either a real or an imaginary part of the system.

Messages, Methods, and Responses

Messages. An object can be accessed only by the private code surrounding the object. One reason to access an object is to send messages to it. Each message consists of a *selector*, which tells the object what to do with the message, and an *argument*. The argument is optional and its purpose is to explain, comment, provide instruction, or clarify the content of the message.

Methods. A method is a private procedure in an object that tells us what to do with the message and how to do it. In other words, it specifies what can be done with the object. Since each object owns its methods, objects respond differently to the same message. This is a powerful property of OOP. The object, based on the available knowledge, knows which is the most appropriate method to use.

Responses. Once a message has been received, the object sends a response to other objects or to the system, based on the selected method.

The World of Objects

Each object is considered a small world unto itself. It contains data and methods (procedures). It can receive and send messages. However, objects are related to other objects through a *hierarchy* of classes and subclasses of objects. Such a world is created by a process called *instantiation*.

Instantiation. In OOP, we may create objects by taking a copy of a preexisting object (called the parent), and then telling that object how it is to behave differently from the parent. For example, a parent object may be a "vehicle." By taking this object and adding a property "can fly," the vehicle becomes a new object, called "airplane." We refer to the airplane as a child (or offspring). We can create more objects from the vehicle (e.g., boat, car, train), and we can create objects from each of the new objects. For example, we can create a sailboat and a motorboat from a boat object. The process of creating new objects is called instantiation.

Another way to look at instantiation is simply by viewing it as *naming* the object or replacing variables by constants. For example, if the object is a bank account, then a balance of, say, $2,000 is an account instance; the balance is a variable. Once we place a value of 2,000, we instantiate the slot called value. If the object is a city, then Nashville is an instance of that object.

Classes and Inheritance. Organisms are grouped by biologists into classes and subclasses. For example, the class "animal" contains subclasses "bird" and "mammal." Classes inherit characteristics from their upper classes. A similar organization is available in OOP, as shown in Figure 14-A.2.

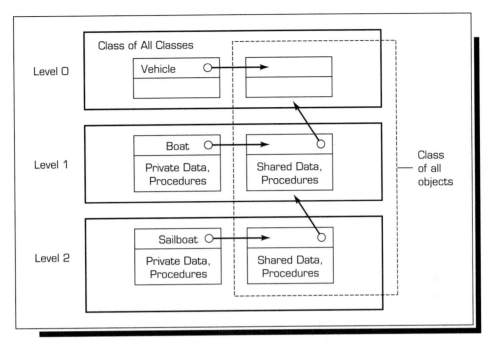

FIGURE 14-A.2 Organization in Object-oriented Programming

When an object is created, it contains two parts. The left portion in Figure 14-A.2 shows the new information unique to those objects. The right side (in broken lines) shows information that points to the parent. Objects in lower levels inherit data and procedures from an upper level, except that private data and procedures are added. The ultimate source of data is the object at the top. It is called the class of all classes (or master object), and it has neither a parent nor private data. Everything held in common between a set of objects is the *class* of the objects.

When a message is sent to an object (say, the sailboat), it checks its private data and procedures to see how to handle the message. If it cannot find such information, it moves to its parent's private file and so on. This may continue, if needed, to the class of all classes whose data and procedures are shared with everybody else. This shared information is what we call the class of the objects.

OOP and Languages

OOP can be written in regular languages such as COBOL or BASIC. However, programming is usually done with special languages.

Smalltalk. Smalltalk is a programming environment within which the boundaries among operating systems, compilers, editors, utilities, data, and application programs become blurred. Hundreds of classes and methods are provided with an extensive use of icons, windows, and a mouse. Related products are Smalltalk-80 and Smalltalk V.

C++. C++ is a C implementation of OOP, specially suited for the UNIX environment. A similar product is Objective C.

LOOPS. LOOPS is a language for object-oriented representation. It also supports rule-based, access-oriented, and procedure-oriented representation methods. Its principal characteristic is the integration of its four programming schemes. For example, rules and rule sets are considered LOOPS objects. The support system contains display-oriented debugging tools, such as break packages and editors.

Other Languages. Several other languages are available, for example Actor, Object Pascal, HyperTalk, and CLOS. For use of OOP in AI, see Retting et al. [2].

Access-oriented Programming

In *access-oriented programming,* gathering or sorting data can cause procedures to be invoked. This complements object-oriented programming. In object-oriented programming, when one object sends a message to another, the receiving object may change its data. Here, when one object changes its data, a message may be sent out. Access programs are composed of two parts: computing and monitoring the computations.

Figure 14-A.3 shows a simulation of city street traffic (based on Stefik et al. [4]). The program includes objects such as city blocks, cars, emergency vehicles, and traffic lights that exchange messages to simulate traffic interactions. The display controller has objects for traffic *icons,* viewing transformations, and windows that display different parts of the city connected to the simulation objects by active values. The simulator represents the dynamics of traffic. The user can interact and control the view in the traffic windows. Access-oriented programming connects the simulation model with its numeric analysis to the graphic display. For example, when a light turns green, a message is sent to certain vehicles to move. The program computes the initial velocity and position. When the cars move, their position on the display is updated. The user can see the cars actually moving. Access-oriented and object-oriented programming provide interactive simulation and animation capabilities.

These representation methods are supported by special software (such as LOOPS) and can be combined with ES shells. An example of such a combination is KEE. For further details, see Stefik et al. [4].

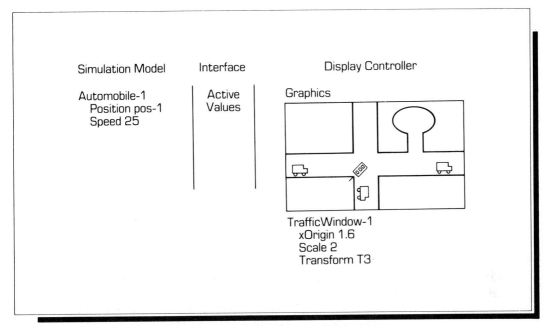

FIGURE 14-A.3   Simulation of a City Street. (*Source:* © 1986, IEEE.)

Questions for Appendix 14-A

1. What is encapsulation? What is its major advantage?
2. Explain how OOP works with respect to messages.
3. What is a class of OOP?
4. How is OOP related to frames?
5. Relate access-oriented programming to object-oriented programming.

References and Bibliography for Appendix 14-A

1. Hinsch, K. et al. "Object-oriented Programming: Its Role in Computing." *Library Software Review* (January-February, 1990).
2. Retting, M., et al. "Object-oriented Programming in AI: New Choices." *AI Expert* (January 1989).
3. Shoemaker, S. "Train. Pas: An Example of Object-Oriented Programming." *PC AI* (September/October, 1990).
4. Stefik, M. J., et al. "Integrating Access-Oriented Programming into a Multi-paradigm Environment." *IEEE Software* (January 1986).
5. Tello, E. R. *Object-oriented Programming for AI*. Reading, MA: Addison-Wesley, 1988.
6. Thomas, D. "What's in an Object." *Byte* (March 1989).

APPENDIX 14-B: How to Build a Knowledge Base (Rule-Based) System

Building a small knowledge base with a shell is fairly simple. Here is an example:

Topic: Using Expert Systems for wine and food pairing

Trying to decide on an appropriate wine match to a certain food is not a simple task. Delegating the decision to a waiter can be a risky proposition in some restaurants (a part-time waiter, who happens to be an undergraduate student, may know very little about wines).

However, this ES can help. Let's build such a system.

Step 1.   Specify the problem. Pairing wine and food at a restaurant.
Step 2.   Name the system (Sommelier in our case).
Step 3.   Write a starting text.
Step 4.   Decide on an appropriate coding for uncertainty situation (e.g., 0 to 10, 0 to 100, −100 to 100, etc.). We will use 0 to 10 in our case.
Step 5.   Decide on any other parameters as required by the shell (e.g., use all rules or only some rules, threshold levels, etc.).
Step 6.   Make a list of the choices or alternatives. In our case, twelve possible wines are considered. They include aged cabernet sauvignon blanc, crisp chardonnay, gewürztraminer, merlot, Pinot noir, and zinfandel.
Step 7.   Build the what-if rules.

Write the rules in the standard format required by the shell (every shell does it differently). EXSYS EL uses the concept of qualifiers. For example, it is known that the wine depends on the menu selection; you may have meat, fish, poultry, or pasta. You may have an appetizer as well.

Each of these is called a qualifier. For example Qualifier No. 1 is the meat menu selection. It can assume the following values: (1) prime rib, (2) grilled steak, and (3) filet mignon. These are labeled the values of the qualifier.

Now let's say that your rule is:

```
IF the meat menu selection is prime rib
      THEN Pinot noir,              confidence = 9/10
   AND merlot,                      confidence = 8/10
   AND aged cabernet sauvignon,     confidence = 6/10
```

To build this rule, you insert the number of the qualifier (No. 1); then you insert the appropriate value (1. for prime rib). This will form, automatically, the IF side of the rule. Then you call the choices (Step 6) and insert the appropriate values in the THEN side with the appropriate confidence level. In this case four different wines are appropriate, but Pinot noir is the best match.

Note: The reason why the system may not recommend Pinot noir is that other rules need to be consulted. For example, what is the appetizer and what is the cost of the wine? In our first prototype we included fourteen rules. Each rule may include notes and references regarding the specific rule. They constitute a knowledge base that is available on a disk from your instructor. Try it; it is not perfect but it works.

Step 8. Prepare any concluding note that you want the user to see at the end of a consultation.

Note: This student project, entitled "Your Sommelier," was done by Lisa Sandoval, a graduate student at California State University, Long Beach, CA.

Chapter 15

Inferences, Explanations, and Uncertainty

In Chapters 13 and 14, we saw how knowledge is acquired and then organized in the knowledge base. In this chapter, we consider the specific reasoning strategies that can be used to draw inferences. We also discuss the central strategies that can be used to guide a knowledge-based system on how to use the stored knowledge and how to communicate with the user. Finally, we show how to make inferences in an uncertain environment. The following topics are addressed in this chapter:

15.1   Inferencing: An Overview

Once the knowledge base is completed it is ready to be used. To do so, we need a computer program that will enable us to access the knowledge for the purpose of making inferences and decisions and for problem solving. This program is an algorithm that controls some reasoning process and it is usually referred to as the inference engine or the control program. In rule-based systems it is also referred to as the rule interpreter.

The control program directs the search through the knowledge base. The process may involve the application of inference rules in what is called pattern matching. The control program decides which rule to investigate, which alternative to eliminate, and which attribute to match. The most popular control programs, forward and backward chaining, are described in this chapter.

Before we examine the specific inferencing techniques used in AI, it might be interesting to see how people, which AI attempts to mimic, reason.

There are several ways in which people reason and solve problems. An interesting way to view the problem-solving process is one in which people draw on "sources of power." Lenat [10] identified nine such sources:

1. Formal methods—formal reasoning methods (e.g., logical deduction)
2. Heuristic reasoning—IF-THEN rules
3. Focus—common sense related toward more or less specific goals
4. Divide and conquer—dividing complex problems into subproblems
5. Parallelism—neural processors (perhaps a million) operating in parallel
6. Representation—ways of organizing pieces of information
7. Analogy—being able to associate and relate concepts
8. Synergy—the whole being greater than the sum of its parts
9. Serendipity—luck, or "fortuitous accidents."

These sources of power range from the purely deductive reasoning best handled by computer systems to inductive reasoning that is more difficult to computerize. Lenat believes that the future of AI lies in finding ways to tap those sources that have only begun to be exploited.

These sources of power are translated to specific reasoning or inference methods. The major inference and control approaches in AI are presented next.

15.2   Categories of Reasoning

Deductive Reasoning

Deductive reasoning is a process in which *general premises* are used to obtain a specific inference. Reasoning moves from a general principle to a specific conclusion. To illustrate this process, let's take a look at an example.

The deductive process generally begins with a statement of the premises and conclusions. It generally consists of three parts: a major premise, a minor premise, and a conclusion. Almost any situation can be put into this form for deductive reasoning purposes:

> Major premise: I do not jog when the temperature exceeds 90 degrees.
> Minor premise: Today the temperature is 93 degrees.
> Conclusion: Therefore, I will not jog today.

To use deductive reasoning, the problem must generally be formatted in this way. Once this format has been achieved, the conclusion must be valid if the premises are true. The whole idea is to develop new knowledge from previously given knowledge.

Inductive Reasoning

Inductive reasoning uses a number of established facts or premises to draw some general conclusion. An example will illustrate this process. Again, a statement is used to express the problem.

> Premise: Faulty diodes cause electronic equipment failure.
> Premise: Defective transistors cause electronic equipment failures.
> Premise: Defective integrated circuits cause electronic equipment
>   malfunction.
> Conclusion: Therefore, defective semiconductor devices are a cause of
>   electronic equipment failure.

The interesting thing about inductive reasoning is that the conclusion may be difficult to arrive at, or it may never be final or absolute. Conclusions can change if new facts are discovered. There will always be some uncertainty in the conclusion unless all possible facts are included in the premises, and this is usually impossible. As a result, the outcome of the inductive reasoning process will frequently contain some measure of uncertainty. That uncertainty will be reduced, however, as more facts or premises are used in the reasoning process. The more knowledge you have, the more conclusive your inferences can be.

Deductive or inductive approaches are used in logic, rule-based systems, and frames.

Analogical Reasoning

Analogical reasoning (which is natural to humans but still difficult to accomplish mechanically) assumes that when a question is asked, the answer can be derived by analogy. For example, if you ask, "What are the working hours of engineers in the company?" the computer may reason that engineers are white-collar employees. Because the computer *knows* that white-collar employees work from 9 to 5, it will infer that engineers work 9 to 5. This is an area of much research, and many new developments should be forthcoming. (For an overview see Owen [19] and Vosniadou and Ortony [26].)

Analogical reasoning, according to Tuthill [25], is a type of verbalization of an internalized learning process. An individual uses processes that require an ability to recognize previously encountered experiences. Because analogical reasoning relates the present with the past in an attempt to relate unrelated objects or concepts, analogical reasoning is similar to commonsense reasoning. For example, a fisherman hooks a fish that fights in a familiar manner. The fisherman recalls the way a fish once ran and the feel of its tail against the line. The fish circled the boat and severed the line in kelp. As a result of that experience the fisherman now has an idea of how the present fish will fight, anticipates its actions, and lands the fish. Thus, the fisherman was able to relate a "feel" on the line to a past experience and a current condition.

The use of this approach has not been exploited yet in the AI field. However, case-based reasoning (see Section 15.8) is an attempt to apply the approach to practical problems.

Formal Reasoning

Formal reasoning involves syntactic manipulation of data structures to deduce new facts, following prescribed rules of inference. A typical example is the mathematical logic used in proving theorems in geometry. Another example is the approach of predicate calculus, which is an effective symbolic representation and deductive technique (see Section 15.3).

Procedural (Numeric) Reasoning

Procedural (numeric) reasoning uses mathematical models or simulation to solve problems. Model-based reasoning (see Section 15.7) is an example of this approach.

Generalization and Abstraction

Generalization and abstraction can be successfully used with both logical and semantic representation of knowledge. For example, if we know that *all* companies have presidents and that *all* brokerage houses are considered companies, then we can infer and generalize that any brokerage house will have a president.

Similarly, if the computer knows that in a certain company all engineers are on a monthly salary, as are the accountants and the system analysts, eventually the computer might conclude that *all* professionals in the company are on a monthly salary.

Metalevel Reasoning

Metalevel reasoning involves "knowledge about what you know" (e.g., about the importance and relevance of certain facts). It could play a major role in developing future ES.

Which approach to use, and how successful the inference will be, depends to a great extent on which knowledge representation method is used. For example, reasoning by analogy can be more successful with semantic networks than with frames.

15.3 Reasoning with Logic

For executing either deductive or inductive reasoning, several basic reasoning rules allow the manipulation of the logical expressions to create new expressions. The most important rule is called **modus ponens.**

Modus Ponens. According to this procedure, if there is a rule "if A, then B," and if we know that A is true, then it is valid to conclude that B is also true. In the terminology of logic, we express this as:

[A AND (A → B)] → B

A and (A → B) are propositions in a knowledge base. Given this expression, we can replace both propositions with the proposition B. In other words, we can use modus ponens to draw the conclusion that B is true if the first two expressions are true. Here's an example:

A: It is sunny.
B: We will go to the beach.
A → B: If it is sunny, then we will go to the beach.

The first premise simply states that it is a sunny day. The second says we will go to the beach. Furthermore, A IMPLIES B. So if both A and A IMPLIES B are true, B is true. Using modus ponens you can then deduce that we will go to the beach.

A different situation is the inference in the case that B is known to be false. This is called *modus tollens.* Another approach is called resolution. For details on these and other methods see Winston [28].

15.4 Inferencing with Rules: Forward and Backward Chaining

Inferencing with rules involves implementation of the modus ponens and other inferencing approaches, which is reflected in the search mechanism with the rule interpreter. Consider the following example:

RULE 1: IF international conflict begins,
THEN the price of gold goes up.

Let us assume that the ES knows that an international conflict just started. This information is stored in the "facts" (assertion) portion of the knowledge base. This means that the premise (IF side) of the rule is *true.* Using modus ponens, the conclusion (consequent) is then accepted as *true.* We say that Rule 1 "fires." **Firing a rule** occurs only when all of the rule's parts are satisfied (being either true or false). Then, the conclusion drawn is stored in the assertion base. In our case, the conclusion (the price of gold goes up) is added to the assertion base, and it could be used to satisfy the premise of other rules. The true (or false) values for either portion of the rules can be obtained by querying the user or by firing other rules. Testing a rule premise or conclusion can be as simple as matching a symbolic pattern in the rule to a similar pattern in the assertion base. This activity is referred to as *pattern matching*.

Every rule in the rule base can be checked to see if its premise or conclusion can be satisfied by previously made assertions. This process may be done in one of two directions, forward or backward, and it will continue until no more rules can fire, or until a goal is achieved.

Forward and Backward Chaining: An Overview

There are two approaches for controlling inference in rule-based ES: forward chaining and backward chaining (each of which has several variations). First, we shall provide an intuitive description of the two approaches; then we shall discuss them in detail.

Example 1. Suppose you want to fly from Denver to Tokyo and there are no direct fights between the two cities. Therefore, you try to find a chain of connecting flights starting from Denver and ending in Tokyo. There are two basic ways you can search for this chain of flights:

1. Start with all the flights that arrive at Tokyo and find the city where each flight originated. Then look up all the flights arriving at those cities and find where they originated. Continue the process until you find Denver. Because you are working backward from your goal (Tokyo), this search process is called **backward chaining** (or goal driven).
2. List all flights leaving Denver and mark their destination (intermediate) cities. Then look up all the flights leaving these intermediate cities and find where they land; continue the process until you find Tokyo. In this case, you are working forward from Denver toward your goal, so this search process is called **forward chaining** (or data driven).

This example also demonstrates the importance of heuristics in expediting the search process. Going either backward or forward, you can use heuristics to make the search more efficient. For example, in the backward approach you can look at flights that go only eastward. Depending on the goals of your trip (e.g., minimize cost, minimize travel time, maximize stopovers), you can develop additional rules to expedite the search even further.

Example 2. Suppose your car will not start. Is it because you are out of gas? Or is it because the starter is broken? Or is it because of some other reason? Your task is to find out why the car won't start. From what you already know (the *consequence:* the car won't start), you go *backward* trying to find the *condition* that caused it. This is a typical application of ES in the area of diagnosis (i.e., the conclusion is known and the causes are sought).

A good example of *forward* chaining is a situation in which a water system is overheating. In this case the goal is to predict the most likely result. After reviewing the rules and checking additional evidence, you can finally find the answer. In forward chaining, you start with a *condition*, or a symptom, which is given as a fact.

As will be shown later, the search process in both cases goes through a set of knowledge rules. After determining which rules are true and which are false, the search will end in a finding (we hope). The word *chaining* signifies the linking of a set of pertinent rules.

The search process is directed by an approach sometimes referred to as **rule interpreter,** which works as follows:

- In forward chaining, if premise clauses match the situation, then the process attempts to assert the conclusion.
- In backward chaining, if the current goal is to determine the fact in the conclusion, then the process attempts to determine whether the premise clauses match the situation.

Backward Chaining

Backward chaining is a *goal-driven* approach in which you start from an expectation of what is to happen (hypothesis), then seek evidence that supports (or contradicts) your expectation. Often this entails formulating and testing intermediate hypotheses (or subhypotheses).

Hypothesis: Total sales are down because of the cold weather.
Subhypothesis: Sales are relatively lower in the northern states.

Now, consider the northern states and compare the sales there with the sales of the remaining states so that the hypothesis can either be accepted or rejected.

On a computer, goal-driven reasoning works the same way. The program starts with a goal to be verified as either true or false. Then it looks for a rule that has that goal in its *conclusion*. It then checks the *premise* of that rule in an attempt to satisfy this rule. It checks the assertion base first. If the search there fails, the ES looks for another rule whose conclusion is the same as that of the premise of the first rule. An attempt is then made to satisfy the second rule. The process continues until all the possibilities that apply are checked or until the first rule is satisfied.

Example. Here is an example of an investment decision. The following variables are involved:

A = Have $10,000
B = Younger than thirty
C = Education at college level
D = Annual income of at least $40,000
E = Invest in securities
F = Invest in growth stocks
G = Invest in IBM stock (the potential goal)

Each of these variables can be answered as true (yes) or false (no).

The facts: Let us assume that an investor has $10,000 (i.e., A is true) and she is twenty-five years old (B is true). She would like advice on investing in IBM stock (yes or no for the *goal*).

The rules: Let us assume that our knowledge base includes these five rules:

R1: IF a person has $10,000 and she has a college degree, THEN she should invest in securities.
R2: IF a person's annual income is at least $40,000 and she has a college degree, THEN she should invest in growth stocks.
R3: IF a person is younger than thirty and if she is investing in securities, THEN she should invest in growth stocks.
R4: IF a person is younger than thirty, THEN she has a college degree.
R5: IF a person wants to invest in growth stock, THEN the stock should be IBM.

These rules can be written as:

R1: IF A, and C, THEN E.
R2: IF D and C, THEN F.
R3: IF B and E, THEN F.
R4: IF B, THEN C.
R5: IF F, THEN G.

Our goal is to find whether or not to invest in IBM stock.

Starting point: In backward chaining we start by looking for a rule that includes the goal (G) in its *conclusion* (THEN) part. Since rule 5 is the only one that qualifies, we start with it. If several rules contain G, then the inference engine will follow procedure to handle the situation.

Step 1: Try to accept or reject G. The ES goes now to the *assertion base* to see if G is there. At the present time, all we have in the assertion base is:

A is true.
B is true.

Therefore, the ES will proceed to step 2.

Step 2: R5 says that if it is *true* that we invest in growth stocks (F), THEN we should invest in IBM (G). If we can conclude that the premise of R5 is either true or false, then we have solved our problem. However, we do not know if F is true. What shall we do now? Note that F, which is the *premise* of R5, is also the *conclusion* of R2 and R3. Therefore, to find out if F is true, we must check these two rules.

Step 3: We try R2 first (arbitrarily); if both D and C are true, then F is true. Now we have a problem. D is not a conclusion of any rule, nor is it a fact. The computer can then either move to another rule or try to find if D is true by asking the investor for whom the consultation is given if her annual income is above $40,000.

What the ES will do depends on the procedures in the inference engine. Usually a user is going to be asked for additional information *only* if the information is not available or it cannot be deduced. We abandon R2 and return to the other rule, R3. This action is called **backtracking** (i.e., knowing that we are in a dead end, we try something else. The computer must be preprogrammed to handle backtracking).

Step 4: Go to R3, test B and E. We know that B is true, because it is a given fact. To prove E, we should go to R1, where E is the conclusion.

Step 5: Examine R1. It is necessary to find if A and C are true. A is true because it is a given fact. To test C, it is necessary to test rule R4 (where C is the conclusion).

Step 6: Rule R4 tells us that C is true (because B is true). Therefore, C becomes a fact (added to the assertion base).

Step 7: If C is true, then E is true, which validates F, which validates our goal (i.e., the advice is to invest in IBM). A negative response to any of the preceding statements would result in a "do not invest in IBM stock."

Notice that during the search the ES moved from the THEN part to the IF part to the THEN part, etc. (Figure 15.1). This is a typical search pattern in *backward chaining.* As will be seen next, the forward chaining starts with the IF part, moves to the THEN part, then to another IF, and so on. Some systems

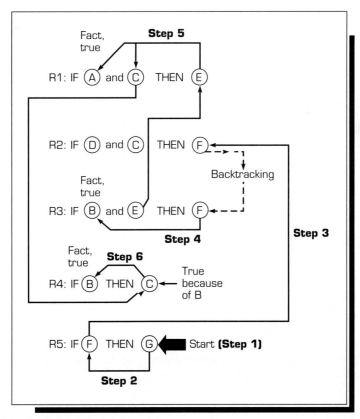

FIGURE 15.1 Backward Chaining

allow a change in the direction of the search during midcourse; that is, they will go from a THEN to THEN (or from IF to IF) if needed.

Forward Chaining

Forward chaining is a *data-driven* approach. In this approach we start from available information as it comes in, or from a basic idea, then try to draw conclusions.

The computer analyzes the problem by looking for the facts that match the IF portion of its IF-THEN rules. For example, if a certain machine is not working, the computer checks the electricity flow to the machine. As each rule is tested, the program works its way toward a conclusion.

Example. Let us use the same example that we introduced in backward chaining. Here we reproduce the rules:

R1: IF A and C, THEN E.
R2: IF D and C, THEN F.
R3: IF B and E, THEN F.
R4: IF B, THEN C.
R5: IF F, THEN G.

and the facts:

A is true (have $10,000) and
B is true (the investor is younger than 30)

Start: Since it is known that A and B are true, the ES starts with one of them (takes A first) and looks for a rule that includes an A in the IF side of the rule. In our case, this is R1. It includes E in its conclusion.

Step 1: The system attempts to verify E. Since A is known (fact, in the assertion base), it is necessary to test C in order to conclude about E. The system tries to find C in the assertion base. Since C is not there, the ES moves to a rule where C is in the THEN side. This is R4.

Step 2: The system tests R4. C is true because it is matched against B, which is known to be true, in the assertion base. Therefore, C is added to the assertion base as being true.

Step 3: Now R1 fires and E is established to be true. This leads to R3 where E is in the IF side.

Step 4: Since B and E are known to be true (they are in the assertion base), then R3 fires, and F is established to be true in the assertion base.

Step 5: Now R5 fires (since F is in its IF side), which establishes G as true. So the expert systems will recommend an investment in IBM stock.

We have seen that an antecedent-consequence rule system can run forward or backward, but which one is better? The answer depends on the purpose of the reasoning and the shape of the search space. For example, if the goal is to discover all that can be deduced from a given set of facts, the system should run forward. In some cases, the two strategies can be mixed (bidirectional).

The execution of the forward and/or backward chaining is done with the aid of a rule interpreter. Its function is to examine production rules to determine which one(s) is capable of being fired and then to fire the rule. The *control strategy* of the rule interpreter (e.g., the backward chaining) determines how the appropriate rules are found and when to apply them. (See Box 15.1.)

Inferencing with rules (as well as with logic) can be very effective, but there are some obvious limitations to these techniques. One reason for this is summarized by the familiar axiom that there is an exception to every rule. For example, consider the following argument:

Proposition 1: Birds can fly.
Proposition 2: An ostrich is a bird.
Conclusion: An ostrich can fly.

The conclusion is perfectly valid but false; ostriches do not cooperate. For this reason, as well as for increased efficiency of the search, we use other inferencing methods.

Box 15.1: The Functions That an Inference Engine Produces

1. Fire the rules.
2. Present the user with a question.
3. Add the answer to the ES "blackboard" (assertion base).
4. Infer a new fact from a rule.
5. Add the inference fact to the blackboard.
6. Match the blackboard to the rules.
7. If there are any matches, fire rules.
8. If there are two further matches, check to see if goal is reached.
9. Fire the lowest numbered unfired rule.

The program works through the knowledge base until it can post a fact (or a partial fact if certainty factors are being used) to the blackboard.

Once a fact has been posted, the system goes back to the knowledge base to infer more facts. This continues until the present goal is achieved or until all rules have been fired.

15.5   The Inference Tree

The **inference tree** (also goal tree, or logical tree) provides a schematic view of the inference process. It is similar to a decision tree. Note that each rule is composed of a premise and a conclusion. In building the inference tree the premises and conclusions are shown as nodes. The branches connect the premises and the conclusions. The operators AND and OR are used to reflect the structures of the rules. There is no deep significance to the construction of such trees—they just provide a better insight into the structure of the rules.

Figure 15.2 presents the logical tree of the example that we used in the previous section. By using the tree, we can visualize the process of inference and movement along the branches of the tree. This is called *tree traversal*. To traverse an AND node, we must traverse all the nodes below it. To traverse an OR node, it is enough to traverse just one of the nodes below.

The inference tree is constructed upside down: the root is at the top and the branches point downward. The tree ends with "leaves" at the bottom. (It can also be constructed from the left to the right, much like a decision tree.)

Inference trees are composed basically of clusters of goals. Each goal may have subgoals (children) and a supergoal (parent).

Single inference trees are always a mixture of AND nodes and OR nodes; they are often called AND/OR trees. The AND node signifies a situation in which a goal is satisfied only when *all* its immediate subgoals are satisfied. The OR node signifies a situation in which a goal is satisfied when *any* of its immediate goals is satisfied. When enough subgoals are satisfied to achieve the primary goal, the tree is said to be *satisfied*. The inference engine contains procedures for expressing this process as a backward and/or forward chaining. These procedures are organized as a set of instructions involving inference rules. They aim at satisfying the inference tree and collectively contribute to the process of goal (problem) reduction. For further discussion see Winston [28].

The inference tree has another big advantage; it provides a guide for answering the *why* and *how* questions in the explanation process. The *how* question is asked by users when they want to know how a certain conclusion has been reached. The computer follows the logic in the inference tree, identifies the goal (conclusion) involved in it and the AND/OR branches, and reports the immediate subgoals. The *why* question is asked by users when they want to know why the computer requests certain information as input. To deal with why questions, the computer identifies the goal involved with the computer-generated query and reports the immediate subgoals.

15.6   Inferencing with Frames

Reasoning with frames is much more complicated than reasoning with rules. The slot provides a mechanism for a kind of reasoning called *expectation-driven*

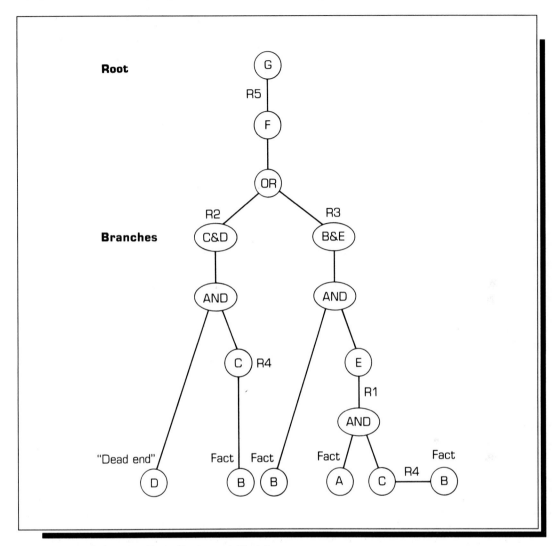

FIGURE 15.2 Inference Tree, Backward Chaining

processing. Empty slots (i.e., unconfirmed expectations) can be filled, subject to certain conditioning, with data that confirm the expectations. Thus, frame-based reasoning looks for confirmation of expectations and often just involves filling in slot values.

Perhaps the simplest way to specify slot values is by default. The default value is attached loosely to the slot so as to be easily displaced by a value that meets the assignment condition. In the absence of information, however, the default value remains attached and expressed.

The reasoning process that takes place with frames is essentially the seeking of confirmation of various expectations. This amounts to filling in the slots and verifying that they match the current situation. With frames, it is easy to make inferences about new objects, events, or situations because the frames provide a base of knowledge drawn from previous experience.

The reasoning in frames can be executed in different ways. Two most common ways are using rules and employing hierarchial reasoning.

Using Rules in Frames

A rule can reason about the characteristics of a frame by referring to its slot values. The following is an example (provided by Walters and Nielsen [27], p. 226).

Example. A route must be planned for driving to a certain destination where a bridge must be avoided if the vehicle is too heavy. A rule such as the following might be placed in the knowledge base:

    RULE 1: IF   WEIGHT of MY-FORD > 3,000 pounds
             THEN take DETOUR around RICKETY BRIDGE

If the value of the WEIGHT slot of the frame MY-FORD is greater than 3,000 pounds, then the plan should include a detour around the rickety bridge.

Rules can be used to process the structural knowledge contained in a taxonomy. The following rule, which might be one of a set for determining at what type of service station the driver should stop to refuel the car, is illustrative:

    RULE 2: IF   ?VEHICLE is MEMBER-OF AUTOMOBILES
             AND   ?VEHICLE has-a ?ENGINE
             AND   ?ENGINE is MEMBER-OF DIESEL
             THEN set REFUEL of ?VEHICLE to TRUCKSTOP

On the first line the inference engine attempts to instantiate the variable ?VEHICLE with every frame, but only those instantiations that are members of the class AUTOMOBILES are kept. At this point, several vehicles might qualify, so several instances of the rule would be established (e.g., with vehicle-2). The second line instantiates the variable ?ENGINE with any frame that ?VEHICLE points to with a has-a relation. Thus, if vehicle-2 had an engine and, say, a fuel-tank, the rule would be instantiated twice—once with ?VEHICLE = vehicle-2 and ?ENGINE = ENGINE, and once with ?VEHICLE = vehicle-2 and ?ENGINE = FUEL-TANK.

The third line of the rule then throws out any instantiation of the rule for which ?ENGINE is not a member of the class DIESEL. The fourth line then sets the slot REFUEL of the associated vehicle to the value TRUCKSTOP.

Reasoning with a knowledge taxonomy is not the exclusive province of rules, *although many frame-based systems use rule-based knowledge extensively.*

Using Hierarchial Reasoning

According to **hierarchial reasoning,** certain alternatives, objects, or events can be *eliminated* at various levels of the search (reasoning) hierarchy. For example, at one level there might be a rule:

RULE: IF   MANUFACTURER of ?VEHICLE is FORD
          THEN ?VEHICLE is NOT MEMBER-OF DIESEL

Assuming Ford does not manufacture any diesel engines, a single rule at this level can eliminate a number of class and subclass possibilities. For details and other methods of elimination see Walters and Nielsen [27].

15.7 Model-based Reasoning

Model-based reasoning is based on knowledge of the structure and behavior of the devices the system is designed to understand. Model-based systems are especially useful in diagnosing equipment problems. The systems include a model of the device to be diagnosed that is then used to identify the cause(s) of the equipment's failure. Because they draw conclusions directly from knowledge of a device's structure and behavior, model-based expert systems are said to *reason from "first principles."* In many cases model-based reasoning is combined with other representation and inferencing methods.

The Hardware Troubleshooting Group in MIT's AI lab assesses the use of model-based ES to diagnose malfunctioning computers. The group uses a computer-repair scenario to contrast the rule-based with the model-based approaches. First, the rule-based approach:

> Consider the likely behavior of an engineer with a great deal of repair experience. He or she simply stares briefly at the console, noting the pattern of lights and error message, then goes over to one of the cabinets, opens it, raps sharply on one of the circuit boards inside, and restarts the machine.

The diagnostic process used in this episode represents the approach that is incorporated in a rule-based expert system. A knowledge engineer formalizes the reasoning process that an expert uses to discover the source of the problem and encodes that procedure in a series of production rules.

A model-based approach, on the other hand, is represented by a scenario such as the following:

> Consider a new engineer who has just completed training. He or she carefully notes the symptoms, gets out a thick book of schematics, and spends the next half hour poring over them. At last he or she looks up, goes over to one of the cabinets, opens it, raps sharply on one of the circuit boards inside, and restarts the machine.

Although in this example the rule-based and model-based approaches resulted in the same actions, the *procedures* used to arrive at the conclusions were very different. Because the novice engineer in the latter scenario could not rely on his or her expertise to diagnose and repair the computer, he or she had to refer to documentation that explained how the computer worked. Similarly, a model-based system depends on knowledge of the structure and behavior of a device, rather than relying on production rules that represent expertise.

One especially attractive feature of a model-based ES is its "transportability." A rule-based ES that incorporates an expert's knowledge of troubleshooting problems with a particular computer might be of no value for repairing a different kind of computer. On the other hand, if a model-based ES included a thorough working knowledge of digital electronic computer circuits, it theoretically could be used to diagnose the problem of *any* computer.

Example. An example of model-based reasoning is given by Fulton and Pepe [3]. Their systems are implemented by NASA at the Kennedy Space Center for troubleshooting. Rule-based systems are not effective in situations where there is a mass of sensor information. Such systems cannot make the necessary association between the set of sensor data and the fault.

The model-based system includes a model that simulates the structure and function of the machinery under diagnosis. Instead of reasoning only from observable values, those systems reason from first principles; that is, the systems know the machinery's internal processes. The systems can *compute* which state the machine is in rather than attempting to match such a state against complex symptoms (which a rule-based system will do).

Once signals are received from the sensors, the expert system activates a simulation program that generates predicted values. These are compared against the information provided by the sensors. As long as the actual data are within the range of the predicted values (the "tolerance"), nothing is done. If the actual data are outside the tolerance, a diagnosis is automatically performed. The result of the diagnosis may activate control commands to prevent the system from entering a dangerous state. This mode of reasoning is very important in intelligent robots.

The models used in this type of reasoning can be either **mathematical models** or **component models.** For example, a mathematical model can simulate the function of a grandfather clock, taking into account the oscillator length, gear size, and so forth. The model can predict the position of the hands after a specific time interval; and with more complexity, can diagnose why the clock is too fast (or too slow). In contrast, a component model contains a functional description of all components and their interactions. As the clock ticked, each component would alter itself, propagate its final position to the relevant components, then allow them to alter their positions.

Special model-based tools are available (they usually involve frames). They are especially helpful in inferencing that involves monitoring production processes (and taking appropriate actions) and diagnosing. A necessary condition for model-based reasoning is the creation of a *complete* and *accurate* model of the system under study. The approach is especially useful in real-time systems. For further details see Davis and Hamscher [1] and Walters and Nielsen [27].

15.8 Case-based Reasoning

Basics

The basic idea of **case-based reasoning** is to adapt solutions that were used to solve old problems and use them for solving new problems. One variation of this approach is the rule-induction method described in Chapter 13. In rule induction the computer examines historical cases and generates rules, which then are chained (forward or backward) to solve problems. Case-based reasoning, on the other hand (according to Riesbeck and Schank [21]), follows a different process; it

- finds those cases in memory that solved problems similar to the current problem, and
- adapts the previous solution or solutions to fit the current problem, taking into account any difference between the current and previous situations.

Finding relevant cases involves

- characterizing the input problem, by assigning the appropriate features to it,
- retrieving the cases from memory with those features, and
- picking the case or cases that match the input best.

The basic justification for the use of case-based reasoning, according to Riesbeck and Schank, is that human thinking does not use logic (or reasoning from first principle). It is basically a processing of the right information retrieved at the right time. So the central problem is the identification of pertinent information whenever needed. This is done in case-based reasoning with the aid of scripts.

Scripts. As you may recall from Chapter 14, **scripts** describe a well-known sequence of events. If a script is available, then you don't have to think much in an attempt to infer the intentions of a waitress. These intentions are either documented in the script or can be inferred from there easily. Therefore, in many cases, it is possible to say that reasoning is no more than applying scripts. The more scripts available to us, the less thinking we need to do. All that is necessary is finding the right script to use. Riesbeck and Schank [21] postulate that given a choice between thinking hard (reworking the problem) and applying an old script, people will choose the script every time. Scripts are found in historical cases, which reflect human experience. The experience can be that of the decision makers or that of others. Case-based reasoning is the essence of how people reason from experience.

TABLE 15.1 Comparison of Case-based and Rule-based Reasoning

Criterion	Rule-based Reasoning	Case-based Reasoning
Knowledge unit	Rule	Case
Granularity	Fine	Coarse
Knowledge acquisition units	Rules, hierarchies	Cases, hierarchies
Explanation mechanism	Backtrack of rule firings	Precedent cases
Characteristic output	Answer, plus confidence measure	Answer, plus precedent cases
Knowledge transfer across problems	High, if backtracking Low, if deterministic	Low
Speed as a function of knowledge base size	Exponential, if backtracking Linear, if deterministic	Logarithmic, if index tree balanced
Domain requirements	Domain vocabulary Good set of inference rules Either few rules or rules apply sequentially Domain mostly obeys rules	Domain vocabulary Database of example cases Stability—a modified good solution is probably still good Many exceptions to rules
Advantages	Flexible use of knowledge Potentially optimal answers	Rapid response Rapid knowledge acquisition Explanation by examples
Disadvantages	Computationally expensive Long development time Black-box answers	Suboptimal solutions Redundant knowledge base

Source: Courtesy of Marc Goodman, Cognitive Systems, Inc. Based on: M. Goodman, "PRISM: A Case-Based Telex Classifier," in *Innovative Applications of Artificial Intelligence,* vol. 11, A. Rappaport and R. Smith, eds. (Cambridge, MA: MIT Press, 1990).

TABLE 15.2 Advantages of Case-based Reasoning.

Knowledge acquisition is improved: easier to build, simpler to maintain, less expensive to develop and support.

Processing time is faster.

Existing data and knowledge are leveraged.

Complete formalized domain knowledge (which is required with rules) is not required.

Experts feel better discussing concrete cases (not general rules).

Explanation becomes easier. Rather than showing many rules, a logical sequence can be shown.

Acquisition of new cases is easy (can be automated). (For an example of knowledge acquisition of cases, see diPiazza and Helsabeck [2].)

Learning can occur from both success and failures.

Case-based reasoning has been proposed as a more psychologically plausible model of the reasoning of an expert than a rule-based model. A theoretical comparison of the two was made by Riesbeck and Schank [21] and a summary is provided in Table 15.1.

Advantages. Case-based reasoning has several potential benefits; they are summarized in Table 15.2.

Process of Case-based Reasoning

The process of case-based reasoning is shown graphically in Figure 15.3. Boxes represent processes and ovals represent knowledge structure. The major steps in the process are described in the following list (reprinted from Slade [23]).

1. *Assign Indexes:* Features of the new event are assigned as indexes characterizing the event. For example, our first air shuttle flight might be characterized as an airplane flight.
2. *Retrieve:* The indexes are used to retrieve a similar past case from memory. The past case contains the prior solution. In our example, we might be reminded of a previous airplane trip.
3. *Modify:* The old solution is modified to conform to the new situation, resulting in a proposed solution. For our airplane case, we would make appropriate modifications to account for changes in various features such as destination, price, purpose of the trip, departure and arrival times, weather, and so on.
4. *Test:* The proposed solution is tried out. It either succeeds or fails. Our airplane reminder generates certain expectations.
5. *Assign and Store:* If the solution succeeds, then assign indexes and store a working solution. The successful plan is then incorporated into the case memory. For a typical airplane trip there will be few expectation failures and, therefore, little to make this new trip memorable. It will be just one more instance of the airplane script.
6. *Explain, Repair, and Test:* If the solution fails, then explain the failure, repair the working solution, and test again. The explanation process identifies the source of the problem. The predictive features of the problem are incorporated into the indexing rules to anticipate this problem in the future. The failed plan is repaired to fix the problem, and the revised solution is then tested. For our air shuttle example, we realize that certain expectations fail. We learn that we do not get an assigned seat and that we do not have to pay ahead of time. We might decide that taking the air shuttle is more like riding on a train. We can then create a new case in memory to handle this new situation and identify predictive features so that we will be reminded of this episode the next time we take the shuttle.

In support of this process are the following types of knowledge structures, represented by ovals in this figure:

Indexing Rules: Indexing rules identify the predictive features in the input that provide appropriate indexes in the case memory. Determining the significant input features is a persistent problem. . . .

Case Memory: Case memory is the episodic memory, which comprises the database of experience.

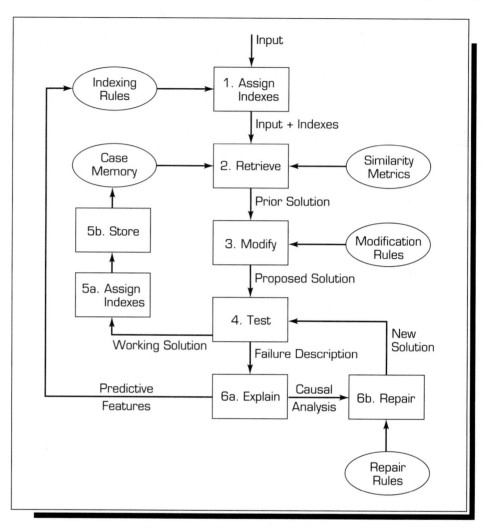

FIGURE 15.3 Case-based Reasoning Flowchart. (*Source: AI Magazine* [Spring 1991], p. 46; based on C. K. Riesback and R. L. Schank, *Inside Case-based Reasoning* [Hillsdale, N J: Lawrence Erlbaum Associates, 1989], p. 32. Copyright © 1989, American Association for Artificial Intelligence. All rights reserved.)

Similarity Metrics: If more than one case is retrieved from episodic memory, the similarity metrics can be used to decide which case is more like the current situation. For example, in the air shuttle case, we might be reminded of both airplane rides and train rides. The similarity rules might initially suggest that we rely on the airplane case.

Modification Rules: No old case is going to be an exact match for a new situation. The old case must be modified to fit. We require knowledge about what kinds of factors can be changed and how to change them. For the airplane ride, it is acceptable to ride in a different seat, but it is usually not advisable to change roles from passenger to pilot.

Repair Rules: Once we identify and explain an expectation failure, we must try to alter our plan to fit the new situation. Again, we have rules for what kinds of changes are permissible. For the air shuttle, we recognize that paying for the ticket on the plane is an acceptable change. We can generate an explanation that recognizes an airplane ride as a type of commercial transaction and suggests that there are alternative acceptable means of paying for services.

Uses, Issues, Applications

Case-based reasoning can be used on its own or it can be combined with other reasoning paradigms. Table 15.3 provides some guidelines. Target application domains, according to Cognitive Systems, Inc., are listed below:

- Tactical planning
- Political analysis
- Situation assessment
- Legal planning
- Diagnosis
- Fraud detection
- Design/configuration
- Message classification.

Case-based reasoning is a new field (started in the mid-1980s) with little practical experience. Therefore, issues and problems may be anticipated. Slade [23] raises the following issues and questions regarding case-based implementation:

- The quality of the results is heavily dependent on the indexes used.
- Automatic case-adaptation rules can be very complex.
- The case base may need to be expanded as the domain model evolves, yet much analysis of the domain may be postponed.
- What makes up a case? How can we represent case memory?

TABLE 15.3   When to Use Case-based Reasoning

Domain cannot be formalized with rules because:
  —domain has weak or unknown causal model
  —domain has underdefined terms
  —contradictory rules apply in different situations
Application requires complex output, e.g., battle plans
Domain is already precedent-based, e.g., law, medical diagnosis, claims settlement
Domain formalization requires too many rules
Domain is dynamic, requiring rapid acquisition of solutions to new problem types
Domain task benefits from records of past solutions, to reuse successful ones and avoid bad ones

Source: Courtesy of Marc Goodman, Cognitive Systems, Inc. Based on: M. Goodman, "PRISM: A Case-Based Telex Classifier," in *Innovative Applications of Artificial Intelligence,* vol. 11, A. Rappaport and R. Smith, eds. (Cambridge, MA: MIT Press, 1990).

- How is memory organized? What are the indexing rules?
- How does memory function in retrieval of relevant information?
- How can we adapt old solutions to new problems? What are the similarity metrics and the modification rules?
- How can we learn from mistakes? What are the repair rules?

Example of Application. This example was provided by Goodman [4]. The application was constructed by Cognitive Systems, Inc., using their case-based reasoning shell. The purpose of the application is to classify incoming telex messages in a bank into one of 109 categories so that they can be processed faster. Also, by proper classification, the receiver can quickly identify if there are some missing data. This application is related to natural language processing. The example includes eight steps:

- *Step 1:* Collection of messages. Messages are collected as they come and are given names. The **case library** consists of over 10,000 sample messages.
- *Step 2:* Expert establishes a hierarchy of telex classifications based on content. Overall, there are 109 types of messages.
- *Step 3:* An expert matches the messages in the case library against the 109 categories.
- *Step 4:* Formulas are used to create *abstract features*, which can either be used to predict a classification or as the classification to be predicted. (For example, a formula determines whether a message is or is not a money transfer.)
- *Step 5:* Lexical patterns, consisting of words, phrases, abbreviations, and synonyms, are established for the domain. These patterns are used to tokenize each message.
- *Step 6:* Each case in the library is then fully represented; that is, its classification, formulas, and features are summarized on one page.
- *Step 7:* By using the case-based reasoning shell, the domain expert applies special techniques to identify possible features that may be important in determining the message category. At the moment (1992), three commercial shells are available (from Cognitive Systems, Inc., Inference Corp., and Esteem Software, Inc.)
- *Step 8:* An incoming message's classification is determined (automatically) by matching the incoming case with similar cases from the case library. Explanations for the match are automatically provided.

15.9   Explanation and Metaknowledge

Explanation

Human experts are often asked to explain their views, recommendations, or decisions. If ES are to mimic humans in performing highly specialized tasks, they need to justify and explain their actions as well. An explanation is an attempt by an ES to clarify its reasoning, recommendations, or other actions (e.g., asking a question). The part of an ES that provides explanations is called an **explanation facility** (or **justifier**). The explanation facility has several specific purposes:

- Make the system more intelligible to the user.
- Uncover the shortcomings of the rules and knowledge base (debugging the systems by the knowledge engineer).
- Explain situations that were unanticipated by the user.
- Satisfy psychological and/or social needs by helping a user feel more assured about the actions of the ES.
- Clarify the assumptions underlying the system's operations, both to the user and the builder.
- Conduct sensitivity analyses (Using the explanation facility, the user can predict and test the effects of changes on the system.).

Explanation in rule-based ES is usually associated with some form of tracing the rules that are fired during the course of a problem-solving session. This is about the closest to a real explanation that today's systems can come, given that their knowledge is usually represented almost exclusively as rules that do not include basic principles necessary for a human-type explanation.

Programs like MYCIN replay the exact rule used when asked for an explanation. DIGITAL ADVISOR is a slight improvement over this. Instead of feeding back the rule verbatim, the ADVISOR determines the generic principle that the rule is based on (at that point in the consultation) and displays that general principle.

In developing large ES, the need for a good explanation facility is essential. Large ES always include more facts and rules than one can easily remember. Often, a new rule added during ES development will interact with other rules and data in unanticipated ways and will make the ES display strange behavior.

Explanation is an extremely important function since understanding depends on explanation (thus making implementation of proposed solutions easier). To understand an event or a situation, you have to explain to yourself exactly what is going on, the role of every participant, and their actions. You need to know the goals of the participants, their intentions, and their potential behavior. Thus, constructing explanations can become a very complex task, especially when done by machines. For this reason most existing explanation facilities provide only two basic types of explanation: the *why* and the *how*.

Why Explanations. A typical *why* question is posed by the user to the computer after the computer asks the user to provide some information. For example, in an investment example (Section 15.4) we may have the following dialog:

COMPUTER: What is your annual income?
    CLIENT: Why? (Why do you need to know?)

COMPUTER: In checking R2, I need to know if your income is above $40,000. If this is true, I will conclude that because you have a college degree, you should invest in growth stocks.

The ES asks for this input when it is unable to find it in the conclusion part of any rule! In the example cited, the computer actually backtracked to another rule and successfully arrived at a final conclusion.

***How* Explanations.** The typical *how* question is posed by users when they would like to know how a certain conclusion or recommendation was reached. Simple systems are limited to the final conclusion. More complex systems can handle intermediate conclusions as well. The system can explain why a certain rule was fired; that is, it shows the chain of rules used to reach the conclusion. In the investment problem the *how* explanation may look like this:

COMPUTER: Invest in IBM stocks.
  CLIENT: How? (How was the conclusion reached?)
COMPUTER: Given that you have $10,000 to invest and you are younger than thirty, then according to rule 4 you have a college degree. If this is the case, then according to R1 you should invest in securities. For a young investor like you, according to R3, you should invest in growth stocks if you are going to invest at all. Finally, in your case, according to R5, if you need to invest in growth stocks, then IBM is your best bet.

The *why* and *how* explanations frequently show the rules in programmed language, and not in a natural language, such as is shown above, because computers cannot speak natural language.

Other Explanations. Some sophisticated ES can provide other explanations. For example, some systems provide a limited *why not* capability. Let us assume that the system selected IBM as a growth stock. The user may ask "Why not GE?" and the system may answer, "Because the annual growth rate of GE is only 7 percent, whereas that of IBM is 11 percent, using rule 78."

This example illustrates a possible connection between the ES and a regular database. In order to provide explanations, the computer may need to go to a database.

Explanation in non-rule-based systems is much more difficult than in rule-based ones because the inference procedures are more complex. For an overview of the topic of explanation see Moore et al. [15].

Metaknowledge

The system's knowledge about how it reasons is called **metaknowledge,** or knowledge about knowledge. The inference rules presented earlier are a special case of metaknowledge. Metaknowledge allows the system to examine the operation of the descriptive (declarative) and procedural knowledge in the knowledge base.

Explanation can be viewed as another aspect of metaknowledge. In the future, metaknowledge will allow ES to do even more. They will be able to create the rationale behind individual rules by reasoning from first principles. They will tailor their explanations to fit the requirements of their audience. And they will be able to change their own internal structure through rule correction, reorganization of the knowledge base, and system reconfiguration.

There are different methods for generating explanations. An easy way to do them is to preinsert pieces of English text in the system. For example, each question that could be asked by the user may have an answer test associated with it. This is called a **static explanation.** Several problems are associated with static explanations. For example, all questions and answers must be anticipated in advance. For large systems this is very difficult. The system also has essentially no idea about what it is saying. In the long run, the program may be modified without changing the text, thus causing inconsistency.

A better form of explanation is a **dynamic explanation,** which is reconstructed according to the execution pattern of the rules. In this method the system reconstructs the reasons for its actions as it evaluates rules.

Most existing explanations fail to meet some of the objectives and requirements listed earlier. The following are some thoughts on this topic (provided by Kidd and Cooper [8]):

The explanation facility of most ES consists of printing out a trace of the rules being used. Explanation is not treated as a task that requires intelligence in itself. If ES are to provide satisfactory explanations, future systems must include not only knowledge of how to solve problems in their respective domains but also knowledge of how to effectively communicate to users their understanding of this problem-solving process. Obviously, the relative balance of these two types of knowledge will vary according to the primary function of the system. Constructing such knowledge bases will involve formalizing the heuristics used in providing good explanations.

With current ES, much of the knowledge vital to providing a good explanation (e.g., knowledge about the system's problem-solving strategy) is not expressed explicitly in rules. Rather, it is implicit in the ordering of certain rule clauses or the way certain hypotheses are linked (i.e., there is a mass of implicit knowledge underpinning each rule and the way groups of rules are structured). Kidd and Cooper have recorded dialogs between experts and their clients in various domains and have found that rules of the form "IF . . . THEN . . . BECAUSE . . ." are used extensively in explanations. Explanations can also be supported graphically.

The purely rule-based representation may be difficult to grasp, especially when the relationships between the rules are not made explicit in the explanation. Kidd and Cooper have developed an explanation facility that can show the inference tree and the parts of it that are relevant to specific queries, thus overcoming some of the deficiencies cited earlier.

15.10   Inferencing with Uncertainty

Uncertainty in AI is treated as a three-step process (according to Kanal and Lemmer [7] and Parsaye and Chignell [20]) as shown in Figure 15.4. In step 1 an expert provides inexact knowledge, that is, in terms of rules with likelihood values. These can be numeric (e.g., a probability value), graphic, or symbolic ("it is most likely that . . .").

In step 2 the inexact knowledge of the basic set of events can be directly used to draw inferences in simple cases (step 3). However, in many cases the various events are interrelated. Therefore, it is necessary to combine the information provided in step 1 into a global value for the system. Several methods can be used for such an integration. The major methods are Bayesian probabilities, theory of evidence, certainty factors, and fuzzy sets.

In step 3 the purpose of the knowledge-based system is to draw inferences. These are derived from the inexact knowledge of step 1 and/or step 2, and usually they are implemented with the inference engine. Working with the inference engine, experts can adjust the input they give in step 1 after viewing the results in steps 2 and 3.

A Note on Uncertainty

Although uncertainty is widespread in the real world, its treatment in the practical world of AI is very limited. As a matter of fact, many real-life knowledge-based systems completely avoid the issue of uncertainty. People feel that representation of uncertainty is not necessary to deal with uncertain knowledge. Why is this so?

The answer given by practitioners is very simple. Even though they recognize the problem of uncertainty, they feel that none of the methods available are

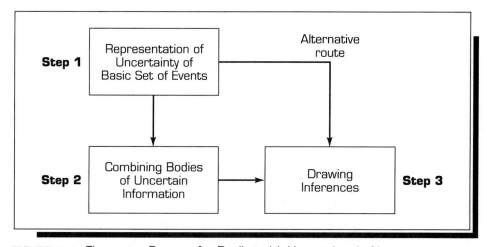

FIGURE 15.4   Three-step Process for Dealing with Uncertainty in AI

accurate or consistent enough to handle the situation. As a matter of fact, some knowledge engineers have experimented with several proposed methods for dealing with uncertainty and either found no significant difference from treating the situation under assumed certainty, or found large differences among the results when using different methods. Does this mean that **uncertainty avoidance** is the best approach and this material should be deleted from this book? Certainly not!

Uncertainty is a serious problem. Avoiding it may not be the best strategy. Instead, we need to improve the methods for dealing with uncertainty. Theoreticians must realize that many of the concepts presented in this chapter are foreign to many practitioners. Even structured methods, such as the Bayesian formula, seem extremely strange and complex to many people.

15.11   Representing Uncertainty

The three basic methods of representing uncertainty are numeric, graphic, and symbolic.

Numeric

The most common method of representing uncertainty is numeric, using a scale with two extreme numbers. For example, 0 may be used to represent complete uncertainty while 1 or 100 represents complete certainty. Although such representation seems to be easy to some people (maybe because it is similar to representation of probabilities), it is very difficult for others.

In addition to the difficulties of using numbers, there are problems with cognitive biases. For example, experts figure the numbers from their own experience and are influenced by their own perceptions. For a discussion of these biases, see Parsaye and Chignell [20]. Finally, people may be inconsistent in providing numeric values at different times.

Graphic

Although many experts can describe uncertainty in terms of numbers, such as "it is 85 percent certain that . . . ," some have difficulties in doing so. By using horizontal bars, for example, it is possible to assist experts in expressing their confidence in certain events. Such a bar is shown in Figure 15.5. Experts are asked to place markers somewhere on the scale. Thus, expert A may express very little confidence in the likelihood of inflation, whereas expert B is more confident that inflation is coming.

Even though graphic presentation is preferred by some experts, the graphs are not as accurate as numbers. Another problem is that most experts do not have experience in marking graphic scales (or setting numbers on the scale). Many experts, especially managers, prefer ranking over either graphic or numeric methods.

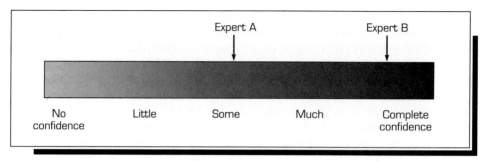

FIGURE 15.5 Confidence Scale about the Occurrence of Inflation

Symbolic

There are several ways to represent uncertainty by using symbols. Many experts use a *Likert scale* approach to express their opinion. For example, an expert may be asked to assess the likelihood of inflation on a five-point scale: very unlikely, unlikely, neutral, likely, and very likely. *Ranking* is a very popular approach among experts with nonquantitative preferences. Ranking can be either ordinal (i.e., listing items by the order of their importance) or cardinal (ranking complemented by numeric values). Managers are especially comfortable with ordinal ranking. When the number of items to be ranked is large, people may have a problem with ranking and also tend to be inconsistent. One method that can be used to alleviate this problem is a pair-wise comparison combined with a consistency checker; that is, rank the items, two at a time, and check for consistencies. One methodology for such ranking, the *analytical hierarchy process*, was described in Chapter 5. For further discussion of ranking, see Parsaye and Chignell [20].

The method of fuzzy logic, which will be presented later, includes a special symbolic representation combined with numbers.

Symbolic representation methods are frequently combined with numbers or are converted to numeric values. For example, it is customary to give weight of one to five to the five options in a Likert-like scale.

15.12   Probabilities and Related Approaches

The Probability Ratio

The degree of belief of confidence in a premise or a conclusion can be expressed as a probability. Probability is the chance that a particular event will occur (or not occur). It is a ratio computed as follows:

$$P(X) = \frac{\text{Number of outcomes favoring the occurrence of}}{\text{Total number of events}}$$

The probability of X occurring, stated as $P(X)$, is the ratio of the number of times X occurs to the total number of events that take place.

Multiple probability values occur in many systems. For example, a rule may have three parts to its antecedent, each with a probability value. The overall probability of the rule can be computed as the product of the individual probabilities, if the parts of the antecedent are independent of one another. In a three-part antecedent, the probabilities may be 0.9, 0.7, and 0.65. The overall probability is:

$$P = (0.9)(0.7)(0.65) = 0.4095$$

The combined probability is about 41 percent. But this is true only if the individual parts of the antecedent do not affect or interrelate to one another.

Sometimes one rule references another. Here, the individual rule probabilities can propagate from one to another. So we need to evaluate the total probability of a sequence of rules or a path through the search tree to determine if a specific rule fires. Or, we may be able to use the combined probability to predict the best path through the search tree.

In knowledge-based systems several approaches for combining probabilities exist. For example, probabilities can be multiplied (i.e., joint probabilities) or averaged out (using a simple or a weighted average); in other instances, only the highest or lowest values are considered. In all such cases, rules and events are considered independent of each other. If there are dependencies in the system, the Bayes extension theorem can be employed.

The Bayesian Extension

Bayes theorem is a mechanism for combining new and existent evidence usually given as subjective probabilities. It is used to *revise* existing *prior probabilities* based on new information.

The Bayesian approach is based on **subjective probabilities;** a subjective probability is provided for each proposition. If E is the evidence (sum of all information available to the system), then each proposition (P) has associated with it a value representing the probability that P holds in the light of all the evidence E, derived by using Bayesian inference. Bayes's theorem provides a way of computing the probability of a particular event given some set of observations we have already made. The main point here is not how this value is derived, but that what we know or have inferred about a proposition is represented by a single value for its likelihood.

Two criticisms may be advanced against this approach. The first is that the single value does not tell us much about its precision, which may be very low when the value is derived from uncertain evidence. To say that the probability of a proposition being true in a given situation is 0.5 (in a range of 0 to 1) usually refers to an *average* figure that is true within a given range. For example, 0.5 plus or minus 0.001 is completely different from 0.5 plus or minus 0.3, yet both may be reported as 0.5. The second criticism is that the single value combines the evidence for and against a proposition without indicating how much there is of each.

The subjective probability expresses the "degree of belief," or how strongly a value or a situation is believed to be true.

The Bayesian approach, with or without new evidence, can be diagrammed as a network.

Dempster-Shafer Theory of Evidence

The Dempster-Shafer *theory of evidence* is a well-known procedure for reasoning with uncertainty in artificial intelligence. (For details see Shafer [22] and Kanal and Lemmer [7].) It can be considered an extension of the Bayesian approach.

The Dempster-Shafer approach distinguishes between uncertainty and ignorance by creating **belief functions.** Belief functions allow us to use our knowledge to bound the assignment of probabilities when these may be unavailable.

The Dempster-Shafer approach is especially appropriate for combining expert opinions, since experts do differ in their opinions with a certain degree of ignorance and, in many situations, at least some *epistemic information* (i.e., one that was constructed from vague perceptions). The Dempster-Shafer approach can be used to handle epistemic information as well as ignorance or lack of information. Unfortunately, the theory assumes that the sources of information to be combined are statistically *independent* of each other. In reality, there are many cases in which the knowledge of experts is overlapping; that is, there are dependencies among sources of information. For such cases the Ling and Rudd [12] extensions are necessary.

15.13   Theory of Certainty (Certainty Factors)

Certainty Factors and Beliefs

Standard statistical methods are based on the assumption that an uncertainty is the probability that an event (or fact) is true or false. In the **certainty theory,** as well as in fuzzy logic, uncertainty is represented as a *degree of belief.* In any nonprobabilistic method of uncertainty one needs to go through two steps. First, it is necessary to be able to express the degree of belief. Second, it is necessary to manipulate (e.g., combine) degrees of belief during the use of knowledge-based systems.

Certainty theory relies on the use of **certainty factors.** Certainty factors (CF) express belief in an event (or fact, or hypothesis) based on evidence (or the expert's assessment). There are several methods of using certainty factors in handling uncertainty in knowledge-based systems. One way is to use 1.0 or 100 for absolute truth (complete confidence) and 0 for certain falsehood. These cer-

tainty factors are not probabilities. For example, when we say there is a 90 percent chance for rain, then there is either rain (90 percent) or no rain (10 percent).
In a nonprobabilistic approach, we can say the certainty factor rain = 90 means
that it is very likely to rain. It does not necessarily mean that we express any
opinion about our argument of no rain. Thus, certainty factors *do not* have to
sum up to 100.

Certainty theory introduces the concepts of *belief* and **disbelief.** These concepts are independent of each other and so cannot be combined as probabilities,
but they can be combined according to the following formula:

$$CF[P,E] = MB[P,E] - MD[P,E]$$

where

$$
\begin{aligned}
CF &= \text{certainty factor} \\
MB &= \text{measure of belief} \\
MD &= \text{measure of disbelief} \\
P &= \text{probability} \\
E &= \text{evidence, or event}
\end{aligned}
$$

Another assumption of the certainty theory is that the knowledge content
of rules is much more important than the algebra of confidences that holds the
system together. Confidence measures correspond to the information evaluations that human experts attach to their conclusions, for example, "it is probably
true" or "it is highly unlikely."

Combining Certainty Factors

Certainty factors can be used to combine different estimates of experts in
several ways. Before using any ES shell make sure that you understand how
certainty factors are combined (for an overview see Kopcso et al. [9]). The most
acceptable way of combining them in rule-based systems is the approach used
in EMYCIN. According to this approach, we can distinguish between the two
cases as described next.

Combining Several Certainty Factors in One Rule. Consider this rule
with an AND operator:

IF inflation is high, CF = 50 percent, (A), and
IF unemployment rate is above 7 percent, CF = 70 percent, (B), and
IF bond prices decline, CF = 100 percent, (C)
THEN stock prices decline

For this type of rule, for the conclusion to be true, all IFs must be true, but in
some cases there is uncertainty as to what is going on. In such cases, the CF of
the conclusion will be the *minimum* CF on the IF side:

$$CF(A, B, \text{ and } C) = \text{minimum}[CF(A), CF(B), CF(C)]$$

In our case, the CF for stock prices to decline will be 50 percent. In other words, the chain is as strong as its weakest link.

Now look at this rule with an OR operator:

IF inflation is low, CF = 70 percent; or
IF bond prices are high, CF = 85 percent
THEN stock prices will be high

In this case it is sufficient that only *one* of the IFs is true for the conclusion to be true. Thus, if *both* IFs are believed to be true (at their certainty factor) then the conclusion will have a CF with the *maximum* of the two:

$$CF \text{ (A or B)} = \text{maximum } [CF \text{ (A)}, CF \text{ (B)}]$$

In our case, CF = 85 percent for stock prices to be high. Note that both cases hold for any number of IFs.

Combining Two or More Rules. When we have a knowledge-based system with several interrelated rules, each of which has the same conclusion but a different certainty factor, then each rule can be viewed as a piece of evidence that supports the joint conclusion. To calculate the certainty factor (or the confidence) of the conclusion, it is necessary to combine the evidences. This is done according to the following procedure (as used in MYCIN).

Let's assume there are two rules:

R1: IF the inflation rate is less than 5 percent
    THEN stock market prices go up (CF = 0.7)
R2: IF unemployment level is less than 7 percent,
    THEN stock market prices go up (CF = 0.6)

Now, let's assume it is predicted that next year the inflation rate will be 4 percent and the unemployment level will be 6.5 percent (i.e., we assume that the premises of the two rules are true). The combined effect is to be computed in the following way:

$$CF(R1,R2) = CF(R1) + CF(R2)[1 - CF(R1)]; \text{ or}$$
$$CF(R1,R2) = CF(R1) + CF(R2) - CF(R1) \times CF(R2)$$

In probabilistic terms, when we combine two dependent probabilities (joint probabilities) we get:

$$CF(R1,R2) = CF(R1) \times CF(R2)$$

Here, we deleted this value from the sum of the two certainty factors, assuming an *independent* relationship between the rules.

Example: Given CF(R1) = 0.7 AND CF(R2) = 0.6, then:
    $$CF(R1,R2) = 0.7 + 0.6(1 - 0.7) = 0.7 + 0.6(0.3) = 0.88$$

That is, the ES will tell us that there is an 88 percent chance that stock prices will increase.

Note: If we just added the CFs of R1 and R2, their combined certainty would be too large. We modify the amount of certainty added by the second certainty factor by multiplying it by (1 − the first certainty factor). Thus the greater the first CF, the less certainty is added by the second. But additional factors always add some confidence.

For a third rule to be added, the following formula may be used:

$$CF(R1,R2,R3) = CF(R1,R2) + CF(R3) [1 - CF(R1,R2)]$$

Assume a third rule is added:

R3: IF bond price increases
     THEN stock prices go up (CF = 0.85)

Now, assuming all rules are true in their IF part, the chance that stock prices will go up is:

$$CF(R1,R2,R3) = 0.88 + 0.85 (1 - 0.88) = 0.88 + 0.85 (.12) = 0.982$$

That is, there is a 98.2 percent chance that stock prices will go up. Note that CF(R1,R2) was computed earlier as 0.88. For more rules, we apply the same formula incrementally.

15.14 Fuzzy Logic

Some AI programs exploit the technique of **inexact (approximate) reasoning.** This technique, which uses the mathematical theory of **fuzzy sets** (e.g., see Zadeh [29] and Negoita [18]), simulates the process of normal human reasoning by allowing the computer to behave less precisely and logically than conventional computers do.

The thinking behind this approach is that decision making isn't always a matter of black and white, true or false; it often involves gray areas and the term *maybe*. In fact, creative decision-making processes are unstructured, playful, contentious, and rambling.

Fuzzy logic can be advantageous for the following reasons:

- *It provides flexibility.* Rigid thinking can often lead to unsatisfactory conclusions. You've locked yourself into a set pattern. Make allowances for the unexpected and you can shift your strategy whenever necessary.
- *It gives you options.* If you're confronted with a number of possibilities, you'll need to consider them all. Then, using facts *and* intuition ("highly unlikely" or "very good"), you can make an educated guess. Even computers are learning to use such rules of thumb.
- *It frees the imagination.* At first you may feel that something simply can't be done—all the facts conspire against it. Why not try asking yourself, "What

if . . . ?" Follow another avenue and see where you end up. You may make a better decision.

- *It's more forgiving.* When you're forced to make black and white decisions, you cannot afford to be wrong, because when you're wrong, you lose completely. The other way is more forgiving. If you figure something is 80 percent gray, but it turns out to be 90 percent gray, you're not going to be penalized very much.
- *It allows for observation.* Literal-minded computers have been known to come up with some peculiar results. For example, when one user instructed her computer to come up with information on smoking in the workplace, the computer diligently churned out an article on a salmon-processing plant. A little fuzzy logic might have helped the computer make a more intelligent choice.

Let's look at an example of a fuzzy set that describes a tall person. Suppose people are asked to define the minimum height that a person must attain before being considered "tall." The answers could range, say, from 5'10" to 6'2". The distribution of answers may look like this:

Height	Proportion Voted for
5'10"	0.05
5'11"	0.10
6'	0.60
6'1"	0.15
6'2"	0.10

Let's assume that Jack is 6 feet tall. In probability theory we can use the cumulative probability and say that there is a 75 percent chance that Jack is tall.

In fuzzy logic we say: Jack's degree of membership within the set of tall people is 0.75. The difference is that in probability terms Jack is perceived to be either tall or not tall and we are not sure completely whether he is tall or not. By contrast, in fuzzy logic we agree that Jack is more or less tall. Then, we can assign a membership function to show the relationship of Jack to the set of tall people (the fuzzy logic set):

$$<\text{Jack}, 0.75> \equiv \text{Tall}$$

This can be expressed in a knowledge-based system as Jack is tall (CF = 75). An important difference from probabilities is that related membership does *not* have to total 1. For example, the statement Jack is short, CF = 15, indicates that the combination is only 90. In probability theory if the probability that Jack is tall is 75 percent, then the probability that he is not tall (i.e., he is short—assuming only two events) must be 25 percent.

In contrast to certainty factors that include two values (e.g., the degree of belief and disbelief), fuzzy sets use a spectrum of possible values. Fuzzy logic has not been used much in ES in the past because it is more complex to develop, it requires more computing power, and it is more difficult to explain to users.

Fuzzy Logic in Rule-based Systems

In a regular rule-based system, a production rule has no concrete effect at all unless the data completely satisfy the antecedent of the rule. The operation of the system proceeds sequentially, with one rule firing at a time; if two rules are simultaneously satisfied, a conflict resolution policy is needed to determine which one takes precedence.

In a fuzzy rule-based system, in contrast, *all* rules are executed during each pass through the system, but with strengths ranging from "not at all" to "completely," depending on the relative degree to which their fuzzy antecedent propositions are satisfied by the data. If the antecedent is satisfied exceptionally well, the result of the rule firing is an assertion that exactly matches the consequent proposition of the rule. If the antecedent fuzzy proposition is only partially satisfied, the result is an assertion resembling the consequent, but made vague in proportion to the fuzziness of the match. If the antecedent is not satisfied at all, the result of the rule firing is a null proposition that puts no restrictions on the possible values of the variables in the consequent.

Applications and Software

Fuzzy logic is difficult to apply when the evidence is provided by people. The problems stem from linguistic vagueness to difficulties in supplying the definitions needed. One example where fuzzy logic is being used extensively is in consumer products where the input is provided by sensors rather than by people. Some examples are air conditioners, cameras, dishwashers, and microwaves. (See also Box 15.2.)

Box 15.2: Fuzzy Logic Applications

Regulating automatic braking systems in cars
Autofocusing in cameras
Automating the operation of laundry machines
Building environmental controls
Controlling the motion of trains
Identifying the dialect of killer whales
Inspecting beverage cans for printing defects
Keeping the shuttle vehicles in one place in space
Matching golf clubs to customer's swings
Trading stocks on the Japanese Nikke stock exchange
Regulating water temperature in shower heads
Controlling the amount of oxygen in cement kilns
Increasing accuracy and speed in industrial quality control applications

Fuzzy sets can be processed with special software packages such as the following representative examples:

- Fuzzy C Compiler (Togai Infralogic Inc.): This product takes text file specifications of computer programs called fuzzy associative memory, a program that processes fuzzy sets, and creates appropriate data structures and source code in C.
- TILSHELL (Togai Infralogic Inc.): This product is a complete development environment featuring window-driven editors for quickly developing the necessary text files.

Limited fuzzy logic capabilities are available in the following ES shells: Gensym, Guru, and OPS-2000.

Chapter Highlights

- Several methods can direct search and reasoning. The major ones are chaining (backward and forward), model-based reasoning, and case-based reasoning.
- Analogical reasoning relates past experiences to a current case.
- Modus ponens is a reasoning procedure that says that in an IF-THEN rule, if one part is true, so is the other.
- Testing rules to find if they are true or false is based on a pattern-matching approach.
- In backward chaining the search starts from a goal. You seek evidence that supports (or contradicts) the acceptance of your goal.
- In forward chaining the search starts from the data (evidence) and tries to arrive at a conclusion.
- The chaining process can be described graphically by an inference tree.
- Inferencing with frames is frequently done with the use of rules.
- In model-based reasoning, a model describes the system. Experimentations are conducted using a what-if approach to solve the problem.
- Case-based reasoning is based on experience with similar situations.
- In a case-based reasoning the attributes of an existing case are compared against critical attributes derived from cases stored in the case library.
- Two types of explanations exist in most ES: the *why* question, which requests an explanation of why certain information is needed, and the *how* question, whose purpose is to find how a certain conclusion was arrived at by the computer.
- Metaknowledge is knowledge about knowledge. It is especially useful in generating explanations.
- An explanation can be static, in which case a canned response is available for a specific configuration.
- An explanation can be dynamic, in which case the explanation is reconstructed according to the execution pattern of the rules.

- In using chaining it is frequently necessary to resolve potential conflicts between rules.
- AI treats uncertainty as a three-step process: First uncertainty is represented, then it is combined, and finally inferences are drawn.
- Three basic methods can be used to represent uncertainty: numeric (probability-like), graphic, and qualitative.
- Disbelief expresses a feeling of what is *not* going to occur.
- Certainty theory combines evidence available in one rule by seeking the *lowest* certainty factor when several certainty factors are added, and the *highest* certainty factor when either one of several factors is used to establish evidence.
- Certainty theory uses a special formula to combine evidences available in two or more rules.
- Fuzzy logic represents uncertainty by using fuzzy sets.
- Fuzzy logic is based on two premises: First, people reason using vague terms (e.g., *tall, young, beautiful*). Boundaries between classes are vague and are subject to interpretation. Second, human quantification is frequently fuzzy.
- Fuzzy sets create sets whose boundaries are well defined and they assign membership values to those items that cannot be defined precisely.

Key Words

analogical reasoning	explanation facility	metaknowledge
backtracking	firing a rule	model-based reasoning
backward chaining	forward chaining	modus ponens
belief function	fuzzy logic	procedural (numeric)
case-based reasoning	fuzzy set	reasoning
case library	hierarchial reasoning	rule interpreter
certainty factor	inductive reasoning	script
certainty theory	inexact (approximate)	static explanation
component model	reasoning	subjective probability
deductive reasoning	inference tree	uncertainty
disbelief	justifier	uncertainty avoidance
dynamic explanation	mathematical model	

Questions for Review

1. List the nine "sources of power." How are they related to problem solving?
2. Define deductive reasoning and contrast it with inductive reasoning.
3. What is meant when we say that a rule "fires"?
4. Define pattern matching. Explain how it is used in rule chaining.
5. Explain why backward chaining is considered goal driven.
6. Explain why forward chaining is considered data driven.
7. Explain the difference between an AND and an OR question.
8. Define backward chaining and contrast it with forward chaining.
9. Define an inference tree. What is its major purpose?
10. Explain this statement: Reasoning with frames may involve hierarchial reasoning.
11. Define model-based reasoning.
12. Define case-based reasoning.
13. List five advantages of case-based reasoning.
14. Review the case-based reasoning processing. Briefly discuss each step.
15. List some of the purposes of the explanation capability.
16. Explanation in current expert systems is done by tracing the rules. Discuss how this is done.
17. What is the *why* question? What is a typical answer to this question?
18. What is the *how* question? What is a typical answer to this question?
19. What is metaknowledge? How is it related to the explanation facility?
20. Define static explanation.
21. Why can knowledge be inexact?
22. Review the general process of dealing with uncertainty.
23. Provide an example that shows why numeric presentation of uncertainty is difficult or even impossible.
24. What are the advantages of the graphic representation of uncertainty? What are the disadvantages?
25. Qualitative methods such as multiple choice (Likert scale) and ranking are popular among experts. Why do they like these methods?
26. What is the role of belief functions in the theory of evidence?
27. What is a degree of disbelief? Give an example.
28. Why does one select a *minimum* value when using AND operator and a *maximum* value when using OR operator in combining certainty factors?
29. What are the basic premises on which the fuzzy logic approach is based?
30. What are the major advantages of fuzzy logic? What are the major disadvantages?

Questions for Discussion

1. Describe analogical reasoning. How is it related to case-based reasoning?
2. What are some of the potential problems with the qualitative method of representing uncertainty?

3. It is said that chaining (backward, forward) is an implementation of modus ponens. Why?
4. Certainty factors are popular in rule-based systems. Why is this so? What unique features does the theory of uncertainty provide?
5. Discuss the major deficiencies of existing explanation facilities. Organize your discussion as a comparison with a potential explanation given by a human.
6. The explanation facility serves the user as well as the developer. Discuss the benefits derived by each.
7. If you had a dialog with a human expert, what questions besides "Why?" and "How?" would you be likely to ask? Give examples.
8. It is said that reasoning with frames almost always involves rules. Explain why.
9. What is meant by "reasoning from first principles"? Give an example. Give an example of reasoning *not* from a first principle.
10. Summarize the major advantages of model-based reasoning. When would you use it?
11. Comment on this statement: "An understander of the world is an explainer of the world."
12. Describe the relationship between metaknowledge and explanations.
13. Fuzzy thinking is said to be advantageous for five reasons. List the reasons and provide an example to support each. If you disagree with a reason, explain why.
14. Explain the basic premise of case-based reasoning.
15. Explain the relationship between scripts and case-based reasoning.
16. Compare and contrast rule-based versus case-based reasoning.
17. Which applications are most suitable for case-based reasoning? Why?
18. List and discuss some of the potential problems of using case-based reasoning.

Exercises

1. You are given a set of rules for this question: Should we buy a house or not?

   R1: IF inflation is low
       THEN interest rates are low
       ELSE interest rates are high
   R2: IF interest rates are high
       THEN housing prices are high
   R3: IF housing prices are high
       THEN do not buy a house
       ELSE buy it

   a. Run a backward chaining with a high inflation rate as given.
   b. Run a forward chaining with a low inflation rate as given.
   c. Prepare an inference tree for the backward chaining case.

2. You are given an ES with the following rules:

   R1: IF interest rate falls
       THEN bond prices increase
   R2: IF interest rate increases
       THEN bond prices decline
   R3: IF interest rate is unchanged
       THEN bond prices remain unchanged
   R4: IF the dollar rises (against other currencies)
       THEN interest rate declines
   R5: IF the dollar falls
       THEN interest rate increases
   R6: IF bond prices decline
       THEN buy bonds

   a. A client just observed that the dollar exchange rate is falling. He wants to know whether to buy bonds. Run a forward and a backward chaining and submit a report to him.
   b. Prepare an inference tree for the backward chaining you did.
   c. A second client observed that the interest rates are unchanged. She asks for advice on investing in bonds. What will the ES tell her? Use forward chaining.

3. Assume you plan to drive from New York to Los Angeles to arrive mid-afternoon for an appointment. You want to drive no more than two hours the day you arrive, but on other days, you're willing to drive eight to ten hours. One logical way to approach this problem is to start at Los Angeles, your goal, and work backward. You would first find a place about two hours from Los Angeles for your final stopover before arrival, then plan the rest of your trip by working backward on a map until your route is completely planned. You have a limited number of days to complete the trip.

   How would you analyze the problem starting from New York? What are the major differences? Which approach would you use? Why?

4. You are given an expert system with seven rules pertaining to interpersonal skills for a job applicant:

   R1: IF the applicant answers questions in a straightforward manner
       THEN he is easy to converse with
   R2: IF the applicant seems honest
       THEN he answers in a straightforward manner
   R3: IF the applicant has items on his resume that are found to be untrue
       THEN he does not seem honest
       ELSE he seems honest
   R4: IF the applicant is able to get an appointment with the executive assistant
       THEN he is able to strike up a conversation with the executive assistant

R5: IF the applicant struck up a conversation with the executive assistant
    and the applicant is easy to converse with
    THEN he is amiable
R6: IF the applicant is amiable
    THEN he has adequate interpersonal skills
R7: IF the applicant has adequate interpersonal skills
    THEN he will get the job

  a. It is known that the applicant answers questions in a straightforward manner. Run a backward chaining analysis to find if the applicant will get the job or not.
  b. Assume that the applicant does not have any items on her resume that are found to be untrue and she is able to get an appointment with the executive assistant. Run a *forward* chaining analysis to find out if she will get the job.
  c. We just discovered that the applicant was able to get an appointment with the executive assistant. It is also known that she is honest. Does she have interpersonal skills, or not?
    Note: a, b, and c are *independent* incidents.

5. Given the following two sets of statements and conclusions, what type of reasoning was used to arrive at the conclusions?

  Case a: Students that do not study do not pass exams.
      Nancy is a student.
      Nancy did not study.
      Conclusion: Nancy will not pass her exam.

  Case b: Jack did not study for the exam.
      Jack is a student.
      Jack did not pass the exam.
      Conclusion: Students who do not study do not pass exams.

6. Review the message classification example in the case-based section of the chapter. Compare the steps to Figure 15.3 and discuss.
7. You are given these rules:

R1: IF inflation is high
    THEN unemployment is high
R2: IF inflation is high and the interest rate is high
    THEN stock prices are low
R3: IF the gold price is high or dollar exchange rate is low
    THEN stock prices are low
R4: IF gold price is high
    THEN unemployment is high

Conduct the following computations and list the rules used.
  a. The certainty factor for high inflation is 0.8 and for high interest rates it is 0.6. Find the certainty factor for stock prices.

b. The certainty factor for a high gold price is 0.5 and that for a low dollar exchange rate is 0.7. Find the certainty factor for stock prices.
c. Given all the information in parts a and b, figure the certainty factor for low stock prices and for high stock prices.
d. Figure the certainty factor for a high unemployment rate given that the inflation rate is high and the gold price is high. (Use the data in parts a and b.)

8. You are given three rules:

   R1: IF blood test results = "yes"
        THEN there is 0.8 evidence that disease is "malaria"
   R2: IF in malaria zone = "yes"
        THEN there is 0.5 evidence that disease is "malaria"
   R3: IF bit by flying bug is "true"
        THEN there is 0.3 evidence that disease is "malaria"

   What certainty factors will be computed for having malaria by the expert system if:
   a. the first two rules are considered to be true
   b. all three rules are considered to be true

9. You are given these rules:

   R1: If you study hard, then you will receive an A in the course. CF = 0.82.
   R2: If you understand the material, then you will receive an A in the course. CF = 0.85.
   R3: If you are very smart, then you will receive an A in the course. CF = 0.90.

   a. What is the chance of getting an A in the course if you study hard and understand the material?
   b. What is the chance of getting an A in the course if all premises of the rules are true?

10. Uncertainty avoidance is a viable strategy, and it is used by many builders of knowledge-based systems. Review the literature and/or conduct an interview with a builder. Prepare statements *for* and *against* uncertainty avoidance.

11. Express the following statements in terms of fuzzy sets:
    a. The chance for rain is 80 percent today. (rain? no rain?)
    b. Mr. Smith is sixty years old. (young?)
    c. The salary of the president of the United States is $200,000 per year. (high? very high?)
    d. The latest survey of economists indicates that they believe that the recession will bottom in April (20 percent), in May (30 percent), or in June (22 percent).

12. Given the following information (problem provided by E. Rivers):
    - Brenda is younger than the dancer, who lives directly west of Ginny.
    - The dancer lives directly north of Miss Quinn, who lives exactly five miles from Helen, who lives exactly two miles from the singer.
    - The pianist is older than Miss Chadwick and Cindy is older than the actress.
    - Helen is older than Miss Howell, who lives exactly three miles from Ginny, who lives directly south of Miss Bien.

    The fact that all four ladies are delightful people has nothing to do with the solution to the following questions.

    a. Represent this knowledge using two of the methods described in your text.
    b. Explain your rationale for selecting the two methods you chose.
    c. What inferencing method would need to be used with each of the two representation methods you selected in order to answer the following questions:
        - How far does Cindy live from Brenda?
        - Which lady is the oldest?
    d. What are your answers to the question in part c?
    e. Of the two methods you selected, which do you prefer (based on your answer to points c and d)? Explain your rationale.

References and Bibliography

1. Davis, R., and W. Hamscher. "Model-Based Reasoning: Troubleshooting." In *Exploring AI: Survey Talks from the National Conference on AI*, H. E. Shrobe, ed. San Mateo, CA: Morgan Kaufman, 1988.
2. diPiazza, J. S., and F. A. Helsabeck. "Laps: Cases to Models to Complete Expert Systems." *AI Magazine* (Fall 1990).
3. Fulton, S. L., and C. O. Pepe. "An Introduction to Model-based Reasoning." *AI Expert* (January 1990).
4. Goodman, M. "PRISM: A Case-Based Telex Classifier." In *Innovative Applications of Artificial Intelligence*, vol. 11, A. Rappaport and R. Smith, eds. Cambridge, MA: MIT Press, 1990.
5. Hammond, K. J. *Case-Based Planning*. New York: Academic Press, 1989.
6. Kameny, I., et al. *Guide for the Management of Expert Systems Development*. Santa Monica, CA: RAND Corp., 1989.
7. Kanal, L., and J. Lemmer. *Uncertainty in Artificial Intelligence*. Amsterdam: North Holland, 1986.
8. Kidd, A. L., and M. B. Cooper. "Man-Machine Interface Issues in the Construction and Use of an Expert System." *International Journal of Man-Machine Studies* 22 (1985).

9. Kopcso, D., et al. "A Comparison of the Manipulation of Certainty Factors by Individuals and Expert Systems Shells." *Journal of Management Information Systems* (Summer 1988).

10. Lenat, D. B. "The Ubiquity of Discovery." *Artificial Intelligence* 19 (no. 2, 1982).

11. Liang, T. P., and E. Turban, eds. *Case-Based Reasoning*, a special issue of *Expert Systems with Applications*, January, 1993.

12. Ling, X., and W. G. Rudd. "Combining Opinions from Several Experts." *Applied AI* 3 (1989).

13. Magill, W. G. W., and A. L. Stewart. "Uncertainty Techniques in Expert Systems Software." *Decision Support Systems* (January 1991).

14. Mishkoff, H. C. *Understanding Artificial Intelligence*. Dallas: Texas Instruments, 1985 (republished by H. W. Sams, 1988).

15. Moore, J. D., et al. "Explanation in Expert Systems—A Survey." In *Proceedings, The First International Symposium on Expert Systems in Business, Finance, and Accounting*. Univ. of Southern California, Los Angeles, September 1988.

16. Nagao, M. *Knowledge and Inference*. New York: Academic Press, 1990.

17. Neapolitan, R. E. *Probabilistic Reasoning in Expert Systems*. New York: John Wiley & Sons, 1990.

18. Negoita, C. F. *Expert Systems and Fuzzy Systems*. Menlo Park, CA: Benjamin-Cummings, 1985.

19. Owen, S. *Analog for Automated Reasoning*. New York: Academic Press, 1990.

20. Parsaye, K., and M. Chignell. *Expert Systems*. New York: John Wiley & Sons, 1988.

21. Riesbeck, C. K., and R. L. Schank. *Inside Case-based Reasoning*. Hillsdale, NJ: Lawrence Erlbaum Associates, 1989.

22. Shafer, G. *A Mathematical Theory of Evidence*. Princeton, NJ: Princeton Univ. Press, 1976.

23. Slade, S. "Case-based Reasoning: A Research Paradigm." *AI Magazine* (Spring 1991).

24. Sombe, L. *Reasoning Under Incomplete Information in Artificial Intelligence*. New York: John Wiley & Sons, 1990.

25. Tuthill, G. S. *Knowledge Engineering*. Blue Ridge Summit, PA: TAB Books, 1990.

26. Vosniadou, S., and A. Ortony, eds. *Similarity and Analogical Reasoning*. Cambridge, MA: Cambridge Press, 1989.

27. Walters, J., and N. R. Nielsen. *Crafting Knowledge Based Systems*. New York: John Wiley & Sons, 1988.

28. Winston, P. H. *Artificial Intelligence*, 2nd ed. Reading, MA: Addison-Wesley, 1984.

29. Zadeh, L. A. "Coping with the Imprecision of the Real World." *Communications of ACM* (April 1984).

APPENDIX 15-A: ES Shells and Uncertainty

This appendix shows how different expert system shells handle uncertainty.*
I. EMYCIN is the classic ES shell (see Chapters 12 and 16).

Given: $-1 \leq CF \leq +1$

1) IF, $CF1 \geq 0$, $CF2 \geq 0$
   THEN, $CFX = CF1 + CF2 - CF1 \times CF2$

2) IF, $CF1 < 0$, $CF2 < 0$
   THEN, $CFX = CF1 + CF2 + CF1 \times CF2$

3) IF, CF1 and CF2 have different signs
   THEN, $CFX = \dfrac{CF1 + CF2}{1 - MIN\,(|CF1|,|CF2|)}$

II. EXSYS is a small rule-based shell. There are two options:

1. Use a scale of 0 through 10, actually 1 through 9; using 0 and 10 will lock the values as either completely true or completely untrue.

   Given: $CF = 0, 1, 2, \ldots, 10$

   IF, either CF1 or CF2 = 0 or 10
   THEN, CFX is the first 0 or 10 found
   ELSE, $CFX = AVG(CF1, CF2)$

2. Use a -100 to $+100$ scale; three suboptions are available
   a. Average the certainty factors:

   Given: $-100 \leq CF \leq 100$

   THEN, $CFX = AVG(CF1, CF2)$

   b. Multiply the certainty factors (similarly to a joint probability):

   Given: $-100 \leq CF \leq 100$

   IF, $CF1 \geq 0$ AND $CF2 \geq 0$
   THEN, $CFX = CF1 \times CF2/100$
   ELSE, UNDEFINED

---

*According to D. Kopcso, et al., "A Comparison of the Manipulation of Certainty Factors by Individuals and Expert System Shells," *Journal of Management Information Systems* (Summer 1988). For additional information see W. G. W. Magill and A. L. Stewart, "Uncertainty Techniques in Expert Systems Software," *Decision Support Systems* (January 1991).

c. Use a certainty-factors-like approach:

Given: $-100 \leq CF \leq 100$

IF, $CF1 \geq 0$ AND $CF2 \geq 0$
THEN, $CFX = 100 - (100 - CF1) \times (100 - CF2)/100$
ELSE, UNDEFINED

III. VP Expert is a small shell.

Given: $0 \leq CF \leq 100$

THEN, $CFX = CF1 + CF2 - CF1 \times CF2/100$

Chapter 16

Building Expert Systems: Process and Tools

This chapter provides an overview of the process of building expert systems. The process, which consists of six major phases and several dozen activities, is executed differently depending on the nature of the system being constructed, the development strategy, and the supporting tools. The following topics form the framework for analyzing the building process:

16.1 Development Life Cycle

An expert system is basically computer software and as such its development follows a software development process. The goal of such a process is to maximize the probability of developing viable, sustainable software within cost limitations and according to schedule. The main functions of a model of this process are to determine the order of the steps (or tasks) involved in the software development and to establish the transition criteria for progressing from one stage to another. Many such models have been proposed; notable is the waterfall model (see Boehm [7]) for a **system development life cycle.**

When expert systems are constructed, some or all of the software development tasks are being performed. The nature of the specific application determines which tasks are going to be performed, in which order, and to what depth. For example, a large-scale ES will be developed according to a complex life-cycle process, whereas a small-scale system for end-users will include only a few of the tasks. (See appendix 16-C.)

The various tasks that are encountered in building expert systems are organized in six phases, as shown in Figure 16.1. Specific explanations of these phases and some of the tasks involved are provided in the remaining sections of this chapter.

Be aware, however, that the process is *not linear;* rather, some tasks are performed together, and as will be shown, a return to previous tasks or even phases happens frequently.

16.2 Phase I: Project Initialization

Finding an appropriate project for ES is not an easy task. Dozens of factors must be considered, and many ES projects fail because of poor front-end analysis. Experts have developed methodologies and checklists for executing the tasks in this phase (e.g., Beckman [5], Carrico et al. [8], Harmon and Sawyer [15], Prerau [26], and Samuell and Jones [28]). In a large-scale project, several participants will probably be involved.

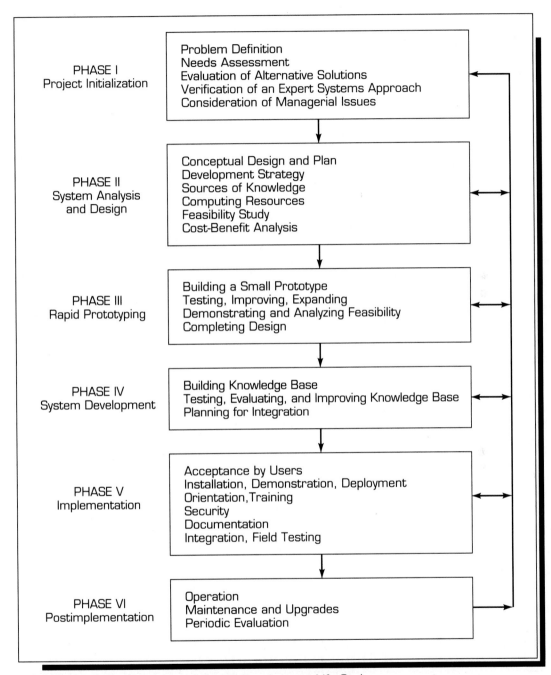

PHASE I Project Initialization	Problem Definition Needs Assessment Evaluation of Alternative Solutions Verification of an Expert Systems Approach Consideration of Managerial Issues
PHASE II System Analysis and Design	Conceptual Design and Plan Development Strategy Sources of Knowledge Computing Resources Feasibility Study Cost-Benefit Analysis
PHASE III Rapid Prototyping	Building a Small Prototype Testing, Improving, Expanding Demonstrating and Analyzing Feasibility Completing Design
PHASE IV System Development	Building Knowledge Base Testing, Evaluating, and Improving Knowledge Base Planning for Integration
PHASE V Implementation	Acceptance by Users Installation, Demonstration, Deployment Orientation, Training Security Documentation Integration, Field Testing
PHASE VI Postimplementation	Operation Maintenance and Upgrades Periodic Evaluation

FIGURE 16.1 Schematic View of the ES Development Life Cycle

TABLE 16.1 Tasks in Project Initialization

Problem definition

Needs assessment

Evaluation of alternative solutions
(availability of experts, education and training, packaged knowledge, conventional software)

Verification of an expert systems approach
(requirements, justification, appropriateness)

Consideration of managerial issues
(project initiator, financing, resources, legal and other constraints, selling the project, identifying a champion)

Ending milestone: Approval of the project in principle

The typical tasks of this phase are shown in Table 16.1. The tasks are inter-related and may not follow any specific sequence. The details of the major tasks are discussed next.

16.3   Problem Definition and Needs Assessment

A clear definition of the problem simplifies the remaining tasks significantly and helps generate a productive program. Defining the problem is a matter of answering some basic questions. Just what is the problem? What are the real needs? Typical business problems could be low productivity, lack of sufficient expert knowledge to go around, information overload, time problems, or people problems. Whatever the problem or need, write a clear statement of it and provide as much supporting information as possible.

Most expert systems are being used to improve an aspect of poor job performance. For example, an employee may not be achieving a desired quantity or quality of work within time or cost constraints. Problems like this can often be traced to a lack of knowledge. The employee must either possess the knowledge or have access to it, whether in the form of an expert person or an expert system. The best way to understand the problem or need is to conduct a kind of formal study called **needs assessment.**

16.4   Evaluation of Alternative Solutions

Before you start a major ES development program, consider alternative solutions to the problem. Lack of knowledge is a problem that could be solved in ways other than with expert systems. Let's consider some examples.

Availability of Experts. If the problem is knowledge related, then someone must have the desired knowledge. One approach may simply be to make an existing or new expert accessible to those needing the expertise.

Education and Training. Another solution is to provide education and training in the desired subject matter for those who need it. Courses, seminars, and related materials are frequently much less expensive to develop than an expert system.

Packaged Knowledge. An alternative to additional education and training is to package the knowledge and related information into printed (or electronic) documentation. Of course, it takes time to generate manuals and job aids. However, they are often fairly inexpensive and a great deal easier to create than an expert system.

Conventional Software. A computer solution may still be best for a problem, but an expert system may not be completely appropriate. Once you've defined a problem, examine the possibility of using standard software packages. For example, a popular spreadsheet or database management system may work.

16.5   Verification of an Expert System Approach

The fact that other alternatives are not appropriate for solving a problem does not mean that an expert system is necessary. A framework for determining a fit with an ES approach was proposed by Waterman [40]. According to this framework (which has been modified in this text), a three-part study should be conducted: requirements, justification, and appropriateness.

Requirements for ES Development. The following twelve requirements are *all* necessary to make ES development successful:

1. The task does not require common sense.
2. The task requires only cognitive, not physical, skills.
3. At least one genuine expert, who is willing to cooperate, exists.
4. Experts involved can articulate their methods of problem solving.
5. Experts involved can agree on the knowledge and the solution approach to the problem.
6. The task is not too difficult.
7. The task is well understood and is defined clearly.
8. The task definition is fairly stable.
9. Conventional (algorithmic) computer solution techniques are not satisfactory.
10. Incorrect or nonoptimal results can be tolerated.
11. Data and test cases are available.
12. The task's vocabulary has no more than a couple of hundred concepts.

Justification for ES Development. Like any other information system, an expert system needs to be justified. Of the following eight factors, at least one must be present to justify an ES:

1. The solution to the problem has a high payoff.
2. The ES can preserve scarce human expertise so it will not be lost.
3. Expertise is needed in many locations.
4. Expertise is needed in hostile or hazardous environments.
5. The expertise improves performance and/or quality.
6. The system can be used for training.
7. The ES solution can be derived faster than that which a human can provide.
8. The ES is more consistent and/or accurate than a human.

The derived benefits in one or more of these areas must be compared against the costs of developing the system. A preliminary justification is conducted in this phase, whereas a detailed analysis is performed in phase II.

Appropriateness of the ES. Three factors should be considered in determining when it is appropriate to develop an ES:

1. Nature of the problem: The problem should have a symbolic structure, and heuristics should be available for its solution. In addition, it is desirable that the task be decomposable.
2. Complexity of the task: The task should be neither too easy nor too difficult for a human expert.
3. Scope of the problem: The problem should be of a manageable size; it also should have some practical value.

Checklists. Several checklists have been developed to assist in finding applications suitable for expert system development:

- An elaborate method with four separate checklists has been suggested by Slagle and Wick [31], who use a weighing point system.
- A checklist approach that attempts to assess the strategic value of an ES has been suggested by Samuell and Jones [28].
- Detailed checklists have been proposed by Prerau [26].

The choice of problem should also take into consideration the generic areas discussed in Chapter 12 where ES have proved to be successful.

16.6 Consideration of Managerial Issues

Expert systems projects do not start by themselves. Sometimes they start because there is an acute need. But in many cases, they start because someone in the organization believes in AI technologies and is willing to support an ES project. A project may start as soon as a decision is made to look for an appropriate project. A project may start because the company has decided to follow a competitor's lead or because one of the company's employees did an ES project as a student. Who starts a project is obviously an important issue but there are several other managerial issues that need to be considered when an ES (or any other AI project) is launched:

- Availability of financing
- Availability of other resources
- Legal and other potential constraints
- Selling the project: All interested parties and especially top management must be convinced of the project's value. (See McCullough [22].)
- Identifying a champion: Someone in top management needs to sponsor the project strongly.

16.7 Phase II: System Analysis and Design

Once the concept of the project has been blessed, a detailed system analysis must be conducted to obtain some idea of how the system is going to look. Many tasks are performed in this phase, which may be supported by an initial prototype. These tasks are listed in Table 16.2.

16.8 Conceptual Design

A conceptual design of an ES is similar to an architectural sketch of a house. It gives you a general idea of what the system will look like and how it is going to solve the problem. The design shows the general capabilities of the system, the interfaces with other computer-based information systems, the areas of risk, the

TABLE 16.2 Tasks in Project Conceptualization and System Analysis

Tasks
Conceptual design and plan
Development strategy
Sources of knowledge
Computing resources
Feasibility study
Cost-benefit analysis
Ending milestone: approved complete project plan

required resources, anticipated cash flow, the composition of the team, and any other information that is necessary for detailed design later. Vendors and consultants may play a major role in this phase because of their experience. The development team is being initiated and the participants start to assume their roles. Once the conceptual design is completed, it is necessary to decide the development strategy.

16.9   Development Strategy

According to Vedder and Turban [38], there are several general classes of AI **development strategies:** do it yourself, hire an outside developer, enter into a joint venture, merge, and attack on all fronts. Although some organizations use a single strategy, others use several. Thus, whenever a new application is developed it can be matched with any of the strategies.

Do It Yourself. This course of action is attractive for organizations that already possess the skills and resources needed for developing AI projects. It is also a strong candidate for companies that want to develop AI applications containing significant amounts of proprietary or sensitive knowledge (Odette [24]). Various options are available in this general class.

First, AI development can be *part of end-user computing.* The principal attraction of this strategy is that it provides a low-cost, low-risk entry into AI technology. It is an attractive option for organizations that are highly decentralized. A typical advocate of this approach is Du Pont, Inc. (Feigenbaum et al. [11]). By 1993, over 1,000 ES were in use for an annual savings of about $30 million.

Second, AI projects can be *completely centralized.* According to this strategy, all AI projects are centralized in a special unit or department. It is a typical strategy in very large organizations that are heavily involved with AI.

Third, AI development can be *decentralized,* but control can be centralized. Systems are developed using the Du Pont strategy but they are registered in a central unit. This unit assures appropriate maintenance, security, documentation, standardization of technologies, and interfaces with other computer-based information systems.

High technology islands are the fourth option. Some companies are using several specialized units for AI; this is the concept of the "technology island."

The fifth option involves utilizing *information centers.* According to this approach, an organization uses the existing information (or help) centers as the vehicles for disseminating ES.

Hire an Outside Developer. The first variation of this strategy is to hire a consulting firm. This is an attractive option for the many firms that do not have (or cannot afford) knowledge engineers in-house. A second variation is to belong to a consortium of clients. An example of this strategy is the development of an ES called Underwriting Advisor (Harmon et al. [14]).

Enter into a Joint Venture. The first variation of this strategy is to form a joint venture with a vendor. In such a strategy, the vendor develops a system for the client while testing its own products and services. A second variation is to sponsor university research and learn from the results. Digital Equipment Corp. built the XCON system, by joining forces with Carnegie-Mellon University, using this strategy.

Merge, Acquire, or Become a Major Stockholder in an AI Company. An old adage applies to this strategy, according to DeSalvo and Liebowitz [10]: If you can't beat them, join them. A company might develop an expert systems capability by merging with or acquiring an AI company or by becoming a major stockholder.

16.10   Selecting an Expert

Experts. Table 16.3 lists some characteristics of human experts. Human experts possess knowledge that is much more complex than what we find in documented sources. It is based on experience, and in many cases it can be expressed in terms of heuristics.

Selection. Expert systems use both documented sources and human experts as sources of knowledge. The more human expertise that is needed, the longer and more complicated the acquisition process will be. Several issues may surface in selecting expert(s).

- Who selects the expert(s)
- How to identify an expert (what characteristics an expert should exhibit)
- What to do if several experts are needed
- How to motivate the expert to cooperate.

The latter issue is briefly discussed next.

Many expert systems that are now functioning had little trouble with expert cooperation. Their experts were researchers, professors, or maintenance experts due to retire soon. The whole idea of ES was challenging, new, and innovative, so experts tended to cooperate. In some systems several experts were engaged, each of whom contributed a small portion of a large knowledge base.

This cooperative situation may change when different types of experts are involved. Experts are starting to ask questions such as, "What's in it for me?" "Why should I contribute my wisdom and risk my job?," and so on. For these reasons, before building an AI system that requires the cooperation of experts, management should ask questions such as these:

- Should experts be compensated for their contributions (e.g., in the form of royalties, a special reward, or payment)?
- How can one tell if the experts are telling the truth about the way they solve problems?

TABLE 16.3 Attributes of an Expert

1. Highly developed *perceptual attention ability*—experts can "see" what others cannot.
2. Awareness of the difference between *relevant* and *irrelevant* information—experts know how to concentrate on what's important.
3. Ability to *simplify* complexities—experts can "make sense out of chaos."
4. A strong set of *communication skills*—experts know how to demonstrate their expertise to others.
5. Knowledge of when to make *exceptions*—experts know when and when *not* to follow decision rules.
6. A strong sense of *responsibility* for their choices—experts are not afraid to stand behind their decisions.
7. *Selectivity* about which problems to solve—experts know which problems are significant and which are not.
8. Outward *confidence* in their decisions—experts believe in themselves and their abilities.
9. Ability to *adapt* to changing task conditions—experts avoid rigidity in decision strategies.
10. Highly developed *content knowledge* about their area—experts know a lot and keep up with the latest developments.
11. Greater *automaticity* of cognitive processes—experts can do habitually what others have to work at.
12. Ability to *tolerate stress*—experts can work effectively under adverse conditions.
13. Capability to be more *creative*—experts are better able to find novel solutions to problems.
14. Inability to *articulate* their decision processes—experts make decisions "on experience."
15. Thorough *familiarity* with the domain, including task expertise built up over a long period of task performance, knowledge of the organizations that will be developing and using the ES, knowledge of the user community, and knowledge of technical and technological alternatives.
16. Knowledge and *reputation* such that if the ES is able to capture a portion of the expert's expertise, the system's output will have credibility and authority.
17. Commitment of a substantial amount of *time* to the development of the system, including temporary relocation to the development site if necessary.
18. Capability of *communicating* his or her knowledge, judgment, and experience.
19. *Cooperative, easy to work with*, and *eager* to work on the project.
20. *Interest in computer systems*, even if he or she is not a computer specialist.

Source: Items 1–14 from S. K. Goyal, et al. "COMPASS: An Expert System for Telephone Switch Maintenance," *Expert Systems* (July 1985) Reprinted from *Expert Systems* with permission of Learned Information, Inc., Medford, NJ. Items 15–20 adapted from J. Shanteau, "Psychological Characteristics of Expert Decision Makers," in *Proceedings, Symposium on Expert Systems and Audit Judgment,* Univ. of Southern California, Los Angeles, February 17–18, 1986.

- How can experts be assured that they will not lose their jobs, or that their jobs will not be deemphasized, once the ES is fully operational?
- Are the experts concerned about other people in the organization whose jobs may suffer because of the introduction of ES, and what can management do in such a case?

In general, management should use some incentives to influence experts so that they will cooperate fully with the knowledge engineer.

16.11 Software Classification: Technology Levels

It's helpful to classify software into five **technology levels:** languages, support tools, shells, hybrid systems, and ES applications (specific ES). The boundaries between the levels are fairly fuzzy, and our classification approach is used mainly for providing an initial understanding of ES software. Figure 16.2 illustrates the levels.

Roughly speaking, the specific application (top of figure) can be constructed with shells, and/or support tools, and/or hybrid systems, and/or languages. Shells and hybrid systems can be constructed with languages and/or support tools, and support tools are constructed with languages.

The higher the level of the software in Figure 16.2, the *less programming* is required. The trade-off is that the higher the level, the *less flexible* is the software. Generally speaking, the use of higher levels of software enables quicker programming (even by end-users). On the other hand, complex and nonstandard applications must be built with lower levels of software.

Description of Levels

Specific Expert Systems. Specific ES are the application products that advise a specific user on a specific issue, for example, a consultation system that diagnoses a malfunction in a locomotive and systems that advise on tax shelters or on buying software.

Shell (Skeletal) Systems. Instead of building an ES from scratch, it is often possible to borrow extensively from a previously built specific ES. This strategy

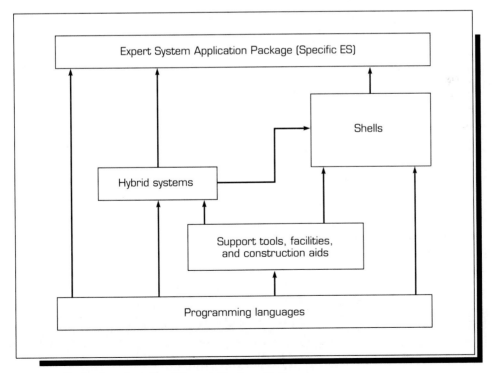

FIGURE 16.2 Technology Levels of Expert System Software

has resulted in several integrated software tools that are described as shell (skel-etal) systems. The expert systems are stripped of their knowledge component, which leaves only a shell—the explanation and inference mechanisms.

Shells are integrated packages in which the major components of the expert systems (except for the knowledge base) are preprogrammed. The programmer needs only to insert the knowledge in order to build a system.

Support Tools. With shells, the system builder needs to construct only the knowledge base. In contrast, many other types of tools help build the various parts of the system. They are aids for knowledge acquisition, knowledge vali-dation and verification, and construction of interfaces to other software pack-ages.

Hybrid Systems (Environments). **Hybrid systems** are composed of several support tools and programming languages. They enable systems to be built faster than they would be built if only programming languages were used. Hy-brid systems provide skilled programmers with a rapid prototyping environ-ment in which they can build shells or specific ES. ART, for example, contains modules from which an inference engine can be assembled. One module pro-vides a procedure for handling measures of uncertainty, while another module provides a Bayesian procedure for handling probabilities. The knowledge engi-neer builds an inference engine and then proceeds to use that engine in con-junction with a knowledge base to build an expert system.

Programming Languages. Expert systems can be constructed with one of many programming languages—ranging from AI languages to standard proce-dural languages (such as COBOL). They can even be programmed with fourth-generation languages such as Lotus 1-2-3. A brief description of the AI program-ming languages, **LISP** and **PROLOG,** is given in Appendix 16-A.

16.12   Building Expert Systems with Tools*

Several software tool kits may simplify the construction of ES. In fact, most knowledge engineers build ES by using some commercial knowledge engineer-ing development software; they add only a problem-specific knowledge base. Over the past twenty years, these tools have evolved from low-level languages to high-level knowledge engineering aids. Now, commercial-quality software tools are becoming available.

A knowledge engineering tool reflects a certain knowledge engineering viewpoint and a specific methodology for building ES. It includes a problem-solving paradigm. It may, for example, reflect a preference for building diag-

*This section is based on Hayes-Roth et al. [17].

nostic ES by capturing an expert's empirical symptom-problem associations. A specific paradigm constitutes a strategy for using knowledge to solve a class of problems.

Each paradigm implies certain design properties for the knowledge system architecture, and a knowledge engineering tool generally builds these properties directly into its knowledge base structure and inference engine. A shell such as EXSYS supports the construction of ES with rule-based, backward-chaining architecture. This may appear restrictive because the design constrains what a knowledge engineer can do and what the specific ES can do. On the other hand, EXSYS exploits its knowledge-system-designed constraints to improve the quality and power of the assistance it gives. Because the knowledge engineering tool "knows" how knowledge is stored within the knowledge base, the detailed operation of the inference engine, and the organization and control of problem-solving activities, it can simplify development tasks considerably. There is an analogy here to any focused software. A spreadsheet, for example, constrains the user to rows and columns, which makes programming a natural and easy process; that is, constraints may be very useful.

Building an ES with knowledge engineering tools involves the following four steps:

1. The builder employs the tool's development engine (Figure 16.3) to load the knowledge base.

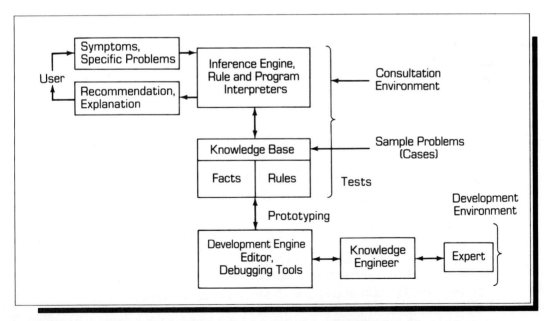

FIGURE 16.3 Building Specific Expert Systems within a Shell (*Source:* Adapted from P. Kinnucan, "Software Tools Speed Expert Systems Development," *High Technology* [March 1985].)

2. The knowledge base is tested on sample problems using the inference engine. The test may suggest additions and changes that could result in an improved knowledge base. This is basically a prototyping step done with the aid of the editor and debugging tools.
3. The process is repeated until the system is operational.
4. The development engine is removed and the specific expert system is ready for its users (using a *run-time* component of the tool).

16.13   Shells and Environments

Shells

Expert systems, as described earlier, are composed of six basic components: knowledge acquisition subsystems, inference engine, explanation facility, interface subsystem (for conducting consultation), knowledge base management facility, and knowledge base. The first five subsystems constitute what is called an expert system **shell.** The knowledge base is the *content,* or the "inside," of the shell. Experience has shown that there is no need to program the first five subsystems of the shell for every application. On the contrary, once a shell is constructed it can be used for many applications; all one has to do is insert the necessary knowledge. By using the shell approach, expert systems can be built much faster. Furthermore, the programming skill required is much lower. All factors together contribute to a cost reduction. The shell concept, which is illustrated in Figure 16.4, is especially useful in rule-based systems.

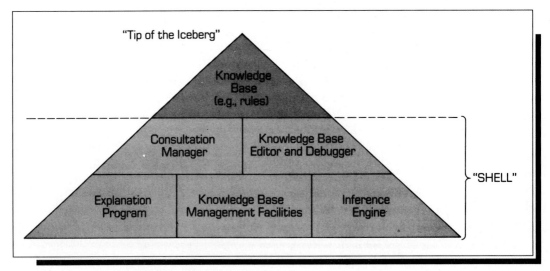

FIGURE 16.4   Shell Concept for Building Expert Systems. (*Source:* B. G. Buchanan in Texas Instruments First Satellite Program)

Here are some examples of rule-based shells:

- Small size: EXSYSEL, VP Expert, Level5
- Medium size: EXSYS Professional, Guru, KES 2.2, Nexpert, Personal Consultant Plus
- Large size: ESE, S.1, AES, IMPACT, SYNTEL, ADS
- Induction: 1st-CLASS, TIMM

For additional information on all types of shells see Gevarter [12] and Harmon et al. [14].

A shell can be extremely useful in developing expert systems for a specific application, provided it is well chosen. Two types of shells exist: general and domain specific. When you select a shell, make sure it can handle the specifics of the application properly (including explanation and interface with databases and other computerized systems).

Shells do have limitations and disadvantages. Because they are inflexible, it may be difficult to fit them to nonstandard problems and tasks. As a result, a builder may use several shells, as well as environments and other tools, even in one application. Such proliferation may cause problems in training and maintenance. Shells also add an interface layer that requires its own resident interpreter. Shells are end-user tools (similar to fourth-generation languages), and their use is subject to the problems of end-user computing (poor documentation, weak security, improper maintenance).

Despite their limitations, shells are being used extensively by many organizations, small and large. In some cases they are used primarily for training or as the starting tool in the prototyping cycle.

Domain-specific tools are designed to be used *only* in the development of a specific area. For example, there are shells for diagnostic systems, shells for configuration, and shells for scheduling. A domain-specific tool may include some rule-based tools, an inductive mechanism, or a knowledge verification component. Domain-specific tools enhance the use of more standard tools by providing special development support and users' interface. Such features permit a much faster construction of applications. Presently, there are only a few commercial domain-specific shells and tools available. They cost much more than general-purpose software. For further discussion see Price [27].

Environments

Development environments are defined by Harmon et al. [14] as development systems that support *several* different ways of representing knowledge and handling inferences. They may use frames, object-oriented programming, semantic networks, rules and metarules, different types of chaining (forward, backward, and bidirectional), nonmonotonic reasoning, a rich variety of inheritance techniques, and more (see Table 16.4). Hybrid systems permit a programming environment that allows for building complex specific systems or complex tools. Initially, hybrid tools were developed for large computers and AI work-

TABLE 16.4 Features of
Hybrid Systems

Backward, forward, and bidirectional chaining
Object-oriented programming, frames
Metarules
Hypothetical reasoning
Complete pattern matching or variable rules
Nonmonotonic reasoning or truth maintenance
Dynamic graphics, icons, visual interactive simulations
High-quality browsing utilities
CASE library facilities
Ability to set breakpoints or interrupt a consultation
Semantic networks
Interfaces to databases, spreadsheets and hypermedia, neural networks
Real-time capabilities

Source: Based on *Expert Systems Strategies* 4 (no. 2, 1988). Published by Harmon Associates.

stations. Now they are available on personal computers. The following are representative packages:

- Large systems: ART, KEE, Knowledge Craft, Aion Development System, KBMS
- PC systems: GoldWorks II, Nexpert Object, ART-IM, Keystone, KEE/PC, Personal Consultant Plus, DAI-SOGEN, Level5 Object, and Kappa PC

Environments are more specialized than languages. Therefore they can increase the productivity of system builders. Although environments require more programming skills than shells, they are more flexible. Hybrid systems are based on two basic tools: Smalltalk and OPS.

Smalltalk was developed initially as an object-oriented programming language. It was expanded to include facilities for data abstraction, message sending, object classification, and interactive development. Now it is a complete development tool kit used for rapid prototyping of AI systems. Smalltalk has many built-in graphic interfaces (e.g., icons).

OPS is a production system programming. Production system techniques are useful when the knowledge related to a programming problem occurs (or can be expressed) in a natural rule structure. The OPS family was used in developing the XCON system. It combines a rule-based language with a conventional procedural programming technique. Two commercial products were developed from the initial research tool: OPS5 (implemented in LISP) and OPS83 (incorporates an imperative sublanguage that resembles Pascal or C). It is now being used in a comprehensive commercial environment known as Knowledge Craft.

Hybrid systems are gaining popularity. Representative examples are:

- *ART* is a comprehensive LISP-based environment; it is a forward-chaining rule-based system. It is based on OPS5, but many features have been added. ART has four main components: rules (mainly for procedural knowledge), facts, schemata, and viewpoints (for declarative knowledge). A related product, ART-IM, is written in C and runs on workstations and personal computers.
- *KEE* is basically an object-oriented-based environment. Thus, the primary knowledge representation method is a frame. In contrast with ART, which approaches problems from a rule-based perspective, KEE begins by conceptualizing a problem in terms of objects and the relationships among them. KEE uses extensive graphics, icons, and windows and can be used on a variety of computers (including advanced personal computers). Related products are KEE/370 (for IBM machines) and KEE/PC.
- Nexpert Object can run on IBM's PC-AT or larger personal computers (386's). Nexpert Object is known for its extensive built-in interfaces.

16.14 Software Selection

Software packages of languages, aids, environments, and shells are plentiful. See Appendix 16-B. You can choose from several hundred commercial packages for knowledge acquisition, representation, browsing, debugging, editing, explaining, and so on. The ES builder is frequently puzzled by what is described as an "ES software jungle." Selecting software, in general, is a complicated matter because of frequent changes in technology and the many criteria against which the alternative packages are compared (see Anderson [2]).

In principle, the selection of a tool is based on a match between the varieties of knowledge to be represented and the built-in features of the tool. In practice, this selection process is complex for several reasons:

- It is difficult to make the transition from problems to tools.
- Tool selection is affected by whatever tool one may already own and the degree of familiarity with ES tools.
- Currently, tools on the market are more similar than they are different.

The major issues involved in the *selection* of ES development software are summarized in Table 16.5. For complex systems a builder may use several software development packages.

Note: The selection of hardware is a problem only when large systems are being constructed. Small systems are routinely developed and implemented on personal computers. Even large systems can be developed on existing workstations.

TABLE 16.5 Representative Issues in Software Selection for Expert System Development

Can the tool be easily obtained and installed? (This includes cost factors, legal arrangements, and compatibility with existing hardware.)

How well is the tool supported by the vendor? Is the current version of the system fairly stable?

How difficult will it be to expand, modify, or add a front-end or a back-end to the tool? Is a source code available or is the system sold only as a black box?

Is it simple to incorporate LISP (or other language) functions to compensate for necessary features that are not built in?

What kind of knowledge representation schemes does the tool provide? (rules? networks? frames? others?) How well do these match the intended application?

Can the tool handle the expected form of the application data? (continuous, error filled, inconsistent, uncertain, time varying, etc.)

Do the inference mechanisms provided match the problem?

Does the allowable granularity of knowledge match what is needed by the problem?

Does the expected speed of the developed system match the problem if real-time use is required?

Is there a delivery (consultation) vehicle available if many copies of the application will be needed?

What is the track record of success of the package?

What are the in-house software capabilities? (Are programmers available and qualified?)

What are the existing programming languages in systems that are likely to interface with the proposed application?

What are the future plans and strategy regarding AI dissemination and the use of languages and tools?

What hardware and networks are present in the organization?

Is this the organization's first ES application? Or have systems been developed before? What software was used in the past?

What is the anticipated maintenance plan? Who is going to do it?

Where is the product going to be used and by whom?

How easy is it to port applications to different hardware environments?

What training is necessary for the builder and for the users?

Source: Modified from S. K. Goyal et al., "COMPASS: An Expert System for Telephone Switch Maintenance," *Expert Systems* (July 1985). Reprinted from *Expert Systems* with permission of Learned Information, Inc., Medford, NJ.

Evaluation Procedures

Several methodologies have been proposed for evaluation of ES software. Generally speaking, these methods develop a set of attributes against which existing packages are compared. In addition, in-depth evaluations of popular packages appear periodically in magazines. One problem is that most of these evaluations are subjective. Also, the capabilities of the packages change rapidly as new versions appear. The following references can be reviewed for both proposed methodologies and actual evaluations: Gevarter [12], Harmon et al. [15], and Mettrey [23]. All other things being equal, cost-effectiveness can be the determining factor in software selection.

Shells Versus Languages. Choosing which software tool to use is a major decision in the development process. Your choice will depend on several important factors. For example, is programming capability available in-house and, if so, which languages are used? What type of computer system will be used to develop the software and what is the user's host computer? The selection of a tool will also be affected by the time and funds available to create the software. Will you use a shell, an AI language, or a conventional programming language?

The fastest and easiest approach is to use a shell. But is there a shell made for your computer? Does the shell format fit the domain of interest? Is the shell large enough and capable enough to handle the project you have in mind?

If this is your first expert system development project, you should strive for a shell. Start by identifying the shells available for your kind of computer. Most shells run on only a few target machines. Dozens of packages are available for IBM personal computers and various compatibles; fewer programs are available for the Apple Macintosh series. Several shells run extremely well on workstations such as Sun Microsystem's products.

If a shell is available for your computers and within budget, you need to determine if its capabilities fit your problem. You may have to do some initial knowledge engineering to see if the domain can be expressed properly in rule format. Match the specifications of the tool to other aspects of the problem, and if there is a fit, by all means make the investment. If a shell does not fit your machine, or if you need extensive interfaces with a conventional software, you should use conventional programming. Expert systems are programmed in COBOL, Pascal, and especially in C.

Another option is to use the AI languages of PROLOG or LISP. LISP and PROLOG interpreters are available for almost any machine. (See Appendix 16-A.)

16.15 Hardware Support

The choice of software packages is frequently determined by the hardware used and its processing and memory power. Efficient LISP execution, for example, may require very specialized hardware architectures. Such architectures have been commercially available under the name **LISP machines.** Although LISP implementations exist for a wide variety of conventional computers (including micros), performance could be marginal for many large-scale or complex commercial applications.

For ES to be more cost-effective, the cost of hardware must be reduced. This could be done, for instance, with a bus-centered architectural design that allows for resource sharing. In addition, it provides an efficient means to augment existing non-AI application software with powerful AI tools. For example, a LISP machine equipped with both LISP and UNIX processors (with full-communication, bus-centered systems) can also furnish an environment for PROLOG and/

or UNIX-based software. This will enable dedicated **AI workstations** to be used for general-purpose computing—a considerable cost reduction to the user.

Some commercial vendors are moving away from LISP or PROLOG and toward conventional languages like C. Another approach is to develop the ES on special hardware, using LISP or PROLOG, then run the ES consultation on a less powerful AI computer or on a standard computer. Many ES can run on regular computers. In general, mainframes or large minicomputers are usually adequate for both AI and other languages, provided that enough memory is available.

AI in the Mainframe Environment. Most ES work in the past was done on workstations and on micros rather than on mainframes. Four reasons account for this situation:

1. There are many more personal computers and users.
2. ES development tools for the personal computer are usually superior.
3. It is easy to buy a low-cost shell and experiment with the technology.
4. An MIS backlog plagues almost every mainframe operation.

Lately, however, a trend has also developed to build ES on the mainframe to exploit the advantages of integrated systems.

Any movement toward mainframe intelligence must be accomplished by a careful understanding, nurturing, and support. ES technology can greatly improve the operation of many mainframe-based information systems. One of the major issues in developing a mainframe ES is where the computerized corporate knowledge base should reside. Such knowledge provides, in many cases, the competitive edge of the corporation and it originates in the heads of experts who usually use microcomputers, not a mainframe. Moreover, there is a considerable amount of information in the corporate database, residing on the mainframe. Experts need to access this information. Therefore, it makes sense to *connect* the personal computers with the mainframe. Users must be able to use ES on mainframes via their personal computers; that is, it is necessary to develop *distributed* ES.

About a dozen companies develop software for the mainframe, usually with the possibility of accessing it from personal computers. Representative examples are listed in Table 16-6. For information about these products see [3] and Schwartz [29].

16.16   Feasibility Study

The **feasibility study** for an ES is similar in structure to a feasibility study for any information system. A proposed outline is shown in Table 16.7 (for details consult books on system analysis and design). The larger the system the more *formal* the steps must be, since approval by top management is required. (For details see Walters and Nielsen [39].)

TABLE 16.6 Examples of ES Development Software for the Mainframe

Product	Vendor
ADS	Aion Corp. (Palo Alto, CA)
Application Expert	Cullinet (Westwood, MA)
ESE, KT, TIRS	IBM Corp. (White Plains, NY)
ART, ART-IM	Inference Corp. (Los Angeles, CA)
KBMS	AI Corp. (Waltham, MA)
KEE, KEE/370	IntelliCorp. (Mountain View, CA)
Nexpert	Neuron Data, Inc. (Palo Alto, CA)
KES	Software A&E (Arlington, VA)
S.1	Teknowledge Corp. (Palo Alto, CA)

16.17 Cost-Benefit Analysis

Each ES project requires an investment of resources (including money), which can be viewed as the cost of the system, in exchange for some expected benefit(s). The viability of a project is determined by comparing the costs with anticipated benefits. This comparison is termed a **cost-benefit analysis,** or cost-effectiveness analysis. In practice, such an analysis may become rather com-

TABLE 16.7 Elements of a Feasibility Study

Economic (financial) feasibility	Cost of system development (itemized)
	Cost of maintenance
	Anticipated payoff
	Cash flow analysis
	Risk analysis
Technical feasibility	Interface requirements
	Networking issues
	Availability of knowledge and data
	Security of confidential knowledge
	Knowledge representation scheme
	Hardware/software availability/compatibility
Operational feasibility and impacts	Availability of human and other resources
	Priority as compared to other projects
	Needs assessment
	Organizational and implementation issues
	Management and user support
	Availability of expert(s) and knowledge engineer(s)
	Legal and other constraints
	Corporate culture
	User environment

plicated. The iterative nature of ES makes it difficult to predict costs and benefits, because the systems are changed constantly. In addition, there are several
factors, which we will now discuss, that complicate the analysis.

Getting a Handle on Development Costs. Expert systems may be expensive to develop and/or maintain. Like most other software projects, you'll make
a major investment of time and money in creating a workable program. Knowing some of the costs involved helps you estimate the payoff.

First, factor in the cost of all development tools, such as languages and
shells. Next, consider what additional hardware you might need. Include the
cost of the expert, especially if that expert is not on your payroll. Usually you'll
need a knowledge engineer and a programmer, although for a simple expert
system you may not need the knowledge engineer, and if a shell is to be used,
you may not need the programmer. Don't forget to include the time needed for
employees to test, debug, and maintain the program. Finally, add in costs for
outside consultants.

The secret to making a *realistic* estimate lies in determining the amount of
time each of the participants will need. It is practically impossible to make a
perfect estimate, but it is essential that an estimate of development costs be
made. Even an educated guess is better than none at all.

A small system with fewer than a hundred rules may take only several
months and require two or three people at most. Still, developing such a project
could cost from $10,000 to $50,000. If you use an inexpensive shell on a personal
computer and create a small expert system, you may be able to do it for several
thousand dollars, assuming that your expert will also do the knowledge engineering and program the knowledge into the shell.

If you are planning a large expert system for a minicomputer or a mainframe, your costs will be more than $100,000 and can be in the millions.

At first sight, the cost of a project seems easy to identify and quantify. In
practice, it is often difficult to relate costs to projects in a precise manner. Allocation of overhead costs is an example. Should they be allocated by volume,
activity level, or value? What about future maintenance costs?

Evaluating the Benefits. The assessment of costs is not easy, but the assessment of benefits is more difficult for the following reasons: First, some benefits
are intangible. Second, frequently a benefit cannot be precisely related to a single cause. Third, results of a certain action may occur over a long period of time.
Fourth, a valuation of benefits includes the assessment of both quantity and
quality. The latter is difficult to measure, especially when service industries are
involved. Fifth, the multiplicity of consequences can pose a major problem for
quantification. Some consequences like goodwill, inconvenience, waiting time,
and pain are also extremely difficult to measure and evaluate.

The key is to identify the appropriate benefits. If the expert system can
solve a problem whose losses are currently known, you have a starting point.
Otherwise, you have to try to calculate a dollar value for the benefits. An expert
system will generate income for you or prevent the loss of income.

When to Justify. Cost justification should be done any time a go-no-go decision is to be made; that is, the justification process occurs throughout the life of the ES. Specifically, cost justification needs to be done (or reexamined) during every phase of the process:

- At the end of phase I, that is, when the project is initially blessed
- At the end of phase II, when the complete design is ready
- After the initial prototype is completed
- Once the full prototype is in operation
- Once field testing is completed (prior to deployment)
- Periodically after the system is in operation (e.g., every six or twelve months).

How to Justify. Justification can be a lengthy, complex process (e.g., see Thompson and Feinstein [35] and Smith and Dagli [32]). Furthermore, several methods are available to compare the costs and the benefits. Be very careful. One method may yield a different go-no-go recommendation than another method.

Several methods can be used to evaluate ES proposals and none of them is perfect. Table 16.8 shows five common methods with the advantages and dis-

TABLE 16.8 Commonly Used Methods of Evaluating ES Proposals

Indicator	Advantages	Disadvantages
Internal rate of return (IRR)	Brings all projects to common footing. Conceptually familiar. No assumed discount rate.	Assumes reinvestment at same rate. Can have multiple roots.
Net present value or net worth (NPV or NW)	Very common. Maximizes value for unconstrained project selection.	Difficult to compare projects of unequal lives or sizes.
Equivalent annuity (EA)	Brings all project NPVs to common footing. Convenient annual figure.	Assumes projects repeat to least common multiple of lives, or imputes salvage value.
Payback period	May be discounted or nondiscounted. Measure of exposure.	Ignores flows after payback is reached. Assumes standard project cash-flow profile.
Benefit-to-cost ratio	Conceptually familiar. Brings all projects to common footing.	May be difficult to classify outlays between expense and investment.

Source: A. Smith and C. Dagli, "An Analysis of Worth: Justifying Funding for Development and Implementation," in *Managing Expert Systems,* E. Turban and J. Liebowitz, eds. (Harrisburg, PA: Idea Group Publishers, 1992).

advantages of each. Smith and Dagli [32] proposed what they call holistic methods of justification. Such methods can better deal with fuzzy environments and multidimensional attributes.

Table 16.9 is an example of a cost-benefit analysis of a small project.

16.18   Phase III: Rapid Prototyping and a Demonstration Prototype

Prototyping has been crucial to the development of many ES. A prototype in ES refers to a small-scale system. It includes representation of the knowledge captured in a manner that enables quick inference and the creation of the major components of an ES on a rudimentary basis. For example, in a rule-based system the prototype may include only fifty rules and it may be built with a shell. This small number of rules is sufficient to produce consultations of a limited nature.

The prototype helps the builder to decide on the structure of the knowledge base before spending a great amount of time on building more rules. Developing the prototype has other advantages, as shown in Table 16.10 on page 656. Rapid prototyping is essential in large systems because the cost of a poorly structured, and then not used, ES can be very high.

The process of rapid prototyping is shown in Figure 16.5 on page 657. We start with the *design* of a small system. The designer determines what aspect (or segment) to prototype, how many rules to use in the first cut, and so on. Then the knowledge is acquired for the first cut and represented in the ES. Next, a test is conducted. The test can be done using historical or hypothetical cases. The expert is asked to judge the results. The knowledge representation methods and the software and hardware effectiveness are also checked. A potential user may be invited to test the system. The results are then analyzed by the knowledge engineer, and if improvement is needed the system is redesigned. Usually the system goes through several iterations with appropriate refinements. The process continues until the system is ready for a formal demonstration. Once the system is demonstrated, it is tested again and improved. This process continues until the final (complete) prototype is ready. For details on the prototyping process see Walters and Nielsen [39].

A prototype is also a good way to prove your concept before investing in a major program. If you use a shell, you can rapidly assemble a small prototype that will tell you if you're on the right track. A demonstration of the prototype can also be a valuable aid in acquiring approval and funding for your project.

One advantage of rule-based systems is that they are modular. Thus you can construct small subdivisions of larger systems and test them one step at a time. You can add to the system in a piecemeal fashion and build to the final system gradually. If each subsection is tested and approved separately, the final system should work the first time.

TABLE 16.9 Cost-Benefit
Analysis of a Small Project

Cost-Benefit Analysis for a Spouse Survivor Benefit Plan

Development costs
1 knowledge engineer
   (4 months half time) $7,230
1 domain expert
   (4 months half time) .... $ 5,453
1 site license for the expert system shell .... $ 5,000

Total costs (excluding maintenance) $17,683

Benefits: (annual)
Reduction in need for overtime .... $ 2,800
Elimination of need to hire two military pay specialists $56,086

Total $58,886

Savings
Year 1 ($58,886 − $17,683) $41,203

Continuing annual savings (before maintenance) $58,886

Tangible benefits
1. Reduction of backlog from 380 cases to fewer than 40 cases.
2. Improvement in turnaround time from over 4 months to 2
   weeks or less.
3. Audit trail, due to printout of consultation.

Intangible benefits
1. Risk reduction. If the only expert becomes unavailable,
   processing can continue.
2. Consistent application of former Spouse Survivor Benefit
   Plan laws.
3. Improved job satisfaction for both the military pay specialist
   and adjudicators.
4. More timely management information on backlogs.
5. Additional information—case status.
6. Legal requirements standardized.
7. Processing standardized.
8. Image improved with customers.

Note: The savings for the first year would be higher if the cost of
the expert system shell software were amortized over many
projects, rather than included in the cost of this project.

Source: T. Tubalkain and J. W. Griesser, "Expert Systems Catching on at the Navy Finance Center," in *Managing Expert Systems*, E. Turban and J. Liebowitz, eds. (Harrisburg, PA: Idea Group Publishers, 1992).

TABLE 16.10 Advantages of the Rapid Prototype

It allows project developers to get a good idea of whether it is feasible to attempt to tackle the full application using expert system technology.

It provides a vehicle through which to study the effectiveness of the knowledge representation.

It provides a vehicle through which to study the effectiveness of the knowledge implementation.

It may disclose important gaps or important problems in the proposed final system.

It yields a tangible product of the project at an early stage.

It gives an opportunity to impress management or system funders with a flashy system demonstration, helping to retain or increase support of the project.

It gives an idea of what the final system will do and will look like to outside experts and potential users.

It allows the possibility of an early midcourse correction of the project direction based on feedback from management, consulting experts, and potential users.

It provides a first system that can be field tested—yielding experience in using and testing the system and, if the tests are successful, credibility that the eventual final system will perform its desired function well.

It might provide a system with enough utility that, although not a final product, may be put in the field on an extended basis. This early deployment of a limited system yields some domain benefits, gives experience to system deployers, system operators, and system maintainers, and might identify potential problems in those areas.

It provides an accelerated process of knowledge acquisition.

It makes it easier for experts to criticize existing programs or provide exceptions to the rules.

It makes selling the system to skeptics easier.

It helps sustain the expert's interest.

It provides an idea of the value of the software and the hardware.

It provides an idea of the degree of the expert's cooperation.

It provides information about the initial definition of the problem domain, the need for the ES, and the like.

It demonstrates the capabilities of the ES.

Source: Based, in part, on D. S. Prerau, *Developing and Managing Expert Systems*, © 1990 by Addison-Wesley Publishing Company. p. 39. Reprinted with permission of the publisher.

The prototyping phase can be short and simple or it can take several months and be fairly complex. Figure 16.6 shows the possible tasks and participants in the process. The lessons learned during rapid prototyping are incorporated into the final design. Also, this is the time when another go-no-go decision is made. If the decision is "go," system development begins.

16.19   Phase IV: System Development

Once the initial prototype is ready and management is satisfied, system development begins. Obviously, a plan must be made about how to continue. At this stage, the development strategy may be changed (e.g., a consultant may be

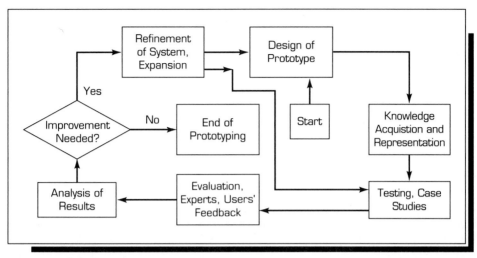

FIGURE 16.5 Rapid Prototyping

hired). The detailed design is also likely to be changed and so are other elements of the plan.

Depending on the nature of the system—its size, the amount of interface with other systems, the dynamics of the knowledge, and the development strategy—one of the following approaches for system development will be utilized:

- Continue with prototyping (evolutionary model)
- Use structured life-cycle approach
- Do both.

System development can be a lengthy and complex process. In this phase, the knowledge base is built and continuous testing, reviews, and improvements are carried out. Other activities include creation of interfaces (e.g., to databases), creating and testing the user's interface, and so on. For a list of tasks and participants, see Figure 16.7.

16.20 Building the Knowledge Base

Building the knowledge base means acquiring knowledge from experts and/or documented sources (as described in chapter 13) and representing this knowledge in an appropriate form in the computer (chapter 14). The following discussion supplements the material in the previous chapters.

Once the knowledge has been acquired from the expert, it has to be formatted into a knowledge base. Here we want to describe the process of organizing that knowledge in such a way that it can be understood and then translated into rules or another form of knowledge representation.

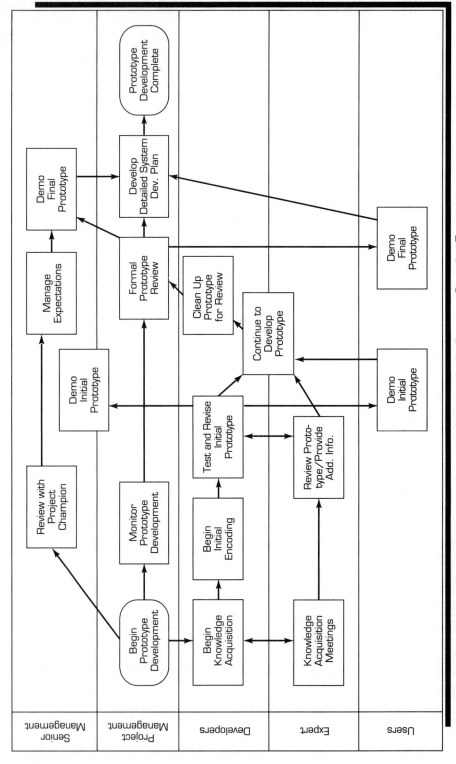

FIGURE 16.6 Prototype Development Effort. (*Source:* P. Harmon and B. Sawyer, *Creating Expert Systems* [New York: John Wiley & Sons, 1990], p. 275. © 1990 John Wiley & Sons. Reprinted by permission.)

658

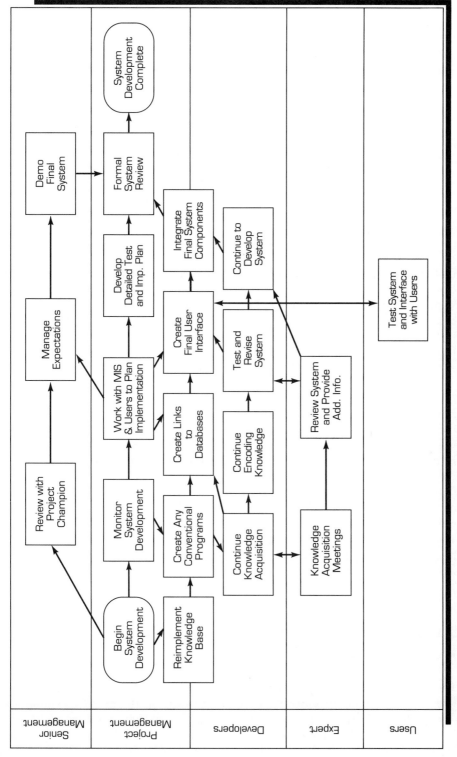

FIGURE 16.7 System Development Effort (Phase IV). (*Source*: P. Harmon and B. Sawyer, *Creating Expert Systems* [New York: John Wiley & Sons, 1990], p. 270. © 1990 John Wiley & Sons. Reprinted by permission.)

Define the Potential Solutions. The first step in organizing your domain knowledge is to list all of the possible solutions, outcomes, answers, choices, or recommendations. If you're using a rule-based system, each potential solution will be in the THEN portion of a rule. At this point, you can begin creating the rules for each outcome. Some simple expert systems have a set of rules that defines each outcome and that's it.

Define the Input Facts. The next step is to identify and list all of the data that will be required by the system. These are the facts (e.g., symptoms) that the user *may* enter into the system. The expert system will actually ask questions to obtain these inputs. For example, the system may ask you how old you are if there is a rule that says that if you are 18 or older you can vote in the federal election. Data provided by the user will be compared to IF statements in the rules to begin or continue the search process.

Develop an Outline. Even though you may know the potential solutions and needed input data, you may have difficulty writing the rules. Large, complex knowledge domains usually require some additional organization. One technique that may be useful is to develop an outline.

Draw a Decision Tree. The elements of knowledge (or portions of it) may be such that they organize themselves quickly into a tree format. If so, you may be able to proceed directly to the construction of a decision or search tree.

Map a Matrix. Some knowledge organizes itself neatly into a matrix showing the various attributes that produce a particular conclusion. Induction shells use this knowledge-formatting technique. If you have selected such a shell, you can proceed immediately to organizing your knowledge as examples.

Develop the Software. Once your rules are written, you can enter them immediately into a shell. Your first objective should be to build a small prototype. Select one small subset of the knowledge base and enter its rules into the shell. You should be able to do this quickly. The result will be a prototype you can test to check your ideas and verify their implementation quickly. If your prototype works, you can proceed with confidence to enter the remainder of the rules.

16.21 Testing, Validating and Verifying, and Improving

The prototype, and later improved versions of the system, are tested and evaluated for performance both in the lab and in the field. Initially, evaluation is done in a simulated environment. The system is exposed to test problems (e.g., historical cases or sample cases provided by users). A close link exists between the evaluation and the refinements of the ES. The evaluation may reveal cases not handled by the system's rules. As a result, new rules are added or old ones are modified. Such changes may have unexpected negative effects on parts of the system. For example, conflict could arise because of inconsistency in rules. A good development tool provides a rapid consistency check for the rules in the knowledge base.

Evaluation also deals with the issue of the quality of the advice rendered. Determining quality can be a very difficult activity if we lack standards for comparison (see Box 16.1 on page 662). Expert systems often give advice in areas where there is no "gold standard," so a simple comparison is impossible.

As a result of these evaluation difficulties, expert systems are being evaluated in less formal and more experimental ways. The principal judge of the system's quality is the domain expert, who can tell if the results are satisfactory. Potential users can also serve as judges in regard to ease of use, comfortable interface, and clarity of explanations.

A common method used to evaluate an ES is to compare its performance to an accepted criterion, such as a human expert's decision. In this approach, called the **Modified Turing Test,** managers are shown two solutions to a problem. One is the result of human judgment and the other of an ES. Without knowing which is which, managers are asked to compare the solutions. There are several problems with this approach. First, the open-endedness of many management problems may make it difficult to describe them to an independent evaluator. The problems may be so complex that even experienced managers may disagree on their proper interpretation and solution. Second, expert systems used by teams of managers should probably be evaluated by teams of managers; hence they may be more difficult to evaluate (because of possible disagreements). Despite such difficulties, an ES might be useful even if its only accomplishment is the reduction of the time needed to perform existing tasks without reduction in quality. Time reduction may be a good initial criterion for evaluation of an ES.

In business settings ES can often be evaluated by experimentation. Say, for example, preventive maintenance is to be performed on several identical machines. An expert system's advice about frequencies of maintenance could be implemented in some of the machines while the rest are scheduled according to the vendor's recommendations. The relative breakdown rates and repair and maintenance costs under the two methods can then be compared to find which one is superior.

An Iterative Process of Evaluation. Each time the system is exposed to a new case, or whenever there are changes in the environment, the system needs a refinement. In a rule-based system, such a refinement is likely to produce more rules. XCON, for example, grew from a couple of hundred to about 20,000 rules in about ten years. Each time a substantial refinement is made, an evaluation should follow.

Evaluation occurs during and after each iteration. Performance is recorded as the system improves its use in either a simulated or real-life environment. Development and evaluation continue as long as improvements are achieved. For further details see Berry and Hart [6], Preece [25], and Suen et al. [33].

Box 16.1: Difficulties in Evaluating an Expert System

The following questions indicate the difficulties that stand in the way of evaluation studies:

1. What characteristics should be evaluated? The performance of the system has been the main characteristic of interest. However, the system's discourse or ease of use may also be key to its acceptance.

2. How should performance be evaluated? Owing to the nature of expert system applications, it is sometimes hard to define a "gold standard" against which to compare the system's performance. For example, a match between the conclusions of the system and the expert may be hard to obtain. Indeed, different experts may disagree on certain details or both the problem and the expert may be wrong. In evaluating performance, should one look only at the conclusion or should the program's line of reasoning be evaluated as well? What form should the evaluation take when the system provides multiple (as opposed to unique) answers?

3. How should the test problems be selected? The fact that the realism of real-world exceptions and irrelevancies can seriously affect the performance of an expert system is well known. However, in certain areas, the supply of realistic studies may be very limited. In the case of PROSPECTOR, for instance, there is only a small number of known ore deposits to draw on, and the time between initial and final characterizations of the deposit could be long. Similar problems occur with rare diseases and other cases when sampling costs are high.

4. How should one evaluate the program's mistakes? In judgmental areas, it is interesting to observe the type of mistakes an expert system may make. One is reminded that the work of Piaget on developmental psychology was prompted by the patterns of mistakes (not the correct responses) in IQ tests taken by children. The same search for error patterns occurs in intelligent tutoring systems, but the implications for evaluation studies appear to be unexplored. Clearly, this issue also relates to the requirement that expert systems "degrade gracefully."

(*Source:* A. A. Assad and B. L. Golden, "Expert Systems, Microcomputers, and Operations Research," *Computers and Operations Research* 131 [1986]. Reprinted with permission)

Box 16.2: Some Requirements of a Good Expert System

1. The ES should be developed to fulfill a recognized and important need.
2. The processing speed of the system should be very high.
3. The ES should be able to increase the expertise of the user.
4. Error correction should be easy to perform.
5. The program should be able to respond to simple questions.
6. The system should be capable of asking questions to gain additional information.
7. Program knowledge should be easily modified (i.e., add, delete, and modify rules).
8. The user should feel that he or she is in control.
9. The degree of effort (both physical and mental) used by the novice should be reasonable.
10. Input requirements (in terms of data) should be clear and simple to obtain.

(*Source:* Based, in part, on D. C. Berry and A. E. Hart, "Evaluating Expert Systems," *Expert Systems* [November 1990].)

The evaluation assures that the system is good (see Box 16.2). It involves both validation and verification. **Validation** refers to the determination of whether the right system was built; that is, whether the system does what it was meant to do and at an acceptable level of accuracy. **Verification** confirms that the ES has been built correctly (according to the specifications).

16.22   Phase V: Implementation

The process of implementing an ES can be long and complex—similar to the implementation of any software project. Here we will briefly touch on several issues; in Chapter 18 implementation problems and strategies are revisited.

Acceptance by the User. Acceptance depends on behavioral and psychological considerations. It is important that the development of specific ES be communicated as widely as possible to foster a climate of acceptance among the people who will use the system.

Installation Approaches. The expert system is ready to be field tested when it reaches a minimal level of stability and quality. In rule-based systems, this may occur when the system can handle 75 percent of the cases and exhibit less than a 5 percent error rate. It can be installed in parallel with a human expert for a short test period.

Demonstration. Demonstrating the fully operational system to the user community is important. Viewers can become believers.

Mode of Deployment. Several deployment modes for ES may be considered. The final system could be delivered to users as a turnkey, stand-alone system; it could be operated as a separate entity but integrated into the users' environment; it could be embedded into another system; or it could be run as a service, with the users' requests and data accessed remotely and results delivered to the users.

The users of the expert system may be responsible for operating it, maintaining it, or neither. The system could be available on a demand, scheduled, or continual basis. It could be available twenty-four hours a day or during selected hours, and it could be run interactively or in batch mode. A single system could service one user, many users in one site, or many users in many sites.

Orientation and Training. Depending on the mode of deployment, the builders must plan appropriate orientation and training. If the users are assigned maintenance responsibilities, the training may be fairly extensive.

Security. Security is a heightened concern in ES. Expert systems may contain the accumulated proprietary knowledge of a firm. Communicating and distributing the end product, protecting the software, and at the same time providing an environment that does not constrain authorized users in its application form a substantial practical problem. Therefore, organizational and hardware and/or software controls assume increased importance in the design and distribution of expert systems.

Documentation. Implementation of ES must include appropriate documentation. Prerau [26] has said:

> There is a tendency to skimp on documentation during system development and then to complete it quickly and sometimes haphazardly at the end of a project. Clearly expert system project leaders should try to avoid this situation.
>
> Standard techniques of documentation can be used where applicable for documenting expert system programs. For example, reports can be written describing for each program module its purpose, inputs, outputs, and so on. But beyond such standard techniques, there are some aspects of expert system implementations that may allow additional types of documentation.
>
> If a knowledge documentation is compiled and kept updated as part of knowledge acquisition, it becomes a significant piece of program documentation. It is a program specification that is constantly up to date and relevant. If the documented knowledge has clear parallels to the implementation (by rule cor-

respondences, naming conventions, specific references, and other means), it can act as a pointer to the program code. (p. 280)

The documentation that will accompany the system might consist of printed manuals, online documentation, or both. There may be levels of documentation for system maintainers, system operators, and system users.

Integration and Field Testing. If the expert system stands alone, it can now be field tested. A system that needs to be integrated is physically added to the existing computer-based information system before testing in the field is conducted. Field testing is extremely important because conditions in the field may differ from those that exist at the developer's lab.

Field tests need to be planned and coordinated. In many cases they last longer than people think. For example, the expert may be needed for some refinements, but he or she may be busy.

16.23   Phase VI: Postimplementation

Several activities are performed once the system is distributed to users. The most important of the activities are system operation, system maintenance, system upgrading and expansion, and system evaluation.

Operations. According to Prerau [26],

If the expert system is to be delivered as a service, a system operations group (or several groups if there are several sites) should be formed and trained. If the system is to be a product run by users, an operator training group may need to be formed, and consideration should be given to providing help for user-operators with problems. . . . If the system is embedded into another system, the operators of the other system should be trained in any new operating procedures required.

Maintenance. Prerau [26] has also said:

A long-term maintenance group (or groups) should be designated or formed and, if necessary, trained. Maintenance encompasses not only fixing problems found during system operation but also revising internal data and knowledge that has changed over time. . . . A decision must be made whether to have centralized maintenance, with program patches and new releases coming from a single source, or a more distributed maintenance.

If the expert system is embedded in another system, some thought should be given to whether one maintenance group will serve the overall system or whether the expert system will be maintained separately. If separate maintenance is chosen, procedures for coordinating the two maintenance groups should be formed. For further discussion of maintenance and upgrading see Agarwal et al. [1] and McCaffrey [21].

Expansion (Upgrading). Expert systems are continuously expanded. All new knowledge needs to be added, and new features and capabilities need to be added as they become available. Also, the ES may be integrated with other systems. Expansion can be carried on by the maintainer, the original builder, or a vendor.

Evaluation. Expert systems need evaluation periodically (e.g., every six or twelve months). In such an evaluation, questions such as these should be answered:

- What is the actual cost of maintaining the system as compared to the actual benefits?
- Is the maintenance provided sufficient to keep the knowledge up to date so that system accuracy remains high?
- Is the system accessible to all users?
- Is acceptance by users increasing?

16.24   Organizing the Development Team

Many expert systems are developed by a team—a team that needs to be organized. Some members of the team (the core) participate in the initial steps (phases I-V); others are added only after the development strategy has been finalized (phase VI).

A typical development team consists of an expert, a knowledge engineer, and a programmer (see Figure 16.8). However, a vendor, a user, or information system specialist may also be included. The knowledge engineer extracts the expert's knowledge and puts it into a suitable form. The programmer writes the codes for putting the knowledge into memory and creates the inference engine and other components as required.

Although the team approach is probably the best development arrangement, it does require a great deal of cooperation and communication among the team members. A large system may require more members. The larger the team, then, the better the organization and management needed to create a workable system. The size of the team and its composition depend on a specific application. Table 16.11 on page 668 lists many of the possible functions and roles that may be found in an ES team. An end-user ES may include only *one* participant who is helped, on a part-time basis, by other people.

Many teams include two additional important players: the project champion and the project leader. The *project champion* is a person with power and influence and a major interest in facilitating the project's successful completion. The project champion provides the authority and the resources. He or she may be a senior vice president of a functional area (e.g., finance, manufacturing) or a corporate generalist. The *project leader* is a specialist who manages the project on a day-to-day basis. The leader is familiar with the application, is user oriented, and understands the technology. This individual manages, coordinates, and runs the project using a particular project management approach.

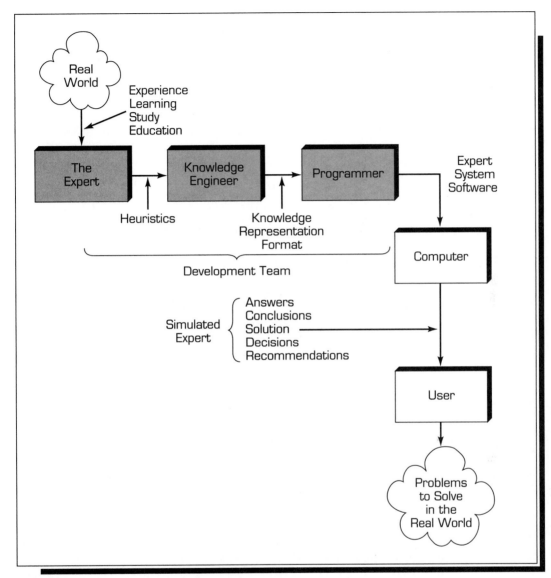

FIGURE 16.8 Expert System Development Team

Chapter Highlights

- Building an expert system is a complex process with six major phases: system initialization, system analysis and design, rapid prototyping, system development, implementation, and postimplementation.
- Defining the problem properly will simplify the remaining development tasks.

TABLE 16.11 Functions and Roles in an Expert System Team

Knowledge engineer	Knowledge acquirer	Technical leader
Expert	Knowledge representor	System engineer
System analyst	Knowledge implementer	Integration specialist
Programmer	Tool developer	Technical demonstrator
Vendor	System tester (evaluator)	Security specialist
End-user	Trainer	Documentation writer
Project champion	System developer	System operator
Project manager	Hardware (software) specialist	
Consultant	Network expert	

Source: Based on D. S. Prerau, *Developing and Managing Expert Systems,* © 1990 by Addison-Wesley Publishing Company. p. 57. Reprinted with permission of the publisher.

- Sometimes conventional technologies do a better job than expert systems.
- Knowledge can be increased by providing training; this classical method is valid in many, many cases.
- Like any other project, an ES must be justified.
- Without the commitment of resources, the ES will fail.
- Top management support is essential from the inception of the project.
- A large ES needs a champion as a sponsor.
- Expert systems can be developed in-house (internally) or can be subcontracted; there are several variations to each option.
- Expert systems developed by end-users can be successful. One system may save little in costs, but many little savings accumulate.
- Selecting experts can be difficult; candidates need to exhibit many different attributes.
- Although ES can be developed with many tools, the trend is to develop the initial prototype with simple (and inexpensive) integrated tools (either shells or hybrid environments).
- Currently, most ES are being developed and run on standard computers (personal computers, workstations, mainframes).
- A feasibility study is essential for the success of any medium- to large-sized ES.
- Expert systems are difficult to justify because of the many intangible factors.
- Justification is done several times during the development process, and so is the go-no-go decision.
- Many ES are being built by creating a small-scale prototype, testing it, and improving and expanding. The process, which can be repeated many times, has many advantages.
- The major aspects of system development are building the knowledge base and evaluating and improving the system.

- Evaluation of expert systems is difficult because of the many attributes that need to be considered and the difficulties in measuring some of them.
- Implementing an ES is similar to implementing any other computer-based information system. However, integration may be difficult to accomplish.
- Once the system is distributed to users, it is necessary to perform several tasks: operation, maintenance, upgrade, and postimplementation evaluation.
- Developing the proper team for ES development can be challenging; size, composition, and leadership are only some of the important factors.

Key Words

AI workstation	feasibility study	needs assessment
cost-benefit analysis	hybrid systems	PROLOG
development	(environments)	shell
environment	LISP	technology level
development life cycle	LISP machines	validation
development strategy	Modified Turing Test	verification
domain-specific tool		

Questions for Review

1. List the phases in the ES development life cycle.
2. Describe the criteria that can be used to justify ES.
3. Give some guidelines for selecting a task suitable for an ES.
4. Describe the activities of project initialization.
5. What is included in a conceptual design of ES?
6. Describe the ES documentation task.
7. Describe the difficulties in finding a good expert.
8. What are the major guidelines for selecting experts?
9. How do shells relate to expert system development?
10. What is a feasibility study? Why is it done?
11. What is the purpose of rapid prototyping?
12. What is meant by a champion?
13. Define postimplementation.
14. List all the activities conducted in implementation.
15. Describe the classification of ES development tools used in this chapter.
16. What is the difference between a shell and a programming environment?
17. Explain how the software packages EMYCIN and MYCIN are related.
18. What are the major components of a shell?
19. Describe the major advantages of a shell; also list the major limitations.
20. What are the differences between domain-specific tools and general-purpose tools?
21. Define environments and discuss their use.
22. Explain the difficulties in selecting ES software packages.
23. List five issues related to software selection.

Questions for Discussion

1. Compare a conceptual design with a final design.
2. Discuss the general classes of AI development strategies.
3. The selection of an *appropriate* ES project is considered most important. Why? Why is it difficult to do it?
4. Review the elements that go into a feasibility study. Why is it difficult to conduct one?
5. Describe some intangible benefits of expert systems.
6. Why is it necessary to conduct cost-benefit analyses several times during the development process?
7. Why is it hard to evaluate expert systems?
8. Distinguish between acceptance by a user and acceptance by a designer.
9. Why is the security issue so important to expert systems?
10. Training is an alternative to an expert system. Under what circumstances would you train rather than use an ES (and vice versa)?
11. Two major development strategies are to do it yourself or to subcontract. Compare and contrast the two approaches.
12. Review the attributes of experts listed in Table 16.3. Which of them, in your opinion, are the five most important ones and why?
13. A shell versus a language is an ongoing debate. Find some material on the topic and prepare a table showing the advantages and disadvantages of each.
14. There are many benefits to prototyping. Can you think of some disadvantages?
15. Review the elements that go into an ES. If you are using a shell, relate these elements to the components of the shells. Report differences in terminology.
16. Most ES shells are geared to deal with diagnosis and prescription of a treatment. Why is this so?
17. Comment on the following statement: "Constraints in software development tools may be very helpful."
18. Review the process of building a specific ES with knowledge engineering tools. Compare it with building any information system with tools (for example, a spreadsheet).
19. Compare a shell with a fourth-generation tool such as Lotus 1-2-3 or dBASE.
20. Some say it is much easier to program with a simple ES shell (e.g., EXSYS or VP Expert) than to program with Lotus 1-2-3. Why?
21. Explain the difference between a domain-specific shell and a general shell. Why is the former more expensive?
22. Why is it difficult to match a problem and ES development tools?
23. Which should be selected first, software or hardware? Why?

Exercises

1. **Feasibility study for expert systems:** Assume that the president of a company or the commander of a military base asks you to prepare a feasibility study

for the introduction of an expert system in the organization. Prepare a report that includes the following information:

  a. Identification of a problem area—go through the process in this chapter

  b. Description of the expert(s) to be involved—their capabilities and willingness to participate

  c. Software and hardware to be used in this project and why you chose them

  d. Development team and why each member is necessary

  e. Timetable for development and implementation

  f. List of the potential difficulties during the construction period

  g. List of managerial problems (related to the *use* of the system) that could appear if the expert system is introduced

  h. Construction and operating budgets

  i. List of the interfaces (if needed) with other computer-based information systems

2. **Starting an ES project:**

  a. Think of a specific problem that could be aided by (or even replaced with) an expert system. Preferably, the problem should be one about which you can obtain the required knowledge from an expert; however, if this is not possible, you may choose a problem in which the knowledge is obtained from published materials. Problems in which you are the expert should be selected only as a last resort. Describe the problem task in general terms.

  b. How is this task normally performed without the aid of an expert system? Who is responsible for the final judgment? What sort of training and/or experience does this person normally have?

  c. Identify the generic category that best describes your problem task and explain why.

3. What types of hardware would you suggest for each of the following situations and why?

  a. Advising on admissions for a medium-sized college

  b. Scheduling maintenance for a major airline

  c. Diagnosing complex problems in a large machine

  d. Advising students on what classes to take.

4. Many software and computer magazines conduct frequent evaluations of ES development tools. Find a recent evaluation and identify all the criteria against which the software is being judged.

5. Obtain a demonstration copy of an ES development tool (or get one from your instructor). What type of software is it? What is its level of classification? What do you like and dislike about it?

References and Bibliography

1. Agarwal, R., et al. "Knowledge Base Maintenance." *Expert Systems: Planning, Implementation, Integration* (Summer 1991).

2. Anderson, E. E. "Choice Models for the Evaluation and Selection of Software Packages." *Journal of MIS* (Spring 1990).

3. *Artificial Intelligence Research*, July 3, 1989 (New Science Associates).

4. Assad, A. A., and B. L. Golden. "Expert Systems, Microcomputers, and Operations Research." *Computers and Operations Research* 13 (no. 2, 1986).

5. Beckman, T. J. "Selecting Expert Systems Applications." *AI Expert* (February 1991).

6. Berry, D. C., and A. E. Hart. "Evaluating Expert Systems." *Expert Systems* (November 1990).

7. Boehm, B. W. *Software Engineering Economics*. Englewood Cliffs, NJ: Prentice-Hall, 1981.

8. Carrico, M. A., et al. *Building Knowledge Systems*. New York: McGraw-Hill, 1989.

9. Clocksin, W. F., and C. S. Mellish. *Programming in PROLOG*. 3rd ed. New York: Springer-Verlag, 1987.

10. DeSalvo, D. A., and J. Liebowitz, eds. *Managing AI and Expert Systems*. Englewood Cliffs, NJ: Yourdon Press/Prentice-Hall, 1990.

11. Feigenbaum, E., et al. *The Rise of the Expert Company*. New York: Random House, 1988.

12. Gevarter, W. B. "The Nature and Evaluation of Commercial Expert Systems Building Tools." *Computer* (May 1987).

13. Goyal, S. K., et al. "COMPASS: An Expert System for Telephone Switch Maintenance." *Expert Systems* (July 1985).

14. Harmon, P., et al. *Expert Systems Tools and Applications*. New York: John Wiley & Sons, 1988.

15. Harmon, P., and B. Sawyer. *Creating Expert Systems*. New York: John Wiley & Sons, 1990.

16. Harrison, P. R. *Common Lisp and Artificial Intelligence*. Englewood Cliffs, NJ: Prentice-Hall, 1990.

17. Hayes-Roth, F., et al. *Building Expert Systems*. Reading, MA: Addison-Wesley, 1983.

18. Liebowitz, J. "Useful Approach for Evaluating Expert Systems." *Expert Systems* (April 1986).

19. Liebowitz, J. "When Is a Prototype an Expert System?" *Expert Systems: Planning, Implementation, Integration* (Spring 1991).

20. Marcellus, D. H. *Expert System Programming in Turbo PROLOG*. Englewood Cliffs, NJ: Prentice-Hall, 1990.

21. McCaffrey, M. J. "Maintenance of Expert Systems—The Upcoming Challenge." In *Managing Expert Systems*, E. Turban and J. Liebowitz, eds. Harrisburg, PA: Idea Group Publishers, 1992.

22. McCullough, T. "Six Steps to Selling AI." *AI Expert* (December 1987).

23. Mettrey, W. "An Assessment of Tools for Building Large Knowledge-Based Systems." *AI Magazine* (Winter 1987).

24. Odette, L. "Expert Systems: When to Make Them, When to Buy Them." In *Proceedings of the 1987 Expert Systems in Business Conference*, J. Feinstein,

J. Liebowitz, H. Look, and B. Sullivan, eds. Medford, NJ: Learned Information, 1987.

25. Preece, A. D. "Towards a Methodology for Evaluating Expert Systems." *Expert Systems* (November 1990).

26. Prerau, D. S. *Developing and Managing Expert Systems.* Reading, MA: Addison-Wesley, 1990.

27. Price, C. J. *Knowledge Engineering Tool Kits.* Englewood Cliffs, NJ: Prentice-Hall, 1990.

28. Samuell, R., III, and W. T. Jones. "A Method for the Strategic Assessment of Expert Systems Applications." *Expert Systems with Applications* (Fall 1990).

29. Schwartz, T. *Expert Systems in a Mainframe Environment.* Special Report. New York: Intelligent Systems and Analyst, 1988.

30. Shanteau, J. "Psychological Characteristics of Expert Decision Makers." In *Proceedings, Symposium on Expert Systems and Audit Judgment.* Univ. of Southern California, Los Angeles, February 17–18, 1986.

31. Slagle, J., and M. Wick. "A Method for Evaluating Candidate Expert Systems Applications." *AI Magazine* (Winter 1988).

32. Smith, A., and C. Dagli. "An Analysis of Worth: Justifying Funding for Development and Implementation." In *Managing Expert Systems,* E. Turban and J. Liebowitz, eds. Harrisburg, PA: Idea Group Publishers, 1992.

33. Suen, C. Y., et al. "Verifying, Validating and Measuring the Performance of Expert Systems." *Expert Systems with Applications* (June 1990).

34. Teft, L. *Programming in Turbo PROLOG with an Introduction to Knowledge-based Systems.* Englewood Cliffs, NJ: Prentice-Hall, 1990.

35. Thompson, D. M., and J. L. Feinstein. "Cost-Justifying Expert Systems." In *Managing AI and Expert Systems,* D. A. DeSalvo and J. Liebowitz, eds. Englewood Cliffs, NJ: Yourdon Press/Prentice-Hall, 1990.

36. Tubalkain, T., and J. W. Griesser. "Expert Systems Catching on at the Navy Finance Center." In *Managing Expert Systems,* E. Turban and J. Liebowitz, eds. Harrisburg, PA: Idea Group Publishers, 1992.

37. Turban, E., and Liebowitz, J. *Managing Expert Systems.* Harrisburg, PA: Idea Group Publishers, 1992.

38. Vedder, R., and E. Turban. "Strategies for Managing Expert Systems Development." In *Managing Expert Systems,* E. Turban and J. Liebowitz, eds. Harrisburg, PA: Idea Group Publishers, 1992.

39. Walters, J., and N. R. Nielsen. *Crafting Knowledge-based Systems.* New York: John Wiley & Sons, 1989.

40. Waterman, D. A. *A Guide to Expert Systems.* Reading, MA: Addison-Wesley, 1985.

41. Weitzel, J. R., and L. Kerschberg. "Developing Knowledge-based Systems: Reorganizing the System Development Life Cycle." *Communications of ACM* (April 1989).

42. Winston, P. H., and B. K. Horn. *LISP,* 2nd ed. Reading, MA: Addison-Wesley, 1985.

APPENDIX 16-A: AI (Symbolic) Languages

The AI, or symbolic manipulation, languages provide an effective way to present AI-type objects. The two major languages are LISP and PROLOG. With these languages, the programming and debugging procedures can frequently be done much faster. The major characteristics of the two languages are described next.

LISP. LISP (for list processor, see Winston and Horn [42]) is one of the oldest general-purpose languages. Developed at MIT by McCarthy in 1958, it is still in active use. LISP's applications include expert systems, natural language processing, robotics, and educational and psychological programming. Its unique features give the programmer the power to develop software that goes far beyond the limitations of other general-purpose languages such as COBOL and Pascal.

Specifically, LISP is oriented toward symbolic computation; the programmer can assign values to terms like *financial* and *liquidity*. Although the values have no direct meaning in LISP, the LISP program can conveniently manipulate such symbols and their relationships. LISP programs also have the ability to modify themselves. In a limited sense, this means that a computer can be programmed to "learn" from its past experiences.

LISP allows programmers to represent objects like rules and nets as "lists"—sequences of numbers, character strings, or other lists. It provides them with operations for splitting lists apart and for making new lists by joining old ones. Conventionally, LISP programmers write lists as bracketed sequences of elements. They often draw them as box-and-arrow diagrams. The accompanying illustration shows a list that represents the sentence "PC is a computer."

In most programming situations, lists contain other lists or sublists as elements. Here is a simple example of list code, a recursive definition of a function that sums two integers:

```
(defun sum (A B)
  (cond ((eq A 0) B)
    (t (sum (minus 1 A) (plus 1 B))))
```

This definition says: "If you have two numbers and the first [A] is 0, then the other [B] is their total. If the first is not 0, then try for the sum (A − 1, B + 1)." In this example, *sum* is a newly defined function, whereas the remaining functions (e.g., defun, cond, minus 1, t) are predefined. LISP programs consist of many such functions.

LISP code is usually executed directly by a LISP interpreter. In some versions the source program is compiled to increase efficiency.

There are numerous variations of LISP. Some include built-in features for special applications. Most notable are COMMON LISP, IQLISP, INTERLISP, MACLISP, ZETALISP, GOLDEN COMMON LISP, and FRANZLISP (UNIX based). Each of these may have several subvariants.

PROLOG. Although LISP is the most popular AI language in the United States, **PROLOG** (for programming in logic) is the most popular AI language in Japan and probably in Europe (see Clocksin and Mellish [9]). Its basic idea is to express statements of logic as statements in programming language. The proof of a theorem using these statements could be thought of as a way of executing those statements. Thus logic itself could be used directly as a programming language. For example, the statements "all dogs are animals" and "Lassie is a dog," and the theorem "Lassie is an animal," could be expressed formally in PROLOG as follows:

PROLOG	Meaning
animal (X):-dog(X)	(X is an animal if X is a dog)
dog (Lassie)	(Lassie is a dog)
?-animal (Lassie)	(Is Lassie an animal?)

PROLOG can then be run to try to prove the theorem, given the two statements. Clearly, it will come to the conclusion that the theorem is true.

There are three basic types of statements in PROLOG:

:-P	means P is a goal (or predicate) to be proven
P.	means P is an assertion or a fact
P:-Q,R,S	means Q, R, and S imply P

To define a goal, several clauses may be required. One of the techniques of knowledge representation is first-order logic. Because PROLOG is based on a subset of first-order logic (predicate calculus), it can use this format of knowledge representation. PROLOG has the additional advantage of having a very powerful inference engine in place. Therefore, the algorithm used in PROLOG is more powerful than the simple pattern-matching algorithms commonly used with LISP in production-rule representations of knowledge.

PROLOG's basis in logic provides its distinctive flavor. Because a PROLOG program is a series of statements in logic, it can be understood declaratively; that is, it can be understood quite separately from considerations of how it will be executed. Traditional languages can be understood only procedurally, that is, by considering what happens when the program is executed on a computer. Representative variants of PROLOG include MPROLOG, ARITY PROLOG, QUINTUS PROLOG, and Turbo PROLOG.

LISP has been and still is the favorite AI language in the United States. To a large extent this is due to the existence of sophisticated programming environments and specialized **AI workstations.** The situation is changing, however, as more sophisticated implementations of PROLOG supported by improved environments are appearing in the market.

PROLOG allows a program to be formulated in smaller units, each with a natural declarative reading; by contrast, the size and multiple nesting of function definitions in LISP are barriers to readability. In addition, PROLOG's built-in pattern-matching capability is an extremely useful device. PROLOG does, however, have certain deficiencies. For example, the use of built-in input/output predicates creates symbols that have no meaning in logic.

The arguments for (and against) LISP and PROLOG are likely to go on for some time. In the meantime, some attempts are being made to combine the two. One such example is a product called POPLOG—a programming environment that combines PROLOG, LISP, and POP-11 (POP-11 is an extension of PROLOG) into a single package. The package is friendlier than its components, and when compiled it runs faster than PROLOG, LISP, or POP-11.

APPENDIX 16-B: Software Sampler

Several hundred software products are available, and they change rapidly. The periodical *PC AI*, for example, has an annual product guide (in its July/August issue). In 1990, the list included about 300 items. This appendix is a representative list of well-known products. It is based on a list that appeared in the May 1991 issue of *AI Expert* and is organized by vendor.

Vendor	Products
AI Technologies	Mercury KBE, ISIU
Aion Corp.	ADS, KBMS, 1st-CLASS, Fusion HT
ARITY Corp.	The Arity/Expert Development Package
ATTAR Software	Xpert Rule
Bell Atlantic Software Systems	Laser
Cullinet Software	Enterprise Expert, Application Expert
Carnegie Group	Test Bench, Knowledge Craft, IMKA Technology
Cogent Software	Personal Hyperbase, Hyperbase Developer
Computer Associates	CA-DB: Expert/VAX, CA-DB Expert/Voice
Computer-Aided KE Systems	Knowledge Analysis Tool Knowledge Quest
Emerald Intelligence	Diagnostic Advisor, Mahogany Helpdesk, Magellan
Expert Systems International	ESP Frame Engine
Experteligence	Action!
Exsys, Inc.	EXSYS EL, EXSYS Professional
Firstmark Technologies	Knowledge Seeker
Gensym Corp.	G2
Ginesys Corp.	K-Base Corporate, K-Base Builder, K-Induction

Vendor	Products
Gold Hill, Inc.	GoldWorks II
The Haley Enterprise	Eclipse DOS Developer's Edition, Eclipse Toolkits
IBM Corp.	TIRS, ESE, AD/Cycle
Inference Engine Technologies	Sienna OPS5
Inference Corp.	ART, ART-IM, CBR Express, Xi Plus
Information Engineering Systems	USER: Expert System, IE-Expert
Information Builders	Level5, Level5 Object
Integrated Systems	RT/Expert
IntelliCorp.	KEE, ProKappa, Kappa PC
Intelligence Ware, Inc.	IXL, Auto-Intelligence
Intelligent Environments, Inc.	CRYSTAL, CRYSTAL Induction
Intellipro, Inc.	OPS-2000
Jordan-Webb Info Systems	EXSYS
KDS Corp.	KDS, KDS/VOX
Knowledge Garden	KnowledgePro
Logicware, Inc.	Twaice
M.I.S. International	Consult-I
Micro Data Base Systems	Guru, Guru Solver
Mystech Assoc.	AURORA
Neuron Data	Nexpert Object, NEXTRA
Norrad	NetLink+
Oxko	Inducprl, Maingen
Paperback Software	VP Expert
Park Row Software, Inc.	Easy Expert
Perceptics, Inc.	Knowledge Shaper
Production Systems Technology	OPS83, RAL
Rosh Intelligent Systems	Knowledge-CAIS, Brief-CAIS, Hyper-CAIS
Softsync, Inc.	SUPEREXPERT
Software Plus	Cxpert
Software A&E	Knowledge Engineering System (KES)
Software Artistry	PC Expert Professional, Knowledge Engine
Symbologic Corp.	Symbologic Adept
Transform Logic	Transform Expert
Wang Laboratories	CommonKnowledge

Appendix 16-C: Developing Small Expert Systems

Small expert systems, like small decision support systems, go through an abbreviated development process. They are usually developed with ES shells, and they are usually rule based. Several suggestions have been made for the short process. For example, Harmon [2] advocates the following seven-step process:

- Phase 1: Identify problem characteristics, analyze cost-effectiveness, and arrange for management support.
- Phase 2: Identify task and knowledge.
- Phase 3: Develop small prototype.
- Phase 4: Develop system (add knowledge as needed).
- Phase 5: Test with actual users.
- Phase 6: Transport to field and train users.
- Phase 7: Update and maintain system.

Another process suggested by Harmon et al. [3] has six phases:

1. Select a tool and implicitly commit yourself to a particular consultation paradigm.
2. Identify a problem and then analyze the knowledge to be included in the system.
3. Design the system on paper with flow diagrams, matrices, and a few rules.
4. Develop a prototype of the system using a tool. This includes creating a knowledge base and testing it by running a number of consultations.
5. Expand, test, and revise the system until it does what you want it to do.
6. Maintain and update as needed.

The relatively low cost that is involved in small systems enables shortcuts that can save development time.

Small expert systems are being developed by end-users. A detailed example is provided by Frenzel [1]. Small expert systems may be subject to the dangers involved in end-user computing. For example, the developers do not have the expertise in developing systems and as a result the systems may have poor (or no) documentation, bad interfaces, an unacceptable security system, and so forth. Despite these dangers, which can be controlled and managed, developing small systems can, at the least, be a good training exercise for the builder; it also could result in significant benefits.

References to Appendix 16-C

1. Frenzel, L. E. *Understanding Expert Systems*. Indianapolis: W. W. Sams, 1987, pp. 171–181.
2. Harmon, P. *Expert Systems Strategies* (January 1986).
3. Harmon, P., et al. *Expert Systems Tools and Applications*. New York: John Wiley & Sons, 1988.

Part 6

Cutting Edge Technologies

The technologies described in the previous chapters are new, but they have already established themselves in the commercial world. In this section we describe two cutting edge technologies that are just beginning to enter the commercial world: neural computing and genetic algorithms. Both technologies are described in Chapter 17, the only chapter in this part.

Chapter 17

Neural Computing and Other Machine Learning Technologies

Neural computing is an approach that attempts to mimic the manner in which our brains work. It is one of several approaches to machine learning. Machine learning refers to computer technologies that can learn from experience (historical cases). This chapter is dedicated mainly to neural computing.* The specific sections are:

*Most of the material on neural computing in this chapter was written by Larry Medsker from the American University, Washington, D.C.

17.1   Machine Learning Overview

Automated problem solving has been a target for generations, long before computers were invented. Consider these examples: statistical models such as regression or forecasting, management science models such as inventory level determination and allocation of resources, and financial models such as make versus buy decisions and equipment replacement schedules. Unfortunately, such methods deal with what is called shallow knowledge, or **knowledge-poor procedures.** When problems are complex, they cannot be solved by these standard models. Instead, additional knowledge is needed. Such knowledge can be provided in some cases by expert systems either by themselves, or when integrated with other CBIS. However, ES employ a *reasoning* approach, and therefore their use is limited to narrow and usually shallow domains. For more complex situations we use a different approach called **machine learning.** Machine learning refers to a set of several methods that attempt to teach machines to solve problems, or to support problem solving, by applying historical cases.

This task, however, is not simple. One problem is that there are many models of learning. Sometimes it is difficult to match the learning model with the type of problem (e.g., in job scheduling) that needs to be solved. Although machine learning is considered to be part of artificial intelligence, some of its technologies do not exhibit the characteristics of AI.

Learning

Until recently, machine learning has not been a major concern for applied AI. Most AI researchers initially felt that it was necessary to concentrate on how to make a computer program exhibit intelligence before figuring out how the program could learn to improve its own performance. Early examples of machine learning are the well-publicized checkers- and chess-playing programs. These programs improve their performance with experience.

Learning is accomplished by analogy, discovery, or special procedures; by observing; or by analyzing examples. Learning can improve the performance of AI products like expert systems and robotics.

Learning is a "support" area of AI because it is an investigation into the basic principles underlying intelligence rather than an application itself. The following four observations are relevant to learning as it relates to AI:

1. Learning systems demonstrate interesting learning behaviors, some of which (e.g., the checkers-playing program) actually challenge the performance of humans.
2. Although human-level learning capabilities are sometimes matched, no claims have been made about being able to learn as well as humans or in the same way that humans do (e.g., the checkers-playing program learns quite differently from humans).
3. Learning systems are not anchored in any formal bedrock; thus their

implications are not well understood. Many systems have been exhaustively tested, but exactly why they succeed or fail is not precisely clear.

4. A common thread running through most AI approaches to learning (and which distinguishes them from non-AI learning approaches) is that learning in AI involves the manipulation of symbols rather than numeric parameters.

Methods

Large numbers of machine learning methods and algorithms have been developed. Most of them are still in research labs. Here are some examples:

- **Neural computing:** This approach (the subject of the chapter) can be used for knowledge acquisition and for inferencing.
- **Inductive learning:** This approach is used in knowledge acquisition (described in Chapter 13).
- **Case-based reasoning and analogical reasoning.** This approach is used in knowledge acquisition and in inferencing. (See Chapter 15.)
- **Genetic algorithms:** Genetic algorithms (described in this chapter) attempt to follow some of the procedures of biological systems, which are excellent learners.
- **Statistical methods:** Although more suitable to knowledge-poor situations, statistical methods have been applied to knowledge acquisition and problem solving.
- **Explanation-based learning:** This approach, as outlined by Mitchell et al. [27], assumes that there is enough existing theory to provide rationalization of why one instance is or is not a prototypical member of a class. This promising approach has not yet been applied in the real world.

17.2   An Overview of Neural Computing

Over the past four decades, the field of artificial intelligence has made great progress toward automating human reasoning. Nevertheless, the tools of AI have been mostly restricted to sequential processing and only certain representations of knowledge and logic. A different approach to intelligent systems involves constructing computers with architectures and processing capabilities that mimic certain processing capabilities of the brain. The results are knowledge representations based on massive parallel processing, fast retrieval of large amounts of information, and the ability to recognize patterns based on experience. The technology that attempts to achieve these results is called **neural computing,** or **artificial neural networks** (ANNs).

Artificial neural networks are an information processing technology inspired by studies of the brain and the nervous system. After falling into disfavor in the 1970s, the field of ANN experienced a dramatic resurgence in the late

1980s. The renewed interest developed because of the need for brainlike information processing, advances in computer technology, and progress in neuroscience toward better understanding of the mechanisms of the brain. Declared the Decade of the Brain by the U.S. government, the 1990s look extremely promising for understanding the brain and the mind.

The topic of neural computing is covered in sections 17.2–17.19.

17.3   The Biology Analogy

Biological Neural Networks

The human brain is composed of special cells called **neurons.** These cells are special because they do not die when a human is injured (all other cells reproduce to replace themselves, then die). This phenomenon may explain why we retain information. Estimates of the number of neurons in a human brain cover a wide range—up to 100 billion—and there are more than a hundred different kinds of neurons. Neurons are separated into groups called networks. Each network contains several thousand neurons that are highly interconnected. Thus, the brain can be viewed as a collection of neural networks.

The ability to learn and react to changes in our environment requires intelligence. Thinking and intelligent behavior are controlled by the brain and the central nervous system. Those who suffer brain damage, for example, have difficulties learning and reacting to changing environments.

A portion of a network composed of two cells is shown in Figure 17.1. The cell itself includes a **nucleus** (at the center). On the left of cell 1, note the **dendrites,** which provide inputs to the cell. On the right is the **axon,** which sends signals (outputs) via the axon terminals to cell 2. These axon terminals are shown merging with the dendrites of cell 2. Signals can be transmitted unchanged, or they can be altered by synapses. A **synapse** is able to increase or decrease its strength of connection and causes excitation or inhibition of a subsequent neuron.

Artificial Neural Networks

An *artificial* neural network is a *model* that emulates a biological neural network. As you will see, today's neural computing uses a very limited set of concepts from biological neural systems. The concepts are used to implement software simulations of massive parallel processes that involve processing elements (also called artificial neurons or neurodes) interconnected in a network architecture. The artificial neuron receives inputs that are analogous to the electrochemical impulses that the dendrites of biological neurons receive from other neurons. The output of the artificial neuron corresponds to signals sent out from a biological neuron over its axon. These artificial signals can be changed similarly to the change occurring at the synapses.

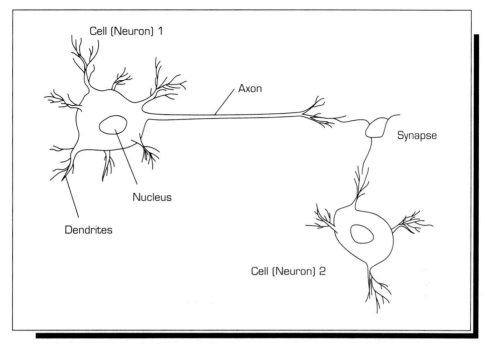

Cell (Neuron) 1

Axon

Synapse

Nucleus

Dendrites

Cell (Neuron) 2

FIGURE 17.1 Portion of a Network: Two Interconnected Biological Cells

The state of the art in neural computing rests on our current understanding of biological neural networks. We are, however, far from having an artificial, brainlike machine. Despite extensive research in neurobiology and psychology, important questions remain about how the brain and the mind work. This is just one reason why neural computing models are not very close to actual biological systems. Nevertheless, research and development in the area of ANNs is producing interesting and useful systems that borrow some features from biological systems.

17.4   Neural Network Fundamentals

Components and Structure

A network is composed of processing elements, organized in different ways to form the network's structure.

Processing Elements. An ANN is composed of artificial neurons (to be referred to as neurons); these are the **processing elements** (PEs). Each of the neurons receives input(s), processes the input(s), and delivers a single output. This

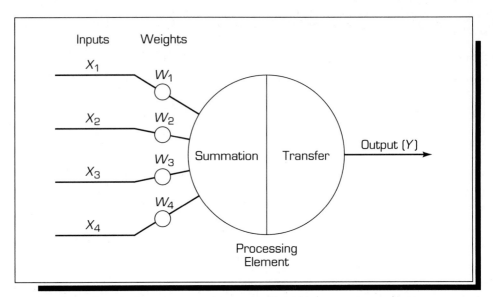

FIGURE 17.2   Processing Information in an Artificial Neuron

process is shown in Figure 17.2. The input can be raw data or output of other processing elements. The output can be the final product or it can be an input to another neuron.

A Network. Each ANN is composed of a collection of neurons that are grouped in layers. A typical structure is shown in Figure 17.3. Note the three layers: input, intermediate (called the **hidden layer**), and output. Several hidden layers can be placed between the input and output layers.

Structure of the Network. Similar to biological networks, an ANN can be organized in several different ways (topologies); that is, the neurons can be interconnected in different ways. Therefore, ANNs appear in many configurations. In processing information, many of the processing elements perform their computations at the same time. This **parallel processing** resembles the way the brain works, and it differs from the serial processing of conventional computing.

Processing Information in the Network

Once the structure of a network is determined, information can be processed. Several major concepts related in the process (see Figure 17.2) are:

Inputs. Each input corresponds to a single attribute. For example, if the problem is to decide on the approval or disapproval of a loan, an attribute can be an income level, age, or ownership of a house. The numeric *value* of an attribute is the input to the network. Several types of data can be used as inputs (see Box 17.1).

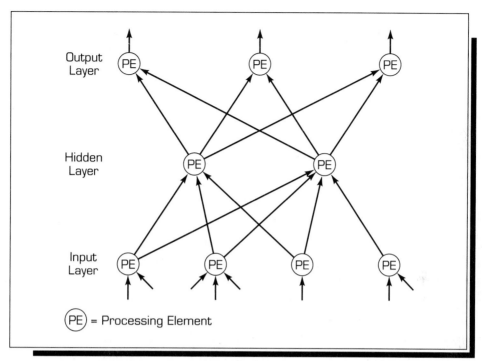

Output Layer

Hidden Layer

Input Layer

(PE) = Processing Element

FIGURE 17.3 Neural Network with One Hidden Layer

Outputs. The output of the network is the solution to a problem. For example, in the case of a loan application it may be "yes" or "no." The ANN assigns numeric values, for example, $+1$ for "yes" and 0 for "no." The purpose of the network is to compute the values of the output.

Box 17.1: Input to Neural Networks

Neural computing can process only numbers. If a problem involves qualitative attributes or pictures, they must be preprocessed to numeric equivalences before they can be treated by the artificial neural network.

Examples of inputs to neural networks are pixel values of characters and other graphics, digitized images and voice patterns, digitized signals from monitoring equipment, and coded data from loan applications. In all cases, an important initial step is the design of a suitable coding system so that the data can be presented to the neural network, commonly as sets of 1s and 0s. For example, a 6-by-8-pixel character would be a 48-bit vector input to the network.

Weights. A key element in an ANN is the **weight.** Weights express the *relative strength* (or mathematical value) of the initial entering data or the various connections that transfer data from layer to layer. In other words, the weights express the *relative importance* of each input to a processing element. Weights are crucial; it is through repeated adjustments of weights that the network "learns."

Summation Function. The **summation function** finds the weighted average of all the input elements entering each processing element. A summation function multiplies each input value (X_i) by its weight (W_i) and totals them together for a weighted sum, Y. The formula for n inputs in one processing element (Figure 17.4a) is:

$$Y = \sum_i^n X_i W_i$$

For several (j) processing neurons (Figure 17.4b), the formula is:

$$Y_j = \sum_j^n X_i W_{ij}$$

Transformation (Transfer) Function. The summation function computes the internal stimulation, or activation level, of the neuron. Based on this level, the neuron may or may not produce an output. The relationship between the internal activation level and the output may be linear or nonlinear. Such relationships are expressed by **transformation (transfer) functions,** and there are several different types of them. The selection of the specific function determines the network's operation. One popular nonlinear transfer function is called a **sigmoid function** (or **logical activation function**):

$$Y_T = \frac{1}{1 + e^{-Y}}$$

where Y_T is the transformed (or normalized) value of Y (see Box 17.2).

The purpose of this transformation is to modify the output levels to a reasonable value (e.g., between zero and one). This transformation is done *before* the output reaches the next level. Without such transformation, the value of the output may be very large, especially when several layers are involved. Sometimes, instead of a transformation function, a *threshold value* is used. For example, any value of 0.5 or less is changed to zero; any value above 0.5 is changed to one.

A transformation can occur at the output of each processing element, or it can be performed at the final output of the network.

Learning

An ANN learns from its experiences. The usual process of learning involves three tasks (Figure 17.5):

1. Compute outputs.

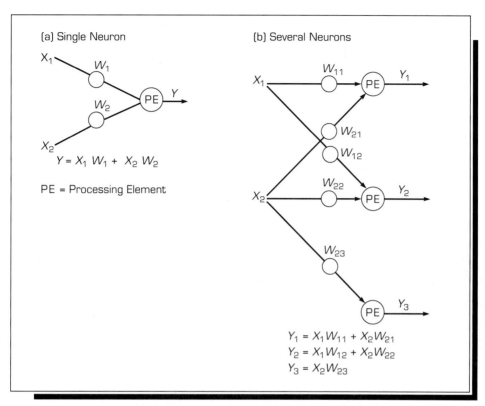

(a) Single Neuron

$Y = X_1 W_1 + X_2 W_2$

PE = Processing Element

(b) Several Neurons

$Y_1 = X_1 W_{11} + X_2 W_{21}$
$Y_2 = X_1 W_{12} + X_2 W_{22}$
$Y_3 = X_2 W_{23}$

FIGURE 17.4 Summation Function for Single Neuron (a) and Several Neurons (b)

Box 17.2: Example of ANN Functions

$X_1 = 3 \quad W_1 = 0.2$

$X_2 = 1 \quad W_2 = 0.4 \quad$ Processing $\quad Y = 1.2$
Element

$X_3 = 2 \quad W_3 = 0.1$

Summation function:

$$Y = 3(0.2) + 1(0.4) + 2(0.1) = 1.2$$

Transformation (transfer) function:

$$Y_T = \frac{1}{1 + e^{-1.2}} = 0.77$$

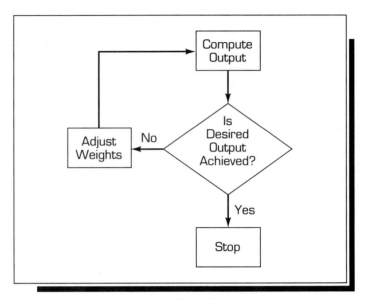

FIGURE 17.5 Learning Process of an Artificial Neural Network

2. Compare outputs with desired targets.
3. Adjust the weights and repeat the process.

The learning process starts by setting the weights by either some rules, or randomly. The difference between the actual output (Y or Y_T) and the desired output (Z) is called the delta. The objective is to minimize the delta (or better, to reduce it to zero). The reduction of the delta is done by changing the weights. The key is to change the weights in the *right* direction, that is, to make changes that further reduce the delta.

Information processing with an ANN consists of an attempt to recognize patterns of activities **(pattern recognition)** (see Box 17.3). During the learning stages, the interconnection weights change in response to training data presented to the system.

Different ANNs compute the delta in different ways, depending on the learning algorithm that is being used. More than a hundred learning algorithms are available for various situations and configurations; these are discussed in Section 17.10.

17.5 Developing Neural Network Applications

Although the development process of ANNs is similar to the structured design methodologies of traditional computer-based information systems, some steps are unique to neural network applications or have additional considerations. In the process described here, we assume that preliminary steps of system devel-

Box 17.3: How Patterns Are Presented and Recognized

This box shows seven ideal desired outputs. Actual cases can be exactly the same, or they can differ. The problem is to clarify each pattern to a class (the interpretation).

The historical cases show how interpretation decisions were made. These cases are divided into two categories: test cases and training cases.

Desired Outputs

Pattern										Interpretation
0	0	0	0	0	0	0	0	0	0	down
1	1	1	1	0	0	0	0	0	0	left
1	1	1	0	0	0	0	1	1	1	valley
0	1	0	1	0	1	0	1	0	1	alternating
0	0	0	0	0	0	1	1	1	1	right
0	0	0	1	1	1	1	0	0	0	hill
1	1	1	1	1	1	1	1	1	1	up

Historical Cases

	Pattern										Interpretation
Test cases											
#1	1	1	0	0	1	1	0	0	1	1	alternating
#2	0	0	0	0	0	1	0	0	0	1	right
#3	1	1	0	1	1	1	0	0	0	0	left
#4	0	0	1	1	0	1	0	1	0	1	alternating
#5	0	0	0	1	1	0	1	1	0	0	alternating
Training cases											
#6	1	1	1	0	1	1	1	0	1	1	alternating
#7	0	0	1	0	0	0	1	1	1	1	right
#8	0	1	0	1	1	0	1	1	0	0	alternating
#9	1	1	1	0	0	0	0	0	0	0	left
#10	1	1	1	1	0	0	1	1	1	1	valley

Notice that the historical cases may deviate from the desired output. The ANN will try to minimize the difference and give an interpretation as close as possible to the desired pattern.

(*Source:* C. W. Engel and M. Cran, "Pattern Classifications: A Neural Network Competes with Humans," *PC AI* [May/June 1991]. Used with permission.)

opment, such as determining information requirements and conducting the feasibility analysis for the project, have been completed successfully. Such steps are generic to *any* information system.

As shown in Figure 17.6, the development process for an ANN application has nine steps. In *step 1* the data to be used for training and testing of the network are collected. Important considerations are that the particular problem is amenable to neural network solution and that adequate data exist and can be obtained. In *step 2* training data must be identified, and a plan must be made for testing the performance of the network.

In *steps 3 and 4* a network architecture and a learning method are selected. The availability of a particular development tool or the capabilities of the development personnel may determine the type of neural network. Important considerations are the particular number of neurons and the number of layers to be used.

Current neural network models have parameters that tune the network to the desired performance level. Part of the process in *step 5* is initialization of the network weights and parameters, followed by modification of the parameters as performance feedback is received. In many cases, the initial values are important for determining the efficiency and length of the training.

The next step, *number 6,* is to transform the application data into the type and format required by the neural network. This may mean writing software for preprocessing the data. Data storage and manipulation techniques and processes need to be designed for conveniently and efficiently retraining the neural network when needed. Also, the way the application data is represented and ordered often determines the efficiency and possibly the accuracy of the results from the network.

In *steps 7 and 8,* training and testing are conducted as an iterative process of presenting input and desired output data to the network. The network computes the actual outputs and adjusts the weights until the actual outputs match what is desired. The desired outputs and their relationships to input data are derived from historical data (a portion of data collected in step 1).

At *step 9* in the process, a stable set of weights is obtained. Now the network can reproduce the desired outputs given inputs like those in the training set. The network is ready for use as a stand-alone system or as part of another software system.

Let's look now at these nine steps in detail.

17.6   Data Collection and Preparation

The first two steps in the ANN development process involve collecting data and separating them into a training set and a test set. The training cases are used to adjust the weight. The test cases are used for validation of the network.

The anticipated structure of the neural network and the learning algorithm determine the data type, such as binary or continuous. High-quality data collec-

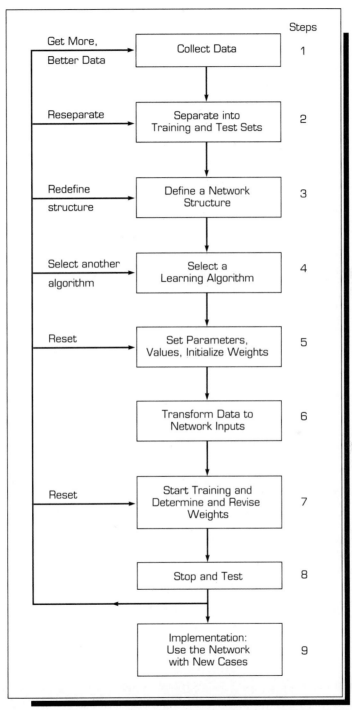

FIGURE 17.6 Flow Diagram of the Development Process of an Artificial Neural Network

tion requires care to minimize ambiguity, errors, and randomness in data. The data should be collected to cover the widest range of the problem domain; data should cover not only routine operations, but also exceptions and conditions at the boundaries of the problem domain.

In general, the more data used, the better—as long as quality is not sacrificed. Larger data sets increase processing times during training, but also improve the accuracy of the training and could lead to faster convergence to a good set of weights.

17.7 Network Structures

Several different neural network models and algorithms are being developed and studied [see 2, 4, 8, 20]. Three representative architectures are shown in Figure 17.7 and are discussed next.

Associative Memory Systems

Associative memory refers to the ability to recall complete situations from partial information. These systems correlate input data with information stored in memory. Information can be recalled from even incomplete or "noisy" input. Associative memory systems (e.g., see Khanna [21]) can detect similarities between new input and stored patterns. (See Box 17.4 and Hopfield [18].)

One type of unsupervised learning, competitive filter associative memory, has capabilities for learning by changing its weights in recognition of categories

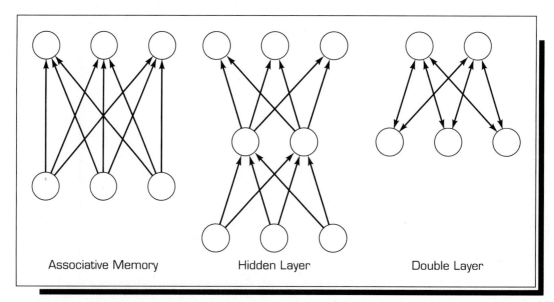

    Associative Memory   Hidden Layer   Double Layer

FIGURE 17.7 Neural Network Structures

Box 17.4: OCR Neural Network

This figure shows how a neural network can recognize characters better than template matching. Sets of neurons extract features from the input image. (Here, neurons extract the locations of vertical, horizontal, and diagonal strokes.) The locations of these features indicate possible choices of the character class. Most of the evidence shows that 6 is the best choice.

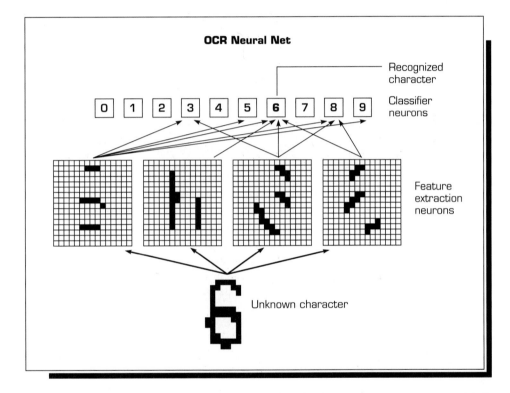

Source: AT&T Technology Magazine, Vol. 6, No. 4, 1991 ©.

of input data without being provided examples by an external trainer. A leading example of such a single-layer, self-organizing system for a fixed number of classes in the inputs is the Kohonen network [see 21].

Hidden Layer

Complex practical applications require one or more (hidden) layers between the input and output neurons and a correspondingly large number of weights.

Most commercial ANNs include three, and sometimes four or five layers, with each containing from 10 to 1,000 processing elements. Some experimental ANNs utilize millions of processing elements. The use of more than three layers is rare in most commercial systems because the amount of computation added with each layer increases exponentially.

Double-Layer Structure

A double-layer structure does not require the knowledge of a precise number of classes in the training data. Instead, it uses feed forward and feed backward approach to adjust parameters as data are analyzed to establish arbitrary numbers of categories that represent the data presented to the system. Parameters can be adjusted to tune the sensitivity of the system and produce meaningful categories.

17.8   Preparation

In preparation for the training, it is necessary first to decide on what learning algorithm to use (step 4, see Figure 17.6). This decision is related to the software development tools that are going to be used. A decision must be made at this stage because the structure and data preparation may have to be adjusted to fit the learning algorithm (especially if a software tool is used).

Selecting a learning algorithm is necessary but not sufficient. Before the training starts, several parameters must be determined (step 5). One parameter determines the rate of learning (as will be shown in section 17.10). It can be set to be high or low. Another parameter is the threshold value that determines the form of the output (an example is given in section 17.10). Finally, the initial values of the weights need to be set. Several other parameters that deal with validation and testing can also be determined during preparation.

The choice of the network's structure (e.g., the number of nodes and layers), as well as the selection of the initial conditions of the network, determines the length of time for the training. Therefore, these choices are important and require careful consideration at the outset of the process.

The last task of preparation is transforming the training and test data to the format required by the network and its algorithm (step 6). This step is especially important when a software development tool is used.

17.9   Training the Network

The training phase (step 7) consists of presenting the training data set to the network so that the weights can be adjusted to produce the desired output for each of the inputs. Weights are adjusted after each input vector is presented, so several iterations of the complete training set will be required until a consistent set of weights that works for *all* the training data is derived.

In the ideal case, the network can learn the features of the input data without learning irrelevant details. Thus, with the presentation of novel inputs that are not identical to those in the training set, the network would be able to make correct classifications.

17.10   Learning Algorithms

An important consideration in ANN is the appropriate use of algorithms for learning (or training). Such algorithms are called **learning algorithms** and there are more than one hundred of them. A taxonomy of these algorithms has been proposed by Lippman [24], who distinguishes between two major categories based on the input format: binary-valued input (0s and 1s) or continuous-valued input. Each of these can be further divided (Figure 17.8) into two basic categories: supervised learning and unsupervised learning.

Supervised learning uses a set of inputs for which the appropriate (desired) outputs are known. In one type, the difference between the desired and actual output is used to calculate corrections to the weights of the neural network. A variation of that approach simply acknowledges for each input trial whether or not the output is correct as the network adjusts weights in an attempt to achieve correct results. Examples of this type of learning are backpropagation and the Hopfield network.

In **unsupervised learning,** only input stimuli are shown to the network. The network is self-organizing; that is, it organizes itself internally so that each hidden processing element responds strategically to a different set of input stimuli

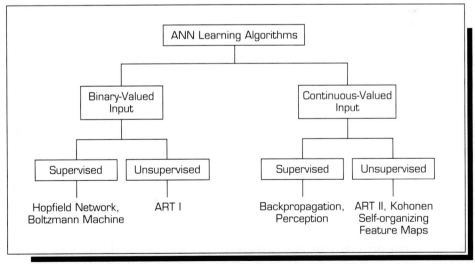

FIGURE 17.8 Taxonomy of Artificial Neural Network Learning Algorithms. (*Source:* Based on R. P. Lippman, "Review of Neural Networks for Speech Recognition," *Neural Computing* 1 (no. 1, 1989).)

(or groups of stimuli). No knowledge is supplied about what classifications (outputs) are correct, and those that the network derives may or may not be meaningful to the person training the network. However, the number of categories into which the network classifies the inputs can be controlled by varying certain parameters in the model. In any case, a human must examine the final categories to assign meaning and to determine the usefulness of the results. Examples of this type of learning are the Adaptive Resonance Theory (ART) and Kohonen **self-organizing** feature maps.

How a Network Learns

Consider a single neuron that learns the inclusive OR operation—a classical problem in symbolic logic. There are two input elements, X_1 and X_2. If either of them or both have a positive value, then the result is also positive. This can be shown as follows:

	Inputs		
Case	X_1	X_2	**Desired Results**
1	0	0	0
2	0	1	1 (positive)
3	1	0	1 (positive)
4	1	1	1 (positive)

The neuron must be trained to recognize the input patterns and classify them to give the corresponding outputs. The procedure is to present to the neuron the sequence of the four input patterns so that the weights are adjusted by the computer after each iteration. This step is repeated until the weights converge to a uniform set of values that allow the neuron to classify correctly each of the four inputs. The results shown in Table 17.1 were produced by using the Excel spreadsheet software to execute the calculations. In this simple example, a step function is used to evaluate the summation of input values. After calculating outputs, a measure of the error (delta) between the output and the desired values is used to update the weights, subsequently reinforcing correct results. At any step in the process for a neuron, j, we get

$$\text{delta} = Z_j - Y_j$$

where Z and Y are the desired and actual outputs, respectively. Then, the updated weights are

$$W_i(\text{final}) = W_i(\text{initial}) + \text{alpha} \times \text{delta} \times X_1$$

where alpha is a parameter that controls how fast the learning takes place.

As shown in Table 17.1, each calculation uses one of the X_1 and X_2 pairs and the corresponding value for the OR operation along with initial values, W_1 and W_2, of the neuron's weights. In this example, the weights are assigned random values at the beginning, and a *learning rate* (a parameter), alpha, is set to be relatively low. Delta is used to derive the final weights, which then become the initial weights in the next row.

TABLE 17.1 Example of Supervised Learning

				Initial				Final	
Step	X_1	X_2	Z	W_1	W_2	Y	Delta	W_1	W_2
1	0	0	0	0.1	0.3	0	0.0	0.1	0.3
	0	1	1	0.1	0.3	0	1.0	0.1	0.5
	1	0	1	0.1	0.5	0	1.0	0.3	0.5
	1	1	1	0.3	0.5	1	0.0	0.3	0.5
2	0	0	0	0.3	0.5	0	0.0	0.3	0.5
	0	1	1	0.3	0.5	0	1.0	0.3	0.7
	1	0	1	0.3	0.7	0	1.0	0.5	0.7
	1	1	1	0.5	0.7	1	0.0	0.5	0.7
3	0	0	0	0.5	0.7	0	0.0	0.5	0.7
	0	1	1	0.5	0.7	1	0.0	0.5	0.7
	1	0	1	0.5	0.7	0	1.0	0.7	0.7
	1	1	1	0.7	0.7	1	0.0	0.7	0.7
4	0	0	0	0.7	0.7	0	0.0	0.7	0.7
	0	1	1	0.7	0.7	1	0.0	0.7	0.7
	1	0	1	0.7	0.7	1	0.0	0.7	0.7
	1	1	1	0.7	0.7	1	0.0	0.7	0.7

Parameters: alpha = 0.2; threshold = 0.5.

The initial values of weights for each input are transformed using the above equation to assign values that are used with the next input (row). The threshold value (another parameter) causes the Y value to be 1 in the next row if the weighted sum of inputs is greater than 0.5; otherwise, the output is set to 0. In this example, in the first step, two of the four outputs are incorrect (delta = 1) and no consistent set of weights has been found. In the subsequent steps, the learning algorithm improves the results until it finally produces a set of weights that give the correct results ($W_1 = W_2$ as in step 4 of Table 17.1). Once determined, a neuron with those weight values can quickly perform the OR operation.

In developing ANN, an attempt is made to fit the problem characteristic to one of the known learning algorithms. Software programs exist for all the different algorithms, but it is best to use a well-known and well-characterized one, such as backpropagation, which will be described next.

17.11 Backpropagation

Backpropagation (short for back-error propagation) is the most widely used learning algorithm (see Hecht-Nielsen [16]). It is a very popular technique that is relatively easy to implement. It does require training data for conditioning the network before using it for processing other data. A backpropagation network includes one or more hidden layers. The network is considered a *feed forward* approach, since there are no interconnections between the output of a processing element and the input of a node on the same layer or on a preceding layer. Externally provided correct patterns are compared with the neural network output during training (i.e., it is a supervised training), and feedback is used to adjust the weights until all training patterns are correctly categorized by the network.

Starting with the output layer, errors between the actual and desired outputs are used to correct the weights for the connections to the previous layer. It has been shown that for any output neuron, j, the error (delta) = $(Z_j - Y_j) \times (df/dx)$, where Z and Y are the desired and actual outputs. It is useful to choose the sigmoid function, $f = [1 + \exp(-x)]^{-1}$, to represent the output of a neuron, where x is proportional to the sum of the weighted inputs to that neuron. In this way, $df/dx = f(1 - f)$ and the error is a simple function of the desired and actual outputs. The factor $f(1 - f)$ is the logistic function, which serves to keep the error correction well bounded. The weights of each input to the jth neuron are then changed in proportion to this calculated error. A more complicated expression can be derived to work backwards in a similar way from the output neurons through the inner layers to calculate the corrections to the associated weights of the inner neurons.

The procedure for executing the learning algorithm is as follows: initialize weights and other parameters by giving them random values. Then read in the input vector and the desired output. Compute actual output via the calculations forward through the layers; change the weights by calculating *backward* from the output layer through the hidden layers. This procedure is repeated for all the input vectors until the desired and actual outputs agree within some predetermined tolerance. Given the amount of calculation for one iteration, a large network can take a very long time to train. Current research is aimed at developing algorithms to improve this process.

17.12   Testing

As the reader may recall, in step 2 of the development process (Figure 17.6), the available data are divided into training and testing data. Now that the training has been performed, it is necessary to test the network. The testing (step 8) examines the performance of the network using the derived weights by measuring the ability of the network to classify the test data correctly. Black-box testing (comparing test results to actual historical results) is the primary approach to verify that inputs produce the appropriate outputs.

In many cases, the network is not expected to perform perfectly, and only a certain level of quality is required. Usually, the neural network application is an alternative to another method that can be used as a standard. For example, a statistical technique or other quantitative methods may be known to classify inputs correctly 70 percent of the time. The neural network implementation often improves on that percentage. If the neural network is replacing manual operations, performance levels of human processing may be the standard for deciding whether the testing phase is successful.

The test plan should include routine cases as well as potentially problematic situations. If the testing reveals large deviations, the training set needs to be reexamined and the training process may have to be reactivated.

In some cases, other methods can supplement black-box testing. For example, the weights can be analyzed statistically to look for unusually large values that indicate overtraining or unusually small weights that indicate unnecessary nodes. Also, certain weights that represent major factors in the input vector can be selectively activated to make sure that corresponding outputs respond properly.

Even at a performance level equal to that of a traditional method, the ANN may have other advantages. For example, the network is easily modified by retraining with new data. Other computerized techniques may require extensive reprogramming when changes are needed.

17.13   Implementation

The implementation of the ANN (step 9) frequently requires proper interfaces with other computer-based information systems and training of the users. Ongoing monitoring and feedback to the developers are recommended for system improvements and long-term success. An important consideration is to gain confidence of the users and management early in the deployment to ensure that the system is accepted and used properly.

If it is a part of a larger system, the ANN will need convenient interfaces to other information systems, input/output (I/O) devices, and manual operations for the users. The system may need I/O manipulation subsystems such as signal digitizers and file conversion modules. Good documentation and user training are necessary to ensure successful integration into the mainstream operations. A convenient procedure must be planned for updating the training sets and initiating periodic retraining of the network. This includes the ability to recognize and include new cases that are discovered when the system is used routinely.

Ongoing monitoring and feedback to the developers is necessary for maintaining the neural network system. Periodic evaluation of system performance may reveal environmental changes or previously missed bugs that require changes in the network. Enhancements may be suggested as users become more familiar with the system, and feedback may be useful in the design of future versions or in new products.

Neural Computing Paradigms. In building an artificial neural network, the builder must make many decisions:

- Size of training and test data
- Learning algorithms
- Topology: number of processing elements and their configurations (inputs, layers, outputs)

- Transformation (transfer) function to be used
- Learning rate for each layer
- Diagnostic and validation tools.

A specific configuration determined by these decisions is referred to as the network's paradigm.

17.14 Programming Neural Networks

Artificial neural networks are basically software applications that need to be programmed. Like any other application, an ANN can be programmed with a programming language, a programming tool, or both.

A major portion of the programming deals with the training algorithms and the transfer and summation functions. It makes sense, therefore, to use development tools in which these standard computations are preprogrammed. Several dozen development tools are on the market (Table 17.2). Some of these tools are similar to expert system shells. Even with the help of tools, however, the job of developing a neural network may not be so simple. Specifically, it may be necessary to program the layout of the database, to partition the data (test data, training data), and to transfer the data to files suitable for input to an ANN tool.

Some development tools can support up to several dozen network paradigms. In addition to the standard products, there are many special products. For example, some products are based on spreadsheets (e.g., NNetSheet). Other products are designed to work with expert systems as hybrid development products (e.g., KnowledgeNet and NeuroSMARTS). For a list of ANN tools, see [19].

TABLE 17.2 Representative Neural Computing Development Tools

Tool	Vendor
BrainMaker	California Scientific Software (Grass Valley, CA)
ExploreNet	Hecht-Nielsen Neurocomputer Corp. (San Diego, CA)
Explorer NeuralWorks: Professional I, II Plus	NeuralWare (Pittsburgh, PA)
Plexi	Lucid Inc. (Menlo Park, CA)
NeuroShell	Ward Systems Group (Frederick, MD)
MacBrain	Neurix (Boston, MA)
N-NETEX, N-NET 600	AI Ware (Cleveland, OH)
Nestor Development System	NESTOR Corp. (Providence, RI)

For a complete list, see "Neural-Net Resource Guide," *AI Expert* (July 1991): 60–68.

The user of ANN tools is constrained by the configuration of the tool. Therefore, builders may prefer to use programming languages such as C or to use spreadsheets to program the model and execute the calculations.

17.15 Neural Network Hardware

Most current neural network applications involve software simulations that run on conventional sequential processors. Simulating a neural network means mathematically defining the nodes and weights assigned to it. So instead of using one CPU for each neuron, one CPU is used for all of the neurons. This simulation may take long processing times. Advances in hardware technology will greatly enhance the performance of future neural network systems by exploiting the inherent advantage of **massive parallel processing.** Hardware improvements will meet the higher requirements for memory and processing speed and thus allow shorter training times of larger networks.

Each processing element computes node outputs from the weights and input signals from other processors. Together, the network of neurons can store information that may be recalled to interpret and classify future inputs to the network.

The computational work of an ANN can consist of hundreds of thousands of manipulations. To increase the computational speed when regular computers are used, one of three approaches is applicable:

1. *Faster machines:* For example, a machine with the Intel 80486 processor supplemented by a math coprocessor can expedite work, but not too much (e.g., between two to ten times faster).
2. *Neural chips:* Most of today's special chips can execute computations very fast, but they cannot be used to train the network. So, it is necessary to "train off the chip." This problem is expected to be corrected soon. (In the interim, acceleration boards are practical.) The idea of a chip is to provide implementation of neural network data structures on a chip— an analog chip (e.g., Intel 80170 Electronically Trainable ANN) or a digital chip, or even an optical one. (See Caudill [6] for details.) Most neural chips are still in the developmental stage.
3. *Acceleration boards:* These are dedicated processors that can be added to regular computers, similar to a math coprocessor. Because they are especially designed for an ANN, they work very fast. (For example, such a processor can be ten to a hundred times faster than the 20 MHZ 80386/387 processor.) Acceleration boards are currently the best approach to speeding up computations. Some examples are BrainMaker Accelerator Board, Balboa/860 boards, and NeuroBoard. The latter is at least a hundred times faster than the 80386/387 processor. Acceleration boards are extremely useful because they reduce training time, which is usually quite long. For example, an independent testing with NeuroBoard showed training time reduced from seven minutes to one second.

17.16   Benefits of Neural Networks

The value of neural network technology includes its usefulness for pattern recognition, learning, classification, generalization and abstraction, and the interpretation of incomplete and noisy inputs. A natural overlap with traditional AI applications thus occurs in the area of pattern recognition for character, speech, and visual recognition. Systems that learn are more natural interfaces to the real world than systems that must be programmed. Speed considerations point to the need to take advantage of parallel processing implementations.

Neural networks have the potential to provide some of the human characteristics of problem solving that are difficult to simulate using the logical, analytical techniques of expert system and standard software technologies. For example, neural networks can analyze large quantities of data to establish patterns and characteristics in situations where rules are not known. Neural networks may be useful for financial applications such as measuring stock fluctuations for determining an appropriate portfolio mix. Likewise, neural networks can provide the human characteristic of making sense of incomplete or noisy data. These features have thus far proven too difficult for the symbolic/logical approach of traditional AI.

Neural networks have several other benefits:

- *Fault tolerance:* Since there are many processing nodes, each with primarily local connections, damage to a few nodes or links does not bring the system to a halt.
- *Generalization:* When a neural network is presented with noisy, incomplete, or previously unseen input, it generates a reasonable response.
- *Adaptability:* The network learns in new environments.

Thus, neural computing differs from traditional computing methods in many ways, and the differences can be exploited by the application developer. Neural networks can be applied in areas where data are multivariate with a high degree of interdependence between attributes, data are noisy or incomplete, or many hypotheses are to be pursued in parallel and high computational rates are required.

Beyond its role as an alternative, neural computing can be combined with conventional software to produce powerful hybrid systems. Such integrated systems could include database, expert system, neural network, and other technologies to produce computerized solutions to complex problems.

17.17   Limitations of Neural Networks

In general, ANNs do not do well at tasks that are not done well by people. For example, arithmetic and data processing tasks are not suitable for ANNs and are best accomplished by conventional computers. Current applications of ANNs excel in the areas of classification and pattern recognition.

Most neural network systems lack explanation facilities. Justifications for results are difficult to obtain because the connection weights do not usually have obvious interpretations. This is particularly true in pattern recognition where it is very difficult or even impossible to explain the logic behind specific decisions. The limitations and expense of current parallel hardware technology restrict most applications to software simulations. With current technologies, training times can be excessive and tedious; thus, the need for frequent retraining may make a particular application impractical. Finally, neural computing usually requires large amounts of training and test data.

17.18   Neural Networks and Expert Systems

When ANNs were revived in recent years, they were labeled by the Japanese as sixth-generation computing. This labeling gave the erroneous impression that the fifth-generation computing, of which expert systems are a major part, is going to be replaced. As a matter of fact, although in some cases ANNs can perform tasks better (or faster) than ES, in most instances the two technologies are not in competition. Furthermore, the characteristics of the technologies are so different that they can *complement* each other rather nicely in some cases.

In principle, expert systems represent a logical, symbolic approach, whereas neural networks use numeric and associative processing to mimic models of biological systems. The main features of each approach are summarized in Table 17.3.

Expert Systems

Expert systems are especially good for closed-system applications for which inputs are literal and precise and lead to logical outputs. They are especially useful for interacting with the client/user to define a specific problem and bring

TABLE 17.3   Major Characteristics of Expert Systems and Artificial Neural Networks

Characteristic	Expert Systems	Neural Networks
Approach	Symbolic (mainly)	Numeric
Reasoning	Logical	Associative
Operations	Mechanical	Biological-like
Explanation	Available	Not available
Processing	Sequential	Parallel
System	Closed	Self-organizing
Validation and verification	Slow, difficult	Fast
Driven by	Knowledge	Data
Maintenance	Difficult	Easy

in facts peculiar to the problem being solved. Expert systems reason by using established facts and preestablished rules.

A major limitation of the expert system approach arises from the fact that experts do not always think in terms of rules. Also, experts may not be able to explain their line of reasoning, or they may explain it incorrectly. Thus, in many cases, it is difficult or even impossible to build the necessary knowledge base. To overcome this and other limitations, neural computing may be attempted instead.

Neural Networks in Knowledge Acquisition

In situations where rules cannot be determined directly, or where it may take too long to solicit them, an ANN can be useful for fast identification of implicit knowledge by automatically analyzing cases of historical data. The ANN analyzes the data sets to identify *patterns* and relationships that may subsequently lead to rules for expert systems. The ANN may be the sole technique for knowledge acquisition or it may supplement explicit rules derived by other techniques (such as interviews or rule induction).

Another possible contribution of ANNs to knowledge acquisition occurs when the interface with an expert may best be accomplished with an expert system module that asks questions and directs the data gathering from the expert efficiently and comprehensively. A trained neural network can then rapidly process information to produce associated facts and consequences. Next, an expert system module can perform further analysis and report results. Thus, fewer explicit rules may be necessary since the neural network contains general knowledge embedded in its connection weights and produces specific knowledge relevant to the user's specific problem.

17.19   Examples of Applications

In financial analysis ANNs can preprocess information from large databases to look for patterns and trends. Results can be used in investment decisions (e.g., see Trippi and Turban [33]).

Artificial neural networks can be useful in the structured models of statistics and operations research/management science. They can help solve very difficult optimization and allocation problems that are not solvable with standard models. Examples include:

1. **Pattern recognition**

   Speech generation—systems that learn phonemes in order to pronounce English text.

   Data transmission—fast matching of patterns of data used in compression techniques for transmission of voice, image, and text.

   Motion detection for military applications—aircraft identification, terrain analysis, recognition of underwater targets from sonar signals.

Robot learning—hand-eye coordination through training for grasping objects; possible use with space-station assembly systems.

Automation of operations in hazardous environments—earth observatory, power plants, undersea vehicles.

Character recognition—typewritten and handwritten, even if distorted; verification of signatures on checks and recognition of zip codes.

Voice recognition systems—voice-activated control of devices, voice typewriter.

Diagnosis of defective equipment—analysis, based on training cases, of monitored data to identify malfunctions in electrical circuits and so forth.

2. **Interpretation of data** *where analytical tools are needed to make generalizations or draw conclusions from large amounts of data from different sources or from sensors:*

Financial services—identification of patterns in stock market data and assistance in bond trading strategies.

Loan application evaluation—judging worthiness of loan applications based on patterns in previous application information.

Jet and rocket engine diagnostics—training neural networks with sensor data.

Medical diagnosis—training neural networks with cases of previous patients.

Credit-card information—fast detection of fraud from purchasing patterns.

DNA sequencing—analysis of patterns in DNA structures and rapid comparison of patterns in new sequences.

Airline forecasting—prediction of seat demand after training with historical data; rapid modification by retraining with new data as it becomes available.

Evaluation of personnel and job candidates—matching personnel data to job requirements and performance criteria; allows flexibility and tolerance of incomplete information.

3. **Optimization.** Several techniques (such as the Boltzmann machine and simulated annealing) can find acceptable solutions to problems involving many parameters.

4. **Resource allocation based on historical, experiential data.**

5. **Standard statistical analyses.** Hybrid systems perform such analyses on data sets selected by the neural network.

17.20   Genetic Algorithms

An algorithm is a set of instructions that is repeated to solve a problem. The word *genetic* refers to a behavior of algorithms that would be similar to biological processes of evolution.

A basic goal of **genetic algorithms** is to develop systems that demonstrate self-organization and adaptation on the sole basis of exposure to the environment, similar to biological organisms. Attaining such a goal would provide special capabilities in pattern recognition, categorization, and association; that is, the system would be able to learn to adapt to changes.

Example: A Game Called Vector

To illustrate how genetic algorithms work, let us review a special game, called Vector, devised by Walbridge [34].

Description. You play this game against an opponent who secretly writes down a string of six digits. Each digit can be either 0 or 1. For this example, the secret number is 001010. You must try to guess this number as quickly as possible. All you can do is present a number to your opponent and he or she will tell you how many of the digits (but not which ones) that you guessed are correct. For example, a guess 110101 has no correct digits (score = 0). A guess 111101 has only one correct digit (the third one). Thus, the score = 1.

Random Trial and Error. There are sixty-four possible six-digit strings of numbers. If you just pick numbers at random, on the average, it will take up to thirty-two guesses to find the right string. Can you do it faster? Sure, if you can make sense of the feedback provided to you by your opponent. This is exactly what the genetic algorithm does.

Genetic Algorithm Solution. *Step 1:* Present to your opponent four strings selected by random trial. Four were selected arbitrarily for this presentation; through experimentation, you may find that five or six would be better. You selected these four:

- (A) 110100, of which you correctly scored 1 digit
- (B) 111101, of which you correctly scored 1 digit
- (C) 011011, of which you correctly scored 4 digits
- (D) 101100, of which you correctly scored 3 digits

Since none of the strings is entirely correct, continue.

Step 2: Delete (A) and (B) for having low scores. Call (C) and (D) parents.

Step 3: Mate the parents' "genes" through *crossover.* This is done by splitting each number as shown:

- (C) 01:1011
- (D) 10:1100

Now, crossover the first two digits of (C) with the last four of (D). The result is (E), the first offspring:

- (E) 011100; score = 3

Similarly, crossover the first two digits of (D) with the last four of (C). The result is (F), the second offspring:

- (F) 101011; score = 4

It looks as though the offspring are not doing much better than the parents.

Step 4: Now copy the original (C) and (D).

Step 5: Mate and crossover the new parents, but use a different split. You get two new offspring (G) and (H):

- (C) 0110:11
- (D) 1011:00
- (G) 0110:00; score = 4
- (H) 1011:11, score = 3

Next, repeat step 2; select the best "couple" to reproduce. We have several options (e.g., G and C). Select (G) and (F) (one of the second bests). Now duplicate and crossover. Here are the results:

- (F) 1:01011
- (G) 0:11000
- (I) 111000; score = 3
- (J) 001011; score = 5

Also, you may generate more offspring:

- (F) 101:011
- (G) 011:000
- (K) 101000; score = 4
- (L) 011011; score = 4

Now repeat the processes with (J) and (K) as parents; duplicate the crossover:

- (J) 00101:1
- (K) 10100:0
- (M) 001010; score = 6

This is it; you reached the solution after thirteen guesses. Not bad when compared to thirty-two for a random guess.

The process exercised in this game is shown in Figure 17.9. *Note:* Using common sense and logic, this problem can be solved faster. However, this example is easy to follow.

Definition and Applications

Grefenstette [13] defines a genetic algorithm as "an iterative procedure maintaining a population of structures that are candidate solutions to specific domain challenges. During each temporal increment (called a *generation*), the structures in the current population are rated for their effectiveness as domain solutions, and on the basis of these evaluations, a new population of candidate

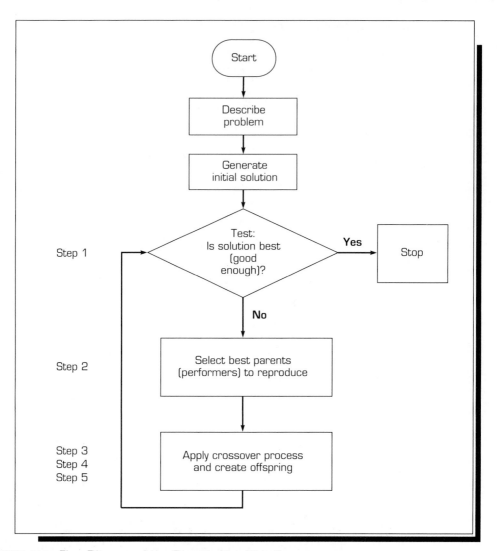

FIGURE 17.9 Flow Diagram of the Genetic Algorithm Process

solutions is formed using specific 'genetic operators' such as reproduction, crossover and mutation."

Most genetic algorithms use three primary operators:

1. **Reproduction:** Through **reproduction** genetic algorithms produce new generations of improved solutions by selecting parents with higher fitness ratings or by giving such parents greater probability to be contributors.

2. **Crossover:** Many genetic algorithms use strings of binary symbols, as in our game, to represent solutions. **Crossover** means choosing a random

position on the string (e.g., after two digits) and exchanging the segments either to the right or to the left of this point with another string partitioned similarly.

3. **Mutation:** This genetic operator was not shown in the game. **Mutation** is an arbitrary change in a situation. Sometimes it is needed to keep the algorithm from getting "stuck." The procedure changes a 1 to 0 or a 0 to 1 instead of duplicating them. However, such a change occurs at a very low probability (say, one in a thousand).

Genetic algorithms can be viewed as a type of machine learning for automatically solving complex problems. They provide a set of efficient, domain-independent search heuristics for a broad spectrum of applications. Austin [1] has indicated some general areas of applications:

- Dynamic process control
- Induction of optimization of rules
- Discovering new connectivity topologies (e.g., neural computing connections)
- Simulating biological models of behavior and evolution
- Complex design of engineering structures
- Pattern recognition.

A genetic algorithm is an exciting tool. It receives information that enables it to reject inferior solutions and to accumulate good ones. Also, genetic algorithms are suitable for parallel processing (see Austin [1]). Finally, genetic algorithms are also related to *fuzzy logic* (see Karr [20]).

Chapter Highlights

- Neural computing attempts to mimic the manner in which the brain works. It uses procedures similar to those that function in biological systems.
- The human brain is composed of billions of cells called neurons, which are grouped in interconnected clusters.
- Neural systems are composed of processing elements called artificial neurons. They are interconnected and receive, process, and deliver information (usually in binary code). A group of connected neurons forms an artificial neural network.
- An artificial neural network can be organized in many different ways, but the major elements are the processing elements, the contacts among the processing elements, the inputs, the outputs, and the weights.
- Weights express the relative strength (or importance) given to input data.
- Each neuron has an activation value that is expressed by summarizing the input values multiplied by their weights.
- An activation value is translated to an output by going through a trans-

formation (transfer) function. The output can be related in a linear or non-linear manner or via a threshold value.

- Artificial neural networks learn from historical cases. The learning (training) produces the required values of the weights, which make the computed outputs equal (or close) to desired outputs.
- The learning process is carried out with algorithms. There are more than a hundred, and they are easy to computerize.
- Supervised learning refers to a situation in which computed outputs are compared to standards that have been input. In unsupervised learning, the network is self-organized to produce categories (patterns) into which a series of inputs falls.
- Testing is done by using historical data and running it on adjusted weights to see if the outputs match the standards.
- Neural computing is frequently integrated with traditional computer-based information systems and with expert systems.
- Most ANNs are being built with tools that include the learning algorithm(s) and other computational procedures.
- Artificial neural networks lend themselves to parallel processing. However, current ANNs are solved on standard computers where multiprocessing is simulated on a single processor.
- Special boards have been developed for expediting the computational work of computers; these boards can be easily added to standard computers.
- Neural computing excels in pattern recognition, learning, classification, generalization and abstraction, and interpretation of incomplete input data.
- Artificial neural networks do well at tasks done well by people and *not* so well at tasks that are done well by traditional computer systems (e.g., transaction processing, nonrepetitive scientific computing).
- Machine learning describes the many techniques that enable computers to learn from experience.
- Machine learning is used in knowledge acquisition as well as in inferencing and problem solving.
- Machines learn differently from the way people do and not as well.
- Genetic algorithms use a three-step iterative process: test a solution to see how good it is, select the best "parents," and generate offspring. The procedure improves the results as knowledge accumulates.

Key Words

artificial neural network	crossover	inductive learning
associative memory	dendrites	knowledge-poor procedures
axon	explanation-based learning	learning algorithm
backpropagation	genetic algorithm	machine learning
case-based reasoning	hidden layer	

massive parallel processing	pattern recognition	supervised learning
mutation	processing element	synapse
neural computing	reproduction	transformation
neuron	self-organizing	(transfer) function
nucleus	sigmoid (logical	unsupervised learning
parallel processing	activation) function	weight
	summation function	

Questions for Review

1. What is an artificial neural network?
2. Explain the following terms: *neuron, axon, dendrite,* and *synapse.*
3. Describe biological and artificial neural networks.
4. What is a hidden layer?
5. How do weights function in an artificial neural network?
6. Describe the role of the summation function.
7. Describe the role of the transformation function.
8. What is a threshold value?
9. Why are learning algorithms important to an ANN?
10. Define associative memory.
11. Briefly describe backpropagation.
12. Explain how acceleration boards aid computers.
13. List the major benefits of neural computing.
14. List the major limitations of neural computing.
15. What is machine learning? List its major technologies.
16. What are the major objectives of machine learning? Why is there such an interest in the topic?
17. Describe the learning process in genetic algorithms. Why is it similar to a biological process?
18. Describe the major genetic algorithm operators.

Questions for Discussion

1. Compare artificial and biological neural networks. What aspects of biological networks are not mimicked by the artificial ones? What aspects are similar?
2. Draw a picture of a neuron and explain the flow of information.
3. Compare and contrast neural computing and conventional computing.
4. Why is parallelism related to ANNs? How can an ANN be developed and run on one processor?
5. Discuss the role of weights in ANNs.
6. Explain the combined effects of the summation and transformation functions.
7. Discuss the relationship between a transformation function and a threshold value.
8. Explain how ANNs learn in a supervised and in an unsupervised mode.
9. Why is an ANN related so closely to pattern recognition?

10. Explain how learning (training) is executed and why there are so many different learning algorithms.
11. Review the development process of ANNs. Compare it to the development process of expert systems.
12. What is meant by "initialization of the parameters of the network"?
13. Discuss the major advantages of ANNs.
14. Explain the difference between a training set and a testing set. Can the same set be used for both purposes? Why or why not?
15. Why is it said that it is much easier to maintain an ANN than an expert system?
16. Compare and contrast a neural chip and an acceleration board.
17. What deficiencies of expert systems can be overcome by artificial neural networks?
18. Explain why a major contribution of ANNs is in knowledge acquisition.
19. Expert systems and ANNs can complement each other very nicely. Explain why and be specific!
20. You are playing a game in which your opponent thinks about an object and you ask questions. Your opponent's answers will guide you to identify the object. To what AI technology is this game similar and why?

Exercises

1. You are trying to identify a specific number in the set of 1 to 16. You can ask questions such as, "Is this number in the set 1–8?" The answer can either be yes or no. In either case, you continue to ask more questions until you can identify the number.*
   a. How many questions are needed, in the worst and the best possible cases, to identify such a number?
   b. Is the problem suitable for parallel processing? Why or why not?
   c. Can you relate this problem to a genetic algorithm?
2. A set of five letters from the alphabet is given to you (say, B, E, M, S, and T). Your task is to compose as many words as possible from these letters. One way to do it is to write a computer program that will try to match each combination of these letters to words in a dictionary.*
   a. Describe the process that a regular computer will go through.
   b. Is the problem suitable for parallel processing? Why or why not?
3. For the following applications, which would be better—neural networks or expert systems? Explain your answers, including possible exceptions or special conditions.
   a. Diagnosis of a well-established, but complex disease
   b. Price-lookup subsystem for a high-volume merchandise sale
   c. Automated voice-inquiry processing system

---

*The problems in exercises 1 and 2 appeared in the April 15, 1988 issue of *AI Week* (contributed by D. B. Hertz).

4. Give possible applications of neural networks for the following:
   a. Character recognition
   b. Transaction processing
   c. Decision support
5. Several companies are flooded by hundreds and even thousands of job applications. Prepare a conceptual design of an integrated ANN and ES that will help in the screening process of a company for which security considerations are important.
6. Review this neural network and compute:

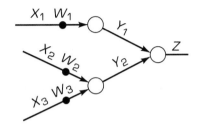

where:

$$X_1 = 15, \ X_2 = 8, \ X_3 = 14$$
$$W_1 = 0.6, \ W_2 = 0.3, \ W_3 = 0.1$$
$$\text{weight for } Y_1 = 0.6, \text{ for } Y_2 = 0.45$$

   a. Compute the value of Z without any transfer function.
   b. Compute the value of Z with a threshold function. If the value is 5 or less, call it 0; otherwise call it 1.
   c. Figure the value of Z with the sigmoid transfer function employed at all neurons.

References and Bibliography

1. Austin, S. "Genetic Solution to XOR Problems." *AI Expert* (December 1990).
2. Bailey, D. L., and D. M. Thompson. "Developing Neural-Network Applications." *AI Expert* (September 1990): 34–41.
3. Beale, R., and T. Jackson. *Neural Computing.* Bristol, England: Adam Hilger, 1990.
4. Caudill, M., and C. Butler. *Naturally Intelligent Systems.* Cambridge, MA: MIT Press, 1990.
5. Caudill, M. "Using Neural Nets" (six parts). *AI Expert* (December 1989, April 1990, June 1990, July 1990, September 1990, December 1990).
6. Caudill, M. "Embedded Neural Networks." *AI Expert* (April 1991).
7. Davis, L. *Handbook of Genetic Algorithms.* New York: Van Nostrand Reinhold, 1989.

8. Dreyfus, H., and S. Dreyfus. *Mind Over Machine*. New York: Free Press, 1986.

9. Eberhart, R., and R. Dobbins. *Neural Network PC Tools*. San Diego: Academic Press, 1990.

10. Engel, C. W., and M. Cran. "Pattern Classifications: A Neural Network Competes with Humans." *PC AI* (May/June 1991).

11. Gallant, S. "Connectionist Expert Systems." *Communications of ACM* (February 1988).

12. Goldberg, D. E. *Genetic Algorithms in Search, Optimization and Machine Learning*. Reading, MA: Addison-Wesley, 1989.

13. Grefenstette, J. "Optimization of Control Parameters for Genetic Algorithms." *IEEE Transactions on Systems Management and Cybernetics* 16 (no. 1, 1982).

14. Guha, R. V., and D. B. Lenat. "CYC: A Mid-Term Report." *AI Magazine* (Fall 1990).

15. Hawley, D. D., et al. "Artificial Neural Systems: A New Tool for Decision Making." *Financial Analyst* 46 (November 1990): 63–72.

16. Hecht-Nielsen, R. *Neurocomputing*. Reading, MA: Addison-Wesley, 1990.

17. Hillman, D. V. "Integrating Neural Networks and Expert Systems." *AI Expert* (June 1990): 54–59.

18. Hopfield, J. "Neural Networks and Physical Systems with Emergent Collective Computational Abilities." *Proc. Natl. Acad. Sci. USA* 79 (1985): 141–152.

19. *Intelligent Software Strategies* 7 (June 1991): 8–12.

20. Karr, C. "Applying Genetics to Fuzzy Logic." *AI Expert* (March 1991).

21. Khanna, T. *Foundations of Neural Networks*. Reading, MA: Addison-Wesley, 1990.

22. Klimasauskas, C. C. "Applying Neural Networks—Part 2." *PC AI* (March/April 1991).

23. Kosko, B. *Neural Nets and Fuzzy Systems*. Englewood Cliffs, NJ: Prentice-Hall, 1991.

24. Lippman, R. P. "Review of Neural Networks for Speech Recognition." *Neural Computing* 1 (no. 1, 1989): 1–38.

25. Medsker, L. R., ed. Special issue of *Expert Systems with Applications* 2 (no. 1, 1991).

26. Minsky, M., and S. A. Papert. *Perceptions*. Cambridge, MA: MIT Press, 1969.

27. Mitchell, T. M., et al. "Explanation-based Generalization: A Unifying View." *Machine Learning* (no. 1, 1986).

28. Parsaye, K., et al. *Intelligent Databases*. New York: John Wiley & Sons, 1989.

29. Rawlins, G., ed. *Foundation of Genetic Algorithms*. San Mateo, CA: Morgan Kaufman, 1991.

30. Schwartz, T. J. "A Neural Chips Survey." *AI Expert* (December 1990).

31. Sejnowski, T., and C. Rosenberg. "Parallel Networks that Learn to Pronounce English Text." *Complex Systems* 1 (1987): 145–168.

32. Sherald, M. "Mission Possible—If You Combine Neural Networks and Expert Systems." *PC AI* (May/June 1991).

33. Trippi, R., and E. Turban. *Neural Network Applications in Investment and Financial Services.* Chicago: Probus Publishers, 1992.

34. Walbridge, C. T. "Genetic Algorithms: What Computers Can Learn From Darwin." *Technology Review* (June 1989).

35. Wasserman, P. "Neural Computing: Theory and Practice." New York: Van Nostrand Reinhold, 1989.

Part 7

Integration and Implementation

The management support systems described in this book can be implemented as stand-alone systems, but they also can be integrated with other computer-based information systems. Certain integrations take place when the systems are in development, whereas others can occur only during implementation. Therefore Part 7, which deals with implementation issues, begins with the topic of integration (Chapter 18). Several modes of integration are described as well as the difficulties and problems.

Since the introduction of MSS technologies may create a significant change in an organization, the implementation process should be designed carefully. Both the generic and unique aspects of MSS implementation are described in Chapter 19. In Chapter 20 we address potential organizational and societal impacts. Of special interest is the issue of AI's effect on employment—a highly debated topic.

Chapter 18

Integrating MSS Technologies

In previous chapters we introduced several MSS technologies as being completely independent of each other, and indeed, many such systems are unrelated. However, there is increasing evidence that integrating these systems with one another and/or with other computer-based information systems (CBIS) may enhance the quality and efficiency of many computerized systems in total. This chapter examines the various issues of MSS integration in the following sections:

18.1   What Is Systems Integration?

Integration of computer-based systems means that the systems are integrated into one facility rather than having separate hardware, software, and communications for each independent system. Integration can be at the development tools level or at the application system level. There are two general types of integration: functional and physical.

Functional integration implies that different support functions are provided as a single system. For example, working with electronic mail, using a spreadsheet, communicating with external databases, creating graphic representations, and storing and manipulating data can all be accomplished at the same workstation. A user can access the appropriate facilities through a single, consistent interface and can switch from one task to another and back again.

Physical integration refers to packaging of the hardware, software, and communication features required to accomplish functional integration. Software integration is determined to a large extent by the hardware integration. The major approaches to physical integration, according to Newman [42], are shown in Figure 18.1 and are summarized next.

Access Approaches

According to the access approach, MSS development tools and/or application programs can *access* each other or access standard applications or development software. The access can be done based on one of three types of hardware configuration: single processor, multiprocessor, or networking.

Single Processor. This simple and most common approach relies on different software operating on the same processor. With this approach, traditional pro-

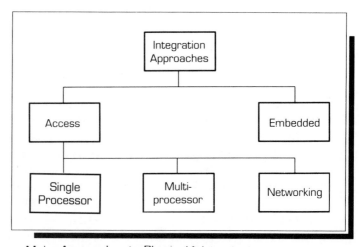

FIGURE 18.1   Major Approaches to Physical Integration

grams and databases are callable from computer memory or from some software package. An example of such an integration is the availability of LISP and/or PROLOG on a single processor with conventional languages. The Hewlett-Packard AI system is a good illustration. It integrates LISP, FORTRAN, C, Pascal, and HP-UX (a version of UNIX). As a result, programmers can edit, compile, test, and debug FORTRAN, C, and Pascal programs incrementally and interactively using either LISP or UNIX without ever leaving the LISP editor. The single-processor approach is not expensive, and the processor can be highly utilized, but it is *not as powerful* as the following two approaches.

Multiprocessors. According to this approach, different software operates on different processors within the same machine. For example, while UNIX is used during data acquisition, LISP can be used for data representation and analysis. Texas Instruments is using such an approach by combining an EXPLORER processor with a Macintosh processor. The multiprocessor approach is much more expensive than the single-processor approach, but it is more flexible and it can assist in faster processing of complex jobs.

Networking. Integration requires some kind of networking if MSS programs and/or conventional systems reside in completely different machines but can interface with each other. Networking permits an easy and quick interface among different software products. An example is General Motors' MAP (for manufacturing automation protocol), which is supported by powerful AI-dedicated workstations. These machines support Transport Control Protocol, Ethernet, Internet Protocol, and SNA, thus enabling a wide range of networking. Texas Instruments' EXPLORER is an example of a dedicated AI workstation that is networked with other systems. Apollo's Domain communication board, for example, is plugged into EXPLORER. The Domain's capabilities allow any computer on the network to store, access, or execute information on any other Domain-network computer as if it were on its own.

Embedded Systems

In this approach to physical integration, the MSS software is embedded in a conventional information system program, e.g., database. **Embedded systems** can be considered the "second generation" of integrating MSS and conventional systems. Such systems embed value-added MSS capabilities in conventional programs. Users see a single application with which they can work; there is no distinction between MSS and conventional parts. An example of an embedded development tool is Guru, which embeds an ES shell and a natural language processor in an environment that supports integrated spreadsheets, text processing, relational DBMS, graphics, report generation, communication, and business computing (for details see Rauch-Hindin [45]). Another example is the Executive Edge (from Comshare Inc.); this tool combines EIS, DSS, and limited ES explanation capabilities.

Embedded systems, which are usually more efficient than systems with access approaches, could be the most important information technologies of the future. Although embedded systems seem to be desirable, they are more difficult and more expensive to construct. On the other hand, there are many standard components on the market that can support the access approaches and can result in savings of time and/or money. Selection of an appropriate integration mode is outside the scope of this chapter; however, it certainly should be considered in the design phase of an integrated project. For further discussion see King [35].

Loose Versus Tight Integration

Another way to describe integration architectures is to distinguish between loose integration (or **loosely coupled** systems) and tight integration (**tightly coupled** systems). Loose integration refers to *two* (or more) *independent systems* that are connected via communication lines (networking). For example, an ES can be tied to a DBMS that serves a database or a decision support system via a communication link. The ES may be used to analyze the data generated by the decision support system. In such a case, the data produced by the decision support system can be stored in an external (text) file that is read by the ES application. A schematic view of such integration is shown in Figure 18.2b. Note that the user sees two systems. Access systems in general are loosely coupled.

Embedded systems, on the other hand, are considered to be tightly coupled. Figure 18.2a shows such an integration system. In such a case, the user sees one system (notice that there is only one user interface). Figure 18.2 is based on an ES shell named KES. Notice that there are no communication links or files in a tightly integrated system.

Expert Systems on a Chip

Computer hardware advances have made possible an expert system embedded in a microprocessor chip, which forms an integrated package of hardware and software. Such an integrated ES can be embedded in a piece of equipment (e.g., a complex electronic gear or robot) to form an intelligent system. One specific example is the EEG Analysis System—an ES embedded in a Motorola MC6801 single-chip, 8-bit microcomputer designed to interpret electroencephalograms recorded from patients with renal diseases.

Computer hardware size and price reductions have made it feasible for complex equipment to contain a dedicated computer and to run an ES that takes care of the equipment in some way. The integrated ES handles tasks such as monitoring and controlling equipment operation, detecting and diagnosing equipment faults, assisting in correcting the faults, and planning ways to work around the faults until they are corrected. The integrated ES is hard-wired into the equipment with direct connections to sensors and switches that allow the ES to monitor and, in some cases, control the equipment. For applications in which dangerous or unexpected situations are likely to arise, the operator could be taken out of the loop completely.

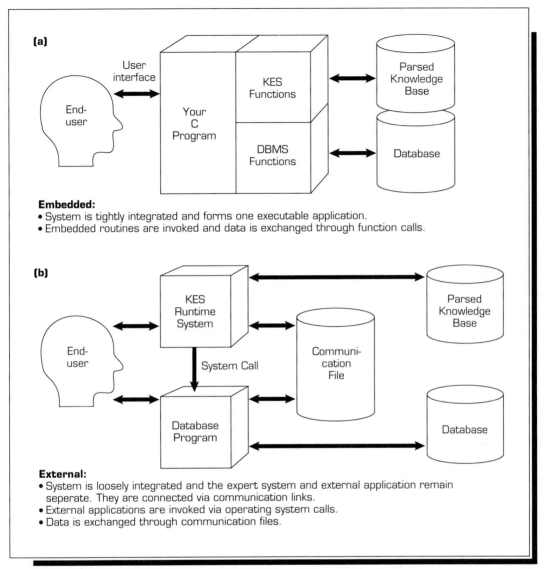

(a)

User interface

End-user

Your C Program

KES Functions

DBMS Functions

Parsed Knowledge Base

Database

Embedded:
- System is tightly integrated and forms one executable application.
- Embedded routines are invoked and data is exchanged through function calls.

(b)

End-user

KES Runtime System

System Call

Database Program

Communi-cation File

Parsed Knowledge Base

Database

External:
- System is loosely integrated and the expert system and external application remain seperate. They are connected via communication links.
- External applications are invoked via operating system calls.
- Data is exchanged through communication files.

FIGURE 18.2 Embedded Versus External (Access) Integration. (*Source:* Courtesy of Software A&E Inc.)

18.2 Integrating the DSS and the ES: An Overview

A decision support system (DSS) is composed of three components: a database and its management, a model base and its management, and a human-machine interface. In the next three sections, we will discuss integration with each of these components. Since databases and interfaces exist in many CBIS, the discussion here is obviously relevant for non-DSS as well.

In certain problem domains, both the ES and the DSS may have distinct advantages that, when combined, yield synergetic results. A DSS typically gives full control to the decision maker about information acquisition, information analysis (quantitatively), and the final decision. As research has shown, human judgmental biases may be present in complex decisions that are supported by a DSS. An ES, on the other hand, is free from acquisition, evaluation, and judgmental biases, at least in the human sense (*if* the knowledge of the expert is properly represented in the ES and *if* the ES is properly designed). The ES can provide intelligence for a particular domain and make a tentative decision. The decision maker can also utilize the DSS in the traditional sense and arrive at a tentative decision. If the results of the ES and DSS could be reconciled and evaluated, the joint effort would probably produce better results than either approach independently. The joint approach is not necessarily constrained by the narrowness of the domain of the ES, because an operational DSS can also be domain specific (e.g., a DSS for routing vehicles in a textile company, or a DSS for determining the allocation of customer engineers to geographic territories). Although typical decision support systems focus on quantitative mathematical and computational reasoning, they should also support qualitative analysis.

18.3   Intelligent Databases and Their Management

Tying expert systems and natural language processors to databases, especially large ones, is one of the most critical and rewarding areas of AI integration. There are several goals and physical modes of such integration into **intelligent databases.**

Goals and Modes

Organizations, private and public, are continuously collecting data, information, and knowledge (all are referred to here as information) and storing it in computerized systems. Updating, retrieving, use, and removal of this information become more complicated as the amount increases. At the same time, the number of individuals who are interacting with this information increases due to networking, end-user computing, and reduced costs of information processing. Working with large databases is becoming a difficult task that requires considerable expertise.

Developing AI applications requires access to databases. For example, without database access it would be difficult to use ES in large MIS applications such as factory automation and credit card authorization.

Expert systems can make the use as well as the management (e.g., updating, deleting, adding, or combining) of databases simpler. One way to do so is to *enhance* the database management system by providing it with an inference capability. Al-Zobaidie and Grimson [4] provide three possible architectures for such a coupling. They also explain how the efficiency and functionality of the DBMS can be enhanced. The contribution of an ES in such a case can be further increased if it is coupled with a natural language processor. For a description of integration of a database, DBMS, ES, and natural language processor, see Harris [22].

Another purpose of ES and DBMS integration is to improve the *management* of the ES's knowledge base (*intelligent knowledge management*). As ES become increasingly complex and diverse, the need for efficient and effective management of their growing knowledge base is apparent. Al-Zobaidie and Grimson [4] proposed an enhanced ES to deal with such situations: this ES will have a special DBMS that can be used to manage its own knowledge base.

A different way of looking at ES and database integration is shown in Figure 18.3. In this case the integration is tight; there is only one user interface. The application program can be driven by data generated by the database directly and/or by data generated by the database and then processed (e.g., interpreted) by the ES.

In addition to the enhanced DBMS and the enhanced ES, it is possible to integrate the ES and the DBMS via a network. Such an integration is discussed by Al-Zobaidie and Grimson [4].

Difficulties in connecting ES to large databases have been a major problem, even for large corporations (e.g., Boeing Co., American Express). Several vendors have recognized the importance of such integration and have developed software products to support it. An example of a product is the Oracle relational DBMS (Oracle Corp.), which incorporates some ES functionality in the form of

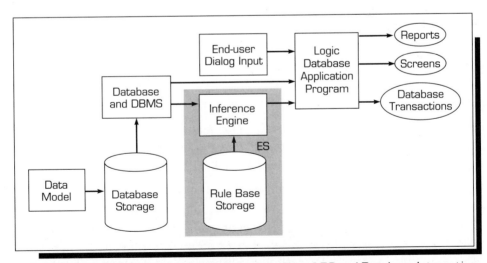

FIGURE 18.3 Intelligent Database Showing One Way of ES and Database Integration. (*Source:* Based on B. Cohen, "Merging Expert Systems and Databases," *AI Expert* [February 1989].)

a *query optimizer* that selects the most efficient path for database queries to travel. In a distributed database, for example, a query optimizer would recognize that it is more efficient to transfer two records to a machine that holds 10,000 records than vice versa. (The optimization is important to users because with such a capability they need to know only a few rules and commands to use the database.) This product includes a knowledge base that can incorporate, for example, rules for selecting which indexes to create or delete.

One of IBM's current main thrusts in commercial AI is providing a knowledge processing subsystem to work with a database and enable users to extract information from the database and pass it to an expert system's knowledge base in several different knowledge representation structures. Another IBM project is easy transferability of data from a typical database format (e.g., COBOL) to an ES format (e.g., LISP) and vice versa.

Another product is the KEE Connection (IntelliCorp.), which translates KEE commands into database queries and automatically keeps track of data passed back and forth between KEE's knowledge base and a relational database using SQL. Other benefits of such integration are the ability to use symbolic representation of data; improvements in the construction, operation, and maintenance of the DBMS (see Jarke and Vassiliou [29]); and the benefit for the ES itself, which is derived from accessibility to a database.

A current issue in database technology is the introduction of the object-oriented approach. Databases now store pictures and sophisticated graphics. Therefore, the management of databases is becoming more difficult and so are the accessibility and retrieval of information. For a discussion of intelligent object-oriented databases see Parsaye et al. [43].

The integration of ES and databases has been the topic of several international and national conferences, books, and dozens of papers. For further information see Brodie and Mylpoulos [8], Cohen [9], Hsu and Skevington [27], Kennedy and Yen [32], Kerschberg [33], Risch et al. [47], and Schur [49].

Online Databases

Commercial online databases are developed independently of each other, with different command languages, file structures, and access protocols. If we add to this the complexity of searching, the proliferation of online databases (several thousand), and the lack of standardization, it is not difficult to see why there is a need for extensive knowledge to use these databases efficiently. Expert systems can be utilized (usually combined with a natural language processor) as interfaces to such databases. The knowledge base of the ES includes knowledge about search strategy. For example, such a system can advise a casual user on how to conduct a simple search or it can guide the more experienced user in accessing databases with complex organizations. In all, the ES can make an online system transparent to the user. Such an integration is extremely important for information systems that use external databases frequently (e.g., executive information systems). For details see Kehoe [31] and Hawkins [23].

18.4   Intelligent Modeling and Model Management

Adding intelligence to the process of modeling (building models or using exist-ing models) and to their management makes lots of sense because some of the tasks involved (e.g., modeling and selecting models) require considerable ex-pertise. The topics of intelligent modeling and *intelligent model management* have attracted significant academic attention in recent years (e.g., see Blanning [7], Elam and Konsynski [13], Fedorowicz and Williams [14], Liang [39], and Vasant and Croker [63]) because the potential benefits could be substantial. It seems, however, that the implementation of such integration is fairly difficult and slow.

Issues in Model Management

Four interrelated subtopics of model management are investigated: problem diagnosis and selection of models, construction of models (formulation), use of models (analysis), and interpretation of the models' output.

Problem Diagnosis and Selection of Models. Several commercial ES are now helping to select appropriate statistical models (e.g., Statistical Navigator). Goul et al. [20] have developed a selection ES for mathematical programming and Courtney et al. [10] have developed an expert system for problem diagnosis. Zahedi [65] has developed a system for model selection. By way of examples, Elam and Konsynski [13] show how future model management systems will work when supported by ES.

Construction of Models. The construction of models for decision making in-volves the simplification of a real-world situation so that a simplified represen-tation of reality can be made. Models can be normative or descriptive and they can be used in various types of computer-based information systems (especially the DSS). Finding an appropriate balance between simplification and represen-tation in modeling requires expertise. The definition of the problem to be mod-eled, the attempt to *select* a prototype model (e.g., linear programming), the data collection, the model validation, and the estimation of certain parameters and relationships are not simple tasks either. For instance, data may be tested for suitability to a certain statistical distribution (e.g., "Does the arrival rate in queuing follow a Poisson distribution?"). The ES could guide the user in select-ing an appropriate test and interpreting its results, which in turn can help in appropriate modeling of the situation.

Use of Models. Once models are constructed they can be put to use. The ap-plication of models may require some judgmental values (e.g., setting an alpha value in exponential smoothing). Experience is also needed to conduct a sensi-tivity analysis as well as to determine what constitutes a significant difference

("Is project A really superior to B?"). Expert systems can be used to provide the user with the necessary guidelines for use of models. In addition, the ES can conduct a cause-effect analysis.

Interpretation of Results. Expert systems are able to provide explanation and interpretation of the models used and the derived results. For example, an ES can trace anomalies in the data. Furthermore, sensitivity analysis may be needed, or the translation of information to a certain format may be the desired result. An ES can advise in all the above.

Quantitative Models

Most experimental ES are *not* being developed according to the four model management issues just discussed. Instead, they are being developed according to the *type* of quantitative model used. Then, some portion of one or more of the four issues may be considered. A representative list of quantitative models is given in Table 18.1 with appropriate references.

For a proposed architecture for a quantitative intelligent model management, see Figure 18.4.

Human experts often use quantitative models to support their experience and expertise. For example, an expert may need to forecast the sales of a certain product or to estimate future cash flow using a corporate planning model. Similarly, many models are used by experts in almost all aspects of engineering. Such a model stands alone (meaning the expert can run the model on a computer as needed), or it can be part of a computer-based information system used by several decision makers and experts.

TABLE 18.1 Quantitative Models and Sources for More Information

Topic	References
Financial models	Turner and Obilichetti [61]
Forecasting	Feng-Yang [15], Kumar and Cheng [36]
Mathematical programming	Goul et al. [20], Murphy and Stohr [41]
Project management	Hosley [25], Sathi et al. [48]
Queuing	Hossein et al. [26]
Simulation	Doukidis [11], Ford and Schroer [16]
Statistics	Hand [21], Gale [17], Gottinger [18]
Strategic planning	Goul et al. [20], Lee and Lee [38]
System dynamics	Wu [64]

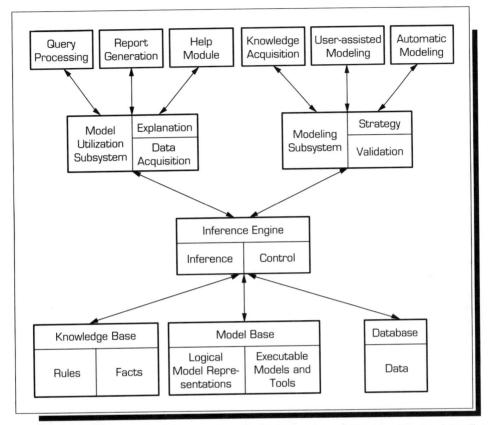

FIGURE 18.4 Software Architecture for Model Management System. The model utilization subsystem (left) directs the effective use of the model. The modeling subsystem (right) helps in increasing the productivity of model building. The inference engine drives the model selection and integration, and the integration of the model base, database, and knowledge base. (*Source:* T. Liang, "Development of a Knowledge-based Model Management System," Reprinted with permission from *Operations Research*, No. 6, 1988, Operations Research Society of America. No further reproduction permitted without the consent of the copyright owner.)

ES contributions in the area of quantitative models and model management can be demonstrated by examining the work of a consultant. A consultant is involved in the following steps:

1. Discussing the nature of the problem with the client
2. Identifying and classifying the problem
3. Constructing a mathematical model of the problem
4. Solving the model
5. Conducting sensitivity analyses with the model

6. Recommending a specific solution
7. Assisting in implementing the solution.

The system involves a decision maker (client), a consultant, and a computer.

If we can codify the knowledge of the consultant in an ES, we can build an intelligent computer-based information system capable of the same process. Unfortunately, relatively little is known about the nature of the cognitive skills that consultants use. However, related research has been done by Goul et al. [20] who have developed a system that attempts to replicate a manager-consultant-computer combination. In their system the computer queries the manager to determine the general category of the managerial problem (e.g., an allocation problem versus inventory management). Next the computer queries the manager to determine the *exact nature* of the problem (e.g., what kind of allocation problem). Then the computer suggests which quantitative model to use (e.g., dynamic programming versus linear programming). The manager can ask the system to define terminology to justify the recommendation made by the machine, and to explain the model used. The decision maker then can formulate the problem using the model, conduct what-if analysis, or use an alternative model. The ES, in this case, helps to identify and classify the managerial problem, acts as a tutor, provides illustrative examples, and selects the model(s) to be used.

Several researchers claim that there is a natural synergy between the prescriptive problem structuring techniques used in the DSS model base and the rule-based program architectures used in ES. In particular, the modeling procedures of the model base are suitable for *initial* problem structuring, whereas ES program architectures are suitable for (1) making the problem structure incrementally modifiable, and (2) developing a user interface that uses terms familiar to users.

Expert systems can be used as an **intelligent interface** between the user and quantitative models. Such an integration is demonstrated by BUMP, a statistical ES (Hand [21]). Large numbers of statistical packages are available on the market to support managerial decision making and research. They contain statistical tests and models that may be included in the model base of a DSS. A major dilemma faced by a nonexpert user is to determine which statistical models to use for what purposes. This is where BUMP is brought into action. This ES selects the appropriate statistical procedure and guides the novice user in using the not-so-friendly statistical packages that usually require a trained statistician for operation.

Several commercial systems are available on the market to assist with statistical analysis. Statistical Navigator (Idea Works, Inc.) is an expert system that helps the user select an appropriate statistical analysis routine from a pool of over 130 routines available in packages such as SPSS, SAS, and SYSTAT. The program does not execute the analysis, but it supplements many of the existing statistical packages. If several routines can do the job, Statistical Navigator ranks them by suitability. The program is built with the EXSYS shell.

18.5   Intelligent Human-Machine Interfaces

If expert systems and natural language processors are integrated with the human-machine interface subsystem, the human-machine dialog is conducted faster and better. Currently, expert systems are being used as front-ends to many application and development software packages. For example, Conversational Advisory System serves as a front-end to several DBMS products, and CLOUT is used as a front-end to R:BASE 5000. For details on this role of ES see Harris [22], Isshikawa [28], and Shafer [51].

In previous sections we discussed the benefits of integrating ES with the three components of a DSS. These benefits are summarized in Table 18.2 to-

TABLE 18.2   Summary of Integrating Expert Systems and DSS

	ES Contribution	DSS Contribution
Database and Database Management Systems (DBMS)	• Improves construction, operation, and maintenance of DBMS [29] • Improves accessibility to large databases • Improves DBMS capabilities [29] • Permits symbolic representation of data	• A database is provided to the ES [29]
Models and Model Base Management Systems	• Improves model management [12] • Helps in selecting models [20, 21] • Provides judgmental elements to models • Improves sensitivity analysis [20] • Generates alternative solutions [46] • Provides heuristics [24] • Simplifies building simulation models • Makes the problem structure incrementally modifiable • Speeds up trial-and-error simulation	• Provides initial problem structure • Provides standard models and computations • Provides facts (data) to models • Stores specialized models constructed by experts in the model base
Interface	• Enables friendlier interface [22, 29] • Provides explanations [24] • Provides terms familiar to user [24] • Acts as a tutor [20] • Provides interactive, dynamic, visual problem-solving capability [5]	• Provides presentations to match individual cognitive styles
System Capabilities (Synergy)	• Provides intelligent advice (faster and cheaper than human) to the DSS or its user • Adds explanation capability [24] • Expands computerization of the decision-making process [20]	• Provides experience in data collection • Provides experience in implementation [24] • Provides individualized advice to users to match their decision styles

gether with the benefits from an overall system integration. In the forthcoming section, we will introduce several models of ES and DSS integration.

18.6   Models of ES and DSS Integration

Several researchers and practitioners have proposed models for integrating expert systems and decision support systems. The following models are described in this chapter: expert systems attached to DSS components, ES as a separate DSS component, sharing in the decision-making process, ES generating alternative solutions for DSSs, and a unified approach.

Expert Systems Attached to DSS Components

Expert systems can be integrated into all DSS components. This arrangement (according to Turban and Watkins [59]) is shown in Figure 18.5. It includes five expert systems:

- ES #1: Database intelligent component
- ES #2: Intelligent agent for the model base and its management
- ES #3: System for improving the user interface
- ES #4: Consultant to DSS builders. In addition to giving advice on constructing the various components of the DSS, this ES gives advice on how to structure a DSS, how to glue the various parts together, how to conduct a feasibility study, and how to execute the many activities that are involved in the construction of a DSS.
- ES #5: Consultant to users. The user of a DSS may need the advice of an expert for complex issues such as the nature of the problem, the environmental conditions, or possible implementation problems. A user also may want an ES that will guide him or her in how to use the DSS and its output.

In many cases, not all five systems are operational. Frequently it is beneficial to attach only one or two expert systems.

ES as a Separate DSS Component

According to this proposal (Turban and Watkins [59]), an ES is added as a separate component. In Figure 18.6 on p. 736 notice that the systems share the interface as well as other resources. However, as indicated by King [35], such an integration is also available via a communication link (networking, as discussed in Section 18.1). There are three possible configurations for such an integration.

ES Output as Input to a DSS. DSS users may direct the ES output as input to the DSS. For example, the ES is used during the initial phase of problem solving to determine the importance of the problem or to identify the problem.

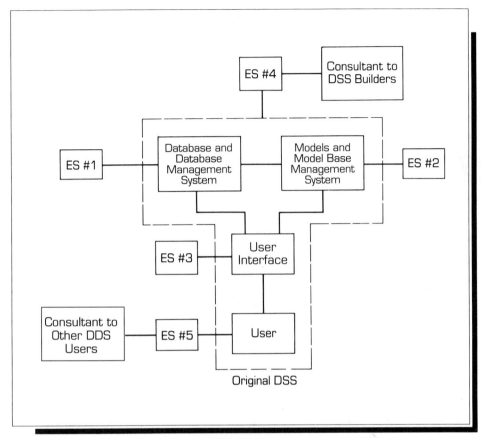

FIGURE 18.5   Integration of ES into All DSS Components

Then the problem is transferred to a DSS for possible solution. For an example see Courtney et al. [10].

DSS Output as Input to ES. In many cases, the results of computerized quantitative analysis provided by a DSS are forwarded to an individual or a group of experts for the purpose of interpretation. Therefore, it would make sense to direct the output of a DSS into an ES that would perform the same function as an expert, whenever it is cheaper and/or faster to do so (especially if the quality of the advice is also superior). An example is a postoptimality analysis of results provided by optimization models (see Lee and Lee [38]).

Feedback. According to this configuration, the output from the ES goes to a DSS, and then the output from the DSS goes back to the original ES.

The three possibilities are illustrated in Figure 18.7 on p. 736.

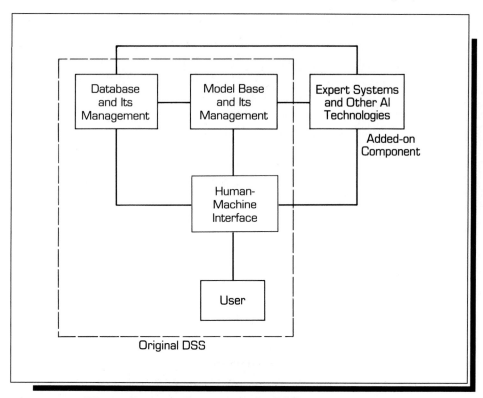

FIGURE 18.6   ES as a Separate Component of a DSS

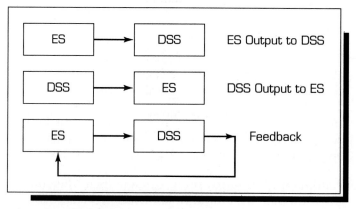

FIGURE 18.7   Interface Possibilities between Expert Systems and Decision Support Systems

Sharing in the Decision-Making Process

According to this approach, ES can complement DSS in one or more of the steps in the decision-making process. An example for such an approach is proposed by Meador, et al. [40]. Decision making is viewed as an eight-step process consisting of:

1. Specification of objectives, parameters, probabilities
2. Retrieval and management of data
3. Generation of decision alternatives
4. Inference of consequences of decision alternatives
5. Assimilation of verbal, numerical, and graphical information
6. Evaluation of sets of consequences
7. Explanation and implementation of decisions
8. Strategy formulation.

The first seven are typical DSS functions, whereas the last one, which requires judgment and creativity, can be done by an ES. Meador et al. [40] suggest that ES might supplement the DSS by using a built-in associative memory with knowledge of business and inferential rules.

Such an integration may be visualized as follows: The user works with the DSS following the first seven DSS steps. On reaching the strategy formulation phase he or she calls on the ES, which will be a completely separate system although it may share the database and perhaps use some of the capabilities of the model base. To better understand this type of integration, we assume that the ES plays the role of a human expert that the user can call on when in need of expertise in strategy formulation. The expert may give an answer immediately, or may conduct some analysis (e.g., forecasting). Such analysis can be accomplished by using the DSS database and its forecasting model.

Generating Alternative Solutions

Reitman [46] points out that most current decision support systems help users evaluate and choose among potential courses of action. Unlike a staff assistant, however, these systems cannot suggest the alternative courses of action that should be considered. He contends that this deficiency might be met by applying concepts and techniques taken from artificial intelligence.

Reitman describes an AI system that plays a game called *Go*. This system is able to work with nonnumeric data to develop alternative game strategies, evaluate them, and select the best alternative. He provides a detailed description of the strategies employed by the system to find or develop courses of action:

- Use of a network of experts at various levels of complexity of the game
- Successful refinement of problems from general to specific
- Assignment of priorities to situations
- Use of an "expert and critic" structure.

Reitman demonstrates how the system tests alternatives and how it limits a search to keep the solution to a manageable task.

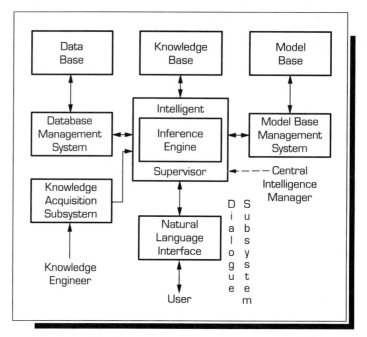

FIGURE 18.8 Unified Architecture for an Intelligent Decision Support System. (*Source:* J. T. C. Cheng, et al., "A Unified Architecture for Intelligent DSS," in *Proceedings, 21st HICSS*, Hawaii, January 1988.)

After describing the *Go* system, Reitman considers how AI-based DSSs might be transferred to systems in a business context. For example, decisions regarding trading futures of commodities appear to be roughly of the same order of complexity as existing AI applications; therefore, they appear to be a promising place to begin exploring the practical use of AI-based DSS.

A Unified Approach

Teng et al. [57] have proposed a unified architecture for ES and DSS integration. The proposal is shown in Figure 18.8. According to this proposal, the ES is placed between the data and the models. Its basic function is to integrate the two components in an intelligent manner.

18.7   Integrating EIS, DSS, and ES

As indicated in Chapter 10, an EIS can be integrated with a DSS. It is especially common for EIS to be used as a source of data for PC-based modeling products. For example, at a large drug company, brand managers download the previous day's orders of their products from Pilot's Command Center (an EIS). The download creates a Lotus-readable file on their PC disk. They then exit to the PC and run a Lotus DSS model against the data to predict where they will be at the end

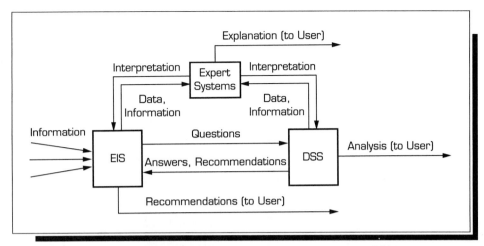

FIGURE 18.9 An Intelligent ESS. (*Source:* Turban and Stevenson [58].)

of the month. The results of this model are then uploaded to the EIS. So, by 11 A.M., senior managers can get on their EIS and see, for example, where each brand manager thinks he or she is going to be at the end of the month.

The integration of EIS and DSS can be accomplished in several ways. Most likely is that the information generated by the EIS is being used as an input to the DSS. More sophisticated systems include feedback to the EIS and even an explanation capability. A schematic view of such a system is given in Figure 18.9; it includes an ES that makes the system intelligent. Such an integration is being researched (e.g., see King [35]).

Generally speaking, the major contribution of ES to EIS can be in making an *interpretation* of the vast amount of information monitored by the EIS, for example, looking at abnormalities or examining potential trends. Another area is the provision of explanations to questions that may be raised by users.

18.8   Integrating Management Support Technologies

Expert systems and natural language processors (NLP) are used extensively in support of managerial decision making. For this reason, expert systems are frequently referred to as expert support systems. Therefore, it is logical to configure AI technologies, and especially ES, with other managerial support systems such as a decision support system and executive information system.

Integration of the various management support technologies can be explored best by viewing the support given by such a system. The major aim of integrated management support is provision of intelligent capabilities by adding an ES (or an intelligent component) to another system.

Figure 18.10 shows the integration of ES for the support of a typical managerial process. It presents the potential use of seven different expert systems; their areas of application are marked from ES 1 to ES 7.

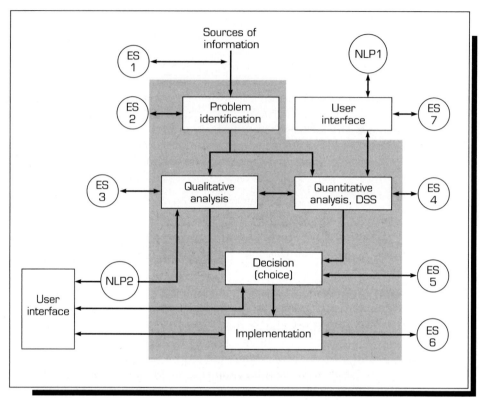

FIGURE 18.10 Expert System Support of the Managerial Process

ES 1. The system can help in the design of the flow of information to managers (e.g., what data to monitor and when) and in the *interpretation* of the collected information. Because some of the information is blurry, a combination of ES, fuzzy logic, and neural computing can be very helpful. The entire area of scanning, monitoring, forecasting (e.g., trends), and assessment (or interpretation) can be helped considerably by automation in general (e.g., electronic mail) and by ES in particular. The expert system can be supported by several natural language processing applications such as summarization of news, understanding of messages, and translation of foreign languages.

ES 2. Based on the information collected, a problem (opportunity) is identified. Expert systems can play an important role in this step in supporting the manager (e.g., see King [35]) and in refining the definition of the identified problem (e.g., see Courtney et al. [10]).

ES 3. Qualitative analysis is based on the use of expertise. Here, experts can be replaced by nonexperts who use the ES, or even by the expert systems themselves. For example, an ES can give advice on legal or tax issues that relate to the problem. Another possible use of ES at this time is for supporting qualitative forecasting methods.

ES 4. The support of ES for quantitative analysis was discussed in detail in Section 18.4. Of special importance is the capability of explaining the results of the analysis that can be executed by staff analysts.

ES 5. A final choice of an alternative can be made by an individual or by a group. Both may need interpretation of information generated during the analysis and execution of additional predictions. These are two typical generic categories of ES. However, the decision makers can also use the ES to help in developing the final design and planning (including an implementation plan) of the proposed action. The role of ES in decisions made by groups (e.g., in a group decision support system, or GDSS) can be extremely important. For further discussion see Agarwal and Prasad [1].

ES 6. Expert systems have been found to be very helpful in increasing the chances of successful implementation. Major benefits could be derived in the areas of explanation and training.

ES 7. A superb user interface is a key to successful implementation of any management support system. Expert systems can improve the interface, especially when they are combined with natural language processors.

Note: In addition to the expert systems one can add natural language processors interfaces (NLP 1 and NLP 2).

18.9   Links with Other Computer-based Information Systems

MSS applications may be linked with others of the same kind. Expert systems may "talk" to each other much like experts do. As a matter of fact, the topic of cooperating expert systems is in its commercial initialization.

An important integration takes place under what is described as computer-integrated manufacturing (CIM). CIM is composed of several computer programs that are used to plan and control different machines, materials handling facilities, robots, and other components. An expert system, for example, can be used to execute production planning in conjunction with some DSS. The planning will attempt to coordinate all activities of the plant, to achieve efficiency in the use of resources, to maximize productivity, to meet delivery dates, and so forth.

Another application of ES is in the area of error recovery. An automated factor is monitored by several sensors and other detecting devices. Any interruption can be detected and interpreted (used in robotics).

Various MSS have been connected to computer-aided design/computer-aided manufacturing (CAD/CAM) systems, sensory systems, materials handling, maintenance, quality control, assembly, and several manufacturing applications software. For further information see Kusiak [37], and Siegel [52]. A comprehensive CIM system is shown in Figure 18.11 and explained in Table 18.3 on page 744.

18.10   Problems and Issues in Integration

Many factors should be considered when MSS systems are integrated. This section describes some of the most important problems and issues.

Need for Integration. Integration may or may not be desirable. A comprehensive *feasibility* study is essential. Technological, economical, organizational, and behavioral aspects need to be analyzed.

Architecture of Integration. Several alternatives are available for executing the integration. Each of these options has some benefits as well as costs and limitations. A careful analysis should be undertaken before the integration.

Justification and Cost-Benefit Analysis. Although integrated systems have many benefits, they also obviously have costs. Making a computer system more intelligent is a novel idea, but someone will have to pay the bill. This issue is very important today since many people are questioning the economics of computerized systems and their alignment with organizational goals.

Peoples' Problems. The integration of MSS technologies among themselves and with conventional computerized systems brings together two different styles: the heuristic-judgmental and the algorithmic-analytical. This combination will certainly mean a change to many people. Builders and other users who are accustomed to working with conventional tools and applications will be asked to be engaged with symbolic processing. How will these people be affected? How will the analytical-type individual react to a heuristic approach? And how will the AI people handle the "burden" of an added structured analysis? Combining the two approaches may not be simple. For example, what if there are preferences for different user-interface modes? These are just some of the questions that need to be answered.

Finding Appropriate Builders. Finding skilled programmers who can work with both MSS technologies and conventional computer systems can be a major task, especially if complex systems are involved. Frequently, use of vendors and/or consultants is the only solution. Therefore companies subcontract most major system integration jobs—frequently a very expensive solution.

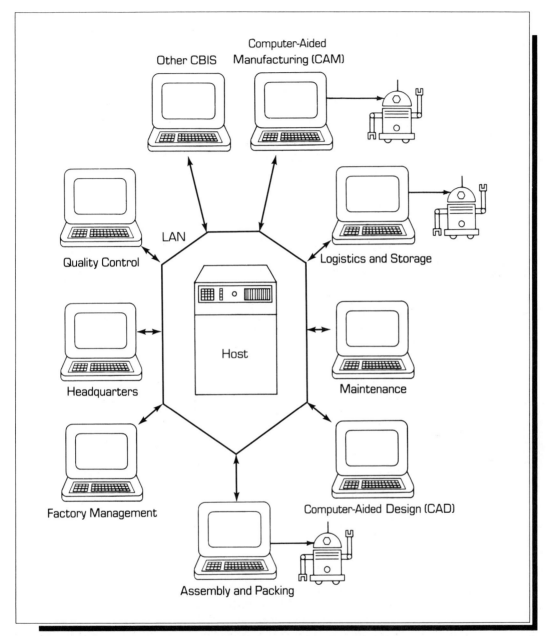

FIGURE 18.11 Computer-integrated Manufacturing in the Factory of the Future

TABLE 18.3   Role of MSS in Computer-integrated Manufacturing—the Factory of the Future

Function Aided by Computers	Description	Supported by			
		ES	**NLP**	**Robots**	**DSS**
Assembly and packaging	Uses robots to put together parts fabricated on site and purchased from outside. Packages ready for shipment.	X	X	X	X
Design (CAD)	Creates a design for a product.	X			
Engineering	Designs the tools, molds, and other facilities needed for manufacturing.	X			
Factory management	Runs the entire production process, coordinates incoming orders, requests components and material, plans and schedules, oversees cost control, arranges deliveries.	X	X		X
Headquarters	Decides what products to make, when, and how much (based on market research, available resources, and strategic planning).	X	X		X
Logistics and storage	Purchases and distributes materials, handles inventory control, removes materials, manages supplies. Shuttles incoming materials and parts, work in process, and final products.	X		X	X
Maintenance	Monitors equipment and processes, makes adjustments when needed, takes care of emergency breakdowns, diagnoses faults, does preventive and corrective maintenance.	X	X	X	
Manufacturing (CAM)	Fabricates metals, plastics, and other materials by molding, machining, welding, etc.	X		X	
Quality control	Tests incoming materials and outgoing products, tests processes in progress, assures quality.	X	X	X	

Attitudes of Information Systems People. Some information systems professionals have not taken MSS seriously, just like they did not take microcomputers seriously for a long time. They are reluctant to learn about these new technologies. They should understand, however, that MSS is a valuable supplement to conventional tools and applications, *not* a substitute for them.

Part of the problem is cultural. The analysis, design, knowledge acquisition, testing, and debugging of MSS and especially ES are much more difficult and time-consuming than the coding itself. The professionals can learn the coding rather fast, but they sometimes do not have the energy to learn all the other activities. Therefore, they depend on MSS experts and therefore may reject opportunities to use MSS.

Development Process. The development process of many CBIS projects follows a sequential life-cycle approach. In contrast, most MSS are prototyped. When the two are combined, a problem of being "out of phase" may be created; that is, the CBIS project may not be ready for the MSS for a long time, and then, when it is ready, the MSS process may slow down the CBIS project due to the needed prototyping.

Organizational Impacts. One of the biggest impacts of MSS could be on the director of information systems. This director needs MSS to better manage conventional CBIS applications. MSS could enhance the director's productivity. The manner in which the director will react to such an opportunity, and the implications on structure, job description, and power distribution within the information systems organization as well as within the entire corporation, need to be considered and researched.

Data Structure Issues. AI applications are centered around symbolic processing, whereas DSS, EIS, ANN, and CBIS projects are built around numeric processing. When these systems are integrated, data will have to flow from one environment to a different one. Databases are structured quite differently from knowledge bases (e.g., see Rauch-Hindin [45]). In a knowledge base, procedural information and declarative information are separated, whereas in a database everything is combined. It is easy to develop a conceptual system with a database and knowledge base and show that the two are interconnected. But somewhere a translation is needed. Who will do it and how?

Data Issues. Several MSS applications, especially expert systems and neural computing, can absorb heterogeneous, partially inconsistent, and incomplete data of different dimensions and accuracy. DSS, EIS, and traditional CBIS applications cannot operate with this kind of input data. When using, for example, an ES as a front-end to a DSS, the incomplete data must be organized and prepared according to the input requirement of the database. The same is true when the DSS output is inputted into an ES.

Connectivity. AI applications, as we have seen, may be programmed with LISP, PROLOG, ES shells, or special knowledge engineering tools, or with a combination of them. The shells may be written in C, FORTRAN, or Pascal, but not necessarily in the *same* language that was used to write the DSS, EIS, or ANN that is being integrated with the AI part. Another problem is that although some AI tool vendors provide interfaces to DBMS, spreadsheets, and so on, these interfaces may not be easy to work with. Furthermore, they may be expensive and will have to be updated constantly (see Pederson [44]).

18.11   Examples of Integrated Systems

Manufacturing

Integrated Manufacturing System. A system called Logistics Management System (LMS) was developed by IBM for operations management (see Sullivan and Fordyce [54]). The system combines expert systems, simulation, and decision support systems. In addition, the system includes computer-aided manufacturing and distributed data processing subsystems. It provides plant manufacturing management a tool to assist it in resolving crises and help in planning. A similar system is used at IBM by financial analysts to simulate long-range financial planning; an ES provides judgmental information and other pertinent factors.

DSS/Decision Simulation (DSIM). DSIM (IBM) is the outcome of combining decision support systems, statistics, operations research, database management, query languages, and artificial intelligence (see Sullivan and Fordyce [54]). AI, especially natural language interfaces and expert systems, provides three things to DSIM:

1. Ease of communication of pertinent information to the computational algorithm or display unit
2. Assistance in finding the appropriate model, computational algorithm, or data set
3. A solution to a problem where the computational algorithm(s) alone is not sufficient to solve the problem, a computational algorithm is not appropriate or applicable, and/or the AI creates the computational algorithm.

Marketing

Promoter. This ES analyzes the effects of promotions and advertisements on sales in the packaged goods industry. It was developed by Management Decision Systems, Inc., and it must be used together with the company's mainframe DSS development tools.

TeleStream. This ES developed by Texas Instruments supports salespersons who work in distributed centers that are selling thousands of products. The system has two parts: Sales Advisor and Sales Assistant. The Sales Advisor tells the salesperson what to offer to the customer. It also describes accessories and supplies. The DSS part attempts to maximize management goals (such as profits and low inventories). The Sales Assistant is an interface that determines the content of the information to be presented to the user and the method of presentation. For details see [2].

Engineering

An integrated system was designed to boost engineers' productivity at Boeing. The DSS portion, called STRUDL (for structured design language), is essentially a passive tool whose effectiveness depends on the user's abilities. By supplying the proper data into the formula or the graphic modeling application, a design engineer can gain insight into the potential of his or her design prototype. Unfortunately, STRUDL cannot help the engineer decide what questions to ask or what data to key in, nor can it give any hints about further actions to take based on the results of analysis. However, an expert system that assumes the role of teacher/partner was added on to do all this.

Financial Services

A large financial services company (see Scott-Morton [50]) uses an integrated system to match its various services with individual customers' needs (e.g., placing a customer's assets into optimal investment packages). Similar applications are being actively developed by large international accounting firms for combining analytical methods and judgment in auditing, and by other business entities for credit evaluation, strategic planning, and related applications. General Dynamic Corp., for example, is using expert systems to support project management analysis.

FINEXPERT* is an intelligent system designed to produce financial reports and analyses of corporations. It was developed in France by EXPERTeam in cooperation with Texas Instruments. Linked to a company's standard accounting system, the ES can produce all the standard financial reports and fifty different charts. Then it performs a financial analysis that includes financial activity, ratio analysis, risk analysis, profitability, and financial equilibrium. Its report satisfies the U.S. Securities and Exchange Commission's requirements for publicly held corporations. The system can run simulations and forecasting models, and a sophisticated explanation facility is available. The system is marketed worldwide as a ready-made system. For further details see [2].

American Express. The 300 American Express employees who authorize credit card purchases may access as many as 13 different databases in making their decision. Now, they are being assisted by an expert system.**

Inference, Inc. (Los Angeles, Calif.) personnel worked with credit authorizers from American Express's Fort Lauderdale site, the credit authorization manager, and details from case histories, to create the expert system. Figure

---

*Based on information provided by Neuron Data, Inc., and by [3].
**Condensed from: Davis, D. B. "Artificial Intelligence Goes To Work," *High Technology,* April 1987, and from Dzierzanowski, J. M., et al. in *Innovation Applications of Expert Systems,* by Schorr, H. and A. Rappaport, eds., Menlo Park, CA: AAAI Press, 1989.

18.12 illustrates the credit authorization process with the authorization expert system assistant.

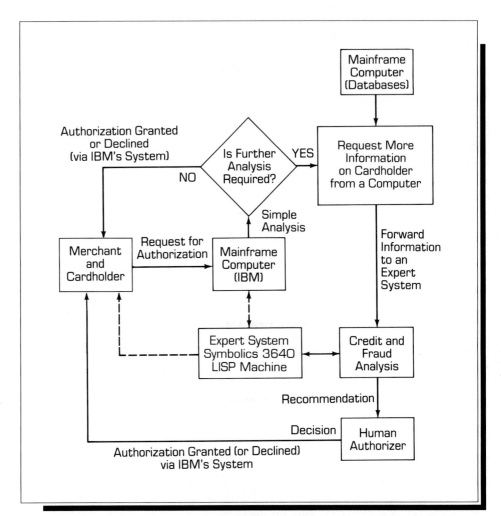

FIGURE 18.12 American Express Authorizer's Assistant. The merchant requests authorization from the mainframe computer. The computer checks the credit availability and performs a simple analysis (e.g., checking the cardholder's normal charging pattern). If no further analysis is needed, the authorization is either granted or declined. If further analysis is necessary, the computer collects more information about the cardholder from another mainframe computer. The initial and new information is forwarded to a rule-based expert system, which was developed with ART (from Inference Corp.). The expert system may request more information from the cardholder if necessary; then it provides a recommendation to the human authorizer (who uses an IBM 327 X terminal). (*Source:* Based on information provided by Inference Corp. and American Express.)

It took one year to build rules, check them, and fix them as necessary. A prototype was unveiled in April 1986 and tested for five months. The expert system was operational in January 1987 with 800 rules.

The only problems experienced with the system so far involve connecting the human credit authorizer's local area networks of IBM PCs with the IBM mainframe in Phoenix, Ariz.

The benefits of the expert system include annual productivity improvements of 20–30 percent, reduced cases of fraud and unpaid charges, and the ability to keep up with the growing number of transactions without increasing the staff.

Retailing

Buyer's Workbench. In retailing, especially in the supermarket industry with its typically small profit margins, the ability to draw on the experience of senior buyers is a key factor in a company's success. Because of the thousands of items that must be tracked for pricing, inventory, and other reasons, buying is often a reactive process. The implementation of an expert system running in tandem with mainframe databases can be an effective tool in changing the process into a proactive one.

A system called Buyer's Workbench* was developed by Deloitte and Touche for Associated Grocers (a supermarket chain in the Northwest). A buyer interacts with the knowledge base via an SQL windows/Microsoft Windows interface. The interface is used to select items that are candidates for action; it also retrieves the data from mainframe databases and analyzes it using an expert system. The expert system contains a large rule base of expert knowledge (obtained from senior buyers) about consumer preferences, vendor characteristics, seasonality, and a variety of other factors (Figure 18.13). The expert system then communicates the results of the analysis to the user via a user interface window.

The Buyer's Workbench takes advantage of the division of functionality inherent in a client-server architecture. The user interface runs on the client machine and the server contains the knowledge base, which is then linked to the mainframe database. Communication between the client and the server is handled via Microsoft Windows' DDE (dynamic data exchange). The client-server model allows flexibility on the client's side by permitting new applications to be integrated via the user interface. Also, the portable nature of the expert system allows the system to be scaled or redeployed to a remote server. In this way, the knowledge base can be expanded without sacrificing connectivity.

---

*Based on material provided by Neuron Data, Inc., and by [3].

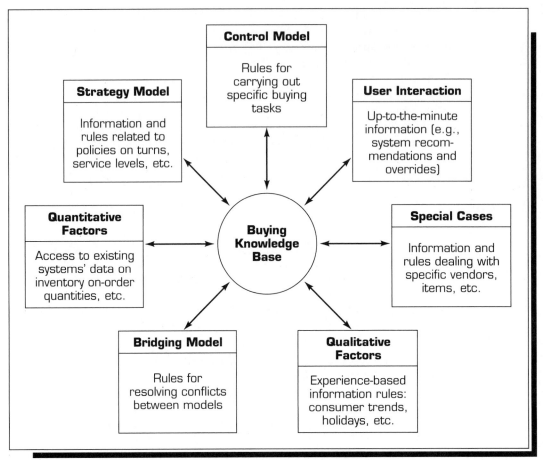

FIGURE 18.13 Categories of Knowledge in Expert System That Is Part of Buyer's Workbench. (*Source: AI Topics*, August 1989 [Deloitte and Touche].)

Commodities Trading

Intelligent Commodities Trading System (ICTS), developed by Fusion Group, integrates the capabilities of expert systems, neural networks, and relational databases in a distributed environment. By examining a set of broad market indicators, the system can make trading recommendations, or optionally execute trades based on its own findings. The indicators watched include rising and falling volume, price movements, and market trends. The rule base applies analytics appropriate to the market situation as characterized by the computed parameters. The analytics employed include moving averages, regression analysis, and probabilities (risk analysis). The neural network is used to perform pattern recognition to forecast price velocity and direction.

ICTS uses Nexpert Object for rule-based processing, the Sybase package for database manipulations, and ANZA Plus as a neurocomputing coprocessor. It also uses Fusion's own Market Data Server to distribute real-time market data. ICTS is designed to run across a variety of UNIX workstations; the current implementation employs hardware from Sun Microsystems Corp., Digital Equipment Corp., Pyramid Technology, and Sony—all connected via a local area network.

Fusion has also developed an interface library to allow the neurocomputing hardware to communicate with the powerful Sybase relational database manager. This interface uses the Sybase Open Server product, which allows an application to respond to the Sybase networking protocol. This allows Nexpert Object to communicate with the ANZA board without additional programming. The data flow diagram for this system is shown in Figure 18.14.

Fifth-generation Project

The efforts of the **Fifth-generation Project** can be used as an example of the movement toward integrating AI with conventional computing. Figure 18.15 presents the conceptual diagram of the software system envisioned by the Japanese. The key elements of the system are the knowledge base and its management system, which would enhance the database, model base, and the DBMS of a conventional CBIS. The problem-solving inference system is the ES aspect, and the intelligent interface system encompasses a natural language interface.

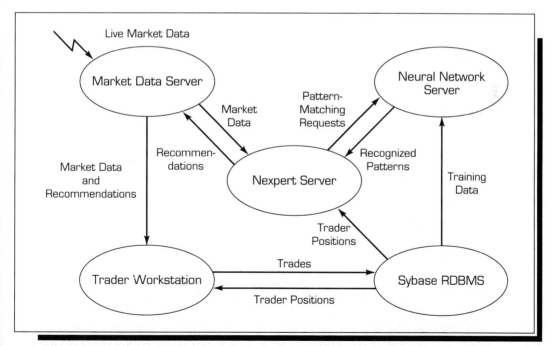

FIGURE 18.14 Data Flow for the Intelligent Commodities Trading System (ICTS). (*Source:* Courtesy of Neuron Data, Inc.)

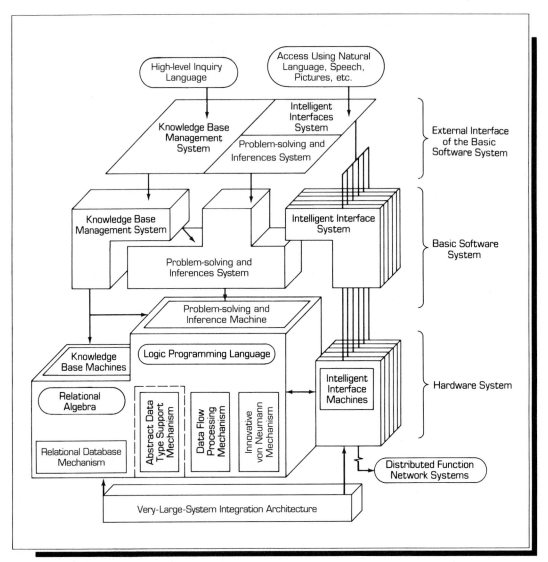

FIGURE 18.15 Basic Configuration of Fifth-generation Computer Systems. (*Source:* Japan Information Processing Development Center)

In addition, intelligent systemization and utility systems are to be developed. The basic application system would then interface with the rest of the components much like a current CBIS. (See Bishop [6].)

Expert systems are related to the Fifth-generation Project in two ways. First, expert systems are viewed as a major application of the new computers, which are intended to tackle a range of nonnumeric processing tasks presently untouched by computers. The new architecture and faster processing speeds will allow much more sophisticated expert systems to be built and will offer researchers ways of solving some of the more difficult problems inherent in the technology. (For further discussion see Johnson [30].)

The second aspect of the relationship between the Fifth-generation Project and expert systems is that expert systems will be an integral part of the new computers. The hardware will be so complicated that it will be impossible for ordinary users to make the best use of it. The users' interface with the computer will be guided by an expert system (or several expert systems), probably using a natural language interface.

18.12   Integration of Tools

Building an integrated, intelligent CBIS can be greatly facilitated by the use of integrated development tools, that is, tools that provide easy interfaces to other tools (such as databases, graphics, and spreadsheets). Many ES development tools offer interfaces to spreadsheets, databases, hypertext technology, graphics, word processing, and the like. Some of them have a natural language interface (e.g., Guru; for details see Rauch-Hindin [45]). Nexpert Object has extensive interfaces with many databases and decision support tools, for example, spreadsheets, communication networks, and database management systems. VP Expert and EXSYS also include a few interfaces. Finally, Level5 Object is fully integrated with a sophisticated DBMS (FOCUS), and it has many interfaces and capabilities.

Chapter Highlights

- When MSS technology is integrated with conventional computer-based information systems, the functionality of the latter is increased.
- Functional integration differs from the physical integration that is required to accomplish it.
- Integration can be achieved by three types of access methods: single processor, multiprocessor, and networking. Alternatively, integration can be embedded.
- An embedded system appears to the user as a single application.
- Another view of integration distinguishes between loosely coupled and tightly coupled systems, intelligent interfaces, and expert command languages.
- The major area of integration is that of databases (and database management systems) with expert systems and natural language processors. The result is intelligent databases.
- Expert systems can be used to simplify accessibility to databases, either corporate or commercial (online).
- The second major area of integration is the use of expert systems to interpret results of data generated by models, particularly quantitative models.

- Expert systems can be used to enhance knowledge management and model management.
- Expert systems are being successfully integrated with decision support systems; the result is many useful applications.
- Several conceptual models of integration are applicable to expert systems and decision support systems.
- Natural language processors, expert systems, and neural computing can be integrated to improve the human-machine interface.
- MSS technologies are being integrated with many computer-based information systems, ranging from CAD/CAM to office automation.
- Many problems exist with respect to the integration of AI technology. They include technical, behavioral, and managerial factors.
- The fifth-generation computer system is the most publicized example of integrating AI technologies with conventional computer-based information systems.
- Several development tools are available to support the construction of AI-integrated applications; well-publicized examples are Guru and Nexpert Object.

Key Words

embedded system	intelligent database	physical integration
Fifth-generation Project	intelligent interface	tight coupling
functional integration	loose coupling	

Questions for Review

1. What is the difference between functional and physical integration?
2. Describe an embedded system.
3. What is the difference between embedded and access integration?
4. DSS and ES integration may result in benefits along what three dimensions?
5. It is said that an ES is an intelligent DSS. Describe their common characteristics. Do you agree with this statement? Why or why not?
6. How can synergy result when decision support systems and expert systems are integrated?
7. What are intelligent databases and why are they so popular?
8. Summarize the benefits a DSS can gain in its database when it is integrated with an ES.
9. How can expert systems enhance knowledge management?
10. Why is an ES needed as an interface to commercial databases?
11. How can the knowledge base of an ES help a DSS?
12. What is model management?
13. Summarize the benefits that an ES can provide to a DSS in the area of models and their management.
14. What is the major capability of BUMP?

15. Summarize the benefits that an ES can provide to a human-machine interface.
16. List various possibilities of integrating decision support systems and expert systems according to the model suggested in Figure 18.6.
17. Give an example of an ES output that can be used as an input to a DSS. Also give an example of the reverse relationship.
18. How can an ES assist in generating alternative courses of action?
19. List some technical issues of integration.
20. List some behavioral issues of integration.
21. List some design issues that may arise during integration.

Questions for Discussion

1. Why may it be difficult to integrate an expert system with an existing information system? Comment on data, people, hardware, and software.
2. Explain this statement and give an example of both cases: Integration of a DSS and an ES can result in benefits during the construction (development) of the systems and during their operation.
3. Compare embedded integration with access integration. What are the major advantages and disadvantages of each?
4. Intelligent databases are considered extremely important. Explain what makes them intelligent and why they are so important.
5. One expert system may be used to consult several decision support systems. What is the logic of such an arrangement? What problems may result when two or more decision support systems share one expert system?
6. Review the work of Goul and associates [20]. Assume they will be successful in developing an ES that will perform as well as a management scientist-consultant. What could be the major implications of such a system? Why is it difficult to build it?
7. Compare the work of Goul and associates with that of Hand [21]. Specifically, what is the major similarity between BUMP and Goul's system?
8. Why is visual problem solving (or visual modeling) considered an integration of decision support systems and expert systems?
9. Explain how the addition of an ES capability can improve the chance of successful implementation of a DSS.
10. Compare Figures 18.5 and 18.6. What are the major differences? What are the similarities? Can Figure 18.6 be viewed as a special case of Figure 18.5? Why or why not?
11. Review current journals and identify a system that you believe is an MSS integration. Analyze the system according to the models suggested in this chapter.
12. Explain why the Fifth-generation Project is viewed as a DSS and ES integration.
13. There are many potential problems in MSS's integration. Find an example of such a problem in a real-life situation (check the journals if you cannot find one in a workplace) and report your findings.

14. In some of our models we suggested that several ES are included in one CBIS. What is the logic of such an arrangement?
15. Modeling involves three activities: construction, use, and interpretation. Give an example of modeling from an area that you are familiar with and explain how an ES can help the process.
16. How can model management be intelligent?

References and Bibliography

1. Agarwal, R., and Prasad, K. "Enhancing the Group Decision Making Process: An Intelligent Systems Architecture." In *Proceedings of the Twenty-second Annual Hawaii International Conference on System Sciences*. Los Alamitos, CA: IEEE Computer Society Press, January 1989.
2. *AI Letter* (June 1988 and April 1989), Texas Instruments.
3. *AI Topics* (August 1989), Deloitte and Touche.
4. Al-Zobaidie, A., and J. B. Grimson. "Expert Systems and Database Systems: How Can They Serve Each Other?" *Expert Systems* (February 1987).
5. Bell, P. C., D. C. Parker, and P. Kirkpatrick. "Visual Interactive Problem Solving—A New Look at Management Problems." *Business Quarterly* (Spring 1984).
6. Bishop, P. *Fifth Generation Computers: Concepts, Implementations, and Uses.* Chichester, England: Ellis Horwood, 1986.
7. Blanning, R. W. "The Application of Artificial Intelligence to Model Management." In *Proceedings of the Twenty-first Annual Hawaii International Conference on System Sciences*. Los Alamitos, CA: January 1988.
8. Brodie, M. L., and J. Mylpoulos. *On Knowledge Base Management Systems: Integrating Artificial Intelligence and Database Techniques.* New York: Springer-Verlag, 1986.
9. Cohen, B. "Merging Expert Systems and Databases." *AI Expert* (February 1989).
10. Courtney, J. F., Jr., et al. "A Knowledge-based DSS for Managerial Problem Diagnosis." *Decision Sciences* (Summer 1987).
11. Doukidis, G. I. "An Analogy on the Homology of Simulation and Artificial Intelligence." *Journal of the Operational Research Society* (August 1987).
12. Dutta, A., and A. Basu. "AI-Based Model Management in DSS." *Computer* (September 1984).
13. Elam, J. J., and B. Konsynski. "Using AI Techniques to Enhance the Capabilities of Model Management System." *Decision Sciences* (Summer 1987).
14. Fedorowicz, J., and G. Williams. "Representing Modeling Knowledge in an Intelligent Decision Support System." *Decision Support Systems* 2 (no. 1, 1986).
15. Feng-Yang, K. "Combining Expert Systems and the Bayesian Approach to Support Forecasting." In *Proceedings, 21st HICSS*. Hawaii, January 1988.
16. Ford, D. R., and B. J. Schroer. "An Expert Manufacturing Simulation System." *Simulation* (May 1987).

17. Gale, W. A. *Artificial Intelligence and Statistics*. Reading, MA: Addison-Wesley, 1986.
18. Gottinger H. W. "Statistical Expert Systems." *Expert Systems* (August 1988).
19. Gallagher, J. P. *Knowledge Systems for Business: Integrating Expert Systems and MIS*. Englewood Cliffs, NJ: Prentice-Hall, 1988.
20. Goul, M., B. Shane, and F. Tonge. "Designing the Expert Component of a Decision Support System." Paper delivered at the ORSA/TIMS meeting. San Francisco, May 1984.
21. Hand, D. J. "Statistical Expert Systems: Design." *Statistician* 33 (October 1984):351–369.
22. Harris, L. R. "The Natural-language Connection; An AI Note." *Information Center* (April 1987).
23. Hawkins, D. T. "Applications of AI and Expert Systems for Online Searching." *Online* (January 1988).
24. Hayes-Roth, F., D. Waterman, and D. Lenat. *Building Expert Systems*. Reading, MA: Addison-Wesley, 1983.
25. Hosley, W. N. "The Application of Artificial Intelligence Software to Project Management." *Project Management Journal* (August 1987).
26. Hossein, J., et al. "Stochastic Queuing Systems, An AI Approach." In *1987 DSI Proceedings*.
27. Hsu, C., and C. Skevington. "Integration of Data and Knowledge in Manufacturing Enterprises; A Conceptual Framework." *Journal of Manufacturing Systems* 6 (April 1987).
28. Isshikawa, H. "KID, Knowledge-based Natural Language Interface for Accessing Database Systems." *IEEE Expert* (Summer 1987).
29. Jarke, M., and Y. Vassiliou. "Coupling Expert Systems with Database Management Systems." In *Artificial Intelligence Applications for Business*, W. Reitman, ed. Norwood, N.J.: Ablex Publishing Corp., 1984.
30. Johnson, R. C. "Japan's AI Computer: The Fifth Generation?" *PC AI* 3 (May/June 1989):54–55.
31. Kehoe, C. A. "Interfaces and Expert Systems for Online Retrieval." *Online Review* (December 1985).
32. Kennedy, A. J., and D. C. Yen. "Enhancing a DBMS Through the Use of Expert Systems." *Journal of Information Systems Management* (Spring 1990).
33. Kerschberg, L., ed. *Expert Database Systems*. Menlo Park, CA: Benjamin-Cummings, 1987.
34. Keyes, J. "Expert Systems and Corporate Databases." *AI Expert* (May 1989).
35. King, D. "Intelligent Decision Support: Strategies for Integrating Decision Support, Database Management, and Expert System Technologies." *Expert Systems with Applications* 1 (no. 1, 1990).
36. Kumar, S., and H. Cheng. "An Expert System Framework for Forecasting Method Selection." In *Proceedings of the Twenty-first Annual Hawaii International Conference on System Sciences*. Los Alamitos, CA: January 1988.
37. Kusiak, A., ed. *Artificial Intelligence, Implication for CIM, IFS*. New York: Springer-Verlag, 1988.

38. Lee, L. K., and H. G. Lee. "Integration of Strategic Planning and Short-term Planning: An Intelligent DSS Approach by the Post Model Analysis Approach." *Decision Support Systems* (1988).

39. Liang, T. "Development of a Knowledge-based Model Management System." *Operations Research* (November-December 1988).

40. Meador, C. L., P. G. Keen, and M. J. Guyote. "Personal Computer and Distribution Decision Support." *Computerworld*, Vol. 18, No. 19 (May 7 1984).

41. Murphy, F., and E. Stohr. "An Intelligent Support for Formulating Linear Programming." *Decision Support Systems* 2 (no. 1, 1986).

42. Newman, W. M. *Designing Integrated Systems for the Office Environment*. New York: McGraw-Hill, 1987.

43. Parsaye, K., et al. *Intelligent Database: Object-Oriented Deductive Hypermedia Technologies*. New York: John Wiley & Sons, 1989.

44. Pederson, K. "Connecting Expert Systems and Conventional Programming." *AI Expert* (May 1988).

45. Rauch-Hindin, W. "Software Integrates AI, Standard Systems." *Mini-Micro Systems* (October 1986).

46. Reitman, W. "Applying Artificial Intelligence to Decision Support." In *Decision Support Systems*, M. J. Ginzberg, W. Reigman, and E. Stohr, eds. Amsterdam: North Holland, 1982.

47. Risch, T., et al. "A Functional Approach to Integrating Database and Expert-Systems." *Communications of ACM* 31 (1989).

48. Sathi, A., et al. "CALLISTO: An Intelligent Project Management System." *AI Magazine* (Winter 1986).

49. Schur, S. "Intelligent Databases." *Database Programming and Design* (June 1988).

50. Scott-Morton, M. "Expert Decision Support Systems." Paper presented in a special DSS conference, Planning Executive Institute and Information Technology Institute. New York, May 21–22, 1984.

51. Shafer, D. *Designing Intelligent Front Ends for Business Software*. New York: John Wiley & Sons, 1989. (Also see *PC AI*, July/August 1990.)

52. Siegel, D. L. "Integrating Expert Systems for Manufacturing." *AI Magazine* (Supplement, Summer 1990).

53. Simos, M. A. "Knowledge-based Systems and Software Engineering: Toward a More Perfect Union." *Expert Systems* (Fall 1989).

54. Sullivan, G., and K. Fordyce. *Decision Simulations, One Outcome of Combining AI and DSS*. Working paper no. 42-395. Poughkeepsie, N.Y.: IBM Corp. 1984.

55. Sullivan, G., and K. Fordyce. "The Role of Artificial Intelligence in Decision Support Systems." Paper delivered at the International Meeting of TIMS. Copenhagen, June 1985.

56. Tannenbaum, A. "Installing AI Tools into Corporate Environments." *AI Expert* (May 1990).

57. Teng, J. T. C., et al. "A Unified Architecture for Intelligent DSS." In *Proceed-*

ings of the Twenty-first Annual Hawaii International Conference on System Sciences. Los Alamitos, CA: January 1988.

58. Turban, E., and D. H. Stevenson. "The EIS-DSS Connection." *Proceedings DSI 89*, New Orleans, November 1989.
59. Turban, E., and P. Watkins. "Integrating Expert Systems and Decision Support Systems." *MIS Quarterly* (June 1986).
60. Turban, E., and H. Watson. "Integrating ES, EIS and DSS." In *DSS '89 Transactions.* San Diego, June 1989.
61. Turner, M., and B. Obilichetti. "Possible Directions in Knowledge-based Financial Modeling Systems." In *DSS '85 Transactions.* Providence, 1985.
62. Van Horn, M. *Understanding Expert Systems.* Toronto: Bantam, 1986.
63. Vasant, D., and A. Croker. "Knowledge-based Decision Support in Business: Issues and a Solution." *IEEE Expert* (Spring 1988).
64. Wu, W. "An Integrated System Based on the Synergy Between System Dynamics and Artificial Intelligence." In *Proceedings, 1988 International Conference of the Systems Dynamics Society.* La Jolla, CA, July 1988.
65. Zahedi, F. "Qualitative Programming for Selection Decisions." *Computers and Operations Research* 14 (no. 5, 1987): 395–407.

Chapter 19

Implementing Management Support Systems

The successful implementation of any computer-based information depends on many social, behavioral, organizational, technical, economic, and environmental factors. MSS technologies are no exception. They, too, depend on many factors, and they may fail as well. What determines the successful implementation of MSS systems? What strategy can be used to increase the chance of successful implementation? This chapter explores these and other questions. Specifically, the following sections are presented:

19.1   Introduction

As with any other computer-based information system, implementation of MSS systems is not always a success story. For example, there is increasing evidence that AI technologies, and especially expert systems, fail at an extremely high rate (e.g., see Keyes [27] and Yorman [47]). Implementation is an ongoing process of preparing an organization for the new system and introducing the system in such a way as to help assure its success.

Implementation in regard to MSS technologies is complex because these systems are not merely information systems that collect, manipulate, and distribute information. Rather, they are linked to tasks that may significantly change the manner in which organizations operate. Nevertheless, many of the implementation factors are common to any information system. Hence much of the discussion in this chapter is based on general experience gained in the implementation of information systems. For an overview see Swanson [44]. This chapter surveys major relevant factors, discusses their impact on implementation, and suggests implementation strategies.

19.2   Implementation: Success and Failure

What Is Implementation?

Machiavelli astutely noted more than 450 years ago that there was "nothing more difficult to carry out, nor more doubtful of success, nor more dangerous to handle, than to initiate a new order of things." The implementation of MSS is, in effect, the initiation of a new order of things, or in contemporary language—the introduction of change.

The definition of implementation is complicated because implementation is a long, involved process with vague boundaries. Implementation can be defined simplistically as getting a newly developed, or significantly changed, system to be used by those for whom it was intended.

According to Lucas [30], the implementation of a CBIS is an ongoing process that takes place during the entire development of the system—from the original suggestion through the feasibility study, systems analysis and design, programming, training, conversion, and installation of the system. Other authors refer to implementation as only the final stage in the system's life cycle. The definition of implementation for MSS systems is more complicated because of the iterative nature of their development.

If the MSS system is intended for a repetitive use, then implementation means a commitment to routine and frequent use of the system, or *institutionalization*. For ad hoc decisions, implementation means the one-time use of the system.

Measuring Implementation Success

The definition of implementation includes the concept of success. A number of possible indicators for a successful information system have been suggested in various implementation studies. Unless a set of success measures is agreed on, it will be difficult to evaluate the success of a system. Dickson and Powers [16] suggest five independent criteria for success:

1. Ratio of actual project execution time to the estimated time
2. Ratio of actual cost to develop the project to the budgeted cost for the project
3. Managerial attitudes toward the system
4. How well managers' information needs are satisfied
5. Impact of the project on the computer operations of the firm.

Other measures for judging the success of MSS include the following:

- Use of the system as measured by the intended and/or the actual use (e.g., the number of inquiries made of an online system)
- User satisfaction (measured with a questionnaire or by an interview—see Swanson [44], Chapter 6)
- Favorable attitudes (either as an objective by itself or as a predictor of use of a system)
- Degree to which a system accomplishes its original objectives (e.g., for an ES: whether it provides reasonable advice)
- Payoff to the organization (through cost reductions, increased sales, etc.)
- Benefits to costs ratios
- Degree of institutionalization of MSS in the organization.

In evaluating the success of expert systems in particular, additional measures of success might be used:

- Degree to which the system agrees with a human expert when both of them are presented with the same cases
- Adequacy of the explanations provided by the system
- Percentage of cases submitted to the system for which advice was not given
- Improvement of the ES on the learning curve, or how fast the system reaches maturity.

Partial Implementation

Feasibility decisions are frequently made on the basis of the payoff shown if *total* implementation is achieved. In reality, a 90 percent, or even 70 percent, implementation is likely. One reason for less than 100 percent implementation is that a change introduced at one place in the system may precipitate compensatory and possibly negative impacts elsewhere. Management may then drop the parts of the project that created the negative impacts. Thus, less than 100 percent of the original project is implemented. Another reason for partial implementation is a reduction in the budget.

Implementation Failures

The implementation of information systems involves several problems that have been subject to extensive research (see Lucas [30] and Meredith [33]). Very little evidence is available, however, to substantiate the true extent and magnitude of the problems. Actual information on implementation failures is a closely held secret in many organizations, especially when millions of dollars have been spent on unimplemented systems.

One DSS researcher, Alter [3], reports that the expected synergy of human and machine in interactive DSS simply hasn't developed and actual instances of managers sitting at a terminal and solving problems are very rare. On investigation, it was found that half the actual DSS users are secretaries or junior analysts. Furthermore, the amount of managerial use of DSS was found to be inversely proportional to the amount of staff help available to the manager.

Frequently, the absence of conditions necessary for successful implementation result in what Dickson and Wetherbe [15] call "tactics of counterimplementation." Counterimplementation at managerial levels includes (1) diverting resources from the project, (2) deflecting the goals of the project, (3) dissipating the energies of the project, and (4) neglecting the project with the hope that it will go away. At an operating level, tactics of counterimplementation take the form of (1) making errors on purpose, (2) using the system for purposes other than those for which it was intended, (3) failing outright to use the system, and (4) relying on old manual procedures whenever possible.

Even an initial *attempt* to implement an information system can trigger a failure. Mohan and Bean [35] report:

> There is considerable evidence that firms . . . experience *severe internal disruptions and change as the new technology* is introduced. In some cases the reactions have been adverse enough to result in temporary rejection of the technology, and a period of three to five years has been necessary for reintroduction.

The initial failure not only postpones progress for a number of years, but it also may make later attempts likely to fail.

Although there is not much formal data available on MSS failures, there are many informal reports on unsuccessful implementation. Why such systems fail and the necessary conditions to minimize failures are dealt with in the following sections.

19.3   Models of Implementation

The importance of the implementation problem has led to extensive research about the determinants of successful implementation. Research began several decades ago with studies conducted by behavioral scientists to examine resistance to change. The management science movement has been occupied with this issue since the late 1950s, and MIS researchers have been studying implementation issues for almost two decades. Considerable numbers of ideas and theories have been accumulated and several models of implementation have been proposed for information systems (see Lucas [30], Meredith [33], and Swanson [44]). Because of the large failure rate of ES, several papers have appeared that attempted to analyze the problems and prescribe remedies. For example, see Badiru [5] and Barsanti [7].

Several dozen factors could determine the degree of success of any information system. The words *factor* or *success factor* refer to a condition present in the organization (such as the support of top management) or to the specific application (such as the use of appropriate software). Success factors can be divided into two categories: the generic factors that relate to any information system and those related specifically to MSS technologies. A methodology for overcoming organizational and behavioral implementation barriers can be found in Dologite and Mockler [17].

The success factors of implementation discussed in this chapter are grouped in eight categories (Figure 19.1). These categories are frequently interrelated and some factors can be classified under two or more categories. Thus, regard this classification as a rough attempt to organize the many factors involved.

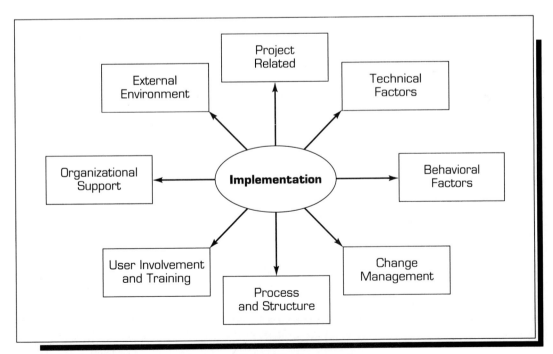

FIGURE 19.1 Determinants of Successful MSS Implementation

19.4   Technical Factors

Technical factors relate to the mechanics of the implementation procedure. Several are of major importance.

Level of Complexity

To maximize the likelihood of successful implementation, the basic rule is to keep the system as simple as possible. The advantages of simplicity for implementation success are many: fewer errors, integrity of design, simpler data requirements, easier user training, managerial transparency, ease of control, and speed of installation. Of course, simplicity must be tempered with another desirable system characteristic: completeness of critical aspects.

System Response Time and Reliability

Situations in which the system reacts too slowly, crashes, or is unavailable when needed have been known to create user dissatisfaction. Slow response time was typical in some expert systems when standard hardware was used (prior to 1987). Response time today is less than a major problem as a result of technological developments.

Inadequate Functions

Limited primary core memory, an imbalance between hardware and software capabilities, poor graphics, complex text manipulation, user-unfriendliness, and inability to deal quickly with changing situations are all examples of inadequate functions that tend to discourage users. In addition to the technical issues just pointed out, several other related issues are listed in Table 19.1.

Technical issues can be classified into two categories: (1) technical constraints, which are due mainly to the limitations of available technology, and (2) technical problems, which are not the result of the technology but are caused by other factors such as scarcity of resources. The first category may disappear when new technologies are developed. The second category can be solved by increasing available resources.

TABLE 19.1 Technical
Implementation Issues

Lack of equipment
Lack of standardization
Problems with the networks
Mismatch of hardware/software
Low level of technical capacity of the project team

19.5   Behavioral Factors

The implementation of computer-based information systems in general, and MSS in particular, is affected by the way people perceive these systems and by how people behave. The topics discussed in this section are decision styles, organizational climate, organizational expectations, and organizational politics. Another important behavioral topic, resistance to change, is presented in the next section.

Decision Styles

Individuals make decisions differently; they have different **decision styles.** They may use different approaches to making decisions, a different sequence of the same steps in the process, or the same sequence but with the steps emphasized differently.

A popular explanation as to why people make decisions differently is that they possess different cognitive styles. A classic distinction is the one between the analytical and heuristic styles. Managers with more analytical styles are usually predisposed to accept traditional computing that involves quantitative analysis. Those with more intuitive styles tend to reject traditional computing; however, they tend to accept ES, especially if the explanation component is effective. The analytical managers can learn to adapt to nonquantitative technologies.

Organizational Climate (Culture)

Sometimes the **organizational climate (culture)** of a company is so hostile to innovation that it is difficult to introduce any changes. If the attitudes of organizational members are poor toward attempts to introduce computer-based systems, then introducing new MSS technologies will be even more difficult. On the positive side, if there is an openness in the organization so that opinions and values are shared, change can be facilitated. Researchers studying organizational change have spoken of a climate that supports mutual trust between the potential users of the system and its developers (e.g., see Zmud and Cox [50]).

In most cases, the influence of senior management is vital in determining organizational climate. If the climate is poor, steps must be taken to improve matters before any attempt is made to introduce change. Typical cases such as the introduction of automation in the U.S. Post Office (see Dickson and Wetherbe [15]) have repeatedly shown that there is strong resistance to change in poor organizational climates.

Organizational Expectations

During the past several years, tremendous publicity has been given to artificial intelligence in general and to expert systems in particular. Now the general level of expectations both by top management and users may be too high.

Overexpectations can be dangerous to the success of any system, especially for initial applications in which the strategy may be to sacrifice potential payoff and speed for effectiveness and quality. If people expect quick, large savings from MSS but do not get it, they will not continue to support such ventures. Therefore, expectations must be maintained at realistic levels.

Organizational Politics

As an organization's growth slows, internal relationships tend to stabilize, division of authority and power is negotiated, and a sense of security and well-being sets in. Implementation of a large-scale MSS project may threaten this equilibrium and arouse opposition toward the project. This is where "politics" frequently enters the picture. The prevalence of politics in organizations, especially large ones, is often underestimated or ignored. However, the successful implementation of a project may well depend on politics. The MSS team leader should be advised not to remain neutral but to become involved, learn the rules, and determine the power centers and cliques of the organization. For further discussion see Markus [31].

19.6   Resistance to Change and How to Manage It

Introducing new technologies into organizations will almost always result in some change. The application of MSS means a change in the manner in which decisions are made, communications are transmitted, control is exercised, and power is distributed. It is only natural to assume that behavioral problems related to such changes will develop, together with some kinds of dysfunctions.

The changes that result from implementing MSS can be social, technical, psychological, structural, or a combination of these factors (see Box 19.1). When managers (or other users) resist the logical arguments presented in defense of MSS, they may not be resisting the technical aspects of the proposed change as much as the perceived social or psychological ramifications. Managers often feel threatened by modern techniques of analysis and sense that a computerized project may take over or jeopardize their job. This fear of change may originate from apprehension that their jobs will be eliminated, that previous performance will prove inefficient relative to the new technique, or that the new technique will result in a downgrading of the status or intrinsic satisfaction of their job. In addition, fears relating to computers (computer phobia) still exist.

Of course, top management may think that such beliefs are absurd. The important point, however, is that what governs the user's behavior is not so much the real threat as the *perceived* threat. A good way for the system introducer to cope with the fear of change is to eliminate the perceived threat. The problem is that some of the perceived threat is probably real (e.g., workers may be laid off and the importance of certain jobs may be reduced). In addition, some of the consequences of the change are uncertain or even unknown in advance.

Sometimes users are afraid of changes in their actual job responsibilities. If job content and meaning are changed, users may be unsure about how they will perform their jobs in the future. They may foresee more responsibility (which many like to avoid), more control, and more accountability. Although users may not want their job to become more challenging, on the other hand, they may not want it to become more routine.

The topic of dealing with resistance to change and its many dimensions (Box 19.1) is gaining momentum in many organizations. **Change management,** as it is frequently called, is emerging as an important discipline, especially for technologically oriented organizations. For information about the nature of the prob-

Box 19.1: Dimensions of Change

CBIS implementation can cause change in an organization in many ways:

- *Rivalries and territorial threats:* The system can increase the power or influence of one department, an individual, or one group over another.
- *Fear of obsolescence:* The system can diminish job responsibilities or contribute to a feeling of loss of esteem.
- *Group cohesiveness leading to resistance to outsiders:* System specialists and/or consultants may be resisted because they are not part of the local group and do not "understand the business."
- *Cultural factors:* The system may be resisted because it does not fit in with present practice or goes against the experience of incumbent managers.
- *Job security:* Concerns arise that jobs will be eliminated or that job duties will be diminished.
- *Information possessiveness:* The system could make information that is presently closely held available to others. Of special concern is the fact that subordinate managers may lose decision autonomy or excuses for poor performance based on a lack of information. Furthermore, data and information are an element of power and must be protected if currently held or sought if not possessed.
- *Job pattern changes:* The system can change communication patterns with peers, present psychic rewards, and affect work group norms.
- *Invasion (or loss) of privacy:* Employees involved with personnel-type information systems anticipate problems with privacy of data.
- *Other:* Fear of the unknown, uncertainties, and disruption of stability are experienced by many employees.

(*Source:* This material is condensed from G. W. Dickson and J. C. Wetherbe, *The Management of Information Systems* [New York: McGraw-Hill, 1985].)

lem and ways to manage the problem, refer to Fallik [18], Ginzberg [20], and Morino [37]. For a list of specific resistors to ES, see Box 19.2. For a discussion of users' perspectives of change in information technology, see Joshi [26].

Overcoming Resistance to Change

Several researchers have viewed implementation as a social change process. They observed that the interpersonal and organizational dynamics of the change process had an overwhelming impact that determines the success of DSS implementation.

Therefore, it was suggested that managing change can enhance successful implementation, and several theories were developed on how to do it. A highly publicized one is that of Lewin and Schein (see Lewin [28]). They focus on the *process* by which change takes place. The Lewin-Schein theory of change is a concise description of this process. The theory states that change consists of three steps:

- *Unfreezing:* creating an awareness of the need for change and a climate of receptivity to change.
- *Moving:* changing the magnitude or direction of the forces that define the initial situation; developing new methods and/or learning new attitudes and behaviors.
- *Refreezing:* reinforcing the changes that have occurred, thereby maintaining and stabilizing a new equilibrium situation.

Box 19.2: The Resistors

- Experts—some fear undue exposure or a reduction in uses for their skills
- Nonexperts—some fear further lack of recognition and even less opportunity to prove themselves
- The generally insecure—some in every organization are routinely insecure
- Technologists—some may fear that if the technology is outside their data processing department, they will lose power and control
- Users—some resist computerization in general and experience problems with the human-machine interface
- Training staff/management—some may fear that self-instruction by interacting with the expert system will diminish their role
- Troublemakers—some in every organization may be envious or just wish to exert power

(*Source:* A. C. Beerel, *Expert Systems: Strategic Implications and Applications* [New York: Ellis Horwood/John Wiley & Sons, 1987], p. 152.)

The Lewin-Schein theory has been used as a change-planning basis to indicate strategies to handle resistance to change in information systems. For example see Dickson and Wetherbe [15]. Their theory of planned change was adapted to DSS by several researchers. For example, Alter [3] and Ginzberg [20] studied the DSS implementation process in its entirety and identified the refreezing phase as being of special importance to CBIS project success or failure. In DSS, the refreezing phase is especially important, because the user must initiate the interaction with the system, and DSS is expected to impact on the decision-making process of users. Furthermore, the relationship between a DSS and its users evolves simultaneously, so the design and implementation of a DSS is an ongoing process.

An important related issue is the role in the refreezing phase of intermediaries, who serve as integrating (change) agents and as human interfaces between the decision makers and the DSS. Thus they can play a major role in implementing DSS.

19.7   Process Factors

The way in which the process of developing and implementing MSS is managed can greatly influence the success of implementation. Topics that are relevant to process factors are top management support, management and user commitment, institutionalization, and length of time users have been using computers. Each of these is discussed in turn.

Top Management Support

Top management support has long been recognized as one of *the* most important ingredients necessary for the introduction of any organizational change. Meredith [33] cites nineteen references that support this phenomenon in computer-based information systems, and it has also been found to be true for expert systems (see DePree [14]).

If top management advocates and devotes full attention to a system, the chances of successful implementation are enhanced. Furthermore, if top management *initiates* the project, the likelihood of success increases markedly.

The support from top management must be meaningful. Top managers must know about the difficulties of the project and the amount of time and resources required to support it. Such support is more likely if the managers have had previous experience with similarly sophisticated projects. It is also helpful if top managers are familiar with the need to accept trade-offs in system designs and are willing to allow a sufficient time span to implement large-scale MSS projects. An important aspect in MSS and especially ES systems is the need for *continuous* financial support to maintain the systems. Without a commitment for such support, projects are doomed. An example is the famous XCON ES, whose maintenance costs became so large that management had to completely reprogram the system at a large one-time charge to reduce the costs and to avoid a failure. (See Barker and O'Connor [6].)

There is danger in advocacy when the support comes primarily from one person. If he or she leaves or is transferred, the support may disappear. Clearly, top management support must be broad based to be meaningful.

Obtaining support is easier said than done. In some cases, top management still views the computer as a tool solely intended for financial and accounting purposes. If the MSS application is in any other functional area, it may not have top management's support.

Extensive research has focused on specific means to gain top management support. Essentially, top management had to be *sold* on the value of the project in terms of the benefits to be gained. This is not a simple task because of the difficulty in measuring intangible benefits and proving savings.

Although there are no specific studies in the literature dealing with methods to increase top management support for MSS, there are several recommendations related to information systems in general. For example, Rockart and Crescenzi [40] have proposed a three-phase process to get senior managers more meaningfully involved in information systems projects: (1) linking management needs of the business to the proposed information system, (2) developing system priorities and gaining confidence in the recommended system, and (3) rapid development of low-risk, managerially useful systems. The third phase is easily attainable for expert systems by use of shells and rapid prototyping. Another model, proposed by Young [48], recommends five activities: (1) receiving executive guidance, (2) forming a steering committee, (3) educating senior management, (4) developing functional budgets, and (5) explaining tactical information system processes to senior managers.

Management and User Commitment

Support, as already described, means understanding issues, participating, and making contributions. It is significantly different, however, from commitment, as demonstrated in the case of the chicken and the pig in Box 19.3. Ginzberg [20] has shown that two kinds of commitment are required for successful implementation. The first is a commitment to the project itself. The second is a commitment to change. Commitment to the project means that during the stages of system development, installation, and use, management ensures that everyone understands the problem the system is being designed to deal with, and that the system developed solves the right problem. Both users and management must develop this commitment to increase the odds that appropriate actions will be taken at each stage of system development. Commitment to change means that management and users are willing to accommodate the change that is likely to be required to implement the system or will be the result of its introduction.

Box 19.3: The Case of the Chicken and the Pig (C&P)

A chicken and a pig grew together from childhood and became very friendly. One day they decided to embark on a new venture. The chicken, who was the quick thinker, suggested that they open a restaurant that serves breakfasts. "Can you imagine," the chicken said, "the comparative advantage that we possess having all the ingredients right here, and we can serve the freshest ham-and-egg meals in the country." The pig, who was a much slower thinker, was at first amazed at the clever idea. However, after some additional thinking the pig said: "My dear friend, what you are proposing does not seem to be a fair partnership. While you will make a *contribution* to the venture, you want me to make a *commitment*."

Institutionalization

Institutionalization is a process through which an information system becomes incorporated as an ongoing part of organizational activities. It can occur in several ways: use of the system by successors to the original users, diffusion of the system to other users, change initiated in the work of employees, and change caused in the structure and processes of the organization. Finally, adding more MSS applications throughout the organization is evidence of institutionalization. All these changes are expected to be permanent. Institutionalization clearly points to successful implementation. It also helps to create a supportive organizational culture for future applications. (See Box 19.4.)

Length of Time Users Have Been Using Computers and MSS

The length of time that a user has been using computers has been shown to be a critical factor contributing to satisfaction with a decision support system (see Sanders and Courtney [43]). In general, the research showed that the longer people use a DSS, the more satisfied they become. We can assume that the same is true for other MSS technologies because both support managerial processes.

19.8   User Involvement and Training

User Involvement

User involvement refers to participation in the system development process by users or representatives of the user group. It is almost an axiom in MIS literature that user involvement is a necessary condition for successful develop-

Box 19.4: The Case of Connoisseur Food Corp.

Management at Connoisseur Foods stated that their real goal is not the implementation of isolated systems or models. Rather, it is the institution of new approaches in corporate decision making. Basically, this means that everyone in the organization should use the new approaches where appropriate and should be able to communicate effectively with either superiors or subordinates concerning recommendations based on these methods. It does not mean that everything should be based on models. Rather, it says that when a model-based analysis suggests a particular course of action in resource allocation, it should be possible to reconcile that suggestion with overall considerations in a much more rigid and disciplined manner.

Movement in a number of directions is increasing the degree of diffusion and acceptance of these models. Visible successes have been attained in a number of applications. Quantitative expertise was developed among Connoisseur Foods personnel, particularly with the hiring of MBAs. Managers were learning to approach situations in a more structured way.

To date, these efforts have had a definite impact on the way some brand managers think about their markets. They have a much deeper understanding of the market process that they are involved in. Previously, they made decisions and monitored their strategies for time intervals of one year. Now they can monitor the quality of a brand's position on a month-to-month basis. For the first time it is possible to see the explicit impact of marketing decisions on the progress of the brand. Furthermore, the organization has become much more aware of the value of DSS because it can now have a much more direct impact on planning decisions, which are an important determinant of sales and profit.

An example of the process of institutionalization can be seen in reviewing the participation of the subsidiaries. The people in the subsidiaries heard about the use of models at the headquarters and felt that this approach might be of value to them. Because the corporate DSS group had had three years of experience with modeling technologies by that time, they felt confident that their personnel could organize and lead the proposed model-building efforts. The result turned out to be one of the most sophisticated applications yet attempted at Connoisseur Foods.

(*Source:* Condensed from Alter [3].)

ment of a CBIS (see Ives and Olson [25]). User involvement with DSS is even more crucial. In expert systems, user involvement is less important because the builder may not know who the users are going to be. It is only in the phases of testing and improving the systems that users' involvement becomes important. In building EIS, user involvement is a *must*, since the system is tailored to the users.

Although there is agreement that user involvement is important, determining when it should occur and how much involvement is appropriate are questions that receive inadequate research attention.

In user-developed systems, the user obviously is very much involved. When teams are used the involvement issue becomes fairly complex, as shown in Table 19.2.

User involvement takes on a slightly different meaning with regard to a DSS than with traditional computer applications. In the latter the users (who frequently are nonmanagement employees) are primarily involved in the planning stage and in testing and evaluation. With regard to DSS development, heavy user involvement is advocated *throughout* the developmental process with a considerable amount of direct management participation. Many researchers advocate not only user involvement, but also user control of (and commitment to) the project, thus requiring continuous involvement and responsibility.

Table 19.3 on page 776 depicts the results of a study, conducted by Hogue and Watson [23], regarding management involvement in six phases of the DSS system development life cycle. The results reveal that there is a substantial involvement in all phases of DSS development. Also evident from the data is that top management had almost no involvement in building and testing the decision support system and played only a small role in its demonstration. Middle management was deeply involved with all phases of the development process. The generally low levels of involvement by lower management can be explained by the fact that the systems studied were almost exclusively designed to support middle- and/or top-management decision making.

The required **training** for building MSS could be very significant. Training may be provided by the information center, by the vendor, or by a university. (See Chrisman and Beccue [12].)

TABLE 19.2 Examples of User Participation

1. **Planning Phase:**
   a. The user initially suggests that the model be built.
   b. The user participates in initial discussions prior to building the model.
   c. The user evaluates the potential cost-benefit ratio for building the model.
   d. The user defines the goals of the model.

2. **Design Phase:**
   a. The user is the team leader in building the model.
   b. The user obtains necessary data to build the model.
   c. The user makes suggestions for improving the model.
   d. The user "smoothes the way/runs interference" during the model design phase.

Source: Brightman and Harris [9].

TABLE 19.3 Management Involvement in the Development of the DSS. Percentage of Companies with Management Involvement at Each Management Level and Development Stage.

Phase in Life Cycle	Management Level			
	Lower	Middle	Top	Any Level
Idea (conceptualization)	0	61.1	61.1	100
Information requirements	0	77.8	61.1	100
Building	11.1	72.2	5.6	77.8
Testing	11.1	72.2	5.6	83.3
Demonstration	11.1	77.8	27.7	88.9
Acceptance of system	0	72.2	66.7	100

Source: Hogue and Watson [23].

Generally speaking, the training required to use MSS technologies is fairly minimal. In some large-scale integrated systems, however, the required training may be substantial. Training should describe the system and explain why it is being installed; it also must teach users how to ask for information and how to use the information they receive. Training is a continuous process: it must be conducted as new people enter the system, and it should take place whenever significant changes are made in the system.

Guidelines for successful MSS training programs are similar to those for other CBIS training. Zmud [49] argues that for online systems, a training routine on the computer is preferred over a formal training program. In most instances, however, formal training is used.

The *organization of the building team* can affect implementation. Organization is reflected by team size and composition, team leadership, the department to which the team reports, the person who controls the team, and how much power the team possesses.

Relationship with the Information Systems Department

Many MSS applications may need to be connected with the organization's database(s). The existing information system must be capable of providing current and historical data. Distributed MSS requires the use of the corporate networks, and some MSS applications need minicomputers or mainframes. Therefore, the relationship with the information systems department may be crucial to the success of MSS.

Note: Although some large scale MSS are being built and operated by the IS department, many MSS are those of end-users.

One aspect of this issue is to whom the MSS project directors report. They may, for example, report to a functional business area or to a technology or research and development department. In such a case, cooperation with the information systems department is vital.

Goals, Plans, and Communications

The mission of the project, the responsibilities, the constraints, and the plans must all be clear. Plans and schedules for the project must be available.

Sufficient information must be accessible to all participants. Formal lines of communication need to be established among all concerned parties.

Selection of Projects

The concept of **organizational validity** developed by Schultz and Slevin [42] implies that for a project to be implemented successfully, it must be compatible with, or "fit," the particular organization. This fit *must* occur at three levels: individual, small group, and organizational. If a project requires an extraordinary amount of change in individual attitudes, small-group dynamics, or organizational structure (i.e., there is no fit), then the probability of successful implementation is reduced. Schultz and Slevin have suggested several methods for measuring the fit. Such information, which should be acquired in the planning stage, can determine the strategy of MSS development and implementation.

19.9   Organizational Factors

Organizational factors may cause systems to fail. Several are particularly important for MSS and are discussed briefly in this section.

Competence (Skills) and Organization of the AI Team

The participants' skills, especially those of the DSS builder and the technical support, were found to be critical for the success of DSS. Table 19.4 on page 778 summarizes the findings of Meador et al. [32] regarding the *perceived* importance of these skills in general and the estimated skill level in the respondents' companies. Note that there is a wide gap between what is believed to exist in organizations and what is perceived as important. These results suggest that adjustments in this area could be very beneficial.

The responsibility for the development and implementation of DSS is also an important factor. Table 19.5 on page 778 shows some empirical results for existing DSS. Notice that most DSS development is controlled by users.

Values and Ethics

Management is responsible for considering the ethics and values involved in implementing an MSS project. Three points are important:

1. *Goals of the project:* Because the process of implementation is based on an attempt to attain organizational or departmental goals, the development team should decide whether the ultimate goals desired are ethical. The

TABLE 19.4 Average Rated Importance and Performance of DSS Participants' Skills (scale: 1 = lowest importance, 7 = highest importance).

	Average Rated Importance (perceived)	Average Rated Performance (estimated)
Sensitivity to users' needs	6.23	4.43
Project management skills (planning and control)	5.64	4.42
Implementation planning: Education, motivation, and training of users	5.49	4.24
Expertise in design of analysis-based systems like DSS	5.47	3.57
Intimate knowledge of your department's operations	5.21	3.82
Willingness to work closely with users in designing new systems	5.09	5.84
Leadership ability, administrative experience, sensitivity to political issues	4.78	4.03

Source: Meador et al. [32]. Reprinted by special permission. Copyright 1984, by the Society for Information Management and the Management Information Systems Research Center at the University of Minnesota.

team should also determine whether the goals are ethical to those people who are crucial to the implementation process.

2. *Implementation process:* Another question the builders should ask is whether the implementation process is ethical, or even legal. Although the goals are ethical, the implementation process itself may not be; for example, consider an attempt to attain a sales goal through violation of a government antitrust law.

TABLE 19.5 Responsibility for DSS Development and Implementation.

Department	Development Responsibility (%)	Implementation Responsibility (%)
Respondent department	55.6	64.9
DP (IS) department	23.7	19.1
Jointly	4.6	5.3
Consultant, vendor	7.7	0.0
Other (head office, outside service)	8.4	10.7
	100.0	100.0

Source: Huff et al. [24].

3. *Possible impact on other systems:* The goals and processes may both be ethical, but the impact of the implemented project on another system may not be.

Adequacy of Resources

The success of any CBIS project depends also on the degree to which organizational arrangements facilitate access to the required computerized system and other resources. Success depends on factors such as availability of terminals and microcomputers, quality of the local area network, accessibility to databases, and user fees. Other factors include support and help facilities (e.g., availability of a help center), maintenance of software (see Swanson [44]), and availability of hardware.

Other Organizational Factors

Other organizational factors important in MSS implementation are the role of the **system advocate** (sponsor) who initiated the project and the compatibility of the system with organizational and personal goals of the participants.

19.10 External Environment

MSS implementation may be affected by factors outside the immediate environment of the development team. The external environment includes legal, social, economic, political, and other factors that could affect the project implementation either positively or negatively.

For example, government regulations regarding telecommunications across international borders may restrict the use of an otherwise successful EIS to a single country. Legal considerations may limit the use of an ES because developers may be afraid of legal action if the advice rendered by the ES leads to damages. (Some legal issues are discussed in the next chapter.) Vendors, research institutions, venture capital organizations, and universities can all play an important role in MSS implementation.

19.11 Project-related Factors

Most of the factors discussed in the previous sections can be considered elements in the implementation climate. Climate consists of the general conditions surrounding any application implementation; that is, climate is independent of any particular project. A favorable climate is helpful, but not sufficient. Each specific project must be evaluated on its own merits, such as its relative importance to the organization and its members. It must also satisfy certain cost-benefit criteria. Evaluation of a project involves several dimensions and requires consideration of several factors. For information systems in general, these factors, according to Meredith [33], can be described as follows:

- An important or major problem that needs to be resolved
- A real opportunity that needs to be evaluated
- Urgency of solving the problem
- High-profit contribution of the problem area
- Contribution of the problem area to growth
- Substantial resources tied to the problem area
- Demonstrable payoff if problem is solved.

Several of these factors will be highlighted in the discussion that follows.

Expectations from a Specific System

Expectations on the part of users as to how a system will contribute to their performance and the resultant rewards can greatly affect which system is utilized (see Robey [39]). **Overexpectations** were observed in AI technologies, which sometimes are presented as magical mystery.

Expectations about a system's value bear some relationship to how the need for a system is perceived. If users don't expect a system to enable them to do their jobs better and increase organizational efficiency, then they are not likely to perceive a great need for the system. Similarly, if users don't expect that the job tasks supported by the system will assist them in achieving their goals, they will be unlikely to use the system. Expectations can be affected by training, experience, and attitudes.

Cost-Benefit Analysis

Any CBIS application can be viewed as an alternative investment. As such, the application should show not only a payoff but also an advantage over other investment alternatives, including the option of "do nothing." Recently, the pressures to justify information systems (e.g., see Allen [2]), including MSS systems, have increased. Effective implementation depends to a great extent on the ability to make such justifications.

Each MSS project requires an investment of resources that can be viewed as the cost of the system in exchange for some expected benefit(s). The viability of a project is determined by comparing the costs with anticipated benefits. This comparison is termed a **cost-benefit analysis,** or cost-effective analysis. In practice, such an analysis may become rather complicated. The iterative nature of DSS and ES, for example, makes it difficult to predict costs and benefits; the systems are changed constantly. For methodologies that can be used in ES, and possibly other MSS, see Turban and Liebowitz [45]. The cost-benefit analysis deals with cost valuation and benefit valuation, discussed next.

Cost Valuation. The costs of a project may seem, at least at first sight, easy to identify and quantify. In practice, it is often difficult to relate costs to projects in a precise manner. Allocation of overhead costs is an example. Should they be allocated by volume, activity level, or value? What about future costs? A well-known "game" is to show the advantages of a certain alternative while neglecting future costs. In addition, there are additional accounting complications, such as the impact of taxation and the selection of a proper interest rate for present-value analysis.

Benefit Valuation. Although the assessment of costs is not easy, the assessment of benefits is even more difficult for several reasons. First, some benefits are intangible. Second, frequently a benefit cannot be related precisely to a single project. Third, results of a certain action may occur over a long period of time, or they may be realized in several portions. Fourth, a valuation of benefits includes the assessment of both quantity and quality. The latter is difficult to measure, especially when service industries are involved. Fifth, the multiplicity of consequences can pose a major problem for quantification. Some consequences like goodwill, inconvenience, waiting time, and pain are extremely difficult to measure and evaluate.

Note: Empirical studies indicate that very few companies conduct a cost-benefit analysis on their DSS (e.g., see Hogue and Watson [23] and Money et al. [36]). Instead, they use a value analysis that includes nonmonetary benefits.

Project Management

Several practical **project management** questions should be answered before implementation of the MSS project:

- Who will be responsible for executing each portion of the project?
- When must each part be completed?
- What resources (in addition to money) will be required?
- What information is needed?

In brief, a complete planning document for implementation should be prepared. With the formal answers to these questions, operating procedures, necessary training, and transitions can be planned beforehand so they do not become implementation problems later. Such planning is difficult to perform in most MSS technologies because of the iterative nature of system development. For further discussion of project management for ES development refer to Turban and Liebowitz [45].

Availability of Financing

All required financing, cash flows, identification of sources, and assurances of funds should be planned in advance. Commitments should be secured so that money will be available when needed. Lack of appropriate financing is frequently cited as a major obstacle to implementation and/or continuous use of large-scale systems.

Timing and Priority

Two interrelated factors in project implementation are timing and priority. For example, an MSS builder may find that an issue considered very important at the time of the feasibility study is not as important at implementation time. Usually, timing and priority are uncontrollable factors as far as the MSS team is concerned.

19.12   Evaluation*

Development of large-scale MSS often requires a great investment of money, time, and personnel. At the same time, results may be neither measurable nor tangible. Therefore, it is advisable to evaluate the success of MSS once they are implemented.

The special characteristics of DSS, particularly the cyclic and evolutionary nature of its implementation, and its impact on decision making call for a special approach to its evaluation. (See Box 19.5.) This special approach must be distinct

---

Box 19.5: The Success of DSS

In a survey conducted by Meador et al. [32], respondents were asked to rate their agreement with several statements indicating the "success of their DSS." These statements included:

1. The DSS fits in well with our planning methods.
2. It fits in well with our reporting methods.
3. It fits in well with our way of thinking about problems.
4. It has improved our way of thinking about problems.
5. It fits in well with the "politics" of how decisions are made around here.
6. Decisions reached with the aid of the DSS are usually implemented.
7. The DSS has resulted in substantial time savings.
8. It has been cost-effective.
9. It has been valuable relative to its cost.
10. It will continue to be useful to our organization for a number of years.
11. It has so far been a success.

---

*The material in Section 19.12 is condensed from Athappilly [4]. From DATA MANAGE-MENT Magazine. Copyright and reprint permission granted, 1985. Data Processing Management Association. ALL RIGHTS RESERVED.

from the usual type of "post implementation audit." Evaluations in that category are cumulative in nature. The intent of these evaluations is only to assess the outcome. In many cases, these cumulative evaluations suffer from "being too little and too late." They do not help the organization by revealing what factors led to those outcomes, and how or why they occurred.

But some evaluations provide useful information in addition to the end-product assessment. They are called *formative evaluations*. In the context of MSS, this formative evaluation has an added dimension, which is its dynamic and evolutionary nature. An example of such evaluation for DSS is given in Figure 19.2. The evaluation is conducted in four phases, as shown in Box 19.6.

The DSS evaluation must be an integral part of the DSS development and implementation, encompassing all phases of the DSS development process. The

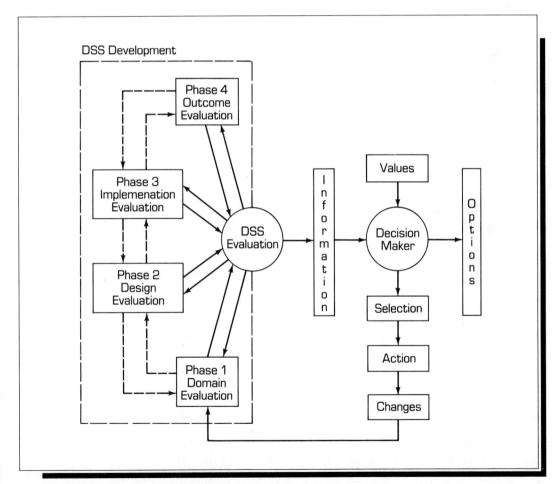

FIGURE 19.2 A Dynamic DSS Evaluation Model. (*Source:* Athappilly [4]. Copyright and reprint permission granted. 1985. Data Processing Management Association. All rights reserved.)

Box 19.6: A Proposal for DSS Evaluation

A proposal for DSS evaluation is shown in Figure 19.2. The evaluation process is composed of four phases: domain, design, implementation, and outcome.

- *Domain.* Analysis of the project, its justification, the opportunities, the constraints, and the objectives of the DSS. This phase is non-quantitative and it includes expert judgment.
- *Design.* Identification of system capabilities, assessment of input data, and suggestions for design. The objective is to select the DSS design and the design of the modifications that result from the iterative process. The evaluation is mainly descriptive, involving resource description, pilot projects, and expert advice.
- *Implementation.* Providing periodic feedback to the implementors. Detecting drawbacks in the procedural design, providing information about the predefined decisions, and maintaining records and procedures. This evaluation is executed with tools such as event logging and routine reports; it results in suggestions for design modifications.
- *Outcome(s).* Outcome(s) of the DSS are measured and interpreted during the construction of the DSS and at the end. Comparison with objectives and plans is executed. Variance analysis is performed. Many tools can be used: cost-benefit, value analysis, system analysis, rating and weighing, cognitive testing, event logging, and outcome assessment. The result of this phase may be the continuation, modification, or termination of the DSS.

(*Source:* Based on Athappilly [4].)

emphasis on decision support must be the focal point of DSS evaluation. See Guimataes et al. [21].

19.13 Implementation Strategies

During the last 25 years there have been many suggestions of implementation strategies for management science (e.g., see Schultz and Slevin [42]) and for information systems (e.g., see Lucas [30] and Meredith [33]). Many of the suggestions are generic and can be used as guidelines in implementing DSS and ES as well. The purpose of this section is to summarize strategies that were developed specifically for DSS and ES.

Implementation Strategies for DSS

The implementation strategies of DSS can be divided into four major categories:

1. Divide the project into manageable pieces.
2. Keep the solution simple.
3. Develop a satisfactory support base.
4. Meet user needs and institutionalize the system.

In general terms, each of these categories may seem obvious. Given a choice, who would want to provide a system that does not meet user needs or that does not have a satisfactory support base? However, a number of distinct strategies exist under each heading. And as outlined in Table 19.6, every one of these strategies has a certain purpose and certain pitfalls, just like strategies for losing weight.

The following topics are especially important in ES implementation:

- Quality of the system
- Cooperation of the expert(s)
- Conditions that justify the need for a particular ES.

A brief discussion of these topics follows.

Quality of the System. The success of ES depends on the quality of the system. Buchanan and Shortliffe [10] believe the following seven features should be presented in a good ES:

1. The ES should be developed to fulfill a recognized need.
2. The ES should be easy to use even by a novice.
3. The ES should be able to increase the expertise of the user.
4. The ES should have exploration capabilities.
5. The program should be able to respond to simple questions.
6. The system should be capable of learning new knowledge (i.e., the system should be able to ask questions to gain additional information).
7. The program knowledge should be easily modified (i.e., add, delete, and modify rules).

These features are necessary but far from being sufficient for a successful ES.

The Cooperation of Expert(s). For an ES to be successfully implemented it must give good advice. Such advice depends, most of all, on the cooperation of

TABLE 19.6 DSS Implementation Strategy

Implementation Strategy	Typical Situation or Purpose	Pitfalls Encountered
1. **Divide project into manageable pieces.**	To minimize the risk of producing a massive system that doesn't work.	
Use prototypes.	Success of the effort hinges on relatively untested concepts. Test these concepts before committing to a full-fledged version.	Reactions to the prototype system (in an experimental setting) may differ from reactions to a final system in day-to-day use.
Use an evolutionary approach.	Implementer attempts to shorten feedback loops between self and clients and between intentions and products.	Requires users to live with continuing change, which some people find annoying.
Develop a series of tools.	To meet ad hoc analysis needs by providing databases and small models that can be created, modified, and discarded.	Limited applicability. Expense of maintaining infrequently used data.
2. **Keep the solution simple.**	To encourage use and to avoid scaring away users.	Although generally beneficial, can lead to misrepresentation, misunderstanding, misuse.
Be simple.	Not an issue for inherently simple systems. For other systems or situations, it may be possible to choose between simple and complicated approaches.	Some business problems are not inherently simple. Insisting on simple solutions may result in skirting the real issue.
Hide complexity.	The system is presented as a "black box" that answers questions using procedures not presented to the user.	Use of "black boxes" by nonexperts can lead to misuse of the results because of misunderstanding of the underlying models and assumptions.
Avoid change.	Given a choice of automating existing practice or developing new methods, choose the former.	New systems may have little real impact. Not applicable to efforts purporting to foster change.
3. **Develop a satisfactory support base.**	One or more components of a user-management support base is missing.	Danger that one support-gaining strategy will be applied without adequate attention to others.
Obtain user participation.	The system effort was not initiated by users. The usage pattern is not obvious in advance.	With multiple users, difficulty of getting everyone involved and incorporating everyone's interests. With sophisticated models, reduced feasibility of user participation in model formulation and interpretation.

Source: Alter (), pp. 166–169 (with permission).

TABLE 19.6 (continued)

Implementation Strategy	Typical Situation or Purpose	Pitfalls Encountered
Obtain user commitment.	The system has been developed without user involvement. The system is to be imposed on users by management.	It is difficult to obtain commitment without some kind of *quid pro quo* or demonstration that the system will help the user.
Obtain management support.	To obtain funding for continuation of the project. To obtain management action in forcing people to comply with the system or use it.	Management enthusiasm may not be shared by users, resulting in perfunctory use or disuse.
Sell the system.	Some potential users were not involved in system development and do not use it. System is not used to full potential by the organization.	Often unsuccessful unless real advantages can be demonstrated convincingly.
4. Meet user needs and institutionalize system.	A system is to have many individual users in an ongoing application.	Since strategies under this heading are somewhat incompatible, emphasis on one may exclude another.
Provide training.	The system is not designed in close cooperation with *all* potential users.	Frequent difficulties in estimating the type and intensity of training that is needed. Initial training programs often require substantial reformulation and elaboration.
Provide ongoing assistance.	The system is used by an intermediary rather than a decision maker. The system is used with the help of an intermediary who handles mechanical details.	If the system is used by an intermediary, the decision maker may not understand the analysis in sufficient detail.
Insist on mandatory use.	The system is a medium for integration and coordination in planning. The system purports to facilitate work of individuals.	Difference between genuine use and half-hearted submission of numbers for a plan. Difficulty in forcing people to think in a particular mold.
Permit voluntary use.	Avoid building resistance to a hard sell by allowing voluntary use.	Generally ineffective unless the system meets a genuine felt need or appeals to an individual intellectually or otherwise.
Rely on diffusion and exposure.	It is hoped that enthusiasts will demonstrate the benefits of a system to their colleagues.	Ineffective: perhaps as much an excuse for lack of positive action as it is a real strategy.
Tailor systems to people's capabilities.	People differ in their ability and/or propensity to use analytic techniques.	Not clear how to do so. In practice, systems seem to be built to people's requirements, not their capabilities.

the domain expert. Most functioning ES had very little trouble with expert co-operation. The following are some questions with regard to experts' cooperation that must be discussed before building an ES:

- Should the experts be compensated for their contribution (e.g., in the form of royalties, a special reward, or payment)?
- How can one tell if the experts are telling the truth about the way they solve problems?
- How can the experts be assured that they will not lose their jobs, or that their jobs will not be deemphasized, once the ES is fully operational?
- Are the experts concerned about other people in the organization whose jobs may suffer because of the introduction of ES, and what can management do in such a case?

In general, management should use some incentives to influence the experts so that they will cooperate fully with the knowledge engineer. The experts have lots of power, which they can even use to sabotage a system; this power must be recognized and respected.

Conditions That Justify an ES. Expert systems are more prone to succeed when one or more of the following conditions prompted the need for the system (based on Van Horn [46]):

- The expert is not always available or is expensive.
- Decisions must be made under pressure, and missing even a single factor could be disastrous.
- There is rapid employee turnover resulting in a constant need to train new people. Such training is costly and time-consuming.
- A huge amount of data must be sifted through.
- A shortage of experts is holding back development and profitability.
- Expertise is needed to augment the knowledge of junior personnel.
- There are too many factors—or possible solutions—for a human to keep in mind at once, even when the problem is broken into smaller pieces.
- The problem requires a knowledge-based approach and cannot be handled by a conventional computational approach.
- Consistency and reliability, not creativity, are paramount.
- Factors are constantly changing, and it is very hard for a person to keep on top of them all and find what is needed at just the right time.
- One type of expertise (e.g., statistics) must be made available to people in different fields (e.g., accounting, marketing) so they can make better decisions.

Chapter Highlights

- Many MSS projects either fail or are not completed.
- Successful implementation is determined by many factors.

- Implementation is an ongoing process.
- Implementation means introducing change.
- Success of implementation can be partial, and it is usually measured by several criteria (e.g., user satisfaction, degree of use, and payoff to the organization).
- Technical success is related to the system's complexity, reliability, and responsiveness; hardware, network, and software compatibilities; and the technical skills of the builders.
- AI uses a symbolic qualitative approach that needs to fit users' decision-making styles.
- Organizational climate and politics can be detrimental to the success of any application.
- There are many dimensions to change and to its resistance; overcoming resistance is a complex process.
- Many individuals may resist MSS for several reasons.
- Managers in many organizations have as their goal to manage change and make it a positive experience for the organization.
- Top management support is crucial; it can be increased through guidance, education, participation, communication, and appropriate budget procedures.
- Institutionalization means that MSS becomes an integral part of the organization.
- Involvement of users at the various stages of system development varies in its importance depending on the MSS technology.
- Training for MSS use is usually minimal, but training for building MSS may be very significant.
- Several organizational factors are important to successful implementation; they range from the profile of the team (organization, size, composition, skill levels) to the relationship with the information systems department.
- Lack of adequate resources means failure.
- Medium and large MSS projects must go through a rigorous cost-benefit analysis. Assessing benefits may be very difficult because many of them are intangible.
- MSS applications are basically information systems and they should, therefore, be developed with appropriate project management techniques.

Key Words

change management	organizational validity	top management
cost-benefit analysis	overexpectations	support
decision style	project management	training
institutionalization	system advocate	user commitment
organizational climate (culture)		

Questions for Review

1. Define implementation in a broad sense.
2. Define implementation in a narrow sense.
3. What is institutionalization?
4. Describe the various criteria for measuring the success of an implemented information system.
5. List several measures for evaluating success of expert systems.
6. Describe the technical factors related to successful implementation.
7. What is meant by system response time?
8. What is a decision style?
9. Explain the difference between analytical and heuristic decision styles.
10. List some of the dimensions of change related to implementation.
11. What is information possessiveness?
12. List some of the potential resistors to ES.
13. Why is the support of top management vital to system implementation?
14. List some of the ways to increase the support of top management.
15. Describe some of the organizational factors that can affect the success of implementation.
16. What are some of the difficulties in conducting cost-benefit analyses of MSS technologies?

Questions for Discussion

1. Why is implementing MSS technologies more complex than implementing MIS technologies?
2. How can an organizational climate influence implementation?
3. What actions can be taken by top management to support MSS application?
4. What is the difference between user involvement and user commitment?
5. Why is the issue of expectation so important in ES implementation?
6. The question of why so many expert systems fail is important. Find an article on this subject and discuss it. (For example, see Chapter 1 in Turban and Liebowitz [45].)
7. Review the XCON case in Chapter 12, Appendix 12-B. Identify factors that could have contributed to the success of this system.

Exercises

1. Given below is a DSS success factor questionnaire (developed by Sanders and Courtney [41]). Administer the following questionnaire to 10 users of DSS in your organization. Assign a "5" to a strongly agree, "4" to agree, "3" to neutral, "2" to disagree, and "1" to strongly disagree. Compute the average results and rank the factors in order of their importance.

   Overall Satisfaction

   _____ I have become dependent on DSS.
   _____ As a result of DSS, I am seen as more valuable in this organization.

_____ I have personally benefited from the existence of DSS in this organization.

_____ I have come to rely on DSS in performing my job.

_____ All in all, I think that DSS is an important system for this organization.

_____ DSS is extremely useful.

Decision-making Satisfaction

_____ Utilization of DSS has enabled me to make better decisions.

_____ As a result of DSS, I am better able to set my priorities in decision making.

_____ Use of data generated by DSS has enabled me to present my arguments more convincingly.

_____ DSS has improved the quality of decisions I make in this organization.

_____ As a result of DSS, the speed at which I analyze decisions has been increased.

_____ As a result of DSS, more relevant information has been available to me for decision making.

_____ DSS has led me to greater use of analytical aids in my decision making.

Comment on the results.

2. Review the Louisiana National Bank DSS case in the Chapter 3 case studies. A number of factors have led to the successful development and use of the DSS, called FPS, at the Louisiana National Bank. A key factor was the support and involvement of top management. They requested the system and have been its primary beneficiaries.

   Another important factor was the characteristics of the system's sponsor. Gil Urban was patient, low-keyed, and determined to maintain a low profile. Although he had the opportunity to build a power base through FPS, he chose not to do so. Other managers knew this and chose to work with him freely.

   The bank offered an excellent organizational environment for the creation of FPS. There was a need for the system, and the bank had a history of innovation. Open communications were encouraged, and the system became a communication vehicle and framework for unified decision making. Bank officers have high morale and pride, which have enabled them to embrace institutional goals over personal goals.

   A transitional development and implementation approach was used. The initial version of FPS provided familiar reports and required little additional understanding. Over time, as trust in the system grew, the system slowly and patiently moved managers from the old to new ways of thinking.

   Finally, FPS provided a unified planning system. It combined three closely related, but often separated, phases of the planning process: forecasting, analysis, and reporting. FPS allows managers to move from one phase to another in an easy, integrated manner.

   a. Identify the major factors that led to the successful implementation of FPS.

   b. Why was the "transitional development and implementation approach" successful?

Case Study: Implementing DSS at Firestone Tire & Rubber Co.*

The short-term goal of "the DSS mission" was simply to support senior executives through DSS implementation. The long-range goal of this mission was to expand DSS use throughout Firestone. The DSS strategy was to support the overall corporate strategic plan and provide management with the analytical tools and capabilities to run the company more successfully.

The issues raised in the initial phase of DSS implementation were manifold: corporate accounting and financial functions were largely decentralized. Firestone executives were also unfamiliar with computers—many could not even type—and they were almost impossible to pin down in terms of a training schedule. The need to provide something usable and useful immediately was critical.

The implementation group quickly reached several key decisions. The first was to limit the scope of the user group. Next, it developed a simple, menu-driven approach to get the user on the system. Third, it decided it should start quickly, so it brought in the Dow Jones & Co., Inc., news service, as a vehicle to acquaint users with the terminals and the system. "Start quickly," Bode, the DSS builder, advised, "while interest is high."

The implementation strategy also included the development of a "straw man" database, along with a DSS conceptual design, based on the user interviews conducted by the group. An executive steering committee was set up to assist in the initial design and also to become educated in the potential of DSS. Finally, the implementation group provided online demonstration DSS systems to enable hands-on DSS processing.

DSS training at Firestone consisted of one-on-one coaching sessions, comprehensive documentation with lots of examples, online help features, telephone hotline user support, and online product enhancement announcements.

The implementation has meant some good news and some bad news. The good DSS news was that the company had a solid base system in place, the executive training and acceptance looked promising, and the alignment of DSS and corporate objectives would serve to solidify the company's position in the marketplace.

The bad news was that overexpansion of DSS could impede the system's ability to respond quickly; getting increased volumes of data onto the system is difficult and the responsibility of database administration is an issue that must be resolved. Specifically the company decided that this responsibility should not be that of the management information systems director but that of the vice president for administration.

By the time the system went up, the executives were comfortable with the terminals and the DSS process, their expectations of the implementation were

---

*Source: Condensed from *Computerworld* (September 27, 1982).

quite realistic, and the users understood the importance of taking the time to learn the system.

Firestone's DSS plans are:

- To expand DSS usage in the analysis of data (graphics capabilities and so forth).
- To expand user groups along the line of internal strategic interests in the company.
- To integrate DSS with other office systems such as word processing functions.

Case Questions

1. Identify the determinants of success in the Firestone case.
2. Which of these are not discussed in this chapter?
3. Identify the major implementation problems cited in the case.
4. What are some unique features about DSS that one can learn from this case?
5. Why was DSS an appropriate tool in this case?
6. Why was the responsibility for database administration delegated to the V.P. for administration?

Case Study: Campbell Soup Puts Expert System to Work in Their Kitchens*

The process of soup making is highly automated from beginning to end, but minor malfunctions do occur. So the Campbell folks decided that expert system approaches could help their repair and maintenance people to anticipate and prevent malfunctions and to diagnose them faster when they occurred.

Campbell worked with Texas Instruments (TI) Corp. to select the first application for an expert system. The application they chose was the diagnosis of malfunctions that can occur in cooker systems (more formally called "hydrostatic sterilizers"). Cookers are the working heart of every Campbell canning plant. The cooker's vital job is to sterilize the food. Elaborate conveyor systems load and unload the cookers. Downtime is expensive and disrupts shipping schedules.

Campbell plant operators and maintenance people are well able to handle day-to-day operation of the cookers and to correct common malfunctions in their many plants worldwide. Occasionally, though, difficulties arise that demand diagnosis by an expert—someone thoroughly versed in the design, installation, and operation of the cookers. The Campbell people wanted to capture this expertise in an inexpensive computer system, so that even their smallest plant could have the expertise available immediately. That would also free their

*Source: Condensed from the *Artificial Intelligence Letter* 1 (no. 5, November 1985). Published by Texas Instruments, Data Systems Group, Austin, TX.

experts to concentrate on design improvements and new processes. A secondary objective was to use the system as a training tool for new maintenance personnel.

The system was developed in 1985 on a microcomputer. The ES can be delivered on any IBM PC (or compatible) because PCs are inexpensive, familiar, and easy to use. The system was developed with the Personal Consultant shell.

The following extract is an example of an English translation of one of the rules in Campbell's expert system.

> IF the cooker's symptom is TEMPERATURE-DEVIATION, and the problem temperature is T30-INTERMEDIATE-COOLING SPRAY, and the input and output air signals for TIC-30 are correct, and the valve on TCV-30 is not open,
>
> THEN the problem with the cooker is that TCV-30 is not working properly. Check the instrumentation and the air signal.

Development of Campbell's first expert system took about six months from initial contact with the human expert to field testing. The history of its development is instructive. On November 5, 1984, the Campbell cooker expert met with TI knowledge engineers for the first time. The expert was understandably skeptical, but completely cooperative. The first four days were devoted to teaching the TI people about the normal operation of the cookers, so they could discuss malfunctions intelligently.

On December 10, TI returned to Campbell with a first-draft system that used thirty-two rules. TI's development philosophy is to get a prototype system up and running as quickly as possible for early evaluation by the clients. It has proven to be the best strategy for eliciting further knowledge. Many people have difficulties in providing their knowledge directly, but can easily provide constructive criticism, which generates knowledge indirectly.

With the wealth of additional knowledge elicited in a three-day review of the prototype with Campbell management, TI enlarged the system to sixty-six rules and presented it to Campbell on January 22, 1985. This time, the review produced no great changes. Rather, some of the terms were refined and some detailed steps were added to certain diagnostic procedures.

Also at this point, the system was demonstrated to potential users—a shift supervisor at Campbell's Camden, N.J., plant, and several operations and maintenance people at Campbell's Napoleon, Ohio, plant. Their consensus was that the system would be useful to have at the plants. During these trips, Campbell also decided to expand the expert system to cover both startup and shutdown procedures.

On February 12, TI presented the next refinement of the system to Campbell. It had now grown to eighty-five rules, plus twelve startup and shutdown procedures. After a few minor flaws were corrected, Campbell declared this first phase of the system ready. A second phase covering rotary cookers had been added by Campbell after the hydrostatic sterilizer system appeared destined for success.

On March 19, an expert system covering hydrostatic cookers, their startup and shutdown procedures, and rotary cookers was presented by TI. The system had now grown to 125 rules. On this visit, the system was demonstrated to a wider circle of Campbell's management, and there was consensus that Campbell's first expert system was nearly ready for field testing. The next month was spent refining the rotary cooker rules and including rules covering a different type of hydrostatic cooker used at only one of Campbell's plants.

By November 1, 1985, the expert system contained 151 rules plus startup and shutdown procedures, and Campbell was fanning out the system to its plants.

Four of the key people in the project—Aldo Cimino and Reuben K. Tyson of Campbell and Richard Herrod and Michael D. Smith of TI—have summarized some of the practical lessons learned or reconfirmed:

- It's more important to put together a prototype fast than to make it complete.
- Extracting knowledge from the human expert is a difficult process for both the expert and the knowledge engineer, and they must guard against discouragement.
- The knowledge engineer must be prepared to accept frequent corrections—and the expert must be willing to give them.
- Because experts are seldom aware of all their thinking processes, each review of a developing system is helpful in uncovering additional needed knowledge.
- The expert must be fully cooperative, even if skeptical.
- Strong management commitment to a project of this type is absolutely essential to its success. An expert's time is in short supply and the project must have a high enough priority to assure adequate access to the expert.
- Early demonstration to potential users is important. Without their feedback about perceived deficiencies, and without their support, even a well-conceived system can end up in a closet collecting dust.
- An expert system must continue to grow to cover unforeseen situations and equipment modifications. Fortunately, it's fairly easy to add new knowledge to an expert system.

Case Questions

1. Trace the development process of this system. List all the measures that were taken to ensure successful implementation.
2. Compare the practical lessons listed at the end of this case with the theoretical approach to successful implementation proposed in this chapter. Discuss similarities and differences.
3. Discuss some of the potential benefits of this system.
4. Development of the system was done by an outside vendor working as a consultant. Discuss the advantages and disadvantages of such an approach from an implementation point of view.
5. User involvement in this case occurred about midway in the development cycle. This is fairly typical in expert systems. In conventional information

systems, on the other hand, users are involved much earlier. Explain the logic behind these two practical approaches. Do you agree with them? Why or why not?

6. A close relationship between the expert and the knowledge engineer is essential to successful implementation. Review the case and point out the incidents of interaction between the two and the lessons learned.

7. Why is it so important to complete the first prototype early? How can it enhance implementation?

References and Bibliography

1. Alavi, M., and E. A. Joachimsthaler. "Revisiting DSS Implementation Research." *MIS Quarterly* (March 1992).
2. Allen, B. "Make Information Services Pay Its Way." *Harvard Business Review* (January–February, 1987).
3. Alter, S. L. *Decision Support Systems, Current Practice and Continuing Challenges.* Reading, MA: Addison-Wesley, 1980.
4. Athappilly, K. "Successful Decision Making Starts With DSS Evaluation." *Data Management* (February 1985).
5. Badiru, A. B. "Successful Initiation of Expert Systems Projects." *IEEE Transactions on Engineering Management* (August 1988).
6. Barker, V., and D. O'Connor. "Expert Systems for Configuration at Digital, XCON and Beyond." *Communications of ACM*, March 1989.
7. Barsanti, J. B. "Expert Systems: Critical Success Factors for Their Implementation." *Information Executive* (Winter 1990).
8. Berry, D., and A. Hart, eds. *Expert Systems: Human Issues.* New York: Chapman and Hall, 1990.
9. Brightman, H. J., and S. E. Harris. "Building Computer Models that Really Work." *Managerial Planning* (January–February 1984).
10. Buchanan, B. G., and E. H. Shortliffe. *Rule-Based Expert Systems: The MYCIN Experiments of the Stanford Heuristic Programming Project.* Reading, MA: Addison-Wesley, 1984.
11. Buswick, T. "AI Training: Myths and Realities." *PC AI* (Spring 1988).
12. Chrisman, C., and B. Beccue. "Training for Users as a Management Issue." *Journal of Information Systems Management* (Summer 1990).
13. Cooper, R. B., and R. W. Zmud. "Information Technology Implementation Research: A Technological Diffusion Approach." *Management Science* (February 1990).
14. DePree, R. "Implementing Expert Systems." *Micro User's Guide* (Summer 1988).
15. Dickson, G. W., and J. C. Wetherbe. *The Management of Information Systems.* New York: McGraw-Hill, 1985.
16. Dickson, G., and R. Powers. "MIS Project Management: Myths, Opinions and Realities." In *Information Systems Administration*, W. McFarlin, et al., eds. New York: Holt, Rinehart & Winston, 1973.

17. Dologite, D. G., and R. J. Mockler. "Developing Effective Knowledge-Based Systems: Overcoming Organizational and Individual Behavioral Barriers." *Information Resource Management Journal* (Winter 1989).

18. Fallik, F. *Managing Organizational Change: Human Factors and Automation.* Philadelphia: Taylor and Francis, 1988.

19. Feigenbaum, E., P. McCorduck, and H. P. Nii. *The Rise of the Expert Company.* New York: Times Books, 1988.

20. Ginzberg, M. J. "Key Recurrent Issues in the MIS Implementation Process." *MIS Quarterly* 5 (no. 2, 1981).

21. Guimataes, T., et al. "The Determinants of DSS Success: An Integrated Model." *Decision Sciences* (March/April 1992).

22. Helton, T. "AI Infusion: Getting Your Company Involved." *AI Expert* 5 (March 1990): 54–59.

23. Hogue, J. T., and H. J. Watson. "Current Practices in the Development of Decision Support Systems." *Information and Management* (May 1985).

24. Huff, S. L., et al. "An Empirical Study of Decision Support Systems." *INFOR* (February 1984).

25. Ives, B., and M. H. Olson. "User Involvement in Information System Development: A Review of Research." *Management Science* 30 (May 1984).

26. Joshi, K. "A Model of User's Perspective on Change: The Case of Information System Technology Implementation." *MIS Quarterly* (June 1987).

27. Keyes, J. "Why Expert Systems Fail." *AI Expert* (November 1989).

28. Lewin, K. "Group Decision and Social Change." In *Readings in Social Psychology,* T. M. Newcomb and E. L. Hartley, eds. New York: Holt, Rinehart & Winston, 1947.

29. Liebowitz, J. *Institutionalizing Expert Systems: A Handbook for Managers.* Englewood Cliffs, NJ: Prentice-Hall, 1991.

30. Lucas, H. C. *Implementation: The Key to Successful Information Systems.* New York: Columbia University Press, 1981.

31. Markus, M. L. "Power, Politics and MIS Interpretation." *Communications of ACM* (June 1983).

32. Meador, C. L., M. J. Guyote, and P. G. W. Keen. "Setting Priorities for DSS Development." *MIS Quarterly,* Vol. 8, No. 2 (June 1984).

33. Meredith, J. R. "The Implementation of Computer-Based Systems." *Journal of Operational Management* (October 1981).

34. Meyer, M. H., and K. F. Curley. "Expert Systems Success Model." *Datamation* (September 1, 1989).

35. Mohan, L., and A. S. Bean. "Introducing OR/MS into Organizations: Normative Implications of Selected Indian Experience." *Decision Sciences* 10 (1979).

36. Money, A., et al. "The Quantification of Decision Support Benefits within the Context of Value Analysis." *MIS Quarterly* (June 1988).

37. Morino, M. M. "Managing and Coping with Change: An IS Challenge." *Journal of Information Systems Management* (Winter 1988).

38. Odette, L. "Expert Systems: When to Make Them, When to Buy Them." In *Proceedings of the 1987 Expert Systems in Business Conference,* J. Feinstein, J.

Liebowitz, H. Look, and B. Sullivan, eds. Medford, NJ: Learned Information, 1987.

39. Robey, D. "User Attitudes and MIS Use." *Academy of Management Journal* 22 (September 1979).

40. Rockart, J. F., and A. D. Crescenzi. "Engaging Top Management in Information Technology." *Journal of Systems Management* (April 1986).

41. Sanders, G. L., and J. F. Courtney. "A Field Study of Organizational Factors Influencing DSS Success." *MIS Quarterly* (March 1985).

42. Schultz, R. L., and D. P. Slevin, eds. *Implementing Operations Research/Management Science.* New York: Elsevier, 1975.

43. Smith, D. L. "Implementing Real World Expert Systems." *AI Expert* (December 1988).

44. Swanson, E. B. *Information System Implementation.* Homewood, IL: Richard D. Irwin, 1988.

45. Turban, E., and Liebowitz, J., eds. *Managing Expert Systems.* Hershey, PA: Idea Group Publishers, 1992.

46. Van Horn, M. *Understanding Expert Systems.* Toronto: Bantam Books, 1986.

47. Yorman, D. "Success Factors for Expert Systems." *Capital PC Monitor* 7 (May 1988).

48. Young , J. "Ways to Win Top Brass Backing." *Computerworld* (November 4, 1987).

49. Zmud, R. W. "Individual Differences and MIS Success: A Review of the Empirical Literature." *Management Science* 25 (no. 10, 1979).

50. Zmud, R. W., and J. F. Cox. "The Implementation Process: A Change Process." *MIS Quarterly* (June 1979).

Chapter 20

Organizational and Societal Impacts of Management Support Systems

In the course of this book we have introduced several applied MSS technologies. If management support systems grow in importance in the information systems market, they could have a profound effect on organizations, people, and society. This chapter deals with some of the potential impacts of such a development in the following sections:

20.1   Introduction

MSS systems are important participants in the Information Revolution, a cultural transformation that most people are only now coming to terms with. Unlike slower revolutions of the past, such as the Industrial Revolution, the Information Revolution is taking place very quickly and affecting every facet of our lives. Inherent in this rapid transformation is a host of managerial and social problems: impact on organizational structure, resistance to change, possible increased unemployment levels, and so on. The MSS share of the computer industry could reach 25 percent by the year 2000, so its impact can be substantial.

Separating the impact of MSS from that of other computerized systems is a difficult task, especially because of the trend to integrate MSS with other computer-based information systems. Very little published information about the impact of MSS technologies exists because the techniques are so new. Some of our discussion thus must relate to computer systems in general. We recognize, however, that MSS technologies do have some unique organizational, social, and cultural implications, which are highlighted throughout this chapter.

MSS can have both micro- and macro-implications: it can affect particular individuals and jobs, the work structure of departments, and units within the organization (microeffects); it can also have significant long-term effects on total organizational structures, entire industries, communities, and society as a whole (macroeffects).

Figure 20.1 presents a framework for research that shows a complete management system. Such a system stays in equilibrium as long as all of its parts are unchanged. When there is a change in one of the components, the change will affect some of the other components. The major change stimuli are strategy and technology, especially computerized systems like a DSS or ES. For further discussion, see Benjamin and Scott-Morton [4] and Wijnhoven and Wassenarr [47].

The purpose of this chapter is to foster a basic understanding of the major organizational and societal impacts of widespread use of MSS.

20.2   Overview of Impacts

The impacts of computers and MSS technology can be divided into two general categories: organizational (microlevel) and societal (macrolevel). Computers have had an impact on organizations in many ways. We cannot discuss all of the ways in this chapter, so we selected those topics that we felt are most relevant to MSS. They are designated in Table 20.1, along with the chapter section in which the topics are discussed.

Computer technology has already changed the world in which we live, and much more change is anticipated. Table 20.2 summarizes some of the major areas of social impact and designates the chapter sections in which they are discussed.

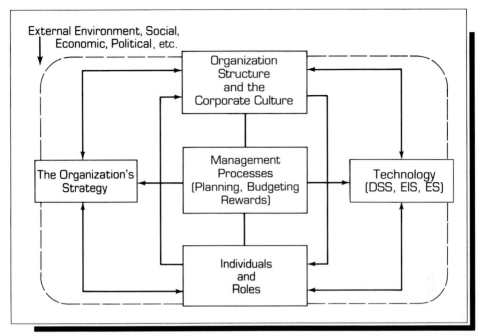

FIGURE 20.1 Framework for Organizational and Societal Impacts of AI Technology. (*Source:* M. Scott-Morton, "DSS Revisited for the 1990s," paper presented at DSS 1986, Washington, D.C., April 1986. Used with permission.)

TABLE 20.1 Organizational Impacts of Computer Technology

Area of Impact	Section in This Chapter
Structure	20.3
Span of control	20.3
Centralization versus decentralization	20.3
Authority, power, and status	20.3
AI special units	20.3
Job content and roles	20.4
Career ladder	20.4
Supervision	20.4
Individuals	20.5
Productivity and competitiveness	20.6
Decision making and the manager's job	20.7
Organizational intelligence	20.8
Issues of legality, ethics, and privacy	20.9
The information center	20.10

TABLE 20.2 Social Impacts of Computer Technology

Area of Impact	Section in This Chapter
Research and development: The Fifth-generation Project	20.11
Employment levels	20.12, 20.13
Education and training	20.14
Work in hazardous environments	20.15
Opportunities for the disabled	20.15
Changing role of women	20.15
Telecommuting (working at home)	20.15
Consumers	20.15
Quality of life	20.15
Computer crime	20.15
Social responsibility	20.16

20.3   Organizational Structure and Related Areas

The organizational impacts of computer technology may be felt along several dimensions, ranging from structure and degree of centralization to distribution of power. Here we deal only with a few of the issues.

Structure

Computer-based systems have already created changes in organizational structures. MSS could further enhance these changes in several ways.

Flatter Organizational Hierarchies. MSS allows increased productivity of managers, an increased **span of control** (less need for supervision), and a decreased number of experts (because of expert systems). It is reasonable to assume, then, that *fewer* managerial levels will exist in many organizations; there will be fewer staff and line managers. This trend is already evidenced by the continuing phenomenon of the "shrinking size of middle management" (e.g., *Fortune* [32]).

Flatter organizational hierarchies will also result from the reduction in the total number of employees as a result of increased productivity and from the ability of lower-level employees to perform higher-level jobs (e.g., by using ES). As one example consider the Bank of America's reorganization (1985) and Citicorp's reorganization (1991), both of which resulted in a smaller corporation and a much flatter structure. The main cause for the changes was the increased use of computers.

Staff-to-Line Ratio. The ratio of staff to line workers in most organizations has increased with the replacement of clerical jobs by computers and with the increased need for information systems specialists. The expansion of MSS, and especially ES, may reverse this trend. Specifically, the number of professionals and specialists could *decline* in relation to the total number of employees in the organization. Similarly, Citicorp's 1991 restructuring resulted in the elimination of two managerial layers.

Centralization of Authority

The relationship between computerized systems and the degree of centralization of authority (and power) in the organizations that these systems serve has been debated extensively, especially since the introduction of microcomputers. It is still difficult, however, to establish a clear pattern. For example, the introduction of ES in General Electric's maintenance area increased the power of the decentralized units because they became less dependent on the company's headquarters. On the other hand, ES can be used as a means of increasing control and centralization.

Computer-based information systems can support either centralization or decentralization of electronic information processing within an organization. For a detailed discussion see Boxes 20.1 and 20.2 and Huber [15]. Although information systems are usually established *after* an organizational structure is completed, it is quite possible that a new or modified information system will change the organizational structure and/or the degree of decentralization.

Because of the trend toward smaller and flatter organizations, centralization may become more popular. However, this trend could be offset by specialization in more decentralized units. Whether extensive use of MSS will result in more centralization or decentralization of business operations and management may depend on top management's philosophy. After all, people can control the direction in which computers take them.

Box 20.1: To Centralize or Decentralize

- *Centralization:* Large, central computer systems, where large MSS systems are developed and used, allow upper management to centralize the decision making formerly done at lower levels of the organization.
- *Decentralization:* Personal computers, data communication networks, and distributed MSS allow top management to delegate more responsibility to middle managers and to increase the number of branch offices (or other company units) while still providing top management with the ability to control the organization.

Box 20.2: Huber's Propositions about Computers' Impacts on Organizations

The use of MSS and other computer-assisted communication technologies leads to the following organizational changes:

1. A large number and variety of people participating as decision sources
2. A decrease in the number and variety of people participating in traditional face-to-face communication
3. Less time in meetings
4. Better chance that a particular organizational level will make a particular decision
5. Greater variation across the organization in the levels at which a particular type of decision is made
6. Fewer organizational levels involved in authorizing actions
7. Fewer intermediate information nodes within the organizational information processing network
8. Fewer levels involved in processing messages
9. More frequent development and use of databases
10. More rapid and more accurate identification of problems and opportunities
11. Organizational intelligence (e.g., scanning, monitoring) that is more accurate, comprehensive, timely, and available
12. Higher-quality decisions
13. Shorter time required to authorize actions
14. Shorter time required to make decisions

(*Source:* Condensed from G. P. Huber, "A Theory of the Effects of Advanced Information Technologies on Organizational Design, Intelligence, and Decision Making." *Academy of Management Review*, 15 [no. 1, 1990].)

Power and Status

Knowledge is power—this fact has been recognized for generations (e.g., see Buckland [6]). The latest developments in computerized systems are changing the power structure within organizations. The struggle over who will control the computers and information resources has become one of the most visible conflicts in many organizations, both private and public. Expert systems, for example, may reduce the power of certain professional groups because their knowledge will become public domain (see Ryan [34]). On the other hand, individuals who control AI application teams may gain considerable prestige, knowledge, power, and status. In contrast with a regular CBIS, the issues at stake in MSS could be much more important and visible, because complex decision situations and upper management may be involved. An intelligent information system may control some of the major decisions in an organization, including long-range strategic ones.

Special Units

Another change in organizational structure is the possibility of creating a DSS department, management support department, and/or AI department. Such a department (or a unit) can be an extension of the information center, can replace a management science unit, or can be a completely new entity.

DSS departments exist in several large corporations. For example, Security Pacific Corp. Bank has a 15-person DSS department in its financial services division. Mead has a corporate DSS applications department at the same level as the IS department. Many companies have a small DSS unit. Several large corporations have already created AI departments. For example, FMC Corp. created one of the earliest and largest AI departments (Box 20.3); Boeing Co. operates a large AI department. In both cases, the departments are involved in extensive training in addition to research, consulting, and application activities. For details on how several corporations structure their AI units see Turban [42].

20.4 Personnel Management Issues

One of the major impacts of MSS, and especially of ES, is on the content of many jobs in both private and public organizations. **Job content** is important not only because it is related to organizational structure, but also because it is interrelated with employee satisfaction, compensation, status, and productivity. The

Box 20.3: Artificial Intelligence at FMC Corp.

FMC Corp. (Santa Clara, Calif.) has made a major commitment to AI. In the mid-1980s the company built a 90-person AI center. Major applications started in the defense area and moved to the industrial machinery (manufacturing and maintenance) area. Initial expert systems were used in oil pumping operations, automotive engine design, and tool design. Applications now range from the operations of chemical plants to machinery manufacturing. Robotics and machine vision technology are being transferred from defense to the manufacturing plants.

To build up the necessary personnel, the company has designed an in-house training program equivalent to a master of science program for the AI specialists. With a rich application environment and strong corporate commitment, the company has become an industrial center of excellence in applied AI.

topics discussed next are other areas in personnel management that could be impacted by MSS.

Role of Employees and Managers

MSS projects could cause major changes in the roles that managers and employees play. For example, many experts in organizations will stop providing routine advice; instead, they will conduct more research and development. The routine advice will be provided online, or by lower skill employees that are supported by ES. At Security Pacific Bank, for example, junior financial analysts at low levels perform some tasks previously done by higher-level employees. Thus, many role definitions will be changed. New jobs such as knowledge engineers will also be created.

On the other hand, some jobs will disappear altogether. For example, an ES that can advise people about what immunizations are required when traveling abroad could eliminate the position of the person who currently gives out this information. Similarly so-called help desk ES have eliminated jobs of employees who provided routine information.

The support staff for top management will generally consist of *information specialists* (e.g., employees of the AI center), whereas today's typical manager has mainly specialists in functional areas (e.g., finance, law, accounting). The need for functional specialization will decrease mainly as a result of the introduction of ES. An interesting change could occur in the jobs of experts who are supported by ES (see Box 20.4). For further discussion on changes in roles and responsibilities see Sviokla [38].

Box 20.4: Change in the Experts' Jobs— The XCON Experience

Before the expert system XCON was available, even experts had to do manual checking, undertake tedious jobs, and handle repetitive, boring tasks. They, too, made mistakes that had to be corrected, and their jobs were given low status.

After XCON became available, the experts' jobs changed. Here is what the experts do:

- They check what XCON does.
- They do the 2 percent that XCON cannot do.
- They update XCON's knowledge base with new information.

Now the experts are considered custodians of XCON's pool of configuration knowledge, and they are accorded high status.

Role Ambiguity and Conflict

Changes in the job content will result in opportunities for promotion and employee development. But these changes could create problems of role conflict and **role ambiguity,** especially in the short run. In addition, there may be considerable resistance to changes in roles, primarily on the part of managers who favor a noncomputerized information system.

Employee Career Ladders

The increased use of MSS in organizations could have a significant and somewhat unexpected impact on career ladders. Today, many highly skilled professionals have developed their abilities through years of experience. This experience is gained by holding a series of positions that expose the person to progressively more difficult and complex situations. The use of MSS and especially ES may "block out" a portion of this learning curve. However, several questions remain unaddressed: How will high-level human expertise be acquired with minimal experience in lower-level tasks? What will be the effect on compensation at all levels of employment? How will human resource development programs be structured? What career plans will be offered to employees?

Changes in Supervision

The fact that an employee's work is performed online and stored electronically introduces the possibility for greater electronic supervision, especially when enhanced by AI technologies. For professional employees whose work is often measured by completion of projects, "remote supervision" implies greater emphasis on completed work and less on personal contacts. This emphasis is especially true if employees work in geographically dispersed locations away from their supervisors. In general, the supervisory process may become more formalized, with greater reliance on procedures and measurable outputs than on informal processes.

Other Considerations

Several other personnel-related issues could surface as a result of using MSS. For example, what will be the impact of MSS on job qualifications, on training requirements, and on worker satisfaction? How can jobs involving the use of MSS tools be designed so they present an acceptable level of challenge to users? How might MSS be used to personalize or enrich jobs? What can be done to make sure that the introduction of MSS does not demean jobs or have other negative impacts from the workers' point of view? What principles should be used to allocate functions to people and machines, especially those functions that can be performed equally well by either one? Should cost or efficiency be the sole or major criterion for such allocation? All these and even more issues could be encountered in any system implementation and should be the subject for research by the academic and business communities.

20.5   Individuals

MSS systems may affect individuals in various ways. What is a benefit to one individual may be a curse to another. What is an added stress today can be a relief tomorrow. Some of the areas where MSS systems may affect individuals, their perceptions and behaviors, are described next.

Job Satisfaction

Although many jobs may become substantially more "enriched" with MSS, other jobs may become more routine and less satisfying. For example, Argyris [2] predicted that computer-based information systems would reduce managerial discretion in decision making and thus create dissatisfied managers.

Inflexibility and Dehumanization

A frequent criticism of traditional data processing systems is their negative effect on people's individuality. Such systems are criticized as being impersonal: they dehumanize and depersonalize activities that have been computerized, because they reduce or eliminate the human element that was present in the noncomputerized systems. Many people feel a loss of identity; they feel like "just another number."

One of the major objectives of MSS is to create *flexible* systems that will allow individuals to input their opinions and knowledge. MSS should be people oriented and user-friendly to make them more easily accepted.

Cooperation of Experts

Human experts who are about to give their knowledge to an ES may have reservations. Consider these examples of thoughts that may enter an expert's mind:

- "The computer may replace me."
- "The computer may make me less important."
- "Why should I tell the computer my secrets? What will I gain?"
- "The computer may find out that I am not as great an expert as people think."

This kind of thinking may cause the expert not to cooperate, or even to give incorrect knowledge to the computer. To deal with such situations, management should motivate (and possibly compensate) experts.

Psychological Impacts

The widespread use of home terminals, for instance, threatens to have an even more isolating influence than television. If people are encouraged to work and shop from their living rooms, some unfortunate psychological effects such as stress and loneliness could develop.

20.6   Productivity and Competitiveness

The major benefits of MSS, which can result in a competitive advantage, are:

- *Increased productivity:* Productivity is increased when workers can accomplish their tasks faster or with fewer interruptions (e.g., see Liebowitz [21] and Sviokla [38]).
- *Increase in quality:* Quality is increased by reduction of errors, by production of more consistent products and services, and by improvements in inspection and quality control (all at a reasonable cost).
- *Cost reduction:* Producing a product or providing a service at a lower cost than competitors (yet with the same quality) provides a competitive edge.
- *Timely production:* Producing products (and providing services) whenever needed results in a competitive advantage.
- *Fast training of employees:* The costs of training can be very high, especially if turnover is high or in cases of rapid technical changes. Training time (and cost) can be reduced drastically with AI (e.g., see Senker [36]).
- *Increased production (service) capacity:* Because they allow improved planning, ES can increase production or service capacity.
- *Unique services:* Voice technology, for example, enables banks and telephone companies to offer new and unique services.

In addition to these benefits, MSS can enhance other computer systems that contribute to increased productivity and competitiveness. For an overview on information technology as a competitive weapon see Wysocki and Young [48]. For a discussion of ES competitiveness see Beerel [3] and Monger [23].

20.7   Decision Making and the Manager's Job

Computer-based information systems have had an impact on the manager's job for about two decades. However, this impact was felt mainly at the lower- and middle-managerial levels. Now MSS could have an impact on the top manager's job as well.

The most important task of managers is making decisions. MSS technologies can change the manner in which many decisions are being made and consequently change the managers' jobs. The impacts of MSS on decision making can be many; the most probable areas are listed here:

- Automation of routine decisions
- Less expertise (experience) required for many decisions
- Faster-made decisions
- Less reliance on experts (staff) to provide support to top executives
- Power redistribution among managers
- Support to complex decisions, making them faster and of better quality.

Many managers have reported that the computer has finally given them time to "get out of the office and into the field." (EIS can save an hour a day for every user.) They also have found that they can spend more time on planning activities instead of "putting out fires." Another aspect of the management challenge lies in the ability of MSS to *support* the decision process in general and strategic planning and control decisions in particular. MSS could change the decision-making process and even decision-making styles. For example, information gathering for decision making will be much quicker. AI technologies are being used now to improve environmental scanning of information (e.g., see Elofson and Konsynski [10]). As a result, managers may change their approach to problem solving. Research indicates (e.g., see Mintzberg [22]) that most managers currently work on a large number of problems simultaneously, moving from one to another as they wait for more information on their current problem or until some external event "interrupts" them. MSS tend to reduce the time necessary to complete any step in the decision-making process. Therefore, managers will work on fewer tasks during the day but complete more of them. The reduction of startup time associated with moving from task to task could be the most important source of increased managerial productivity.

Another possible impact on the manager's job could be a change in leadership requirements. What are generally considered to be good qualities of leadership may be significantly altered with the use of MSS. For example, when face-to-face communication is replaced by electronic mail and computerized conferencing, leadership qualities attributed to physical appearance could be less important.

Even if managers' jobs do not change dramatically, the methods that managers use to do their jobs will. For example, an increasing number of CEOs no longer use intermediaries; instead, they work directly with computers. Once voice understanding is economically feasible, we may see a real revolution in the manner in which computers are used by managers.

20.8 Institutional—Information Bases

The availability of MSS implies the possible development of very large and complex data and information bases that require trained expertise to use and maintain. (For a detailed discussion see Holsapple and Whinston [14].) In other words, *organizational intelligence* will become a critical issue.

Institutional information bases are maintained by written documentation and experts in methods of accessing and interpreting information. The information that makes up these data and knowledge bases is accumulating at an ever-increasing rate. The ability of humans to work with this information base is becoming strained. In many cases, such ability is limited to a few individuals who have a tremendous amount of training and experience. The use of AI could greatly facilitate both the maintenance and use of institutional information bases.

As system integration continues to expand in organizations, the volume of accessible data and knowledge will grow considerably. Powerful filtering and reporting systems that can be used by nonprogrammers will be a necessity. Problem determination and analysis will be much faster than what is now available with the traditional MIS approach. Some questions that need to be addressed include the following:

- How will the availability of knowledge affect strategic plans?
- How will the communication stream be affected? Will results of decisions be as readily communicated to peers, subordinates, and superiors by managers, who may assume that these people *have* and *take advantage* of the access to information bases?
- How will managers be trained to make *effective* use of these new tools?
- What needs to be done to assess the current competency of managers and to match the tools of these competencies?

20.9 Issues of Legality, Privacy, and Ethics

Legality

The introduction of MSS, and especially ES, may compound a host of legal issues already relevant to computer systems. The expensive, prolonged litigation of IBM's antitrust case and the restructuring of AT&T are two prominent examples. Questions concerning liability for the actions of intelligent machines are just beginning to be considered. The issue of a computer as a form of unfair competition in business has already been raised in a recent dispute over the practices of airline reservation systems.

In addition to resolving disputes over the unexpected and possibly damaging results of some MSS systems, other complex issues may surface. For example, who is liable if an enterprise finds itself bankrupt as a result of using the advice of ES? Will the enterprise itself be held responsible for not testing such systems adequately before entrusting them with sensitive issues? Will auditing and accounting firms, which are just beginning to use AI, share the liability for failing to apply adequate auditing tests? Will the manufacturers of such systems be jointly liable? Consider these specific issues that may be encountered:

- What is the value of an expert opinion in court when the expert is a computer?
- Who is liable for wrong advice (or information) provided by an ES? For example, what happens if a physician accepts an incorrect diagnosis made by a computer and performs an act that results in the death of a patient?
- What happens if a manager enters an incorrect judgment value into an MSS and the result is damage or a disaster?
- Who owns the knowledge in a knowledge base?
- Should royalties be paid to experts, and if so how much?
- Can management force experts to contribute their expertise?

For a discussion of these and other issues consult Mykytyn et al. [24] and Tuthill [44].

Privacy

The issue of privacy, which is important to other computer-based information systems as well, will surface in MSS and become even more difficult to control because there will be knowledge bases in addition to corporate databases.

Modern computer systems can economically collect, store, integrate, interchange, and retrieve information and knowledge. This ability can affect every individual's right to privacy. Confidential information on individuals contained in information bases could be misused and result in invasion of privacy and other injustices.

The use of AI technologies in the administration and enforcement of laws and regulations may increase public concern regarding privacy of information. These fears, generated by the perceived abilities of AI, whether real or not, will have to be addressed at the outset of almost any AI development efforts.

Ethics

Ethical issues in MSS are similar to those within other information systems. Representative issues that could be of interest in MSS implementations are:

- Computer abuse and misuse
- Electronic surveillance
- Software piracy
- Invasion of individuals' privacy
- Use of proprietary databases
- Exposure of employees to unsafe environments related to computers
- Computer accessibility for workers with disabilities
- Accuracy
- Accessibility to information
- Liability of programmers and other IS employees
- Use of corporate computers for private purposes.

In the area of MSS one may examine the following issue:

- How much decision making to delegate to computers (see Exercise 4, end of this chapter).

The following are some references related to ethical issues:

1. Dejoie, R. et al. *Ethical Issues in Information Systems*, Boston, MA: Boyd and Fraser, 1991.
2. Lachat, M. R. "Artificial Intelligence and Ethics: An Exercise in the Moral Imagination." *AI Magazine*, Vol. 7, No. 2 (1986).
3. McFarland, M. C. "Ethics and the Safety of Computer Systems." *Computer*, (February 1991).

4. Ottensmeyer, E. J. and Heroux, M. A. "Ethics, Public Policy, and Managing Advanced Technologies: The Case of Electronic Surveillance." *Journal of Business Ethics*, vol. 10 (1991): 519–526.

5. Straub, D. W., Jr., and Collins, R. W. "Key Information Liability Issues Facing Managers: Software Privacy, Proprietary Database and Individual Rights to Privacy." *MIS Quarterly* (June, 1990): 143–154.

20.10   The Information Center

One of the most interesting changes in organizational structure related to computer technology is the introduction of the **information center** (IC).* The concept of the IC was conceived (by IBM, Canada, see Hammond [13]) as a response to the increased number of end-user requests for new computer applications. This demand created a huge backlog of work in the DP department,** and users had to wait several years to get their systems built.

Information centers are groups of employees specially trained in the use of MSS building tools (such as DBMS, spreadsheet technology, and ES shells) and applications software. The IC's primary task is to provide fast turnaround on users' requests for information, data analyses, special reports, and other one-time information needs. Some people regard IC as the DSS department.

Purposes and Activities

The three main functions of an IC are (1) to provide assistance to end-users in dealing with computing problems, (2) to provide general technical assistance, and (3) to provide general support services. Each function should fulfill the following requirements (per Jacobson, H., and Cardullo, J., "Information Centers: Boon or Bane," *Management Technology*, September 1983):

End-user computing:
- Training and education
- Assisting in software (application) development
- Developing prototype programs
- Establishing configuration for standardization
- Debugging assistance
- Identifying networking requirements
- Consulting with the user to determine if a particular application is appropriate for end-user development
- Providing a formal means for users' communication with management and with the traditional data processing staff

---

*Other names for a similar organizational unit are information resource center and users' service center.

**The name *Data Processing* (DP) *department* is still used by many organizations. However, this name is being slowly replaced by new names such as *Information Systems* (IS) *department*.

- Cooperating with database administrators to improve shared-data resources
- Generating a catalog or library of existing applications for future use
- Managing software documentation for specific applications (e.g., for specific DSS).

Technical assistance:
- Provide guidance in the selection of hardware and software
- Help in the selection and evaluation of application packages, DSS generators, ES shells, and other building tools
- Software installation and updates
- Assistance in using query and report languages and/or packages
- Hardware installation and use
- Communication devices, installation, and use
- Establishing database (or file) backup, recovery, and archive guidelines.

General support services:
- Providing clearinghouse functions for receiving and disseminating information on relevant personal computing issues
- Establishing a "hotline" for interrupt-driven user requests for information on software, hardware, or application systems
- Chairing user group meetings on a regular and ad hoc basis.

Staffing

Information centers should be staffed by people with the following attributes:

- Business knowledge (usually MBAs)
- Analytical skills
- Current knowledge of software development packages
- Current basic hardware knowledge
- Knowledge of where to go to find needed information
- Patience and enthusiasm
- Good interpersonal communication skills
- Programming skills (especially in 4GLs)
- Drive and motivation to complete programs without direct supervision
- End-user and service orientation.

Problem Areas

The purposes and activities of the IC as described above are a utopian vision: Executives get the information they need *when* they need it; the data processing department is *freed* from mundane programming to work on important projects. As for other managers and professionals in an organization, there is a wealth of information that can be easily tapped for the benefit of the corporation. All this is coordinated at the IC, where users and IC personnel work together to meet everyone's needs. Reality, however, may be quite different. Although many tend to agree that the IC is the best way to control and capitalize on the sweep of new information technology, it is evident that many organizations have also found that the path to the utopian vision is a rocky one. The following are some potential problem areas in IC operations:

- Opposition comes from the IS department (power struggle and ego problems).
- Users do not have enough computer knowledge, yet they set up their own IC. This may result in low-quality service.
- Corporate management anticipates that the IC will be an expensive new unit with its hardware and software. Because it is difficult to conduct a cost-benefit analysis of an IC, management may be reluctant to establish one.
- There may be resistance from noncomputer-oriented users who fear that the IC will help computer-oriented users.
- Security problems (e.g., more company data in more hands) may occur.
- The struggle regarding to whom the IC should report and who should control it may occur.
- Senior management support may be lacking.
- Staffing the IC with individuals who do not possess the specified attributes discussed earlier may be a problem.
- Potential backlog for IC-developed or assisted applications can occur.
- Proliferation of PCs may have resulted in "uncontrolled" purchases, which may mean supporting multiple vendors' products and incompatibility of equipment.
- There can be redundancy of effort if IC operations are not coordinated (several IC-like groups may emerge and duplicate one another's efforts).

Despite the problem areas, the information center is becoming an extremely important support for user-developed DSS. See Box 20.5.

The Roles of the Information Systems (IS) Department

One of the major purposes of end-user computing is to ease the pressure on the IS department. And indeed, very few of the early DSS were constructed by the IS department. Furthermore, the organization's IS group was initially seen, by DSS builders, as the "enemy." With the introduction of the information center's concepts, it seemed that the role of the IS department in constructing MSS would diminish. However, it is recognized that constructing MSS can provide status and power to the builders, and therefore IS departments may struggle to participate and even control such development projects. Therefore, it is not surprising that Huff et al. [16] found that the IS department had the main development responsibility in 23.7 percent of 133 DSS.

Box 20.5: The Chesebrough-Pond's Case

A typical example of an information center that works with DSS extensively is Chesebrough-Pond's, Inc., a large, diversified producer of consumer goods (food, apparel, health/beauty).

Chesebrough-Pond's (Trumbull, CT) started an information center in 1981 after conducting a year-long study to determine how to decrease both the high cost of computerized (time-sharing) systems and the long development backlog. Then a users' survey was conducted to determine needs and to set up and prioritize decision analysis criteria.

The initial software selected was

- EXPRESS (as a comprehensive DSS generator)
- FOCUS (for data management)
- FCS/EPS (for financial planning and modeling).

The operating environment was IBM's VM/CMS. The selection of software was based primarily on the following criteria: "what-if" capability, reporting capability, ease of use, and the reputation of the vendor. Vendors were selected because they had large user bases (the company decided not to "blaze trails" with an untested vendor). The selectors looked at technical assistance and stable vendorship.

The info center was staffed with analytically skilled people with MBA-type backgrounds, good communication skills, service orientation, self-motivation, and experience. The company decided *not* to use people out of the MIS department. ("These people often are not oriented to the end-user environment.") The center not only responded to people but also played a proactive role (e.g., by showing management the progress of various systems through prototyping and by searching for opportunities for DSS).

(*Source:* Condensed from *Computerworld*, October 25, 1982.)

20.11   Research and Development: The Fifth-generation Project

The Fifth-generation Project was announced in 1982 by the Japanese government. The Japanese have marshaled an impressive array of resources in an attempt to change their image from implementors of technology to developers and innovators (see Box 20.6). By the time it is complete, the Fifth-generation Project may require more than $1 billion in a typical Japanese combination of public and private funding.

Box 20.6: The Japanese—Only Implementors of Others' Innovations?

The United States traditionally has been the greatest source of techno-logical innovation in the world. More recently, the Japanese have founded their own "tradition" in what has been called their "economic miracle"; dur-ing the years since World War II, they have become the acknowledged leaders at the implementation of technology. The following examples will probably be familiar:

- The automobile was first mass-produced in the United States; but by applying American technology and management techniques in in-novative ways, Japanese automobile manufacturers have made an impact on the American automobile industry that is dramatic and irrevocable.
- It is becoming increasingly difficult to purchase a high-quality stereo, television, or other electronic device that is not manufac-tured in Japan.
- Although handheld calculators and digital watches were invented in the United States, creative Japanese competition has driven nearly every American manufacturer out of those markets.
- The process of electronic miniaturization was created in the United States, first with transistors and then with integrated circuits. Japanese companies are now among the largest producers of chips in the world and may be on the verge of dominating that market.
- The manufacture of cameras and other optical instruments, previ-ously dominated by Germany, is now dominated by Japan.

If these kinds of trends were to continue, you might expect the Japanese to wait until American manufacturers had commercialized AI successfully and developed a wide range of AI products. Then, according to past sce-narios, Japanese companies would develop clever, creative, and inexpen-sive products based on the mature American technology. This time, however, the Japanese have served notice that they are no longer con-tent to create innovative uses for American technology. This time they intend to develop the technology themselves; this time, they plan to make their own discoveries. (*Note:* The Japanese are already using fuzzy-logic-based expert systems in many consumer products.)

Fifth-generation Technology

The ultimate aim of the project is the development of fifth-generation com-puters. To achieve this goal, the Japanese have divided the project into the fol-lowing four parts.

Data Access. MSS programs typically require large amounts of data. The ability to retrieve information as needed is just as important as the ability to store the information in the first place. The Fifth-generation Project has developed a prototype computer, called the Relational Database Machine, that is designed specifically to facilitate the storage and retrieval of information.

Inference. An inference engine is an essential component of a knowledge-based system. The Fifth-generation Project is developing a prototype computer, known as the Personal Sequential Inference Machine, to provide inference capabilities in PROLOG. When ready, the inference machine will be used by researchers as a tool to write programs for other parts of the project.

Ease of Use. The Fifth-generation Project includes research in several areas of AI that investigate ways of making computers easier to use: computer vision, speech understanding, and natural language processing.

Intelligent Programming. Intelligent computer programming tools are being developed to expedite the programming efforts in all phases of the project.

Knowledge Is Power

Why are the Japanese so intent on supplanting the United States by becoming the world leader in computer technology? What is it about intelligent machines that is leading them to devote so many resources to their development? Why is it so important to be first?

Quite simply, the Japanese believe that knowledge, supplied by a new generation of intelligent machines, is poised to become the basis of a new economic order. They believe that the world is evolving toward a postindustrial society in which the wealth of nations will be measured not in terms of gold or oil, but information. The Japanese believe the nation that is first to commercialize AI technology successfully will gain an enormous economic advantage over other nations. First place will not only give that nation an obvious advantage in the computer industry, it will have repercussions throughout a wide range of human affairs.

The United States currently dominates the worldwide processing of information by computers. Because information processing in the United States is a $200 billion industry (annually), it is a dominance that the country can scarcely afford to lose. Gaining the preeminent position in the computer industry might be just the tip of the iceberg for Japan, merely the most obvious of the widespread economic advantages that the Japanese hope the Fifth-generation Project (as well as the Sixth- and the Seventh-generation Projects) will provide them. The successful development, implementation, and proliferation of AI technology (according to Feigenbaum and McCorduck [11]) could render all Japanese products so much better than their competitors', thanks to the degree of knowledge that will be brought to bear on their design and manufacture, that the Japanese will dominate markets in conventional products, too.

20.12 Automation and Employment*

The Industrial Revolution of the eighteenth century saw machines replace muscle power. This was the beginning of automation: the automatic transfer and positioning of work by machines, or the automatic operation and control of a production process by machines. The assembly line operation of automobile manufacturing is a typical example of automation.

The impact of computers on employment and productivity is directly related to the use of computers for achieving automation. There can be no doubt that computers have created new jobs and increased productivity; they have also, however, caused a significant reduction in some types of job opportunities. Computers used for office information processing or for numeric control of machine tools are accomplishing tasks formerly performed by clerks and machinists. Jobs created by computers require different types of skills and education than those jobs eliminated by computers. Therefore, specific individuals will become unemployed unless they are retrained for new positions or new responsibilities.

The productivity of many individual workers has been increased significantly by computerization. The time required to perform certain tasks has been drastically reduced. Increased productivity has led to lower costs and prices, which in turn have increased demand for products and services and, thus, have increased employment. The higher profits caused by increases in productivity also have stimulated more investment in the expansion of production facilities, resulting in further increased employment.

Another point to remember is that the higher standard of living caused by increased productivity generates *more* rather than *less* demand for more types and amounts of goods and services (at least up to a certain limit). "Yesterday's luxuries become today's necessities" is a statement that emphasizes the almost unlimited demand for goods and services our society seems to exhibit. This phenomenon is related to the impact of computers on employment, because a desire to increase the standard of living leads to an expanded demand for goods and services, and results in an increase in employment opportunities.

The computer industry has created a host of new job opportunities for the manufacture, sale, and maintenance of computer hardware, software, and other computer services. Many new jobs (system analysts, knowledge engineers, computer operators) have been created. Additional jobs have been created because the computer makes possible the production of complex industrial and technical goods and services that would otherwise be impossible or uneconomical to produce.

The controversy over the effect of computers on employment will continue as long as activities formerly performed by people are computerized. Unemployment figures are more than statistics; office and factory workers whose jobs

---

*This section is based on O'Brien's work [27].

have been eliminated by computerization are real people with real employment needs. Such people will take little comfort in the fact that computers have many beneficial effects on employment in general. Business firms and other computer-using organizations, labor unions, and government agencies must continue to provide job opportunities for people displaced by computers. This includes transfers to other positions, relocation to other facilities, or training for new responsibilities. Only if society continues to take positive steps to provide jobs for people displaced by computers can we take pride in the increase in employment caused by computer usage. Finally, education, starting at elementary schools and ending at universities, must keep up with technology to prevent massive unemployment.

20.13   AI and Employment

The previous section presented an overview of the issue of computer systems, productivity, and employment. There is very little information on the relationship of MSS to these topics. However, both AI and ES have the potential of significantly affecting the productivity and employment of many types of employees. The material in this section summarizes the position of some of the country's top experts with regard to the potential impact of AI on productivity and unemployment.*

Although the impact of AI may take decades to materialize, there is agreement among researchers that AI in general, and ES in particular, will increase the productivity of **knowledge workers.** Technology will be relatively inexpensive and thus create substantial shifts in jobs and job contents. Researchers disagree about the potential impact of AI technologies on the aggregate employment (or unemployment) level. The two extreme positions are (1) massive unemployment and (2) increased employment (or at worst, no change in the employment level). These positions have been supported by two Nobel prize winners; Wassily Leontief [20], who supports the massive unemployment argument, and Herbert Simon, who takes the other position. Now, let us examine the major arguments of the opposing parties.

Massive Unemployment

Massive unemployment (see Box 20.7) as a result of AI is predicted for the following seven reasons:

1. The need for human labor will be reduced significantly.
2. The skill levels of people performing jobs with the help of AI will be low.
3. AI will affect both blue- and white-collar employees (professionals and managers, too) in all sectors, including service industries and high-

*This discussion is based on Nilsson [26]. For extended discussion see Partridge [31].

Box 20.7: Survey: Computers Cause Joblessness

Unemployment is the greatest concern among a polled population in France, Germany, Great Britain, Norway, Spain, and the United States. And in every one of those countries—except the United States—respondents believed that increased use of computers would worsen the unemployment problem.

The poll further showed Japan as the exception: respondents did *not* believe unemployment was "the greatest concern for yourself and your country today."

The poll, titled "The Impact of Technological Change in the Industrial Democracies," was conducted by Louis Harris International for the Atlantic Institute. The study also indicated a large measure of agreement in all the countries polled that the use of computer data banks would facilitate infringement on personal privacy.

The conclusions that the Atlantic Institute made from the data are "unexpected." According to the Atlantic Institute, France, Britain, Spain, and, to a lesser extent, Italy reflect a high degree of optimism about computer and word processing systems, whereas Japan and Germany seem to generate considerable and widespread negativism about their use. The United States, it feels, is a case apart, with Americans already much more attuned to the perceived advantages of the technologies. The Atlantic Institute for International Affairs, headquartered in Paris, is a private, independent, nongovernment center for research and discussion.

(*Source:* Condensed from *MIS Week*, August 28, 1985.)

technology companies. In the past, service industries and the high-technology sector absorbed employees replaced by computers in other sectors.

4. In the past few years, and especially in 1991, several industries ranging from banking and insurance to computers and automotive have laid off many employees.

5. Industry, government, and services already have a substantial amount of **hidden unemployment;** that is, companies retain many employees who are not needed or fully utilized for humanitarian reasons, union pressures, or government policies.

6. Unemployment levels have grown steadily in the past decade in spite of increased computerization.

7. The per capita amount of goods and services that people can consume is limited and sooner or later may stop growing.

Unemployment is a matter of concern to all of us (see Box 20.7), yet many believe that computerization will increase employment rather than unemployment.

Increased Employment Levels

Increased employment levels are predicted for several reasons:

1. Historically, automation has always resulted in increased employment, by creating new occupations (see Box 20.8).
2. Unemployment is worse in unindustrialized countries.
3. Work, especially the professional and managerial kind, can always be expanded, so there will be work for everyone.
4. The task of converting to automated factories and offices is complex and may take several generations.
5. Many tasks cannot be fully automated (e.g., top management, nursing, marriage counseling, surgery, the performing arts, and the creative arts).
6. Machines and people can be fully employed, each where its comparative advantage is strongest.
7. Real wages may be reduced, however, because people will have income from other sources (assuming that the government will control the distribution of wealth); people will have enough money to spend and thus will help create more jobs.
8. The cost of goods and services will be so low that the demand for them will increase significantly. Automation will never catch up with the increased demand.

This debate about how AI will affect employment raises a few other questions: Is some unemployment really socially desirable? (People could have more leisure time.) Should the government intervene more in the distribution of income and in the determination of the employment level? Can the "invisible hand" in the economy, which has worked so well in the past, continue to be successful in the future? Will AI make most of us idle but wealthy? (Robots will

---

Box 20.8: New or Expanded AI-related Jobs

- AI computer lawyer
- AI headhunter
- AI project manager
- AI hardware architecture specialist
- AI venture capitalist
- AI user training specialist
- Expert system shell developer and vendor
- Industrial robotics supervisor/manager
- Knowledge acquisition and maintenance specialist
- Robotic maintenance engineer.

(*Source:* J. Liebowitz, "Possible Societal Impacts of Artificial Intelligence," *Information Age* [July 1989].)

do the work; people will enjoy life.) Should the issue of income be completely separated from that of employment?

20.14   Training, Retraining, and Education

As indicated earlier, extensive training may be needed to retrain people who lose their jobs to computerization.

People react differently to the need for training according to factors such as their education, time elapsed since previous educational experience, time since previous training, job security, proximity to retirement, ability to ignore competing commitments, age, family status, and income needs. Because of these influences, questions such as the following arise: What kind of employment policies are most conducive to successful training for new technology? If it is in the national interest to foster rapid, well-integrated technical change, should the government finance and assist massive training efforts? What roles should private and public educational institutions play in these efforts? These and other questions are being considered by management, unions, and the government.

Management's Position

The position of management varies from company to company. Some companies (e.g., the auto industry) have instituted extensive retraining programs. In other cases, nothing is being done. Management's position could be influenced by the position taken by unions.

Trade Union's Position

Most unions respond to technological change with opposition or at best with unwilling acceptance. Very few unions welcome technological change (see Rosow [33]). However, studies indicate that union opposition is usually followed by adjustment and accommodation. A union is likely to adapt when satisfactory trade-offs can be made. Union accommodation usually occurs under the following circumstances:

- Union leadership sees that the technological change is inevitable.
- The membership base is notably larger than the group affected by technological changes.
- Management has given detailed consideration to the union's political circumstances and has developed trade-off routes into which union response can be channeled.

Several techniques are commonly used to lessen the impact of unemployment:

- Early warning systems regarding layoffs linked to business planning (at least six months to one year ahead)

- Work force reduction accomplished only by voluntary resignation or early retirement
- Contractually provided special rights to training and retraining, transfer to other jobs or other functions (including relocation), wage retention after bumping or transfer ("red circling"). For example, the federal government grants two-year pay protection.
- Severance pay, supplemental unemployment benefits, and integration with unemployment insurance programs

Government's Position

The federal government has not been active in the area of training and retraining. It considers the problem that of the states, counties, and cities. One of the few government programs that is related to unemployment is the **Job Training Partnership Act** (JTPA). The JTPA supplements the federal Comprehensive Employment and Training Act (CETA). Although primarily targeted at the economically and culturally disadvantaged, the JTPA includes provisions (Title III) for retraining displaced workers. In essence, the act provides grants to the states, which, in cooperation with the private sector, set up and run local training programs. A main goal of the JTPA is to move retraining and job creation into the private sector, in contrast to CETA, which focused on public-sector support and positions. The JTPA represents the first time that the federal government, through national legislation, has identified dislocated workers as a pervasive problem.

20.15   Other Societal Impacts

Several other positive and negative social implications of MSS and especially AI systems could be far-reaching. (For an overview see Partridge [31].) MSS already have had many direct beneficial effects on society when they have been used for complicated human and social problems such as medical diagnosis, computer-assisted instruction, government program planning, environmental quality control, and law enforcement. Problems in these areas could not have been solved economically (or solved at all) by other types of computer systems. Specific examples of *potential* impact are described next.

Work in Hazardous Environment. Expert systems, especially when combined with sensors and robots, can reduce or even eliminate the need for a human presence in dangerous or uncomfortable environments (e.g., see Oxman's work on cleaning chemical spills [29]).

Opportunities for the Disabled. The integration of some AI technologies (speech recognition, vision recognition) into a CBIS could create new employment opportunities for disabled people. For example, those who cannot type would be able to use a voice-operated typewriter, and those who cannot travel could work at home. Boeing Co. is developing several ES that help disabled employees perform useful tasks.

Changing Role of Women. MSS could change the "traditional" role of women at the workplace. For example, the opportunity to work at home and the need for less travel (e.g., due to teleconferencing) could help women with young children assume more responsible (and demanding) managerial positions in organizations.

Working at Home (Telecommuting). Another trend gaining momentum is working at home. This phenomenon, called **cottage industry** in the past, is now referred to as **telecommuting.** Employees work at home on a computer or a terminal linked to their place of employment. The first telecommuters to work at home were typists and bookkeepers, but now a growing number of professionals do a significant part of their work at home (see Newman [25], Cross and Raizman [7], and O'Leary [28]). The advantages of telecommuting are more flexible hours, less time spent traveling, less need for office and parking space, and the ability of the housebound to hold a job. As usual, there are some disadvantages: difficulties in supervising work, lack of human interaction, and increased isolation. (For a discussion of these and other negative factors see [45].)

Improvements in Health. Several early expert systems were designed to improve the delivery of health care (e.g., MYCIN). Since that time we have seen a growing role for AI technologies in supporting various tasks carried out by physicians and other health-care workers. Of special interest are expert systems that support diagnosis of diseases and the use of machine vision in radiology.

Aids for the Consumer. Several AI products are in place, and many more will be developed, to help the layperson perform skilled or not so desirable tasks. For example, Taxcut is an ES that can help in tax preparation; Willmaster is an ES that helps a layperson draft a simple will; and Wines on Disk advises the consumer on how to select wines. Intelligent robots will clean the house and mow the lawn. These and many other improvements will contribute to the quality of life.

Quality of Life. On a broader scale, MSS have implications for the **quality of life** in general (see Krout et al. [19]). Improved organizational efficiency may result in more leisure time. The workplace can be expanded from the traditional nine to five at a central location to twenty-four hours a day at *any* location. This expansion provides flexibility that can significantly improve the quality of leisure time, even if the total amount of leisure time is not increased.

Negative Effects

Introduction of MSS technologies may be accompanied by some negative effects. In addition to unemployment and the creation of large economic gaps among people, MSS technologies may result in other negative situations, some of which are common to other computer systems.

Computer Crime. Fraud and embezzlement by "electronic criminals" is increasing. The American Bar Association estimates that losses from theft of tangible and intangible assets (including software), destruction of data, embezzlement of funds, and fraud at as much as $45 billion annually [1]. With ES, there is a possibility of deliberately providing bad advice (e.g., to advise employees to opt for early retirement in cases in which they really should stay on). On the other hand, ES can be used to prevent computer crimes. For a discussion, see Tener [40].

Too Much Power. Distributed MSS may allow greater centralization in decision making and control of an organization. This may give some individuals or governmental agencies too much power over other people. Power may be used in an unethical manner; see Dejoie et al. [8].

Blaming the Computer Phenomenon. Many people tend to blame the computer in order to cover up human errors or wrongdoing. You may hear "but the expert system told us to do it" to justify some action that otherwise would be unjustifiable.

20.16 Managerial Implications and Social Responsibilities

The potential societal as well as organizational impacts of MSS discussed in this chapter raise the issue of what management can do about all the changes. How do we anticipate the broad societal effects of MSS and the things it makes possible? What can we do to ensure that people's attitudes toward MSS are well founded and that their expectations about what these systems can and cannot do are accurate? How do we determine the potential positive and negative effects of MSS before they become realities?

Social Responsibility. Organizations need to be motivated to utilize MSS to improve the quality of life in general. They should design their MSS to minimize negative working conditions. This challenge relates not only to companies that produce MSS hardware and software, but also to companies that use these technologies. Properly designed systems can be implemented and used in ways that are either positive or negative.

Public Pressure. Increased exposure to the concepts and actual use of MSS will bring some pressure on public agencies and corporations to employ the latest capabilities for solving social problems. At the same time, conflicting public pressures may rise to suppress the use of MSS because of concerns about privacy and "big brother" government.

Computer and Staff Resources. Obvious implications of the introduction of MSS involve the increased need for computer resources and people with computer skills. MSS may not be the dominant factor in the expected future growth of computer resources, but it will be a significant one. Depending on the level of involvement in MSS, significant impacts could be expected on the recruitment of personnel and training.

Planning. Management must be ready for all the potential impacts of MSS—especially that of ES—and AI. They may come faster than most of us think. Managers should plan the introduction of these emerging technologies after analyzing their potential impacts (see Weitz [46]). Smart machines can change our world (see Zuboff [49]); let's be ready to make the best of them.

Chapter Highlights

- MSS can affect organizations in many ways, either as stand-alone systems and/or integrated with other computer-based information systems.
- Flatter organizational hierarchies are expected, but the ratio of staff to line workers may decrease.
- The impact of MSS on the degree of centralization of power and authority is inconclusive. Distributed MSS may increase decentralization.
- MSS could cause a power redistribution. Advisory professionals may be the losers as power shifts to administrators and managers.
- Special AI units and departments are likely to appear in many organizations.
- Many jobs will require fewer skills when supported by MSS.
- The job of the surviving expert will become more important as it becomes one of custodian of the expert system and the knowledge base.
- Expertise will be much easier to acquire (shorter time).
- MSS could reduce the need for supervision by providing more guidelines to employees through electronic means.
- The impact of MSS on individuals is unclear; it can be either positive or negative.
- Organizational data and knowledge bases will be critical issues as MSS becomes more available.
- Serious legal issues may develop with the introduction of AI; liability and privacy are the dominant problem areas.
- In one view, AI will cause massive unemployment because of increased productivity, reduced required skill levels, and impacts on all sectors of the economy.
- In another view, AI will increase employment levels because automation makes products and services more affordable and so demand increases, and the process of disseminating automation is slow enough to allow the economy to adjust to AI technologies.

■ Training and retraining for new technologies are important concerns and should be supported by organizations and governments.
■ Many positive social implications can be expected from MSS. They range from providing opportunities to the handicapped to reducing the exposure of people to hazardous situations.
■ Quality of life, both of work and at home, is likely to improve as a result of MSS.
■ Managers need to plan for the MSS of the future so they are ready to make the best of them.

Key Words

cottage industry	Job Training	role ambiguity
hidden unemployment	Partnership Act	span of control
information center	knowledge workers	telecommuting
job content	quality of life	

Questions for Review

1. Explain why organizations might have fewer managerial layers (or levels) because of MSS. Give at least two reasons.
2. Why might the ratio of staff to line workers decrease in the future?
3. How can MSS increase the trend toward decentralization?
4. Explain the impact of microcomputers on the degree of organizational decentralization.
5. List some of the major forces that created user-oriented computing.
6. Describe the potential power shift in organizations when expert systems are used.
7. Describe some potential changes in jobs and job descriptions in organizations that plan to use MSS extensively.
8. What are some of the issues related to human-computer interactions?
9. List some of the reasons why an expert may not be able or willing to contribute his or her expertise to an ES.
10. Why will managers in the future work on fewer problems simultaneously?
11. List the major ethical issues related to MSS.
12. Describe some of the legal implications of ES.
13. List three reasons why AI could result in massive unemployment.
14. Give three arguments to counter the arguments in the previous question.
15. What actions can management take to reduce the impact of employee replacement by a computer?
16. What is the Job Training Partnership Act?
17. List some potential social benefits of MSS.
18. Why could work done at home be increased through AI?
19. How can telecommuting improve the quality of life?
20. List some possible negative effects of MSS technologies.

21. Could MSS provide more managerial opportunities for the handicapped and minorities? Why or why not?

Questions for Discussion

1. Some say MSS in general and ES in particular dehumanize managerial activities and others say they don't. Discuss arguments for both points of view.
2. Explain why you agree or disagree with the following statement: technologies will increase organizational productivity.
3. Describe the manager of the future in a workplace that uses MSS extensively.
4. Should top managers who use ES instead of a human assistant be paid more or less for their job? Why?
5. How can an ES increase the span of control of a manager?
6. The following excerpt was published in the November 1974 issue of *Infosystems:*

   I've seen the ablest executives insist on increased productivity by a plant manager, lean on accounting for improved performance, and lay it on purchasing in no uncertain terms to cut its staff. But when these same executives turn to EDP they stumble to an uncertain halt, baffled by the blizzard of computer jargon. They accept the presumed sophistication and differences that are said to make EDP activities somehow immune from normal management demands. They are stopped by all this nonsense, uncertainty about what's reasonable to expect, and what they can insist upon. They become confused and then retreat, uttering about how to get a handle on this blasted situation.

   Discuss how MSS technologies can change such a situation.
7. The Department of Transportation in a large metropolitan area has an expert system that advises an investigator about whether to open an investigation on a reported car accident. (This system, which includes 300 rules, was developed by Dr. Nagy at George Washington University.) Discuss the following questions:
   a. Should the people involved in an accident be informed that a machine decides the future of an investigation?
   b. What are some of the potential legal implications?
   c. In general, what do you think of such a system?
8. Diagnosing infections and prescribing pharmaceuticals are weak points of many practicing physicians (according to Dr. Shortliffe, one of the developers of MYCIN). It seems, therefore, that society would be well served if MYCIN (and other expert systems) were used extensively. But few physicians use MYCIN. Discuss these questions:
   a. Why do you think MYCIN is little used by physicians?
   b. Assume that you are a hospital administrator whose physicians are salaried and report to you. What would you do to influence and persuade these physicians to use MYCIN?
   c. If the potential benefits to society are so great, can society do something that will increase the use of MYCIN by doctors?

Exercises

1. Write a short essay that describes the major similarities and differences between the Industrial Revolution and the Information Revolution.
2. Read the article "The Molting of America" by J. Cook in *Forbes*, November 22, 1982. Relate the development of AI to the future of America as projected in this article. Specifically, consider the national benefits of AI.
3. Debate the following issues:
   a. Are we relying too much on computers?
   b. Are we becoming too dependent on intelligent computers that are doing all the thinking?
   c. Many jobs will require fewer skills when supported by AI. Debate the positive and negative implications of such an impact.
   d. Telecommuting is liked by many, but others think that it is undesirable and unprofitable. Present the positions of both sides.
   e. The skill requirements for many jobs performed with AI support will be reduced. For example, a technician will be able to do the job of an engineer. Should we pay the technician more than he or she is making today, the same, or less? (Refer to Senker [36].)
4. Several hospitals are considering the introduction of an "intelligent bedside assistant" that will provide a patient records database for diagnosis and prognosis to physicians and staff. The system will provide any information required from the patients' medical records, as well as determine diagnosis, based on symptoms, and prescribe medications and other treatments. The system includes an expert system as well as a DSS.

   You are a hospital administrator and you are very excited about the benefits for the patients. However, when you called a staff meeting, the following questions were raised: "What if the system malfunctions? What if there is an undetected error in the program or the rules?" The system once implemented will take full responsibility for patient care since physicians will rely on it. A loss of data or error in the program may result in disaster. For example, suppose there is a bug in the database program and as a result a critical piece of information is missing from the patient's record. The physician who relies on the system could prescribe a drug that is based on incomplete data. The consequence of this mistake may be life threatening. Another possibility is that some of the rules in the knowledge base are not accurate for all patients.

   Would you implement such a system or not?

References and Bibliography

1. American Bar Association Computer Crime Task Force, White Collar Crime Committee, Criminal Justice Section. *Report on Computer Crime.* Washington, DC: American Bar Association, 1984.

2. Argyris, C. "Management Information Systems: The Challenge to Rationality and Emotionality." *Management Science* (February 1971).

3. Beerel, A. C. *Expert Systems: Strategic Implications and Applications.* New York: Ellis Horwood/John Wiley & Sons, 1987.

4. Benjamin, R. I., and M. S. Scott-Morton. "Information Technology Integration and Organizational Change." *Interfaces* (May-June 1988).

5. Berry, D., and A. Hart. *Expert Systems: Human Issues.* Cambridge, MA: MIT Press, 1990.

6. Buckland, M. K. "Information Handling, Organizational Structure, and Power." *Journal of American Society of Information Science* (September 1989).

7. Cross, T. B., and M. Raizman. *Telecommuting: The Future Technology at Work.* Homewood, IL: Dow-Jones/Irwin, 1986.

8. Dejoie, R. M., et al. *Ethical Issues in Information Systems.* Cincinnati: Boyd & Fraser Publishing, 1991.

9. Doctor, R. D., "Information Technology and Social Equity Confronting the Revolution." *Journal of the American Society for Information* (April 1991).

10. Elofson, G. S., and B. R. Konsynski. "Supporting Knowledge Sharing in Environment Scanning." In *Proceedings of the Twenty-Third Annual Hawaii International Conference on System Sciences,* Los Alamitos, CA: IEEE Computer Society Press, January 1990.

11. Feigenbaum, E. A., and E. P. McCorduck. *The Fifth Generation Computer.* Reading, MA: Addison-Wesley, 1983.

12. Gill, K. S. *Artificial Intelligence and Society.* New York: John Wiley & Sons, 1986.

13. Hammond, L. W. "Management Consideration for an Information Center." *IBM System Journal,* Vol. 21, No. 2 (1982).

14. Holsapple, C. W., and A. B. Whinston. *Business Expert Systems.* Homewood, IL: Richard D. Irwin, 1987.

15. Huber, G. P. "A Theory of the Effects of Advanced Information Technologies on Organizational Design, Intelligence, and Decision Making." *Academy of Management Review* 15 (no. 1, 1990).

16. Huff, S. L., et al. "An Empirical Study of Decision Support Systems." *INFOR* (February 1984).

17. Katz, D., and R. L. Kahn. *The Social Psychology of Organizations,* 4th ed. New York: John Wiley & Sons, 1986.

18. Keyes, J. "Expert Help Desks: Expert Help for the 90's." *AI Expert* (September 1990).

19. Krout, R., et al. "Computerization, Productivity and Quality of Work Life." *Communications of ACM* (February 1989).

20. Leontief, W. *The Future Impact of Automation on Workers.* Oxford: Oxford Univ. Press, 1986.

21. Liebowitz, J. "Possible Societal Impacts of Artificial Intelligence." *Information Age* (July 1989).

22. Mintzberg, H. *The Nature of Managerial Work.* New York: Harper & Row, 1973.

23. Monger, R. F. "AI Applications: What's Their Competitive Potential?" *Journal of Information Systems Management* (Summer 1988).
24. Mykytyn, K., et al. "Expert Systems: A Question of Liability?" *MIS Quarterly* (March 1990).
25. Newman, S. "Telecommuters Bring the Office Home." *Management Review* (December 1989).
26. Nilsson, N. I. "Artificial Intelligence: Employment and Income." *AI Magazine* (Summer 1984).
27. O'Brien, J. A. *Computers in Business Management*, 6th ed. Homewood, IL: Richard D. Irwin, 1991.
28. O'Leary, M. "Home Sweet Office (Telecommuting)." *CIO* (July 1991).
29. Oxman, S. W. "Reporting Chemical Spills: An Expert Solution." *AI Expert* (May 1991).
30. Paradice, D. "Ethical Decision-Making Process of Information Systems Workers." *Journal of Business Ethics*, Vol. 10, No. 4 (1991).
31. Partridge, D. "Social Implication of AI." In *AI Principles and Applications*, M. Yazdani, ed. New York: Chapman and Hall, 1988.
32. "The Recovery Skips Middle Managers." *Fortune* (February 6, 1984).
33. Rosow, J. M. "People vs. High Tech: Adapting New Technologies to the Workplace." *Management Review* (September 1984).
34. Ryan, J. "Expert Systems in the Future: The Redistribution of Power." *Journal of Systems Management* (April 1988).
35. Scott-Morton, M. "DSS Revisited for the 1990s." Paper presented at DSS 1986. Washington, D.C., April 1986.
36. Senker, P. "Implications of Expert Systems for Skill Requirements and Working Life." *AI and Society* 3 (1989).
37. Sharma, R. S. "A Socio-Technical Model for Deploying Expert Systems—Part I: The General Theory." *IEEE Transactions on Engineering Management* (February 1991).
38. Sviokla, J. J. "An Examination of the Impact of Expert Systems on the Firm: The Case XCON." *MIS Quarterly* (June 1990).
39. Szewczak, E. J., et al. *Management Impacts of Information Technology*. Hershey, PA: Idea Group Publishers, 1991.
40. Tener, W. T. "Expert Systems for Computer Security." *Expert Systems Review* (March 1988).
41. Trappl, R., ed. *Impacts of AI: Scientific, Technological, Military, Economic, Social, Cultural, Political*. New York: Elsevier, 1986.
42. Turban, E. *Expert Systems and Applied Artificial Intelligence*. New York: Macmillan, 1992.
43. Turban, E., and J. Liebowitz. *Managing Expert Systems*. Hershey, PA: Idea Group Publishers, 1991.
44. Tuthill, S. G. "Legal Liabilities and Expert Systems." *AI Expert* (March 1991).
45. *Wall Street Journal*, March 30, 1986, p. 25.
46. Weitz, R. R. "Technology, Work and the Organization: The Impact of Expert Systems." *AI Magazine* (Summer 1990).

47. Wijnhoven, A.B.J.M., and D. A. Wassenarr. "Impact of Information Technology on Organizations: The State of the Art." *International Journal of Information Management* 10 (1990).

48. Wysocki, R. K., and J. Young. *Information Systems: Management Principles in Action.* New York: John Wiley & Sons, 1990.

49. Zuboff, S. *In the Age of the Smart Machine.* New York: Basic Books, 1988.

Glossary

Action Language User's action (e.g., input data, query, etc.).

Active DSS A special type of intelligent DSS that can respond to changes and is viewed as proactive rather than reactive.

AI Workstations *See* LISP Machines.

Algorithm A step-by-step search, where improvement is made in every step until the best solution is found.

Analogical Reasoning Determining the outcome of a problem by the use of analogies. A procedure for drawing conclusions about a problem by using past experience.

Artificial Intelligence (AI) The subfield of computer science that is concerned with symbolic reasoning and problem solving.

Artificial Neural Network (ANN) *See* Associative Memory Technology.

Assembly Language Computer language that replaces the binary digits of machine language with abbreviations to indicate processing operations.

Assertion The database or fact part of the knowledge base. It includes rules that are known to be true or false and any other information.

Associative Memory Technology An experimental computer technology that attempts to build computers that will operate like a human brain. The machines possess simultaneous memory storage, and work with ambiguous information. (*See* Neural Computing Networks.)

Axon   Outgoing terminal from a biological neuron.

Backpropagation   The most known learning algorithm in neural computing. Learning is done by comparing inputs to desired outputs of historical cases.

Backtracking   A technique used in tree searches. The process of working backward from a failed objective or an incorrect result to examine unexplored alternatives.

Backward Chaining   A search technique used in production ("IF-THEN" rule) systems that begins with the action clause of a rule and works "backward" through a chain of rules in an attempt to find a verifiable set of condition clauses.

Belief Function   Representation of uncertainty without the need to specify exact probabilities.

Blind Search   A search approach that makes use of no knowledge or heuristics to help speed up the search process. A time-consuming and arbitrary search process that attempts to exhaust all possibilities.

Brainstorming (Electronic)   Methodology of idea generation by association. This group process uses analogy and synergy. In this text it is computer supported.

Breadth–first Search   A search technique that evaluates every item at a given level of the search space before proceeding to the next level.

Case-based Reasoning   Methodology in which knowledge and/or inferences are derived from historical cases.

Certainty Factor   A percentage supplied by an expert system that indicates the probability that the conclusion reached by the system is correct. Also, the degree of belief of the expert that a certain conclusion will occur if a certain premise is true.

Chunk of Information   A collection of facts stored and retrieved as a single unit. The limitations of working memory are usually defined in terms of the number of chunks that can be handled simultaneously.

Class   Term used in object-oriented programming to designate a group of items with the same characteristics. (For example, the car Mustang is in a class of transportation.)

Classification Model (for ES)   A model used in building expert systems that uses production rules and covers a highly bounded problem.

Client/Server Architecture   A network system where several PCs (client) share the memory and other capabilities of a larger computer (the server).

Cognitive Style (Cognition)   The subjective process through which individuals organize and change information during the decision-making process.

Combinatorial Explosion   Problem in which adding one variable, or even one value to a variable, increases the size of the problem exponentially, resulting in an astronomical number of potential solutions to the problem.

Complete DSS   A strategy for constructing a full-service DSS generator and an organization to manage it. Contrasted with a quick-hit strategy.

Complete Enumeration Process of checking *every* feasible solution to a problem.

Computer-aided Instruction In general, the use of the computer as a teaching tool. Synonymous with Computer-based Instruction, Computer-assisted Learning, and Computer-based Training.

Computer Graphics The presentation of data in the form of bar charts, histograms, pie charts, or grids on a display screen or plotter to highlight data variations. Graphics are available in black and white or in color and can be presented in two or three dimensions.

Conflict Resolution (of Rules) Selecting a procedure from a conflicting set of applicable competing procedures or rules.

Consultation Environment The part of the expert system that is used by the nonexpert to obtain expert knowledge and advice. It includes the workplace, inference engine, explanation facility, the recommended action, and the user interface.

Controllable Variables Decision variables such as quantity to produce, amounts of resources to be allocated, etc. that can be changed and manipulated by the decision maker.

Cottage Industry Factory employees who are doing the work in their homes. The modern version of the cottage industry is telecommuting.

Critical Success Factors (CSF) A methodology developed at MIT for identifying the factors that are most critical to the success of an organization.

Crossover Combination of parts from two superior solutions in a genetic algorithm in an attempt to produce even better solutions.

Database The organizing of files into related units that are then viewed as a single storage concept. The data are then made available to a wide range of users.

Database Management System (DBMS) The software to establish, update, or query a database.

Decision Room An arrangement for a group DSS in which terminals are available to some or all participants. The objective is to enhance the decision-making process (e.g., by tabulating secret ballots).

Decision Styles The manner in which decision makers think and react to problems. It includes their perceptions, cognitive responses, values, and beliefs.

Decision Support Systems (DSS) Computer-based information systems that combine models and data in an attempt to solve nonstructured problems with extensive user involvement.

Decision Table Table that is used to represent knowledge and prepare it for analysis.

Decision Tree A graphical presentation of a sequence of interrelated decisions to be made under assumed risk.

Declarative Knowledge Representation Representation of facts and assertions.

Deductive Reasoning   In logic, reasoning from the general to the specific. Conclusions follow premises. Consequent reasoning.

Deep Representation   Model that captures all the forms of knowledge used by experts in their reasoning.

Default Value   A value given to a symbol or variable automatically if no other value is defined by the programmer or user.

Delphi   A qualitative forecasting methodology using anonymous questionnaires. Effective for technological forecasting and forecasting involving sensitive issues.

Demon   A procedure that is automatically activated if a specific, predefined state is recognized.

Dependent Variables   Systems' measure of effectiveness.

Depth-first Search   A search procedure that explores each branch of a search tree to its full vertical length. Each branch is searched for a solution and if none is found, a new vertical branch is searched to its depth, and so on.

Descriptive Models   Models that describe things as they are.

Deterministic Models   Models that are constructed under assumed certainty, namely, there is only one possible (and known) result to each alternative course or action.

Development Environment   That part of the expert system that is used by the builder. It includes the knowledge base, the inference engine, knowledge acquisition, and improving reasoning capability. The knowledge engineer and the expert are considered a part of this environment.

Dialog Generation and Management System (DGMS)   A software management package in a DSS whose functions in the dialog subsystem are similar to that of a DBMS in a database.

Dialog Style   The combination of the action languages, the display language, and knowledge base that determines input and provides output. Examples of styles include menu-driven and command language.

Dialog System   The hardware and software that provide the user interface for DSS. It also includes the ease-of-use, accessibility, and human-machine interface.

Disbelief   Degree of belief that something is *not* going to happen.

Distributed AI   Splitting of a problem to multiple cooperating systems for deriving a solution.

Drill Down   The ability to investigate information in details. For example, find not only total sales, but also sales by region, by product, or by salesperson.

DSS Generator   Computer software (sometimes with hardware) that provides a set of capabilities to quickly build a specific DSS.

DSS Tools   Software elements (such as languages) that facilitate the development of a DSS, or a DSS generator.

Dynamic Models   Models whose input data are being changed over time; for example, a five-year profit (loss) projection.

Editor   A software tool to aid in modifying a software program.

Effectiveness   The degree of goal attainment. Doing the right things.

Efficiency   Ratio of output to input. Appropriate use of resources.

Electronic Data Processing (EDP)   Processing of data largely performed by electronic devices.

Embedded Systems   Inclusion of one system inside another one. No distinction among the composing parts is visible.

EMYCIN   Nonspecific part (called shell) of MYCIN consisting of what is left when the knowledge is removed. EMYCIN becomes a new problem solver by adding the knowledge (using rules) for a different problem domain.

Encapsulation   Coupling of data and procedures in object-oriented programming.

End-user Computing   Development of one's own information system by a computer user.

English-like Language   A computer language that is very similar to the everyday, ordinary English.

Enumeration (Complete)   A listing of *all* possible solutions and the comparison of their results in order to find the best solution.

Evolutionary (Iterative) Process   A systematic process for system development that is used in DSS. A portion of the system is quickly constructed, then tested, improved, and enlarged in steps. Similar to prototyping.

Exception Reporting   Reports that call attention to deviation larger than an agreed upon threshold (e.g. 10 percent, or $200,000).

Executive Information Systems (EIS)   Computerized systems that are specifically designed to support executive work.

Executive Support System   An executive information system that includes some analytical capabilities.

Expert System (ES)   Computer system that applies reasoning methodologies on knowledge in a specific domain in order to render advice or recommendations, much like a human expert. A computer system that achieves a high level of performance in task areas that, for human beings, require years of special education and training.

Expertise   The set of capabilities that underlines the performance of human experts, including extensive domain knowledge, heuristic rules that simplify and improve approaches to problem-solving, metaknowledge and metacognition, and compiled forms of behavior that afford great economy in skilled performance.

Explanation Facility   The component of an expert system that can explain the system's reasoning and justify its conclusions.

Extraction   To capture data from several sources, synthesize them, summarize, find the relevant data, and organize them.

Facet   An attribute or a feature that describes the content of a slot in a frame.

Factory of the Future   Highly automated factory that is managed and controlled by intelligent computers.

Fault-tolerance   A computing system that continues to operate satisfactorily in the presence of faults.

Feasibility Study   A preliminary investigation to develop plans for construc-

tion of a new information system. The major aspects of the study are cost/
benefit, technological, human, organizational, and financial.

Federal Privacy Act　Federal legislation (1974) that prohibits governmental
agencies from providing information about individuals without the consent
of the individuals.

Fifth-generation Languages　Artificial Intelligence languages such as LISP
and PROLOG and their variants.

Fifth-generation Project　The research project in which the Japanese are investigating parallel processing and other advanced computing techniques
in an attempt to develop a "fifth generation" of computer systems, which
will be both efficient and intelligent.

Firing a Rule　Obtaining information on either the IF or THEN part of a rule,
which makes this rule an assertation.

Flexibility in DSS　System ability to react to changes in the environment,
tasks, or users of the DSS. It is the ability to modify, adapt, solve problems,
and evolve.

Form Interaction　Input data into designated spaces (fields) in forms displayed on the CRT.

Forward Chaining　Data-driven search in a rule-based system.

Fourth-generation Languages (4GLs)　Nonprocedural, user-oriented languages that enable quick programming by specifying only the desired results.

Frames　A knowledge representation scheme that associates one or more features with an object in terms of various slots and particular slot values.

Front-end Systems　Software systems (sometimes with hardware) that are
used to simplify the accessibility to other computerized systems (e.g., to a
database).

Fuzzy Logic　Ways of reasoning that can cope with uncertain or partial information; characteristic of human thinking and many expert systems.

Garbage Collection　A technique for recycling computer memory cells no
longer in use.

General-purpose Problem Solver　A procedure developed by Newell and
Simon in an attempt to create an intelligent computer. Although unsuccessful, the concept itself made a valuable contribution to the AI field.

Generators　Software packages designed to expedite the programming efforts
that are required to build information systems.

Genetic Algorithm　Software program that learns from experience in a similar (simplified) manner to the way in which biological systems learn.

Goal-seeking　The capability of asking the computer what values certain variables must have in order to attain desired goals.

Graphical User Interface (GUI)　An interactive user-friendly interface, in
which by using icons and similar devices the user can control the communication with the computer.

Group DSS　An interactive, computer-based system that facilitates solution of unstructured problems by a set of decision makers working together as a group.

Groupware Several computerized technologies and methods that aim to support the work of people working in groups.

Hardware The physical equipment of a computer system, including processor, memory, input/output devices, and other components.

Heuristics Informal, judgmental knowledge of an application area that constitutes the "rules of good judgement" in the field. Heuristics also encompass the knowledge of how to solve problems efficiently and effectively, how to plan steps in solving a complex problem, how to improve performance, and so forth.

Hidden Layer Middle layer of an artificial neural network with three or more layers.

Hidden Unemployment Refers to cases in which people are considered employed but are working only part of the time. Thus, the same amount of work can be executed by fewer employees.

Highlight Charts Summary displays that show only important information based on the user's own judgment.

Human-Machine Interface *See* User Interface.

Hybrid Environment A software package for expediting the construction of expert systems that includes several knowledge representation schemes.

Hypermedia Combination of several types of media such as text, graphics, audio, and video.

Hypertext An approach for handling text and other information by allowing the user to jump from a given topic, whenever he or she wishes, to related topics.

Icon A visual, graphic representation of an object, word, or concept.

Iconic Model A physical, scaled replica.

Idea Generation A process of generating ideas by people, usually supported by some software. For example, developing alternative solutions to a problem.

IF-THEN A conditional rule in which a certain action is taken only if some condition is satisfied.

Implementation The introduction of a change; putting things to work.

Independent Variables Variables in a model that are controlled by the decision maker and/or by the environment and that determine the result of a decision (also called Input Variables).

Inductive Reasoning In logic, reasoning from the specific to the general. Conditional or antecedent reasoning.

Inexact (Approximate) Reasoning Used when the expert system must make decisions based on partial or incomplete information.

Inference The process of drawing a conclusion from given evidence. To reach a decision by reasoning.

Inference Engine That part of an expert system that actually performs the reasoning function.

Inference Tree A schematic view of the inference process that shows the order in which rules are being tested.

Influence Diagram A diagram that shows the various types of variables (decision, independent, result) in a problem and how they are related to each other.

Information Center Facility with end-user tools that is staffed by end-user oriented specialists who first train and then support business users.

Information Overload Large amounts of information; too heavy a load.

Inheritance The process by which one object takes on or is assigned the characteristics of another object higher up in a hierarchy.

Inputs The resources introduced into a system for transformation into outputs.

Instantiation The process of assigning (or substituting) a specific value or name to a variable in a frame (or in a logic expression) making it a particular "instance" of that variable.

Institutional MSS One that is a permanent fixture in the organization with continuing financial support. It deals with decisions of a recurring nature.

Institutionalization The process through which an MSS system becomes incorporated as an ongoing part of organizational procedures.

Integrated Circuits Circuits composed of many tiny transistors that have been placed together in a single physical element, typically into a silicon chip.

Integrated Computer Systems Software packages that perform several different functions. For example Lotus 1-2-3 provides modeling capability, database management, and graphics.

Intelligent Agent Expert or knowledge-based system that is embedded in computer-based information systems (or their components) to make them smarter.

Intelligent Computer-aided Instruction (ICAI) Using AI techniques for training or teaching with a computer.

Intelligent DSS A DSS that includes one or more components of expert systems or other AI technologies. This component makes the DSS behave in a better (more "intelligent") manner.

Interactive Visual Decision Making (IVDM) Graphic animation in which systems and processes are presented dynamically to the decision maker. It enables visualization of the results of different potential actions.

Interactive Visual Simulation A special case of IVDM in which a simulation approach is used in the decision-making process.

Interdependent Decisions A series of interrelated decisions. Sequential decisions are usually interdependent.

Interface The portion of a computer system that interacts with the user, accepting commands from the computer keyboard and displaying the results generated by other portions of the computer system.

Intermediary   A person who uses the computer to fulfill requests made by other people. Example: a financial analyst uses the computer to answer questions for top management.

Iterative Process   *See* Evolutionary Process.

Justification Facility   *See* Explanation Facility. Also called justifier.

Key Performance Indicators (KPI)   Specific measures of the critical success factors.

Knowledge   Understanding, awareness, or familiarity acquired through education or experience. Anything that has been learned, perceived, discovered, inferred, or understood. The ability to use information.

Knowledge Acquisition   The extraction and formulation of knowledge derived from various sources, especially from experts.

Knowledge Base   A collection of facts, rules, and procedures organized into schemas. The assembly of all of the information and knowledge of a specific field of interest.

Knowledge-based Management   Management of the stored knowledge in terms of storing, accessing, updating, and reasoning with (analogous to a database management system).

Knowledge Engineer   An AI specialist responsible for the technical side of developing an expert system. The knowledge engineer works closely with the domain expert to capture the expert's knowledge in a knowledge base.

Knowledge Engineering (KE)   The engineering discipline whereby knowledge is integrated into computer systems in order to solve complex problems normally requiring a high level of human expertise.

Knowledge Refining   The ability of the program to analyze its own performance, learn, and improve itself for future consultations.

Knowledge Representation   A formalism for representing facts and rules in the computer about a subject or a specialty.

Knowledge System   Computer systems that embody knowledge, including inexact, heuristic, and subjective knowledge; the results of knowledge engineering.

Knowledge Worker   Employee who uses knowledge as a significant input to his or her work.

Lexicon   A dictionary.

Life Cycle (in System Development)   Structured approach to the development of information systems with several distinct steps.

Linear Programming   A mathematical model for optimal solution of resource allocation problems.

LISP (List Processor)   An AI programming language, created by AI pioneer John McCarthy, that is especially popular in the United States.

LISP Machines (or AI Workstations)   A single-user computer designed primarily to expedite the development of AI programs. Recently these machines were extended to serve several users simultaneously.

Logical Inferences Per Second (LIPS)   A means of measuring the speed of computers used for AI applications.

Machine Language   A language for writing instructions in a form to be executed directly by the computer. The language is composed of two values: zeros and ones.

Machine Learning   Computer that can learn from experience (e.g., programs that can learn from historical cases).

Management by Exception   A control system in which performance is monitored and action is taken only if the performance is outside a designated range.

Management Information Systems (MIS)   A business information system designed to provide past, present, and future information appropriate for planning, organizing, and controlling the operations of the organization.

Management Science (MS)   The application of scientific approach and mathematical models to the analysis and solution of managerial decision problems.

Mathematical Model   A system of symbols and expressions representing a real situation.

Megachip   Chip with more than 1 million components.

Metaknowledge   Knowledge in an expert system about how the system operates or reasons. More generally, knowledge about knowledge.

Metarules   A rule that describes how other rules should be used or modified.

Microcomputers   A complete computer system based on a microprocessor.

Microelectronics   Miniaturization of electronic circuits and components.

Microelectronics and Computer Technology Corporation (MCC)   A consortium of American companies involved in AI and other advanced computer research.

Model Base   A collection of preprogrammed quantitative models (e.g., statistical, financial, optimization) organized as a single unit.

Model Base Management System (MBMS)   A software to establish, update, combine, etc. a model base.

Model-based System (or Reasoning)   Application whose knowledge is derived by mathematical (or other type of) model.

Model Building Blocks   Preprogrammed software elements that can be used to build computerized models. For example, a random number generator can be used in the construction of a simulation model.

Modeling Tools   Software programs that enable the building of mathematical models quickly. A spreadsheet and a planning language are modeling tools.

Modified Turing Test   Test in which a manager is shown two solutions, one derived by a computer and one by a human, and is asked to compare the two.

Modus Ponens   An inference rule type which from "A implies B" justifies B by the existence of A.

Monte Carlo Simulation   A mechanism that uses random numbers in order to predict the behavior of an event whose probabilities are known.

Multimedia   Several human-machine communication media (e.g., voice, text).

Multiple Experts   A case in which two or more experts are used as the source of knowledge for an expert system.

Multiple Goals   A decision situation in which alteratives are being evaluated in light of several sometimes conflicting goals.

Mutation   Genetic operator that causes a change in a situation.

MYCIN   Early rule-based expert system, developed by Dr. Edward H. Short-liffe, that helps to determine the exact identity of an infection of the blood and that helps to prescribe the appropriate antibiotic.

Natural Language   A language spoken by humans on a daily basis, such as English, French, Japanese, or German.

Natural Language Processors (NLP)   An AI-based user interface that allows the user to carry on a conversation with a computer-based system in much the same way as he or she would converse with another human.

Neural Computing Networks   An experimental computer design that aims at building intelligent computers that will operate much like the human brain.

Nonprocedural Languages   The programmer specifies only the desired results rather than the detailed steps of how to get there.

Normative   Prescribes how a system should operate.

Numerical Processing   The traditional use of computers to manipulate numbers.

O-A-V Triplet   Objects, attributes (of the objects), and values (of the attributes). It is a fundamental concept in object-oriented programming and frame representation.

Object-oriented Programming   A language for representing objects and processing those representations by sending messages and activating methods.

Open System   Computer systems on a network, which permit the software and hardware of any vendor to be used by any user.

Operations Research   *See* Management Science.

Optimization   Identification of the best possible solution.

Organizational Culture (Climate)   The aggregate attitudes in the organization concerning a certain issue (such as technology, computers, and DSS).

Organizational DSS   A network DSS that serves people, at several locations, usually dealing with several decisions.

Parallel Processing   An advanced computer processing technique that allows the computer to perform multiple processes at the same time, in "parallel."

Parsing   The process of breaking down a character string of natural language input into its component parts so that it can be more readily analyzed, interpreted, or understood.

Pattern Matching   *See* Pattern Recognition. However, sometimes it refers specifically to matching the IF and THEN parts in rule-based systems. In such a case, pattern matching can be considered as one area of pattern recognition.

Pattern Recognition   The technique of matching an external pattern to one stored within a computer's memory, used in inference engines, image processing, neural computing, and speech recognition (e.g., the process of classifying data into predetermined categories).

Planning Language   A software package designed to expedite the construction of a financial and/or operational computerized planning system.

Predicate Calculus   A logical system of reasoning used in AI programs to indicate relationships among data items. The basis for the computer language PROLOG.

Presentation Language   The information displayed; output.

Principle of Choice   The criterion for making a choice among alternatives.

Problem Solving   A process in which one starts from an initial state and proceeds to search through a problem space in order to identify a desired goal.

Procedural Knowledge (contrasted with Declarative Knowledge)   Information about courses of action.

Procedural Languages   A language in which the programmer must define the detailed procedures that the computer is to follow.

Production Rules   A knowledge representation method in which knowledge is formalized into "rules" containing an IF part and a THEN part (also called a condition and an action).

Productivity   The ratio of outputs (results) to inputs (resources).

PROLOG   A high-level computer language designed around the concepts of predicate calculus.

Propositional Logic   A formal logical system of reasoning in which conclusions are drawn from a series of statements according to a strict set of rules.

Protocols   A set of instructions governing the format and control of data in moving from one medium to another.

Prototyping   A strategy in system development in which a scaled-down system or portion of a system is constructed in a short time, tested, and improved in several iterations.

Query Language   A language provided as part of a DBMS for easy access to data in the database.

Random Number   A number sampled from a uniform distribution in an unbiased manner (each number has exactly the same chance of being selected).

Rapid Prototyping   In expert systems development, a prototype is an initial version of an expert system, usually a system with 25 to 200 rules, that is quickly developed to test the effectiveness of the overall knowledge representation and inference mechanisms being employed to solve a particular problem.

Ready-made Expert System Mass-produced packages that may be purchased from software companies. These are very general in nature.

Real-time In synchronization with the actual occurrence of events; results are given rapidly enough to be useful in directly controlling a physical process or guiding a human user.

Relational Database A database whose records are organized into tables that can be processed by either relational algebra or relational calculus.

Report Generation The ability to use a few commands to generate an entire report. At the extreme, one command can generate an entire report patterned according to a template.

Repertory Grid Technique A tool used by psychologists to represent a person's view of a problem in terms of its elements and constructs.

Reusability Self-sufficiency of an object that enables it to be used as an independent component (in object-oriented programming).

Risk Analysis Analysis of decision situations in which results are dependent on events whose probabilities of occurrence are assumed to be known.

Robotics The science of using a machine (a robot) to perform manual functions without human intervention.

Role Ambiguity A situation in which the role to be performed by an employee is not clear. Lack of job description and changing conditions often result in role ambiguity.

ROMC (Representation, Operations, Memory Aids, Mechanism Control) A systematic approach for developing large-scale DSS. It is a user-oriented approach for articulating system performance requirements.

Rule A formal way of specifying a recommendation, directive, or strategy, expressed as IF premise THEN conclusion.

Rule-based System A system in which knowledge is represented completely in terms of rules (e.g., a system based on production rules).

Rule Induction Rules are created by a computer from examples of problems where the outcome is known in a process called *induction*. These rules are generalized to other cases.

Rule Interpreter Inference mechanism in a rule-based system.

Runtime System Part of an expert system shell that provides a consultation by interfacing with a user and an *existing knowledge base* and inference engine.

Satisfice A process during which one seeks a solution that will satisfy a set of constraints. In contrast to optimization, which seeks the best possible solution; when one satisfices, one simply seeks a solution that will work. (Good enough.)

Scenario A statement of assumptions and configurations concerning the operating environment of a particular system at a particular time.

Schema   A data structure for knowledge representation. Examples of schemas are frames and rules.

Script   Framelike structure representing stereotyped sequences of events (such as eating at a restaurant).

Search Space   Set of all possible solutions to a problem.

Search Tree   Graphic presentation that shows the problem, its alternative solutions, and the progress of a search for the best (acceptable) solution.

Self-evolving DSS   A special type of intelligent DSS.

Semantic Networks   A knowledge representation method consisting of a network of nodes, standing for concepts or objects, connected by arcs describing the relations between the nodes.

Semantics   The meaning in language. The relationship between words and sentences.

Semistructured Decisions   Decisions in which some aspects of the problem are structured and others are unstructured.

Sensitivity Analysis   A study of the effect of a change in one or more input variables on a proposed solution.

Sensory System   Any system that monitors the external environment for a computer.

Sequential Processing   The traditional computer processing technique of performing actions one at a time, in a sequence.

Shallow (Surface) Representation   Model that does not capture all of the forms of knowledge used by experts in their reasoning. Contrasted with Deep Representation.

Shell   A complete expert system stripped of its specific knowledge. In rule-based systems, it is a kind of expert system development tool consisting of two stand-alone pieces of software: a rule set manager and an inference engine capable of reasoning with the rule set built with the rule set manager.

Sigmoid Function   Transfer function of an S shape in the range of zero to one.

Simulation   An imitation of reality.

Slot   A sub-element of a frame of an object. A particular characteristic, specification, or definition used in forming a knowledge base.

Specific DSS   A system that actually accomplishes a specific task. It is similar to "application software" in conventional MIS.

Specific Expert Systems   An expert system that advises users on a specific issue.

Speech Understanding   An area of AI research that attempts to allow computers to recognize words or phrases of human speech.

Spreadsheet (Electronic)   Computer technology that is similar to columns-and-rows worksheets used by accountants. It is a modeling tool.

SQL (Structured Query Language)   A data definition and management language of relational databases. It front-ends most relational DBMS.

Status Access   Rapid access to current information, provided by a computer.

Structured Decisions   Standard or repetitive decision situations for which solution techniques are already available.

Suboptimal   Best for a subsystem of the total system.

Symbolic Processing   Use of symbols, rather than numbers, combined with rules of thumb (or heuristics), in order to process information and solve problems.

Syntax   The manner in which words are assembled to form phrases and sentences. Putting words in a specific order.

System   A set of elements that is considered to act as a single, goal-oriented entity.

System Analysis   The investigation and recording of existing systems and the conceptual design and feasibility study of new systems.

System Design   Specification of appropriate hardware and software components required to implement an information system.

System Development Life Cycle (SDLC)   A systematic process for constructing large information systems in an effective manner.

Telecommunication   The transfer of information over distance by means of telephone, radio, or other transmission.

Telecommuting   Employees work at home, usually using a computer or a terminal that is linked to their place of employment.

Template   A piece of presentation knowledge that indicates the visual layout of a report's contents and the sources of values that can appear in particular locations.

Templates (for Spreadsheets)   Preprogrammed, reusable spreadsheet models with built-in titles and formulas, developed for specific applications.

Time-series Analysis   A technique that analyzes historical data over a period of a few years and then makes a forecast.

Turing Test   A test that is designed to measure the degree of a computer's "intelligence."

Uncertainty   In the context of expert systems, uncertainty refers to a value that cannot be determined during a consultation. Many expert systems can accommodate uncertainty. That is, they allow the user to indicate if he or she does not know the answer.

Uncontrollable Variations   Factors that affect the result of a decision but are not under the control of the decision maker. These can be internal (technology, policies) or external (legal, climate).

Unstructured Decisions   Complex decisions for which no standard solutions exist.

User-friendly   Term used to describe a facility designed to make interaction with a computer system easy and comfortable for the user.

User Interface (or Human-Machine Interface)   The component of a computer system that allows bidirectional communication between the system and its user.

Validation   Determination of whether the right system was built.

Verification   Confirmation that the system was built to specifications (correctly).

Virtual Reality   A 3-D interactive technology which provides the user a feeling that he or she is physically present in the real world.

Visual Simulation   *See* Interactive Visual Simulation.

VLSI (Very-Large-Scale Integration)   The process of combining several hundred thousand electronic components into a single integrated circuit (chip).

Voice Recognition   The ability of a computer to understand the meaning of spoken words (sentences as input).

Voice Synthesis   A transformation of computer output to an audio (voice); for example, a telephone number given as a response to a request from 411.

Weight   Value assigned on each connection at the input to a neuron. Analogous to a synapse in the brain. Weights control the inflow to the processing element.

"What-If" Analysis   The capability of "asking" the computer what the effect will be of changing some of the input data.

Workplace (or Blackboard)   A globally accessible database used in expert systems for recording intermediate, partial results of problem solving.

WYSIWYG   "What you see is what you get." A capability of creating reports (or other outputs) on the computer screen and then printing the results in the format seen on the screen.

Appendix A

The Interactive Financial Planning System (IFPS)*

A-1 Why IFPS?

The Interactive Financial Planning System (IFPS) is a nonprocedural fourth-generation computer language developed by Execucom Systems Corporation of Austin, Texas as a mainframe tool in the early 1970s. Like spreadsheet packages its principal output is a spreadsheet of numbers. Unlike those languages, which are cell oriented, IFPS is a modeling language oriented to communicating with managers. It allows you to represent your ideas in a near natural language form. Because it is a modeling language, the users can see what is in the model and can understand the assumptions that were made in creating it.

IFPS provides a number of other features that help in the communications process:

- Instructions are written in natural language form, with no restrictions on the lengths of names. Thus, for example, you can write

    PROFIT BEFORE TAX = SALES − COST OF GOODS SOLD

    which is much more understandable than, say, PBT = S − C.

---

*Prepared by Paul Gray, The Claremont Graduate School.

- There are no order restrictions. Ideas can be written in the order in which you and your managers feel comfortable in thinking about them, as long as each variable is defined at some point in your model. The computer takes care of computing things in the right order.
- The interface allows you to create either spreadsheet output or graphic output or to create custom reports that are in the format people in your organization use.
- The user can easily write models in such a way that the assumptions made are pointed out explicitly.
- Command files allow creation of large models that can be operated simply and with little knowledge of IFPS by managers and others in the organization.
- An optional module can be added to perform linear and nonlinear programming optimizations.
- The mainframe version of IFPS includes an expert's system component, called the *explanation facility*, that helps to explain how and why specific results are obtained. The PC version is called IFPS/PC*

Communication is improved further by the ability to ask "what-if" questions. These questions can be in the form of altering assumed values, asking for sensitivity to specific ranges of variables, and performing goal seeking.

The mainframe version of IFPS also allows you to undertake risk analysis because it allows you to perform Monte Carlo simulations.

Finally, IFPS is a full-featured language. It contains a variety of built-in functions. It allows use of databases, consolidation of spreadsheets, full-page editing, and much more.

A-2 The Structure of IFPS

IFPS consists of six subsystems: the executive subsystem, the modeling language subsystem, the database subsystem, the report generator subsystem, the data file subsystem, and the command file subsystem.

The *executive subsystem* is the highest level of IFPS operation. It is used to accomplish the following activities:

- Specify permanent files.
- List models and reports.
- Delete models and reports.
- Combine models.
- Consolidate models and data files.
- Copy models and reports.
- Call other subsystems.

*For instruction on using the PC version see Gray [2]. Abbreviated instructions are given in the instructor's manual to this text. IFPS/Personal is menu driven and is very user friendly.

The *modeling language subsystem* is called by issuing a MODEL command. The modeling language subsystem is the primary vehicle for analyzing the situation of interest to the IFPS user. The following activities are performed in the modeling language subsystem:

- Create new models.
- Edit models.
- Produce solutions to the model.
- Plot model results.
- Print complete reports.
- Ask "what-if" questions.
- Perform goal seeking.
- Perform risk analysis.

The *database subsystem* is a relational data manager for IFPS applications. It supports multidimensional modeling, reporting, and querying using the structured query language, SQL.

The *report generator subsystem* is called by issuing a REPORT command. This subsystem is used for the following purposes:

- Creation of special report definitions
- Editing of special report definitions.

The *data file subsystem* is entered by issuing a DATAFILE command. The data file subsystem is used for

- Creation of IFPS data files
- Editing and maintenance of IFPS data files.

The *command file subsystem* is entered by issuing a CMDFILE command. This subsystem allows the user to create stacks of commands that may be executed with a single command.

A-3　A Simple IFPS Model

The easiest way to learn IFPS is to study a simple model and its output. Figure A.1 shows a model that computes the dividends expected to be paid out by a firm from 1991 through 1995 under a set of highly simplifying assumptions about income and costs:

- Half of the net profit after tax each year is declared as dividend.
- Selling price will be $5.00 in 1991 and will increase by 5 percent per year, compounded annually.
- Cost of goods sold (COGS) includes all expenses and will be 80 percent of sales.
- Tax rate will be 28 percent and taxes will be paid on the excess of sales over cost of goods sold.

```
 10 COLUMNS 1991..1995
 20 \
 30 \              IFPS MODEL FOR COMPUTING DIVIDEND FORECAST
 40 \
 50 DIVIDENDS = .50*NET PROFIT AFTER TAX
 60 NET PROFIT AFTER TAX = SALES - COGS - TAXES
 70 SALES = SELLING PRICE*QUANTITY SOLD
 80 COGS = 0.8*SALES
 90 TAXES = TAX RATE*(SALES-COGS)
100 \
110 \ ASSUMPTIONS
120 \
130 SELLING PRICE = 5, PREVIOUS*1.05
140 TAX RATE = 28%
150 QUANTITY SOLD = 1000 FOR 2. 1250 FOR 2. 1450
```

FIGURE A.1   Simple IFPS Model

■ Quantity sold in 1991 and 1992 will be 1000. It is expected to increase to 1250 for 1993 and 1994 and to increase again in 1995 to 1450.

IFPS models are like spreadsheets, containing rows and columns. The first line must tell IFPS how many columns you want and what to name them. The first number represents the starting year (1991) and the second number the ending year (1995). The two dots tell IFPS to include all years in between. Alternatively, writing COLUMNS 1..6 would have specified that the columns should be called 1 through 6. If the column titles are to have names rather than numbers (e.g., YEAR1 to TOTAL), they must be spelled out individually.

Each line begins with a line number. You do not need to type in these numbers when you create a model. IFPS can assign line numbers automatically for you. Line numbers are used in mainframe IFPS but not in IFPS/Personal.

```
 20 \
 30 \        IFPS MODEL FOR COMPUTING DIVIDEND FORECAST
 40 \
```

The \ symbol tells IFPS that this line is a comment. Thus, lines 20 through 40 in Figure A.1 are comments. Comments are printed verbatim. That is, the output specified by these three lines consists of a blank line followed by a line that prints the heading IFPS MODEL FOR COMPUTING DIVIDEND FORE-CAST and another blank line. The backslash is not printed. These comment lines allow a primitive form of labeling and formatting.

50 DIVIDENDS = .50 * NET PROFIT AFTER TAX

Dividends are defined as being 50 percent of net profit after tax. In IFPS, a single variable name appears to the left of the equal sign and an expression appears on the right. Multiplication is specified by the *. Addition, subtraction, and division are specified by +, −, and /.

Unlike procedural programming languages, it is possible to use a variable in IFPS before it is defined. Variable names are not restricted in length and can include multiple words.

60 NET PROFIT AFTER TAX = SALES − COGS − TAXES

This line is an accounting relation. It defines NET PROFIT AFTER TAX as being income (SALES) less cost of goods sold (COGS) and taxes.

70 SALES = SELLING PRICE * QUANTITY SOLD

Sales is the dollar income resulting from multiplying the selling price for each unit by the quantity sold. Both selling price (line 130) and quantity sold (line 150) are *assumptions* of the model.

80 COGS = 0.8 * SALES

This arithmetic statement contains the assumption that cost of goods sold will be 80 percent of sales.

90 TAXES = TAX RATE * (SALES − COGS)

Taxes are paid at a given tax rate on the excess of sales revenue over cost. Note that this statement could contain a modeling error if, in any year, costs exceed sales and a loss is incurred. You could guard against such a mistake by writing line 90 as

90 TAXES = IF (SALES − COGS) .GT. 0 THEN'
95 TAX RATE * (SALES − COGS) ELSE 0

In this form, IFPS first tests to see if (SALES − COGS) is greater than 0. If it is, the previous definition of TAXES is used; if it is not then taxes are 0. Note that the apostrophe on line 90 allows "continuation" of the model statement onto the next line.

100 \
110 \ ASSUMPTIONS
120 \

Lines 100 through 120 are comment lines to indicate that what follows are assumptions of the model.

```
130  SELLING PRICE = 5, PREVIOUS * 1.05
140  TAX RATE = 28%
150  QUANTITY SOLD = 1000 FOR 2, 1250 FOR 2, 1450
```

The last three lines specify the assumptions of the model.

Selling price is forecasted to have an initial value of 5 in 1991 and then to increase by 5 percent each year. The way this is done is to put a comma between the value in the first column (selling price) and what follows. In general, a comma separates column values in a model. The next statement introduces the important concept of PREVIOUS. PREVIOUS is a reserved word that refers to the value in the previous column of the model. Thus, in 1992, the value of the selling price in 1991 is used; in 1993, the sales in 1992; and so on. IFPS also has the reserved word FUTURE which allows you to refer to values in the succeeding column. If you want to refer to something three periods ago, you use PREVIOUS 3; if you want to refer to something two periods from now, use FUTURE 2. Multiplying the previous value by 1.05 increases it by 5 percent. This is a convenient way of computing an annual growth rate. For line 130, selling price, only one comma separates column 1 and column 2. IFPS therefore assumes that the expression in column 2 is to be extended through to the last column, 1995. There is no need to repeatedly type this expression for every column in this model.

A continuation of a 28 percent effective tax rate for the company is assumed throughout the time interval, and the specified quantity sold. Note that in a case such as that of "quantity sold" we can repeat values over more than one column by using the IFPS reserved word FOR. Thus, writing 1000 FOR 2 is the same as writing 1000, 1000.

A-4   Output from the Simple IFPS Model

The output from the Simple IFPS Model is shown in Figure A.2. The output is obtained by asking IFPS to SOLVE the model. We have actually done more than that as can be seen from the dialog shown as follows:

```
?solve
MODEL SIMPLE VERSION OF 7/21/92  13:00-5 COLUMNS 8 VARIABLES
ENTER SOLVE OPTIONS
?width 78 20 8 2
?all
```

Note: As a convention, model definitions and output from the computer are shown in capital letters but what you type is shown in small letters. Thus, in this example, you type *solve* and the computer responds with *MODEL SIMPLE*, etc.

```
MODEL SIMPLE VERSION OF 07/21/92 13:00 — 5 COLUMNS 8 VARIABLES

ENTER SOLVE OPTIONS
?WIDTH 78 20 8 2
?ALL
                              1991      1992      1993      1994      1995

             IFPS MODEL FOR COMPUTING DIVIDEND FORECAST

DIVIDENDS                   360.00    378.00    496.13    520.93    634.49
NET PROFIT AFTER TAX        720.00    756.00    992.25   1041.86   1268.99
SALES                      5000.00   5250.00   6890.63   7235.16   8812.42
COGS                       4000.00   4200.00   5512.50   5788.13   7049.94
TAXES                       280.00    294.00    385.88    405.17    493.50

   ASSUMPTIONS

SELLING PRICE                 5.00      5.25      5.51      5.79      6.08
TAX RATE                      0.28      0.28      0.28      0.28      0.28
QUANTITY SOLD              1000.00   1000.00   1250.00   1250.00   1450.00
```

FIGURE A.2 Output of a Simple IFPS Model

In response to a question mark from the computer, we first told IFPS to *solve* the model. It came back and asked for solve options. These options allow you some additional simple formatting capabilities. In our case, we wrote *width 78 20 8 2* to tell IFPS that we wanted output that was 78 spaces wide, that used 20 of those spaces for the names of variables, 8 spaces for each column, and gave all numbers two decimal points.

We next specified ALL to indicate that we wanted output for all columns and all variables. IFPS responded by printing out all five columns and all variables and comment lines. If we had specified COLUMNS 1,3,5, for example, only 1991, 1993, and 1995 would have been printed. If we had specified DIVIDENDS, SALES THROUGH TAXES only the DIVIDENDS, SALES, COGS, and TAXES lines would have printed.

Study the output. It shows that, as specified by the IFPS model, selling price is $5.00 initially and grows by 5 percent each year thereafter. In each case, COGS is 80 percent of the SALES value and TAXES are 28 percent of the excess of SALES over COGS. In looking at this forecast as a stockholder you would be pleased that your dividends are going to increase.

A-5 Exploring IFPS Output—"What-If" and Goal Seeking

As a stockholder, you may want to explore the assumptions made by your company about its future dividend payments. Although the model lists only three assumptions, we know there are others. Figure A.3 shows a revision of the model that makes all the assumptions explicit.

Here, all numeric values have been deleted from the model itself (lines 50, 80, 130) and replaced with variable names. Specifically, the assumptions of a 50 percent dividend payout rate, a 5 percent annual selling price growth rate, and an 80 percent sales cost rate are made explicit by replacing these numbers with their variable names in the model and recording the variable names and their values in the assumptions section of the model (lines 140 through 200). Using variable names rather than numbers in your model is good practice and should be followed as a basic principle.

"What-If." The model in the form shown in Figure A.3 is better suited for asking questions. Let us begin by challenging the selling price assumptions. Suppose you are pessimistic about the selling price and believe selling price will reach only $4.50 per unit and increase only 3 percent per year. You do not need to redo the model to see the effect these changes could have. Rather, you would have the following dialog with the computer:

```
ENTER SOLVE OPTIONS
? what if
ENTER STATEMENTS
? selling price = 4.50, previous * selling price growth rate
? selling price growth rate = 1.03
? solve
ENTER SOLVE OPTIONS
? all
```

What you do is create a "what-if" case. To do so, you type WHAT IF in response to a question mark. IFPS responds with ENTER STATEMENTS. You then write the new assumptions. To do so, you write the complete IFPS line as you want it to read. In a "what-if" case, IFPS *temporarily* replaces each variable by its new definition. You enter one change at a time. When you have finished, you ask IFPS to SOLVE and then give it the solve options desired. The result of this "what-if" dialog is shown in Figure A.4. In examining Figure A.4 you see that the selling price and the selling price growth rate have been replaced according to our instructions and the calculations reflect the changes in the assumption.

As a second "what-if" test, assume that not only will sales performance be poorer but that the SALES COST RATE, which had been assumed constant for five years at 80 percent, will go up starting in 1993 to 90 percent because increased advertising will be needed to sustain sales growth. The dialog required follows:

```
ENTER SOLVE OPTIONS
? what if continue
? what if case 2
ENTER STATEMENTS
? sales cost rate = 0.80 for 2, 0.90
```

```
MODEL SIMPLE1 VERSION OF 07/21/92 12:46
 10   COLUMNS 1991. .1995
 20 \
 30 \              IFPS MODEL FOR COMPUTING DIVIDEND FORECAST
 40 \
 50   DIVIDENDS = DIVIDEND PAYOUT RATE*NET PROFIT AFTER TAX
 60   NET PROFIT AFTER TAX = SALES – COGS – TAXES
 70   SALES = SELLING PRICE*QUANTITY SOLD
 80   COGS = SALES COST RATE*SALES
 90   TAXES = TAX RATE*(SALES–COGS)
100 \
110 \ ASSUMPTIONS
120 \
130   SELLING PRICE = 5,PREVIOUS*1.05
140   TAX RATE = 28%
150   DIVIDEND PAYOUT RATE = 0.50
170   SALES COST RATE = 0.80
180   QUANTITY SOLD = 1000 FOR 2, 1250 FOR 2, 1450
190   SELLING PRICE = 5, PREVIOUS * SELLING PRICE GROWTH RATE
200   SELLING PRICE GROWTH RATE = 1.05
END OF MODEL
```

FIGURE A.3　Simple IFPS Model with All Assumptions Stated Explicitly.

```
? solve
ENTER SOLVE OPTIONS
? all
```

By writing *what if continue* you are telling IFPS that you want to keep the immediately preceding WHAT IF conditions and add new ones.

Goal Seeking. Goal seeking involves specifying the outcome and IFPS tells you what needs to occur to achieve this outcome. For example, under the original assumptions of Figure A.2 the dividend is 360 in the first year, but it grows slowly thereafter.

To cope with anticipated inflation, a more appropriate goal might be an annual dividend increase of 20 percent from the previous year. What quantity sold is necessary to achieve this goal? You would have the following dialog with IFPS:

```
ENTER SOLVE OPTIONS
? base case
? goal seek
GOAL SEEKING CASE 1
ENTER NAME OF VARIABLE(S) TO BE ADJUSTED TO ACHIEVE PERFORMANCE
? quantity sold
ENTER 1 COMPUTATIONAL STATEMENT(S) FOR PERFORMANCE
? dividends = 360,  previous * 1.20
```

```
***** WHAT IF CASE 1 *****
2 WHAT IS STATEMENTS PROCESSED
```

	1991	1992	1993	1994	1995
IFPS MODEL FOR COMPUTING DIVIDEND FORECAST					
DIVIDENDS	324.00	333.72	429.66	442.55	528.76
NET PROFIT AFTER TAX	648.00	667.44	859.33	885.11	1057.53
SALES	4500.00	4635.00	5967.56	6146.59	7343.94
COGS	3600.00	3708.00	4774.56	4917.27	5875.16
TAXES	252.00	259.56	334.18	344.21	411.26
ASSUMPTIONS					
TAX RATE	0.28	0.28	0.28	0.28	0.28
DIVIDEND PAYOUT RATE	0.50	0.50	0.50	0.50	0.50
SALES COST RATE	0.80	0.80	0.80	0.80	0.80
QUANTITY SOLD	1000.00	1000.00	1250.00	1250.00	1450.00
SELLING PRICE	4.50	4.64	4.77	4.92	5.06
SELLING PRICE GROWTH RATE	1.03	1.03	1.03	1.03	1.03

```
ENTER SOLVE OPTIONS
?
```

FIGURE A.4 Results of First What-If Case

The first instruction, base case, is designed to reinstate the original assumptions. (If you do not include it, IFPS will perform goal seeking on the current "what-if" case.) When you ask for *goal seek,* IFPS asks you first which variable you want changed to achieve the desired goal and then to specify the goal as an IFPS statement. The results of the dialog are shown in Figure A.5.

Goal seeking provides output only on the variable adjusted (sales in Figure A.5). However, IFPS does follow that up immediately with the ever-present *ENTER SOLVE OPTIONS.* You can gain additional information by typing ALL in response to the question mark or, as is done in Figure A.6, listing specific variables for which output is wanted (dividends and net profit after tax in Figure A.6).

The foregoing discussion has centered on a relatively simple situation. IFPS can be used to model much more complex situations. A variety of models from finance, statistics, operations management, and decision making are illustrated in Gray [1] and in Plane [3].

```
***** GOAL SEEKING CASE 1 *****

                     1991      1992      1993      1994      1995

QUANTITY SOLD      1000.00   1142.86   1306.12   1492.71   1705.96
```

FIGURE A.5   Goal Seeking

A-6   IFPS Built-In Functions and Subroutines

IFPS contains a large number of preprogrammed functions and subroutines to make your work easier. The functions include financial functions (for computing net present value, internal rate of return, etc.), mathematical functions, and trend extrapolation functions. The subroutines provide amortization and depreciation capabilities. For example, suppose you wanted to find out the net present worth and the growth rate associated with the stream of dividends in our simple model. You would add the following statements to Figure A.3:

```
92 NET PRESENT WORTH OF DIVIDENDS = NPVC (DIVIDENDS, .12, 0)
94 DIVIDEND GROWTH PERCENTAGE = GROWTHRATE (DIVIDENDS)
```

The NPVC function asks you to specify the cash inflow, the discount rate, and the cash outflow. In our case, the inflows are the dividends. The discount rate is 12 percent, and there are no (zero) outflows. The output of the NPVC function is the cumulative net present value of the dividends. The GROWTHRATE function measures the annual percentage growth in the variable; in our case, in dividends.

```
ENTER SOLVE OPTIONS
?DIVIDENDS, NET PROFIT AFTER TAX

                       1991      1992      1993      1994      1995

DIVIDENDS            360.00    432.00    518.40    622.08    746.50
NET PROFIT AFTER TAX 720.00    864.00   1036.80   1244.16   1493.00
```

FIGURE A.6   Obtaining Additional Output from Goal Seeking

NPVC and GROWTHRATE are just two of the functions and subroutines available in IFPS. Table A.1 lists the subroutines and Table A.2 lists the built-in functions.

A-7   Uncertainty and Risk Analysis

Probability Distributions. In many situations, something is known about the uncertainties being faced. For example, in our dividend example, the manager may not be sure about the selling price but can estimate, say, based on market surveys, that the initial selling price is not likely to be less than 2.50 nor more than 7.50. Furthermore, the manager may estimate the selling price growth rate to be between 3 and 7 percent per year. These estimates can be expressed as probability distributions. IFPS provides three standard built-in probability distributions (uniform, triangular, and normal) and *two ways* to create custom distributions. The built-in distributions are shown in Figure A.7. Here we show

- A uniform distribution between 3 and 7 and a normal distribution with mean 1.05 and standard deviation of 0.02. One of these distributions might represent the manager's view of the uncertainty about the selling price growth rate.
- A triangular distribution between 2.50 and 7.50 with most likely value (peak) at 5.00. Triangular distributions can be specified in terms of their peak and either the end points or their 10th and 90th percentile points (triangle c in Figure A.7).

Example. Suppose we choose NORRAND to represent the initial selling price growth rate and T1090RAND to represent selling price. Then the quantities used in line 70 in Figure A.3

        70 SALES = SELLING PRICE * QUANTITY SOLD

TABLE A.1   IFPS Subroutines

Name	Description
ACRS DEPR	Accelerated cost recovery depreciation
AMORT	Amortization
DECBAL	Declining balance depreciation
GENDECBAL DEPR	General declining balance
STLINEDEPR	Straight line depreciation
SUM DEPR	Sum of the years digits depreciation

TABLE A.2 Built-in Functions in IFPS

Name	Description	Name	Description
\multicolumn{4}{c}{**Financial**}			
BCRATIO	Benefit/cost ratio for given discount rate	NPV	Net present value of future earnings from one investment
CIRR	Internal rate of return from continuous cash flows and compounding	NPVC	Present value from future earnings and investments
IRR	Internal rate of return	NTV	Terminal value of future earnings and investments
MDIRR	Internal rate of return assuming mid-period cash flows		
\multicolumn{4}{c}{**Mathematical**}			
ABS	Absolute value	NATLOG	Natural logarithm
DEFINITION	Defines probability distribution	ROUND	Rounds decimals to nearest integer
GROWTHRATE	Compound growth rate of variable	ROUNDUP	Rounds decimal to next highest integer
LOG10	Logarithm to base 10	STDDEV	Standard deviation of variable
MATRIX	Selects row and column element	STEP	Step function
MAXIMUM	Maximum of a list	SUM	Adds values in row or column
MINIMUM	Minimum of a list		
MEAN	Average of a variable	TRUNCATE	Deletes decimal part of number
MEDIAN	Median of a variable	VMATRIX	Selects row and column where column number is computed
NATEXP	e to the power x	XPOWERY	Raises x to the power y
\multicolumn{4}{c}{**Extrapolation**}			
MOVAVG	Moving average	TREND	Fits a trend line
POLYFIT	Fits a polynomial curve		

would be written as:

```
190 SELLING PRICE = T1090RAND (2.50, 5.00, 7.50)'
195 PREVIOUS * SELLING PRICE GROWTH RATE
200 SELLING PRICE GROWTH RATE = NORRANDR (1.05, 0.02)
```

To use T1090RAND, three numbers must be specified: the 10 percent point (2.50), the maximum of the triangle (5.00), and the 90 percent point (7.50). In

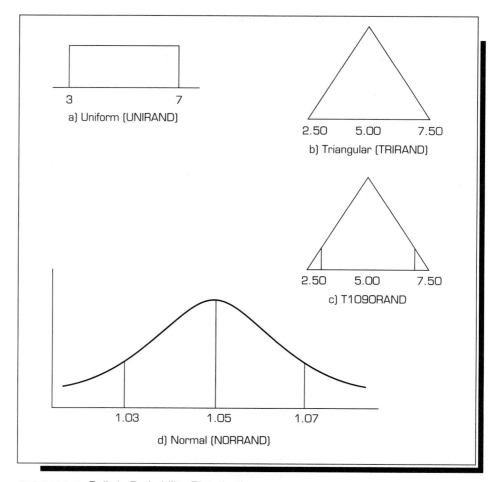

FIGURE A.7   Built-in Probability Distributions

the case of NORRANDR we specified the mean (1.05) and the standard deviation (0.02). (*Note:* NORRANDR was used rather than NORRAND because, by
adding R, IFPS selects a different value each period from the distribution. If we
had specified NORRAND, IFPS would have chosen a value in period 1 and kept
the same value for every period thereafter. Do you see the difference?)

Simulation. A simulation procedure is used with a model that includes probability distributions. The basic idea in simulation is that the model is run many
times, with each replication using a different combination of values drawn randomly from the probability distributions. The objective is to obtain not only the

average (i.e., the mean) outcome, but also information on the distribution of the possible results to be anticipated.

If you tell IFPS to SOLVE, as was done in the previous sections, IFPS finds and uses the mean of each distribution to obtain an answer. If, however, you ask for MONTE CARLO, IFPS runs a simulation. MONTE CARLO requires specifying how many replications are to be run and which variables are to be printed out. The following "what-if" dialog adds two probability distributions to the model of Figure A.3, runs 100 replications, and prints out selected data.

```
? what if
MODEL SIMPLE VERSION 01/01/93 19:16—5 COLUMNS 10 VARIABLES
WHAT IF CASE 1
ENTER STATEMENTS
? selling price = t1090rand(2.50,  5.00,  7.50),
previous * selling price growth rate
? selling price growth rate = norrandr (1.05,  .02)
? monte carlo 100
ENTER MONTE CARLO OPTIONS OR NONE
? columns 1991, 1995
ENTER MONTE CARLO OPTIONS OR NONE
? hist dividends, freq sales
ENTER MONTE CARLO OPTIONS OR NONE
? none
```

After entering the "what-if" statements, you specify MONTE CARLO 100 to tell IFPS to run 100 replications (i.e., a sample size of 100).

IFPS asks you to specify the Monte Carlo options. These options involve the columns and variables to be recorded and printed. Because IFPS must store data for each option you want, you should use them sparingly. If you do not specify columns, IFPS uses the last column as the default value. In the example, we asked for both 1991 and 1995 to show you the effects of the two probability distributions. The results obtained are shown in Figure A.8 (the histogram for 1995 has been omitted).

By performing risk analysis in IFPS, you develop a better understanding of the range of outcomes that can occur. By using simulation, you can calculate the risks associated with a venture.

A-8   Optimization

The IFPS "what-if" and goal seeking capabilities show what can be achieved under specific assumptions. However, they cannot be used to find out what the optimum policy should be unless a large number of trial and error cases are run.

```
***** WHAT IF CASE 1 *****

                            FREQUENCY TABLE

              PROBABILITY OF VALUE BEING GREATER THAN INDICATED

           90      80      70      60      50      40      30      20      10

DIVIDENDS
1991      203     239     270     301     330     360     388     458     553
1995      294     346     392     436     478     522     562     663     802


SALES
1991     2819    3313    3751    4174    4582    5000    5384    6355    7685
1995     4087    4804    5439    6053    6643    7250    7806    9215   11144

        SAMPLE STATISTICS

          MEAN   STD DEV  SKEWNESS   KURTOSIS   10PC CONF MEAN    90PC

DIVIDENDS
1991     345.8   134.1      .4         2.7          328.6        362.9
1995     501.3   194.4      .4         2.7          476.5        526.2


SALES
1991     4802    1862       .4         2.7          4564         5040
1995     6963    2700       .4         2.7          6617         7309

       HISTOGRAM FOR COLUMN 1991 OF DIVIDENDS
      19- 20              *
      17- 18            *  *
      15- 16            *  *  *
      13- 14         *  *  *  *
      11- 12         *  *  *  *
       9- 10         *  *  *  *
       7-  8         *  *  *  *  *
       5-  6      *  *  *  *  *  *  *  *  *
       3-  4      *  *  *  *  *  *  *  *  *  *
       1-  2      *  *  *  *  *  *  *  *  *  *
              _____
                    2      4      6
                 9     7      4      2
                 9     3      7      1
      START       70.0  STOP     650.0 SIZE OF INTERVAL      58.00
```

FIGURE A.8   Results of Monte Carlo Simulation

For example, in the simple IFPS model shown in Figures A.1 and A.3, the dividend payout rate was assumed to be 50 percent every quarter. Is this payout rate optimal? The answer depends on what the objective is. For simplicity of illustration, assume that

- The firm's objective is to maximize the net present worth of the total dividend payout over the time horizon.
- Sales growth depends on advertising. Each dollar diverted from dividends to advertising is estimated to result in $10 of additional sales. Since each dollar of sales results in 14.4 cents of net profit after tax, a dollar invested in advertising results in $1.44 of additional net profit.

To deal with the possibility of advertising, the model has to be revised to take the facts just stated into account. (See Exercise 3 at the end of this Appendix.) The problem now involves a tradeoff. Paying out more dividends reduces sales in the future because less money is available for advertising, and hence profit and dividends are reduced in the future. Paying out less dividends now increases sales now, and profit and potentially dividends in the future. What is the optimal policy?

What we have formulated is an optimization problem faced by managers. A separate module of IFPS/Plus for the mainframe, IFPS/Optimum, is available for solving optimization problems using mathematical programming.

A-9   Command Files

Command files provide a user-friendly way of using IFPS models without knowing much about IFPS. They automate the command sequences that otherwise have to be performed manually in IFPS. The simplest way of thinking about command files is that they contain a list of the commands that you would enter in an interactive session.

A command file consists of *instructions* and *directives*. Instructions are the commands given to IFPS during an interactive session such as LIST or SOLVE. Directives are specific to command files. They consist of an exclamation point followed by a keyword.

Exercises

1. Modify line 50 in the program shown in Figure A.1 so that it checks to see if NET PROFIT AFTER TAX is positive. If it is not, arrange to pay zero dividends.

2. How would the output of the program in Figure A.1 be affected if line 130 were written as SELLING PRICE = 5?

3. Suppose you can reinvest some or all of the dividend money to advertise. That is, modify the model in Figure A.3 as follows:

ADVERTISING = ADVERTISING RATE * PREVIOUS NET PROFIT
                    AFTER TAX
NET PROFIT AFTER TAX = SALES − COGS − TAXES − ADVERTISING
SALES = (SELLING PRICE * QUANTITY SOLD)
            + ADVERTISING LEVERAGE * ADVERTISING

Here, ADVERTISING RATE indicates the fraction of the previous year's net profit invested into advertising and advertising leverage is the number of dollars of sales achieved from each dollar invested in advertising. Add the following assumptions:

ADVERTISING RATE = 0.2
ADVERTISING LEVERAGE = 5

To determine effectiveness of the advertising policy, compute the net present worth of the dividends from the statement:

NET PRESENT WORTH OF DIVIDENDS = NPVC(DIVIDENDS,.12, 0)

SOLVE the model. Then run a series of WHAT IF cases.

a. Vary ADVERTISING RATE between 0 and 0.5 in steps of 0.1.
b. Vary ADVERTISING RATE between 0.6 and 0.9 in steps of 0.1 and, in addition, set

DIVIDEND PAYOUT RATE = (1 − FUTURE ADVERTISING RATE)
FOR 4, 0.5.

(*Note:* Changing the DIVIDEND PAYOUT RATE is required to make funds available for advertising.)
Use the data you obtain to draw a graph showing the Net Present Value of Dividends as a function of the Advertising Rate. What is the optimal advertising rate?

4. *Income Statement Exercise.*
    Given: A company is producing and selling several products for a gross sales (income) of 2.15 million dollars (in 1992). Returns and allowances are 3 percent of gross sales, reducing the income to net sales. Marketing expenses, management, and general (MM&G) are figured to be 20 percent of net sales. Cost of goods sold is the sum of labor ($325,000), materials ($600,000) and overhead. Overhead is figured to be 30 percent of the combined cost of labor and materials plus $70,000.
    Gross profit is the difference between the net sales and the cost of goods sold. To figure the profit before tax, the MM&G expenses need to be subtracted from the gross profit. Finally, there is a 28 percent federal tax and 7 percent state tax that needs to be considered.
    a. Prepare an income statement and compute the taxes and profit after tax, for 1992. (Figures in thousands of dollars.)

    b. Find the profit after tax if gross sales decline to $1.9 million.

    c. Find the federal tax paid if the tax rate is 32 percent. (Use original data.)

    d. Find the gross sales needed to generate a profit after tax of $1,000,000 (net profit). (Use original data.)

5. *Five-Year Projection Exercise.* Use the original data of Exercise 4 to prepare a five-year projection (1993–1997) using the following growth assumptions:

- Gross sales increases 6 percent per year.
- Labor increases 5 percent per year.
- Material increases 7 percent per year.
- The fixed overhead increases $10,000 per year.

    a. Prepare a five-year projection.

    b. Show the net profit if labor increases 10 percent.

    c. Show *graphically* the net profit under "a" and "b." Use bars if IFPS/Personal is used.

6. *Personnel Hiring Policy Exercise.* The 1993 employment mix in the City of Hope is: Asians 15 percent, Blacks 8 percent, Latinos 7 percent, and Caucasians 70 percent. There is a total of 500 employees. Each year 10 percent of the employees, in each category, leave the city. Replacement is done according to a hiring policy. The city is considering two hiring policys (in percent):

	Asians	Blacks	Latinos	Caucasians
Policy A	20	20	30	30
Policy B	30	15	25	30

Prepare a five-year (1994–1998) hiring plan for vacant positions using the two policies. Show the number of people to be hired and the total number of employees.

Note:

    a. The city expects a growth rate of 7 percent per year in its total employment.

    b. Work with two decimals accuracy level.

7. A company's marketing research group prepared the following report on a proposed new product:

It is difficult to assess with certainty how any new product will do. The best we can do is quantify the risk. We believe that the proposed new product has an economically useful lifetime of five years. The total market at the time of introduction should be 500,000 units per year, and this market should grow at a rate of 10 percent per year. At a price of $9/unit we believe that the product can capture a significant share of the market, most likely 5 percent. We expect that we can produce the product for $6.75 per unit and that annual overhead cost will be $12,000. Engineering advises that an initial investment of $95,000 will be required to create the product. As you know, we use a discount rate of 15 percent for analyzing all new product proposals.

Based on our analysis, we recommend going ahead with this product since, based on the foregoing assumptions, the net present value for this product is over $88,000.

Your task is to check whether the marketing research group's claim that the anticipated net present value is over $88,000 is correct.

8. The vice president of marketing who received the report described in the previous exercise was quite risk averse. He felt that the uncertainties referred to by the marketing group were real and that they should introduce these uncertainties into their model. He called the head of the marketing research group into his office and they agreed that the following uncertainties existed:

   ■ Market share is normally distributed with a mean of 5 percent and a standard deviation of 1 percent.
   ■ Overhead may be as low as $10,000/year and as high as $15,000/year, but is most likely to be $12,000/year. A triangular distribution should describe this uncertainty.
   ■ Unit costs can also be described by a triangular distribution. The range is from $6.50 to $7.25, with $6.75 as the most likely unit cost.
   ■ Initial investment requirements are uniformly distributed between $90,000 and $100,000.

   It is your job, using Monte Carlo analysis in IFPS, to determine whether the company should proceed under these uncertainties. The vice president of marketing is unwilling to proceed if there is even a 10 percent chance that the net present value will be negative. Based on your results, what decision will he reach?

9. When the proposal reached the CEO, she became concerned about the assumptions because the company had experienced recent overruns in production cost. She felt that a "what-if" analysis should be done using a triangular distribution with a range from $7 to $8 per unit and a most likely value of $7.50. She was, however, less risk averse than the vice president of marketing and was willing to go ahead with the product if there was at least a 70 percent chance that the net present value would be positive.

   Your assignment is to make the "what-if" analysis requested. Based on your data, would she give a go-ahead decision?

10. Refer to the EOQ example of Chapter 5 (Appendix 5-A) solved with Lotus 1-2-3.
    a. Write an IFPS program for the same problem.
    b. Solve the model.
    c. Find the new EOQ if the annual usage changes to 1100.
    d. Find the required discount (in %) that will make the total cost of the discount option equal to that of the EOQ.
    e. Compare the Lotus versus the IFPS solutions and procedures.

11. Find the present value of
    a. Investment today is $3500. Discount rate is 12 percent, and return for year 1 to year 5 is $1000, $1500, $2000, $1200, and $1000.
    b. Adjust initial investment (using goal seeking) in order to get NPV = $2500 at year 5.
    c. What if investment is $4000?

12. Find the growth of return value of (use Growthrate built-in function)
    a. Investment today is $3500. The cumulative returns for year 1 to year 5 are $1000, $2500, $4500, $5700, and $6700. Discount rate is 10 percent.
    b. What if returns for the first three years are $1000, $1555, and $1800?
    c. Adjust returns in order to get growth of return equals to 125 percent (every year).

13. Find internal rate of return of
    a. Investment is $3500. Return for year 1 to year 5 is $1000, $1500, $2000, $1200, and $1000.
    b. What if investment is $1000?

14. Find the value of benefit cost ratio of
    a. Investment is $3500. Return for year 1 to year 5 is $1000, $1500, $2000, $1200, and $1000. Discount rate is 10 percent.
    b. What if investment is $2500?
    c. How high does the initial investment have to be if the benefit-to-cost ratio equals 1.03 at year 5?

15. Find the cumulative straight line depreciation of:
    a. Investment is $3500, salvage value is 0.04. The life is 5 years.
    b. Adjust investment in order to get a period depreciation of 900.

16. Find the cumulative straight line depreciation of:
    a. Investment is $3500. Category is 5. Purchase year is 1992.
    b. What if investment equals $2000?

17. Find the cumulative depreciation using declining balance method of:
    a. Investment is $3500. Salvage is 0.04. The life is 5 years. Acceleration constant is 1.4.
    b. What if investment is $2800 and salvage is 0.05?

18. Given demand, in thousands of units for the last seven years, per quarter.

Years	Quarter 1	Q2	Q3	Q4
1	12	20	16	15
2	11	15	19	18
3	15	12	16	20
4	18	18	14	26
5	13	16	17	17
6	10	13	22	20
7	14	13	15	23

Use IFPS to write a program that will compute:
a. The mean, median, and standard deviation of the demand
b. Moving average (basis = 4 quarters)
c. Centered moving average (basis = 3 quarters)
d. Linear regression; find the equation and the projected demand in the 20th and the 40th quarters
e. The seasonal index
f. The cyclical elements for each period
g. Random variations (trendline, mean, median)
h. Show the graphics, for the above, for the first six periods.

19. *To hedge or not to hedge.* Farmers in Eastern Illinois grow corn that they can sell either at prevailing market prices or at a predetermined contract price. Mike Orange owns a small farm (net worth $500,000) that produces 150,000 bushels of corn in a normal year, 200,000 bushels in a good year, and 80,000 bushels in a poor year. Prices in the open market vary from $3.50 to $5.60 per bushel. The most likely price is $4.10. The statistical distribution of the above data approximates a *triangular* shape. The cost of producing corn is $0.70/bushel in addition to a fixed cost of $300,000/year for the upkeep of the farm.

   The tax schedule on farms is such that no tax is paid on an annual profit of $42,000 (depreciation is to be disregarded); 42,001 − 65,000 profit results in an 18 percent tax on this amount. Any profit above 65,000 is subject to 28 percent tax.

   As stated earlier, the farmer can sell at the market price or at the contract price. Currently the contract price is $4.10/bushel for either a quantity of 60,000 bushels or 120,000 bushels. In such a case the farmer must deliver the entire quantity. If the crop is lower than that amount he must buy the difference, in the open market, at the prevailing price.
   a. Build an IFPS model to describe the farmer's problem.
   b. Prepare an influence diagram.
   c. Find which alternative is superior.
   (You need the IFPS mainframe version; use the TRIRAND and INTERPO-LATION function.)

References and Bibliography to Appendix A

1. Gray, P. *Guide to IFPS,* 2nd ed. New York: McGraw-Hill, 1987.
2. Gray, P. *Guide to IFPS/Personal.* New York: McGraw-Hill, 1988.
3. Plane, D.R. *Quantitative Tools for Decision Making Using IFPS.* Reading, MA: Addison-Wesley, 1986.

Appendix B

Lockheed-Georgia Company: Executive Information Systems*

When Ken Cannestra, president of Lockheed-Georgia Company, arrived at the office at 7:30 A.M. on September 3, 1987, he turned on his computer to review the status of key company projects. Using a specially designed input device, Cannestra scanned screen after screen of program update information. Then he accessed the companywide electronic mail system to read messages from Lockheed-Georgia and other companies throughout the Lockheed Corporation. Half an hour later he checked his electronic calendar for meetings scheduled during the day.

---

*An article by George Houdeshel and Hugh Watson entitled "The Management Information and Decision Support (MIDS) System at Lockheed-Georgia," *Management Information Systems Quarterly,* Spring, 1987, provides helpful background information for the case.

This case was prepared by Professor Lynda M. Applegate at Harvard University as the basis for class discussion rather than to illustrate either effective or ineffective handling of an administrative situation. A supplement (#9-187-147) is available to accompany this case, and provides sample color displays from the executive information system discussed in this case.

On the agenda was a meeting with Bob Pittman, manager of Management Information and Control Services; George Houdeshel, supervisor of Management Information and Decision Support; and Stephen Beer, manager of Distributed Data Processing and User Support. These individuals were responsible for developing and maintaining the Management Information and Decision Support (MIDS) system—the executive information system that Cannestra had just finished using.

In the 8 years since MIDS had been introduced, the size and scope of the system and the number of users had grown steadily. MIDS had become tightly linked into the management and control processes of the company. However, the impending reorganization of Lockheed Corporation, which would be announced that day, would require a restructuring of Lockheed-Georgia and a change in their management systems. The meeting was being held to discuss the future of MIDS in the new organization.

Company Background

Lockheed Corporation was a major competitor in the nation's $90 billion aerospace industry. (See Exhibit 9 for a competitive profile of the aerospace industry.) In 1987, Lockheed Corporation's primary business was research, development, and production of aerospace products and systems. Of the corporation's 1985 sales, programs for the U.S. government accounted for 88 percent, sales to foreign governments 7 percent, and commercial customers, domestic and foreign sales, 5 percent. (Exhibit 1 presents the Lockheed Corporation organization chart. Exhibit 2 presents a financial summary for 1985.)

Lockheed-Georgia Company

Lockheed-Georgia Company, organized around four business segments, reported to the Lockheed Corporation through the Aeronautical Systems Group. The Lockheed-Georgia Company was formed in 1951 to bring the dormant World War II Air Force Plant #6 in Marietta, Georgia, back on line to modify B-29 bombers for the growing Korean conflict. The company was known for its success in developing cargo aircraft. Beginning with the C-130 Hercules and continuing with the C-141 Starlifter and the C-5 Galaxy, Lockheed-Georgia became a major competitor in airlift design and manufacturing. Lockheed-Georgia's primary competitors were Boeing, McDonnell Douglas, and Airbus.

A unique feature of the aerospace industry was the strategic dependence of each company on a limited number of multi-billion dollar products. In 1987, Lockheed-Georgia depended on three major airplane programs and research for its survival. (See Exhibit 3 for the Lockheed-Georgia organization chart.)

Described as the "bread and butter" of Lockheed-Georgia, the C-130 Hercules had been in production since 1954. In 1986, production was three planes per month and each plane sold for between $15–20 million.

EXHIBIT 1 Lockheed Corporation Organization Chart, January 1987

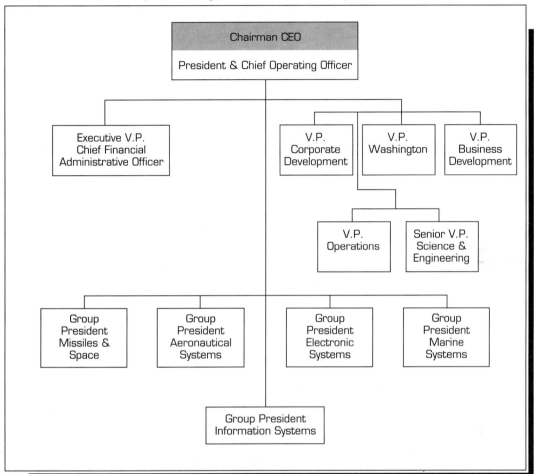

Production of the C-5 Galaxy began in 1966, and 81 C-5As were built before the line ended in 1973. In December 1982, Lockheed-Georgia won an Air Force contract to build 50 updated versions of the airplane, designated the C-5B. The $6.9 billion program was scheduled for completion in 1989. In 1987, approximately one C-5B per month was produced. Ken Cannestra emphasized the importance of finding follow-up contracts for the C-5 or new products to replace it when he said:

> When I consider the future of the company one of the things that I worry about the most is how we will manage if we do not find something to replace the C-5B contract as the program winds down in the late 1980s. Tremendous declines in personnel, sales and profits would occur if we do not act now to develop new products or new markets for our existing products.

EXHIBIT 2 Lockheed Corp. Financial Summary for 1985 (in millions except per share data)

Operating Results

	1986	1985	1984	1983	1982	1981
Sales						
Missiles, space, and electronic systems[a]	$5,337	$4,982	$3,883	$2,898	$2,782	$2,422
Aeronautical systems	4,389	4,130	3,779	3,159	2,518	2,541
Marine systems	161	230	330	365	293	200
Information systems	386	193	121	68	20	13
Total Sales	$10,273	$9,535	$8,113	$6,490	$5,613	$5,176
Program profits						
Missiles, space, and electronic systems	320	284	253	182	168	161
Aeronautical systems	455	437	373	297	261	275
Marine systems	(10)	8	13	39	26	22
Information systems	(2)	4	11	9	2	3
Total Program Profits	763	733	650	527	457	461
Interest expense	66	53	62	66	130	186
Net earnings (loss)	$ 408	$ 401	$ 344	$ 263	$ 207	$ (289)
Earnings (loss) per share of common stock						
Primary						
Continuing operations	$ 6.18	$ 6.10	$ 5.28	$ 4.18	$ 3.65	$ 3.09
Average number of common and common equivalent shares outstanding	66.0	65.7	64.9	62.4	55.9	48.7
Dividends per share of common stock	$ .95	$ .75	$ .45			

[a]The Missiles and Space and Electronic Systems Group was split into two separate groups in 1986.

In March 1961, Lockheed-Georgia won the Air Force competition to design and build the C-141 StarLifter, the world's first pure jet transport plane. While no new C-141s were being produced in 1987, Lockheed-Georgia actively pursued opportunities to modify existing C-141s.

High technology research represented the final business segment for the Lockheed-Georgia Company. Under government contracts, the company's engineers tested advanced airplane designs and new material, such as composites, and developed new aerospace products.

Management Information and Control Services

The Management Information and Control Services department, under the direction of Bob Pittman, was responsible for design, implementation, and ongoing maintenance and management of the MIDS system. (See Exhibit 4.) The department was organized around four major activities. Graphics Arts and Cost Reduction, made up of a supervisor and two technical illustrators, developed graphics for presentations by company executives. These employees worked closely with three employees in Organization Planning and Control, and Re-

EXHIBIT 3 Lockheed-Georgia Organization Chart, January 1987

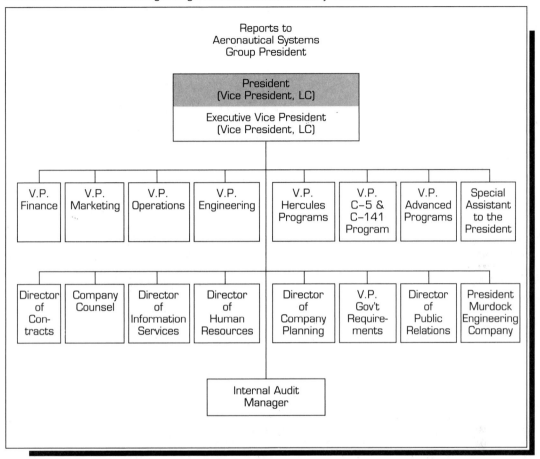

ports and Presentations, who wrote speeches and companywide reports for company executives. Finally, Management Information and Decision Support consisted of nine employees who were responsible for the daily flow of information from the functional/program areas to the top executives via the MIDS system.

Information Technology at Lockheed-Georgia

The highly technical, engineering focus of Lockheed-Georgia contributed to a heavy reliance on information technology throughout the company including robotics, artificial intelligence, computer-aided design, and computer-aided manufacturing. Many functional areas (e.g., engineering, manufacturing) had their own information systems technology group within the functional group. These groups were additional to a centralized information services group that

EXHIBIT 4   Management Information and Control Services Organization Chart, January 1987

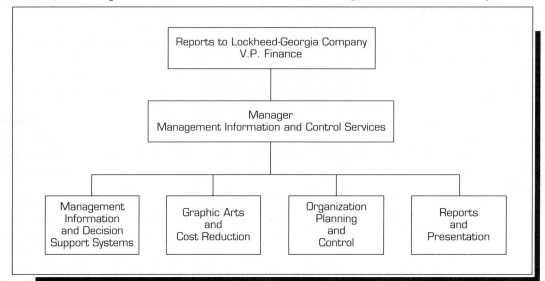

reported directly to the president through the director of Information Services. (See Exhibit 5.) Technical support to the MIDS system was a responsibility of the Distributed Computing and User Support Department in the centralized Information Services area.

MIDS Implementation and Description

Bob Pittman started at Lockheed-Georgia Company in 1951 "on the drawing boards" preparing speeches and presentations for the executives. Because of his companywide knowledge and perspective, he was eventually promoted to his present position. Over the years, he gained the confidence and respect of company executives as a reliable information source because he was diligent in collecting information and unbiased in reporting that information in a form that focused on the needs of executives. In 1975 when the company president, Robert B. Ormsby, requested a personal, automated system for daily information reporting, it seemed natural that he would turn to Bob Pittman to direct the development of the system.

Ormsby's directive to Pittman was for an online status reporting system to provide information that was concise, timely, complete, easy to access, relevant to his needs, and could eventually be used by other executives. Lockheed-Georgia's existing information systems provided large quantities of data, but Ormsby found it difficult to quickly locate information relevant to a given problem. In addition, reports did not contain up-to-date data and organizational

EXHIBIT 5 Information Services Organization Chart, January 1987

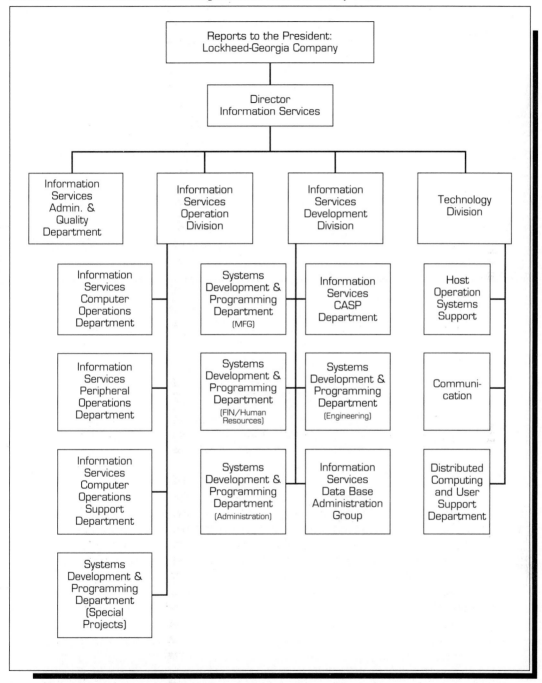

units were basing decisions on data which should have been the same but was not. Pittman recalled that first request:

> Bob Ormsby made his way to the presidency through the engineering area as chief engineer and vice president of Engineering. He was a tinkerer and engineer at heart. It was no surprise to us that he would welcome the chance to use the latest technology. But this was 1975 and we had a difficult time finding the technology needed to support the color graphics and information intensive nature of the system he wanted. Ormsby kept asking us about the system and we kept explaining that we were having trouble locating the right hardware. One day in 1978, as Ormsby was walking through the electronics lab, he saw a newly developed microcomputer being used for color graphics research. He immediately wanted to know why that computer could not be used for his information reporting system. It took three years to identify the appropriate computer but only six months from that time to get a computer with the first prototype of the MIDS system on the president's desk.

Once Ormsby had identified the computer to use for the MIDS system, Bob Pittman immediately began to gather a team to work on the project. He approached George Houdeshel, an industrial engineer, to identify a project supervisor. Houdeshel was intrigued by the potential of the project and decided to accept the assignment himself. Houdeshel realized, however, that he would have to work with the Information Services department to design and implement the system. In the past, attempts to coordinate software development projects with the Information Services group were besieged by problems. He recalled his concerns with the project:

> In past projects, a programmer or team of programmers would be assigned to work with me on a project. They always had other duties to perform and I had no say in the determination of priorities. In addition, once we had finally developed a good working relationship where the programmers understood what I wanted, they would be transferred to a different project.

Houdeshel informed Pittman that he would supervise the MIDS project, and he recommended that the Information Services personnel assigned to the project be responsible to the Management Information and Control Services department and be physically located in that area. Pittman contacted Steve Beer who would be responsible for the MIDS project in the Information Services department. Beer and Pittman worked out an arrangement where the programmers assigned to the MIDS project would relocate to the Management Information and Control Services department and would report to Houdeshel as project supervisor and to Beer as functional manager.

The original MIDS project team consisted of two people from the Management Information and Control Services staff and one person from the Information Services staff. The Management Information and Control Services personnel were needed for their experience in preparing company reports and presentations for Lockheed executives. They were responsible for determining the system content, screen designs, and operational requirements. The Information Services personnel were responsible for hardware selection and acquisition, and for software development.

The MIDS team began by exploring the information requirements of Ormsby and his staff. This included determining what information was needed, in what form, at what level of detail, and how often it would need to be updated. The next step was to determine data sources for the MIDS system. Houdeshel explained how data was selected for use in MIDS.

> We selected raw data that had not already been analyzed and filtered. We wanted the information to meet the needs of different executives and to minimize the bias that could be introduced through previous analysis.

The initial version of MIDS provided Ormsby with 31 information displays. Ormsby was very enthusiastic about the prototype system, and requested that the system be made available immediately to the top executives at Lockheed-Georgia.

Growth of the MIDS System

During the 8 years following the development of the prototype, MIDS evolved to the point where, in 1987, it offered over 1,400 displays for 87 users. Five Information Analysts were responsible for maintaining the information within the MIDS system, and three Computer Analysts were responsible for developing and modifying the software. The system design also evolved over the 8-year period.

The original MIDS system was designed to run on a stand-alone microcomputer in each executive's office. Each executive was provided with a floppy disk that contained the MIDS control program and the information displays that the executive was authorized to view. Each day, the Information Analysts would update the floppy disks containing the displays. As more executives were given access to MIDS, updating each executive's floppy disk separately became impractical, and the decision was made to store the displays centrally on a DEC VAX 11/780.

Although the decision to move to a centralized system made it easier to maintain MIDS, a new problem arose. Pittman summarized the situation:

> The decision to change to a centralized MIDS system solved the update and maintenance problems but introduced the problem of how to control access to screens so that executives could view only the information they were authorized to see. We decided to use a password-based security procedure in which each display was assigned to one of three classes: private data, reserved data, and open data. Two authorization tables were then used to profile each user's authorization privileges. In addition, the password was linked

to a specific terminal requiring the user to be in his or her office to use MIDS with full password authorization privileges. Although this placed some limitations on the functionality of the system, we believed that the highly sensitive and important nature of the information demanded extra precautions.

As system use filtered down to the level of the functional managers, a second problem arose. Pittman explained the problem:

> Early in the development of MIDS, we [the MIDS staff] were forced to confront two important policy issues. First, and most important, was a determination of who owned the data in the MIDS system. The second issue concerned the determination of who would be responsible for controlling access to information within the system and how that control would be enforced. We felt that a key factor in the success of the system was that each executive feel confident that the information received from MIDS was unbiased and did not reflect the usual filtering that comes when the information source is in a position of defending his/her organizational unit's performance. We wanted functional area managers to have the same confidence in the system.

The MIDS staff, with the approval of Ormsby, decided that individual managers should control access to information specific to their functional area. To enforce this policy, the MIDS system was partitioned into two levels. The Executive MIDS system contained information available to all of the top executives of the company, based on their authorization status. MIDS subsystems were developed by specific functional managers who controlled access to the subsystem data. No executive could view information in a MIDS subsystem without the approval of the subsystem manager. Access to a MIDS subsystem by other functional managers was controlled in a similar manner. Based on authorization status, managers were given access to portions of the Executive MIDS system.

Bob Pittman and George Houdeshel were granted authority to enforce this policy. Enforcing the policy was not always easy, but Pittman and Houdeshel believed that the success of MIDS hinged on the ability to ensure security, privacy, and confidence in the information. They recounted one of the most difficult challenges to the policy.

> Paul Frech assumed the presidency of the Lockheed-Georgia Company in June, 1984 when Ormsby was promoted to group president. Frech's background was in manufacturing. By this time the manufacturing control area had developed their own MIDS subsystem and Frech was anxious to gain access to it so he could monitor manufacturing data. The manufacturing manager, however, did not want the president or any other chief executive to be able to have free access to this information. At least six times Frech asked to be granted access to the Manufacturing Subsystem of MIDS. Six times we had to carefully explain to him the reason for the policy and offer to update the Executive MIDS with any manufacturing information that he wanted to track on a regular basis. We also recommended that he talk with the manager of Manufacturing Control to discuss specific MIDS displays that he wished to see.

The Executive's Use of MIDS

Each executive gained access to MIDS through an IBM PC/XT located in his or her office by entering a password. Upon entry into the system, the executive was given the option to: (1) view a specific MIDS display, (2) view a previously defined sequence of displays, (3) obtain a listing of all screens that had been updated, (4) obtain a listing of all persons having access to the system, (5) enter the PROFS electronic mail system, (6) access an external database (e.g. CompuServ). The user was also given a number of options for viewing a specific display. Users familiar with the MIDS system commands could use keystroke commands to call up any screen for which authorization was available. A maximum of four keystrokes was all that was required to view any screen in the MIDS system. A keyword index was also available instead of keystroke commands to call up a screen. The keyword index, containing the words most commonly used by the executives, was revised regularly based on monitoring the executives' use of the system. Finally, users could view a specific display by accessing the MIDS Major Category Menu. (See Exhibit 6.) This menu provided an overview of the major categories of information contained in the system.

Information for a particular subject area was organized in a top-down fashion within a single display or in a series of displays. A summary graph was always presented first, either at the top of a screen of a single display or as the first display in a series of displays. Supporting graphs, tables, and text followed

EXHIBIT 6 MIDS Major Category Menu

MIDS MAJOR CATEGORY MENU

□ TO RECALL THIS DISPLAY AT ANY TIME HIT 'RETURN-ENTER' KEY.
□ FOR LATEST UPDATES SEE S1.

A MANAGEMENT CONTROL
     OBJECTIVES; ORGANIZATIONS; TRAVEL/
     AVAILABILITY/EVENTS SCHED.

  CP CAPTURE PLANS INDEX

B C-5B ALL PROGRAM ACTIVITIES

C HERCULES ALL PROGRAM ACTIVITIES

E ENGINEERING
     COST OF NEW BUSINESS; R & T

F FINANCIAL CONTROL
     BASIC FINANCIAL DATA; COST REDUCTION;
     FIXED ASSETS; OFFSET; OVERHEAD;
     OVERTIME; PERSONNEL

H HUMAN RESOURCES
     CO-OP PROGRAM, EMPLOYEE STATISTICS &
     PARTICIPATION

M MARKETING
     ASSIGNMENTS; PROSPECTS; SIGN-UPS;
     PRODUCT SUPPORT; TRAVEL

O OPERATIONS
     MATERIEL; OPERATIONS SUPPORT;
     PRODUCTION OPERATIONS; PRODUCT
     ASSURANCE & SAFETY

P PROGRAM CONTROL
     FINANCIAL & SCHEDULE PERFORMANCE
   MS MASTER SCHEDULING MENU

S SPECIAL ITEMS
     DAILY DIARY; SPECIAL PROGRAMS

U UTILITY
     SPECIAL FUNCTIONS AVAILABLE

T Q I P

EXHIBIT 7   MIDS Users, Displays, and Displays Viewed[a]

| | | Number of Displays | | Mean Number of |
Year	Number of Users	Executive MIDS	Subsystems	Displays Viewed Per User/Per Day
1979	12	69	N/A	N/A
1980	24	231	N/A	N/A
1981	27	327	N/A	N/A
1982	31	397	16	3
1983	31	441	21	4
1984	49	620	415	4.2
1985	70	710	530	5.5
1986	87	726	750	5.2

[a]From Houdeshel and Watson (1987).

providing more detail. The MIDS staff found that the executives preferred to have as much information as possible on a single display even if it appeared "busy."

All displays contained a screen number, title, date when it was last updated, and the name and telephone number for the source(s) of the information presented. Knowing the information source and the identity of the responsible staff member within a specific organizational unit was important for ensuring accountability for the information contained in the system. This also provided the executive with access to the specific person(s) that could answer more detailed questions about the information.

Standards were developed for the terms used, color codes, and graphic designs. Pittman explained how MIDS helped standardize communication within the company:

> The importance of standard definitions can be illustrated by the use of the word "signup." In general, the term refers to a customer's agreement to buy an aircraft. Before MIDS, organizational units used the term differently. To marketing people, a signup was the receipt of a letter of intent to buy. Legal services considered it receipt of a signed contract. Finance interpreted it as the receipt of a down payment. In MIDS we defined a signup as a signed contract with a nonrefundable down payment. Over the years, we noticed that gradually all of the organizational units began to use the term signup in the same way that it was defined in MIDS. This was true for many other terms where, before MIDS, the definition was vague and subject to wide ranges of interpretation.

Color was also used in a standard way in the MIDS system. The traffic light pattern was adopted to convey project status. Green corresponded to a favorable evaluation; yellow to a marginal evaluation; and red to an unfavorable evaluation. For example, if a project was under budget or ahead of schedule, it was displayed in green; on budget or on schedule was displayed in yellow; and over budget or behind schedule was displayed in red. Special markings were used to differentiate color for executives with color differentiation problems. All displays were designed to provide both black and white and color hard copy output. Color transparencies were also available.

Comments were added to the displays to explain abnormal conditions, provide graphic analysis, reference related displays, and provide information about pending changes. Houdeshel provided an example of the use of comments to enhance display interpretation:

> A recent display showed that May signups were three less than forecasted. The Information Analyst responsible for the display knew, however, that a downpayment from a customer for three aircraft was en route and due to arrive at any moment. The Information Analyst added this information as a comment. Without these comments, the display would have been what we call a "paper tiger." This is a situation that appears to require managerial attention but really does not. This is a good example of how MIDS is designed to convey information for decision-making—not just to transmit data.

Executives were taught to use MIDS in a 15-minute tutorial by the Information Analysts. Written instructions for the system were not used.

All executives did not use MIDS in the same way. Some browsed through displays while others regularly viewed a specific sequence of displays. An important feature for browsing through the system was the ability to stop the generation of a display on the screen with a single keystroke when it was of no further interest. Special programs were also created to allow executives to page through a series of displays in a predefined sequence. These "sequence files" could be created by the user, requested by the user and prepared by the MIDS staff, or offered to a user by the MIDS staff after observing viewing habits.

Ken Cannestra described his use of MIDS. See Exhibit 10 for sample MIDS displays used by the president and executives.

> On a typical day, I log into MIDS when I arrive at work. I start out by viewing the update screen. This allows me to quickly obtain up-to-date information on all of our major programs and projects. Once I've finished with the update screen, I usually review some of the sequences of screens that contain information that I monitor on a regular basis. Some, like the C-5 project, I will review each day. Others I review on a regular basis but not necessarily every day. I usually end the session by checking my mail, most of which comes from corporate.

When asked to evaluate MIDS, Cannestra stated:

> MIDS increases my efficiency and I feel that I am better informed. If I didn't have MIDS I would probably have to spend more time in routine meetings with my staff and the functional managers to get the information that I need. In addition, I would probably have to wade through a lot more reports just to keep up-to-date.

EXHIBIT 8 Corporate Special Bulletin

___

September 3, 1987

LOCKHEED INTEGRATES THREE AIRCRAFT DIVISIONS
INTO SINGLE COMPANY TO MEET CHALLENGES OF FUTURE

Today we are publicly announcing the immediate integration of the Lockheed-Georgia Company, Lockheed-California Company, and Lockheed Aircraft Service Company into a single operating company, Lockheed Aeronautical Systems Company (LASC), headquartered in Burbank, California.

Although we have a strong aeronautical company today, the business environment in which we operate is changing significantly. Analysis of the projected aeronautical line of business reveals very few major program starts in the next 5 to 10 years.

Therefore, we must better utilize our resources and our talented people and their capabilities to compete in significant second-source and subcontracting opportunities as well as major programs when they materialize:

Focusing the use of our people and financial resources will make us a stronger competitor. Market opportunities not previously available because of noncompetitive costs will then be open to us.

Modernizing our facilities and redesigning our cost structure will offer us the opportunity to create jobs as we enter this new competitive arena.

Consolidating our research, technology and engineering capabilities into one primary organization will further strengthen our technical excellence.

Preserving and supporting the Advanced Development Projects (ADP) organization will further strengthen our unique product development capabilities.

Concentrating leadership and resources to win the Advanced Tactical Fighter (ATF) program will secure our position in advanced aeronautical systems development and production into the next century.

Our primary intent in taking these actions is to expand the possibility of winning new business in a depressed market, thus creating a challenging and more stable future for our employees.

Effective immediately the management structure of Lockheed Aeronautical Systems Company is as follows:

- John C. Brizendine is appointed president of LASC.
- Harold T. Bowling is appointed executive vice president-LASC and general manager of the Ontario Division.

EXHIBIT 8 (continued)

- Kenneth W. Cannestra is appointed executive vice president-LASC and general manager of the Georgia Division.
- E. Lloyd Graham is appointed executive vice president-LASC and general manager of headquarters operations.
- R. Richard Heppe is appointed executive vice president-president-LASC and general manager of Advanced Tactical Fighter programs.
- Ben R. Rich is appointed executive vice president-LASC and general manager of ADP.
- Robert W. Berry is appointed vice president-finance and contracts, LASC.
- Robert B. Corlett is appointed vice president-human resources, LASC.
- Willard H. Mitchell is appointed vice president-Washington office, LASC.

Other management positions, including a new position of executive vice president of LASC and general manager of research, technology and engineering, will be announced as integration progresses.

The goals of LASC will be accomplished by recasting the objectives of our aeronautical divisions:

- Burbank and its supporting facilities will be responsible for research and development, full systems acquisition, and certain production capabilities.
- Marietta and its supporting facilities will be responsible for primary production for LASC, second source production, major subcontracting, and major aircraft modification.
- Ontario and its supporting facilities continue to be responsible for their existing lines of business with research and development assistance provided by Burbank.

All current locations will remain in operation with no immediate effect on employment other than that caused by the normal fluctuations of business.

Performance on all existing contracts will not be interrupted at present locations as we continue to provide our customers excellent products and services.

It will take time to accomplish full integration, but we expect to have the job done by the end of 1988. We will keep you informed of the progress being made.

With your continued support and commitment, we are confident the new Lockheed Aeronautical Systems Company will achieve solid success.

L. O. Kitchen
Chairman
and Chief Executive Officer

EXHIBIT 8 (continued)   Organizational Structure of the Lockheed Aeronautical Systems Co., September 3, 1987

Lockheed Corporation

L.O. Kitchen
Chairman and C.E.O.

R.A. Fuhrman
President and C.O.O.

Lockheed Aeronautical Systems Company

J.C. Brizendine
President

Washington Office

Human Resources

Finance & Contracts

New Business Development and Plans

Administration

Facilities

ATF Programs

R.R. Heppe
Executive V.P.-LASC and General Manager

Georgia Division

K.W. Cannestra
Executive V.P.-LASC and General Manager

Ontario Division

H.T. Bowling
Executive V.P.-LASC and General Manager

LASC HQ Operations

E.L. Graham
Executive V.P.-LASC and General Manager

Advanced Development Projects

B.R. Rich
Executive V.P.-LASC and General Manager

Research Technology and Engineering

(*)
Executive V.P.-LASC and General Manager

* To be announced

EXHIBIT 9   Competitive Profile of the Aerospace Industry

The aerospace industry is segmented along two dimensions. The most basic seg-mentation is according to customer market with approximately half of sales to cus-tomers in the U.S. government market (military and NASA contracts) and the other half to customers in nongovernment, commercial, and general aviation markets. The industry also is structured according to relative engineering and production capability with only five or six of the leading companies having the thousands of engineers and scientists and the massive plant facilities necessary to produce sophisticated military and commercial aircraft. The key success criteria in both the military and commercial markets are performance and cost competitiveness.

In contrast to other industries (e.g., the auto industry), the aircraft industry pro-duces relatively few, highly specialized, high-cost units per year, each incorporating millions of detail parts and thousands of customer-specific modifications. Federal regu-lations require complete documentation and traceability of each of the part numbers in-corporated in an aircraft. Sales are principally under fixed-price, long-term contracts that are negotiated before actual production begins. Management, therefore, has to de-termine in advance sales volumes and manufacturing costs to accurately price a prod-uct. Several other factors combine to make effective management of aircraft manufac-turing very difficult. First, the product is not made for inventory but is produced only to fill a firm order. Second, the customer typically waits until the last possible minute before committing to purchase a plane for delivery at a certain date. Third, most of the complex subassemblies entering into the assembly flow have enormous lead times. The critical path, from the earliest order of metal stock to delivery of the plane to the cus-tomer, may take as long as 4 years.

For a military or commercial aircraft production program, a major aerospace com-pany serves as the prime contractor and designs, develops, produces, markets, and services the product. Start-up costs for a new airplane are $1 to $3 billion. Because of the enormous human and financial resources put into any one program, a company will generally have only three or four programs in progress at one time. Production rates are on the order of one to eight planes per month. Costs, including R&D and avionics equipment, vary from $8 million for a relatively inexpensive military jet to ap-proximately $50 million for jumbo jet airliner. A particular airplane program, with mod-ifications, stays in production for either a very short time or for an extended period of time (15 to 20 years). Because of the high fixed cost associated with each product, any interruption in production time can be very costly.

This industry note (Exhibit 9) was adapted from Harvard Business School Case #9–679–037 en-titled, "The Lockheed-California Company."

Dick Martin, director of public relations, was first introduced to MIDS in his previous position as manager of Public Relations.

I arrive at the office at 6:30 most mornings. The first thing that I do is to check PROFS and review my mail. Most of the mail is from outside the com-pany and involves requests for information. I print out the mail file and either answer the requests myself or request one of my staff to handle it. Once I am done with the mail, I review the update screen, which tells me what has changed since I last logged on. Then I review the daily diary which informs me of company news. After scanning the general information, I look at specific

EXHIBIT 10   Sample MIDS Displays (pp. A40–A46)

S1	Major Update Items	* restricted

Date	Item/Event	Display	
3/16	Hercules major subcontracted assemblies	044	
3/16	Corporate staff schedule	A56	>F
3/16	Environmental protection activities	083	>F
3/16	Controlled inventory through February	F51	>F
3/16	Company airplane schedule	A21	>F
3/13	Fixed asset commitments	F34	>F
3/13	Initial placements: small/disadvantaged business	042	
3/13	Status of C-5A operational aircraft	P41	>F
3/13	FY-88 congressional activity	M75	
3/13	Weekly cash receipts *	F28	>F
3/13	Hercules major subcontracted assemblies	044	
3/13	— sign-up — two Hercules A/C for Japan – – – – – – – – – –	M7	
3/13	Employee participation	H2	
3/13	Product support sales & sign-ups	M17	
3/12	Production operations direct labor performance summary	01	>F
3/12	Hercules weekly overtime summary	P15	
3/12	Personnel through February	F31	>F
3/12	R & T sign-ups *	E34	>F

continued >

Gelac Daily Diary
March 11, 1987

- First flight of the modified GII PTA aircraft occurred Friday, March 6, at 3:40 pm. No problems arose during the 1 hr 42 min flight. The aircraft is expected to be ferried to Gelac by the end of this week.

- LAC 6089, the fifth C-141 center wing aircraft, DD250'd at 7:30 pm on March 10.

EXHIBIT 10 (continued)

A44	Stock Performance as of noon/March 19, 1987						Source: 1st Interstate Trad'g-CA (213) S14-3207	
Company	Prior Close	Open	High	Low	Noon	Change	Volume
Boeing	$51\frac{3}{4}$	$51\frac{5}{8}$	$51\frac{7}{8}$	$51\frac{1}{2}$	$51\frac{7}{8}$	$+\ \frac{1}{8}$	225,800
General Dyn.	$75\frac{3}{8}$	$75\frac{1}{4}$	$75\frac{3}{8}$	$74\frac{5}{8}$	$74\frac{7}{8}$	$-\ \frac{1}{2}$	62,800
Lockheed	$50\frac{3}{4}$	$50\frac{5}{8}$	$51\frac{1}{4}$	$50\frac{1}{2}$	51	$+\ \frac{1}{4}$	296,400
McDonnell D.	$78\frac{7}{8}$	$78\frac{3}{8}$	79	$78\frac{3}{8}$	$78\frac{7}{8}$	0	45,600
Northrop	$48\frac{1}{2}$	$48\frac{3}{4}$	$50\frac{3}{8}$	$48\frac{3}{4}$	$50\frac{3}{8}$	$+1\frac{7}{8}$	469,200
Rockwell N.A.	56	56	$56\frac{1}{2}$	$55\frac{7}{8}$	$56\frac{3}{8}$	$+\ \frac{3}{8}$	109,000
Dow Jones Industrial Average -----------------------						+5.26	109.3M

Note: Change equals prior day's close vs. noon.
      For Lockheed trend see A44A
      For industry tends see A44B,C

>F

D4	Hercules Prospects Index sample for demo	Source: Bill Cook 5683

Air Reserve	M7	France - SFAIR	M29
Alaska Int'l Air	M15	Independent	M75
Bolivia	M51	Indonesia - AF	M74
Brazil	M5	Japan - JDA	M34
Cameroon	M4	Malaysia - AF	M14
Canada	M52	Marine Corps	M33
Coast Guard	M53	Nigeria - AF	M42
Colombia	M54	Panama	M61
Eastern	M55	Peru . . . . (D5)	M59
Ecuador - AF	M56	Portugal - AF	M28
Ecuador - Army	M57	Saudi Arabia	M23
Egypt	M41	Venezuela	M58

Note: D5 demo display for Peru

EXHIBIT 10 (continued)

D5		**Peru** rep: Dick Sigler			Source: Bud Lawler 5431 Jim Certain 2265

	Mon	Tue	Wed	Thr	Fri	Sat	Sun
Rep location if away				Caracas, Venezuela -------------			

Forecast – Three L–100–30's   Prev. Herc. Buy — 8

Next event — Finalizing financing

Key person — Certain

Sign-up — Next month

Probability — Good

ROM Value — $60M

A/C Delivery: 4th QTR

As of today: Meetings continue among potential lending institutions, insurers, and Gelac's international marketing/finance/legal team to discuss requirements and conditions for financing. Gelac representatives will be in Lima Monday to lay groundwork for final negotiations. No problems expected.

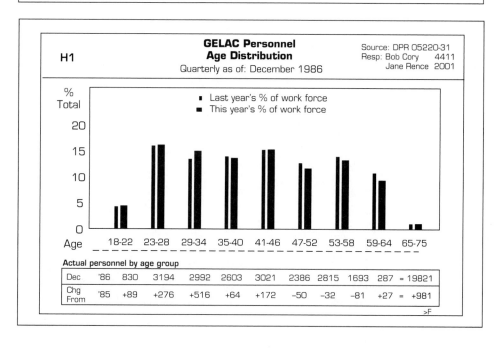

H1		**GELAC Personnel Age Distribution** Quarterly as of: December 1986		Source: DPR 05220-31 Resp: Bob Cory 4411 Jane Rence 2001

%
Total

■ Last year's % of work force
■ This year's % of work force

20

15

10

5

0

Age   18-22   23-28   29-34   35-40   41-46   47-52   53-58   59-64   65-75

Actual personnel by age group

Dec	'86	830	3194	2992	2603	3021	2386	2815	1693	287	= 19821
Chg From	'85	+89	+276	+516	+64	+172	–50	–32	–81	+27	= +981

>F

EXHIBIT 10 (continued)

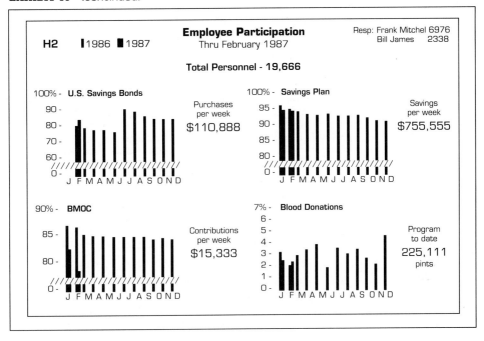

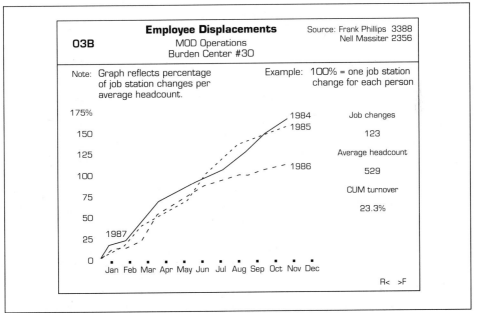

EXHIBIT 10 (contined)

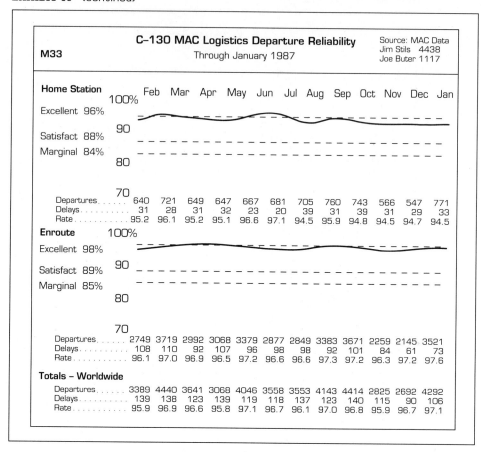

screens that I need to answer specific questions, to use for press responses or to prepare a report. The total time I spend in the morning is about 15 or 20 minutes. During the day I check into PROFS about once an hour if I am in the office, or as soon as I return to the office if I have been away to see if I have any mail. In addition, I will use MIDS five to ten times per day to answer specific questions that have come to me from PROFS or through phone calls.

When asked to evaluate MIDS, Martin stated:

MIDS really saves me time. I no longer have to go through files in my drawer to find information only to find that I haven't saved the most current report. In addition, I no longer have to call all the different offices to find the information I need. In the past, I would often call the same office two or three times during a day to get information to handle requests as they came in. Often the line would be busy or, if I did get through, the person I needed to talk with was out to lunch or off sick. Finally, PROFS has really helped to make my communications with the outside more efficient. Corporate is on the west coast and, in the past, we were always having trouble getting in touch with one another because of the time difference.

EXHIBIT 10 (continued)

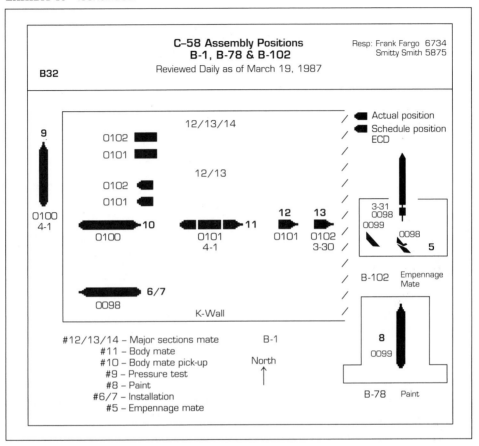

MIDS Organization and Personnel

By 1987, the MIDS staff had grown from two to nine. Approximately 170 Executive MIDS system displays were updated daily. Maintaining the MIDS subsystem displays was left to the functional organizational unit for which the subsystem was developed. In the case of the MIDS subsystems, the MIDS staff provided the functional organizational unit with the tools and training needed to develop and maintain the subsystem, and with space on the mainframe for storing and running the subsystem, and enforced the MIDS system standards and policies.

Each of the five Information Analysts were assigned to specific functional and program areas. They were responsible for attending meetings and developing effective information channels to assure that they "knew everything that was going on in that program or area." In short, they were responsible for *actively* gathering information throughout the company and developing and main-

EXHIBIT 10 (continued)

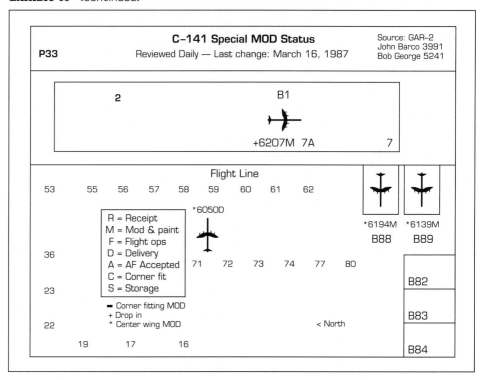

taining the displays in a manner that best suited the information scanning style and content required by each executive. As Pittman explained:

> It is imperative that the Information Analysts understand the information that they enter into the system. Several actions are taken to ensure that this is the case. Most of the Information Analysts have work experience and/or training in their areas of responsibility. They are encouraged to take courses which provide a better understanding of the users' areas and they frequently attend functional area meetings, often serving as an important resource on the companywide perspective. They must determine what to include in MIDS, how to present the information, other data that are necessary to fully understand a display and finally, how to classify the information for access and control.

Over the years, job descriptions and a career path were developed. By 1987 four positions of increasing responsibility had been identified. The Information Associate was an entry-level position with a salary range of approximately $17,000 to $32,000. An undergraduate degree, preferably in MIS, or in-house experience in an information-intensive position was required. Employees at this level were responsible for updating and maintaining existing displays and creating simple displays based on previous samples. The Information Analyst position had a salary range of approximately $20,000 to $38,000. At this level, employees were expected to possess sufficient knowledge, skills, and experience to assume complete responsibility for complex, critical information areas of the company and to create new information displays. The Information Representative had a salary range of approximately $24,000 to $45,000. At this level, the employee was expected to possess proficiency as an analyst and the broad information systems knowledge and skills necessary to direct MIDS system integration at both a technical and organizational level. Finally, the Information Coordinator had a salary range of approximately $26,000 to $50,000. Employees at this level were expected to be capable of identifying and managing the development of new directions for MIDS based on a thorough knowledge of state-of-the-art information technologies and the Lockheed organization.

In 1987, Myra Fowler was one of the Information Analysts working on the MIDS project. Fowler started at Lockheed-Georgia in 1956 upon graduation from high school. Prior to joining the MIDS group in May 1983, she had worked in a number of departments in a variety of secretarial roles. She found her past experience at Lockheed was critical for helping her to perform her role as an Information Analyst.

> As a secretary I was very involved with managing information for the departments in which I worked. Initially this was done without the use of the computer. When I saw the computer being used more and more around the company, I went back to school and took courses in data processing, math, and accounting.

Bobbie Patterson had been an Information Analyst for the past four years. She described her orientation to the position in the following manner.

> At first I was mainly responsible for doing updates for simple displays and doing system backups. This helped me to learn the ropes on less complicated parts of the job. It took approximately 1 year for me to really understand the job and feel comfortable with the broad picture that was needed to function fully in this role.

Cost/Benefit Analysis

When asked to justify the MIDS system, Pittman and Houdeshel pointed to system usage and the satisfaction of the users. They found it difficult, however, to perform a formal cost/benefit analysis. They stated:

> We were never asked to justify costs. We have been fortunate to always have the president as a major champion of the system. It would be very difficult to "sell" the system to a president who was not convinced. The closest we came was "selling" MIDS to Paul Frech, the president after Ormsby.
>
> MIDS was first offered to Frech when he was vice president of manufacturing operations. He had little interest in the system because he felt that he was

very knowledgeable about Lockheed operations and had already established information channels to support his decision-making and job responsibilities. Shortly afterwards, Frech was promoted and moved to corporate headquarters in California. When he was again promoted and returned as president of Lockheed-Georgia, MIDS had become the standard communication channel for executive information and he was reintroduced to the system. At first he was not a regular user. But as time went on he saw the value of the system firsthand. He found that MIDS was an excellent tool for getting up to speed in areas with which he was not personally familiar (e.g., engineering) and to update his knowledge of the status of operations during his absence from Lockheed-Georgia.

Pittman and Houdeshel also compiled data on the number of users and displays and the mean number of displays viewed per day by each executive and how that data changed over time. They felt that this information reflected the benefits of the system because, in their words: "When a user can choose whether or not to use a system, frequency of use can be a measure of success." Exhibit 7 presents the data collected on frequency and patterns of use.

Lockheed Corp. Restructuring—What Now?

Ken Cannestra put down the report on the MIDS system that he had just finished reading and picked up the announcement that all employees of Lockheed Corporation would be receiving that day. (See Exhibit 8.) The reorganization of Lockheed Corporation, detailed in the announcement, would be effective immediately. Lockheed-Georgia would no longer operate as an independent company. Instead, it would be run as a separate division of a newly formed company called Lockheed Aeronautical Systems Company (LASC), which consolidated Lockheed-Georgia, Lockheed-California, and the Lockheed Aircraft Service Company. The new company would be headquartered in Burbank, California. Cannestra's title would change from president of Lockheed-Georgia Company to general manager of LASC—Georgia Division. In this role he would have direct control over manufacturing operations, but he would now have only dotted-line control over the majority of other functional areas (e.g., finance, marketing, human resources, information systems). These functions would be consolidated in LASC, and Cannestra assumed that the majority of the staff would move to California. MIDS, which reported through the finance organization, would be directly affected by the reorganization. Brizendine, the newly announced president of the consolidated LASC, had already expressed interest in expanding MIDS for use throughout the new company. The meeting with Pittman, Houdeshel, and Beer was called to discuss the technical and organizational issues that would need to be resolved if MIDS was to be used as the basis for management decision support and control throughout LASC.

Questions for Discussion

1. Identify the main issue that this case points out. That is, why was this case written, and what does it try to tell us?
2. Listed below are several typical IS issues. Identify those which are *referred to* in the case and *briefly* comment on each of them.
   a. Information security
   b. What support is provided to executives
   c. Expert Systems
   d. Interfaces to other users and information systems
   e. Is the EIS effective (cost/benefit)?
   f. Access and control of information (information "ownership")
   g. Centralization versus decentralization of information services and of MIDS
3. In building EIS there are several key issues. Based on the case, on additional readings, and your own experience, answer the following two questions:
   a. How do you find the *information needs* of executives?
   b. How do you measure the *success* of an EIS?
4. The EIS has been blamed for the corporate snafu. Explain why the EIS is being blamed for the problem. What issues can be identified as a result of the snafu? (Ask your professor for information about this issue.)
5. Evaluate the MIDS staffing strategy.
6. Was the EIS a success or a failure?

Appendix C

Du Pont's Artificial Intelligence Implementation Strategy

It was late spring, 1988, and Ed Mahler was thinking about future directions for the Artificial Intelligence (AI) Task Force. He planned to discuss future strategies he headed at his next meeting with Ray Cairns, vice president for Du Pont's Information Systems Department (ISD). Mahler was convinced that the small systems approach was the way to go and that his group had enough success stories to prove it. At the moment, he was more concerned with how to maintain the enthusiasm and momentum behind the task force. Mahler worried that with very few people reporting directly to him, sustaining the informal networks he had established within the company would be difficult. The AI Task Force had been around for more than two years, and Mahler wondered if "the bloom was off the rose."

For his part, Cairns reflected on Mahler's performance:

> Ed Mahler is doing a terrific job with the AI Task Force. If you had asked me two years ago how far we'd be at this point, I would have said no more than

---

Research Associate Mark Keil prepared this case under the supervision of Assistant Professor John Sviokla of Harvard University as the basis for class discussion rather than to illustrate either effective or ineffective handling of an administrative situation.

ten expert systems would be running in the company. Yet now we have over 200 systems in routine use. Much of the credit for that accomplishment goes to Ed.

Ed really understands the culture of this company and that has certainly helped him. Now, Ed and I agree on a lot of things and we disagree on some things. One area where we disagree, for example, is how much attention we should be spending on the larger, more complex, expert systems. I happen to think we should be spending more effort in this area, while Ed is focused on the small systems. Ed has begun to move slowly toward the bigger systems. His group has offered to fund the development of a large system, but so far no one has submitted a proposal.

The Du Pont Company

Eleuthere Irenee duPont began by manufacturing gunpowder along the banks of the Brandywine River in Wilmington, Delaware, in 1902.[1] The Du Pont company later branched out into pigments, fibers, plastics, and other chemicals, and is today a large, diversified, corporation whose broad product earned a net income of nearly $1.8 billion on 1987 sales of more than $30 billion, placing it tenth in sales and eighth in earnings among *BusinessWeek*'s top 1000 U.S. companies for that year.[2] With more than 100 manufacturing plants worldwide and more than 40 percent of its sales occurring outside the United States, Du Pont had become a global enterprise.

Du Pont's tradition of innovation and technical excellence (by the late 1980s, its annual R&D budget exceeded $1 billion) saw the development of products like neopren, freon, nylon, and teflon. While continuing to fund new opportunities through a set of core businesses that included automotive paints, coal, fibers, films and resins, industrial chemicals, petroleum, and white pigments,[3] Du Pont began to focus on expanding its presence in such high-growth or high-margin businesses as agricultural chemicals, biomedical products, electronics, imaging systems, specialty fibers, and polymers.

Du Pont, like many other U.S. companies at the time was struggling to reduce costs and improve its competitive position. Part of its cost reduction effort, a series of early retirement incentives instituted in 1982, reduced Du Pont's work force to 146,000 employees by 1987. Inasmuch as many of the employees who chose to retire were older and more experienced, this more than 20 percent reduction probably understated the loss of expertise. At the same time, Du Pont was promoting organizational effectiveness. There was an effort to push decision making and responsibility down to the lowest level possible and renewed emphasis on the importance of marketing and customer service.

---

[1] See *Du Pont: The Autobiography of an American Enterprise* (New York: Charles Scribner's Sons) 1952, for a complete history of the company.
[2] "The BusinessWeek Top 1000," *BusinessWeek*, April 15, 1988.
[3] 1987 Du Pont Annual Report.

The Du Pont organization comprised three broad categories: operating departments, technical staff, and other corporate staff. (See Exhibit 1.) The company was highly decentralized, its operating departments being run almost as separate companies, each with its own manufacturing and R&D divisions, and information systems (I/S) group. Corporate technical staff, which included the Central Research and Development, Engineering, and the Information Systems departments provided some centralization and pooling of resources. Du Pont employed a matrix-like structure whereby, for example, an operating department's I/S group reported through the Information Systems Department (ISD) as well as the operating department's management.

ISD had an annual budget of several hundred million dollars and employed more than 900 people. Its reporting structure shown is in Exhibit 2. Historically, ISD had not received much attention from top management, a situation Ray Cairns was trying to change. Cairns was clear on his role as vice president of ISD, a position he held for 9 of his 25 years with Du Pont. "If you asked me to name one thing my job is, I would say it's a marketing job. My job is to sell information systems to upper management."[4]

Cairns's job was not easy. The ISD he joined in the early 1960s was not highly regarded, its systems mostly built from scratch, often failing to meet end users' needs. Cairns's efforts to link ISD's activities more closely to various Du Pont businesses were paying off. ISD's stature within Du Pont was beginning to improve.

Ed Mahler and Artificial Intelligence at Du Pont

In 18 years with Du Pont, Ed Mahler had served in a variety of positions in research and manufacturing, including a five-year stint in corporate planning, where he evaluated emerging technologies that might be useful to Du Pont. It was in this capacity that Mahler became intrigued with the possibilities of artificial intelligence (AI).

But several months of investigation convinced Mahler that at least AI technology was not commercially ready. The specialized LISP machines and expensive programmers needed to develop expert systems were not widely available within the company. Mahler believed the LISP hardware was too expensive, complicated, and unreliable for Du Pont's production environments and end users, and he saw a massive wall of training, software, hardware, jargon, and mysticism standing between the industrial end-user and AI applications. One contract offered to Du Pont for training 40 LISP programmers, including hardware and software, had a price tag of $30 million. Even if Du Pont were to train and support 40 people, Mahler wondered whether a staff that size would have a measurable impact on a company with such a large and decentralized knowl-

---

[4]Clinton Wilder and Nell Margolis, "Information on a Global Scale," *Computerworld*, May 23, 1988, p. 1.

EXHIBIT 1 Du Pont Organizational Chart*

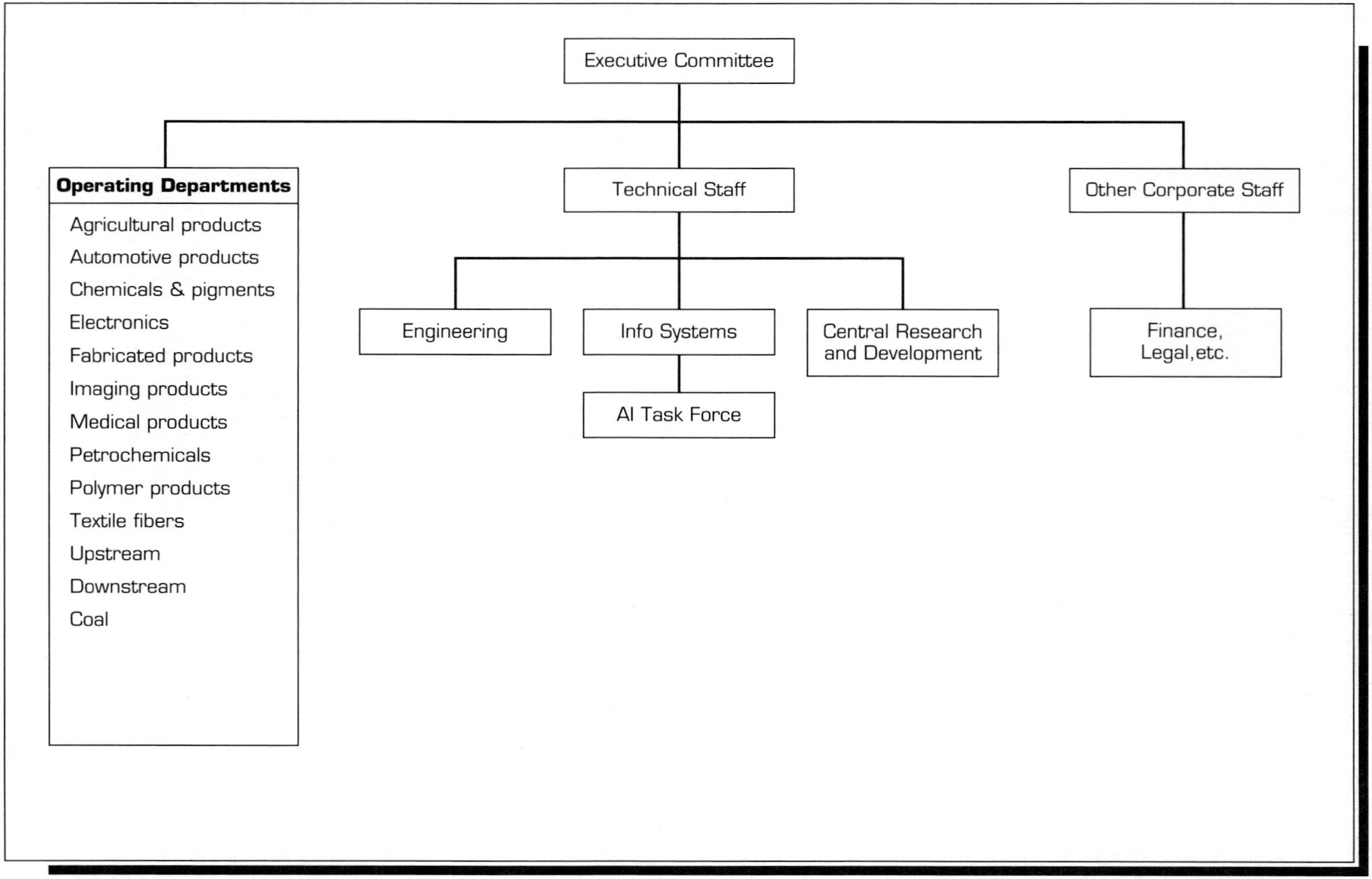

*Adapted from slide presentation given by Ed Mahler.

EXHIBIT 2 Du Pont's Information Systems Department Reporting Structure*

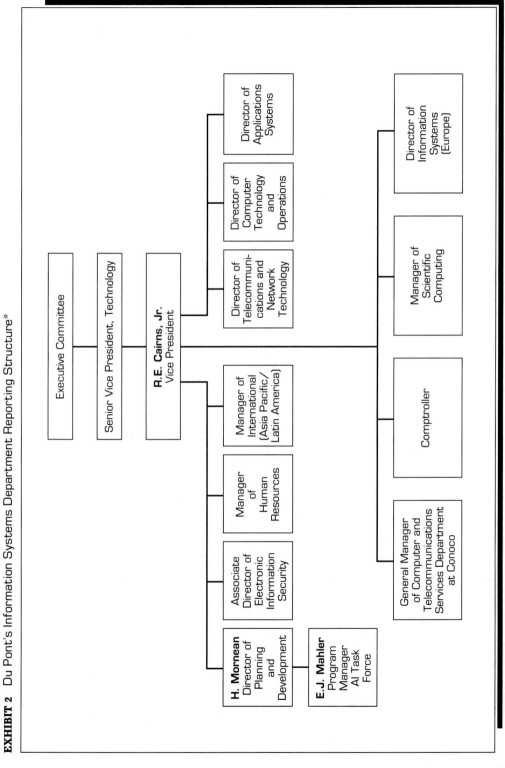

*Adapted from *Computerworld*, May 23, 1988, p. 61.

edge profile. Finally, not one of the more than 30 demonstrations he had seen by AI vendors had run perfectly from start to finish.

In the summer of 1985, two researchers in Du Pont's central research facility, Dave Pensak and John Turner, recognized the potential value of AI, but had difficulty finding business teams to sponsor development of AI applications.

Formation of the AI Task Force

Mahler, just as he was about to give up on AI, heard about the development and decided to investigate the feasibility of AI tools for personal computers. In October 1985, he convinced other managers to loan the people to form a six-member task force.

> Back when we didn't have anything, we went to guys in my old-boy network who knew me personally and who would take a risk on my word. I picked friends who were in different functions and in different environments. There were no formally trained AI experts going into this, although a couple had dabbled in it on their own.

> When we began our first experimental work in the fall of 1985, I intentionally rounded up folks with various backgrounds. Some of the degrees and backgrounds in the group when it was originally formed were electrical engineering and process control, marketing research, computer science, classical systems support, hard-line computer research, agricultural chemistry, and a physics major who spent most of his time in photochemistry. I wanted a bunch of old boy networks that didn't overlap that much, so we would have a broad influence base.[5]

> I really had three criteria for selecting people for the task force, Mahler explained. One, they had to have recognized technical competence within their peer group. Two, they had to have been around Du Pont for a while so that they would have a significant old-boy network. Finally, they had to be willing to take risks and to be committed to the vision.

Between October 1985 and February 1986, Mahler's group began working on a few applications in order to evaluate and gain experience with commercially available expert system shells. "We were testing for both power and dispersability," Mahler observed. "We wanted to know if these systems were powerful enough to serve as general-purpose tools and if they had the necessary features to solve real business problems. We were also interested in dispersability—whether the tools were teachable and compatible with the people and hardware at Du Pont."

By March 1988, the six members of the AI Task Force who reported to Mahler were supplemented by six additional people on loan from other Du Pont

---

[5]"Artificial Intelligence Spotlight," *Computerworld*, November 23, 1987, p. 59.

organizations. Though most worked at the Task Force's Wilmington headquarters, a few were located in the field.

Mahler's enthusiasm for the PC-based tools derived in part from his estimate that there were more than 30,000 "Lotus-literate" people in Du Pont—people who couldn't necessarily program but who were familiar with PC technology. Mahler reasoned that if they could use a spreadsheet application they might also benefit from the PC-based expert-system building tools his group was evaluating.

Mahler became convinced that with a few PC-based shells and a set of internally developed tools for VAX computers, he could use existing hardware and expert-systems technology to solve real business problems. In February 1986, he proposed that his group be formalized. Mahler recalled the formalization process.

> Most new businesses at Du Pont were started within an operating department and did not involve members of the Executive Committee. This situation was different because there was no operating department sponsoring the effort. I assembled a number of top managers from ISD, Engineering, Central Research, and Corporate Plans, to meet with a subset of Du Pont's Executive Committee. Prior to this meeting, Cairns had emerged as a potential ally and sponsor. After a series of management discussions, ISD created a formal group and supplied $2 million annually in seed money, headcount, and, most important of all, the freedom to try some novel management approaches towards implementing a new technology.

"Ed looked at the opportunities at three plants and multiplied by 50," said Doug Reece, a member of the AI Task Force, of Mahler's approach. "His analysis wasn't rigorous—you had to make a leap of faith. When Ed spoke to the Executive Committee, his track record, personality, and background were more influential than his analysis. There's not a lot of folks with the guts to stick their necks out that far."

Mahler's Strategy

In Mahler's opinion, knowledge that could not be applied to what he called "a point of attack" had no value. To Mahler, an expert system was just a computer program for capturing valuable knowledge and delivering it to the point of attack.

Mahler's vision of using PC-based expert systems to solve real business problems ran counter to conventional wisdom. In 1985, people in the AI community, in light of early attempts to build expert systems that had taken five or more man years,[6] were advocating big systems that could provide the big payoffs needed to justify such an expense.

---

[6]Davis, R., "Amplifying Expertise with Expert Systems," in *The AI Business: The Commercial Uses of Artificial Intelligence*, edited by P.H. Winston and K.A. Prendergast, Cambridge, MA: The MIT Press, 1984.

Unlike the large systems touted in the AI literature, which required specialized hardware and were usually built from scratch using flexible, but complex, programming environments, the smaller, less flexible PC-based tools provided a structured environment that made them easier to use. Mahler believed that 90 percent of Du Pont's problems could be solved using standard hardware and PC-based tools, allowing Du Pont to lower its hardware and software costs, while spreading the technology throughout the company. "A lot of people," Mahler said, "say that Du Pont is just building toy systems because we are going after smaller and more approachable problems. They say we'd get a lot more bang for our buck if we went after the large complex systems. I argue for building systems that are just the right size to solve the business problem." Mahler's goal was to lower the entry barriers by building on existing hardware, using low-cost applications-oriented software, training the users on-site, and providing follow-up consulting.

In June 1986, the AI Task Force offered its first training course. Mahler's strategy was to have end-users build their own systems. "We made a fundamental principle," he explained, "that he would not build expert systems centrally. We will help people build them and teach them how to build others or maintain the ones they have, but we will not build any."[7]

Mahler held that this strategy fit the culture of the corporation and fostered ownership on the part of end-users, engendering broad organizational support. The mission of the AI Task Force, according to Mahler, was to "catalyze the implementation of artificial intelligence, particularly knowledge-based systems, broadly and effectively throughout Du Pont."

A site coordinator network, established by Mahler in September 1986 had grown to about 100 people throughout the company. Site coordinators who did not report to Mahler but relied on his group for program direction on expert systems, became experts on the types of systems at particular Du Pont sites. They met every other month to discuss new technical tools and issues of broad concern, such as copyright and patent protection.

In keeping with Mahler's grassroots approach, the expert-system user community, which by 1988 numbered 1,500, conducted its own two-day users' meeting every other month. These meetings, which included a panel discussion on implementing different systems, usually attracted about 50 people. Task Force members, in addition to attending these meetings, spent 50 percent of their time traveling to train and consult with end-users.

By July 1988, Mahler's staff recorded over 200 systems in routine use and another 500 in development. Mahler reported that systems developed to date had saved Du Pont $10 million in 1987, and he envisioned more than 2,000 systems in use by 1991, with annual earnings contribution of more than $100 million. "When Ed came up with the idea that expert systems could be built like spreadsheet applications, they really changed our thinking," observed Hank

---

[7]"Artificial Intelligence Spotlight," *Computerworld*, November 23, 1987, p. 59.

Morneau, director of ISD's planning and development. "It was a whole new way of looking at the problem. So far, it has been a tremendous success, but I think the jury is still out on whether the PC-based systems are the way to go for all of our diverse needs. In the area of production scheduling systems, for example, there are a number of people who feel that a single, large generic system could handle many of our scheduling needs, but it is hard to ignore his success even in this area, so far."

Ray Cairns, vice president of ISD, contrasted Mahler's management strategy with that which prevailed in the rest of ISD. "I don't think the AI group could have existed five years ago," Cairns observed:

> Things have changed significantly as a result of competitive pressures and a streamlining of our work force. But, there is a difference between the AI group and the rest of ISD. The rest of ISD is changing as well, but there's still an attitude that is really a carryover from the way we used to build systems. The major thrust in the past was leveraging our investment by making one system to fit a variety of needs, or combining separate systems to be more efficient. Now, I think the focus is more on functionality and less on efficiency.

Mahler's Management Style

Mahler's fourth-floor office was spacious but simple. He had no secretary, just an answering machine. Behind his desk was an Apple Macintosh computer and an oversized monitor that looked like a 26-inch television. Mahler embraced a philosophy that systems should be "inspection usable"; there was not an open software manual in sight.

Mahler commented briefly on his management style:

> If you're going to lead, you need to do three things: (1) help the group develop a vision, (2) develop a productive work environment, and (3) create a sense of urgency and in that order!

Doug Reece, a member of the AI Task Force since its inception, characterized Ed Mahler as both a visionary and a charismatic leader. Ed had the vision of applying artificial intelligence using standard hardware that was already in place (DEC VAXs and PCs). He saw the need for simpler systems and better interfaces. This ran counter to the conventional wisdom that led others to develop systems that were so complex that only the experts could understand the results. So, Ed had a vision that was different.

Ed also has a different managerial style. This group is very highly self-managed. Du Pont as a whole is not a self-managed organization. We all came from groups where work was parceled out by bosses. When we first had a meeting to talk about individual responsibilities on the AI Task Force, Ed said, "Well, y'all work this out." After that I remember people saying, "I'll do this," until we had things taken care of. Ed doesn't come in and say, "Do this, do that." People set their own goals.

Mahler put much effort into fostering informal relationships. From time to time he arrived at the office at 6 A.M. Whomever he found there at that hour, he would take out to breakfast. "One of Ed's beliefs," observed Paul Soper, another member of the AI Task Force, "is that a lot of things get done through the old-boy network, and now we have an old-boy network for AI."

John Hegarty, also a member of the AI Task Force, was impressed with the work environment that Ed Mahler had created. "Ed is so different from other managers in ISD—they might want to be like him but they find it difficult because of traditional habits," Hegarty explained:

> ISD, in my tenure, was closely managed; the dollars were watched very carefully. I came here from an environment that was restrictive and I found the atmosphere much more comfortable here. We're not in the business of thrusting things on people. We give people a money-back guarantee. When people deal with the AI Task Force, they're very satisfied.

"It's been a very strong marketing tool for us," Mahler said of the money-back guarantee, "and it's the right way to do business. If you buy something at Sears and it doesn't work, what do you do? You take it back. If you run a service business and someone's not satisfied with it, they shouldn't have to pay for it, should they?"

As of July 1988, none of the Task Force had asked for their money back. Mahler took this as evidence that his group was providing quality service.

AI Task Force Activities

AI Task Force efforts focused on five major areas in 1988, training; advisory expert systems; process control applications; production scheduling applications; and technology exploration.

Training. The AI Task Force had trained more than 1,700 people since 1986. Every week, another 50 people received training, and there was still a strong demand. Courses were evaluated and upgraded, if necessary, on a monthly basis. And the task force often developed new courses to meet emerging needs in the user community. The content of the course had changed considerably over the past two years. A course that focused on people issues associated with implementing expert systems was being developed in the summer of 1988.

Training was provided at cost, the philosophy that this was the best way to extract value from the investment in site-licensed software. Exhibit 3 describes the types of training courses offered. A typical training session involved twenty participants and produced $10,000 in billings for the AI Task Force. In many cases, participants left their training with a prototype expert system.

Advisory Expert Systems. Most of the systems that had been developed fell under the category of advisory expert systems. Generally, these were small sys-

EXHIBIT 3   Training Courses Offered by the Artificial Intelligence Task Force at Du Pont

---

Management Awareness Overview (1–2 hours): This presentation, designed for management, discusses Du Pont's artificial intelligence technologies and its rationale for its strategies for implementing them. It also addressed a number of organizational questions, such as: where were expert systems to be found and how much did they cost; what people, money, time, and equipment resources were needed to get started in AI; what sorts of help was available; and what benefits could be expected! Some Du Pont developed expert systems were demonstrated.

An Introduction to Expert Systems (3 hours): This course, designed for middle managers, supervisors, and professionals interested in learning about expert systems, described expert systems technologies and the kinds of problems they addressed best. It explained how to identify potential applications and demonstrated applications in use around Du Pont. Steps in the development of, and some of the software available in the company for writing expert systems, were also discussed.

Knowledge Engineering for Expert Systems Development (2 days): This course, intended for the people who actually develop expert systems, was offered in two versions, one for those interested in business applications, and one for those interested in technical applications. Both versions covered knowledge acquisition techniques and the use of various software tools for expert systems development. Students were expected to be ready to start developing expert systems at the end of the course. An Introduction to Expert Systems was a prerequisite for this course.

Knowledge Engineering II (2 days): The course focused student concentration on developing and refining skills used in the structuring of knowledge. It was divided into three segments: organizing knowledge, structuring knowledge, and converting knowledge to rule sets. Skills used in the acquisition of knowledge—e.g., communications, interviewing, listening, and interacting with experts—were also discussed. Course structure varied across lectures, discussions, group activities, and a hands-on lab. Specific case studies (some related to Du Pont activities) were covered.

---

tems used within Du Pont, although a number of systems had been developed for use outside the company. The Packaging Advisor™ was such a system.

Selar OH Plus belonged to a family of materials widely used in the manufacture of food containers because they prolonged shelf life by providing a barrier against oxygen permeation. Du Pont's Selar OH Plus provided a three- to fivefold improvement over the oxygen impermeability of conventional products. But as a relatively new entrant in this market, Du Pont faced the difficult challenge of differentiating its new product from conventional materials. Al Topolski, development programs manager for Du Pont's barrier resins, pushed for the development of the Packaging Advisor as a marketing tool to introduce Selar OH Plus.

The Packaging Advisor helped Du Pont customers choose appropriate materials for specific packaging requirements. Users input values for parameters such as shelf life and storage temperature, and the system would provide an evaluation of the cost and performance levels of a wide range of available barrier resins, including materials supplied by Du Pont competitors. "The marketing benefits of this program had been substantial," remarked Topolski, who was convinced that the Packaging Advisor had made an impact. "We've taken the Packaging Advisor out to customers who were so-so on being ready to buy our resin. But they wanted this program. It was enough to kick 'em over and say, 'Let's talk to the purchasing agent and let's get an order in so we can get this program.'"

Process Control Applications. Roughly 20 systems had been developed for real-time process control applications in manufacturing. An example was the Purge Expert developed at Du Pont's Corpus Christi freon plant.

Freon manufacturing involved a distillation step to remove impurities. Some of the mixture in the distillation column, containing both good product and impurities, was purged to improve product quality.[8] The challenge was to maximize the purging of impurities while minimizing loss of good product. Inadequate purging of impurities resulted in a batch of product that had to be reworked. Too much purging wasted valuable product. The performance of human operators who carried out the purging process varied greatly.

The Purge Expert, developed with the aid of the AI Task Force to automate the purging of impurities, produced savings of more than $120,000 per year based on raw material savings alone.[9]

Production Scheduling. A subgroup of the AI Task Force had been formed to develop and implement scheduling systems that integrated concepts from AI and operations research. This relatively new effort was aimed at realizing larger systems designed to better coordinate manufacturing and marketing across Du Pont's wide range of products. In the spring of 1988, the task force added 30 additional people on loan from various departments to work on production scheduling applications.

Technology Exploration. Some technology exploration was going on in AI, as well, including high-end tool evaluation and work on improved user interfaces. One member of the task force, for example, was studying frame-based AI tools; others were following developments in neural networks.

Future Challenges

Different people saw different challenges facing the AI Task Force. Of greatest concern were maintaining task force momentum, monitoring performance, maintaining and tracking existing systems, supporting end-users, and developing better AI tools.

---

[8]J.J. Bailey, "Economic Evaluation of Knowledge-Based Systems," M.I.T. Master's Thesis, 1987.
[9]Ibid.

Maintaining Program Momentum. Ed Mahler was concerned about growth in the number of systems and in system and organizational complexity. "In the beginning, people were attracted to the task force because it was something new and exciting," he observed. "In the early days, it was like guerrilla warfare. But now we've shown the business value of the technology. We're going through a transition from an embryonic state to a growth business that must compete for resources with all the other technologies."

"The territory out there is still relatively untapped and we can still do a lot with existing expert system shells," added another task force member. "As we turn the earth over, occasionally we find a big worm like scheduling—but basically, we're still an R&D outfit groping our way around looking for applications. Somewhere along the line this experimentation will have to diminish."

Monitoring Task Force Performance. Mahler is interested in monitoring the performance of the AI Task Force, as by surveying the user community, which led him to form an oversight committee, composed of senior level technical people and some site coordinators, to provide feedback on program direction. Mahler was concerned about the quality of the feedback he was getting from the oversight committee. "The people on the committee are very competent and dedicated, but they are not at levels of the organization to get plugged into the kind of information they need," he observed. "It was an interesting experiment, but it hasn't worked out very well so far." Mahler wanted to redirect the committee by adding some new people.

Maintaining Existing Systems. As a matter of policy, the task force did not become heavily involved in maintaining existing systems. "We almost demand that they do their own support," Hegarty said. "We turn it over to them and we fully expect them to maintain their own system. They can call our help line if they need assistance, but we do not undertake the support of any expert system."

Paul Soper's concern about systems becoming obsolete was echoed by others; "There are already lots of systems out there that have some type of life-cycle," observed one task force member, "and underneath each one there is a maintenance issue."

Tracking Existing Systems. John Hegarty saw the cataloging and monitoring of the expert systems proliferating throughout Du Pont as a growing challenge.

In previous months, he had been developing a database of existing systems. (Exhibit 4 shows the type of information that Hegarty was collecting.) Basically, we're looking for data that indicate how well we're doing in terms of spreading the gospel," Hegarty explained. "Also, with all the seeds Ed is planting, there is a great need to prevent duplication. We want to prevent reinvention of the wheel. We have only a vague idea what's out there." By July 1988, Hegarty's database included 266 expert systems in use within Du Pont. The actual number of systems was believed to be even higher.

EXHIBIT 4 Types of Information in Hegarty's Database at Du Pont

EXPERT SYSTEM NAME

BUSINESS SECTOR
(Administrative, Engineering, Financial, Manufacturing, Marketing, Research & Development)

TYPE OF SYSTEM
(Advisory, Customer Service, Planning, Process Control, Safety, Sales, Scheduling, Support, Training, Troubleshooting)

PRIMARY/EXPERT-SYSTEM TOOL (Level5, RS/1, etc.)

TYPE OF HARDWARE (PC, Minicomputer, Mainframe)

USES DATABASE(S) (Y or N)

USES GRAPHICS (Y or N)

USES ONLINE PROCESS DATA (Y or N)

SIZE (number of rules)

STAGE OF DEVELOPMENT[a]

ESTIMATED ANNUAL BENEFIT ($)

PERSON HOURS INVESTED

DOLLARS INVESTED

DEPARTMENT WHERE DEVELOPED (e.g. ISD)

SITE (e.g., Corpus Christi)

PRODUCT INVOLVED (e.g., polyethylene)

TARGET USER (e.g., lab technician)

DATE SYSTEM IDENTIFIED

DEVELOPER'S NAME

CONTACT PERSON'S NAME

CONTACT PERSON'S PHONE

CONTACT PERSON'S ELECTRONIC MAIL ADDRESS

DESCRIPTION OF EXPERT SYSTEM

[a]The AI Task Force used a five-stage development nomenclature. Stages ranged from identification of the system to routine use of the system.

Each week, Hegarty received one or two inquiries from people thinking of building an expert system. In each case, he would check the database, and in some cases was able to respond to the inquiry with the name of someone who had developed a similar system.

Although the training sessions organized by the task force stressed the importance of the database, many system builders were not supplying the information Hegarty wanted, particularly cost to develop the system and estimates of annual savings. Though Hegarty was not alone in feeling that the task force had a right to demand this type of information, others viewed it as a violation of the task force's policy of catalytic unobtrusiveness. Until this issue was resolved, Hegarty was forced to rely on site coordinators to feed information into the database.

Mahler favored a more informal alternative to a central database, something as simple as anyone who wanted to build an expert system first sending electronic mail message to the rest of the user community. "Everybody thinks it's a great idea," Mahler said on the database, "until they try to do it. It's an unrepresentative sample that is difficult to keep current and difficult to access. It's too much of an intrusion on the user. People perceived it to be some kind of corporate audit."

Mahler proposed a simple one-page check-the-boxes survey, the first of which he administered in March 1988. (The survey is shown in Exhibit 5.)

Supporting End Users. Several task force members were concerned about the level of support provided to users. Hegarty explained: "We are pledged to help people be successful. We feel we're successful when a system is commercialized—that it's being used by several end-users. Users would like us to become totally active in what they are doing, but that's not practical."

Users were pressuring the task force to participate more actively in the development process. Mahler conceded that more central support and activity was required on bigger systems. "There are some projects where this is needed because of integration with other systems," he acknowledged, "but the vast majority of systems we are doing are still zero to 10 percent participation by the AI Task Force."

Developing Better Tools. Paul Soper also commented on the need for better AI tools. "We want to develop easier tools so that more people can use them. The current tools are still too close to programming. We talk about tools that would be inspection usable. Ed's definition of inspection-usable is a Coke machine. The ideal tools would work the same way; you put in your knowledge and out pops an expert system."

Mahler's Concerns

As he charted the future direction of the task force, Mahler pondered the growing organizational complexity required to support the growing number of export systems. Worried that there might be a danger in becoming too locked

EXHIBIT 5 Mahler's Survey at Du Pont

---

1. Did you take any expert systems courses offered by Du Pont?
   yes _____   no _____

2. Have you worked on developing an expert system during the past year?
   yes _____   no _____   (if no, skip to question 6)

3. If so, how many systems have you worked on? _____

4. A. Of those systems, how many are under development? _____
   B. How many have been discontinued? _____
   C. How many are completed, but not in routine use? _____
      (e.g., demos for trade shows, etc.)
   D. How many are in routine use? _____

5. Did any of the AI Task Force members participate in the development of these
   systems?
   yes _____   no _____

6. Have you ever developed any systems which might have broad applicability across
   the company?   yes _____   no _____

7. If you wish to have a system included in the network, please give the name and a
   brief description of the system. (Optional; attach second sheet if necessary.)

8. Please indicate the cumulative total estimated annual savings or earnings impact for
   any systems you have developed.
0–$25M _____	$25–$50M _____	$50–$100M _____
$100–$250M _____	$250–$500M _____	$500–$1MM _____
Over $1MM _____	Intangible Benefit _____	

   Your Name: Dept.:   Function:
   (optional)   Site:

---

into the current generation of AI tools, Mahler wondered how to strike a balance
between applying today's tools and investing in the inspection-usable tools that
were probably on the horizon. Mahler wondered if there was a danger of getting
too locked in with the current generation of AI tools. He was aware of the pressure to tackle larger systems, and of the growth effects this would have on the
task force, and the management challenges it would present for him.

Student Project 1

Frazee Paint, Inc.— An Example of a Student-developed DSS*

The San Diego area is inundated with colorful vans belonging to Frazee Paint, Inc., a retailer of paint and wallpaper supplies. This developing company uses its vans to tell you, in vivid colors, about their products and services. In addition, the company is advertising in newspapers, TV, and on the radio. The company's sales have been increasing slowly. These increases are believed to be linked to the advertising budget and the population growth. Some relevant information is shown in Table 1.

The company was recently acquired by Worldwide Decorating, Inc. The first task of its new management was to prepare a six-year financial plan. The plan is based on the following assumptions:

a. The population growth rate will be the same as in the past.
b. The advertising budget will be $150,000 for the first year, increasing 10 percent per year thereafter.
c. The cost of goods sold is 75 percent of the sales plus a fixed cost of $500,000. The cost of goods sold in any particular department is $250,000 plus 75 percent of the sales in that department.
d. Sales will increase at the same rate as in the past and will be influenced by both the population and the advertising budget.
e. Taxes are about 35 percent of gross profit.

---

*This case is based on a paper written by Ken Campbell and Fred Orton, then doctoral candidates at United States International University, San Diego, CA.

TABLE 1 Historical Data

Year	Sales ($ thousands)	Population in Territory (thousands)	Advertising Budget ($ thousands)
1985	$40,898	806	$ 25
1986	47,472	840	85
1987	47,722	880	135
1988	52,043	925	120
1989	50,186	980	150
1990	55,340	1,048	180

Note: Dollars are constant for 1985.

Part A

On preliminary analysis, which you conducted, the company realized that sales would reach only $64.14 million in 6 years with a net income of just above $9.9 million. These results were unacceptable to the new owners, who aspired to a sales level of $110.68 million in 5 years (double the sales realized in 1990).
Questions:

1. What is the managerial problem?
2. Build a model that will allow you to compute the projected sales and net income for the next 6 years.
3. Attempt to solve the model. (Hint: You will need to execute a statistical analysis in order to generate the input data for the model.) Show how the sales and income projections quoted earlier were derived.
4. Do you have any suggestions about how management can attain their sales goal? (Use only information provided in this case.)

Solutions to Part A

1. The problem is how to increase sales over the next 6 years.
2. and 3. In order to build such a model, one can use several methods.
Our approach is to use a DSS modeling approach. First, an influence diagram is built (Figure 1). Then, execute the following steps:
   a. Employ a simple linear regression on the data in Table 1 using population as the dependent variable and years as the independent variable. The result is:

   Population (thousands) = 745.667 + 47.86 time (years)

   b. Use a multiple linear regression on the data in Table 1. Independent variables: population, advertising budget. Dependent variables: sales.
   The result: Sales (in thousands of dollars) = 22741 + 47.938 × advertising budget (in thousands of dollars) + 22.607 × population (thousands).

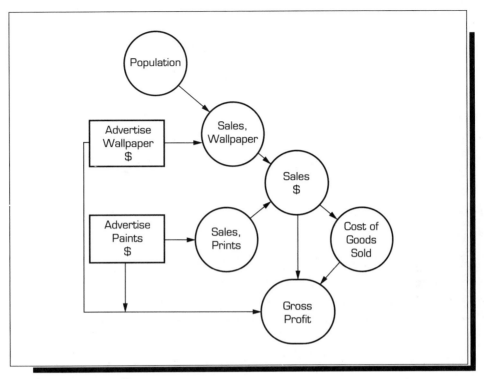

FIGURE 1   Influence Diagram

      c. Build a 5-year income and profit model (use IFPS or Lotus 1-2-3). The IFPS model and its solution are given in Table 2.
The results indicate that the projected sales in 1996 are $64.14 million and the net income is $9.94 million. These projected sales are *not* acceptable to management.
4. The only thing that management can do to improve the situation is to increase advertising (other alternatives could be considered but they are outside the scope of this case). Since population is an uncontrollable variable, it cannot be changed by management.

    To find the necessary increase in advertising, we conducted a goal-seeking analysis, using IFPS. The sales goal in 1996 was set as $110.68 million, doubling the sales of 1990. We "adjusted" the advertising as of 1991. In this manner, we get a gradual growth in sales. The results are impressive (see Table 3).

Part B

In an attempt to conduct a fine-tuned analysis, management decided to separate both historical sales data and advertising expenditures along their major prod-

TABLE 2 Six-year Sales Forecast with Current Advertising Budget (all in thousands of dollars)

	1991	**1992**	**1993**	**1994**	**1995**	**1996**
Time period	7	8	9	10	11	12
Population	1080.687	1128.547	1176.407	1224.267	1272.127	1319.987
Advertising	150	165	181.5	199.65	219.615	241.5765
Sales	54349.87	56150.01	58021.99	59973.01	62010.97	64144.56
Cost of goods sold	41262.4	42612.5	44016.49	45479.76	47008.23	48608.42
Gross profit	12937.47	13372.5	13824	14293.6	14783.13	15294.56
Taxes	4528.114	4680.376	4838.399	5002.761	5174.095	5353.098
Net income	8409.354	8692.126	8985.599	9290.842	9609.033	9941.467

Time = 7,8,9,10,11,12
Population = 745.667 + 47.86 * TIME
Advertising = 150, 1.1 * PREVIOUS
Sales = 22.6 * Population + 47.9 * Advertising + 22741.344
Cost of goods sold = 500 + .75 * SALES
Gross profit = Sales − Cost of goods sold − Advertising
Taxes = .35 * Gross Profit
Net Income = Gross Profit − Taxes

uct lines: paint and wallcover supplies. Table 4 shows the available information.

Management was interested in finding the effect of splitting the advertising budget between the two departments. They want to find out what would happen over the next five years if the proposed advertising budget of Table 3 is split 50–50; if the budget is divided ⅓ and ⅔; if the budget is divided ⅔ and ⅓; and if 100 percent goes to each department. The idea is to find out, using trial and error, what is the best budget allocation between paint and wallcover supplies. [Results are not given here.]

TABLE 3 Required Advertising to Double Sales by 1996 (in thousands of dollars)

	1991	**1992**	**1993**	**1994**	**1995**	**1996**
Time period	7.00	8.00	9.00	10.00	11.00	12.00
Population	1080.69	1128.55	1176.41	1224.27	1272.13	1319.99
Advertising	753.23	828.56	911.41	1002.55	1102.81	1213.09
Sales	83244.71	87934.33	92984.75	98432.05	104315.91	110680.00
Cost of goods sold	62933.54	66450.75	70238.57	74324.04	78736.94	83510.00
Gross profit	19557.95	20655.03	21834.78	23105.46	24476.17	25956.91
Taxes	6845.28	7229.26	7642.17	8086.91	8566.66	9084.92
Net income	12712.66	13425.77	14192.60	15018.55	15909.51	16871.99

Goal-seeking Solution: Goal: Sales (1996) = 110680
                          Adjust: Advertising (1991)

TABLE 4 Detailed Historical Data

	1	2	3	4	5	6	7
Year	Pop. (000)	Paint Advert ($K)	Wallcov Advert ($K)	Total Advert ($K)	Paint Sales ($K)	Wallcov Sales ($K)	Total Sales ($K)
1985	806	10	15	25	20465	20433	40898
1986	840	50	100	150	21468	26004	47472
1987	880	50	85	135	24321	23401	47722
1988	925	50	70	120	24798	27245	52043
1989	980	65	85	150	25432	24754	50186
1990	1048	80	100	180	28102	27238	55340

Part C: Allocation of the Money Among Various Media Options (Third Iteration)

Once the total amount of advertisement dollars is determined, as well as its distribution between paint and wallpaper, it is necessary to decide on the appropriate media. That is, determine how much to spend on advertising in TV, direct mail, newspapers, et cetera. Historical data are available on the exposure of potential customers to the various media and on the success of such exposure. In such an event we can use an optimization approach utilizing linear programming. A hypothetical example for the advertisement of paints follows:

The Frazee Company plans to allocate some or all of its advertising budget of $82,000 in the San Diego Metropolitan area. It can purchase local radio spots at $120 per spot, local TV spots at $600 per spot, and local newspaper advertising at $220 per insertion.

The company's policy requirements specify that the company must spend at least $40,000 on TV and allow newspaper expenditures up to either $60,000 or 50 percent of the TV expenditures, whichever is more profitable, overall, for the company.

The payoff from each advertising medium is a function of the size of its audience. The general experience of the firm is that the values of insertions and spots in terms of "audience points" (an arbitrary unit) are as follows:

Radio	40 audience points per spot
TV	180 audience points per spot
Newspapers	320 audience points per insertion

It is necessary to find the optimal allocation of advertising expenditures among the three media. A linear programming model is used in this case:

Formulation

1. The decision variables

$$x_1 = \text{No. of spots allocated to radio}$$
$$x_2 = \text{No. of spots allocated to TV}$$
$$x_3 = \text{No. of insertions allocated to newspapers}$$

2. The objective function

$$\text{maximize } z = 40x_1 + 180x_2 + 320x_3$$

3. The constraints

$$120x_1 + 600x_2 + 220x_3 \le 82{,}000 \tag{1}$$
$$600x_2 \ge 40{,}000 \tag{2}$$

and either

$$220x_3 \le 60{,}000 \tag{3a}$$

or

$$220x_3 \le 300x_2 \tag{3b}$$

where x_1, x_2, x_3 are integers.

The Solution

The problem must be solved twice, once for each set of "either/or" constraints, and the better solution selected. Either

$$x_2 = 66.67, \quad x_3 = 190.9, \quad z = 73{,}090.9 \text{ for (3a)}$$

or

$$x_2 = 91.1, \quad x_3 = 124.24, \quad z = 56{,}177.6 \text{ for (3b)}$$

The first solution is better. Rounding to integers:

$$x_2 = 66 \text{ (spots on radio)}$$
$$x_3 = 191 \text{ (spots in newspaper)}$$
$$z = 73{,}000 \text{ (audience)}$$

Note: the solution was derived by an LP package since the student version of IFPS does not have optimization capabilities.

Exercises

1. Run a six-year projection under the five budget allocation policies. Comment on the results.
2. Was it logical to split the analysis as was done in part B? Why?
3. Frazee's customers are either individuals or contractors. If individuals are thought to be highly influenced by advertising, would they buy more paint or more wallpaper products than the average for the company? Or would they buy the same? Explain.
4. Can an optimal solution be found to this (part B) allocation problem?

Student Project 2

Expert Telephone Configuration System Case*

Introduction

Tripler Army Medical Center Expert Telephone Configuration System (EXTELC-SYS) was designed to aid Tripler Information Management Division personnel, U.S. Army Information Systems Command Signal Battalion Liaison personnel, and telephone users. It helps them select appropriate telephone equipment and configure a hospital department, division, or separate service telephone system to meet users' needs within constraints imposed by Army regulations, budget, equipment available, and the ongoing hospital renovation project.

The system was developed using EXSYS during the summer of 1988. Knowledge required to develop the system rules was acquired from the Army's information systems personnel and from the system developer. The system was installed on a PC. The liaison office staff uses the system to develop, modify, or confirm telephone equipment configurations associated with telephone move and change requests received from Tripler customers.

---

*The project was developed by Major Gary Gilbert, formerly a graduate student at the University of Southern California. He also wrote this case.

A75

EXTELCSYS simplifies training required for new personnel as well as expedites processing of telephone moves and changes associated with the hospital renovation project. Future enhancements planned for the system include adding the capability to produce a consolidated listing of all the equipment required, by room number, for an entire department or division telephone system.

Problem Domain

The Tripler Army Medical Center Information Management Division in Hawaii is responsible for overseeing all aspects of the five components of the Army's Information Mission Area within the medical center. These include automation, communications, visual information, records management, and printing/publishing. Communications support is provided to the medical center by the Army Information Systems Command Signal Battalion–Hawaii. Voice, data, and radio communications support are included.

By far, the biggest job of the signal liaison office staff is to review requests for telephone moves and changes associated with the massive 10-year hospital renovation project.

Because each hospital activity must move one or more times on an interim or permanent basis, hundreds of telephone move or change requests are generated.

Two different telephone companies provide service to the hospital. The old sections of the hospital and the outlying buildings are serviced by Hawaiian Telephone Company. The newly renovated sections of the hospital are serviced by Tel-a-Com Hawaii. Telephone configurations are complicated by the two-contractor situation. All telephone lines provided by Hawaiian Telephone in the old and outlying areas must be serviced by the new Tel-a-Com Hawaii switch, and all off-post (nonmilitary) and commercial access requires access to trunks provided by Hawaiian Telephone Company. Telephone equipment provided by Tel-a-Com Hawaii is made by Rolm, Inc.; telephone equipment provided by Hawaiian Telephone is made by GTE. In addition, the Hawaiian Telephone equipment is all analog equipment, while the new switch and the majority of the Tel-a-Com Hawaii telephone equipment is digital. Digital instruments will not work on analog lines and vice versa.

A significant amount of training and experience is required to familiarize the signal liaison personnel with the complicated hospital telephone system so they can do an adequate job of configuring telephones.

Because the signal liaison personnel and the information management officer are military, their tenure is limited to the length of their assignments in Hawaii. In addition, military career management practices favor reassigning officers and noncommissioned officers after 18 months to 2 years in a job in order to broaden their experience. The result is a significant problem in maintaining sufficient expertise within the signal liaison and the information management staffs to be able to competently configure telephones. Therefore, the purpose of this expert system is to "capture" and maintain telephone configuration expertise. To save money and to develop the system rapidly, an ES shell called EXSYS was used.

Feasibility Study

Necessary Requirements for Expert System Development

Six specific requirements were validated before the development of the expert system.

1. The task requires real knowledge about the various Tripler telephone systems, the renovation project, budget and regulatory constraints, and interdepartmental politics along with the ability to make heuristic judgments and/or decisions based on that knowledge.
2. The task requires only cognitive skills, rather than physical or mechanical skills.
3. The signal liaison officer, noncommissioned officer, and information management officer (system designer and author of this case) are sufficiently knowledgeable and experienced to be considered "experts" in this narrow area of telephone communication engineering.
4. The telephone configuration process is just application of a variety of "rules" to the specific requirements and constraints of a particular situation.
5. The task is well understood and is clearly defined. The current experienced experts previously mentioned solve the telephone configuration problems every day. The problem is sufficiently narrow in scope.
6. Computer equipment and staff resources or funding were available to complete the project. The system developer is sufficiently trained to use the EXSYS development tool, and computer-assisted tutorials are available for both development and operational training.

In summary, all the ingredients for successful implementation existed. The system was justified and the ES technology was found to be appropriate.

EXTELCSYS

Conceptual Design and Feasibility

Selection of an Expert. The liaison officer, noncommissioned officer, and information management officer are sufficiently knowledgeable to be considered experts in this narrowly focused problem area.

System Developer. The system developer has a master's degree in management of computer systems applications, 10 years of Automation management and computer system design experience, and 3 years of experience at preparing, reviewing, and/or approving telephone configurations at Tripler.

Development Strategy. Rapid prototyping was used to develop the system. At the first cut, a fifteen-rule system was developed. The system was then revised and expanded to include more features and situations until enough rules were included to provide satisfactory results in at least 90 percent of the specific consultations tested.

Selection of Hardware and Software. The system was developed on a laptop Zenith 184 microcomputer using EXSYS. Once completed, the system was transported and operated on a Zenith 248 microcomputer.

Project Development Costs

Hardware

Zenith 248 PC with dot matrix printer	$1,900

Software

EXSYS program	$395
DOS (bundled with hardware)	0
Total	$2,295

Personnel person-hours (military personnel provided)

Information management officer	25
Signal liaison staff experts	12
Total person-hours	37

Cost/Benefit Analysis. This system is very inexpensive, especially since the computer hardware is already in place, and military personnel are used for both the development and knowledge acquisition. Even if those costs are included, the benefits of this system far outweigh the costs. Most significant are the reduction in training requirements and the reduction in time required by the signal liaison staff to prepare telephone configurations and by the information management officer to review and approve them. If the increase in quality and consistency of the final product is also considered, this system will pay for itself in less than a month.

Knowledge Acquisition Methodology

In the development of EXTELCSYS, the system developer is also an expert. This is an excellent example of a user-developed system in which the expert's task is to capture his or her own expertise. Often, this type of expert system development results in a better product than one in which the system developer or knowledge engineer must extract the knowledge from some expert, especially if the expert is uncooperative.

Since pooling knowledge from several experts could result in synergy, the EXTELCSYS system developer also interviewed the other experts from the signal liaison staff to add information to the knowledge base. The developer also tested the system with the staff during and after completion of development to ensure that rules were clearly stated, accurate, and unambiguous.

Rapid Prototyping Procedures

EXTELCSYS was built using the rapid prototyping methodology. A simple prototype was built using fifteen rules and ten choices. This prototype was able to determine many features: what type of instrument should be installed (digital or analog); what make (Rolm or GTE); what model (multi- or single-line, pushbutton or rotary dial, etc.); if the line(s) should be capable of receiving incoming calls from off post (direct inward dial); how it should be installed (wall mounted or on a desk) depending on the required location within the medical center; and a selection of user requirements. Seven qualifiers were used in the first prototype. The basic rules, choices, and qualifiers still exist in the final version of the system, although they have been significantly modified.

After the first prototype was tested, new rules, qualifiers, variables, values, choices, and so forth, were continually added until all the basic features and/or requirements known to the experts were included. Some features that are automatically included with installation of a new telephone were not included.

The final (1988) system includes fifty rules, fifteen qualifiers, four mathematical variables, and thirty-five choices.* The user (or the inference engine) can select from seventeen different features, including headset, speaker phones, commercial long distance, military long distance (called AUTOVON), internal department and/or hospitalwide intercom, group teleconferencing, computer modem, telefax, autoanswering machine, hunt groups (rings the next line in an office when one is busy), pick groups (enables any line in an office to be answered from any telephone), digital radio paging, and a 25-foot extension cord.

Training and Implementation Plan

Implementation of EXTELCSYS involves three steps: (1) transporting the system to the Zenith 248 personal computer in the signal liaison office; (2) training the signal liaison staff on the system; and (3) changing the standing operating pro-

---

*After the completion of the case, the system was further developed before it was fielded. It includes more than a hundred rules in its fielded version.

cedures for processing telephone moves and changes or preparing and reviewing telephone configuration plans.

1. Transporting EXTELCSYS simply requires that a copy of EXSYS "runtime" and EXTELCSYS rules and text files be loaded on the Zenith 248.

2. The signal liaison staff are the primary users. Initial training was conducted by the information management officer. Training of new personnel will be conducted by the signal liaison staff. The EXSYS help features and the tutorial demos will also be used for refresher or remedial training. The information management officer will train his replacement and cross-train another information management division staff member on both operation and maintenance of the system. EXSYS demo tutorials will also be used to conduct system maintenance training.

3. The information management officer issued instructions to the staff for updating standard operation procedures. A complete EXSYS/EXTELCSYS consultation printout for each recommended telephone instrument configuration is required to be included with all telephone move or change requests, which are forwarded to the information management officer by the signal liaison staff for approval.

Documentation, Maintenance, and Continued Program Plans

Documentation

EXTELCSYS user documentation consists of the EXSYS user documentation itself, the starting and ending texts (see Appendix 1 to this case), sample consultation printouts (Appendix 2 to this case), and printouts of the choices (possible recommendations) and rules (Appendix 3 and 4 to this case). The EXSYS "runtime" module also has built-in help modules that can be printed or called up by the user during a consultation. System maintenance documentation consists of the EDITXS user documentation, the EDITDEMO tutorials and software, the user documentation listed previously and contained in the appendices, plus the EXTELCSYS rules and text files.

System Maintenance

System maintenance consists of updating the rules, choices, qualifiers, or variables to meet new user needs or changes in procedures, regulations, or equipment available. Maintenance will be performed by the information management officer rather than by the signal liaison user personnel. This will enable the officer to maintain control of and familiarity with the rules, choices, and qualifiers, which are the basis for system recommendations. For this plan to be successful, the information management officer must consult regularly with the signal liaison user personnel to ensure that rules are revised or new rules are developed for any situation for which the system does not produce a satisfactory recommendation.

Continued Program Plans

The information management officer will continue to revise and expand EXTELCSYS to incorporate rules and choices for configuring those standard features not included in the current version. Although those features (transfer, call forward, hold, camp-on-busy, park, conference, system speed dial, etc.) are automatically included with each telephone configuration, the user does have an option of including a button for each feature on his or her instrument or using a series of pound sign (#) or star (*) commands to execute them. For the sake of system development expedience, these options were not included in the current version. In addition, the information management officer plans to expand the system to enable signal liaison personnel to run EXTELCSYS for an entire department at one time and produce a consolidated listing of all telephone instrument configurations required for a department. The current version must be run individually for each instrument required. This extension will require increased use of the EXSYS math functions and interface to a database. Finally, the information management officer plans to produce a database of all telephone equipment currently installed or in storage. EXTELCSYS would then be modified to automatically update the database any time a telephone move or change is approved and executed.

Security and Integrity

EXTELCSYS does not contain any sensitive information; therefore, security of the system is not of great concern. The software is of some value because several person-hours have gone into producing it. However, it can easily be developed again if lost or destroyed. The knowledge base, however, cannot be recreated if the experts are no longer available because they have been reassigned (which will occur shortly). Therefore, security of the system entails carefully backing up the knowledge base rules and text files and storing backups in a secure location away from the work site. Complete copies of the EXTELCSYS files and documentation are stored in the Tripler Data Processing Center computer magnetic media library and at Tripler's alternate storage site at the Fort Shafter Data Processing Center.

System integrity will be maintained by providing only the EXSYS runtime module and the EXTELCSYS rules and text files to the signal liaison staff personnel. They are not provided the EDITXS or EDITDEMO editing software. They will thereby be unable to modify the rules or choices without contacting the information management officer. The information management officer will occasionally require the signal liaison staff to provide an expanded consultation printout that includes the rules used by EXSYS to make the recommendations. The officer will then be able to spot-check the rules to make sure no unauthorized changes have been made to the system.

Problems and Lessons Learned

Conversion of heuristic rules of thumb into IF-THEN-ELSE rules is not easy, even when a system such as EXTELCSYS is well suited for a rule-based expert system. It is difficult even if the developer, knowledge engineer, and expert are all the same person; it is even more difficult when they are different persons.

Since the EDITDEMO (student) version of EXSYS was available to the developer during development of the initial prototype, the knowledge base includes only fifty rules. The full-blown EDITXS is needed to expand and include the additional requirements and telephone feature options mentioned.

Because the EXSYS inference engine uses backward chaining exclusively, there are some situations that occur within EXTELCSYS in which user input to EXSYS questions does not result in all the appropriate choices being selected. This usually occurs after the system has determined its own answers to some qualifier without asking the user, and then asks the user a question that would allow him or her to add a requirement for a feature that may have been inadvertently omitted earlier. Examples are rules No. 34–44 which, before modification, asked the user about modem, telefax, or answering machine features. A rule could have been invoked because the user selected an answering machine but not a modem or telefax machine. However, when the user saw the qualifier's fifteen questions, which included answers pertaining only to modems or telefax machines, he or she may have remembered that a modem was needed and selected some answers that pertain to modems. This situation required the rules to be modified.

Maintenance of backup copies of the rules and text files during development can save redoing development work because the master rule or text files become corrupted. This occasionally happens while files are being saved to disk. Again, failure to follow this simple rule resulted in extra work during the EXTELCSYS development effort.

Conclusion

EXTELCSYS provides the Tripler Army Medical Center Information Management Division staff with a workable expert system that reduces the time involved in preparing and reviewing telephone configurations. Expertise previously available only from existing staff members has been preserved.

Note: This project was extremely helpful to its developer and his organization. However, for a better student project, interfaces for databases and/or spreadsheets are desirable.

Questions for Discussion

1. What are the factors that created the need for this system?
2. Describe the process of requesting equipment and approving it. Explain how the ES is used in this process.
3. List some of the necessary requirements (feasibility) for this project.
4. What are the project's major justification points?
5. Describe how rapid prototyping was executed.
6. Discuss the implementation and training plan. Can it be improved?
7. Briefly summarize the lessons learned from this project.
8. The grade for this project was an A. What would you do to elevate it to an A$^+$?
9. The use of multiple experts in this case was beneficial. How does it differ from a typical multiple expert case?

Appendix 1:   Starting and Ending Texts

Starting Text

Tripler Army Medical Center Expert Telephone Configuration System (EXTELCSYS) is designed to aid information management division personnel, signal battalion liaison personnel, and telephone users in configuring an office telephone system to meet their department, division, or separate service needs. The system is designed to select an appropriate telephone instrument with features required to perform the functions desired by the user depending on the user's office, clinic, or ward location within the medical center installation. It is to be used to plan telephone moves and changes associated with the renovation program. In many cases user activities will be converted from the existing rotary dial analog telephone system provided under lease contract from Hawaiian Telephone Company to the digital telephone system being installed by Tel-a-Com Hawaii Corp. For those activity moves that are only temporary, the existing rotary equipment will be moved or an electronic key push-button system may be temporarily leased from Hawaiian Telephone if funds are available.

EXTELCSYS should be run for each new telephone you need and/or for each old telephone you are moving. The system will recommend the type of telephone and associated features which will best fit the needs of the user in the new location.

Instructions: Select *one* or *more* answers to each question EXTELCSYS asks you, and enter the numbers of the selections separated by commas.

Ending Text

EXTELCSYS will now recommend the type of telephone instrument and associated features best suited to the user's needs as provided by the answers you gave to the questions the system asked of you. *Remember,* this is only a recommendation. If the user is not satisfied, he or she may submit a request for exception with justification to the chief, information management division.

To see why EXTELCSYS made a recommendation, enter the number of the recommendation.

Appendix 2:   Sample Consultation

This appendix contains a sample of EXTELCSYS consultations for which the computer screens have been printed out as they would appear to the user.

Example: The user is asked the following:

1. Instrument location is
    1. in new/renovated section of main hospital
    2. in old section of main hospital
    3. in outlying buildings of Medical Center installation
    4. in an office
    5. in a reception area
    6. in a treatment room
    7. in a patient room
    8. on a desk
    9. mounted on the wall
    10. unknown at this time
    11. in a conference room

    2, 4, 8 = answer

2. Feature(s) desired is/are
    1. push-button dial
    2. headset
    3. pick group
    4. external speaker
    5. microphone
    6. commercial long distance
    7. AUTOVON
    8. off-post dialing
    9. ability to receive calls from off post
    10. internal (activity) intercom
    11. group teleconferencing with speaker phone
    12. computer modem
    13. telefax machine
    14. answering machine
    15. 25-foot extension cord
    16. digital paging
    17. hunt group
    18. none of the above

    7, 8, 9, 12, 16, 17 = answer

3. User is
   1. a department or division chief
   2. not a department or division chief
   3. status unknown

1 = answer

Based on the answers to these, and if needed more questions, a recommendation (Table 1) is generated by the system.

Results and Sensitivity Analysis

Results. Twelve items are recommended, starting with CF (certainty factor) = 100 (Hawaiian Telephone rotary instrument) to CF = 10 for item 12 (in the column titled Original Value). It is now up to the liaison office staff to determine what to approve.

Sensitivity Analysis. By pressing "C" it is possible to change any of the input data. As an illustration, we changed the location from the old location to the renovated one. The system asked us more questions and then displayed new recommendations side by side with the original one (column titled New was added in Table 1). Notice that new items appear on the list and negative values appear on some of the original items. These items should *not* be included in the package.

TABLE 1 Recommendation Made by EXTELCSYS

Values Based on − 100 to + 100 System	Original Value	New
1. Hawaiian Telephone rotary instrument	100	− 90
2. RJ 11 jack required	80	80
3. Primary line is Priority AUTOVON (AVP)	70	70
4. Additional line is Direct Inward Dial (DID)	70	70
5. External keypad	60	60
6. Primary line is Direct Inward Dial (DID)	60	None
7. Additional C line	55	55
8. Hunt group	50	50
9. Primary line is extension	50	− 20
10. PAX Intercom required	50	50
11. Additional line is an extension line	20	20
12. Department/Division/Activity Intercom	10	10
13. Analog extension required	None	80
14. Rolm single-line digital instrument	None	100

Appendix 3:   Sample Choices (Out of 35)

Choices

1. Hawaiian Telephone rotary instrument
   Used in rule(s): (0005) (0006) (0007) (0009) (0010) (0011) (0049)
2. Hawaiian Telephone electronic push-button instrument
   Used in rule(s): (0009) (0010)
3. Rolm single-line digital instrument
   Used in rule(s): (0006) (0024)

Appendix 4:   Sample Rules (Out of 50)

RULE 1
IF   Instrument location is in old section of main hospital or in outlying buildings of
         medical center installation
THEN the instrument type is analog
         AND
         Equipment make is GTE (Hawaiian Telephone)
         AND
         Primary line is extension—probability = 50/100
         AND
         Primary line is private—probability = −20/100
ELSE Equipment make is Rolm
         AND
         Primary line is private—probability = 20/100
         AND
         Primary line is extension—probability = −20/100

Note: Digital Rolm phones cannot be installed in outlying buildings because existing cables will not support the digital system. Digital Rolm phones will not be installed in the old part of the hospital.

Reference: TAMC Telephone Switch Installation Contract

RULE 2
IF   Instrument location is in old section of main hospital
         AND
         Instrument location is in patient room
THEN Telephones will not be installed in patient rooms located in the old hospital or
         outlying building

Index

I1